The C++ Graphics Programming Handbook

LIMITED WARRANTY AND DISCLAIMER OF LIABILITY

ACADEMIC PRESS, INC. ("AP") AND ANYONE ELSE WHO HAS BEEN INVOLVED IN THE CREATION OR PRODUCTION OF THE ACCOMPANYING CODE ("THE PRODUCT") CANNOT AND DO NOT WARRANT THE PERFORMANCE OR RESULTS THAT MAY BE OBTAINED BY USING THE PRODUCT. THE PRODUCT IS SOLD "AS IS" WITHOUT WARRANTY OF ANY KIND (EXCEPT AS HEREAFTER DESCRIBED), EITHER EXPRESSED OR IMPLIED, INCLUDING, BUT NOT LIMITED TO, ANY WARRANTY OF PERFORMANCE OR ANY IMPLIED WARRANTY OF MERCHANTABILITY OR FITNESS FOR ANY PARTICULAR PURPOSE. AP WARRANTS ONLY THAT THE MAGNETIC DISKETTE(S) ON WHICH THE CODE IS RECORDED IS FREE FROM DEFECTS IN MATERIAL AND FAULTY WORKMANSHIP UNDER THE NORMAL USE AND SERVICE FOR A PERIOD OF NINETY (90) DAYS FROM THE DATE THE PRODUCT IS DELIVERED. THE PURCHASER'S SOLE AND EXCLUSIVE REMEDY IN THE EVENT OF A DEFECT IS EXPRESSLY LIMITED TO EITHER REPLACEMENT OF THE DISKETTE(S) OR REFUND OF THE PURCHASE PRICE, AT AP'S SOLE DISCRETION.

IN NO EVENT, WHETHER AS A RESULT OF BREACH OF CONTRACT, WARRANTY OR TORT (INCLUDING NEGLIGENCE), WILL AP OR ANYONE WHO HAS BEEN INVOLVED IN THE CREATION OR PRODUCTION OF THE PRODUCT BE LIABLE TO PURCHASER FOR ANY DAMAGES, INCLUDING ANY LOST PROFITS, LOST SAVINGS OR OTHER INCIDENTAL OR CONSEQUENTIAL DAMAGES ARISING OUT OF THE USE OR INABILITY TO USE THE PRODUCT OR ANY MODIFICATIONS THEREOF, OR DUE TO THE CONTENTS OF THE CODE, EVEN IF AP HAS BEEN ADVISED OF THE POSSIBILITY OF SUCH DAMAGES, OR FOR ANY CLAIM BY ANY OTHER PARTY.

Any request for replacement of a defective diskette must be postage prepaid and must be accompanied by the original defective diskette, your mailing address and telephone number, and proof of date of purchase and purchase price. Send such requests, stating the nature of the problem, to Academic Press Customer Service, 6277 Sea Harbor Drive, Orlando, FL 32887, 1-800-321-5068. APP shall have no obligation to refund the purchase price or to replace a diskette based on claims of defects in the nature or operation of the Product.

Some states do not allow limitation on how long an implied warranty lasts, nor exclusions or limitations of incidental or consequential damage, so the above limitations and exclusions may not apply to you. This Warranty gives you specific legal rights, and you may also have other rights which vary from jurisdiction to jurisdiction.

THE RE-EXPORT OF UNITED STATES ORIGIN SOFTWARE IS SUBJECT TO THE UNITED STATES LAWS UNDER THE EXPORT ADMINISTRATION ACT OF 1969 AS AMENDED. ANY FURTHER SALE OF THE PRODUCT SHALL BE IN COMPLIANCE WITH THE UNITED STATES DEPARTMENT OF COMMERCE ADMINISTRATION REGULATIONS. COMPLIANCE WITH SUCH REGULATIONS IS YOUR RESPONSIBILITY AND NOT THE RESPONSIBILITY OF AP.

The C++ Graphics Programming Handbook

Roger Stevens
Rio Rancho, NM

AP Professional
AP Professional is a Division of Academic Press, Inc.

Boston San Diego New York
London Sydney Tokyo Toronto

AP PROFESSIONAL

An Imprint of ACADEMIC PRESS, INC.
A Division of HARCOURT BRACE & COMPANY

ORDERS (USA and Canada): 1-800-3131-APP or APP@ACAD.COM
AP Professional Orders: 6277 Sea Harbor Dr., Orlando, FL 32821-9816

Europe/Middle East/Africa: 0-11-44 (0) 181-300-3322
Orders: AP Professional 24-28 Oval Rd., London NW1 7DX

Japan/Korea: 03-3234-3911-5
Orders: Harcourt Brace Japan, Inc., Ichibancho Central Building 22-1, Ichibancho Chiyoda-Ku, Tokyo 102

Australia: 02-517-8999
Orders: Harcourt Brace & Co. Australia, Locked Bag 16, Marrickville, NSW 2204 Australia

Other International: (407) 345-3800
AP Professional Orders: 6277 Sea Harbor Dr., Orlando FL 32821-9816

Editorial: 1300 Boylston St., Chestnut Hill, MA 02167 (617)232-0500

Web: http://www.apnet.com/approfessional

This book is printed on acid-free paper. ♾

United Kingdom Edition published by
ACADEMIC PRESS LIMITED
24–28 Oval Road, London NW1 7DX

The C++ Graphics Programming Handbook
p. cm.
ISBN 0-12-668340-9
1. C++ (computer program language) 2. Computer graphics.
QA76.73.C153C13 1996
006.6'6—dc20

96-23725
CIP

Printed in the United States of America
96 97 98 99 CP 9 8 7 6 5 4 3 2 1

Table of Contents

Part 1

Basic Graphics Programming

1

Introduction

New computers, display adapters, C++ compilers, and operating systems are appearing so fast these days that it is almost impossible for the individual user to keep up with them. It's easy to become confused, particularly since any packaged system that you get is unlikely to have software that fully utilizes your hardware capabilities. If you are satisfied with one of the commercial drawing packages, you can get by nicely, but if you want to make the fullest use of the high-color or true-color modes of a modern Super VGA card, you need to get back to basics and create your own graphics programs. The emergence of many new C++ compilers makes this a lot easier than it used to be. However, the new techniques require a lot more learning on your part. To get the best graphics displays, you'll have to learn how to implement Super VGA high-resolution multicolor modes, which are just beginning to be standardized. You may find it very useful to understand some of the undocumented display modes. You'll need to be able to save graphics displays to a disk file in a number of different standard formats and to restore the disk file data to a screen display. An overview of three-dimensional techniques won't do any harm, either.

Another important aspect of implementing graphics that is highly personal is the trade-off between flexibility and speed. Every commercial graphics package has to compromise speed to be capable of working with almost any conceivable type of hardware. If you understand the fundamentals, you can write software that is lightning fast but only works with your particular collection of hardware. Alternately, you can provide a lot more flexibility in different display modes if speed is not a concern. In other words, if you design your own graphics functions, you can tailor each function to do exactly the job that you want it to and no more. For example, say you want to draw an ellipse after specifying the coordinates of the center, the x and y axes length, and the color. No problem; you can design your ellipse drawing function to work exactly this way. On the other hand, if you want to specify the top left and bottom right coordinates of a rectangle and draw your ellipse inside this box, your function can just as easily be designed to use this mode of operation. You don't need to create an omnibus ellipse drawing function that will use all of the possible modes of specifying the ellipse parameters, but you can if you want to. Nor do you need to hold committee meetings to determine which method of specifying the ellipse will satisfy the greatest number of users. You can design your function to do what is right for you. Similarly, you don't need to create a huge function that will draw ellipses for every graphics display mode ever thought up by the human mind, nor do you need to make it work with every type of display adapter card ever designed. Instead, you can make the function work with only your hardware configuration and the display mode that you want to use. The function will be much simpler and much faster. You can also be more flexible than the commercial graphics packages. For example, Borland C++ allows you to draw lines that are either 1 pixel wide or 3 pixels wide. What if you want to draw a line 10 pixels wide? Sorry, you're just out of luck. Now, if you want to draw only 1- or 3-pixel-wide lines, you have no problem with the standard graphics package. However, if you want to draw 10- or 20- or 30-pixel-wide lines, you can easily include in your own graphics programs a feature that allows you to make lines of any desired width.

Programming Style

Every programmer has his or her own style. When you're writing a book like this, that style is ideally one that will enable the reader to use the programs and functions with minimal effort. One thing that I have done to encourage this is put every curly bracket on a separate line and match the indentation of the beginning and ending curly brackets for a section of code. This ensures that you can look at a listing and tell which curly brackets encompass each section. For example:

```
for (i=0; i<10; i++)
{
    for (j=0; j<12; j++)
    {
        if (m[i][j] < i*j)
        {
            m[i][j] = 0;
            n[i][j] = i*j;
        }
        else
        {
            m[i][j] = i*j;
            n[i][j] = 0;
        }
    }
}
```

Another thing that I have done, that many programmers disagree with, is eliminate almost all comments from the code listing itself. I've done this for several reasons. First, I've tried to keep each function and program simple enough so that continual comments are unnecessary to understand the code. Any additional exposition that is needed is included in the accompanying text. Second, if you're are trying to type in some of the code into your computer, you'll be eternally grateful for all those thousands of comment characters that you didn't have to type and that, if you had typed, would make no contribution to running the code itself. Finally, if you are actually working with the listings, you will often want to comment out some sections of code. For example, if you decide to make major modifications of the code, you'll probably want to copy the entire section you are working with, using the editor, and then comment it out. Then if your modifications mess up the original section of program beyond recovery, you can always return to the section that you copied and at least be back where you started. But if a section of the program already contains a lot of comments that use the original C /* opening and */ closing symbols, you can't just put comment symbols at the beginning and end of a section to comment it out; instead you have to go down through and modify each comment that is within the block. Fortunately, with C++ you can use // to indicate that the rest of the line is a comment and these can be overridden for an entire block by the old original comment symbols, which makes commenting a lot easier.

An Overview of the Book

In this book, we want to supply you with a variety of ways of performing basic graphics operations such as plotting points, drawing lines, and drawing and filling polygons and ellipses. We also want you to have a good understanding of display modes and of the use of the ROM BIOS video services. Along with most types of functions, test programs will be included that permit you to see the functions in action and analyze the advantages and disadvantages of different techniques for performing an operation. We also want you to have a good understanding of how to use extended high-resolution modes of the Super VGAs. The number of Super VGAs is increasing every day, and up until recently there was little or no standardization of high-resolution modes. Finally, however, the Video Electronics Standards Association (VESA) has specified a set of standards that new Super VGA cards follow that enable one to write high-resolution multicolor applications that will work with any Super VGA. You'll find the procedures explained fully in the material that follows. Finally, we've given detailed information on three accepted formats for storing display information on a disk file and retrieving this information. The ultimate goal is to provide you with all of the information that you need to develop your own customized set of graphics routines and to provide test programs that can be used to verify that your graphics functions are working in the way that you intended.

Hardware Considerations

A few years ago, there were such significant differences in motherboards and other computer hardware that a PC compatible was usually not quite compatible. Thus a great deal of effort was needed to ensure that software routines would work with a widely varied set of hardware considerations. It was also usually a good idea to list the actual hardware that made up the test computer configuration so that readers would have a baseline reference point if things went wrong. Today, most of the obvious hardware compatibility problems have been solved, but with both hardware and software becoming more complex, you can encounter all kinds of subtle incompatibilities. In developing the software in this book, I used a NexGen computer that uses a 586 microprocessor and an ATI Graphics Xpression Super VGA board and a computer featuring an AMA 486 DX4 100 microprocessor with an STB PowerGraph Super VGA board. If my software works with both of these slightly offbeat systems it should be a snap to work with any Intel 486- or Pentium-based system.

Basic Graphics Programming

This book is divided into seven sections. The first, *Basic Graphics Programming*, begins with this introduction. Chapter 2 describes the inner working of the VGA and Super VGA card hardware. It will help you a lot in graphics programming and in troubleshooting if you go over this chapter and gain familiarity with the VGA hardware.

There's a lot of pressure these days to program everything to work as a Windows program. If you're planning to write some programs that draw particular graphics, you can save a lot of trouble by just writing them to work with DOS. The neat features of Windows just aren't needed to create a desired graphic. This isn't to say that you need to throw out Windows. Even if you're using Windows 95, you have a couple of options available. You can either start Windows 95 in a DOS mode or run a full-sized DOS window from Windows 95. Chapter 3, *Writing and Compiling C++ Code*, describes how to use the different operating systems and C++ compilers and some of the features of writing programs with C++.

Communicating with the Display Adapter Card

This section tells you everything you need to know about using the VGA card to produce displays. Proper programming of a display adapter requires an intimate knowledge of the workings of its internal registers. These control the display timing and the way that display memory interacts to produce various colors on the screen. This is particularly true if you are interested in using unusual display modes that are off the beaten track of what is handled by the ROM BIOS video services or if you need more speed than you can get from the ROM BIOS services. Chapter 4 describes the contents and functions of the EGA/VGA registers in detail.

One of the primary considerations in creating computer graphics is determining the display mode that is to be used. Display adapter cards have a number of modes that are supported by the ROM BIOS video services and others that are not documented but can be created through judicious manipulation of the display adapter card registers. In addition many new modes have been standardized by VESA and are supported by most Super

VGAs. Chapter 5 describes all these modes, the resolutions and colors involved, memory requirements, and character cell sizes for text. With this information, you can select the mode that is most suited to your graphics purposes within the limitations of your equipment configuration.

Although the ROM BIOS video services provide a means for plotting a pixel on the screen in any of the regular video modes, this service is usually too slow and may also be inadequate for some purposes. In fact, VESA has assumed that no one will ever use the ROM BIOS point-plotting service again, so it is not supported for VESA modes. Chapter 6 describes several methods of plotting a pixel to the screen through direct access of the VGA registers. Methods are included for 16-color, 256-color, high-color, and true-color modes.

The ROM BIOS video services provide a number of methods of direct access to the display adapter cards. A basic set of these services is common to every VGA and Super VGA card. There is also a set of ROM BIOS extensions specified by VESA that are available on every Super VGA card that supports VESA. Chapter 7 documents all of these services for the original display adapter cards (CGA, EGA, and VGA). Chapter 8 documents all of the VESA ROM BIOS extensions.

Positioning Graphics

This section investigates some considerations about positioning graphics on the screen that need to be taken up before we begin drawing actual graphics figures. Some graphics functions, such as those that draw circles or squares, work properly only when the pixels are square (the amount of the screen covered by a pixel is the same in the horizontal and vertical directions). If this is not the case, circles will appear as ellipses and squares as rectangles. Since not all display modes have a square pixel system, it is a good idea to configure a set of system coordinates for your graphics work and then convert them to the actual screen coordinates at appropriate places in the program. Another good reason for configuring a set of system coordinates is that screen coordinate systems usually have their origin at the top lefthand corner of the screen, with increasingly positive values of x going toward the right and increasingly positive values of y going downward, which is totally unlike most mathematical coordinate systems. Finally, if we set up system coordinates that have as high a resolution as the highest-resolution display we will be using, and properly handle our coordinate conversion, we can change a display mode with a single statement and have the display appear in the new mode without having to make a lot of individual coordinate changes. Chapter 9 describes how to set up coordinate systems, how and where to perform the conversion to screen coordinates, and the relationships that must exist between system and screen coordinates in order to ensure that unfortunate interactions do not occur to degrade the display.

It is often possible to design programs in such a way that calls to graphics functions that draw points, lines, circles, etc., on the screen never designate points that are outside the screen boundaries. If this is the case, you don't need to worry about clipping, and your functions will be the fastest that are achievable. There are other times, however, when points may be outside the screen boundaries and, if no precautions are taken, may produce disturbing and unwanted displays. Finally, there may be cases where you want to confine your graphics to a small window on the screen. In any of these cases, clipping operations are necessary to prevent any attempts at displaying points outside the desired clipping boundaries. On the most primitive level, this means checking every pixel to be displayed against the boundary parameters. It is often possible, however, to modify line endpoints to ensure that all points are within the screen boundaries. This is a much faster way of performing necessary clipping. Chapter 10 describes the clipping problem and shows various solutions that may be used.

Drawing Primitive Graphics Figures

This section describes how to draw and fill some of the basic graphics figures. We have used C++ to set up a series of classes that include the functions and variables needed to draw these figures. Chapter 11 lists the code for these classes, which are common to most of the programs that will be described in the following chapters. Chapter 11 also describes how the generic graphics functions that we use work. A lot of primitive geometric figures are included in the listing of Chapter 11, but detailed explanations are deferred to later chapters.

Line drawing is one of the more important aspects of graphics. Not only can the line-drawing function be used for drawing straight lines, but complicated curves can also be drawn in the form of tiny line segments. Chapter 12 goes into the details of line drawing. In addition to general-purpose line drawing functions, a fast horizontal line drawing function is described that can be used for fast filling of various geometric shapes. Methods for drawing wide lines and dotted, dashed, and other stylized lines are given. The chapter also discusses how to join straight-line segments appropriately.

Drawing and filling circles using a rectangular coordinate system is a difficult problem, particularly if the circle boundary is a wide line that needs to be completely filled in. Using Bresenham's algorithm, there are a number of ways of solving this problem. Chapter 13 shows some of the best and fastest methods of drawing and filling circles.

One good aspect of drawing circles is that the circle has a symmetry such that we need only compute one-eighth of the circle and then draw this repeatedly to complete the figure. Unfortunately, this is not true of ellipses, so that the problem becomes much more complicated. Furthermore, we may not be satisfied with ellipses oriented along the coordinate axes, but may want to tilt them in various ways. Chapter 14 describes the solutions for various ellipse drawing and filling problems.

Given that we have a good function for drawing circles, and that we know the beginning and ending angles of an arc, we can draw that arc if we figure out how the function can know which points on the circle it calculates are within the arc and therefore should be drawn, and which are not and therefore should be skipped. Filling an arc may seem meaningless to you at first; what we mean is that we draw lines from the center of the circle to the endpoints of the arc and then fill the area enclosed by the arc and these two lines. This is useful in making pie charts. Chapter 15 describes how we approach these arc problems and provides functions to perform the desired operations.

Drawing an irregular polygon is simply a process of drawing a series of line segments and making sure that there is a closing connection from the last set of coordinates specified to the first. There are different ways to handle the passing of the points to the drawing function, however. The best method may depend upon the nature of the polygons and how many pairs of coordinates are used to define it. Filling an irregular polygon is much more complicated, since even if we have collected the coordinate pairs of all the points that make up the polygon boundary, we still have to figure out whether we are inside or outside the polygon if each fill line is to be drawn correctly. Finally, if a polygon, or other closed figure, is bounded by lines whose exact location is not known to us, we need a fill technique that starts somewhere within the closed surface and keeps on filling until everything up to the boundary line is filled, no matter how peculiar the shape of the boundary is. Chapter 16 discusses these problems and lists some fast functions for performing the various operations.

A rectangle with its corners rounded makes a nice background for displaying menus or text panels. It also turns out to be rather easy to create a rounded rectangle outline or a filled rounded rectangle by using a combination of the functions developed for circles and rectangles. Chapter 17 describes how to do this.

Chapter 18 addresses the problem of how to draw a nicely shaped curve when several reference points are given to specify the curve shape. We don't want to just connect the specified points with line segments; instead we want a curve whose shape is both smooth and pleasing to the eye. Two mathematical methods are given for doing this: the Bezier curve and the B-Spline curve.

More Complicated Displays

The ROM BIOS for a VGA card contains several character sets for use in displaying characters on the screen. If you know how to use the character sets properly, you can overcome quite a few limitations that are built in to their normal use. For example, the usual C routines for printing characters to the screen won't work properly when you have moved to a portion of the display outside the normal screen boundaries, but a custom routine will enable you to place characters anywhere you desire. A custom function will also let you place alphanumerics on a screen generated by one of the undocumented display modes, which is impossible with the regular functions. You can also make functions to display large characters or vertical characters. Finally, you can mix 8 × 8 and 8 × 16 characters (to make superscripts, for example). Chapter 19 shows you how to do all of these things.

Our chapter on ellipses introduced the notion of rotating a figure. Chapter 20 takes a more general approach to the problem of coordinate rotation and geometric figure rotation and gives the matrices that may be used to perform these operations.

Advanced Graphics Topics

Chapter 21 extends coordinate rotation and translation to cover three dimensions and also presents the mathematics of projecting a three-dimensional figure onto a two-dimensional screen. Chapter 22 uses the three-dimensional mathematical techniques to provide all of the functions needed to define three-dimensional figures; rotate, translate, and scale them; determine the lighting of facets and identify which facets are visible; and finally project the resulting figure as a realistic two-dimensional display.

Chapter 23 describes some of the basic principles of ray tracing. A complete ray-tracing program is too long to include in this book, but with the information given here you can make intelligent use of one of the readily available raytracing programs.

If you look at some of the straight lines drawn in earlier chapters, you'll notice discernible steps, or "jaggies." This is puzzling, since when you look at a photographic reproduction such steps are not seen. Chapter 24 describes a technique known as anti-aliasing that can be used to essentially eliminate the stepping effect.

In Chapter 25 we show an example of how to put together everything we've learned up to now to create a complicated graphics display.

Chapter 26 introduces the techniques of warping and morphing. Warping can be used to correct a distorted image. Morphing transforms one image into another through a series of distortions.

Saving, Restoring, and Converting Displays

If you have some photographs available in digital format, or if you have generated a graphics display using the techniques described in this book, you may want to save the display in one of the standard graphics formats, or you may want to convert from one format to another. Chapter 27 describes how to display and store pictures using the *PCX* format. This is one of the most popular display storage formats; it handles 16 colors, 256 colors, or 24-bit color and performs some compression. Chapter 28 provides the same information for *BMP* files. This is the format used for Windows graphics. It doesn't perform compression, but handles all kinds of color information very quickly. Chapter 29 provides similar information on Targa files.

2

How Display Adapter Card Hardware Works

If you can program in C++, you don't have to be a hardware expert to create breathtaking displays with a PC and an SVGA card and monitor. However, the graphics capabilities of most C++ compilers are limited and don't keep up with the latest developments in monitors and graphics adapter cards. Therefore, you need to know how the computer, display adapter card, and monitor work together to produce various types of graphics displays. Each particular hardware configuration has its strengths and limitations. Sometimes there are hidden features that you can exploit or ways to work around limitations if you know how the whole system works. Furthermore, if you decide to upgrade your PC with a new display adapter card and monitor, it is important to know just what you are getting for your money. In this chapter, we're going to look at the basics of display adapter card and monitor hardware. By the time we're through, you should have a good idea of how hardware works.

The Monitor

First, we're going to look at the monitor, whose resolution and color-handling capabilities determine the quality of your computer display. Display adapter cards exist simply to supply the monitor with the signals that it needs to produce a useful display. All desktop computers use a monitor whose display device is a cathode ray tube (CRT). Most color CRTs have a florescent screen that when examined under a microscope is seen to consist of a lot of groups of red, green, and blue dots. Three electron guns at the base of the tube are arranged with a set of optics so that the red gun can only impinge upon red dots, the green gun on green dots, and the blue gun on blue dots. Which clump of dots is illuminated at any time is determined by a deflection yoke, which surrounds the neck of the CRT and provides magnetic fields that independently bend the electron beam in the horizontal and vertical directions.

The usual method of scanning the screen is to deflect the beam from the top lefthand corner of the screen toward the right. When the beam reaches the right edge of the screen, one horizontal scan line is complete, and the beam is blanked and returned as quickly as possible to the left side of the screen to begin another line. (This quick return is called *horizontal retrace*.) Meanwhile, the vertical deflection is changing at a much slower rate, so that by the time the next horizontal scan line starts, the beam is positioned just below the previous line. (You can see that the horizontal scan lines are not quite horizontal; they slant downward just a little bit because of the changing vertical deflection.) When all the horizontal scan lines are completed, a vertical retrace takes place, in which the beam is blanked and returned as quickly as possible to the top of the screen.

How does all this relate to resolution? In order for the picture on the screen to be refreshed often enough so that there is no objectionable flicker, we need a vertical refresh rate of about 50 to 90 Hertz. Vertical resolution is related to the number of horizontal scan lines that occur in a complete vertical scan. Multiply this number by the vertical refresh rate and you'll get the horizontal frequency (scan rate). As you can see, the higher the vertical resolution, the higher the horizontal frequency must be. The circuitry needed to do horizontal scanning gets more and more expensive as the horizontal scan rate increases, which is one of the reasons why high-resolution monitors cost more than low-resolution ones.

The horizontal resolution depends upon the number of clumps of phospher dots across the screen and upon how quickly the beams that illuminate these clumps can be turned on and off during a horizontal scan. This determines the required video amplifier frequency, which is 4.5 megaHertz for a television set but can be many times this for a high-resolution monitor (another reason for increased cost). A final factor in resolution is the dot pitch (the size of the dot clumps on the picture tube). No matter what you do, you can't get a pixel to be smaller than the dot pitch. We'll get into more detail on this later.

Early monitors and current TV sets have a single resolution specification, using fixed horizontal and vertical frequencies. Modern computer monitors must be capable of handling a number of different resolutions and consequently are capable of variable scan rates.

Another thing to be considered is the concept of interlace. This is used on all current TV sets. Suppose, for example, that a vertical scan rate of 60 Hertz is needed to avoid flicker that is objectionable to the human eye. Now suppose we fool the eye by scanning only every other horizontal line of the picture during one vertical scan and then scanning the in-between lines on the next vertical scan. The eye thinks the vertical refresh rate is 60 Hertz and does not perceive any objectionable flicker, but the actual rate to scan a complete picture is 30 Hertz, causing the frequencies to be halved and thus the cost reduced. This technique is called interlacing. Its success depends upon very precise positioning of the scan lines. In TV, a vertical scan consists of 262.5 lines. The first scan begins at the top left of the screen, but the next one begins midway vertically between the first two lines of the original scan and halfway across the screen horizontally. Thus the half line of the 262.5 lines is at the end of the first vertical scan and at the beginning of the second vertical scan. It's best to avoid interlacing if you can. Any jitter in the CRT deflection circuits is much more evident when the interlacing technique is used. This doesn't matter too much on a television, because most of the jitter is at the power line frequency and the vertical display frequency is synched to this; it is much more of a problem with computer displays, where the vertical frequency and the power line frequency are different. Thus you'll find that a noninterlaced picture is usually better than an interlaced one.

If you're going to buy a new monitor, you ought to get one with a variable scan frequency, a maximum resolution of at least 1024 768 pixels (the horizontal resolution is normally given first), and a dot pitch of no more than 0.28 mm. The higher the resolution and lower the dot pitch, the better.

Before going into how a display is created, let's look a little deeper into the constraints of the CRT deflection system. Cost is not the only factor in selecting horizontal and vertical scan frequencies. The horizontal and vertical deflection yokes that comprise the CRT beam deflection system can be designed to work efficiently only over a very narrow range of frequencies. The driver circuits for these deflection circuits are designed as an integral part of the whole deflection system to match the yoke frequency constraints. In television sets, the deflection system frequency ranges are very narrow; the only control of the exact frequencies is by horizontal and vertical sync signals that are sent from the display adapter card. If the sync signals are close enough in frequency to the natural frequencies of the TV deflection system, they will lock the deflection system to their exact frequencies, and everything will be fine. If they are too far off, the TV deflection system will go its own merry way, and all that will appear on your screen is a meaningless jumble.

What about multi-sync monitors? Such modern computer monitors have deflection systems that can be synched to a number of different sets of frequencies. You need to be sure, however, that your display adapter card doesn't send synchronization information to the monitor at frequencies for which it wasn't designed. If it does, you'll at least get an unreadable scramble on the screen, and in the worst cases, the monitor can self-destruct. Multi-sync deflection takes place electronically or through relays that switch when a different frequency is recognized. In either case, more sophisticated and more expensive circuits are required, and that is another reason why multi-sync monitors cost more. It would be nice if the specs for a monitor told you how good the method for changing frequencies was and whether the monitor was subject to self-destruction if the wrong sync frequencies are applied. Since this is the kind of information that manufacturers don't want to talk about, the only way to be sure of a new monitor is to watch a demo unit in operation for all of the display modes that you are interested in using. If there are disturbing clunks when shifting from one mode to another, if there are strange flashes and changes in display size, or if you just don't like the appearance of the display, try another model.

We now know how the deflection system works, but just sweeping a beam across the face of a CRT doesn't result in a display. What happens is that while the beam position is being swept across the face of the CRT, signals applied to the red, green, and blue electron guns determine how large a stream of electrons hits the florescent dots on the front of the screen. If you don't want anything displayed on the screen at a particular point, you make sure that all beams are off at that point; if you want a brilliant red at a particular point, you make sure the red gun is on full and the other two are off, and so forth. The VGA card takes care of determining what signals are sent to what guns. (The VGA requires an analog monitor, which means that the gun signals can take on any value over some specified range, giving a lot more color combinations than the EGA, which uses a digital monitor that has only a few discrete levels possible for each color gun signal.) To paint two adjacent pixels on the CRT screen in different colors, you have to be able to switch the gun levels in the time required for the deflection system to move the beams from one pixel location to another. This time can be determined by the fact that we know how many pixels are in a line, how many lines are in a screen, and how many screens are displayed in a second. The reciprocal of the pixel time determines the video frequency at which all of the monitor circuitry that carries red, green, and blue signals from the monitor inputs to the electron guns must work. You don't have to worry about this; it is a problem for the engineers who designed the monitor. However, you should note that the higher the video frequency, the more expensive the video circuits are to build, so that this also causes the price of high-resolution monitors to go up. It is possible to design a monitor with a video frequency bandwidth that is too small for the resolutions that are to be supported. This makes the monitor cheaper (this is done all the time with television sets), but you'll notice the difference in the blurring of your high-resolution displays.

Finally, no matter how good the frequency response (and consequently the resolution) of your video system, the ultimate limit to how good the resolution on the screen can be is the size of the florescent dots on the front of the screen. Most high-resolution multi-sync monitors have dot sizes of 0.28 mm to 0.31 mm. In this case, the smaller the dot size, the better resolution you get. Of course if you are using nothing but the very lowest resolution modes, small dot size is a waste, since it will just give you a display with a lot of black space between dots, but generally, as graphics capabilities improve, you're going to want all of the resolution you can get.

The Video Graphics Array (VGA) Card

The Video Graphics Array (VGA) card accepts digital data from the computer, converts it in various ways, stores it in four memory planes, and converts it to analog signals for transmission to the red, green, and blue inputs of the monitor. It also sets up all the proper timing relationships and sends the horizontal and vertical sync signals to the monitor. Figure 2-1 shows a block diagram of the VGA circuitry.

Figure 2-1. Block Diagram of Video Graphics Array (VGA)

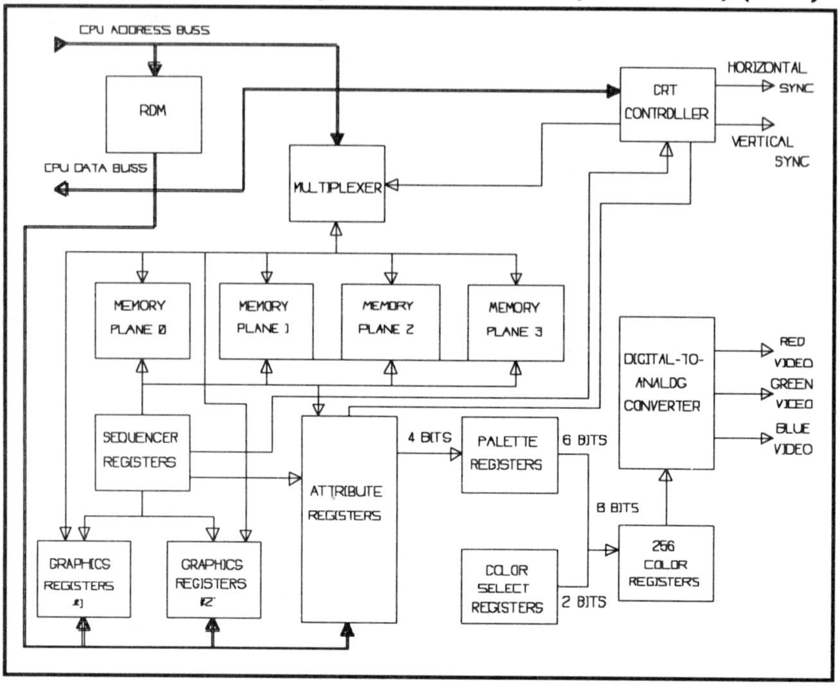

All of the operations of the VGA are controlled by registers on the card that store critical parameters. Chapter 3 will describe these registers and their contents in detail. Here, we're just giving an overview. The CRT controller registers, shown at the upper right of the block diagram, determine all of the timing parameters for the card and monitor. For any supported display mode, they send the proper horizontal and vertical sync signals to the monitor. These are derived from a high-frequency master clock, which also produces the proper timing signals that are used by the digital-to-analog converter to convert the color information for each pixel into analog red, green, and blue voltages for output to the monitor. The remainder of the card consists of four memory planes and the control circuits needed to process data to and from memory.

The reason for four memory planes is that the original EGA modes required 256K of memory to store the data for the highest-resolution screen, whereas only 64K of computer memory space was available. Consequently, IBM broke the necessary memory up into four planes, all four being addressed by the same 64K memory address space. Through the use of the graphics, sequencer, and attribute registers, data from the computer for a particular memory address is routed to those of the four memory planes that must be activated for a particular color. In order to be backward compatible, the VGA uses the same four memory planes in 16 color modes. Super VGA boards now use much more than 256K of memory (1-Megabyte boards are common) so that additional paging schemes are needed to fit into the 64K computer memory address space.

In 16 color modes with default color selection, the four memory planes correspond to the red, green, blue, and intensity portions of the color signal, but as colors or modes are changed, this is more often an abstraction than a reality. To get back to the reality of colors, there are 256 color registers, each of which contains 18 bits-6 bits for red, 6 bits for green, and 6 bits for blue. Consequently, a color register can define one of 262,144 shades of color. For 256-color display modes, the information from the memory planes selects one of these 256 registers, and that register in turn controls generation of the proper voltages for the monitor color inputs. For the 16-color display modes, the information from the memory planes selects one of 16 palette registers. Each palette register can contain a value from 0 to 63 (6 bits), which is combined with 2 bits of information from the color select registers to create an 8-bit signal that selects one of the 256-color registers to control the color of a designated pixel. Thus, by changing the palette register contents, it is possible to select 16 from 64 possible choices and then, by resetting the color select registers, it is possible to choose any one of four different sets of color registers designated by the same palette register assignments.

This gives you some idea of how all of the registers and hardware tie together. In the next chapter, we give details of the register assignments and usages, which will bring you a lot closer to making use of some of the interesting features that are hidden in the register capabilities.

The Enhanced Graphics Adapter (EGA)

The Enhanced Graphics Adapter (EGA) is just like the VGA if you chop off the digital-to-analog converter, the 256 color registers, and the color select register. The EGA has no 256-color modes. For the 16-color modes, the outputs from the palette registers are used directly to select 16 of 64 possible colors. The six bits from the palette registers correspond to 25% levels of red, green, and blue and 75% levels of red, green, and blue, respectively. Thus four levels of each color are possible, 0, 25%, 75%, and 100%, by the right combinations of these bits. These bits are sent directly to the monitor which has digital inputs for the six bits.

3

Writing and Compiling C++ Graphics Code

The information in this book is designed to let you get right down to the basics of how your computer works with the graphics adapter card and display monitor. It will enable you to create breathtakingly beautiful displays that keep up with the graphics state of the art. This is done by avoiding any interface programs that are limited by current technology. Unfortunately, hardware design for PCs is moving so fast that such interface programs are usually obsolete before you buy them. You are quite likely to have a graphics adapter card and monitor that can produce display having higher resolution and more colors than the interface program ever conceived of. You can make full use of your new capabilities with minor modifications of the programs in this book. However, you do need to learn how to navigate through the maze of operating systems and C++ compilers that are currently available. This chapter will describe the mechanics of that process, which can be quite bewildering when you encounter some of the complexities for the first time.

Compiling and Running C++ Programs from DOS

If you're a devoted fan of the Disk Operating System (DOS), don't dispair. Technology has not yet passed you by. In fact, if your aim is to produce a beautiful graphics display, you're probably better off with DOS than anything else. Windows, for example, sets up a display mode for your graphics card and would prefer to stick with it. It's not too happy when you attempt to override this selection. And why would you want to anyway? You want to produce a full display screen in some particular graphics mode; that's what DOS does best. If you're running DOS, just load your C++ compiler and you're off and running.

Compiling and Running C++ Programs from Windows

What if you're running Windows? If you use Windows 3.1, no problem. Just exit Windows and return to DOS. If you're running Windows 95, you may have one of the newer C++ compilers that run from Windows anyway. You'll be able to compile your programs and then run them without difficulty. But suppose you have a compiler such as Borland C++ version 3.1 that runs from DOS. In this case, you have three options. The easiest is to run the compiler from a DOS window. You can select the *My Computer* on your Windows display by clicking with your mouse and then navigate through the paths to run the compiler. Typically this might require you to select drive C, the *BORLANDC* directory, the *BIN* directly within that, and finally the compiler program *BCC*. If you're going to be doing this very often, create a shortcut when you get to the program by holding down the left mouse button and dragging the program icon to the *Start* icon. Now you can run the program as a DOS session within Windows 95. The keys Alt-Enter (pressed simultaneously) enable you to toggle between viewing the program in a window and viewing it full screen. While you're working with the compiler, if you want to run another program, you may need to press these keys to get to the windowed mode so that you can find the proper icons for the new program that you want to run. On the other hand, when you are ready to compile and run your program, you'll want to be in the full-screen mode; if you aren't, you may get an error message telling you that you are trying to use display memory in a way that is incompatible with the windowed mode.

Some Super VGA boards won't properly create displays for the programs in this book if run in a DOS window within Windows. If yours is one of these, or if for some other reason, you aren't comfortable running in Windows 95, there are still two ways to get to a DOS kernel without Windows 95 running at all. If you're already in Windows 95, click your mouse on *Shut Down*. From the menu that comes up, select *Restart Your Computer in MS-DOS Mode*. The computer will reboot and you will be in the MS-DOS mode. Alternately, if you are just booting up your computer for the day, You can hold down the F8 key just before the computer starts to load Windows 95. In this case you'll get a menu of various ways to load Windows. Select the item that says *DOS Prompt only* and you'll soon be running in DOS.

Compiling and Running C++ Programs from OS-2

Finally, let's consider OS-2. If you're a devoted fan of this operating system, you should be able to run the C++ compilers from a DOS window within it. As an alternative, many OS-2 systems are set up with a dual-boot feature that allows you to boot up in either OS-2 or DOS. If you have this feature, boot up in DOS and avoid any problems.

Turbo C++ or Borland C++ through Version 3.1

Borland C++ version 3.1 is the latest version of Borland C++ oriented primarily for the DOS environment. If you can get hold of a copy of this compiler, you'll like it and find it the easiest to use in compiling the programs in this book. Furthermore, I've found that when I compile a program from this book with Borland C++ version 3.1, the resulting program runs much faster than the same C++ code compiled using MicroSoft C++ version 7.0. Here's all you have to do:

1. Go to the directory that contains your Borland C++ compiler and then go to the *BIN* subdirectory. Type *BC*. The compiler will load and start running.

2. Select the *File* menu with your mouse or by hitting Alt-F. If you're going to be creating a new program, choose *New* from the menu that appears. If you want to load an existing program, choose *Open* and then type in the path and file name of the file you want to work with. If you choose *New*, Borland will create a file in the *BIN* sub-directory having the name *NONAME00.CPP*. If you want the file somewhere else or you want it to have a different name, go to the *File* menu and choose *Save as*. When prompted, type in the path and file name you want to use. The file will be saved accordingly and the heading at the top of the display will change to indicate that you are working with this new file. If you load a file from a different directory, be aware that when Borland compiles it, the results are still placed in the *BIN* sub-directory. So, if you load a file *C:\MYDIR\MYFILE.CPP*, and then modify it, compile it, and run it, the files *MYFILE.OBJ*, and *MYFILE.EXE* will be in the *BIN* sub-directory.

3. The default setting does not save any changes you've made in the file if you opt to run it. This may be what you want if you think there is a possibility that the changes you're making may screw things up to the point where you want to get back to the original file. On the other hand, if something goes wrong while you're running, you may lose all your changes. This is particularly true if you're using Windows 95 and find that you need to stop your program in the midst of a run with Ctrl-Break. If you happen to hit this key combination at the wrong time, Windows 95 will come up with an error message and all your changes are gone forever. You can select the option for Borland C++ to save your source file before running each time you select *Run*. In this case your latest version of the file will replace the original file. The original file will still be stored with the extension *BAK*.

4. If one run is unsuccessful and you decide you want the old file version back, now is the time to recovber it from the *BAK* file and rename it to your original name or something else. If you make a couple more minor changes and run again, the *BAK* file will contain your source code as modified, except for the latest minor changes, and the original will be gone forever.

5. Finally, once the source code is set up the way you want it, you simply select the *Run* menu and the *Run* item under it and the program will compile and run. All programs in this book have been tested with Borland C++ version 3.1.

Borland C++ Version 4.0 and Beyond

The later versions of Borland C++ are designed to run in Windows and have Windows programming in mind. There are three ways that this directly affects you if you're writing a DOS program. First, you'll have to create a project file; you can't just compile and run your program directly. Second, if you're running in Windows 95, you either need to be in the DOS mode or in the full-window mode; otherwise when you get ready to run your program, it will fail. If you start running the C++ compiler and it does not fill up the entire screen, you can toggle to the full-screen mode by hitting the key combination Alt-Enter. If at some point you decide you'd like to run another program for awhile without turning of your C++ compiler, you can hit Alt-Enter again to get back to a window that will allow you to access other Windows capabilities. Third, when your program has run to completion, it may return to a Window and you'll get an error message telling you that you can't run the program from a window. No problem. The same Alt-Enter key combination will get you back to the full screen again.

When the Borland C++ version 4.0 compiler begins running, you may have a previous program listing displayed or you may have a blank screen. Here's what you do to compile and run a file.

1. Select the *File* item from the menu with your mouse or by hitting Alt-F. From the menu now displayed, select *Open*. Then find, or type in the full path for and name of your source file. (You don't need the path if your source file is in the same directory that contains the C++ compiler. (If you haven't started a file yet, select *New* from the menu.) Now, you'll have the source file on the screen and can add to, delete, or edit it.

2. Before you compile and run a program, you're going to need to set up a project file. (If you've already done that for a previous run of this same program, you can select *Project* and then *Open*.) Otherwise, select *New* from the *Project* menu. You'll be asked to select a project name. You may choose any eight-letter name followed by the extension *.IDE*. To avoid getting confused, it's a good idea to choose a name that, without the extension, is the same as your principal source file. After typing in the file name, you should select a platform. The correct platform for DOS programs is *DOS Standard*. Then you'll need to choose a target model. All the programs in this book will run with the *Compact* target model. If your source code file is in a directory other that the *BIN* sub-directory where your compiler resides, you'll need to take a couple extra steps. First, select the *Options* menu item. From the menu that appears, select *Project*. A new screen will appear that has a block on the right labeled *Source Directories*. Choose the one marked *Source:* and type in the path for your source code file. Then select *OK*. You'll now be back in the main menu.

3. Select *Debug* and under this choose *Run*. The program should now compile and run. Except for the graphics file viewing

programs, all programs in this book have been tested with Borland C++ version 4.0.

MicroSoft C++ Version 7.0

The MicroSoft C++ version 7.0 compiler is not as Windows oriented as Borland C++ version 4.0, but there are some similarities. One of these is that you will need a project file in order to compile and run your program.

Here's how to get going.

1. From the menu that appears when the program begins to run, choose the menu item *Project*. Under this, if you already have a project file set up, select *Open*; otherwise choose *New*. You'll now find yourself in a new menu at the point where you are asked to select a project name. The path to the compiler sub-directory will already appear in the window. Hit the right-arrow key once to avoid erasing this path when you make your next entry. Then back up to just after the last backslash on the right and enter your project name. Again, it saves confusion to have the main part of the project name the same as that of your main source code file. The proper extension to use for a MicroSoft C++ project is *.IDE*.

2. You next need to choose the item *Select Project Template*. Under this, for run-time support, you want to select *C++*. Then, from the options available choose *DOS.EXE*. You'll now be asked to select the source code files needed for the project. The file names from which you can choose are all in the *BIN* sub-directory that contains your C++ compiler. Don't be fooled by the fact that you can type in a full path name and file name; when the file name is included in your project file, it will be stripped of any path you type in. Therefore, before starting a project, you need to make sure that you have copied the source code files to the *BIN* sub-directory. Once you have selected all source code file names for the project list, you can select the *Save List* item. This will save the project file listing and return you to the main menu.

3. Now you can select the *Project* item and choose the *Build All* option. The compiler will then compile your file. If there are no errors, a screen will appear having an option *Run Program*. Select this to run the program. If there are errors, you need to select the *View Results* item, which will enable you to view a list of the errors. You can switch back and forth between this list and your source code listing and insert the needed corrections. When you think you've fixed everything, select *Project* and *Build All* to recompile. Eventually you'll get rid of all the errors and have a running program. Except for the graphics file viewing programs, all programs in this book have been tested with MicroSoft C++ version 7.0.

MicroSoft Visual C++

Version 4.0 of MicroSoft Visual C++ is designed only to create Windows programs; it will not work for creating and compiling DOS programs. However, along with the Visual C++ version 4.0 CD-ROM, you should have received another CD-ROM that contains MicroSoft Visual C++ Version 1.52, which can create DOS programs. It's best to have your C++ source code in the same sub-directory as the C++ compiler, namely *C:\MVC\BIN*. You can then go through the following process:

1. To begin, you need to choose *Project* from the menu and then select *New*. You'll then be shown a menu that allows you to select the *Project Name* (it can be the same name as your source file without the extension) and the *Project Type*. The type should be *MS-DOS application (.EXE)*. When both of these are correct, you click the mouse on *OK*.

2. You'll now be switched to a menu that allows you to specify the source code files that are to be a part of your project. Note that you have to make sure you have the right directory and sub-directory selected. Then the available source code files will come up in the main window of the menu. Highlight the one you want with a mouse click and then click on the *ADD* button. Then click *Close* to return to the original menu.

3. Select *Project* again and this time select the *Build* item. The compiler will now compile and link your program. If there are

errors or warnings, they will appear in a new window, when the compiler is finished. You can then edit the file to make any necessary corrections and then select *Project* and *Build* again to recompile.

4. When you get all of your own errors corrected, you'll still see one error listed; you'll be told that the program cannot find the library *mafxord.lib*. Just ignore this. Instead of making any further corrections, just return to DOS (or select the *MSDOS Prompt* option from Windows 95).

5. Now go to the directory that contains the compiled version of your program. (It should be the same directory that holds your source code.) You'll recognize the compiled file because it will have the same name as your project, but with the extension *.EXE*. Typing this name and a *Return* should run the program for you.

Part 2

Communicating with the Display Adapter Card

4

VGA/EGA Display Adapter Card Registers

All operations of every PC display adapter card, be it the Monochrome Graphics Adapter (MGA), the Color Graphics Adapter (CGA), the Enhanced Graphics Adapter (EGA), the Video Graphics Array (VGA), or one of the super VGAs, can be controlled by directly accessing a series of registers through the computer input/output ports. These registers store information used to determine the display resolution, color properties, and many other parameters that are needed to generate the proper display mode. The original IBM PC display adapters (MGA and CGA) as well as the Hercules Graphics Adapter (HGA) made use of the Motorola 6845 integrated circuit to control display operations. This integrated circuit has a set of basic registers for display control. All display adapters developed since then have similar sets of registers so that downward compatibility can be maintained (at least at the ROM BIOS level). Improvements in display resolution, etc., have made some of the 6845 registers inadequate, so the EGA, VGA, and Super VGAs have some changes and additions to the CRT controller register set (which mimics the 6845 registers) as well as many added registers. The changes and additions to the CRT controller registers have been made in such a way that any software developed for the MGA, CGA, or HGA that works through the ROM BIOS will work equally well with one of the more advanced display adapter cards. However, software designed to send commands directly to the registers of the MGA, CGA, or HGA may need modification to work with EGA, VGA, or Super VGAs to achieve the same type of display that would have been produced on the screen by one of the original 6845-equipped adapters. Later, when you look at the detailed comparison of the EGA/VGA controller registers and the 6845 in Table 4-2, you'll note some differences that can cause trouble in conversion. This will provide a starting point if difficulties occur when trying to use very old software packages with a new display adapter card.

The new registers that have been added to the EGA and VGA are used for such things as manipulating the display memory planes, determining which colors are to be output to the screen, and selecting new color modes. The newer, so-called Super VGA cards have additional registers besides those specified for the EGA and VGA. Unfortunately, there is no standardization of Super VGA characteristics, so that the added registers and their uses differ for each different manufacturer of a Super VGA chip set. Furthermore, manufacturers of these chip sets are continually coming up with improved versions, in which the additional registers and how they operate may have changed from the previous version. All this means is that, first, we can't possibly describe in this book the operation of all the chip sets currently on the market and, second, even if we could, the information could very well be obsolete by the time you get it. Fortunately, the Video Electronic Standards Association (VESA) has defined a standard set of ROM BIOS video services that will enable you to set video modes and do about everything else you need to do with a display adapter card except actually write a color to a pixel on the screen. Furthermore, one of the VESA services allows you to read information from the display adapter card that allows you to write a pixel to the screen by communicating directly with the internal registers of the display adapter card, without knowing in detail just how these registers work. If you have a recent Super VGA card, the VESA services will work for you. These VESA services will be described in detail in Chapter 7.

If you have an early Super VGA card that was produced before the VESA standard was established, or was designed to an earlier version of the VESA standard, you may need to get the manufacturer's technical data on how the chip set works and devise your own programs. Sometimes this is easy, but more often you will find that you have to buy a technical manual containing this information, and even finding out where to get it may require several letters or phone calls.

The remainder of this chapter will be devoted to a detailed description of the registers that are used in the standard VGA card and how to use them. This will include those registers that are a part of the earlier cards and an indication of differences you should be aware of if you are programming for an earlier card or if you want your programs to be able to run on any display adapter that a potential user may have in his system.

Accessing Display Adapter Card Registers

Before getting into the details of the individual registers, let's look at how one communicates with an output port in general. Each I/O port is assigned a number. If you are using a MicroSoft C or C++ compiler, the proper command to read the contents of a port is

```
bbbb = inp(aaaa);
```

where *aaaa* is a byte giving the port number and *bbbb* is the name of a variable to which a byte of information from the port will be transferred. This variable may be of type *char* or *int*. If you use a different type, you're likely to get in trouble. Writing to a port with MicroSoft C or C++ compilers is done with the command

```
outp(aaaa,bbbb);
```

where *aaaa* is the port number and *bbbb* is the byte which is sent to the port.

If you are using a Borland C or C++ compiler you may also use these commands or you may use the commands

```
bbbb = inportb(aaaa);
```

and

```
outportb(aaaa, bbbb);
```

If you use this latter set of commands, however, you won't be compatible with MicroSoft compilers.

In communicating with display adapter card registers, you will mostly find that they consist of sets of registers assigned to a pair of I/O ports. How does this work? Suppose, for example, that you want to communicate with one of the CRT controller registers, which are assigned to ports 3D4H and 3D5H. You first determine the number of the CRT controller register you want to talk to. Let's suppose it's number 12H. You now output this to the index register port 3D4H as follows:

```
outp(0x3D4, 0x12);
```

(Note that throughout the text, when we give a hexadecimal number, we follow it by an *H*, whereas in programming for a C or C++ compiler, a hexadecimal number is identified by preceeding it by *0x*.) This statement selects the register to be addressed so that you can then use another *inp* or *outp* command, addressing the data register port (3D5H). For example

```
outp(0x3d5, dddd);
```

where *dddd* is the byte you wish to send to the register.

So far, we've dealt with input and output commands that transfer a single byte through a port. There are also commands that take a word (two bytes) and transmit it to two adjacent ports (the least significant byte of the word to the port specified and the most significant byte of the word to the next adjacent port. Suppose we use the command

```
outpw(0x3d4, 0x1254);
```

This transmits 12H to port 3d4H and 54H to port 3d5H. It is the same as the two commands:

```
outp(0x3d4, 0x12);
outp(0x3d5, 0x54);
```

The same word command may be used with MicroSoft C and C++ and Borland C and C++. In addition, Borland C and C++ compilers have the equivalent command *outport*.

Now that you know how to communicate with the registers in programming with C or C++, let's see what information needs to be sent to or received from the display adapter registers.

General Registers

Table 4-1 lists the general registers included with the EGA/VGA. There are five such registers, each with its own port address, so no indexing is necessary. Please note that one port address may be used both to write to one register and to read from a different one when the first register is write-only and the second register is read-only. Similarly, one port address may be used to write to a register and another port address use to read the contents of the same register.

TABLE 4-1. GENERAL REGISTERS MISCELLANEOUS OUTPUT REGISTER

Write Register Address: 3C2H

Read Register Address: 3CCH

Bit 7	Bit 6	Bit 5	Bit 4	Bit 3	Bit 2	Bit 1	Bit 0
Sync Polarity.		Odd/ Even Page.	Disable Video.	Clock Select.		Enable RAM. 0= disable1 = enable.	I/O Address Select. 0=3BxH 1=3DxH

The **Sync Polarity** bits control the polarity of the sync signals that are sent to the monitor. VGA monitors not only use the sync signals to lock in the line and frame frequencies, but also make use of the polarity information to determine how many lines make up a frame. The number of lines per frame is shown in the following table:

Bits 7 and 6	Resolution
11	480 lines.
10	350 lines.
01	400 lines.
00	Reserved.

The **Odd/Even Page** bit selects which page (0 or 1) is used for display when in modes 0, 1, 2, 3, and 7.

The **Disable Video** bit enables the video drivers for normal operation or disables them for control of the display through the feature connector.

The **Clock Select** bits determine the clock frequency. They have the following meaning:

Bits 3 and 2	EGA Clock Frequency	VGA Clock Frequency
11	Reserved.	Reserved.
10	External Clock.	Reserved (may be used on super VGAs).
01	16.257 MHz.	28.322 MHz.
00	14.161 MHz.	25.175 MHz.

The **Enable RAM** bit determines whether display memory can be accessed by the processor.

The **I/O Address Select** bit determines whether the display adapter registers are at the monochrome display address block (3BxH) or the color display address block (3DxH).

FEATURE CONTROL REGISTER

Register Write Address:
Monochrome Adapters: 3BAH
Color Adapters: 3DAH

Register Read Address (VGA Only): 3CAH

Bit 7	Bit 6	Bit 5	Bit 4	Bit 3	Bit 2	Bit 1	Bit 0
				Reserved.		Feature Control Bit 1.	Feature Control Bit 0.

The two **Feature Control** bits, when set to 1, cause the corre-sponding bits on the feature connector to go high; when set to 0, these bits cause the corresponding bits on the feature connector to go low.

INPUT STATUS REGISTER ZERO

Read Register Address: 3C2H (Read Only)

Bit 7	Bit 6	Bit 5	Bit 4	Bit 3	Bit 2	Bit 1	Bit 0
CRT Vertical Retrace Pending.	Feature Connector Bit 1.	Feature Connector Bit 0.	Switch Sense.				

The **Vertical Retrace Pending** bit, when 1, indicates that a vertical retrace interrupt is being processed; when set to 0, the vertical retrace interrupt has been cleared.

Feature Connector bit 1 indicates the status of the feature control bit 1 on pin 20 (for EGA) or pin 17 (VGA) of the feature connector; feature connector bit 0 indicates the setting of the feature control bit 0 on pin 21 (EGA) or pin 19 (VGA) of the feature connector.

The **Sense Switch** bit reports the status of a selected sense switch (0 = off; 1 = on). There are four sense switches; the one that is read is determined by the clock select bits (bits 3 and 2) of the miscellaneous output register.

INPUT STATUS REGISTER ONE

Read Register Address: (Read Only)
Monochrome Adapters: 3BAH
Color Adapters: 3DAH

Bit 7	Bit 6	Bit 5	Bit 4	Bit 3	Bit 2	Bit 1	Bit 0
		Diagnos-tic 1.	Diagnos-tic 0.	Vertical Retrace.			Display Enable

The **Diagnostic** bits are connected to two of the eight-color outputs of the attribute controller. The color plane enable (bits 5 and 4 of attribute register 12H) determines which color outputs appear at these bits as follows:

Color Plane Register		Input Status Register One	
Bit 5	Bit 4	Bit 5	Bit 4
0	0	P2	P0
0	1	P5	P4
1	0	P3	P1
1	1	P7	P6

When using the EGA, the only method for determining the contents of the color lookup table in the attribute controller is through the use of these diagnostic bits. With the VGA, the attribute register contents can be read directly.

The **Display Enable** bit, when 0, indicates that the display is in the display mode. When this bit is 1, the display is not in the display mode (either horizontal or vertical retrace is occurring).

CRT Controller Registers

The CRT controller registers are the only registers that were used in early display adapter boards. Table 4-2 describes the CRT controller registers, comparing the 6845 version with the EGA/VGA version. If you are trying to convert programs that have direct access to the 6845 to use with the EGA or VGA, you need to note particularly the differences in registers 3, 4, 5, 6, 7, and 8.

TABLE 4-2. CRT CONTROLLER REGISTERS

Index Register Address:
Monochrome Adapters: 3B4H
Color Adapters: 3D4H

Data Register Address:
Monochrome Adapters: 3B5H
Color Adapters: 3D5H

Register Number	6845 Register Description	EGA/VGA Register Description
00H	Total Horizontal Columns	Total Horizontal Columns
01H	Horizontal Display End	Horizontal Display End
02H	Horizontal Sync Position	Start Horizontal Blank
03H	Horizontal Sync Width	End Horizontal Blank
04H	Total Vertical Lines	Horizontal Sync Start
05H	Vertical Adjust	Horizontal Sync End
06H	Vertical Displayed	Vertical Total
07H	Vertical Sync Position	Overflow
08H	Interlace Mode	Initial Row Address
09H	Max Scan Line Address	Max Row Address
0AH	Cursor Start Register	Cursor Start Position
0BH	Cursor End Register	Cursor End Position
0CH	Screen Start Address (MSB)	Start Address (MSB)
0DH	Screen Start Address (MSB)	Start Address (MSB)
0EH	Cursor Address (MSB)	Cursor Location (MSB)
0FH	Cursor Address (LSB)	Cursor Location (LSB)
10H	Light Pen Register (MSB)	Vertical Sync Start
11H	Light Pen Register (LSB)	Vertical Sync End
12H		Vertical Display End
13H		Row Offset
14H		Underline Row address
15H		Start Vertical Blank
16H		End Vertical Blank
17H		CRTC Model Control
18H		Line Compare

A number of the CRT controller registers are devoted to the timing of the display. The horizontal timing descriptors are shown in Figure 4-1. They include the total length of a horizontal line in characters, the beginning and end of the horizontal blanking and retrace signals, and the length of the displayed portion of the line. They are defined a little differently than one might ordinarily think of doing it, so look at the diagram carefully when you are adjusting the contents of these registers. Figure 4-2 shows the vertical timing descriptors. These differ from the horizontal ones in that they are measured in terms of scan lines rather than characters.

CRT CONTROLLER REGISTER 00H—HORIZONTAL TOTAL

Index Register Address:
Monochrome Adapters: 3B4H
Color Adapters: 3D4H
Data Register Address:
Monochrome Adapters: 3B5H
Color Adapters: 3D5H

Index = 0

Bit 7	Bit 6	Bit 5	Bit 4	Bit 3	Bit 2	Bit 1	Bit 0
Total number of character times per horizontal scan minus 5 for VGA. Total number of character times per horizontal scan minus 2 for EGA.							

This register contains the number of characters that make up a total scan line, including border and blanked character positions. For obscure reasons, the actual number in the register is two less than the actual total for the EGA and five less for the VGA.

CRT CONTROLLER REGISTER 01H—HORIZONTAL DISPLAY END

Index Register Address:
Monochrome Adapters: 3B4H
Color Adapters: 3D4H
Data Register Address:
Monochrome Adapters: 3B5H
Color Adapters: 3D5H

Index = 1

Bit 7	Bit 6	Bit 5	Bit 4	Bit 3	Bit 2	Bit 1	Bit 0
Character count at which horizontal display is to end minus 1.							

Figure 4-1. Horizontal Timing Diagram

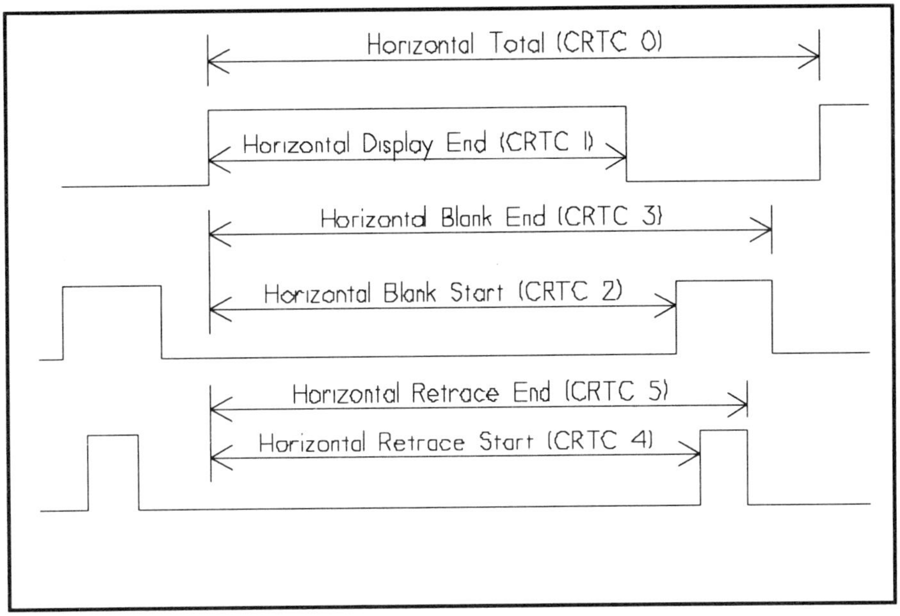

Figure 4-2. Vertical Timing Diagram

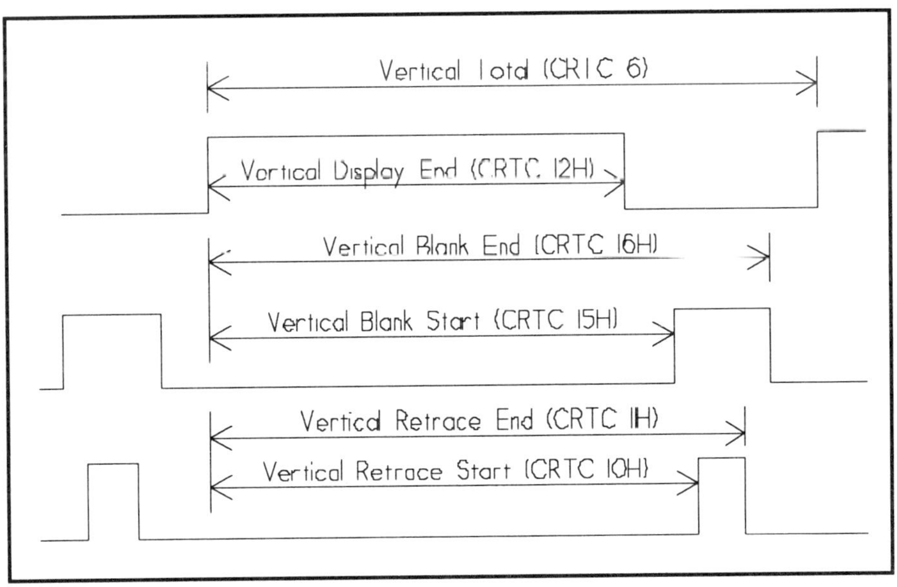

This is the total number of characters actually displayed minus one. Note that the character is defined as consisting of 8 pixels, so that with a one-byte register we can have a resolution of up to 2040 pixels, which is more than adequate for all display systems currently available.

CRT CONTROLLER REGISTER 02H—HORIZONTAL BLANK START

Index Register Address: Index = 2
Monochrome Adapters: 3B4H
Color Adapters: 3D4H
Data Register Address:
Monochrome Adapters: 3B5H
Color Adapters: 3D5H

Bit 7	Bit 6	Bit 5	Bit 4	Bit 3	Bit 2	Bit 1	Bit 0
Character count at which horizontal blanking is to start.							

The horizontal blanking pulse will begin at the start of the character whose number is given in this register.

CRT CONTROLLER REGISTER 03H—HORIZONTAL BLANK END

Index Register Address: Index = 3
Monochrome Adapters: 3B4H
Color Adapters: 3D4H
Data Register Address:
Monochrome Adapters: 3B5H
Color Adapters: 3D5H

Bit 7	Bit 6	Bit 5	Bit 4	Bit 3	Bit 2	Bit 1	Bit 0
Test bit. Normally set to 1.	Horizontal display enable skew. 00 = 0 character clocks. 01 = 1 character clock. 10 = 2 character clocks. 11 = 3 character clocks.		Character count for end of horizontal blanking modulo 32 for EGA. Character count for end of horizontal blanking modulo 64 for VGA (the most significant bit is found in bit 7 of CRTC Register 5 — Horizontal Sync End).				

The **Test** bit should always be set to 1 for normal operation.

The **Horizontal Enable Skew** bits determine the number of character times to skew (delay) the horizontal timing to obtain proper synchronization.

The **End Horizontal Blanking** bits determine the character position for the end of the horizontal blanking pulse. Actually, only the five least significant bits of this value are given. The display adapter begins checking character position values after the blanking pulse begins, and as soon as the last five bits match, the blanking pulse is terminated. For the VGA there is a sixth (most significant) bit for this quantity, which is found in CRT Controller Register 05H—Horizontal Sync End register.

CRT CONTROLLER REGISTER 04H—HORIZONTAL SYNC START

Index = 4

Index Register Address:
Monochrome Adapters: 3B4H
Color Adapters: 3D4H
Data Register Address:
Monochrome Adapters: 3B5H
Color Adapters: 3D5H

Bit 7	Bit 6	Bit 5	Bit 4	Bit 3	Bit 2	Bit 1	Bit 0
Character count at which horizontal sync (retrace) begins.							

This is the character count at which the horizontal sync (retrace) pulse begins. The monitor uses a sawtooth waveform to scan the screen horizontally. The voltage of this waveform starts at zero and increases at a constant rate to sweep the trace across the monitor screen. When the end of the horizontal line is reached, there is a sudden drop to zero, which causes the trace to jump back to the beginning of the line. This pulse provides the signal that it is time for that jump to begin.

CRT CONTROLLER REGISTER 05H—HORIZONTAL SYNC END

Index Register Address:
Monochrome Adapters: 3B4H
Color Adapters: 3D4H
Data Register Address:
Monochrome Adapters: 3B5H
Color Adapters: 3D5H

Index = 5

Bit 7	Bit 6	Bit 5	Bit 4	Bit 3	Bit 2	Bit 1	Bit 0
Bit 5 of Hori-zontal Blank End for VGA modes	Horizontal sync skew 00 = 0 character clocks. 01 = 1 character clock. 10 = 2 character clocks. 11 = 3 character clocks.		Horizontal sync end. Character count for horizontal sync (retrace) end modulo 32.				

The **Horizontal Blank End** bit is the most significant bit of the horizontal blank end value given in CRT Controller Register 03H—Horizontal Blank End Register for VGAs only.

The **Horizontal Sync Skew** bits determine the number of character times to delay the horizontal sync to obtain proper synchronization.

The **Horizontal Sync End** bits determine the character position for the end of the horizontal sync pulse. Actually only the five least significant bits of this value are given. The display adapter begins checking character position values after the blanking pulse begins, and as soon as the last five bits match, the horizontal sync pulse is terminated.

CRT CONTROLLER REGISTER 06H—VERTICAL TOTAL

Index = 6

Index Register Address:
Monochrome Adapters: 3B4H
Color Adapters: 3D4H
Data Register Address:
Monochrome Adapters: 3B5H
Color Adapters: 3D5H

Bit 7	Bit 6	Bit 5	Bit 4	Bit 3	Bit 2	Bit 1	Bit 0
VGA modes: Horizontal scan lines per vertical frame - 2. (Eight least significant bits. Most significant bits are found in bit 5 and bit 0 of CRT Controller Register 07H—Overflow Register.) EGA modes: Horizontal scan lines per vertical frame - 1. (Eight least significant bits. Most significant bits are found in bit 5 and bit 0 of CRT Controller Register 07H—Overflow Register.)							

This register contains the eight least significant bits of the total number of horizontal scan lines that make up a vertical frame (minus 2 for the VGA and minus 1 for the EGA). The most significant bit is bit 5, and the next most significant bit is bit 0 in the CRT Controller Register 07H—Overflow Register.

CRT CONTROLLER REGISTER 07H—OVERFLOW

Index = 7

Index Register Address:
Monochrome Adapters: 3B4H
Color Adapters: 3D4H
Data Register Address:
Monochrome Adapters: 3B5H
Color Adapters: 3D5H

Bit 7	Bit 6	Bit 5	Bit 4	Bit 3	Bit 2	Bit 1	Bit 0
Vertical Sync Start (bit 9).	Vertical Display Enable End (bit 9).	Vertical Total (bit 9).	Line Com-pare (Split Screen) (bit 8).	Vertical Blank Start (bit 8).	Vertical Sync Start (bit 8).	Vertical Display Enable End (bit 8).	Vertical Total (bit 8).

The overflow register provides a place to store additional bits needed to expand quantities contained in other registers that need to be expanded for the EGA/VGA. The designations of the bits are shown in the table; a full description of each quantity is given in connection with the register where its main portion is stored.

CRT CONTROLLER REGISTER 08H—
PRESET ROW SCAN/INITIAL ROW ADDRESS

Index Register Address: Index = 8
Monochrome Adapters: 3B4H
Color Adapters: 3D4H
Data Register Address:
Monochrome Adapters: 3B5H
Color Adapters: 3D5H

Bit 7	Bit 6	Bit 5	Bit 4	Bit 3	Bit 2	Bit 1	Bit 0
Reserved.	Byte Panning Control. Number of bytes to pan for horizontal panning.		Preset Row Scan. Starting row for first character to be displayed on screen (normally 0).				

The **Reserved** bit should not be used.

The **Byte Panning Control** bits indicate the number of bytes to pan during a horizontal panning operation.

The **Preset Row Scan** bits indicate the starting row of the character box for the first line of characters to be displayed at the top of the screen. Normally, this is 0, to display the full characters. If one desires to provide a smooth scrolling of the display vertically, rather than having the display scroll by jumping a row of characters at a time, then the beginning row of the character box of the first character line must change incrementally. This is done by incrementing the number in this section of this register.

CRT CONTROLLER REGISTER 09H—MAXIMUM ROW ADDRESS

Index Register Address: Index = 9
Monochrome Adapters: 3B4H
Color Adapters: 3D4H
Data Register Address:
Monochrome Adapters: 3B5H
Color Adapters: 3D5H

Bit 7	Bit 6	Bit 5	Bit 4	Bit 3	Bit 2	Bit 1	Bit 0
Enable Double Scan. 0 = normal 200-line scan. 1 = converts 200-line scan to 400-line scan.	Line compare. (Split Screen) (bit 9).	Vertical Blank Start (bit 9).	Number of scan lines per character row minus 1.				

The **Enable Double Scan** bit, when set to 1, divides the clock in the row scan counter by two so that each horizontal line is displayed twice, enabling a 200-line resolution display to be displayed in 400 lines. (This gives better apparent resolution than an ordinary 200-line display.) When this bit is set to 0, the normal 200-line display is produced.

The **Line Compare** bit is the most significant bit for the line compare value, which is described under CRT Controller Register 18H—Line Compare Register.

The **Vertical Blank Start** bit is the most significant bit for the vertical blank start value, which is described under CRT Controller Register 15H—Vertical Blank Start.

The **Number of Scan Lines Per Character Row** bits define the height of character row in scan lines.

CRT CONTROLLER REGISTER 0AH—CURSOR START ROW ADDRESS

Index Register Address:Index = 0AH
Monochrome Adapters: 3B4H
Color Adapters: 3D4H
Data Register Address:
Monochrome Adapters: 3B5H
Color Adapters: 3D5H

Bit 7	Bit 6	Bit 5	Bit 4	Bit 3	Bit 2	Bit 1	Bit 0
Reserved.		Cursor on/off. 0 = cursor on. 1 = cursor off.	Cursor Start Row Address. Address of first character scan line at which cursor is enabled.				

The **Cursor On/Off** bit determines if the cursor will be displayed.

The **Cursor Start Row Address** bits indicate the cursor start line of the character cell.

CRT CONTROLLER REGISTER 0BH—CURSOR END ROW ADDRESS

Index Register Address: Index = 0BH
Monochrome Adapters: 3B4H
Color Adapters: 3D4H
Data Register Address:
Monochrome Adapters: 3B5H
Color Adapters: 3D5H

Bit 7	Bit 6	Bit 5	Bit 4	Bit 3	Bit 2	Bit 1	Bit 0
Reserved	Cursor skew 00 = 0 character clocks 01 = 1 character clock 10 = 2 character clocks 11 = 3 character clocks		Address of character scan line at which cursor is disabled				

The **Reserved** bit should not be used.

The **Cursor Skew** bit defines the skew of the cursor signal in character clocks.

The **Cursor End Row Address** bits indicate the line of the character cell at which the cursor should stop being enabled.

CRT CONTROLLER REGISTER 0CH—START ADDRESS HIGH

Index Register Address: Index = 0CH
Monochrome Adapters: 3B4H
Color Adapters: 3D4H
Data Register Address:
Monochrome Adapters: 3B5H
Color Adapters: 3D5H

Bit 7	Bit 6	Bit 5	Bit 4	Bit 3	Bit 2	Bit 1	Bit 0
Display memory address of top lefthand pixel on the screen. This is a 16-bit address. This register contains bits 8–15 of the address. Bits 0–7 are found in CRT Controller Register 0DH—Start Address Low.							

This is the high byte of the 16-bit display memory address of the top lefthand pixel on the screen.

CRT CONTROLLER REGISTER 0DH—START ADDRESS LOW

Index Register Address: Index = 0DH
Monochrome Adapters: 3B4H
Color Adapters: 3D4H
Data Register Address:
Monochrome Adapters: 3B5H
Color Adapters: 3D5H

Bit 7	Bit 6	Bit 5	Bit 4	Bit 3	Bit 2	Bit 1	Bit 0
Display memory address of top lefthand pixel on the screen. This is a 16-bit address. This register contains bits 0–7 of the address. Bits 8–15 are found in CRT Controller Register 0CH—Start Address High.							

This is the low byte of the 16-bit display memory address of the top lefthand pixel on the screen.

CRT CONTROLLER REGISTER 0EH—CURSOR LOCATION HIGH

Index Register Address:
Monochrome Adapters: 3B4H
Color Adapters: 3D4H
Data Register Address:
Monochrome Adapters: 3B5H
Color Adapters: 3D5H

Index = 0EH

Bit 7	Bit 6	Bit 5	Bit 4	Bit 3	Bit 2	Bit 1	Bit 0
Display memory address of cursor location on the screen. This is a 16-bit address. This register contains bits 8–15 of the address. Bits 0–7 are found in CRT Controller Register 0FH—Cursor Location Low.							

This is the high byte of the 16-bit display memory address of the cursor location on the screen.

CRT CONTROLLER REGISTER 0FH—CURSOR LOCATION LOW

Index Register Address:
Monochrome Adapters: 3B4H
Color Adapters: 3D4H
Data Register Address:
Monochrome Adapters: 3B5H
Color Adapters: 3D5H

Index = 0FH

Bit 7	Bit 6	Bit 5	Bit 4	Bit 3	Bit 2	Bit 1	Bit 0
Display memory address of the cursor location on the screen. This is a 16-bit address. This register contains bits 0–7 of the address. Bits 8–15 are found in CRT Controller Register 0EH—Cursor Location High.							

This is the low byte of the 16-bit display memory address of the cursor location on the screen.

CRT CONTROLLER REGISTER 10H—VERTICAL SYNC START

Index Register Address: Index = 10H
Monochrome Adapters: 3B4H
Color Adapters: 3D4H
Data Register Address:
Monochrome Adapters: 3B5H
Color Adapters: 3D5H

Bit 7	Bit 6	Bit 5	Bit 4	Bit 3	Bit 2	Bit 1	Bit 0
These are the lower 8 bits of a 10-bit number specifying the value of the internal line counter when the vertical sync (retrace) pulse begins. Bit 8 of this number is found in bit 2 and bit 9 is found in bit 7 of CRT Controller Register 07H—Overflow.							

These are the eight least significant bytes of the number of the scan line at which vertical retrace starts. The two most significant bytes are in CRT controller register 7.

CRT CONTROLLER REGISTER 11H—VERTICAL SYNC END

Index Register Address: Index = 11H
Monochrome Adapters: 3B4H
Color Adapters: 3D4H
Data Register Address:
Monochrome Adapters: 3B5H
Color Adapters: 3D5H

Bit 7	Bit 6	Bit 5	Bit 4	Bit 3	Bit 2	Bit 1	Bit 0
Protection Bit. 0=can write to CRTC registers 0-7. 1=cannot write to CRTC registers 0-7.	Reserved	Vertical interrupt enable. 0=vertical interrupt can occur. 1=vertical interrupt cannot occur.	Vertical interrupt clear. 0=clear vertical interrupt. 1=no effect.	Scan line at which vertical sync ends modulo 16. Compared with 4 LSB of line counter after vertical sync begins to determine when vertical sync should end.			

It is important to note that if the **Protection** bit is not set to 0, you will not be able to write any data to CRT controller registers 0 to 7 (described previously). This make it impossible to inadvertently change the contents of these registers and thereby damage your monitor. To write to these registers, you must first set the protection bit to 0. When writing is complete, you should reset the protection bit to 1.

The **Reserved** bit should not be used.

The **Vertical Interrupt Enable** bit, when set to zero, causes the INTL line to be asserted when the vertical interrupt signal becomes true.

The **Clear Vertical Interrupt** bit should be set to 0 to clear the vertical interrupt after a vertical interrupt is processed and before interrupts are reenabled.

The **Vertical Sync End** bits determine the value of the internal line counter for the end of the vertical sync (retrace) pulse. Actually, only the four least significant bits of this value are given. The display adapter begins checking the line counter values after the vertical sync pulse begins, and as soon as the last four bits match, the vertical sync pulse is terminated.

CRT CONTROLLER REGISTER 12H—VERTICAL DISPLAY END

Index Register Address: Index = 12H
  Monochrome Adapters: 3B4H
  Color Adapters: 3D4H
Data Register Address:
  Monochrome Adapters: 3B5H
  Color Adapters: 3D5H

Bit 7	Bit 6	Bit 5	Bit 4	Bit 3	Bit 2	Bit 1	Bit 0
These are the lower 8 bits of a 10-bit number specifying the number of the last scan line displayed vertically. Bit 8 of this number is found in bit 1 and bit 9 is found in bit 6 of CRT Controller Register 07H—Overflow Register.							

This register contains the eight least significant bits of the number of the last horizontal line that is displayed at the bottom of the screen. The two most significant bits of this number are found as bits 6 and 1, respectively, of CRT Controller Register 07H—Overflow Register.

CRT CONTROLLER REGISTER 13H—ROW OFFSET

Index Register Address: Index = 13H
Monochrome Adapters: 3B4H
Color Adapters: 3D4H
Data Register Address:
Monochrome Adapters: 3B5H
Color Adapters: 3D5H

Bit 7	Bit 6	Bit 5	Bit 4	Bit 3	Bit 2	Bit 1	Bit 0
Display width (difference in memory addresses of two adjacent vertical pixels) in 16-bit words (if bit 6 of CRTC register 17H—Mode is 1) or in 32-bit double words (if bit 6 of CRTC register 17H—Mode is 0).							

This register specifies the amount that is to be added to the current display memory address to advance from one screen row to the next. This amount is in 16-bit words if bit 6 of CRT Controller Register 17H—Mode Register is set to 1 or in 32-bit double words if bit 6 of CRT Controller Register 17H—Mode Register is set to 0. For example, in a 640-pixel, 16-color mode, each pixel on the screen occupies 1 bit in the memory addressing space. Thus one line requires 80 bytes, so in mode 1, this register would be programmed to 80/2 or 40 (28H) words. For a 320-pixel, 256-color mode, each pixel on the screen occupies one byte in the memory addressing space. Thus one line requires 320 bytes, so in mode 0, this register would be programmed to 320/4 or 80 (50H) double words.

Actually, this register can define a virtual screen that is wider than the actual displayed screen. The display screen can then be considered a window looking at part of this virtual screen, and the horizontal panning capability of the display adapter card can be used to move the window back and forth to display different portions of this virtual screen.

CRT CONTROLLER REGISTER 14H—UNDERLINE ROW ADDRESS

Index Register Address: Index = 14H
Monochrome Adapters: 3B4H
Color Adapters: 3D4H
Data Register Address:
Monochrome Adapters: 3B5H
Color Adapters: 3D5H

Bit 7	Bit 6	Bit 5	Bit 4	Bit 3	Bit 2	Bit 1	Bit 0
Reserved = 0.	Double-Word Mode. 0 = normal word memory addressing. 1 = double word memory addressing.	Count by 4. 0 = normal clocking of memory address counter. 1 = memory address counter is character clock divided by four.	Row address at which underline will occur.				

The **Reserved** bit should always be zero.

The **Double-Word Mode** bit indicates whether the display memory is to be addressed in words or double words.

The **Count by 4** bit clocks the memory address counter with the character clock when set to 0. When set to 1, the memory address counter is clocked by the character clock divided by four (for proper timing when double-word addressing is used). If bit 3 of CRT Controller Register 17H—Mode Register is set to 1, the linear counter will increment twice for each character.

CRT CONTROLLER REGISTER 15H—VERTICAL BLANK START

Index Register Address: Index = 15H
Monochrome Adapters: 3B4H
Color Adapters: 3D4H
Data Register Address:
Monochrome Adapters: 3B5H
Color Adapters: 3D5H

Bit 7	Bit 6	Bit 5	Bit 4	Bit 3	Bit 2	Bit 1	Bit 0
The 8 LSB of a 10 bit-number specifying the value of the line counter at which the vertical blanking interval should start minus one. The ninth bit is found as bit 3 of CRTC Register 07H—Overflow Register and the tenth bit is found as bit 5 of CRTC Register 09H—Maximum Row Address Register.							

These are the eight least significant bits of the number of the scan line at which vertical blanking starts. The ninth bit is in CRT Controller Register 07H—Overflow Register and the tenth bit is found in CRT Controller Register 09H—Maximum Row Address Register.

CRT CONTROLLER REGISTER 16H—VERTICAL BLANK END

Index Register Address: Index = 16H
Monochrome Adapters: 3B4H
Color Adapters: 3D4H
Data Register Address:
Monochrome Adapters: 3B5H
Color Adapters: 3D5H

Bit 7	Bit 6	Bit 5	Bit 4	Bit 3	Bit 2	Bit 1	Bit 0
Scan line at which vertical blanking ends modulo 256. Vertical blanking ends when the eight LSB of the line counter first matches this number after vertical blanking has begun.							

The **Vertical Blanking End** bits determine the value of the internal line counter for the end of the vertical blanking signal. This register contains the eight least significant bits of this value. The display adapter begins checking the line counter values after the vertical blanking signal begins, and as soon as the last eight bits match, the vertical blanking signal is terminated.

CRT CONTROLLER REGISTER 17H—MODE

Index Register Address: Index = 17H
Monochrome Adapters: 3B4H
Color Adapters: 3D4H
Data Register Address:
Monochrome Adapters: 3B5H
Color Adapters: 3D5H

Bit 7	Retrace enable. 0 = places all horizontal and vertical timings in a hold state. 1 = enables horizontal and vertical control signals.
Bit 6	Word/Byte mode 0 = word mode. 1 = byte mode.
Bit 5	Address wrap when in word mode. 0 = address bit 13 sent to LSB of display memory (scan lines separated by 8K bytes). 1 = address bit 15 sent to LSB of display memory (scan lines separated by 32K bytes).
Bit 4	Memory address output control. 0 = enable EGA output drivers. 1 = disable EGA output drivers. Useage varies for different VGA boards.
Bit 3	Linear counter. 0 = memory address counter clocked by character clock. 1 = memory address counter clocked by every other character clock.
Bit 2	Line counter. 0 = clock scan line counter with every horizontal retrace. 1 = clock scan line counter with every other horizontal retrace.

Bit 1	Select row scan counter. 0 = row scan counter bit 1 is placed on memory address bus bit 14 during active display time. 1 = memory addresses are output sequentially. This provides Hercules GA compatibility.
Bit 0	Compatibility mode support. 0 = row scan counter bit 0 is placed on memory bus bit 13 during active display time. 1 = memory addresses are output sequentially. This provides Hercules GA compatibility.

The **Retrace Enable** bit disables all horizontal and vertical timing signals when set to 0. When set to 1, all timing signals are enabled.

The **Word/Byte Mode** bit, when set to 0, permits CGA emulation by shifting the display memory address one position to the left and then placing either address bit 13 or 15 (depending upon the setting of the address wrap bit) in the least significant bit position. When set to 1, addresses are transferred to display memory unaltered. To understand how this works, we need to look at how the CGA is designed. When sending consecutively displayed data to the CGA, all odd-numbered bytes are sent to consecutive display memory addresses, beginning with B8000H. Even-numbered bytes are sent to consecutive display memory addresses starting at BA000H. If we have data addressed to the CGA like this and want to use it with the EGA or VGA, we set the word/byte mode bit to 1, which shifts the addresses one bit to the left and then moves bit 13 (or 15) to the LSB, causing all of the data now to be addressed consecutively as needed for the EGA/VGA.

The **Address Wrap** bit determines whether address bit 13 or 15 should be output to the display memory least significant address line when in the word mode.

The **Memory Address Output Control** bit, when set to 1, disables the EGA display memory drivers. Usage varies on VGA boards. Consult the literature from the manufacturer of your VGA board to determine the use of this bit.

The **Linear Counter** bit increments the linear counter at each character clock when set to 0. When set to 1, the linear counter is incremented on every other character clock.

The **Line Counter** bit increments the line counter at each scan line when set to 0. When set to 1, the line counter is incremented on every other scan line, thereby doubling the vertical timings without affecting the horizontal timings.

The **Select Row Scan Counter** bit, when set to 0, permits compatibility with the Hercules Graphics Adapter (HGA), which uses a four-bank memory, by using the contents of address bit 14 to drive display address bit 1.

The **Compatibility Mode Support** bit, when set to 0, permits compatibility with the CGA, which uses a two-bank memory, by using the contents of address bit 13 to drive display address bit 0.

CRT CONTROLLER REGISTER 18H—LINE COMPARE

Index Register Address: Index = 18H
Monochrome Adapters: 3B4H
Color Adapters: 3D4H
Data Register Address:
Monochrome Adapters: 3B5H
Color Adapters: 3D5H

Bit 7	Bit 6	Bit 5	Bit 4	Bit 3	Bit 2	Bit 1	Bit 0
Display address of start of second window of split-screen display. This is a 10-bit address. The 8 least significant bits (bits 0–7) are in this register. Bit 8 is bit 4 of CRTC Register 07H—Overflow and bit 9 is bit 5 of CRTC Register 09H—Maximum Row Address.							

The display is divided into two windows by clearing the display memory address counter when the horizontal line counter reaches this register's value.

Sequencer Registers

Table 4-3 describes the sequencer registers. These registers control timing and access to the planes of the display memory. To access one of the registers, one first outputs the index number of the register to port 3C4H. The indexed register is then available at port 3C5H.

TABLE 4-3. SEQUENCER REGISTERS

Index Register Address: 3C4H — Data Register Address: 3C5H

Register Name	Index	Status
Reset Register	00H	Read/Write
Clock Mode Register	01H	Read/Write
Write Plane Enable Register	02H	Read/Write
Font Select Register	03H	Read/Write
Memory Mode Register	04H	Read/Write

SEQUENCER REGISTER 00H—RESET

Index Register Address: 3C4H — Index = 0

Data Register Address: 3C5H

Bit 7	Bit 6	Bit 5	Bit 4	Bit 3	Bit 2	Bit 1	Bit 0
						Synchronous Reset and Halt.	Asynchronous Reset and Halt.
						Both must be 1 for sequencer to operate	

Bit 1 commands the timing synchronizer to synchronously clear and halt. Bit 0 commands the timing synchronizer to asynchronously clear and halt. Both bits should be set to 1 for the display to run. Bit 1 should be set to 0 while selecting a new clock frequency. If the synchronous reset period is too long, data may be lost from display memory.

SEQUENCER REGISTER 01H—CLOCKING MODE

Index Register Address: 3C4H
Data Register Address: 3C5H

Index = 1

Bit 7	Bit 6	Bit 5	Bit 4	Bit 3	Bit 2	Bit 1	Bit 0
		Display off. 0 = screen is turned off. 1 = screen is turned on.	32-bit fetch. 0 = load video shifter input latches at normal clock rate. 1 = load video shifter input latches at quarter of clock rate.	Divide by 2. 0 = normal dot clock. 1 = dot clock is master dot clock /2.	16-bit fetch. 0 = load video shifter input latches at normal clock rate. 1 = load video shifter at half of clock rate. (This bit only active if bit 4 is 0.)	Reserved.	8/9 Dot Clocks. 0 = 9 dot clocks per character. 1 = 8 dot clocks per character.

The **Display Off** bit, when set to 0, turns off the screen and picture-generating logic. Since refreshing of the screen is not taking place, memory access by the processor is faster, permitting speedier rewrite of screen data.

The **32-Bit Fetch** bit allows the video serializer to be loaded at quarter rate, which is necessary if dealing with 32-bit double words. This bit is normally not set.

The **Divide by 2** bit when set to 1, causes the dot clock to be divided by two. This causes the EGA/VGA to operate at the 320-pixel-per-scan-line rate. If set to 0, the normal dot clock rate is used, resulting in 640 pixels per scan line.

SEQUENCER REGISTER 02H—MAP MASK

Index Register Address: 3C4H
Data Register Address: 3C5H

Index = 2

Bit 7	Bit 6	Bit 5	Bit 4	Bit 3	Bit 2	Bit 1	Bit 0
				0 = Disable memory plane 3. 1 = Enable memory plane 3.	0 = Disable memory plane 2. 1 = Enable memory plane 2.	0 = Disable memory plane 1. 1 = Enable memory plane 1.	0 = Disable memory plane 0. 1 = Enable memory plane 0.

The **Write Enable** bits enable or disable write access to the respective memory planes on a plane-by-plane basis. This is useful only when the memory planes are not chained. When the planes are chained (as for the 256-color mode) all these bits should be set to 1.

SEQUENCER REGISTER 03H—CHARACTER MAP SELECT

Index Register Address: 3C4H
Data Register Address: 3C5H

Index = 3

Bit 7	Bit 6	Bit 5	Bit 4	Bit 3	Bit 2	Bit 1	Bit 0
		Character map select A (VGA high bit)	Character map select B (VGA high bit)	Character map select A		Character map select B	
		EGA Character Mapping: 00=First 8K of bank 0 (0–7K). 01=First 8K of bank 1 (16–23K). 10=First 8K of bank 2 (32K-39K). 11=First 8K of bank 3 (48K-55K).					
		VGA Character Mapping 000=Address offset of 1st character 0K. 001=Address offset of 1st character 16K. 010=Address offset of 1st character 32K. 011=Address offset of 1st character 48K. 100=Address offset of 1st character 8K. 101=Address offset of 1st character 24K. 110=Address offset of 1st character 40K. 111=Address offset of 1st character 56K.					

In the text modes, the **Character Select A** bits select which character set will be used for a character whose attribute bit 3 is set to 0. The **Character**

Select B bits select which character set will be used for a character whose attribute bit 3 is set to 1.

SEQUENCER REGISTER 04H—MEMORY MODE

Index Register Address: 3C4H   Index = 4
Data Register Address: 3C5H

Bit 7	Bit 6	Bit 5	Bit 4	Bit 3	Bit 2	Bit 1	Bit 0
Reserved.				Chain 4. 0 = display planes not chained. 1 = display planes chained.	Odd/Even. 0 = odd/even storage. 1 = sequential storage.	Extended memory. 0 = no memory extension. 1 = memory extension.	Alpha/Graphics Mode. 0 = graphics mode. 1 = text mode.

The **Reserved** bits should not be used.

The **Chain 4** bit controls the way in which display memory planes are accessed. When set to 0, the planes are not chained together; any combination of the four display memory planes may be accessed by Sequencer Register 02H—Map Mask Register. When this bit is set to 1, the four memory planes are chained together. In this case, the two least significant bits of the memory address are used to select one of the four memory planes. Thus only every fourth byte of each memory plane is used.

The **Odd/Even** bit, when set to 0, causes odd memory addresses to access odd memory planes and even memory addresses to access even memory planes. When set to 1, memory planes are written to according to the map mask register.

The **Extended Memory** bit indicates whether display memory is greater or less than 64K bytes.

The **Alpha/Graphics Mode** bit, when set to 0, indicates that a graphics display mode has been selected. When set to 1, this bit indicates that an alphanumerics display mode has been selected.

Graphics Registers

The graphics registers are described in Table 4-4. The graphics controller forms the interface between the processor and the display memory and determines how data is transferred to the four memory planes.

TABLE 4-4. GRAPHICS REGISTERS

Index Register Address: 3CEH

Data Register Address: 3CFH

Register Name	Index	Status
Set/Reset Register	00H	Read/Write
Set/Reset Enable Register	01H	Read/Write
Color Compare Register	02H	Read/Write
Data Rotate/Function Select	03H	Read/Write
Read Plane Select Register	04H	Read/Write
Mode Register	05H	Read/Write
Miscellaneous Register	06H	Read/Write
Color Don't Care Register	07H	Read/Write
Bit Mask Register	08H	Read/Write

GRAPHICS REGISTER 00H—SET/RESET

Index Register Address: 3CEH
Data Register Address: 3CFH

Index = 0

Bit 7	Bit 6	Bit 5	Bit 4	Bit 3	Bit 2	Bit 1	Bit 0
				Fill data for memory plane 3.	Fill data for memory plane 2.	Fill data for memory plane 1.	Fill data for memory plane 0.

If a memory plane is enabled by Graphics Controller Register 01H— Enable Set/Reset and the write mode is 0 (Graphics Controller Register 05H—

Mode), then a write to a memory address will cause the entire byte in the selected memory plane to be filled by the value (1 or 0) in that plane's bit in this register.

GRAPHICS REGISTER 01H—ENABLE SET/RESET

Index Register Address: 3CEH
Data Register Address: 3CFH

Index = 1

Bit 7	Bit 6	Bit 5	Bit 4	Bit 3	Bit 2	Bit 1	Bit 0
				0=Disable memory plane 3 Set/Reset. 1=Enable memory plane 3 Set/Reset.	0=Disable memory plane 2 Set/Reset. 1=Enable memory plane 2 Set/Reset.	0=Disable memory plane 1 Set/Reset. 1=Enable memory plane 1 Set/Reset.	0=Disable memory plane 0 Set/Reset. 1=Enable memory plane 0 Set/Reset.

This register selects those memory planes for which Graphics Controller Register 0—Set/Reset supplies color data in write mode 0.

GRAPHICS REGISTER 02H—COLOR COMPARE

Index Register Address: 3CEH
Data Register Address: 3CFH

Index = 2

Bit 7	Bit 6	Bit 5	Bit 4	Bit 3	Bit 2	Bit 1	Bit 0
				Color compare value for memory plane 3.	Color compare value for memory plane 2.	Color compare value for memory plane 1.	Color compare value for memory plane 0.

This register establishes a reference color against which data for each pixel from all four memory planes may be compared during a memory read cycle. The return from the memory read is a byte representing eight consecutive pixels beginning at the memory address. Each bit in this byte that is set to 1 indicates that the appropriate pixel matches the color established in this register; each bit that is set to 0 indicates no match. This read mode is set by setting bit 3 of Graphics Controller Register 05H—Mode to 1.

GRAPHICS REGISTER 03H—DATA ROTATE/FUNCTION SELECT

Index Register Address: 3CEH
Data Register Address: 3CFH

Index = 3

Bit 7	Bit 6	Bit 5	Bit 4	Bit 3	Bit 2	Bit 1	Bit 0
			Function Select. 00 = Data overwritten in specified color. 01 = Data ANDED with latched data. 10 = Data ORed with latched data. 11 = Data XORed with latched data.		Rotate Count. Binary representation of the number of bit positions to rotate processor data to the right.		

The **Function Select** bits determine how the data sent to display memory by the processor is combined with the existing data at that memory location before the data is actually transferred to display memory. The processor data may overwrite the existing data or be logically combined with it in some way.

The **Rotate Count** bits determine how many bit positions (from 0 to 7) data is rotated to the right before being written to display memory when in write mode 0.

GRAPHICS REGISTER 04H—READ MAP SELECT

Index Register Address: 3CEH
Data Register Address: 3CFH

Index = 4

Bit 7	Bit 6	Bit 5	Bit 4	Bit 3	Bit 2	Bit 1	Bit 0
						Binary representation of the number of the memory plane to be read by the processor.	

This register determines which color plane is enabled for reading by the processor (when not in the color compare mode).

GRAPHICS REGISTER 05H—MODE

Index Register Address: 3CEH
Data Register Address: 3CFH

Index = 5

Bit 7	Bit 6	Bit 5	Bit 4	Bit 3	Bit 2	Bit 1	Bit 0
	Shift register mode. 00=output data in serial fashion (standard EGA format). 01=CGA compatible output (modes 4 and 5). 11 or 10=output data 8 bits at a time from four memory planes (256-color VGA modes).		Odd/even. 0 = normal EGA/VGA operating mode. 1 = CGA compatible; even addresses access planes 0 and 2, odd addresses access planes 1 and 3.	Read mode. 0 = read from plane selected by graphics data register 4. 1 = do color compare.	Test condition. 0 = Normal operation. 1 = Put all outputs in high impedance state for testing.	Write mode. 00 = Direct write (modified by data rotate and set/reset as applicable). 01 = Write with contents of processor latches. 10 = Memory plane 0–3 filled with 8 bits of of data bit 0–3. 11 = Write with (rotated, if applicable) write data ANDed with Bit Mask (graphics data register 8). Set/reset enabled for all planes.	

The **Shift Register Mode** bits determine how data from the shift registers is transferred to create the serial display output. When bit 6 is set to 1, the serial output is the four most significant bits of plane 0 followed by the four least significant bits from plane 0. This is followed by the four most significant bits of plane 1, and so forth, cycling through the four planes. Each byte selects one of the 256 digital-to-analog registers to output its color selections to the red, green, and blue guns of the cathode ray tube. This method is used for display mode 13H, the 320 × 200 pixel × 256-color mode. When bit 6 is set to 0, the shift register mode is determined by bit 5. When it is set to 0, the digital-to-analog register is selected by the value in the palette register and the value in the color select register. The proper palette register (1 of 16) is selected by four bits, one from each bit plane. This is the 16-color EGA/VGA mode. When bit 5 is 1, the contents of memory planes 0 and 1 are output on both the plane 0 and plane 1 serial outputs and the contents of memory planes 2 and 3 are output on both the plane 2 and plane 3 serial outputs. This is the CGA compatible mode of transferring color information.

The **Odd/Even** bit determines which display map data is routed to the processor data bus on a memory read when Sequencer Register 04H—Memory Mode bit 2 is set to 1 (the odd/even mode). If bit 4 is set to 0, a normal EGA/VGA memory read occurs. If bit 4 is set to 1, odd memory addresses read data from an even memory map if the address LSB is 0 and from an odd memory map if the address LSB is 1.

The **Read Mode** bit, if set to 0, reads data from the memory plane selected by Graphics Controller Register 04H—Read Map Select. When set to 1, a data read operation performs the color compare (see Graphics Controller Register 02H—Color Compare).

The **Write Mode** bits select the write mode as indicated in the following table:

Bit 1	Bit 0	Write Mode
0	0	0
0	1	1
1	0	2
1	1	3

Write Mode 0. The data addressed to display memory is rotated by the current rotation setting (Graphics Register 03H—Data Rotate/Function Select) and then combined with the latched data for each memory plane in accordance with the current logical function selected (Graphics Register 03H—Data Rotate/Function Select) for each bit for which the bit mask (Graphics Register 08H—Bit Mask) is set to 1. If the bit mask is set to 0, the latched bits are returned to their appropriate memory planes unchanged. If the set/reset function is enabled for any memory plane (Graphics Register 01H—Enable Set/Reset) then the set/reset value for that memory plane that is contained in Graphics Controller Register 02H—Color Compare will be written to every unmasked bit of the addressed byte, ignoring the data written by the processor.

Write Mode 1. The data in the memory latches is written to all memory planes at the addressed byte. The bit map, selected logical function and set/reset function are ignored. This mode permits fast transfer of data within the display memory, since a single read operation at one address will fill the latches with the data from all four memory planes at that address and then a single write to another memory address will transfer this data to the new address.

Write Mode 2. Each of the four least significant bits (bits 0–3) of the processor data is extended to a byte and written to the corresponding memory plane. Thus bit 0 forms the byte written to memory plane 0, bit 1 forms the byte written to memory plane 1, etc. The newly created byte is operated upon by the bit mask, the selected logical function, and the set/reset registers, as described for write mode 0. Graphics Register 03H—Data Rotate/Function Select has no effect.

Write Mode 3. The processor data is operated upon by Graphics Register 03H—Data Rotate/Function Select and the resulting byte is ANDed with the data from Graphics Register 08H—Bit Mask. The result is used as the bit mask in writing eight bits of the value in Graphics Register 00H—Set/Reset to each memory plane.

GRAPHICS REGISTER 06H—MISCELLANEOUS

Index Register Address: 3CEH Index = 6
Data Register Address: 3CFH

Bit 7	Bit 6	Bit 5	Bit 4	Bit 3	Bit 2	Bit 1	Bit 0
Reserved.				Memory map 00 = A0000H for 128K bytes 01 = A0000H for 64K bytes 10 = B0000H for 32K bytes 11 = B8000H for 32K bytes		Chain odd maps to even	Display mode. 0 = Text mode 1 = Graphics mode

The **Reserved** bits must all be set to 0.

The **Memory Map** bits determine the size of the display memory window in the processor memory addressing space and the initial address for this window. Note that if you are in a mode that is addressed at A0000H and then shift to a mode that is addressed at B0000H without clearing the memory, then whatever data you had in memory at A0000H will now be at memory address B0000H; you're not getting a new, unused section of memory as you might wish.

The **Chain Odd/Even** bit, when set to 1, enables an odd/even mode in which the least significant bit of the processor memory address is used to select an odd or even memory plane, and this bit is then replaced by a high-order bit of the address data before the display memory is actually addressed. This provides CGA compatibility. When this bit is set to 0, normal display memory addressing occurs.

The **Display Mode** bit, when set to 0, enables the text mode of display. When set to 1, the graphics display mode is enabled.

GRAPHICS REGISTER 07H—COLOR DON'T CARE

Index Register Address: 3CEH
Data Register Address: 3CFH

Index = 7

Bit 7	Bit 6	Bit 5	Bit 4	Bit 3	Bit 2	Bit 1	Bit 0
Reserved.				0=compare color plane 3. 1=color plane 3 don't care.	0=compare color plane 2. 1=color plane 2 don't care.	0=compare color plane 1. 1=color plane 1 don't care.	0=compare color plane 0. 1=color plane 0 don't care.

Bits 0 to 3 determine which display memory planes will be used in a read-mode 1-color comparison. If a bit is set to 1, the corresponding color plane will be used in the color comparison; it the bit is set to 0, it will not be used.

GRAPHICS REGISTER 08H—BIT MASK

Index Register Address: 3CEH
Data Register Address: 3CFH

Index = 8

Bit 7	Bit 6	Bit 5	Bit 4	Bit 3	Bit 2	Bit 1	Bit 0
For each bit position containing a 0, that bit position is immune to change in each memory plane for a write to the same address that was last read. For each bit position containing a 1, that bit position in the memory plane is written to upon a write to the same address that was last read.							

This register determines which bit positions are immune to change when a display memory write action takes place.

Attribute Registers

Table 4-5 describes the attribute registers. There are 20 registers for the EGA and 21 for the VGA. They are primarily concerned with determining the colors to be displayed on the screen. There is no separate port address for the index register. Instead, a toggle action occurs at the common port address of 3C0H. The first port access sends an index. The next port access writes to the register just indexed. The next port address sends another index, and so forth. If you don't know which toggle state the port is in, you can force it to the state of accepting an index by doing a read of port 3D2H. With the VGA, you can read from the indexed register by reading port 3C1H.

TABLE 4-5. ATTRIBUTE REGISTERS

Address: 3C0H toggles between index and data registers. Toggle set to index by read of 3D2H.

Register Name	Index	Status
Palette Registers	00H to 0FH	Read/Write
Mode Control Register	10H	Read/Write
Overscan Color Register	11H	Read/Write
Color Plane Enable	12H	Read/Write
Horizontal Pixel Scanning Register	13H	Read/Write
Color Select Register	14H	Read/Write

ATTRIBUTE REGISTERS 00H TO 0FH—PALETTE

Write Index Register Address: 3C0H
Write Data Register Address: 3C0H
Read Index Register Address: 3C1H (VGA only)
Read Data Register Address: 3C1H (VGA only)
16 Registers—one to define each of the 16 EGA colors

Index = 00H to 0FH

Bit 7	Bit 6	Bit 5	Bit 4	Bit 3	Bit 2	Bit 1	Bit 0
		Red 2/3 saturation.	Green 2/3 saturation.	Blue 2/3 saturation.	Red 1/3 saturation.	Green 1/3 saturation.	Blue 1/3 saturation.
		Note that when the 2/3 saturation and 1/3 saturation bits for a given color are both on, the result is 3/3 or 100% saturation.					

Each of these registers determines 1 of the 16 colors that can be displayed simultaneously in the 16-color modes. For the VGA, the six-bit color value in the palette register selects one of 64 colors whose components are shown in the table. For the VGA, the six-bit value in the palette register selects one of the first 64 color registers, whose colors are the same as the EGA colors in the default condition.

ATTRIBUTE REGISTER 10H—MODE CONTROL

Write Index Register Address: 3C0H
Write Data Register Address: 3C0H
Read Index Register Address: 3C1H (VGA only)
Read Data Register Address: 3C1H (VGA only)

Index = 10H

Bit 7	Bit 6	Bit 5	Bit 4	Bit 3	Bit 2	Bit 1	Bit 0
Source select. 0=palette register source of color bits 4 & 5. 1=color select register source of color bits 4 & 5.	Clock select. 0=pixel changes at each dot clock. 1=pixel changes every other dot clock.	Panning. 0=enables split-screen mode pixel panning. 1=disables split-screen mode pixel panning.		Blinking. 0=bit 7 of character attribute sets background color. 1=bit 7 of character attribute selects blinking.	Character codes. 0=9th dot same as background. 1=9th dot same as 8th dot.	Display Type. 0= monochrome.1 = color.	Display mode. 0 = text. 1 = graphics.

The **Source Select** bit (bit 7) selects the source for outputs to bits 4 and 5 of the digital-to-analog converters. When set to 0, the 256-color registers of the VGA are segmented as four groups of 64 registers each. The six bits in a palette register are the address of 1 of the 64 registers in the segment selected by bits 6 and 7 of Attribute Register 14H—Color Select. If bit 7 is set to 1, the 256-color registers are segmented into 16 groups of 16 registers each. The first four bits from a palette register select 1 of the 16 registers in a segment selected by bits 4, 5, 6, and 7 of Attribute Register 14H—Color Select.

The **Clock Select** bit controls clocking of the pixel data. When set to 1, it allows eight bits of data to select one of 256 colors, by changing pixel data on every other clock cycle. At this setting, bits 5 and 6 of Graphics Controller Register 05H—Mode must be set to 1 to permit the eight bits of data to be loaded to the shift registers in two successive operations. When set to 0, the normal clock rate is used, transferring four bits to the shift registers for 16-color modes.

The **Panning** bit, when set to 1, enables the operation of CRT Controller Register 18H—Line Compare, which permits one part of a split screen to be scrolled while the other part remains stationary. When set to 0, independent panning is prevented.

The **Blinking** bit, when set to 1, causes a 1 in the most significant bit of a character attribute to make the character blink on the display. When this bit is set to 0, the most significant bit of the character attribute causes the character background to be high intensity when it is 1.

The **Character Codes** bit, when set to 1, sets the ninth horizontal pixel of a character to be the same as the eighth pixel when a nine-pixel-wide character cell is used with an eight-pixel-wide character set. Under the same circumstances, setting the bit to 0 will cause the ninth pixel to be the same color as the background.

The **Display Type** bit, when set to 0, causes display attributes to be displayed as color attributes; when set to 1, display attributes are displayed as monochrome attributes (as defined for the IBM Monochrome Display Adapter).

The **Display Mode** bit determines whether the display is to be text (alphanumerics) or graphics.

ATTRIBUTE REGISTER 11H—OVERSCAN COLOR

Write Index Register Address: 3C0H Index = 11H
Write Data Register Address: 3C0H
Read Index Register Address: 3C1H (VGA only)
Read Data Register Address: 3C1H (VGA only)

Bit 7	Bit 6	Bit 5	Bit 4	Bit 3	Bit 2	Bit 1	Bit 0
		1 = secondary red border.	1 = secondary green border.	1 = secondary blue border.	1 = red border.	1 = green border.	1 = blue border.

This register determines the color for the overscan region, which is the space on the display between the end of blanking and the beginning of the display at the top and left and between the end of the display and the beginning of blanking at the bottom and right. The color selection is the same as described for attribute registers 00–0FH (palette registers). Unfortunately, for most EGA and VGA implementations, this feature does not work properly if the color is set to anything other than black (00).

ATTRIBUTE REGISTER 12H—COLOR PLANE ENABLE

Write Index Register Address: 3C0H
Write Data Register Address: 3C0H
Read Index Register Address: 3C1H (VGA only)
Read Data Register Address: 3C1H (VGA only)

Index = 12H

Bit 7	Bit 6	Bit 5	Bit 4	Bit 3	Bit 2	Bit 1	Bit 0
		Video status multiplex		Enable color plane 3	Enable color plane 2	Enable color plane 1	Enable color plane 0

The **Video Status Multiplex** bits select which two of eight color outputs are returned by the diagnostic bits of input status register one, as follows:

Attribute Register 12H		Input Status Register One	
Bit 5	Bit 4	Bit 5	Bit 4
0	0	Primary red	Primary blue
0	1	Secondary green	Secondary blue
1	0	Primary intensity	Primary green
1	1	Secondary intensity	Secondary red

The **Enable Color Plane** bits determine which color planes are enabled in the 16-color configurations.

In some Super VGAs this register is not supported and accessing it causes the screen to go blank. Therefore, try to avoid using it in your programs.

ATTRIBUTE REGISTER 13H—HORIZONTAL PIXEL PANNING

Write Index Register Address: 3C0H Index = 13H
Write Data Register Address: 3C0H
Read Index Register Address: 3C1H (VGA only)
Read Data Register Address: 3C1H (VGA only)

Bit 7	Bit 6	Bit 5	Bit 4	Bit 3	Bit 2	Bit 1	Bit 0
				Horizontal pixel panning. Binary representation of number of pixels to shift character to the left.			

The **Horizontal Pixel Panning** bits specify the number of pixels to the left that the video data is to be shifted. The relationship of the number in this field to the number of pixels the character is to be shifted depends upon the specified width of the character, as follows:

Dots / Pixel	Horizontal Panning Value															
	0	1	2	3	4	5	6	7	8	9	A	B	C	D	E	F
6																
8	0	1	2	3	4	5	6	7	-	-	-	-	-	-	-	-
9	8	0	1	2	3	4	5	6	7	-	-	-	-	-	-	-
12	B	A	9	8	0	1	2	3	4	5	6	7	-	-	-	-
16	F	E	D	C	B	A	9	8	0	1	2	3	4	5	6	7

This pixel by-pixel shifting permits sliding the display to the left smoothly rather than having to jump character by character.

ATTRIBUTE REGISTER 14H—COLOR SELECT

Write Index Register Address: 3C0H Index = 14H
Write Data Register Address: 3C0H
Read Index Register Address: 3C1H (VGA only)
Read Data Register Address: 3C1H (VGA only)

Bit 7	Bit 6	Bit 5	Bit 4	Bit 3	Bit 2	Bit 1	Bit 0
				Color bit 7.	Color bit 6.	Color bit 5.	Color bit 4.

Color bits 7 and 6 are used as the high order bits of the eight-bit address for selecting which of the 256 color registers are used for colors in the 16 color modes. Therefore by changing these bits, one may select one of four sets of 64 color registers.

Color bits 4 and 5 are are used along with **Color bits 6 and 7** to select 1 of 16 sets of 16-color registers in the 16 color modes when Attribute Register 10H—Mode Control bit 7 is set to 1.

Video Digital-to-Analog Converter Registers

Table 4-6 presents an overview of the video digital-to-analog converter registers. There are 256 internal color registers that store the 256 VGA colors. Each is 18 bits long, containing 6 bits of red data, 6 bits of green data, and 6 bits of blue data. There are five registers used to communicate with these internal color registers. They are the color data register write index register, the color data register read index register (write-only), the DAC state register (read-only), the pixel data register, and the pixel mask register. Descriptions of these registers follow.

TABLE 4-6. VIDEO DIGITAL-TO-ANALOG CONVERTER REGISTERS

Register	Address	Status
Color Data Register Write Index Register.	3C8H	Read/Write.
Color Data Register Read Index Register.	3C7H	Write-Only.
DAC State.	3C7H	Read-Only.
Pixel Data Register.	3C9H	Read/Write.
Pixel Mask Register.	3C6H	Read/Write.

COLOR DATA REGISTER WRITE INDEX REGISTER

Write Data Register Address: 3C8H
Read Data Register Address: 3C8H

Bit 7	Bit 6	Bit 5	Bit 4	Bit 3	Bit 2	Bit 1	Bit 0
Address of color register during write mode.							

This register contains the address used to access 1 of the 256 color registers for a write operation. A write operation consists of three inputs to the pixel data register, to load red, green, and blue values. When these three inputs are complete, the register address is incremented so that the programmer does not need to supply a new index value to this register for the next set of color inputs.

COLOR DATA REGISTER READ INDEX REGISTER

Write Data Register Address: 3C7H

Bit 7	Bit 6	Bit 5	Bit 4	Bit 3	Bit 2	Bit 1	Bit 0
Address of color register during read mode.							

This register contains the address used to access one of the 256 color registers for a read operation, which consists of reading three bytes from the pixel data register to obtain red, green, and blue values from the register. When these three bytes have been read, the address in this register is incremented to point to the next color register in case successive color register values are to be read.

PIXEL DATA REGISTER

Write Data Register Address: 3C9H
Read Data Register Address: 3C9H

Bit 7	Bit 6	Bit 5	Bit 4	Bit 3	Bit 2	Bit 1	Bit 0
		Color Data.					

This register provides the interface to the 256 18-bit-color register that is addressed by one of the two preceding registers. For write operations, six color data bits sent to this register on three successive write operations are transferred to the red, green, and blue portions of the color data register addressed by the color data register write index register. That register is then incremented to address the next color data register. For a read operation, three successive reads of this register will obtain the red, green, and blue color information from the color data register addressed by the color data register read index register, after which the register is incremented to address the next color data register.

DAC STATE REGISTER

Read Data Register Address: 3C7H

Bit 7	Bit 6	Bit 5	Bit 4	Bit 3	Bit 2	Bit 1	Bit 0
						DAC State. 0 = Color Data Register Index Read Register was accessed last. 3 = Color Data Register Index Write Register was accessed last.	

This register indicates whether a read or write operation to the color data registers is in effect.

PIXEL MASK REGISTER

Write Data Register Address: 3C6H
Read Data Register Address: 3C6H

Bit 7	Bit 6	Bit 5	Bit 4	Bit 3	Bit 2	Bit 1	Bit 0
Set to FFH by BIOS mode call.							

This register should not be modified by the programmer.

5

Display Modes

When the first IBM PCs were produced in 1981, they were offerred with either of two graphics adapter cards, the Monochrome Display Adapter (MDA), which had a reasonably good text display with a 720 × 400 pixel resolution (which IBM believed would be used by most business-type applications), and the Color Graphics Adapter (CGA), which had the horrible resolution of 320 × 200 pixels and the choice of one of two four-color palettes (IBM believed it would be used only for games). The PC had the capability of addressing a huge 1 megabyte of memory, of which IBM reserved 64K between A0000H and AFFFFH for monochrome text display memory and 64K between B0000H and BFFFFH for color display memory. Using actual computer memory to drive the monitor permitted the computer to update displays by changing the memory contents and at the same time allowed the transfer of the memory contents to the monitor without direct computer intervention at a rate fast enough to refresh the monitor display without flicker. The text display memory stores codes for characters that are generated by a character generator as the information is transferred to the monitor; the color display memory contains actual pixel values.

In 1984, IBM introduced the improved PC XT. The display capabilities were upgraded; the new Enhanced Graphics Adapter (EGA) included a 640 × 350 pixel display mode that could display any 16 from a palette of 64 colors. This mode required 112,000 bytes of memory to store the pixel information. The new display adapter had to be backward compatible with previous systems, so IBM was stuck with the 64K color display memory window. To get around this, a complicated system was created in which a pixel was represented by one bit in each of four memory planes within the card, which as far as the outside world was concerned were all at the same address. This reduced the addressing requirement to 28,000 bytes, which fit within the 64K window. It did, however, involve some very complex programming to set a pixel value, as we shall see later. The latest video upgrade sponsered by IBM that was generally accepted by the industry occurred in 1987 when the Video Graphics Array (VGA) was released as the video standard for the IBM PC-2. It included a 640 × 480 pixel 16-color mode and a new 256-color mode having a resolution of 320 × 200 pixels. The 16-color mode used the same four-plane memory structure used by the EGA; the 256-color mode, at least externally, appeared to simply have a series of 8-bit pixels strung together in memory. Since then, a lot of Super VGA cards have appeared. The early ones used all kinds of register structures to contain higher-resolution displays with more color capability; their only compatibility was that through various paging techniques they contained display memory within the originally specified 64K memory windows. More recently, the Video Electronics Standards Association (VESA) has standardized Super VGA display modes and interfaces with them, so that if you have a fairly new Super VGA card, you will be able to use the techniques described in this book, regardless of who manufactured your card.

Standard VGA Modes

Table 5-1 lists the display modes that are defined for the standard VGA adapter card and are also supported by all Super VGAs. The table includes all of the earlier modes that were available for the MDA, CGA, and EGA, as well as modes unique to the VGA. In Chapters 6 and 7, we'll go into detail on how to generate our own graphics functions for such things as setting the display mode and plotting a pixel to the screen for EGA, VGA, and Super VGA modes. We won't show you how to program for the CGA or for the once popular Hercules Graphics Adapter, since these cards are now obsolete. For the moment, look at lines 54 through 60 of the *colchart* program listed in Listing 5-1 below. They delineate the *setMode* function, which uses ROM BIOS video service 0 to select the desired mode and set up the internal operations of the VGA card to work in the desired mode. This is typical of how you would program to use one of the ROM BIOS video services, that are described in detail in Chapter 7. The process involves setting the contents of various microprocessor registers and then calling the video services interrupt 10H. Most compilers make use of a union *REGS* that contains two

Mode (Hex)	Type	Colors	Resolution
0,1	Text	16/256K	360x400
2,3	Text	16/256K	720x400
4,5	Graphics	4/256K	320x200
6	Graphics	2/256K	640x200
7	Text	mono	720x400
D	Graphics	16/256K	320x200
E	Graphics	16/256K	640x200
F	Graphics	mono	640x350
10	Graphics	16/256K	640x350
11	Graphics	2/256K	640x480
12	Graphics	16/256K	640x480
13	Graphics	256/256K	320x200

equivalent structures. These are defined as:

```
struct
{
    unsigned int ax, bx, cx, dx, si, di, cflag,
    flags;
} WORDREG;
```

and

```
struct
{
    unsigned char al, ah, bl, bh, cl, ch, dl, dh;
} BYTEREGS;
```

The first version of the union is used to read or write 16-bit words to the registers using the *.x* version, and the second version is used to read or write 8-bit characters to the lower or upper half of a register using the *.h* version. Line 54 of the *setMode* function defines the function and the fact that an integer parameter is passed to it. Line 56 defines the union *reg* to be of type *REGS*. Line 57 fills the member of this union corresponding to the upper half of register *a* with a zero, the designation for the ROM BIOS video service that sets the display mode. Line 58 fills the member of the union corresponding to the lower half of the *a* register with the desired display mode number. In line 59, *int86* is called. This activates an interrupt. The parameters passed to this function are first, the number of the interrupt (in this case 10H for the video services interrupt; second, the address of the structure that contains data to be sent to the microprocessor registers (in this case *reg*); and finally, the address of the structure that will contain the contents of microprocessor registers when the *int86* function returns to the calling program. (In this case, we used the same structure that was used to send data to the registers, but you can use two different sets of variables if you want to preserve the data that you sent to the registers. After this function has performed its work, the screen is blanked and set for the new display mode.

There are 16 default colors that normally are activated when you set a 16-color mode. There are 256 colors that are activated when you set up the 256-color mode. The first 16 of these are the same as the colors for the 16-color mode, for compatibility's sake. They are followed by a number of shades of gray for gray-scale use, and then various additional colors. If you're programming, you may need to know just what colors are represented by the various palette register or color register numbers. The program in Listing 5-1 will first set your screen to mode 12H and display the 16 default colors for 16-color modes. Hitting any key will then set the screen to mode 13H and display the 256 default colors for the 256-color mode. This program will enable you to look at all of the available colors. We won't describe it in detail, since the functions that are performed will be described in later chapters.

Undocumented VGA Display Modes

In recent years, a number of undocumented VGA display modes have been discovered by John Bridges and documented in various articles by Michael Abrash. These modes all have the same color capability as mode 13H of 256 colors out of a possible 256K, but have different resolutions. To do this, they make better but more complex use of the four internal memory planes. These modes are listed in Table 5-2. The numbers assigned to these modes are arbitrary. These arbitrary

Listing 5-1. Program to Generate Color Charts

```
/*
╔══════════════════════════════════════════════════════════════╗
║                                                              ║
║       colchart = Program to show default colors              ║
║            By Roger T. Stevens   11-22-95                    ║
║                                                              ║
╚══════════════════════════════════════════════════════════════╝
*/

#include <stdio.h>
#include <string.h>
#include <dos.h>
#include <conio.h>

void cls(char colors);
void setMode(int mode);

#define graph_out(index,val)  {outp(0x3CE,index);\
                               outp(0x3CF,val);}

void main(void)
{
   union REGS reg;

   int i,j,k,color;
   char far *address;
   char dummy;

   setMode(0x12);
   cls(7);
   for (i=0; i<16; i++)
   {
      for (j=0; j<20; j++)
      {
         for (k=0; k<4; k++)
         {
            address = (char far *)
               0xA0000000L
               + 80*(j+50) + i*4 + k+10;
            outport(0x3CE,0x0205);
            dummy = *address;
            *address = i;
            outport(0x3CE,0x0005);
         }
      }
   }
   getch();
   setMode(0x13);
     cls(7);
   for (i=0; i<256; i++)
   {
      for (j=0; j<10; j++)
      {
         for (k=0; k<16; k++)
```

```
                {
                    address = (char far *)
                        00xA0000000L
                        + 320*(j+2+12*(i/
                        16)) +
                        (i%16)*16 + k+10;
                    *address = i;
                }
            }
        }
        getch();
        setMode(0x03);
    }
/*

                setMode() = Sets Video Mode

*/

    void setMode(int mode)
    {
        union REGS reg;

        reg.h.ah = 0;
        reg.h.al = mode;
        int86 (0x10,&reg,&reg);
    }

/*

        cls() = Clears the Screen to a specified color

*/

    void cls(char colors)
    {
        union REGS reg;

        reg.x.dx = 0x2384F;
        reg.h.bh = colors;
        reg.x.ax = 0x0600;
        reg.x.cx = 0;
        int86(0x10,&reg,&reg);
        gotoxy(0,0);
    }
```

numbers will be used throughout the book when dealing with the undocumented display modes. If you use them, the programs in the book will remain compatible; if you want to assign different numbers to undocumented modes, you'll need to make various changes to make everything compatible.

First, we define a "documented display mode" to mean a display mode that can be initialized through the ROM BIOS (usually by BIOS extensions that are included in the VGA card). Particularly, most documented display modes can be initialized through the use of ROM BIOS video service 00. All of these documented modes were described in the previous section. Due to the large number of registers internal to VGA cards, and the flexibility of these registers, it is possible to create a lot of different display modes that are not supported by the ROM BIOS video services. This is particularly true of the Super VGA cards, where the video modes that are supported by the manufacturer only begin to scratch the surface of what might be created. The undocumented display modes described in this and the following sections have the characteristic in common that they provide higher-resolution 256-color modes than mode 19 (the 320 × 200 pixel × 256-color mode), without requiring any additional memory in the VGA card. They also have the unique characteristic that the data for four pixels is stored in two adjacent bytes of memory address space, with two adjacent bytes in memory plane 0 used to store the first of the four pixels, two adjacent bytes in memory plane 1 used to store the next pixel, etc. Starting with the modes described here, with a good understanding of how the display adapter card registers work (as described in Chapter 4), you are ready to start creating your own display modes. There are two cautions to observe, however. First, make sure that you are not attempting to create a display mode that exceeds the memory capabilities of your VGA card. Furthermore, even if your card has adequate memory, you may need to institute a paging scheme if you exceed a 64K memory window. Second, you should be very careful if you attempt to create a display mode that changes the horizontal or vertical sweep rates from those used with one of the documented modes for your card. Many monitors are very limited in the sweep rates that they will accept, and some of them self-destruct if they are fed sweep rates outside the range they are capable of handling.

You'll note quite a little repetition in the undocumented mode descriptions that follow. This is done deliberately, so that if you are

Table 5-2. Undocumented VGA Display Modes

Mode (Hex)	Type	Colors	Resolution
F0	Graphics	256/256K	320×400
F1	Graphics	256/256K	320×240
F2	Graphics	256/256K	320×480
F3	Graphics	256/256K	360×400
F4	Graphics	256/256K	360×480

interested in implementing only one of the undocumented modes you will have all of the necessary information together in one block and will not have to look through a lot of sections, hunting for pieces of it.

We are going to modify the *setMode* function given above so that it can set up any one of five undocumented modes as well as all of the documented modes. The new function is listed in Listing 5-2. The five undocumented modes have been numbered F0H, F1H, F2H, F3H, and F4H to match Table 5-2. The function begins by setting the *ah* register to 0, which selects the ROM BIOS video service for setting the display mode. Next, an *if* statement determines whether the mode number is less than 7FH. If so, the mode is placed in register *al* and *int86* is called to set the mode. The function then returns to the calling program. If the mode number is greater than 7FH, the function first sets register *al* to mode 13H (which is the mode initially used for all the undocumented modes) and then calls *int86*. This sets everything up for the 320 × 200 pixel × 256-color mode, including clearing the display memory and setting the color registers to their default colors. The function then enters a *switch* statement that determines what actions are to be taken with the registers for whatever mode was chosen. There is a case for each of the undocumented modes. In each case, we modify some of the VGA registers to achieve the new VGA mode. After the registers are modified the function leaves the *switch* statement and then sends 0FH to Sequencer Register 2—Map Mask to enable all four color planes. It then enters a *for* loop that zeroes 64K of memory for each of the four display memory planes. We have to clear more memory than was automatically cleared in setting mode 13H, since the undocumented

Listing 5-2. Function to Set Documented and Undocumented Display Modes.

```
/*
 setMode() = Sets Video Mode (includes undocumented VGA
                          modes.)
*/

void setMode(int mode)
{
    char result;
    unsigned int params[17] = 5
{0x6b00,0x5901,0x5a02,0x8e03,0x5e04,
        0x8a05,0x4009,0x0014,0xe317,0x0d06,
        0x3e07,0xea10,0xac11,0xdf12,0xe715,
        0x0616,0x4109};
    char far * address;
    long int i;

    reg.h.ah = 0;
    if (mode<0x7F)
    {
        reg.h.al = mode;
        int86 (0x10,&reg,&reg);
        return;
    }
    reg.h.al = 0x13;
    int86 (0x10,&reg,&reg);
    switch(mode)
    {
        case 0xF0:  /* 320 x 400 pixels */
            outport(0x3c4,0x0604);
            outportb(0x3d4,0x11);
            result = inportb(0x3d5);
            outportb(0x3d5,result & 0x7f);
            for (i=6; i<9; i++)
                outport(0x3d4,params[i]);
            break;

        case 0xF1:  /* 320 x 240 pixels */
            outport(0x3c4,0x0604);
            outport(0x3c4,0x0100);
            outportb(0x3c2,0xc3);
            outport(0x3c4,0x300);
            outportb(0x3d4,0x11);
            result = inportb(0x3d5);
            outportb(0x3d5,result & 0x7f);
            for (i=7; i<17; i++)
                outport(0x3d4,params[i]);
            break;

        case 0xF2:  /* 320 x 480 pixels */
```

```
                outport(0x3c4,0x0604);
                outport(0x3c4,0x0100);
                outportb(0x3c2,0xc3);
                outport(0x3c4,0x300);
                outportb(0x3d4,0x11);
                result = inportb(0x3d5);
                outportb(0x3d5,result & 0x7f);
                for (i=6; i<16; i++)
                    outport(0x3d4,params[i]);
                outport(0x3d4,0x4009);
                break;

            case 0xF3:  /* 360 x 400 pixels */
                outport(0x3c4,0x0604);
                outport(0x3c4,0x0100);
                outportb(0x3c2,0x67);
                outport(0x3c4,0x300);
                outportb(0x3d4,0x11);
                result = inportb(0x3d5);
                outportb(0x3d5,result & 0x7f);
                for (i=0; i<9; i++)
                    outport(0x3d4,params[i]);
                outport(0x3d4,0x2d13);
                break;

            case 0xF4:  /* 360 x 480 pixels */
                outport(0x3c4,0x0604);
                outport(0x3c4,0x0100);
                outportb(0x3c2,0xe7);
                outport(0x3c4,0x300);
                outportb(0x3d4,0x11);
                result = inportb(0x3d5);
                outportb(0x3d5,result & 0x7f);
                for (i=0; i<16; i++)
                    outport(0x3d4,params[i]);
                outport(0x3d4,0x2d13);
                break;
        }
        outport(0x3c4,0x0f02);  // enable writes to
                        // all four planes
        for(i=0; i<0xFFFF; i++)
        {
            address = (char far *) 0xA0000000L + i;
            *address = 0x00;
        }
    }
```

modes have more resolution and therefore use more memory than mode 13H. Thus to avoid strange things appearing on a supposedly cleared screen in the undocumented modes, we must zero all of thecurrent window of display memory. The function then returns to the calling program.

Before leaving this function, let's look in detail at what we do to the VGA registers for each of the undocumented modes. For the 320 × 240 pixel mode

(F0H), the first thing that we do is to send an 06H to Sequencer Register 04H—Memory Mode. This sets up the register so that the display planes are not chained (they were chained by mode 13H), sequential storage is used, and memory greater than 64K is allowed. Mode 13H set things up to accept a byte (eight bits) of color information for each pixel. When the memory planes were chained together, the two least significant bits of the display memory offset from the base address were used to select which memory plane the color information was to be sent to and the remainder of the offset (shifted two bits to the right) became the actual offset from the base display memory address. This caused adjacent pixels to actually be stored in different memory planes, but this internal complication was transparent to the user, who could treat the mode as if all data were stored in adjacent bytes in a single memory plane. As soon as we unchain the memory planes, the eight bits of color information are transferred to the four memory planes in sequence, the first two going to the first plane, the second two to the next, and so forth, with the first two bits of the next pixel again going to the first memory plane. Next, we select CRT Controller Register 11H. First we read the contents of this register and then OR it with 7FH and write it back again. This preserves all of the contents of the register except bit 7, which is changed to 0, thereby permitting us to write to CRT controller registers 00H to 07H. Next, we enter a *for* loop that outputs data to selected CRT controller registers from an array called *params*. For this mode, we do the following:

1. Set CRT Controller Register 09H–Maximum Row Address to 40H. The critical change here is to set bit 0 to 0, to allow one scan line per character row.
2. Set CRT Controller Register 14H—Underline Row Address to 00H. This changes from double-word addressing to normal addressing, allowing scanning of all four memory planes.
3. Set CRT Controller Register 17H—Mode to E3H. The change here from mode 13H is in setting bit 6 to 1, so that we are in byte mode as for mode 12H, rather than in the word mode that was used in mode 13H.

For the 320 × 240 pixel × 256-color undocumented mode (F1H) we first send an 06H to Sequencer Register 04H—Memory Mode. This sets up the register so that the display planes are not chained (they were chained by mode 13H), sequential storage is used, and memory greater than 64K is allowed. Mode 13H set things up to accept a byte (eight bits) of color information for each pixel. When the memory planes were chained together, the two least significant bits of the display memory offset from the base address were used to select which memory plane the color information was to be sent to and the remainder of the offset (shifted two bits to the right) became the actual offset from the base display memory address. As soon as we unchain the memory planes, the eight bits of color information are transferred to the four memory planes in sequence, two to each plane. We then send 01H to Sequencer Register 00H—Reset to synchro-nously disable the timing signals while we change the clock frequency. Then we send C3H to the miscellaneous output register to change the sync polarities to indicate to the display that there are 480 lines in a vertical frame. (Because mode 13H is already set to write each scan line twice, we are actually in a 240-line mode, with each line being repeated to obtain the 480 lines.) We then send 03H to Sequencer Register 00H—Reset to restart the timing signals. Next, we select CRT Controller Register 11H. First we read the contents of this register and then OR it with 7FH and write it back again. This preserves all of the contents of the register except bit 7, which is changed to zero, thereby permitting us to write to CRT Controller Registers 00H to 07H. Next, we enter a *for* loop, which outputs data to selected CRT controller registers from an array called *params*. For this mode, we do the following:

1. Set CRT Controller Register 14H—Underline Row Address to 00H. This changes from double-word addressing to normal addressing, allowing scanning of all four memory planes.
2. Set CRT Controller Register 17H—Mode to E3H. The change here from mode 13H is in setting bit 6 to 1, so that we are in byte mode as for mode 12H, rather than in the word mode that was used in mode 13H.
3. Set CRT Controller Register 06H—Vertical Total to 0DH. This changes the vertical total to look for 240 scan lines rather than 200.
4. Set CRT Controller Register 07H—Vertical Sync Position to 3EH. A new value is required to properly set the vertical timing for 240 lines.
5. Set CRT Controller Register 10H—Vertical Sync Start to EAH. A new value is required to properly set the vertical timing for 240 lines.
6. Set CRT Controller Register 11H—Vertical Sync End to ACH. A new value is required to properly set the vertical timing for 240 lines.

7. Set CRT Controller Register 12H—Vertical Display End to DFH. A new value is required to properly set the vertical timing for 240 lines.
8. Set CRT Controller Register 15H—Start Vertical Blank to E7H. A new value is required to properly set the vertical timing for 240 lines.
9. Set CRT Controller Register 16H—End Vertical Blank to 06H. A new value is required to properly set the vertical timing for 240 lines.
10. Set CRT Controller Register 09H—Max Row Address to 41H.

For the 320 × 480 pixel × 256-color undocumented mode (F2H) we first send an 06H to sequencer register 4 (memory mode register). This sets up the register so that the display planes are not chained (they were chained by mode 13H), sequential storage is used, and memory greater than 64K is allowed. Mode 13 set things up to accept a byte (eight bits) of color information for each pixel. When the memory planes were chained together, the two least significant bits of the display memory offset from the base address were used to select which memory plane the color information was to be sent to and the remainder of the offset (shifted two bits to the right) became the actual offset from the base display memory address. As soon as we unchain the memory planes, the eight bits of color information are transferred to the four memory planes in sequence, two bits to each plane. We then send 01H to sequencer register 0 (reset register) to synchronously disable the timing signals while we change the clock frequency. Then we send C3H to miscellaneous output register to change the sync polarities to indicate to the display that there are 480 lines in a vertical frame. We then send 03H to sequencer register 0 (reset register) to restart the timing signals. Next, we select CRT controller register 11H. First we read the contents of this register and then OR it with 7FH and write it back again. This preserves all of the contents of the register except bit 7, which is changed to 0, thereby permitting us to write to CRT controller registers 0 to 7. Next, we enter a *for* loop that outputs data to selected CRT controller registers from an array called *params*. For this mode, we do the following:

1. Set CRT Controller Register 09H—Maximum Row Address to 40H. The critical change here is to set bit 0 to 0, to allow one scan line per character row.

2. Set CRT Controller Register 14H—Underline Row Address to 00H. This changes from double-word addressing to normal addressing, allowing scanning of all four memory planes.
3. Set CRT Controller Register 17H—Mode to E3H. The change here from mode 13H is in setting bit 6 to 1, so that we are in byte mode as for mode 12H, rather than in the word mode that was used in mode 13H.
4. Set CRT Controller Register 06H—Vertical Total to 0DH. This changes the vertical total to look for 480 scan lines rather than 400.
5. Set CRT Controller Register 07H—Vertical Sync Position to 3EH. A new value is required to properly set the vertical timing for 480 lines.
6. Set CRT Controller Register 10H—Vertical Sync Start to EAH. A new value is required to properly set the vertical timing for 480 lines.
7. Set CRT Controller Register 11H—Vertical Sync End to ACH. A new value is required to properly set the vertical timing for 480 lines.
8. Set CRT Controller Register 12H—Vertical Display End to DFH. A new value is required to properly set the vertical timing for 480 lines.
9. Set CRT Controller Register 15H—Start Vertical Blank to E7H. A new value is required to properly set the vertical timing for 480 lines.
10. Set CRT Controller Register 16H—End Vertical Blank to 06H. A new value is required to properly set the vertical timing for 480 lines.
11. Set CRT Controller Register 09H—Max Row Address to 41H.

For the 360 × 400 pixel × 256-color undocumented mode (F3H) we first send an 06H to Sequencer Register 04H—Memory mode. This sets up the register so that the display planes are not chained (they were chained by mode 13H), sequential storage is used and memory greater than 64K is allowed. Mode 13H set things up to accept a byte (eight bits) of color information for each pixel. When the memory planes were chained together, the two least significant bits of the display memory offset from the base address were used to select which memory plane the color information was to be sent to and the remainder of the offset (shifted two bits to the right) became the actual offset from the base display memory address. As soon as we unchain the memory planes, the eight bits of color information are transferred to the four memory planes in sequence, two bits to each memory plane. We then send 01H to sequencer register 0 (reset register) to synchronously disable the timing signals while we change the clock frequency. Then we send 67H to miscellaneous output register to change the sync polarities to indicate to the display that there are 400 lines in a vertical frame and set the clock frequency for 90 characters (360 pixels) per scan line. We then send 03H to sequencer register 0 (reset register) to restart the timing signals. Next, we select CRT controller register 11H. First we read the contents of this register and then OR it with 7FH and write it back again. This preserves all of the contents of the register except bit 7, which is changed to 0, thereby permitting us to write to CRT controller registers 0 to 7. Next, we enter a *for* loop that outputs data to selected CRT controller registers from an array called *params*. For this mode, we do the following:

1. Set CRT Controller Register 00H—Total Horizontal Column to 6BH. This is required to adjust the horizontal timing signals for 360 pixels per line.
2. Set CRT Controller Register 01H—Horizontal Display End to 59H. This is required to adjust the horizontal timing signals for 360 pixels per line.
3. Set CRT Controller Register 02H—Start Horizontal Blank to 5AH. This is required to adjust the horizontal timing signals for 360 pixels per line.
4. Set CRT Controller Register 03H—End Horizontal Blank to 8EH. This is required to adjust the horizontal timing signals for 360 pixels per line.
5. Set CRT Controller Register 04H—Horizontal Sync Start to 5EH. This is required to adjust the horizontal timing signals for 360 pixels per line.
6. Set CRT Controller Register 05H—Horizontal Sync End to 8AH. This is required to adjust the horizontal timing signals for 360 pixels per line.
7. Set CRT Controller Register 09H—Maximum Row Address to 40H. The critical change here is to set bit 0 to 0, to allow one scan line per character row.
8. Set CRT Controller Register 14H—Underline Row Address to 00H. This changes from double-word addressing to normal addressing, allowing scanning of all four memory planes.

9. Set CRT Controller Register 17H—Mode to E3H. The change here from mode 13H is in setting bit 6 to 1, so that we are in byte mode as for mode 12H rather than in the word mode that was used in mode 13H.

For the 360 × 480 pixel × 256-color undocumented mode (F4H) we first send an 06H to Sequencer Register 04H—Memory Mode. This sets up the register so that the display planes are not chained (they were chained by mode 13H), sequential storage is used and memory greater than 64K is allowed. Mode 13H set things up to accept a byte (eight bits) of color information for each pixel. When the memory planes were chained together, the two least significant bits of the display memory offset from the base address were used to select which memory plane the color information was to be sent to and the remainder of the offset (shifted two bits to the right) became the actual offset from the base display memory address. As soon as we unchain the memory planes, the eight bits of color information are transferred to the four memory planes in sequence, two bits to each plane. We then send 01H to sequencer register 0 (reset register) to synchronously disable the timing signals while we change the clock frequency. Then we send E7H to miscellaneous output register to change the sync polarities to indicate to the display that there are 480 lines in a vertical frame and set the clock frequency for 90 characters (360 pixels) per scan line. We then send 03H to sequencer register 0 (reset register) to restart the timing signals. Next, we select CRT controller register 11H. First we read the contents of this register and then OR it with 7FH and write it back again. This preserves all of the contents of the register except bit 7, which is changed to 0, thereby permitting us to write to CRT controller registers 0 to 7. Next, we enter a *for* loop that outputs data to selected CRT controller registers from an array called *params*. For this mode, we do the following:

1. Set CRT Controller Register 00H—Total Horizontal Column to 6BH. This is required to adjust the horizontal timing signals for 360 pixels per line.
2. Set CRT Controller Register 01H—Horizontal Display End to 59H. This is required to adjust the horizontal timing signals for 360 pixels per line.
3. Set CRT Controller Register 02H—Start Horizontal Blank to 5AH. This is required to adjust the horizontal timing signals for 360 pixels per line.

4. Set CRT Controller Register 03H—End Horizontal Blank to 8EH. This is required to adjust the horizontal timing signals for 360 pixels per line.
5. Set CRT Controller Register 04H—Horizontal Sync Start to 5EH. This is required to adjust the horizontal timing signals for 360 pixels per line.
6. Set CRT Controller Register 05H—Horizontal Sync End to 8AH. This is required to adjust the horizontal timing signals for 360 pixels per line.
7. Set CRT Controller Register 09H—Maximum Row Address to 40H. The critical change here is to set bit 0 to 0, to allow one scan line per character row.
8. Set CRT Controller Register 14H—Underline Row Address to 00H. This changes from double-word addressing to normal addressing, allowing scanning of all four memory planes.
9. Set CRT Controller Register 17H—Mode to E3H. This changes from the mode 13H setting of bit 6 as 1 to put us in byte mode as for mode 12H rather than in the word mode that was used in mode 13H.
10. Set CRT Controller Register 06H—Vertical Total to 0DH. This changes the vertical total to look for 480 scan lines rather than 400.
11. Set CRT Controller Register 07H—Vertical Sync Position to 3EH. A new value is required to properly set the vertical timing for 480 lines.
12. Set CRT Controller Register 10H—Vertical Sync Start to EAH. A new value is required to properly set the vertical timing for 480 lines.
13. Set CRT Controller Register 11H—Vertical Sync End to ACH. A new value is required to properly set the vertical timing for 480 lines.
14. Set CRT Controller Register 12H—Vertical Display End to DFH. A new value is required to properly set the vertical timing for 480 lines.
15. Set CRT Controller Register 15H—Start Vertical Blank to E7H. A new value is required to properly set the vertical timing for 480 lines.
16. Set CRT Controller Register 16H—End Vertical Blank to 06H. A new value is required to properly set the vertical timing for 480 lines.

17. Set CRT Controller Register 09H—Max Row Address to 41H.

The xmodetst.cpp Program

The *xmodetst.cpp* program will enable you to draw a pattern of lines in mode 13H and in each of the undocumented modes to test how these modes work with your VGA card and VGA monitor. The program is given in Listing 5-3. You need to include the *setMode* function listed in Listing 5-2 when you compile and run this program. Several functions and parts of this program are described in detail in subsequent chapters and therefore will not be described here. We've included the program, somewhat out of sequence, in this chapter so that you can try out the undocumented modes at this point. If you are interested in further details, consult Chapter 6 on plotting points to the graphics screen and Chapter 9 on drawing lines and rectangles. The program makes use of a variant of the line pattern display that is part of the *Linetest.cpp* program described in Chapter 9. This program draws a wide rectangular border around the screen and then draws four sets of lines, each set radiating from one of the corners of the rectangle. Each line is a different color. (If there are more than 256 lines for the resolution specified, then the colors start repeating.) There are five different undocumented display modes. You will observe that the module for creating a pattern of lines for each display mode is the same as all the others except for the mode that is selected by the *setMode* function and for the values of *xres* and *yres* that are set to the horizontal and vertical resolutions respectively of the desired mode. The function for setting the VGA color registers *(setVGApalette)* is called at the beginning of each module, so that the module can be taken out and run as a self-contained program, if desired. If you don't care to do this, one statement at the beginning of the program to set the color registers is sufficient.

VESA Super VGA Display Modes

In an attempt to achieve some kind of standardization, the VESA Super VGA BIOS Extension standard was developed by a group of manufacturers working together. The Video Electronics Standards Association is the international, non-profit organization which sets and supports industry-wide video graphics standards for the benefit of the end user. VESA's membership consists of manufacturers of

Listing 5-3. The xmodetst.cpp *Program to Demonstrate Undocumented 256 Color Modes*

```
/*

        xmodetst.cpp = Program to do line test for all
          undocumented VGA graphics display modes.

               By Roger T. Stevens   12-4-95

*/

#include <dos.h>
#include <stdio.h>
#include <stdlib.h>
#include <mem.h>
#include <conio.h>

void plot(int x, int y, int color);
void setMode(int mode);
void drawLine(int xs, int ys, int xe, int ye, int color);
void setVGApalette(unsigned char *buffer);

typedef struct
{
      unsigned char red;
      unsigned char green;
      unsigned char blue;
} RGB;

RGB palette[256];

int color, hue, i, j, k, LINEWIDTH = 3;
int xres, yres, mode;
unsigned long int PATTERN = 0xFFFFFFFF;

union REGS reg;

void main(void)
{
      palette[0].red = 0;
      palette[0].green = 0;
      palette[0].blue = 0;
      for (i=0; i<6; i++)
      {
          for(j=0; j<6; j++)
          {
              for (k=1; k<8; k++)
              {
                  palette[42*i+7*j+k].red = i*12+1;
                  palette[42*i+7*j+k].green = j*12+1;
                  palette[42*i+7*j+k].blue = 10*(k-1)+1;
              }
          }
```

```
        }
/*
            Mode 13H = 320 x 200 pixels x 256 colors
*/

        mode = 0x13;
        setMode(mode);
        setVGApalette(&palette[0].red);
        LINEWIDTH = 3;
        xres = 320; yres = 200;
        drawLine(6,8,xres-5,8,42);
        drawLine(6,yres-4,xres-5,yres-4,42);
        drawLine(7,8,7,yres-4,42);
        drawLine(xres-6,8,xres-6,yres-4,42);
        LINEWIDTH = 1;
        hue = 250;
        for (i=30; i< yres-10; i+=20)
        {
            drawLine(10,10,xres-8,i, hue--);
            drawLine(xres-8,yres-6,10,i, hue--);
            drawLine(10,yres-6,xres-8,i, hue--);
            drawLine(xres-8,10,10,i, hue--);
        }
        getch();

/*
            Mode F0H = 320 x 400 pixels x 256 colors
*/

        mode = 0xF0;
        setMode(mode);
        setVGApalette(&palette[0].red);
        LINEWIDTH = 3;
        xres = 320; yres = 400;
        drawLine(6,8,xres-5,8,42);
        drawLine(6,yres-4,xres-5,yres-4,42);
        drawLine(7,8,7,yres-4,42);
        drawLine(xres-6,8,xres-6,yres-4,42);
        LINEWIDTH = 1;
        hue = 250;
        for (i=30; i< yres-10; i+=20)
        {
            drawLine(10,10,xres-8,i, hue--);
            drawLine(xres-8,yres-6,10,i, hue--);
            drawLine(10,yres-6,xres-8,i, hue--);
            drawLine(xres-8,10,10,i, hue--);
        }
        getch();
```

```
/*
        Mode F1H = 320 x 240 pixels x 256 colors
*/
        mode = 0xF1;
        setMode(mode);
        setVGApalette(&palette[0].red);
        LINEWIDTH = 3;
        xres = 320; yres = 240;
        drawLine(6,8,xres-5,8,42);
        drawLine(6,yres-4,xres-5,yres-4,42);
        drawLine(7,8,7,yres-4,42);
        drawLine(xres-6,8,xres-6,yres-4,42);
        LINEWIDTH = 1;
        hue = 250;
        for (i=30; i< yres-10; i+=20)
        {
            drawLine(10,10,xres-8,i, hue--);
            drawLine(xres-8,yres-6,10,i, hue--);
            drawLine(10,yres-6,xres-8,i, hue--);
            drawLine(xres-8,10,10,i, hue--);
        }
        getch();
/*
        Mode F2H = 320 x 480 pixels x 256 colors
*/

        mode = 0xF2;
        setMode(mode);
        setVGApalette(&palette[0].red);
        LINEWIDTH = 3;
        xres = 320; yres = 480;
        drawLine(6,8,xres-5,8,42);
        drawLine(6,yres-4,xres-5,yres-4,42);
        drawLine(7,8,7,yres-4,42);
        drawLine(xres-6,8,xres-6,yres-4,42);
        LINEWIDTH = 1;
        hue = 250;
        for (i=30; i< yres-10; i+=20)
        {
            drawLine(10,10,xres-8,i, hue--);
            drawLine(xres-8,yres-6,10,i, hue--);
            drawLine(10,yres-6,xres-8,i, hue--);
            drawLine(xres-8,10,10,i, hue--);
        }
        getch();
```

```
/*

        Mode F3H = 360 x 400 pixels x 256 colors

*/

            mode = 0xF3;
            setMode(mode);
            setVGApalette(&palette[0].red);
            LINEWIDTH = 3;
            xres = 360; yres = 400;
            drawLine(6,8,xres-5,8,42);
            drawLine(6,yres-4,xres-5,yres-4,42);
            drawLine(7,8,7,yres-4,42);
            drawLine(xres-6,8,xres-6,yres-4,42);
            LINEWIDTH = 1;
            hue = 250;
            for (i=30; i< yres-10; i+=20)
            {
                drawLine(10,10,xres-8,i, hue--);
                drawLine(xres-8,yres-6,10,i, hue--);
                drawLine(10,yres-6,xres-8,i, hue--);
                drawLine(xres-8,10,10,i, hue--);
            }
            getch();

/*

        Mode F4H = 360 x 480 pixels x 256 colors

*/

            mode = 0xF4;
            setMode(mode);
            setVGApalette(&palette[0].red);
            LINEWIDTH = 3;
            xres = 360; yres = 480;
            drawLine(6,8,xres-5,8,42);
            drawLine(6,yres-4,xres-5,yres-4,42);
            drawLine(7,8,7,yres-4,42);
            drawLine(xres-6,8,xres-6,yres-4,42);
            LINEWIDTH = 1;
            hue = 250;
            for (i=30; i< yres-10; i+=20)
            {
                drawLine(10,10,xres-8,i, hue--);
                drawLine(xres-8,yres-6,10,i, hue--);
                drawLine(10,yres-6,xres-8,i, hue--);
                drawLine(xres-8,10,10,i, hue--);
            }
            getch();
            setMode(0x03);
    }
```

```
/*
        drawLine() = Draws a line from one set of coordinates to
                      another in designated color
*/

void drawLine(int xs, int ys, int xe, int ye, int color)
{
        extern int LINEWIDTH;
        extern unsigned long int PATTERN;
        extern unsigned long int PATTERN;

        int temp, dx, dy, i, j, x, y, x_sign, y_sign,
        decision;
        unsigned long int mask;
        dx = abs(xe - xs);
        dy = abs(ye - ys);
        if (((dx > dy) && (xs > xe)) ||
            ((dy > dx) && (ys > ye)))
        {
            temp = xs;
            xs = xe;
            xe = temp;
            temp = ys;
            ys = ye;
            ye = temp;
        }
        if ((ye - ys) < 0)
            y_sign = -1;
        else
            y_sign = 1;
        if ((xe - xs) < 0)
            x_sign = -1;
        else
            x_sign = 1;
        if (dx > dy)
        {
            for (x=xs,y=ys,decision=0; x<=xe; x++,decision+=dy)
            {
                mask = (mask !=1) ? mask >> 1 : 0x80000000;
                if (decision>=dx)
                {
                    decision -= dx;
                    y+= y_sign;
                }
                if (PATTERN & mask)
                    for (j=-LINEWIDTH/2; j<=LINEWIDTH/2; j++)
                    plot(x,y+j,color);
            }
        }
        else
        {
            for (x=xs,y=ys,decision=0; y<=ye; y++,decision+=dx)
            {
```

```
                mask = mask !=1 ? mask >> 1 : 0x80000000;
                if (decision>=dy)
                {
                    decision -= dy;
                    x += x_sign;
                }
                if (PATTERN & mask)
                    for (j=-LINEWIDTH/2; j<=LINEWIDTH/2; j++)
                        plot(x+j,y,color);
            }
        }
}

/*

    plot() = Function to plot point to VGA 256 Color Screen
                using X mode (320 x 240 pixels)

*/

#define seq_out(index,val) {outp(0x3c4, index);\
                            outp(0x3c5, val);}
void plot(int x, int y, int color)
{
      unsigned long int offset;
      char far *address;
      unsigned int plane;

      offset = (long)xres * y + x;
      if (mode > 0x7F)
      {
          plane = (0x01 << (offset % 4));
          seq_out(2,plane);
          offset >>= 2;
      }
      address = (char far *)(0xA0000000L + offset);
      *address = color;
      seq_out(2,0xFF);
}

/*

    setVGApalette() = Function to set all 256 color registers

*/

void setVGApalette(unsigned char *buffer)
{
      struct SREGS inreg;
      union REGS reg;

      reg.x.ax = 0x1012;
      segread(&inreg);
```

```
        inreg.es = inreg.ds;
        reg.x.bx = 0;
        reg.x.cx = 256;
        reg.x.dx = (int)&buffer[0];
        int86x(0x10,&reg,&reg,&inreg);
        }
```

monitors, peripherals, systems, and software products. The VESA offices are located at 2150 North First Street, Suite 440, San Jose, CA 95131-2029, and can be reached at 408-435-0333, FAX 408-435-8225. The current VESA BIOS extension standard is VBE version 1.2. While these standards are a very large step toward achieving compatibility, and while most current Super VGA boards support at least some of the VESA display modes, there are still display modes on some Super VGA boards that are not VESA compatible and not all Super VGA boards support all VESA display modes.

Table 5-3 shows the Super VGA modes that have been standardized by VESA. Please note that this is a list of all VESA modes but VESA does not require your Super VGA card to support all of these modes. In future chapters, we'll show you how to use information stored on the Super VGA card to determine which modes your card supports so that you can program in ways that are compatible with all cards. If you have a rather old Super VGA card, it may not support the most recent VESA standards, in which case you may find that some of the software described doesn't work properly. If you insist on continuing to work with such a card, you'll need to get information from the manufacturer on how the internal registers of your card work and write programs that access at the register level. To avoid this added time and expense, you'd probably be better off to buy a new Super VGA card.

Each Super VGA card that complies with VESA standards has a built-in supplement to the ROM BIOS that supports various VESA-defined functions. These are defined as sub-functions under the generic video service designation

Table 5-3. VESA Super VGA Display Modes

Mode (Hex)	Type	Colors	Resolution
100	Graphics	256/256K	640×400
101	Graphics	256/256K	640×480
102 or 6A	Graphics	16/256K	800×600
103	Graphics	256/256K	800×600
104	Graphics	16/256K	1024×768
105	Graphics	256/256K	1024×768
106	Graphics	16/256K	1280×1024
107	Graphics	256/256K	1280×1024
108	Text	16/256K	80×60 ch 640×480
109	Text	16/256K	132×25 ch 1188×400
10A	Text	16/256K	132×43 ch 1188×387
10B	Text	16/256K	132×50 ch 1056×400
10C	Text	16/256K	132×60 ch 1056×480
10D	Graphics	32K	320x200
10E	Graphics	64K	320x200
10F	Graphics	16.8M	320×200
110	Graphics	32K	640×400
111	Graphics	64K	640×480
112	Graphics	16.8M	640×480

Table 5-3. VESA Super VGA Display Modes (cont.)

Mode (Hex)	Type	Colors	Resolution
113	Graphics	32K	800×600
114	Graphics	64K	800×600
115	Graphics	16.8M	800×600
116	Graphics	32K	1024×768
117	Graphics	64K	1024×768
118	Graphics	16.8M	1024×768
119	Graphics	32K	1280×1024
11A	Graphics	64K	1280×1024
11B	Graphics	16.8M	1280×1024

4FH (normally entered in register *ah*). The sub-function 02H is the VESA set display mode function. Thus, for all VESA supporting VGA and Super VGA cards, the function corres-ponding to the *setMode* function that occupies lines 54 to 60 of Listing 5-1 is rewritten in Listing 5-4. This function will work for all VGA modes and VESA modes if your Super VGA card is VESA compatible. However, if you use it in a piece of software and then attempt to run the software on a system using non-VESA VGA card, it won't work. So if you're trying to make your software compatible with a lot of different cards, you need to combine this code with that of Listing 5-1 so that the VESA routine is used for VESA compatible cards and the function of Listing 5-1 for regular cards. We'll get into more details about how to do this in Chapter 8.

Listing 5-4. VESA Function for Setting Display Modes

```
/*
                    setMode() = Sets Video Mode
*/
        void setMode(int mode)
        {
        union REGS reg;

        reg.h.ah = 0x4F;
        reg.h.al = 0x02;
        reg.x.bx = mode;
        int86 (0x10,&reg,&reg);
        }
```

6

Plotting a Point on the Graphics Screen

Fortunately, in graphics programming you do not often have to probe the overwhelming array of graphics adapter card registers described in the previous chapters. Most of the graphics operations that you will want to perform can be done with functions from the ROM BIOS video services, which will be described in Chapter 7. A prominent and often used exception to this is the actual plotting of points to the display screen. Using the ROM BIOS video service, with its interrupt-driven structure, just slows things up too much when many points have to be displayed. Therefore, in this chapter we're going to show you how to plot points directly. As you study the software given, you'll begin to get the feel for how to work with the display adapter registers if you have some exotic application that can't be done with the ordinary video services.

Creating a graphics display usually involves plotting one pixel at a time to the screen until the display is complete. A point is plotted by determining its location in display memory and then taking actions that depend upon the display mode being used. The number of pixels on the screen differs widely for the different graphics modes. At the low end, the most used CGA color graphics mode is Mode 04H, which is 320 × 200 pixels × 4 colors. Thus for this mode, the screen has 64,000 pixels, each of which can be represented by two bits, yielding a total memory requirement of 16,000 bytes. The most common EGA color graphics mode is Mode 10H which is 640 × 350 pixels × 16 colors. This screen has 224,000 pixels. Because of the four-plane memory structure, only one bit per pixel is needed, so the memory requirement is 28,000 bytes. At the high end are such super VGA modes as 1024 × 768 pixels

× 256 colors. This screen has 786,432 pixels, each represented by a full byte, so that 786,432 bytes of memory are required. Since this far exceeds the allocated 64K of graphics display memory, some paging technique is needed. Plotting this number of pixels one by one is pretty slow, but fortunately we can usually use one operation to set up a background color that takes care of many pixels and then call a point-plotting function only to plot those pixels that differ from the background. Nevertheless, you can see that we are going to be using the point plotting routine many times in the course of creating a graphics display. Therefore, it is important to plot each pixel as fast as possible so as to minimize the amount of time required to create a graphics display.

Plotting a Point on the CGA

The original CGA color modes such as mode 4 are now obsolete; you're only likely to encounter them when running old game programs. However, these modes are still supported by the VGA, to keep it backward compatible with older programs. You certainly won't want to program in this mode, but you may like to know how it works. Mode 4 consists of 320 × 200 pixels × 4 colors. In mode 4, the CGA has one page of graphics data located at address B8000H, so there is no need to worry about changing pages. (However, the page limitation is based upon the limited amount of memory that comes with a standard CGA; if you are using an EGA or VGA you may have enough memory to access more than one page in this mode and may wish to modify the plotting function to handle the additional pages.) Beginning at the top lefthand corner of the screen, each pixel is represented by two bits in video memory, which form a binary number from 0 to 3, representing the pixel color from 0 to 3, as defined by the selected palette. (For palette 0, color 0 is the current background color and the other three colors in numerical order are green, red, and brown. For palette 1, the colors are the current background color followed in numerical order by cyan, magenta, and white.)

The arrangement of the bits in memory begins with pixel 0 (at the top lefthand corner of the screen), which is stored in the 2 most significant bits of memory address B8000H. The next pixel (pixel 1) in line 0 is stored in the next 2 memory bits, and so forth, until a complete line (320 pixels) has been stored (using up 80 bytes at 2 bits per pixel and 8 bits per byte). The first pixel in the next line (line 1) is stored in the 2 most significant bits of memory address BA000H. The process continues, with pixels for even lines stored consecutively in the memory section beginning at address B8000H and pixels for odd lines stored consecutively in the memory section beginning at address BA000H. Using this information, we can create the point-plotting function listed in Listing 6-1. (The C language does not use line numbers; they are given here for your convenience in referencing the data, but should be removed from an actual program.) Before we look at the actual function, we need to note how C compilers handle data of the type *char far* *, which represents a far address. The compiler uses the four most significant hexadecimal digits to set the segment register and the lower four hexadecimal digits to set the memory address. Thus when we define an address as 0xA0000000L, the actual memory address is A0000H. This can be a little confusing if you don't fully understand that an address is defined by the contents of the segment register multiplied by 16 and added to the contents of the address byte. The function begins in line 5 by computing the offset of the memory address from the base address of B8000H. Note that we use the number of lines modula 2 to add an offset of 2000H for odd lines, but not for even ones. Then we add in 80 bytes for each pair of lines plus the column value divided by four (since four pixels use up only one byte of memory). In line 6, we add this offset to the base graphics display memory address to obtain the address of the display memory byte that contains the pixel we want to write. Next, in line 7, we create a mask consisting of ones at two adjacent bit positions and zeroes elsewhere and shift it to line up with the proper bit positions for the pixel we want to write. In line 8, we shift the *color* data to line up with the mask position. In line 9, we AND the contents of the selected memory address with the inverse of the mask, leaving the original color data for all except the pixel to be changed, whose two bits are now zero. We then OR this with the combination of the shifted color data ANDed with the mask to create the new value of the contents of the selected memory address, which has the changed pixel in the new color and the other pixels unchanged. Note that if we are sure the *color* information is always a value between 0 and 3, we don't need to perform the operation of ANDing the shifted color with the mask; this simply protects us against a wrong color value upsetting adjacent pixel values. The result is that the memory address contains new data for the two pixels at the selected address, and the original data for the three unchanged pixels.

Listing 6-1. Plot Function for CGA (Mode 4) Using Direct Memory Access

```
/*

plot() = Plots a point at (x,y) in selected color usingCGA
     mode 4, sending data directly to display memory.

*/

void  plot (int x, int y, int color)
{
    int offset, mask, temp;
    char far *address;

    offset = 0x2000*(y%2) + 80*(y>>1) + (x>>2);
    address = (char far *) (0xB8000000L + offset);
    mask = 0xC0 >> ((x%4)<<1);
    temp = color<<(6-((x%4)<<1));
    *address = (*address & ~mask) | (temp & mask);
}
```

Point Plotting in 16-Color Modes

Plotting points in 16-color modes is complicated because of the 4-plane memory structure and the fact that doing a read or write to a graphics memory address does not actually read from or write to the addressed memory byte, but instead initiates a series of actions on data that depends upon the settings of the internal registers of the display adapter card. Listing 6-2 is a program that draws a number of vertical lines on the screen, using six different plot functions that utilize various write modes. (You'll see, as we progress, that when writing pixels to the screen, unless we take a masking action, a whole byte, representing 8 adjacent pixels, is plotted. Our program plots vertical lines so that if any mistake is made in the masking it will be obvious as a line that is more than 1 pixel wide. If we were drawing horizontal lines, such an error might result in 8-pixel-wide lines being plotted and overlapping each other, which might not be obvious to the observer.) We'll describe each of the plot functions in following sections. First, however, let's look at the main program. In line 24, we use the setMode function (which will be described in Chapter 7) to set the display to the 640 x 480 pixel x 16-color mode. Then, in line 25, we enter a *for* loop that iterates from 0 to 479 to set the *y* coordinate for each vertical line to be drawn. Within this loop, we plot a series of vertical lines, using different methods for pixel plotting.

Listing 6-2. Program for Testing Plotting Functions

```
/*
╔══════════════════════════════════════════════════════════════╗
║                                                              ║
║   plottest = PROGRAM TO TEST POINT PLOTTING ROUTINES         ║
║              By Roger T. Stevens  11-1-95                    ║
║                                                              ║
╚══════════════════════════════════════════════════════════════╝
*/

#include <stdarg.h>
#include <stdio.h>
#include <stdlib.h>
#include <string.h>
#include <math.h>
#include <dos.h>
#include <conio.h>
#include <ctype.h>
#include <dir.h>

void plot1(int x, int y, char color);
void plot2(int x, int y, char color);
void plot3(int x, int y, char color);
void plot4(int x, int y, char color);
void plot5(int x1, int y1, int x2, int y2);
void plot6(int x, int y, char color);
void plot7(int x, int y, char color);
void setMode(int mode);

#define seq_outw(index,val) {outpw(0x3C4,index | \
(val<<8));}
#define graph_outw(index,val) {outpw(0x3CE,index | \
              (val<<8));}
#define seq_out(index,val)  {outp(0x3C4,index);\
               outp(0x3C5,val);}

#define graph_out(index,val) \ {outp(0x3CE,index);\
               outp(0x3CF,val);}

int xres = 80;

void main(void)
{
    int i;
    setMode(0x12);
    for (i=0; i<=479; i++)
    {
        plot1(260,i,13);
        plot2(280,i,10);
        plot2(300,i,15);
        plot3(300,i,9);
        plot2(320,i,15);
```

```
            plot4(320,i,11);
            plot5(260,i,340,i);
            plot6(360,i,12);
            plot7(380,i,14);
        }
        getch();
    }

/*

plot1() = plots a point on the screen at designated system
 coordinates using sequencer register to select a desired
              color. Uses write mode 0.

*/

    void plot1(int x, int y, char color)
    {

        extern int xres;
        unsigned int offset;
        char dummy, mask;
        char far * mem_address;

        offset = (long int)y * xres + ((long int)x / 8L);
        mem_address = (char far *) (0xA0000000L +
            (long int)offset);
        mask = 0x80 >> (x % 8);
        graph_out(8,mask);
        dummy = *mem_address;
        seq_out(2,color);
        *mem_address = 0xFF;
        seq_out(2,0x0F);
        graph_out(0,0xFF);
        graph_out(8,0xFF);
    }

/*

plot2() = plots a point on the screen at designated system
 coordinates using sequencer register to select a desired
     color and using word outputs.Uses write mode 0.

*/

    void plot2(int x, int y, char color)
    {
        extern int xres;
        unsigned int offset;
        char dummy, mask;
```

```
        char far * mem_address;

        offset = (long int)y * xres + ((long int)x / 8L);
        mem_address = (char far *) (0xA0000000L +
                (long)offset);
        mask = 0x80 >> (x % 8);
        graph_outw(8,mask);
        dummy = *mem_address;
        seq_outw(2,color);
        *mem_address = 0xFF;
        seq_outw(2,0x0F);
        graph_outw(8,0xFF);
    }

/*

plot3() = plots a point on the screen at designated system
  coordinates using graphics register to select a desired
                color. Uses write mode 0.

*/

    void plot3(int x, int y, char color)
    {
        unsigned int offset;
        char dummy, mask;
        char far * mem_address;

        offset = (long int)y * xres + ((long int)x / 8L);
        mem_address = (char far *) (0xA0000000L +
            (long)offset);
        dummy = *mem_address;
        mask = 0x80 >> (x % 8);
        graph_outw(8,mask);
        graph_outw(0,0x0F);
        graph_outw(1, color);
        *mem_address = 0x00;
        graph_outw(1,0x00);
        graph_outw(8,0xFF);
    }
```

```
/*
plot4() = plots a point on the screen at
 designated system coordinates using graphics register to
        select a desired color. Uses writemode 0.
*/

void plot4(int x, int y, char color)
{
    unsigned int offset;
    char dummy, mask;
    char far * mem_address;

    offset = (long int)y * xres + ((long int)x / 8L);
    mem_address = (char far *) (0xA0000000L +
        (long)offset);
    dummy = *mem_address;
    mask = 0x80 >> (x % 8);
    graph_outw(8,mask);
    graph_outw(0,0x00);
    graph_outw(1,~color);
    *mem_address = 0xFF;
    graph_outw(0,0x00);
    graph_outw(1,0x00);
    graph_outw(8,0xFF);
}

/*
 plot5() = copies a byte (8 pixels) on the screen at the
 display coordinates (x1,y1) to the display coordinates
            (x2, y2) using write mode 1.
*/

void plot5(int x1, int y1, int x2, int y2)
{
    extern int xres;
    unsigned int offset1, offset2;
    char far * mem_address1;
    char far * mem_address2;
    char dummy;

    offset1 = (long int)y1 * xres + ((long int)x1 / 8L);
    mem_address1 = (char far *) (0xA0000000L +
        (long)offset1);
    offset2 = (long)y2 * xres + ((long)x2 / 8L);
    mem_address2 = (char far *) (0xA0000000L +
        (long)offset2);
    graph_outw(5,1);
    dummy = *mem_address1;
    *mem_address2 = 0xFF;
    graph_outw(5,0);
```

```
}

/*
plot6() = writes a pixel to the screen using write mode 2.
*/

void plot6(int x, int y, char color)
{
    extern xres;
    unsigned int offset;
    char far * mem_address;
    char dummy, mask;

    offset = (long)y * xres + ((long)x / 8L);
    mem_address = (char far *) (0xA0000000L +
        (long)offset);
    mask = 0x80 >> (x % 8);
    graph_outw(8,mask);
    graph_outw(5,2);
    dummy = *mem_address;
    *mem_address = color;
    graph_outw(8,0xFF);
    graph_outw(5,0);
}

/*
plot7() = plots a point on the screen at designated system
  coordinates using graphics register to select a desired
                color. Uses write mode 3.
*/

void plot7(int x, int y, char color)
{
    unsigned int offset;
    char dummy, mask;
    char far * mem_address;

    offset = (long)y * xres + ((long)x / 8L);
    mem_address = (char far *) (0xA0000000L +
        (long)offset);
    dummy = *mem_address;
    mask = 0x80 >> (x % 8);
    graph_outw(5,3);
    graph_outw(1,0x0F);
    graph_outw(0,color);
    *mem_address = mask;
    graph_outw(5,0);
    graph_outw(0,0x00);
    graph_outw(1,0x00);
```

```
        graph_outw(8,0xFF);
    }

/*
                setMode() = Sets Video Mode
*/

    void setMode(int mode)
    {
        union REGS reg;

        reg.x.ax = mode;
        int86 (0x10,&reg,&reg);
    }
```

Point Plotting with 16-Color EGA/VGA Modes Using the Sequencer Registers and Byte Outputs to the Registers

Because 16-color display modes are characterized by the four-plane display memory structure already described, we cannot directly write a pixel to a memory address. In the default condition of the graphics adapter card registers, (write mode 1) writing to a memory address in the 16-color modes causes the byte written to be sent to every one of the four display memory planes, resulting in a bright white pixel being written at each of eight adjacent pixel locations corresponding to a 1 in the written byte and a black pixel being written to each of the eight adjacent pixel locations corresponding to a 0 in the written byte. Usually, this isn't very useful. Fortunately, we can do some things to the registers that will enable us to do what we want in this situation. The first thing to observe is that in the default write mode of 0, we can send a byte to graphics register 8 that defines which pixels are to be modified in the writing process. If we're just going to write one pixel to the screen, this byte will contain only a single 1 at the desired pixel location. Second, we can send a byte to sequencer register 2 that determines which of the color planes are to be written to. By sending a color value from 0 to 15, we can write the pixel in the desired color. Now, look at the function *plot1* to see how this is done.

In order to properly determine the memory address at which a pixel is to be written, the *extern* parameter *xres* must be set to the number of bytes needed to store a full line of pixels, which is the number of pixels in a line. For example, a 16-color mode that has a resolution of 640 pixels per line requires that *xres* be set to 80. (Since 1 bit is allocated for each pixel and there are 8 bits in a byte, 80 bytes are required to store 640 pixels.) In line 45, the function calculates the offset of the pixel address from the base display memory address by multiplying the number of lines (*y*) by the number of bytes per line (*xres*) and adding the column number (*x*) of the pixel divided by 8. In lines 46 and 47, this offset is added to the base memory address (*0xA0000000L*) to obtain the display memory address of the pixel (*mem_address*). Note that this is the address for all eight pixels that make up a byte. In line 48, a byte containing only one bit, in the most significant position, is shifted right by the *x* modulo 8 (the remainder when *x* is divided by 8) to find the position within the byte occupied by the desired pixel, which is set up in *mask*. Now, let's look for a moment at line 19, which defines the macro *graph_out*. This macro outputs a byte (*index*) to port 3CEH to select the number of a graphics register to be used and then outputs a value (*val*) to port 3CFH to set it in the selected graphics register. Now, back at line 49, we use this macro to send the *mask* to graphics register 8. Now, if we write to a memory address, only the bit in each memory plane represented by the 1 in the mask will be affected; all other bits in the selected byte will be filled with the contents of the display memory plane storage registers. Consequently, before we do anything else, we perform a dummy read of the selected display memory address, so that the registers just mentioned are filled with the contents of the display memory at that address. We then put the pixel *color* parameter into sequencer register 2 with the *seq_out* macro (defined in line 18). This determines that the masked bit will be set to 1 for only the storage registers for the planes having 1's in the color parameter; that bit in the other color planes will be set to 0. Finally, in line 52, we write a full byte of 1's to the selected memory address. This doesn't go directly to display memory, however; it is controlled by various internal registers that decide what will actually be sent to the address for each memory plane. For all but the masked bit, the contents of the memory storage registers are returned to the actual memory plane, so that the unselected pixels are rewritten with their original contents and do not change. For the masked bit (or bits) the original value is changed to that sent to the memory address (always a 1 in this case) for those memory planes selected by sequencer register 2 and to a 0 for those planes not selected. The result of all this is that a pixel of the selected color appears at the desired location.

Point Plotting with 16-Color EGA/VGA Modes Using the Sequencer Registers and Word Outputs to the Registers

The second line in the display is drawn by the function *plot2*. This function is listed in lines 57 to 72. It is just the same as *plot1* except that the macro *seq_outw* is used instead of *seq_out* and the macro *graph_outw* is used instead of *graph_out*. The first of these macros is defined in line 16 and the second in line 17. Both make use of the function *outpw*. This function passes two parameters, a port address, and a word value. The eight least significant bits of the word are sent to the port address and the eight most significant bits of the word are sent to the next higher port address. This works well for those registers of the graphics adapter card where a port address is assigned to contain the register number and the next higher adjacent port address is sent the value to be put in the register. (As noted in the previous chapter, some registers have only one port access address, which toggles between the register number and register value. This method wouldn't work for sending data to them, but it works just fine for sending data to the sequencer and graphics registers.) All we have to do in the macro before calling *outpw* is to assemble the value word by putting the index value into a word-length variable and then ORing it with the desired value for the register shifted eight bits to the left. As you will see from running the program, this technique produces just the same results as the first plot function.

Point Plotting with 16-Color EGA/VGA Modes Using the Graphics Registers

Another way of plotting a point to the EGA/VGA card in the 16-color mode is to use Graphics Register 01H—Enable Set/Reset and Graphics Register 00H—Set/Reset to control the color instead of using Sequencer Register 02H—Map Mask. It may appear at first glance that Graphics Register 01H and Sequencer Register 02H do the same thing, but this is not true. In Write Mode 0, assuming that Graphics Register 01H is at its default value of 00H, the data that is sent to the memory bits selected by Graphics Register 08H—Bit Mask by writing to the memory address normally goes to every one of the four memory planes, thereby writing a white pixel. We have just seen that using Sequencer Register 02H to activate only those planes needed to produce a given color causes the memory write to produce a pixel of the desired color. Now, suppose that instead of sending the color data to Sequencer Register 02H, we send it instead to Graphics Register 01H. Now, each 1 in the color value (4 bits) set to Graphics Register 01H causes the data for the entire memory byte in that memory plane to be 1's or 0's depending upon whether the bit for that memory plane is a 1 or 0 in Graphics Register 1. Each 0 in the color value sent to Graphics Register 01H causes the memory byte in that memory plane to be the value written to the display memory address. Again, the affected bits are determined by Graphics Register 08H—Bit Mask.

So suppose the bit-mask register maintains its default value of FFH and we set Graphics Register 01H to 09H. We also set Graphics Register 00H to 0FH and write 81H to the memory address. The byte of 8 pixels at the memory address is changed as follows. For memory plane 0 and memory plane 3 the 1 in that memory plane position causes the 1 in that plane position in Graphics Register 00H to be controlling and the entire byte is filled with 1's. For the other two memory planes, the byte is filled with the 81H written to the memory address. The result is that the first and last bits are 1 in every memory plane and the intermediate bits are 1 only in planes 0 and 3. Consequently, a row of eight pixels is displayed on the screen, with the first and last bright white and the intermediate ones bright blue.

The function *plot3* shows one way of using these graphics registers to write single pixels in various colors. You will observe that lines 73 through 83 are just the same as for the function *plot2*. In line 84, we set Graphics Register 00H to 0FH. (This is just for safety—it is the default value of the register, so we shouldn't really have to change it.) Then, in line 85, we set Graphics Register 01H to the desired color. Now, the bits selected by the mask will be filled with 1's for each plane designated by *color*. We then write a byte of 0's to the memory address in line 86. This causes the masked bits to be set to 0 for color planes that are not designated by a 1 in Graphics Register 01H. The result is that the selected pixel is displayed in the designated color.

The function *plot4* is another way of doing the same thing. It is mostly the same as *plot3*. The differences are that in line 101 we put 0's in Graphics Register 00H, so that when this is selected, a byte of 0's is set to the designated registers. Then, in line 102, we send the inverse of the color to Graphics Register 01H, so that the memory data for planes that have a 0 in the original color take their data from Graphics Register 00H. Finally, in line 103, we write a byte of 1's to the memory address, so that they are transferred to display memory for color planes where the original color had a 1. The result as far as the displayed pixel is concerned is just the same as for the function *plot3*.

Plotting with 16-Color EGA/VGA Modes Using Write Mode 1

Write mode 1 is an extremely fast method for transferring a byte of data (a block of eight adjacent pixels) from one place in display memory to another. The only problem with this mode is that it doesn't use the mask register, so you are stuck with moving blocks of eight pixels. The function *plot5* accepts as input parameters the *x* and *y* coordinates of a location to read a byte from and a location to write the same byte to. Looking at lines 108 through 117, you'll see that we compute a display memory address in just the same way as for previous plot functions. This address is the address from which we are extracting the data for the block of pixels. Next, in lines 118 through 120 we compute the display memory address for the data destination in the same way. Line 121 sets the Graphics Register 05H—Mode to write mode 1. In line 122, we do a dummy read of the first address. This transfers the color data for a byte from each of the four memory planes to its associated processor register in a single operation. In line 123, we do a write to the destination display memory address, causing the contents of all four processor registers to be transferred to their associated memory planes in a single operation. In the demonstration program, we have used this function to transfer to a new location a series of 8-pixel-wide blocks of data that form a single-pixel-wide line and the background pixels that surround it. Since write mode 1 is much faster than any other way of writing pixel data, you can substantially speed up your graphics programs by figuring out ways to use this mode in creating your graphics displays.

Point Plotting with 16-Color EGA/VGA Modes Using Write Mode 2

A third way of plotting a point to the EGA/VGA card in the 16-color mode is to use write mode 2, where color data transferred to memory is sent directly to the color planes. The function *plot6* does this. Like the previous functions, the first thing that the function does (in line 132) is compute the offset from the base memory address by multiplying the number of lines by xres and then adding in the number of bytes required to reach the byte containing the desired pixel information. Next (in lines 133 and 134) the address is determined by adding this offset to the base memory address. In line 135 the function sets up a mask that has a 1 only in the bit position representing the pixel being selected. In line 136, the function sends this mask out to Graphics Register 08H—Bit Mask. Line 137 sets Graphics Register 05H—Mode to write mode 2. IBM says that in this mode, when a write operation takes place, each bit in the character that is written is expanded to eight identical bits and transferred to one of the color planes. For example, if bit 1 is 1 and bit 0 is 0, then 11111111B would be sent to the selected address in the green memory plane and 00000000B would be sent to the address in the blue memory plane. However, we have set up the mask so that actually only one bit is sent to each color plane. Line 138 does a dummy read of the selected address to transfer the display memory data from the four planes to the corresponding processor registers. When a write to display memory occurs in line 139, the bits in the addressed word in each of the four bit planes that correspond in position to 0 in the bit mask register are immune to change. Where there is a 1 in the bit mask register, the bits in each of the bit planes are changed by the write operation to the bit sent to that memory plane by the write operation. This function should be faster than the previous ones using write mode 0.

Point Plotting with 16-Color EGA/VGA Modes Using Write Mode 3

Write mode 3 uses Graphics Register 03H—Data Rotation/Function Select and Graphics Register 08H—Bit Mask to operate upon the data written to the display memory address in the same way as write mode 1, but then uses the result as a mask in writing eight bits of the value in Graphics Register 00H—Set/Reset to each memory plane. The function *plot7* is an example of this. Lines 143 through 152 are the same as for *plot3*. Line 153 sets Graphics Register 05H—Mode to write mode 3. Line 154 sets Graphics Register 01H to a 1 for each memory plane to select all data from Graphics Register 00H. Line 155 sets Graphics Register 00H to have 1's for only those planes that have 1's in the selected color. Line 156 writes the mask to the display memory address, causing a pixel of the desired color to be written to the screen at the designated location.

Point Plotting Using Assembly Language

It is possible to interface C code with assembly language to speed up the operation of a function. The amount of speedup that is achieved depends primarily on the efficiency of your C compiler. A function similar to that of *plot1* but using assembly language is listed in Listing 6-3. In order to compile it, you will need to have an assembler as well as a C++ or C compiler. Furthermore, some C++ and C compilers cannot handle assembly language instructions from within the integrated environment. If you are including the function in a program that is to be compiled with such a compiler, you will have to use the command line version of the compiler. I have used the regular C and assembly language versions of the plot function with a lot of different programs and have never really noticed any significant difference in speed. Therefore, I suggest that you stick with the regular C++ and C versions of the plot functions unless you have a really compelling reason to do otherwise.

Listing 6-3. Function to Plot a Point to the EGA/VGA Board in 16-Color Mode 16 Using Sequencer Registers and Assembly Language

```
/*

 plot() = Plots a point at (x,y) in selected color for EGA/
      VGA 16 color modes using C port output functions,
         sequencer register 2, and assembly language.

*/

void plot (int x, int y, int color)
{
       extern xres;
       unsigned int offset;
       int dummy, mask;
       char far *address;
       offset = (long)y*xres + (x>>3);
       mask = 0x80 >> (x%8);
       _ES = 0xA000;
       _BX = offset;
       _CX = color;
       _AX = mask;
       asm MOVAH,AL
       asm MOVAL,08
       asm MOVDX,03CEH
       asm OUTDX,AX
       asm MOVAX,0FF02H
       asm MOVDL,0C4H
       asm OUTDX,AX
       asm ORES:[BX],CH
       asm MOVBYTE PTR ES:[BX],00
       asm MOVAH,CL
       asm OUTDX,AX
       asm MOVBYTE PTR ES:[BX],0FFH
       asm MOVAH,0FFH
       asm OUTDX,AX
       asm MOVDL,0CEH
       asm MOVAX,0003
       asm OUTDX,AX
       asm MOVAX,0FF08H
       asm OUTDX,AX
}
```

Point Plotting for 256-Color VGA Modes

The VGA mode 19 is 320 × 200 pixels × 256 colors. The four planes of display memory on the VGA board are used in a very different manner when in this display mode. As far as the user is concerned, all pixels are stored in display memory consecutively, with one byte allocated to describe the color of each pixel. The first byte (at the base memory address A0000H) represents the pixel at the top lefthand corner of the screen. As the memory address increases, pixels are stored for the first line until the right side is reached. The next address is that of the first pixel at the left of the next line, and so forth. Inside the VGA board, data is actually being rotated through the four memory planes, so that in any particular memory plane, only every fourth byte is actually used. However, this internal manipulation is completely transparent to the user, who may go ahead and treat the display memory as an ordinary block of memory. Listing 6-4 is a function to plot a point in VGA mode 19. The function first computes the offset from the base memory address of the desired pixel by taking 320 bytes per line plus the number of columns. This is then added to the base memory address to obtain the actual address of the pixel. The color number of the pixel is then sent to that address. The principle is the same for extended Super VGA 256-color modes.

Listing 6-4. Function to Plot a Point with VGA Mode 19 (320 × 200 Pixels × 256 Colors)

```
/*

 plot() = Function to plot a point at (x,y) using VGA mode
         19 with a specified color from 0 to 255.

*/

void plot (int x, int y, int color)
{
      unsigned int offset
      char far *address;

      offset = 320*y + x;
      address = (char far *)(0xA0000000L + offset);
      *address = color;
}
```

Plotting a Point to the Screen with Undocumented Modes

The function *plot* paints a point to the screen in the designated color of 256 colors at the selected coordinates using any of the undocumented modes described in Chapter 5. You'll observe some similarities but also some startling differences from the plot functions previously given. Before we begin describing the function, we need to review how pixels are stored in display memory for the undocumented modes. Mode 13H chained all of the memory planes together and used the two least significant bits of the address sent to display memory to select which plane was to receive the eight bits of pixel color information. The color information was then sent to the display memory address represented by the rest of the address word (shifted two bits to the right) and to the plane represented by the two least significant bits. Two things resulted from this. First, data rotated through the four planes, with the actual internal memory address increasing only after every fourth pixel. Second, because only 14 bits were left for the display memory address, only 16K of the 64K memory window could be used in this mode. All this is happening internally in the VGA board. As far as the user is concerned, he simply assumes that each pixel uses one byte of memory and that the pixels fill adjacent addresses in display memory, with the top lefthand pixel being in the base display memory address (A0000H). When we disable the memory plane chaining for the undocumented modes, the addressing again works in straightforward, normal fashion.

We are going to need a full byte to store 256-color information. We'll store four adjacent pixels at the same address, one each in memory planes 0 through 3. The fifth pixel will be stored in memory plane 0 at the next adjacent display memory address, and so forth. A *plot* function to do the job is listed in Listing 6-5. Line 9 sets up the parameter offset that would occur from the base memory display address if one byte were allowed for each pixel. In line 10, we take the parameter 01H and shift it to the left by *offset* modula 4 to find the number of the memory plane where this pixel's color data is to be stored. We output the result of this operation to Sequencer Register 02H—Map Mask to enable only the desired memory plane, using the sequencer register output function defined in lines 3 to 5. In line 12 the *offset* is shifted two places to the left (divided by four). Since four planes store four pixels at the same memory address, the actual memory address offset is only one-fourth of that calculated previously. In line 13, this new *offset* is added to the base memory address. In line 14 we output the color value to display memory, and the VGA card takes care of putting it into the correct memory plane. The registers have already been set up so that the memory planes are scanned properly to transfer the color information to the monitor screen.

Listing 6-5. Function to Plot a Point to the VGA Board in 256-Color Undocumented Modes

```
/*
        plot() = Function to plot point to VGA 256 color screen
                      using undocumented modes.
*/

void plot(int x, int y, int color)
{
      #define seq_out(index,val) \ 4 {outp(0x3c4,index);\
                  outp(0x3c5, val);}

      unsigned long int offset;
      char far *address;
      unsigned int plane;

      offset = (long)xres * y + x;
      plane = (0x01 << (offset % 4));
      seq_out(2,plane);
      offset >>= 2;
      address = (char far *)(0xA0000000L + offset);
      *address = color;
}
```

Plotting a Point to the Screen in VESA Graphics Modes

Chapter 8 is going to give you a lot more detail on how to use the VESA extensions to the regular VGA modes. To complete the pixel-plotting modes of this chapter, we'll show you here how to plot a pixel in one of the high-color VESA graphics modes. The function is shown in Listing 6-6. We assume that color data is passed to this function in three seperate bytes, one for red, one for green, and one for blue. The function begins in line 7 with a *switch* statement that switches on the selected video mode. The first set of cases, in lines 9 through 13, is for modes having 32K colors. In lines 14 through 16 the five most significant bits of each color are selected and repositioned with shift operators so that we end up with a color word *data* whose most significant bit is 0, followed by five bits of red information followed by five bits of green information followed by five bits of blue information. Next, in lines 17 and 18, we compute the *offset*, using a global parameter *BytesPerScanLine* as the row multiplier. For many Super VGA cards, this value is two times the horizontal pixel resolution, but it doesn't have to be. We'll show you in Chapter 8 how to get the value of this parameter from the Super VGA card, if you want to write some universal software. The parameter *offset* is stored in the form of a long unsigned integer, so that values of greater than 64K will be preserved. This parameter is transferred to the function *setBank* (where the part above 64K is used to set the correct page of display memory) in line 19. Lines 20 and 21 compute the actual display memory address for the selected pixel. Note that by converting *offset* to an *unsigned int* type, we actually use only the part below 64K. In line 22, the eight least significant bits of the *data* color word are written to display memory and the display memory address is then incremented. The eight most significant bits of the *data* color word are then shifted 8 places to the left and transferred to the display memory address.

Lines 25 through 39 peform the above operations for 64K-color modes. The only difference between this and the 32K-color modes is that the data color word consists of five bits of red followed by six bits of green followed by five bits of blue.

Lines 41 through 45 define the cases for 16.8 million-color modes. We are using three bytes per pixel for color information in these modes. The *offset* parameter, computed in lines 46 and 47, again uses a row multiplier *BytesPerScanLine*, but this parameter is now normally 3

Listing 6-6. Function to Plot a Point to a Super VGA Board in the VESA High Color Modes

```
/*

    plot() = Function to plot multicolor point to Super VGA in
                         VESA supported modes.

*/

1      void plot(int x, int y, int red, int green, int 2blue)
3      {
4          unsigned long int offset;
5          char far *address;
6          int data;
```

```
    switch(mode)
    {
        case 0x10D:
        case 0x110:
        case 0x113:
        case 0x116:
        case 0x119:
            data = (int)(red & 0xF8) << 7 |
                (int)(green & 0xF8) << 2 |
                 (int)(blue & 0xF8) >> 3;
            offset = (long int)y *
                 BytesPerScanLine + 2 * x;
            setBank(offset);
            address = (char far *)(0xA0000000L
                + (unsigned int)offset);
            *(address++) = data & 0xFF;
            *address = data >> 8;
            break;
        case 0x10E:
        case 0x111:
        case 0x114:
        case 0x117:
        case 0x11A:
            data = (int)(red & 0xF8) << 8 |
                (int)(green & 0xFC) << 3 |
                (int)(blue & 0xF8) >> 3;
            offset = (long int)y *
                 BytesPerScanLine + 2 * x;
            setBank(offset);
            address = (char far *)(0xA0000000L
                + (unsigned int)offset);
            *(address++) = data & 0xFF;
            *address = data >> 8;
            break;
        case 0x10F:
        case 0x112:
        case 0x115:
        case 0x118:
        case 0x11B:
            offset = (long int)y *
                 BytesPerScanLine + 3 * x;
            setBank(offset);
            address = (char far *)(0xA0000000L
                + (unsigned int)offset);
            *address = blue;
            offset++;
            setBank(offset);
            address = (char far *)(0xA0000000L
                + (unsigned int)offset);
            *address = green;
            offset++;
            setBank(offset);
            address = (char far *)(0xA0000000L
                + (unsigned int)offset);
            *address = red;
    }
}
```

times the horizontal resolution instead of 2 times as with the previous cases. Also the x value is multiplied by 3 instead of 2. In line 48, the *setBank* function is called to set the proper display memory page. Lines 49 and 50 compute the display memory address for the beginning of the pixel, and in Line 51 the blue value is stored there. The *offset* parameter is incremented, and the process is then repeated for the green value in lines 53 through 56. The *offset* parameter is then incremented again in line 57, and the process repeated in lines 58 through 61 for red. You will notice that in the 32K- and 64K-color cases, we only computed the address once and then incremented it for storing the second byte of color data. We can do this because a memory page change never occurs between the two bytes of the *data* word. For the 16.8 million-color cases, a page change can occur between bytes of a color pixel, so we need to set the bank after each byte to be safe.

The program shown in Listing 6-7 plots line patterns using each of the three high-color modes with 640 × 480 resolution and then with 800 × 600 resolution. You need to include the *plot* function of Listing 6-6 in it for the listing to be complete. We won't describe the program in detail, since several of the functions used are described in detial elsewhere. You should observe that there is a function *colorchange*, which is simply used to change the color each time a new line is drawn. Also note that the parameter *BytesPerScanLine* is set to the most commonly used value for each resolution. If your Super VGA card doesn't use any of these values, you will have to change the parameter to the proper value.

Listing 6-7. Program to Plot Line Patterns in VESA High Color Modes

```
/*

    hicolor = Program to do line test for high color VESA
                        supported modes.

              By Roger T. Stevens   12-7-95

*/

#include <dos.h>
#include <stdio.h>
#include <stdlib.h>
#include <mem.h>
```

```
#include <conio.h>

void colorchange(void);
void plot(int x, int y, int red, int green, int 8blue);
void setBank(unsigned long int offset);
void setMode(int mode);
void drawLine(int xs, int ys, int xe, int ye, int
    red, int green, int blue);

int red=255, green=255, blue=255;
int color, hue, i, j, k, LINEWIDTH = 3;
int xres, yres, mode;
unsigned long int PATTERN = 0xFFFFFFFF;
int BytesPerScanLine;

union REGS reg;

void main()
{

/*

Mode 110H = 640 x 480 pixels x 32K colors

*/
    BytesPerScanLine = 1280;
    mode = 0x110;
    setMode(mode);
    LINEWIDTH = 3;
    xres = 640; yres = 480;
    drawLine(6,8,xres-5,8,0,255,255);
    drawLine(6,yres-4,xres-5,yres-4,0,255,255);
    drawLine(7,8,7,yres-4,0,255,255);
    drawLine(xres-6,8,xres-6,yres-4,0,255,255);
    LINEWIDTH = 1;
    for (i=30; i< yres-10; i+=20)
    {
        drawLine(10,10,xres-8,i, red, green,
            blue);
        colorchange();
        drawLine(xres-8,yres-6,10,i, red, green,
            blue);
        colorchange();
        drawLine(10,yres-6,xres-8,i, red, green,
            blue);
        colorchange();
        drawLine(xres-8,10,10,i, red, green,
            blue);
        colorchange();
    }
    getch();
```

```
/*
        Mode 111H = 640 x 480 pixels x 64K colors
*/
        BytesPerScanLine = 1280;
        mode = 0x111;
        setMode(mode);
        LINEWIDTH = 3;
        xres = 640; yres = 480;
        drawLine(6,8,xres-5,8,0,255,255);
        drawLine(6,yres-4,xres-5,yres-4,0,255,255);
        drawLine(7,8,7,yres-4,0,255,255);
        drawLine(xres-6,8,xres-6,yres-4,0,255,255);
        LINEWIDTH = 1;
        for (i=30; i< yres-10; i+=20)
        {
            drawLine(10,10,xres-8,i, red, green,
                blue);
            colorchange();
            drawLine(xres-8,yres-6,10,i, red, green,
                blue);
            colorchange();
            drawLine(10,yres-6,xres-8,i, red, green,
                blue);
            colorchange();
            drawLine(xres-8,10,10,i, red, green,
                blue);
            colorchange();
        }
        getch();

/*
        Mode 112H = 640 x 480 pixels x 16.8 M colors
*/

        BytesPerScanLine = 1920;
        mode = 0x112;
        setMode(mode);
        LINEWIDTH = 3;
        xres = 640; yres = 480;
        drawLine(6,8,xres-5,8,0,255,255);
        drawLine(6,yres-4,xres-5,yres-4,0,255,255);
        drawLine(7,8,7,yres-4,0,255,255);
        drawLine(xres-6,8,xres-6,yres-4,0,255,255);
        LINEWIDTH = 1;
        for (i=30; i< yres-10; i+=20)
        {
            drawLine(10,10,xres-8,i, red, green,
                blue);
            colorchange();
```

```
            drawLine(xres-8,yres-6,10,i, red, green,
                blue);
            colorchange();
            drawLine(10,yres-6,xres-8,i, red, green,
                blue);
            colorchange();
            drawLine(xres-8,10,10,i, red, green,
                blue);
            colorchange();
        }
        getch();

/*

        Mode 113H = 800 x 600 pixels x 32K colors

*/

        BytesPerScanLine = 1600;
        mode = 0x113;
        setMode(mode);
        LINEWIDTH = 3;
        xres = 800; yres = 600;
        drawLine(6,8,xres-5,8,0,255,255);
        drawLine(6,yres-4,xres-5,yres-4,0,255,255);
        drawLine(7,8,7,yres-4,0,255,255);
        drawLine(xres-6,8,xres-6,yres-4,0,255,255);
        LINEWIDTH = 1;
        for (i=30; i< yres-10; i+=20)
        {
            drawLine(10,10,xres-8,i, red, green,
                blue);
            colorchange();
            drawLine(xres-8,yres-6,10,i, red, green,
               blue);
            colorchange();
            drawLine(10,yres-6,xres-8,i, red, green,
               blue);
            colorchange();
            drawLine(xres-8,10,10,i, red, green,
                blue);
            colorchange();
        }
        getch();

/*

Mode 114H = 800 x 600 pixels x 64K colors

*/

        BytesPerScanLine = 1600;
        mode = 0x114;
        setMode(mode);
```

```
        LINEWIDTH = 3;
        xres = 800; yres = 600;
        drawLine(6,8,xres-5,8,0,255,255);
        drawLine(6,yres-4,xres-5,yres-4,0,255,255);
        drawLine(7,8,7,yres-4,0,255,255);
        drawLine(xres-6,8,xres-6,yres-4,0,255,255);
        LINEWIDTH = 1;
        for (i=30; i< yres-10; i+=20)
        {
            drawLine(10,10,xres-8,i, red, green,
                 blue);
            colorchange();
            drawLine(xres-8,yres-6,10,i, red, green,
                blue);
            colorchange();
            drawLine(10,yres-6,xres-8,i, red, green,
                blue);
            colorchange();
            drawLine(xres-8,10,10,i, red, green,
                 blue);
            colorchange();
        }
        getch();

/*

        Mode 115H = 800 x 600 pixels x 16.8M colors

*/

        BytesPerScanLine = 2400;
        mode = 0x115;
        setMode(mode);
        LINEWIDTH = 3;
        xres = 800; yres = 600;
        drawLine(6,8,xres-5,8,0,255,255);
        drawLine(6,yres-4,xres-5,yres-4,0,255,255);
        drawLine(7,8,7,yres-4,0,255,255);
        drawLine(xres-6,8,xres-6,yres-4,0,255,255);
        LINEWIDTH = 1;
        for (i=30; i< yres-10; i+=20)
        {
            drawLine(10,10,xres-8,i, red, green,
                 blue);
            colorchange();
            drawLine(xres-8,yres-6,10,i, red, green,
                blue);
            colorchange();
            drawLine(10,yres-6,xres-8,i, red, green,
                blue);
            colorchange();
            drawLine(xres-8,10,10,i, red, green,
                 blue);
            colorchange();
```

```
     }
     getch();

     setMode(0x03);
}

/*
     colorchange() = Changes line drawing color
*/

void colorchange(void)
{
     blue -= 48;
     if (blue < 0)
     {
          blue = 255;
          green -= 48;
          if (green < 0)
          {
               green = 255;
               red -= 48;
               if (red < 0)
               {
                    red = 255;
                    green = 255;
                    blue = 255;
               }
          }
     }
}

/*
     drawLine() = Draws a line from one set of coordinates
          to another in designated color
*/

void drawLine(int xs, int ys, int xe, int ye, int
     red, int green, int blue)
{
     extern int LINEWIDTH;
     extern unsigned long int PATTERN;
     int temp, dx, dy, i, j, x, y, x_sign, y_sign,
          decision;
     unsigned long int mask;

     dx = abs(xe - xs);
     dy = abs(ye - ys);
```

```
        if (((dx > dy) && (xs > xe)) || ((dy > dx) &&
             (ys > ye)))
        {
            temp = xs;
            xs = xe;
            xe = temp;
            temp = ys;
            ys = ye;
            ye = temp;
        }
        if ((ye - ys) < 0)
            y_sign = -1;
        else
            y_sign = 1;
        if ((xe - xs) < 0)
            x_sign = -1;
        else
            x_sign = 1;
        if (dx > dy)
        {
            for (x=xs,y=ys,decision=0; x<=xe;
                 x++,decision+=dy)
            {
                mask = mask !=1 ? mask >> 1 :
                    0x80000000;
                if (decision>=dx)
                {
                    decision -= dx;
                    y+= y_sign;
                }
                if (PATTERN & mask)
                    for (j=-LINEWIDTH/2;
                        j<=LINEWIDTH/2; j++)
                        plot(x, y+j, red,
                            green, blue);
            }
        }
        else
        {
            for (x=xs,y=ys,decision=0; y<=ye;
                 y++,decision+=dx)
            {
                mask = (mask !=1) ? mask >> 1 :
                    0x80000000;
                if (decision>=dy)
                {
                    decision -= dy;
                    x += x_sign;
                }
                if (PATTERN & mask)
                    for (j=-LINEWIDTH/2;
                        j<=LINEWIDTH/2; j++)
                        plot(x+j, y, red,
                            green, blue);
            }
        }
    }
```

```
/*
    setMode() = Sets video mode for VESA compatible Super
                          VGA boards
*/

void setMode(int mode)
{
    reg.x.ax = 0x4F02;
    reg.x.bx = mode;
    int86 (0x10,&reg,&reg);
}

/*
          setBank() = Sets video memory bank
*/

void setBank(unsigned long int offset)
{
    static int bank, old_bank;

    old_bank = reg.x.dx;
    bank = offset >> 16;
    if (bank == old_bank)
        return;
    reg.x.dx = bank;
    old_bank = bank;
    reg.x.ax = 0x4F05;
    reg.x.bx = 0;
    int86(0x10, &reg, &reg);
}
```

7

EGA/VGA BIOS Functions

In the previous chapter, you saw some of the complications of programming that directly uses the internal registers of a display adapter card. This is necessary if you're plotting points to the display, because other techniques are not fast enough, and it is necessary if you are using special display modes or characteristics that are not normally supported by your operating system. Otherwise, you'll probably want to avoid a lot of complications by using the Basic Input Output System (BIOS) that resides in Read Only Memory (ROM) on the display adapter card. It is addressed at the computer memory space between C0000H and C4000H and becomes a part of the overall computer BIOS automatically. (On boot-up, the computer scans a designated memory space that includes the area just designated, looking for a header at 2K intervals. When a designated header is found, it indicates the existence of a BIOS extension, which is then incorporated into the computer BIOS where it can be accessed for all appropriate operations.) The BIOS extension consists of three sections. The first performs hardware checks when the computer is booted up, reporting VGA or Super VGA failures with various audible beep codes. (It is assumed that, if there are display hardware problems, it will be impossible to display any error code on the screen; therefore the audible error codes are used.) If all is well, the BIOS then initializes the display hardware and the monitor so that normal display operations can take place.

The next section of the BIOS extension contains a number of functions that are useful for manipulating the display. These are all accessed through an interrupt, 10H. The address of the interrupt-handler code is stored in the interrupt vector table at memory address 40H. Because these functions must be addressed through the interrupt route, they tend to be relatively slow compared with direct access functions. When the interrupt is called, the computer must first store the contents of all its registers. It then loads some pertinent registers with new data. Next it gets the address of the interrupt handler from the interrupt vector table and jumps there. According to the register contents, it jumps to a selected function and performs the necessary actions. It saves some of the resulting register contents and then restores the original register contents. Finally, it returns to the calling program. All of this additional overhead doesn't matter very much when you are performing an operation that occurs only occasionally, such as setting a display mode. In fact, for any display operation except for actually writing pixels to or reading them from the screen, using the ROM BIOS Video Services (through interrupt 10H) is perfectly adequate and relatively simple. When you are plotting thousands of pixels to the screen to create a display, or when you are reading these pixels, you'll usually want to use functions that access the display memory directly if you want the program to run at an acceptable speed. These were described in Chapter 6.

The final section of the VGA or Super VGA BIOS contains character tables. These include 8 × 8 pixel, 8 × 14 pixel, and 8 × 16 pixel character tables. Extensions are also available to make 9-pixel-wide characters. The appropriate character table is selected for use automatically when a display mode is selected. You can access the tables, however, and do interesting things like writing different size characters to a display or writing characters vertically to the screen. How to do all this will be described in Chapter 18.

In the remainder of this chapter, we are going to list all of the VGA BIOS functions and describe what they do. Along with most function descriptions, we're going to supply samples of functions written in C that make use of that BIOS function. The Borland family of C and C++ compilers has several ways of calling the interrupt-driven functions. These include the function calls *int86*, *int86x*, *intr*, and *geninterrupt*. The first of these is useful when we have a function that uses only the normal registers *a* through *d*. This function also enables you to access the high and low bytes of each register separately, if that is desireable. The *int86x* function also makes use of the segment and pointer registers, when they are needed by the function. Both these functions are also supported by MicroSoft Visual C++. The *intr* function often provides a simpler way to communicate with a BIOS function that requires segment and pointer registers. We will use it to illustrate some applications in various functions, but if you are using MicroSoft Visual C++, you should be aware that it does not support this function and should modify your programs accordingly. We won't use the *geninterrupt* call at all, since it doesn't guarantee the condition of registers when it returns, which can sometimes cause some subtle complications that are hard to troubleshoot. The functions in this chapter have all been tested with Turbo C++ and Borland C++.

Incidently, I highly recommend that you upgrade to a Super VGA display adapter card and a multi-sync color monitor if you don't already have one. Many of the programs in this book are designed to give you the best color display of which a PC is capable; if you have an outdated display adapter card and monitor, you won't be able to run them, and you'll be missing the most exciting capability of your PC. There are some additional ROM BIOS video services that have been defined by VESA to provide advanced display capabilities for Super VGA cards. These will be described in Chapter 8. This chapter describes the ROM BIOS video services available for regular VGA cards. (They also work with all Super VGA cards.)

Setting Display Modes (VGA Video Service 00H)

Register Inputs	Register Outputs
AX = Video mode	None

Chapter 4 describes the display modes in great detail, so we won't list or discuss them here. This BIOS video service supports all of the standard VGA modes. You can also use a mode call to clear the screen and return it to a clear black background. However, this method of clearing can be slow on some computers, and you'll find later that we have a better screen-clearing technique that also lets you set the background color. Normally, the most significant bit of the lower register byte is 0. This causes the screen to be cleared when the mode is changed. If you OR the video mode with 80H to set the most significant bit of the lower register byte to 1, the mode change is made without clearing display memory. You might think that this would be a great way to switch from a graphics display to a text menu of some sort and then recover the graphics display, but it doesn't work out that way. First, although the text is addressed at a different place in memory than the graphics, only the addressing really changes; the actual memory locations overlap, so that whatever you do in the text mode will mess up the graphics display. Furthermore, even if you just reset the same graphics mode without clearing, it will do weird things to your display. Here is a function to set the display mode.

```
/*
        setMode() = Function to set display mode
*/

1       void setMode(int mode)
2       {
3           union REGS regs;

4           regs.x.ax = mode;
5           int86(0x10,&regs,&regs);
6       }
```

Line 1 defines the function *setMode* and indicates that the integer parameter *mode* is passed to it. Line 3 defines the union *regs* to be of the type *REGS*, which is defined in the compiler's *DOS* header file. This union is used by the C++ function *int86* to transfer data to the microprocessor registers. It defines two structures: one with word-length data for each of the microprocessor 16-bit registers and the other with byte length data for each of the 8-bit microprocessor registers. You should be aware that the microprocessor registers *A, B, C,* and *D* may be treated as word-length registers by using the name of the union defined by *REGS*, followed by *.x*, followed by the register name, followed by *x*, as for example *regs.x.ax*. They may also be treated as byte-length registers *AH, AL, BH, BL, CH, CL, DH*, and *DL* by using the union name followed by *.h*, followed by the register name, followed by *h*, as for example *regs.h.ah*. The same four basic microprocessor registers are used, but each half can be accessed separately to transfer a byte of data. In this particular case, the upper half of the *A* register (*AH*) is set to 00H to indicate the *setMode* service and the lower half (*AL*) is set to the desired display mode. (Since just putting the mode into *AX* will automatically set *AL* to the mode and zero *AH*, only this one operation is really necessary. The register data is set up in line 4. Line 5 calls the *int86* function, which activates the video service 10H. The second parameter passed to the function is the address of the *regs* structure that contains the register data to be used by the interrupt, and the third parameter is the address of the *regs* structure that returns the register data after the interrupt is complete. If you wanted to, you could have separate structures for the input and output register data, but in this case a single structure is sufficient.

Here is an alternate method of doing the *setMode* function that uses the *intr* function (available only in Borland versions of C++ compilers) to perform the video service interrupt:

```
/*
            setMode() = Function to set display mode
*/

void setMode(int mode)
{
    struct REGPACK regs;

    regs.r_ax = mode;
    intr(0x10, &regs);
}
```

Setting the Cursor Shape (EGA/VGA Video Service 01H)

Register Inputs	Register Outputs
AH = 01H CH = Scan line for start of cursor CL = Scan line for end of cursor	None

This video service sets the shape of the cursor by specifying the beginning and ending scan lines for which the cursor is to be displayed. The default cursor is a blinking single line, which is the last (bottom) line of the character box. The cursor is displayed only in the text modes; in the graphics modes it is not shown, but the BIOS does keep track of its position. If you enter a starting line (register CH) of 20H, the cursor will be turned off. Other than this, you should not enter values higher than the last line of the character box (which is 8, 14, or 16, depending upon the display mode selected). If you enter an ending line value that is less than the starting line value, for the EGA, this will result in the cursor beginning at the specified line and continuing to the bottom of the character box and then starting again at the top of the character box and continuing to the specified ending line. This results in a two-part cursor with a space in the middle. If you try this same thing with the VGA, the cursor will simply not be displayed. In addition to controlling the shape of the cursor, this function stores the starting line value in memory location 461H and the ending line value in memory location 460H. The following is a C function to set the cursor shape:

```
/*
        setCursorShape() = Function to set the shape of the
                                cursor
*/

1       void setCursorShape (int start_line, int end_line)
2       {
3           union REGS regs;
4           regs.h.ah = 0x01;
5           regs.h.ch = start_line;
6           regs.h.cl = end_line;
7           int86(&regs,&regs);
8       }
```

In line 1, we set up a function to define the starting and ending lines of the cursor and pass the *start_line* and *end_line* parameters to it. Line 4 sets register *AH* to 01H to define the video service. Lines 5 and 6 load the start and end line information into the registers, and line 7 calls the *int86* function to activate the interrupt.

Setting the Cursor Position (EGA/VGA Video Service 02H)

Register Inputs	Register Outputs
AH = 02H BH = Page number DH = Display row (y) DL = Display column (x)	None

This service establishes the cursor position at the specified column and row of the stated page. If you are in a text mode, the cursor will then appear at the specified position if you are viewing the stated page. The BIOS keeps track of the cursor position separately for each page and switches the cursor to the new position when you change pages. The number of pages for a particular display mode depends upon the amount of memory installed in your EGA/VGA card. If you are using a graphics mode, the cursor will not appear, but if you write out text, it will begin at the current cursor position. The first cursor position, at the top lefthand corner of the display, is (0,0).

The last position at the bottom right depends upon the display mode. For display mode 10H, for example, the resolution is 640 × 350 pixels and the characters displayed are 80 × 25. Thus the last cursor position for this mode is (79,24). Note that the Borland C family has a *gotoxy* function that sets the cursor position, but it is referenced to the top lefthand corner of any window that has been specified. If the window is specified as the whole screen, the *gotoxy* function coordinates for the first position are (1,1) and for the example given earlier, the last position is (80,25). Therefore, if you interchange it with functions that use the BIOS system of numbering, there will be a slight difference in position.The cursor location information is stored in memory in the memory locations beginning at 450H. The cursor column position for a given page is stored in location 450H + page number × 2 and the cursor row position for a given page is stored in location 451H + page number × 2. You have three choices when you write a function in C to set the cursor position. You can ignore the page number problem altogether and always set the cursor for page 0. In many cases, you'll be using only page 0 and this works just fine. Second, you can specify the desired page and write the cursor position to it. This gives the most flexibility, but requires passing an extra parameter. Third, you can have the function determine the current page and always write the cursor position to it. In this case, you are constrained to the page you are on. The function to do this first uses the video service 0FH to get the active page number. It returns in register BH, which is just where you want it for the cursor-positioning service. The three functions follow:

```
/*

     gotoXY() = Function to set cursor position on page 0

*/

void gotoXY (int x, int y)
{
    union REGS regs;

    regs.h.ah = 0x03;
    regs.h.bh = 0;
    regs.h.dl = x;
    regs.h.dh = y;
    int86(0x10,&regs,&regs);
}
```

By now, you should have a good idea of how to load the registers and call the *int86* function to run one of the ROM BIOS video services. The listing just given passes only two parameters—the *x* and *y* coordinates (in terms of character position, not pixel position). In this function, the page number is set to zero by so setting register *BH*. In the function below, the page is also passed as a parameter, permitting the setting of cursor position for any page.

```
/*
    gotoXY() = Function to set cursor position on a
                    selected page.
*/

void gotoXY (int x, int y, int page)
{
    union REGS regs;

    regs.h.ah = 0x03;
    regs.h.bh = page;
    regs.h.dl = x;
    regs.h.dh = y;
    int86(0x10,&regs,&regs);
}
```

The following function uses ROM BIOS video service 0FH to get the current page number in register *BH* (this service will be described in detail later) and then uses the same code as just given to set the cursor position for this page.

```
/*
    gotoXY() = Function to set cursor position on current
                    page
*/

void gotoXY (int x, int y)
{
    union REGS regs;

    regs.h.ah = 0x0F;
    int86 (0x10,&regs,&regs);
    regs.h.ah = 0x03;
    regs.h.dl = x;
    regs.h.dh = y;
    int86(0x10,&regs,&regs);
}
```

Reading the Cursor Position (EGA/VGA Video Service 03H)

Register Inputs	Register Outputs
AH = 03H BH = Page number	DL = Column DH = Row CH = Start line for cursor CL = End line for cursor

This is a double purpose video service that returns the cursor location and cursor shape (in terms of start and stop lines). The descriptions of the two previous services pointed out where this information is stored in memory, and you can, if you desire, write a program to extract the information directly from memory. However, using this video service is usually easier. You'll probably never have a reason for reading information on the cursor shape. If it's visible (text mode), you can see what the shape is, and if it's invisible (graphics mode), the shape doesn't really matter. Similarly to the previous video service, you have the option of writing a function that will read the cursor position from page 0, from a specified page, or from the current page. We won't list all varieties this time; you can see from the previous examples how to write the function you want. Function calls in C don't really handle returning two parameters very well. There are three basic ways to handle this situation. The first is to have two separate functions to get the cursor data. This works as follows:

```
/*

        getx = Function to get cursor x position

*/

int getx (void)
{
    union REGS regs;

    regs.h.ah = 0x03;
    int86(0x10,&regs,&regs);
    return (regs.h.dh);
}
```

```
/*
        gety = Function to get cursor y position
*/

int gety (void)
{
    union REGS regs;
    regs.h.ah = 0x03;
    int86(0x10,&regs,&regs);
    return (regs.h.dl);
}
```

The next approach is to pass pointers to the function. This works as follows:

```
/*
        getxy = Function to get cursor position
*/

1    int getxy (int *x, int *y)
2    {
3        union REGS regs;
4        regs.h.ah = 0x03;
5        int86(0x10,&regs,&regs);
6        *x = regs.h.dh;
7        *y = regs.h.dl;
8    }
```

If we had passed *x* and *y* directly to the function, actually only copies of the values would have been written to the function. These copies are modified by the function, but there is no way the modified values can get back to the calling program. So instead we pass the addresses of the two parameters. In lines 6 and 7, the register data is transferred to become the contents of the memory at the addresses for *x* and *y*. They remain in these addresses when the function returns so that the new values can be used by the calling program.

Finally, we can make use of a *define* statement in connection with the first pair of functions that we listed above. This works as follows:

```
/*
        getxy() = Gets the position of the cursor
*/

         #define getxy(x,y) {x=getx(); y=gety();}
```

This looks like an ordinary function, but the values of *x* and *y* are replaced with the new cursor position just as if both functions could be returned by a function call.

Reading the Light Pen Position (EGA/VGA Video Service 04H)

Register Inputs	Register Outputs
AH = 04H	AH = 0: Light pen triggered = 1: Light pen not triggered DL = Column DH = Row CH = Pixel line number (old graphics modes) CX = Pixel line number (New EGA and VGA graphics modes BX = Pixel column number

When the IBM PC first came out, it seemed as if light pens were going to be a great way to communicate information to the computer. They never became very popular, however, and have been virtually replaced by the mouse or the trackball. Consequently, VGA cards do not support this video service, although it remains on the EGA as a relic from the past. If you ever come across a light pen, this is how it works. The light pen contains a light sensor. When you hold it up to the face of the monitor CRT, as the scanning electron beam passes the position where the light pen is being held, a pulse of light is emitted by the CRT's phosphorescent screen, which triggers the light pen circuits. This sets them to the light-pen-triggered mode and stores the coordinates of the position occupied by the beam when the trigger occurred. This video service reports back the fact that the system is in the triggered state and reports the position in terms of *x* and *y* graphics pixels as well as text column and row. Once the report is made, the circuits are cleared of position data and returned to the not- triggered mode to wait for the next light pen trigger.

Selecting the Display Page (EGA/VGA Video Service 05H)

Register Inputs	Register Outputs
AH = 04H AL = Page to become active	None

Depending upon the display mode that has been selected, and the amount of video memory that is on the EGA or VGA card, there may be enough video memory to provide one to eight pages of text or full-screen video graphics. However, only one page can be displayed at a time on the monitor. This video service determines which page will be displayed (the active page). The number of available pages for each mode and memory combination is listed in Chapter 4. However, that chapter gave the number of pages for a normal VGA with 256K of memory; if you have a Super VGA card, there may be more pages available and you may need to experiment a bit to find how many pages you have to work with in any given mode. The number of the active page is stored at memory location 462H, and the address of the starting location of the active page in memory is stored in memory locations 44EH and 44FH. The active page can be changed by the following function:

```
/*

        setPage() = Function to set the active page

*/

void setPage (int page)
{
    union REGS regs;

    regs.h.ah = 0x05;
    regs.h.al = page;
    int86 (0x10,&regs, &regs);
}
```

Scrolling a Window up (EGA/VGA Video Service 06H)

Register Inputs	Register Outputs
AH = 06H AL = Number of character rows to scroll up BH = Attribute (color) to be used on new blank lines entering the window from the bottom CH = The number of the upper left character row of the window CL = The number of the upper left character column of the window DH = The number of the lower right character row of the window DL = The number of the lower right character column of the window	None

This video service defines a window on the screen and scrolls by moving all character rows within the window up (the top one(s) are removed from the screen) and inserting new blank rows having the specified attribute at the bottom. The term *attribute* is misleading, what is actually meant is the color of the lines that are inserted. This color is in terms of the colors from 0 to 16 that were defined in Chapter 5 (or whichever of the 64 available colors you have substituted for them) for the 16 EGA palettes when you are in a 16-color mode, or the 256 colors of the 256-color modes. This is not really a background color but a foreground color. Consequently, if you do a *printf* command to one of these blank lines, whatever color you used for the blank lines in the window will be replaced with a background of black and a foreground of white for each printed character. If you enter a zero for the number of lines scanned, the entire window will be blanked to the specified color. This is about the fastest means of clearing the screen. If you're writing a scrolling function and don't want your entire screen to be blanked, you need to make sure that you don't allow the *AL* register to be set to zero to specify no lines scrolled.

One of the interesting things that we can use this function for is to clear the entire screen and change the background color. We do this by setting *AL* to zero and choosing a lower righthand corner that encompasses the whole screen. To do this, we need to know what coordinates mark the bottom right corner. Remember that for this function, this is specified in terms of character rows and columns rather than pixel rows and columns. So the pixel information given for each display mode won't help too much. Note that we can specify 8 × 8 pixel characters, 8 × 14 pixel characters, 9 × 14 pixel characters, 8 × 16 pixel characters, or 9 × 14 pixel characters and 9 × 16 pixel characters and for each mode and for each of these 6 character types, the coordinates of the bottom right corner are different. We will compromise by assuming an 8 × 8 pixel character; if the characters are bigger than this, our bottom right coordinates will be a little too big, but it isn't likely to bother things too much. The resulting function is listed below:

```
/*

        cls() = Clears the screen to designated color

*/

void cls(int color)
{
union REGS regs;
extern xres, yres;
regs.x.ax = 0x0600;
regs.x.cx = 0;
regs.h.dh = yres >> 3;
regs.h.dl = xres >> 3;
regs.h.bh = color;
int86(0x10,&regs,&regs);
}
```

The external variables *xres* and *yres* are the *x* and *y* resolutions of the selected display mode, respectively. Shifting three places to the right gives the number of 8-pixel characters. This function is guaranteed to work for all regular EGA/VGA modes, but it isn't supported by VESA for their higher resolution and higher number of color modes, so it's anybody's guess what may happen if you try it with them. I've found that it will work with some Super VGA cards with some VESA modes, but the best, safest technique for these modes is just to fill the screen with the desired color a pixel at a time.

Next, let's consider the situation where we want to create the background for a scene that has blue sky at the top and green grass at the bottom. We can use this same video service to clear the screen to two colors, one above a certain character row and the other below it. The function that does this follows. This version is tailored for mode 12H, but you can easily modify it to handle other display modes by following the examples shown previously. Note, however, that the line of demarcation between colors will not be at the same place on the screen for every display mode, since the total number of character rows may change for different modes. Hence, if a particular character row number is specified for the color change, this make take different vertical positions on the screen for different display modes. Two colors and a boundary row are passed to the function. The function works by simply calling video service 06H twice. The first time the window from the top of the screen to the boundary row is blanked to the first color. The second time, the window from the boundary row to the bottom of the screen is blanked to the second color.

```
/*

    set_screen() = Sets the screen background colors for
                        display mode 12H

*/

void set_screen(int top_color, int bottom_color,
        int boundary)
{
        union REGS regs;

        regs.h.ah = 0x06;
        regs.h.al = boundary;
        regs.x.cx = 0;
        regs.x.dx = 0x1D4F;
        regs.h.bh = top_color;
        int86(0x10,&regs,&regs);
        regs.h.ah = 0x06;
        regs.h.al = 30 - boundary;
        regs.h.bh = bottom_color;
        int86(0x10,&regs,&regs);
}
```

Next, let's look at a function that creates a window on a part of your screen. The top left and bottom right corners are defined in terms of character column and row coordinates. In line 7, we set up the top half of the *A* register to be 06H to define the video service and the bottom half to zero. Because the *AL* register (bottom byte of *AX*) is 0, the entire window is filled with blank lines of the designated color. As mentioned earlier, you can write characters to this window, but you need a function that will let you designate the character's background color; the *printf* function won't hack it since it draws white colors on a black background, no matter what color you have made the window. In lines 8, 9, 10, and 11, the window top left and bottom right coordinates in terms of character rows and columns are sent to the *C* and *D* registers and are also stored in a set of global variables, so that your calling program will know what the window size is. These parameters are defined as external in lines 5 and 6; you must also define them in the usual way in your calling program. You could also define them as global variables, in which case the *extern* statement of lines 5 and 6 is not necessary. Alternately, you may put these parameters in a structure if you wish to do so.

```
/*
    window() = Makes a window on the display screen for
      display mode 12H at specified rectangle corners
                   in a specified color
*/

1   void window(int xl, int yt, int xr, int yb, int
2         color)
3   {
4         union REGS regs;
5         extern int window_xl, window_yt, window_xr,
6             window_yb, window_color;

7         regs.x.ax = 0x0600;
8         window_xl = regs.h.cl = xl;
9         window_yt = regs.h.ch = yt;
10        window_xr = regs.h.dl = xr;
11        window_yb = regs.h.dh = yb;
12        window_color = regs.h.bh = color;
13        int86(0x10,&regs,&regs);
14  }
```

Once you have written to an empty window, you can use the scroll-up video service to scroll everything up and add blank lines at the bottom. The following function is very similar to the preceding one except that it puts the number of rows to be scrolled into the *AL* register instead of a 0. Since very strange things happen if the scrolled window doesn't have the same dimensions and color as the window that you first created with the *window* function, the window parameters that were stored in global variables by the *window* function are used to define this window, instead of allowing you to pass any values that you want to the function. You can simplify this function a bit by limiting it to scrolling up a single line. Then you don't need to pass any parameters to it; instead you set the *AL* register to one within the function.

```
/*
scroll_up() = Scrolls a window on the display screen by
    a specified number of character rows for display
    mode 12H using coordinates and color specified
              for window function
*/

void scroll_up(int rows)
{
    union REGS regs;

    extern int window_xl, window_yt, window_xr,
        window_yb, window_color;

    regs.h.ah = 0x06;
    regs.h.al = rows;
    regs.h.cl = window_xl;
    regs.h.ch = window_yt;
    regs.h.dl = window_xr;
    regs.h.dh = window_yb;
    regs.h.bh = window_color;
    int86(0x10,&regs,&regs);
}
```

Scrolling a Window down (EGA/VGA Video Service 07H)

Register Inputs	Register Outputs
AH = 07H AL = Number of character rows to scroll down BH = Attribute (color) to be used on new blank lines entering the window from the top CH = The number of the upper left character rowof the window CL = The number of the upper left character column of the window DH = The number of the lower right character row of the window DL = The number of the lower right character column of the window	None

This video service is just the same as the one just described except that blank lines are added at the top instead of at the bottom and all lines within the window are moved downward, with the bottom lines dropping out of the window. All the functions described for scrolling up work equally well when scrolling down.

Reading a Character and Its Attribute from the Screen (EGA/VGA Video Service 08H)

Register Inputs	Register Outputs
AH = 08H BH = Active page	AH = Attribute of text character AL = ASCII value of text character, if found

This video service attempts to read the character that is at the current cursor position. For text modes, the character code for each character on the screen is stored in display memory plane 0 and the character attribute is stored in display memory plane 1. These locations are simply read and returned by the video service. (A blank area of the screen contains space codes (20H).) In the graphics mode, things are much more complicated because we have control over every pixel on the display and can create patterns that are almost but not quite alphanumeric characters. In this case, the video service compares the contents of the character cell pointed to by the cursor and compares it with the character patterns stored in the BIOS for the lower 128 characters of the 256-character set. If a match is found, the character code is returned in register *AL*; otherwise this register is set to zero. (You can't read a space in the graphics mode; a zero is returned to indicate no match was found.) The returned contents of register *AH* are meaningless for graphics modes. If you need to read characters from 128 to 255 in the graphics mode, you will need to run video service 11H, subservice 20H, to set the pointer to the character table to the upper half of the table. This service and subservice will be described later.

When it comes to writing a C function to read a character from the screen, if we want to read text characters we have the same old problem—C can return only one value from a function. We can handle this in two ways. The first is rather awkward; it returns the character directly and passes a pointer to the attribute to the function so that the variable pointed to will contain the attribute when we return. This function is as follows:

```
/*
    getChar() = Reads a character and its attribute from
                            the screen
*/

char getChar (int page, char *attribute)
{
   union REGS regs;

   regs.h.ah = 0x08;
   regs.bh = page;
   int86 (0x10,&regs,&regs);
   *attribute = regs.h.ah;
   return (regs.h.al)
}
```

Here is a nicer way to do the same thing:

```
/*
    getChar() = Reads a character and its attribute from
                            the screen
*/

#define getChar(page,ch,attribute) {ch = get_ch(page);\
   attribute = get_attr(page);}

char get_ch (int page)
{
   union REGS regs;

   regs.h.ah = 0x08;
   regs.bh = page;
   int86 (0x10,&regs,&regs);
   return (regs.h.al)
}

char get_attr (int page)
{
   union REGS regs;

   regs.h.ah = 0x08;
   regs.h.bh = page;
   int86 (0x10,&regs,&regs);
   return (regs.h.ah)
}
```

If you are going to use this function only when in the graphics modes, you don't need to worry about the attribute at all, so you can use this simple function:

```
/*
        getChar() = Reads a character from the screen
*/

char getChar (int page)
{
    union REGS regs;

    regs.h.ah = 0x08;
    regs.bh = page;
    int86 (0x10,&regs,&regs);
    return (regs.h.al)
}
```

Furthermore, if you want to work only with page 0, you don't need to pass the page parameter, but can set register *BH* to 0 instead.

Writing a Character and Its Attribute to the Screen (EGA/VGA Video Service 09H)

Register Inputs	Register Outputs
AH = 09H AL = ASCII character code of character to be written to the screen BL = Attribute of character to be written to screen BH = Active page CX = Number of times to write character and attribute to the screen	None

This service turns out to be quite different, depending upon whether you are writing a character in the text modes, the 16-color graphics modes, or the 256-color modes. For text modes, both foreground and background colors are written to the screen. However, the background can only be one of the 8 nonintensified colors, since only palette numbers 0–7 are allowed. These can be the default colors or whichever of the 64 available colors you have set the palettes to. The foreground can be any of the 16 available palette colors (either default or as selected). The most significant bit determines whether the character will blink or not. The attribute byte for text modes is this:

Bit 7	Bit 6	Bit 5	Bit 4	Bit 3	Bit 2	Bit 1	Bit 0
Blink.	Background palette number (0–7).			Foreground palette number (0–15).			

In the 16-color graphics modes, only the foreground of the character is drawn; the background remains unchanged from the existing background color (whatever color is assigned to palette 0). This doesn't mean that you can write a character over a picture on the screen and have the background of the character remain unchanged, because the background of the character cell is rewritten to the current background color (which is usually black). The character itself is written in whichever of the 16 palette colors is selected. The most significant bit, when on, causes the character to be exclusive ORed with the current data. In this mode, nothing will appear different if you are writing to a background area of the screen. However, if you write the same character again in the same place, it will disappear. If you write on a varigated area of the screen, the color of various parts of the character may vary, depending upon the original character-cell contents. Writing the same character a second time to the same place will cause the picture to return to its original contents. The attribute byte for 16-color graphics modes is this:

Bit 7	Bit 6	Bit 5	Bit 4	Bit 3	Bit 2	Bit 1	Bit 0
0 = overwrite character. 1 = XOR character with existing data.	Not used.			Foreground palette number (0–15).			

In the 256-color graphics mode, only the foreground of the character is drawn; the background remains unchanged from the existing background color (whatever color is assigned to color register 0). This doesn't mean that you can write a character over a picture on the screen and have the background of the character remain unchanged, because the background of the character cell is rewritten to the current background color (which is usually black). The entire attribute byte is used to specify which of the 256 color registers should be used for the color of the character itself. The attribute byte for the 256-color graphics mode is this:

Bit 7	Bit 6	Bit 5	Bit 4	Bit 3	Bit 2	Bit 1	Bit 0
Foreground color register number.							

Note that whichever case you are using, you must be sure to set a value for register *CX* since this determines how many characters will be written to the screen. Normally this is set to 1, but it can be set to a different value if you want to fill an area with the same character. For text modes, this number should be no greater than the number of characters from the current cursor position to the end of the display screen. For graphics modes, this number should be no greater than the number of characters from the current cursor position to the end of the current line. If you use larger numbers than this, you won't like what happens. Strange spacings, overwrites, and blankings will occur. If you leave it at the default value of 0, you'll like what happens even less. Multiple partial characters will write and rewrite the screen.

A simple function to write a character to the screen using this video service is this:

```
/*

        write_c() = Writes a character to the screen

*/

void write_c(char ch, int attribute, int page)
{
    union REGS regs;

    regs.h.ah = 0x09;
    regs.h.al = ch;
    regs.h.bl = attribute;
    regs.h.bh = page;
    regs.x.cx = 1;
    int86(0x10,&regs,&regs);
}
```

Listing 7-1 is a program that uses the above function to write some text to the screen using text mode 03H. Then, hitting any key will change to 16-color graphics mode 12H and write the same text to the screen. Finally, hitting another key will shift to 256-color graphics mode 13H and write the same text to the screen.

Listing 7-1. Program to Write Text in Various Modes

```
/*

     charwrit = Program to test using Video Service 09H

               By Roger T. Stevens   11-22-95

*/

#include <stdio.h>
#include <string.h>
#include <dos.h>
#include <conio.h>

void setMode(int mode);
void main(void)
{
    union REGS reg;

    int i,j,k;
    char st[128] = {"Now is the time for all good"\
        men to come to the aid of their country"\
        or their party or whatever...."};
    int mode[3] = {0x03, 0x12, 0x13}, length[3] =
         {79, 79, 39};
    for (j=0; j<3; j++)
    {
        setMode(mode[j]);
        printf("This is a test....");
        getch();
        for (i=0; i<110; i++)
        {
            gotoxy(i%length[j]+1,
                10+(i/length[j]));
            if (j == 2)
                write_c(st[i],0x09,0);
            else
                write_c(st[i],0x79,0);
            getch();
        }
        setMode(0x03);
    }
}
```

```
/*
   ┌──────────────────────────────────────────┐
   │                                          │
   │       setMode() = Sets Video Mode        │
   │                                          │
   └──────────────────────────────────────────┘
*/

33    void setMode(int mode)
34    {
35        union REGS reg;

36        reg.h.ah = 0;
37        reg.h.al = mode;
38        int86 (0x10,&reg,&reg);
39    }
```

The program begins in lines 10, 11, and 12 by defining a character string *st* and filling it with some text. Next, in lines 13 and 14, we define *mode*, an array that contains the mode number for each of the three modes to be used, and *length*, an array that contains the number of characters we are going to write before beginning a new line, for each mode. In line 15, we begin a *for* loop, which iterates once for each mode. The loop begins in line 17 by setting the desired display mode. Next, in line 18, we use the usual *printf* function to print out the words *This is a test.....* In line 19, the program waits until a key is struck. Then another *for* loop is entered in line 20, which iterates once for each key to be written. This loop starts in line 22 and 23, by using the *gotoxy* function to position the cursor on the display. We are most interested in what happens with the attribute byte, the contents of register *BL* in the *write_c* function. Lines 24, 25, 26, and 27 use an *if* statement to set the attribute to 09H for the 256-color mode and 79H otherwise. In the text mode, an attribute of 79H sets the background color to 7 (light gray) and the foreground color to 9 (light blue). We keep the same setting for the 16-color graphics mode, but the result is that the 7 is ignored and the original background is kept (black) while the character is written in the foreground color 9 (bright blue). Finally, if we were to keep the same setting of 79 for the 256-color mode, the background would remain black and the character would be written in color 79, which turns out to be a green. We don't want that, so for this mode we set the attribute to 09H, which results in using color 09H, which is bright blue, to write the character.

The only trouble with the *write_c* function is that if you just repeat it a number of times to write a bunch of characters, they will all be written on top of each other at the current cursor location. This is a real peculiarity of this

BIOS video service, since if you set the CX register to write several characters, they will be written side by side rather than on top of each other, but the cursor position will not be changed, so the next time you write you'll start at the same location as the first character unless you change the cursor position. The following function increments the cursor position each time it writes a character and also moves it to the beginning of the next line when the end of the line is reached. When the last character on the page is written, it sets the cursor to the top lefthand corner of the page. The function requires two external variables, which contain the values of the number of characters in a line and the number of lines on the screen.

```
/*

        write_c() = Writes a character to the screen

*/

1      void write_c(char ch, int attribute, int page)
2      {
3          union REGS regs;
4          extern int no_of_rows;
5          extern int no_of_cols;

6          regs.h.ah = 0x09;
7          regs.h.al = ch;
8          regs.h.bl = attribute;
9          regs.h.bh = page;
10         regs.x.cx = 1;
11         int86(0x10,&regs,&regs);
12         regs.h.ah = 0x03;
13         int86(0x10,&regs,&regs);
14         regs.h.dl++;
15         if (regs.h.dl >= no_of_cols)
16         {
17             regs.h.dl = 0;
18             regs.h.dh = (regs.h.dh + 1) % no_of_rows;
19         }
20         regs.h.ah = 0x02;
21         int86(0x10,&regs,&regs);
22     }
```

Lines 6 through 11 use video service 9 to write a character at the current cursor position. Lines 12 and 13 use video service 3 to obtain the cursor coordinates in the character coordinate system and place the column in register *DL* and the row in register *DH*. The column value is incremented in line 14. Lines 15 through 19 compare the new column value with the maximum number of columns in the display; if it is greater, the column is set to zero and the row is incremented and the new value taken modula the total number of rows, so that when we get to the end of the bottom row, we restart at the top left of the screen. Line 20 sets the *AH* register for video service 2 and line 21 calls this service to update the cursor position.

Now that you have a character-writing function that takes care of the cursor position, you can create a string-writing function that calls the character-writing function, or you can build the character-writing function right into the string-writing function. The former is the simplest way; the latter is the fastest. Here are the two techniques:

```
/*
    write_s() = Writes a string to the screen using write_c
*/

void write_s(char *string, int attribute, int page)
{
    int i = 0;

    while (string[i])
        write_c(string[i], attribute, page);
}

/*
    write_c() = Writes a character to the screen (self-
                        contained)
*/

void write_s(char *string ch, int attribute, int page)
{
    union REGS regs;

    extern int no_of_rows;
    extern int no_of_cols;
    int i = 0;

    while (string[i])
    {
        regs.h.ah = 0x09;
        regs.h.al = string[i];
        regs.h.bl = attribute;
        regs.h.bh = page;
        regs.x.cx = 1;
        int86(0x10,&regs,&regs);
        regs.h.ah = 0x03;
```

```
            int86(0x10,&regs,&regs);
            regs.h.dl++;
            if (regs.h.dl >= no_of_cols)
            {
                regs.h.dl = 0;
                regs.h.dh = (regs.h.dh + 1) %
                    no_of_rows;
            }
            regs.h.ah = 0x02;
            int86(0x10,&regs,&regs);
        }
    }
```

Writing a Character to the Screen (EGA/VGA Video Service 0AH)

Register Inputs	Register Outputs
AH = 0AH AL = ASCII character code of character to be written to the screen BL = Attribute of character to be written to screen for graphics modes (not used for text modes) BH = Active page CX = Number of times to write character and attribute to the screen	None

This video service is just the same as the previous one for graphics modes. For text modes, the only difference from the previous service is that it uses the current attribute instead of the one that is in register *BL*.

Setting the CGA Color Palette (EGA/VGA Video Service 0BH)

Register Inputs	Register Outputs
AH = 0BH BH = Palette color ID. 0 = Set background color. BL 1 = Set CGA Palette. = Background color when BH = 0. Palette (0 or 1) when BH = 1.	None

This video service should be used only for video modes 4 and 5, where the EGA/VGA is emulating a CGA. If used in EGA/VGA graphics modes, its effect on colors is unpredictable. When register *BH* is set to 0, the value set to register *BL* sets the background color to one of the 16 EGA palette colors. When register *BH* is set to 1, register *BL* may be set to 0 or 1 to select CGA palette 0 or 1, respectively. Each CGA palette consists of only four colors. These are as follows:

CGA Palette 0		CGA Palette 1	
Screen Color	**Equivalent EGA Palette Number**	**Screen Color**	**Equivalent EGA Palette Number**
0 = background color	—	0 = background color	—
1 = green	2	1 = cyan	11
2 = red	4	2 = magenta	13
3 = brown	6	3 = white	15

The following is a C function that may be used to set the CGA background color or to choose the palette. This function first checks the mode and inputs to ensure that they are in the proper range of acceptable values. Consequently, the function is executed only if you are in display mode 4 or 5. Note that for register *BH* set to 0, register *BL* is limited to a palette number from 0 to 15 and that for register *BH* set to 1, register *BL* is limited to the palette numbers 0 or 1.

```
/*
    setCGApalette() = Function to set CGA palette and
                      background color
*/

void setCGApalette(int id, int color)
{
    union REGS regs;
    char mode;

    regs.h.ah = 0x0F;
    if ((mode != 4) && (mode != 5)
        return;
    if (((id == 0) && (color >= 0) &&
        (color < 16)) || ((id != 1) &&
        (color >= 0) && (color < 2)))
    {
        regs.h.ah = 0x0B;
        regs.h.bh = id;
        regs.h.bl = color;
        int86 (0x10,&regs,&regs);
    }
}
```

Writing a Pixel to the Screen (EGA/VGA Video Service 0CH)

Register Inputs	Register Outputs
AH = 0CH AL = Pixel color and write method for 16-color modes. Pixel color for 256-color mode. BH = Page CX = Pixel x position DX = Pixel y position	None

This service writes a pixel to the screen in graphics modes, but is usually much too slow to be of any real value. Note that you can write the pixel to any page, not just the active one. Therefore, you can view one page while writing to another. If you are viewing one page and have plenty of time to construct another page for future viewing, you might want to use this service. In the 16-color graphics modes, the most significant bit, when on, causes the character to be exclusive ORed with the current data. The rest of the register contents determine which of the 16 EGA palette colors will be used to write the pixel. The register contents byte for 16-color graphics modes is this:

Bit 7	Bit 6	Bit 5	Bit 4	Bit 3	Bit 2	Bit 1	Bit 0
0 = overwrite character. 1 = XOR character with existing data.	Not used.			Foreground palette number (0–15).			

In the 256-color graphics mode, the color byte represents any one of the 256 color registers, and the pixel is written in that color. The byte content is:198

Bit 7	Bit 6	Bit 5	Bit 4	Bit 3	Bit 2	Bit 1	Bit 0
Foreground color register number.							

The following is a function to write a pixel to a display page. This function will work for any supported EGA/VGA mode, but, as pointed out in Chapter 6, it is very slow if you're going to plot very many pixels.

```
/*
        plot() = Plots a pixel to the specified page at
             coordinates (x,y) in designated color
*/

void plot(int x, int y, int page, int color)
{
    union REGS regs;
    regs.h.ah = 0x0C;
    regs.h.al = color;
    regs.h.bh = page;
    regs.x.cx = x;
    regs.x.dx = y;
    int86 (0x10,&regs,&regs);
}
```

Reading a Pixel from the Screen (EGA/VGA Video Service 0DH)

Register Inputs	Register Outputs
AH = 0DH BH = Page CX = Pixel x position DX = Pixel y position	AL = Pixel color

Note that you don't have to read the pixel from the active page; it can be on any designated display page. For 16-color modes, this service returns a four-bit number (0 to 15), representing the number of the EGA palette that was used to write the pixel to the page. For the 256-color mode, the service returns an eight-bit number (0 to 255) representing the color register that was used to write the pixel to the page. The following is a C function to read a pixel using this service:

```
/*

        getPixel() = Function to read a pixel from the
                         designated page

*/

int getPixel (int x, int y, int page)
{
    union REGS regs;
    regs.h.ah = 0x0D;
    regs.h.bh = page;
    regs.x.cx = x;
    regs.x.dx = y;
    int86 (0x10,&regs,&regs);
    return (regs.h.al);
}
```

Writing a TTY Character to the Active Page (EGA/VGA Video Service 0EH)

Register Inputs	Register Outputs
AH = 0EH AL = ASCII character to be written to the active page BH = Active page BL = Foreground color of character for the graphics modes	None

This video service is designed to permit your display to emulate a TTY-type terminal. The page that is specified becomes the active page. The service writes a character to the screen (the active page) at the current cursor location. It then automatically advances the cursor position one character column and, if the end of the line has been reached, moves it to the beginning of the next line. When the end of the screen is reached the entire display is scrolled upward one line. The new bottom line has the same color as the previous line. For text modes, the color parameter is ignored and the character is displayed in white. For 16-color modes, the character is displayed with the color designated by the EGA palette number (0 to 15) that is specified. For 256-color modes, the character is displayed in the color designated by the color register whose number is specified (0 to 255). The service intercepts the carriage return, line feed, backspace, and bell characters and uses them to act on the display. These actions are as follows:

ASCII Number	Symbol	Name	Action
0DH	CR	Carriage return	Moves cursor to column zero of next character row
0AH	LF	Line feed	Moves cursor down one character row
08H	BS	Backspace	Moves cursor one character position to the left
07H	BELL	Bell	Generates a beep in the system speaker

The following is a C function to make use of this video service:

```
/*
    writeTTY() = Writes a character to the active page in
     TTY mode (using specified color for graphics modes)
*/

void writeTTY (char ch, int color, int page)
{
    union REGS regs;

    regs.h.ah = 0x0E;
    regs.h.al = ch;
    regs.h.bh = page;
    regs.h.bl = color;
    int86 (0x10,&regs,&regs);
}
```

Determining the Current Video Display Mode (EGA/VGA Video Service 0FH)

Register Inputs	Register Outputs
AH = 0FH	AL = Current video display mode AH = Number of characters per row BH = Number of active display page

This video service, which was used in some of the C functions previously described, reports back the current display mode. The most significant bit of this word is 0 if the display was cleared during the latest mode set and 1 if it was not cleared. The service also reports the current number of characters in a row and the number of the active display page. Probably you'll never need to determine the number of characters in a row. You can obtain the display mode and active page separately using the following C functions:

```
/*
    getMode() = Function to get current display mode
*/
int getMode (void)
{
    union REGS regs;
```

```
        regs.h.ah = 0x0F;
        int86 (0x10,&regs,&regs);
        return (regs.h.al & 0x7F);
    }
```

```
/*
getPage() = Function to get current active display page
*/
```

```
    int getPage (void)
    {
        union REGS regs;

        regs.h.ah = 0x0F;
        int86 (0x10,&regs,&regs);
        return (regs.h.bh);
    }
```

Setting an EGA Palette Register (EGA/VGA Video Service 10H, Subservice 00H)

Register Inputs	Register Outputs
AH = 10H AL = 00H BH = Color BL = Palette number	None

This service selects the color for an individual palette register. There are 64 available colors and 16 available palette registers. This service should be used with the 16-color display modes only; do not use it with the 256-color mode. A C function to use this service follows:

```
/*
setEGApalette() = Sets the color of an EGA/VGA palette
                  register
*/
```

```
    void setEGApalette(char palette, char color)
    {
        union REGS regs;
        regs.x.ax = 0x1000;
```

```
        regs.h.bl = palette;
        regs.h.bh = color;
        int86 (0x10,&regs,&regs);
    }
```

Setting the Border Color (EGA/VGA Video Service 10H, Subservice 01H)

Register Inputs	Register Outputs
AH = 10H AL = 01H BH = Border color	None

It's best to leave this service alone, as it can be a little erratic. The EGA doesn't work well in the 350-line graphics modes if the border is set to any color but black. The service works for the VGA only for 80-character-per-line modes; in these modes the border is restricted to 1 character wide.

Setting the Palette and Border Registers All at Once (EGA/VGA Video Service 10H, Subservice 02H)

Register Inputs	Register Outputs
AH = 10H AL = 02H ES:DX = Pointer to a 17-byte table of palette register and border register values	None

This video service permits setting all of the EGA palette registers and the border register in a single operation. A C function that uses this service follows. This function requires a global variable *char pal_color[17]* that is filled with the color values for the 16 palette registers and the overscan (border) register before the function is called. Note that because this video service makes use of the *ES* register to set the address of the table of palette register values, the function below has to make use of the *intr86* function rather than the *int86* function (which doesn't include the *ES* register). Consequently, instead of the union *REGS* used in previous functions, we make use of two structures, *REGPACK* and *SREGS*.

```
/*

     setAllEGApals() = Sets all the EGA palette registers
                       and the border register

*/

void setAllEGApals(char *pal_colors)
{
    struct REGPACK regs;
    struct SREGS sregs;

    regs.r_ax = 0x1002;
    segread(&sregs);
    regs.r_es = sregs.ds;
    regs.r_dx = (int)pal_colors;
    intr (0x10,&regs);
}
```

Toggling the Blink/Intensity Bit (EGA/VGA Video Service 10H, Subservice 03H)

Register Inputs	Register Outputs
AH = 10H AL = 03H BL = 0 Attribute bit 7 is intensity = 1 Attribute bit 7 is blink	None

This video service applies to the text-display modes only. In the default condition, the attribute byte, when writing characters to a page, can define only eight background colors. The most significant bit of the attribute byte, when set to 1, causes the character to blink. If this service is run with register *BL* set to 0, the most significant attribute bit becomes part of the background color definition, permitting display of 16 background colors. Running the service with register *BL* set to 1 returns to the default state. A C function to perform this operation follows:

```
/*
    setBlink() = Sets EGA/VGA for most significant
      attribute bit to represent blink or color
*/

void setBlink (char blink)
{
   union REGS regs;

   regs.h.ah = 0x10;
   regs.h.al = 0x03;
   regs.h.bl = blink;
   int86 (0x10, &regs, &regs);
}
```

Reading a Palette Color (EGA/VGA Video Service 10H, Subservice 07H)

Register Inputs	Register Outputs
AH = 10H AL = 07H BL = Number of palette register	BH = color value of designated palette register

This video service works with the VGA only. The EGA palette registers are write-only, so the color information cannot be recovered from them. A C function to utilize this service follows:

```
/*
    getPalette() = Returns the palette register color
*/

char getPalette (char palette)
{
   union REGS regs;

   regs.h.ah = 0x10;
   regs.h.al = 0x07;
   regs.h.bl = palette;
   int86 (0x10, &regs, &regs);
   return (regs.h.bh);
}
```

Reading the Overscan (Border) Register (EGA/VGA Video Service 10H, Subservice 08H)

Register Inputs	Register Outputs
AH = 10H AL = 08H	BH = Color value of overscan (border) register

This video service works with the VGA only. The EGA overscan register is write-only so its value cannot be recovered. A C function to utilize this service follows:

```
/*

    getOverscan() = Returns color of the overscan register

*/

char getOverscan (void)
{
    union REGS regs;

    regs.h.ah = 0x10;
    regs.h.al = 0x08;
    int86 (0x10, &regs, &regs);
    return (regs.h.bh);
}
```

Getting the Palette and Border Registers All at Once (EGA/VGA Video Service 10H, Subservice 09H)

Register Inputs	Register Outputs
AH = 10H AL = 09H ES:DX = Pointer to a 17-byte table of palette register and border register values	Data is returned to a 17-byte table pointed to by ES:DX

This video service permits getting all of the palette registers and the border register in a single operation. It works only with the VGA, since the EGA registers are write-only. The 17-byte table to contain the values must be established in the calling program or as a global variable. A C function that uses this service follows:

```
/*
    getAllEGApals() = Gets all the palette register and the
                      border register color values
*/

void getAllEGApals(char *pal_colors)
{
    struct REGPACK regs;
    struct SREGS sregs;

    regs.r_ax = 0x1009;
    segread(&sregs);
    regs.r_es = sregs.ds;
    regs.r_dx = (int)pal_colors;
    intr (0x10,&regs);
}
```

Setting a VGA Color Register (EGA/VGA Video Service 10H, Subservice 10H)

Register Inputs	Register Outputs
AH = 10H AL = 10H BX = Number of color register DH = Red value CH = Green value CL = Blue value	None

This video service permits setting the value of a single VGA color register. It is not applicable to the EGA, which doesn't have color registers. The red, green, and blue register values can be individually set to a value between 0 and 63. In the 256-color modes, all 256 colors can be displayed on the screen. In the 16-color modes, the 16 palette registers can be assigned to groups of 16 or 64 color registers, permitting rapid changes of the entire color palette without changing the color registers. A C function that uses this service to set the value of a single color register follows:

```
/*
    setColorReg() = Sets a VGA color register
*/

void setColorReg(char reg_no, char red, char green,
    char blue)
{
    union REGS regs;

    regs.x.ax = 0x1010;
    regs.h.bh = reg_no;
    regs.h.dh = red;
    regs.h.ch = green;
    regs.h.cl = blue;
    int86 (0x10,&regs,&regs);
}
```

Setting a Block of VGA Color Registers All at Once (EGA/VGA Video Service 10H, Subservice 12H)

Register Inputs	Register Outputs
AH = 10H AL = 12H BX = Number of first color register to be changed CX = Number of color registers to be changed ES:DX = Pointer to table of color values	None

This video service permits setting a block of VGA color registers in a single operation. The service requires a table of color values established either in the calling program or as a global array. The table should be of type *char* and should contain 768 members (3 for each of the maximum of 256 colors). The colors are entered in the table as triplets, in the order red, green, blue, red, green, blue, etc. A C function that uses this service follows:

```
/*
        setVGAcolors() = Sets the colors of a block of VGA
                         color registers
*/

void setVGAcolors(char first_reg, char number, char
    *pal_colors)
{
    struct REGPACK regs;
    struct SREGS sregs;

    regs.r_ax = 0x1012;
    segread(&sregs);
    regs.r_es = sregs.ds;
    regs.r_dx = (int)pal_colors;
    regs.r_bx = first_reg;
    regs.r_cx = number;
    intr (0x10,&regs);
}
```

Normally you'll have an array *pal_colors* large enough to hold a triplet for each of the 256 color registers. Thus the triplet for register 0 will be in array members 0, 1, and 2, the triplet for register 1 will be in members 3, 4, and 5, and so forth. If you are going to change a block of color registers beginning somewhere beyond register 0, you need to make sure that the array address passed to its function is the address of the member of the array that corresponds to the first register to be changed. You can't just pass the address of the beginning of the array.

Selecting the Color Page (EGA/VGA Video Service 10H, Subservice 13H)

Register Inputs	Register Outputs
AH = 10H AL = 13H BL = 0 Select paging mode: BH = 0–4 pages of 64- color registers BH = 1–16 pages of 16- color registers BL = 1 Select page BH = page number (0–3 for paging mode 0) (0–15 for paging mode 1)	None

This video service works only with the VGA. It determines how the 16 EGA palette registers will interact with the 256 VGA color registers for the 16-color display modes. The default mode is paging mode 0 and page 0. This enables the EGA palette registers to be set to any of the first 64 color registers. By setting the page to 1, 2, or 3, the corresponding color registers in the second, third, or fourth set of 64 color registers will be assigned to the palette registers. In paging mode 1, the palette registers should be set to 0 through 15, which correspond to the first 16 color registers. The color register table increases by 16 for each increase in page number, so as to assign the palette registers to the next group of 16 color registers. A C function to set up the paging mode and page follows:

```
/*

        setVGApaging() = Sets the VGA page mode or page

*/

void setVGApaging(char mode, char page)
{
    union REGS regs;

    regs.x.ax = 0x1013;
    regs.h.bl = mode;
    regs.b.bh = page;
    int86(0x10,&regs,&regs);
}
```

Reading a VGA Color Register (EGA/VGA Video Service 10H, Subservice 15H)

Register Inputs	Register Outputs
AH = 10H AL = 15H BX = Number of color register	DH = Red value CH = Green value CL = Blue value

This video service permits reading the value of a single VGA color register. It is not applicable to the EGA, which doesn't have color registers. We want to return the three color components from the register. However, function calls in C don't really handle returning three parameters very well. There are three basic ways to handle this situation. The first is to have three separate functions to get the color data. This works as follows:

```
/*

    get_red = Function to get red register value

*/

char get_red (char color_reg)
{
    union REGS regs;

    regs.x.ax = 0x1015;
    regs.x.bx = color_reg;
    int86(0x10,&regs,&regs);
    return (regs.h.dh);
}

/*

    get_green = Function to get green register value

*/

char get_green (char color_reg)
{
    union REGS regs;
    regs.x.ax = 0x1015;
    regs.x.bx = color_reg;
    int86(0x10,&regs,&regs);
    return (regs.h.ch);
}
```

```
/*
        get_blue = Function to get blue register value
*/

char get_blue (char color_reg)
{
    union REGS regs;
    regs.x.ax = 0x1015;
    regs.x.bx = color_reg;
    int86(0x10,&regs,&regs);
    return (regs.h.cl);
}
```

Another method is to pass pointers to the color variables to the function. This works as follows:

```
/*
        get_colors = Function to get colors from a color
                             register
*/

int get_colors (char reg_no, char *red, char *green,
char *blue)
    {
        union REGS regs;
        regs.x.ax = 0x1015;
        regs.x.bx = reg_no;
        int86(0x10,&regs,&regs);
        *red = regs.h.dh;
        *green = regs.h.ch;
        *blue = regs.h.cl;
    }
```

Finally, we can make use of a *define* statement in connection with the first three functions just described. This works as follows:

```
/*
    get_colors = Function to get colors from a color
                         register
*/

#define get_colors(red,green,blue) {red=get_red(); \
      green=get_green(); blue=get_blue();}
```

This looks just like an ordinary function, but the values of *red*, *green* and *blue* are replaced with the values from the color register just as if both functions could be returned by a function call.

Reading a Block of VGA Color Registers All at Once (EGA/VGA Video Service 10H, Subservice 17H)

Register Inputs	Register Outputs
AH = 10H AL = 17H BX = Number of first color register to be changed CX = Number of color registers to read ES:DX = Pointer to table of color values	Data returned in table pointed to by ES:DX

This video service permits reading a block of VGA color registers in a single operation. The service requires a table of color values established either in the calling program or as a global array. The table should be of type *char* and should contain 768 members (3 for each of the maximum of 256 colors). The colors are returned to the table as triplets, in the order red, green, blue, red, green, blue, etc. A C function that uses this service follows:

```
/*
    getVGAcolors() = Gets the colors of a block of VGA
                        color registers
*/
```

```
void getVGAcolors(char first_reg, char number, char
    *pal_colors)
{
    struct REGPACK regs;
    struct SREGS sregs;

    regs.r_ax = 0x1017;
    segread(&sregs);
    regs.r_es = sregs.ds;
    regs.r_dx = (int)pal_colors;
    regs.r_bx = first_reg;
    regs.r_cx = number;
    intr (0x10,&regs);
}
```

Getting the Current Color Page and Paging Mode (EGA/VGA Video Service 10H, Subservice 1AH)

Register Inputs	Register Outputs
AH = 10H AL = 1AH	BH = Current page BL = Current paging mode

This video service works only with the VGA. It determines how the 16 EGA palette registers are currently set to interact with the 256 VGA color registers for the 16-color display modes. A C function to set up the paging mode and page follows:

```
/*

        getVGApage() = Gets the VGA page mode and page

*/
```

```
void getVGApage(char *mode, char *page)
{
    union REGS regs;

    regs.x.ax = 0x101A;
    *mode = regs.h.bl;
    *page = regs.b.bh;
    int86(0x10,&regs,&regs);
}
```

Summing Color Values to Gray-Scale (EGA/VGA Video Service 10H, Subservice 1BH)

Register Inputs	Register Outputs
AH = 10H AL = 1BH BX = Number of first color register to be summed CX = Number of registers to sum	None

This video service works only with the VGA. It sums the color values of each color register that is operated upon to a gray value by the equation:

$$\text{gray-scale} = (0.30 \times \text{red}) + (0.59 \times \text{green}) + (0.11 \times \text{blue})$$

The resulting gray intensity value is placed in the red, green, and blue portions of the color register. If the original color register values result in a realistic color picture, the new gray scale values will produce a realistic black-and-white reproduction. A C function to use this video service follows:

```
/*

        setGrayScale() = Sets color registers to gray values

*/

void setGrayScale(char first_reg, char number)
{
    union REGS regs;

    regs.x.ax = 0x101B;
    regs.x.bx = first_reg;
    regs.x.cx = number;
    int86(0x10,&regs,&regs);
}
```

Loading a User Character Font (EGA/VGA Video Service 11H, Subservice 00H)

Register Inputs	Register Outputs
AH = 11H AL = 00H BL = Number of character block in display memory to load BH = Number of bytes per character CX = Number of characters to load DX = Character offset into memory block ES:BP = Pointer to the user character table	None

This video service works with text modes only. In the text modes, the EGA/VGA uses display memory plane 2 and/or 3 to store character fonts. The EGA has four memory blocks of 16K bytes each, which are dedicated to holding character sets, but only the first 8K of each block may hold a font. The VGA has eight memory blocks of 8K each, which can all be used to store character fonts. This service loads a user-defined character font, stored in a memory array, to be transferred to the designated character block in display memory. An offset may be designated for the beginning of the load.

Loading the ROM Monochrome Character Set (EGA/VGA Video Service 11H, Subservice 01H)

Register Inputs	Register Outputs
AH = 11H AL = 01H BL = Number of character block in display memory to load	None

This video service works with text modes only. It loads a monochrome character set (8 × 14 character cell) from ROM into the designated character block in display memory.

Loading the ROM 8 × 8 Double-Dot Character Set (EGA/VGA Video Service 11H, Subservice 02H)

Register Inputs	Register Outputs
AH = 11H AL = 02H BL = Number of character block in display memory to load	None

This video service works with text modes only. It loads the 8 × 8 character cell double-dot character set from ROM into the designated character block in display memory. A C function to utilize this service follows:

```
/*
            font_8x8() = Load 8 x 8 font
*/

void font_8x8 (int block)
{
    union REGS regs;
    regs.x.ax = 0x1102;
    regs.x.bx = block;
    int86(0x10,&regs,&regs);
}
```

Setting the Block Specifier (EGA/VGA Video Service 11H, Subservice 03H)

Register Inputs	Register Outputs
AH = 11H AL = 03H BL = Character generator block specifier	None

This video service works with text modes only. When block A and block B are designated to be the same, then bit 3 of the attribute byte of each character is the most significant bit of the foreground color description, thereby permitting the foreground color to be any of the 16 colors available in the 16-color display modes. When block A is different from block B, bit 3 of the attribute byte of each character is the block selector, selecting the font from block A when 0 and the character font from block B when 1. The bits representing each block are as follows:

Bit 7	Bit 6	Bit 5	Bit 4	Bit 3	Bit 2	Bit 1	Bit 0
		Block B Bit 2	Block A Bit 2	Block B Bit 1	Block B Bit 0	Block A Bit 1	Block A Bit 0

If you use attribute bit 3 to switch font blocks, you need to be aware that it will still be considered a color bit. Therefore, if you stick to the default colors, all second-font-block colors will be the bright color set. If you are switching back and forth between font blocks and want all your characters to have the same color, you need to set palette registers 8 through 15 to the same colors as registers 0 through 7. The *setEGApalette* function shown below will do the job for you.

The following is a C function that sets two blocks as the active fonts:

```
/*

    block_select() = Allows attribute 3 of character to
                     select font block instead of color

*/

      void block_select (char block_1, char block_2)
      {
          union REGS regs;

          regs.x.ax = 0x1103;
          regs.h.bl = (block_1&0x03) | ((block_1&0x04)<<2)
              | ((block_2&0x03) << 2) |
              ((block_2&0x04)<<3);
          int86(0x10,&regs,&regs);
      }
```

Listing 7-2 is a C program that will permit you to test using two fonts on a single display.

Listing 7-2. Testing Two Character Fonts

```
/*

    charsize = Program to test using two character fonts

             By Roger T. Stevens    11-22-95

*/

#include <stdio.h>
#include <string.h>
#include <dos.h>

void block_select (char block_1, char block_2);
void font_8x8 (int block);
void font_8x16 (int block);
void setEGApalette(int palette, int color);
void setMode(int mode);
void write_c(char ch, int attribute, int page, int
     replic);
void write_s(int x, int y, char *string, char color);

int no_of_cols = 80, no_of_rows = 30;

void main(void)
{
   union REGS regs;

   int i,j,k;
   char st[128] = {"Now is the time for all good"\
       " men to come to the aid of their"\
       " country or their party or "\
       " whatever...."};

   setMode(0x03);
   printf("This is a test....");
   getch();
   write_s(1,10,st,31);
   getch();
   setEGApalette(9,1);
   font_8x8(1);
   font_8x16(2);
   block_select(1,2);
   regs.x.ax = 0x1103;
   regs.x.bx = 0x0009;
   int86(0x10,&regs,&regs);
   for (i=0; i<40; i++)
```

```
        {
            gotoxy(2+i,2);
            write_c(st[i],0x21,0,1);
        }
        for (i=0; i<40; i++)
        {
            gotoxy(2+i,6);
            write_c(st[i],0x29,0,1);
        }
        for (i=41; i<79; i++)
        {
            gotoxy(2+i,6);
            write_c(st[i],0x21,0,1);
        }
        gotoxy(2,8);
        write_c('a',0x29,0,1);
        gotoxy(3,8);
        write_c('2',0x21,0,1);
        gotoxy(4,8);
        write_c(' ',0x29,0,1);
        gotoxy(5,8);
        write_c('+',0x29,0,1);
        gotoxy(6,8);
        write_c(' ',0x29,0,1);
        gotoxy(7,8);
        write_c('b',0x29,0,1);
        gotoxy(8,8);
        write_c('2',0x21,0,1);
        gotoxy(9,8);
        write_c(' ',0x29,0,1);
        gotoxy(10,8);
        write_c('=',0x29,0,1);
        gotoxy(11,8);
        write_c(' ',0x29,0,1);
        gotoxy(12,8);
        write_c('c',0x29,0,1);
        gotoxy(13,8);
        write_c('2',0x21,0,1);
        getch();
        setMode(0x03);
    }

/*

    setEGApalette() = sets the color for an EGA palette

*/

    void setEGApalette(int palette, int color)
    {
        union REGS reg;

        reg.h.ah = 0x10;
        reg.h.al = 0;
        reg.h.bh = color;
```

```
        reg.h.bl = palette;
        int86(0x10,&reg,&reg);
    }

/*
            setMode() = Sets Video Mode
*/

    void setMode(int mode)
    {
        union REGS reg;

        reg.h.ah = 0;
        reg.h.al = mode;
        int86 (0x10,&reg,&reg);
    }

/*
            font_8x8() = Load 8 x 8 font
*/

    void font_8x8 (int block)
    {
        union REGS regs;

        regs.x.ax = 0x1102;
        regs.x.bx = block;
        int86(0x10,&regs,&regs);
    }

/*
            font_8x16() = Load 8 x 16 font
*/
    void font_8x16 (int block)
    {
        union REGS regs;

        regs.x.ax = 0x1104;
        regs.x.bx = block;
        int86(0x10,&regs,&regs);
    }
```

```
/*
     block_select() = Allows attribute 3 of character
                      to select font block
*/

void block_select (char block_1, char block_2)
{
    union REGS regs;

    regs.x.ax = 0x1103;
    regs.h.bl = (block_1 & 0x03) | ((block_1 & 0x04)
        << 2) | ((block_2 & 0x03) << 2) |
        ((block_2 & 0x04) << 3);
    int86(0x10,&regs,&regs);
}

/*
     write_c() = Writes a character to the screen
*/

void write_c(char ch, int attribute, int page, int
    replic)
{
    union REGS reg;

    reg.h.ah = 0x09;
    reg.h.al = ch;
    reg.h.bl = attribute;
    reg.h.bh = page;
    reg.x.cx = replic;
    int86(0x10,&reg,&reg);
    reg.h.ah = 0x03;
    int86(0x10,&reg,&reg);
    reg.h.dl++;
    if (reg.h.dl >= no_of_cols)
    {
        reg.h.dl = 0;
        reg.h.dh = (reg.h.dh + 1) % no_of_rows;
    }
    reg.h.ah = 0x02;
    int86(0x10,&reg,&reg);
}

/*
  write_s() = Writes a string to the screen in TTY mode
```

```
*/

void write_s(int x, int y, char *string, char color)
{
    struct REGPACK regs;
    struct SREGS segregs;

    segread(&segregs);
    regs.r_es = segregs.ds;
    regs.r_bp = (int) string;
    regs.r_ax = 0x1301;
    regs.r_bx = color;
    regs.r_cx = strlen(string);
    regs.r_dx = (y<<8) | x;
    intr(0x10,&regs);
}
```

Loading the ROM 8 × 16 Character Set (EGA/VGA Video Service 11H, Subservice 04H)

Register Inputs	Register Outputs
AH = 11H AL = 04H BL = Number of character block in display memory to load	None

This video service works with text modes only. In the text modes, the EGA/VGA uses display memory plane 2 or 3 (or both) to store character fonts. The EGA has four memory blocks (of 16K bytes each), which are dedicated to holding character sets, but only the first 8K of each block may hold a font. The VGA has eight memory blocks of 8K each, which can all be used to store character fonts. This service loads the 8 × 16 character cell character set from ROM into the designated character block in display memory. A C function to utilize this service follows:

```
/*

            font_8x16() = Load 8 x 16 font

*/

void font_8x16 (int block)
{
    union REGS regs;
```

```
        regs.x.ax = 0x1104;
        regs.x.bx = block;
        int86(0x10,&regs,&regs);
    }
```

Loading a User Character Font (EGA/VGA Video Service 11H, Subservice 10H)

Register Inputs	Register Outputs
AH = 11H AL = 10H BL = Number of character block in display memory to load BH = Number of bytes per character CX = Number of characters to load DX = Character offset into memory block ES:BP = Pointer to the user character table	None

This video service is identical to subservice 00H except that it changes the values of several of the CRT controller registers to match the selected character size and that it does not automatically execute a set mode before the character set is downloaded. Thus you should run a set mode BIOS call before running this service. In addition, this service can be invoked only if the active display page is page 0. This service transfers a user-defined character font, stored in a memory array, to the designated character block in display memory. An offset may be designated for the beginning of the load. The following are the CRT controller registers affected by this service:

Register	New Contents
Maximum Row Register (09H)	Number of scan lines per character (bytes per character minus one).
Cursor Start Register (0AH)	EGA = Bytes per character minus one. VGA = Bytes per character minus two.
Cursor End Register (0BH)	EGA = 0 (cursor fills character cell). VGA = Bytes per character minus one (cursor fills bottom two lines of character cell).
Vertical Display End Register (12H)	350- or 480-line screen = (number of rows plus one) multiplied by (number of bytes per character) minus one. 200-line screen = (number of rows plus one) multiplied by (number of bytes per character) multiplied by two minus one.
Overflow Register (07H)	Bit 8 of the Vertical Display End value computed above is bit 1 of this register. VGA = Bit 9 of the Vertical Display End value computed previously is bit 6 of this register.

Loading the ROM Monochrome Character Set (EGA/VGA Video Service 11H, Subservice 11H)

Register Inputs	Register Outputs
AH = 11H AL = 11H BL = Number of character block in display memory to load	None

This video service is identical to subservice 01H except that it changes the values of several of the CRT controller registers to match the selected character size and that it does not automatically execute a set mode before the character set is downloaded. Thus you should run a set mode BIOS call before running this service. In addition, this service can be invoked only if the active display page is page 0. This service loads a monochrome character set (8 × 14 character cell) from ROM into the designated character block in display memory.

Loading the ROM 8 × 8 Double-Dot Character Set (EGA/VGA Video Service 11H, Subservice 12H)

Register Inputs	Register Outputs
AH = 11H AL = 12H BL = Number of character block in display memory to load	None

This video service is identical to subservice 02H except that it changes the values of several of the CRT controller registers to match the selected character size and that it does not automatically execute a set mode before the character set is downloaded. Thus you should run a set mode BIOS call before running this service. In addition, this service can be invoked only if the active display page is page 0. This service loads the 8 × 8 character cell double-dot character set from ROM into the designated character block in display memory.

Loading the ROM 8 × 16 Character Set (EGA/VGA Video Service 11H, Subservice 14H)

Register Inputs	Register Outputs
AH = 11H AL = 14H BL = Number of character block in display memory to load	None

This video service is identical to subservice 04H except that it changes the values of several of the CRT controller registers to match the selected character size and that it does not automatically execute a set mode before the character set is downloaded. Thus you should run a set mode BIOS call before running this service. In addition, this service can only be invoked if the active display page is page 0. This service loads the 8 × 16 character cell character set from ROM into the designated character block in display memory.

Setting a Pointer for User Graphics Characters (EGA/VGA Video Service 11H, Subservice 20H)

Register Inputs	Register Outputs
AH = 11H AL = 20H ES:SP = Pointer to user table for characters having ASCII codes from 128 to 255	None

This video service only works with modes 4, 5, and 6. It loads a pointer to an 8 × 8 user-defined character set for characters having ASCII codes from 128 to 255. For graphics modes, these characters have to be stored in regular computer memory, since all display memory is used by the graphics modes. The service requires an array of eight bytes for each of the 128 high-order characters. A C function to perform this service follows:

```
/*

    setHighOrder() = Sets pointer to high order graphics
                              table

*/

void setHighOrder (int *high_order)
{
    struct REGPACK regs;
    struct SREGS sregs;

    regs.r_ax = 0x1120;
    segread(&sregs);
    regs.r_es = sregs.ds;
    regs.r_bp = (int)high_order;
    intr (0x10,&regs);
}
```

Setting a Pointer for User Custom Character Set (EGA/VGA Video Service 11H, Subservice 21H)

Register Inputs	Register Outputs
AH = 11H AL = 21H BL = 0 (EGA Only) Number of character rows is in register DL = 1 = 14 character rows = 2 = 25 character rows = 3 = 43 character rows CX = Number of bytes per character ES:SP = Pointer to user custom character table	None

This video service loads a pointer to a variable-size array of user-defined characters. For graphics modes, these characters have to be stored in regular computer memory, since all display memory is used by the graphics modes. The service requires an array of eight bytes for each custom character.

Setting a Pointer for the 8 × 14 Character Set (EGA/VGA Video Service 11H, Subservice 22H)

Register Inputs	Register Outputs
AH = 11H AL = 22H BL = 0 (EGA only) Number of character rows is in register DL = 1 = 14 character rows = 2 = 25 character rows = 3 = 43 character rows	None

This video service loads a pointer to the 8 × 14 character set located in the EGA/VGA BIOS ROM. For graphics modes, these characters have to remain stored in ROM, since all display memory is used by the graphics modes.

Setting a Pointer for the 8 × 8 Double-Dot Character Set (EGA/VGA Video Service 11H, Subservice 23H)

Register Inputs	Register Outputs
AH = 11H AL = 23H BL = 0 (EGA only) Number of character rows is in register DL = 1 = 14 character rows = 2 = 25 character rows = 3 = 43 character rows	None

This video service loads a pointer to the 8 x 8 double-dot character set located in the EGA/VGA BIOS ROM. For graphics modes, these characters have to remain stored in ROM, since all display memory is used by the graphics modes.

Setting a Pointer for the 8 × 16 Character Set (EGA/VGA Video Service 11H, Subservice 24H)

Register Inputs	Register Outputs
AH = 11H AL = 24H BL = 0 (EGA only) Number of character rows is in register DL = 1 = 14 character rows = 2 = 25 character rows = 3 = 43 character rows	None

This video service loads a pointer to the 8 × 16 character set located in the EGA/VGA BIOS ROM. For graphics modes, these characters have to remain stored in ROM, since all display memory is used by the graphics modes.

Getting Character Generation Information (EGA/VGA Video Service 11H, Subservice 30H)

Register Inputs		Register Outputs
AH =	11H	CX = Bytes per character
AL =	30H	DL = EGA—Number of character rows on screen VGA—Number of character rows on screen minus one
BH =0 =	Get pointer to interrupt 1F (use 8 × 8 character set—upper 128 characters)	ES:BP Pointer requested by BH setting
= 1=	Get pointer to interrupt 43H (use 8 × 8 character set—lower 128 characters)	
= 2=	Get pointer to ROM 8 × 14 character set	
= 3 =	Get pointer to ROM 8 × 8 character set	
= 4 =	Get pointer to upper half of ROM 8 × 8 character set	
= 5 =	Get pointer to ROM alternate 9 × 14 monochrome characters	
= 6 =	Get pointer to ROM 8 × 16 character set	
= 7 =	Get pointer to ROM alternate 9 × 16 characters	

There are a lot of interesting things that you can do with characters in the graphics modes if you have full control of your character-writing functions. You could, of course, include in such functions complete tables of characters, but it is usually more efficient to make use of those that are already in ROM BIOS. The EGA ROM BIOS extensions have three character tables, and the VGA ROM BIOS extensions have five character tables. This video service makes it possible to obtain the address of a desired character table, as well as the number of bytes per character and the number of lines that make up a display screen. The C function *findChar* permits you to get any character table address that you want by specifying the parameter *type*, which is the number that goes into the *BH* register in the preceding table to choose which table address you want. The function returns the table address. It also passes pointers to the parameters *lines* and *bytes_per_char*, which contain the number of lines in the display and the number of bytes per character, respectively, when the function returns. This function is included in the program in Listing 7-3 which writes a string to the graphics screen with full control of the foreground and background colors. We won't describe the program in detail, since it is covered in Chapter 19. Meanwhile, you can try it out to get an idea of how to use video service.

Listing 7-3. Program to Test Reading Character Table Address

```
/*

    charread = Program to test reading character table
                          address

            By Roger T. Stevens    10-13-91

*/

#include <stdio.h>
#include <dos.h>

void display(unsigned long int address, int
    color_plane,
    unsigned char ch);
    unsigned char far *findChar (int type, int
     *lines, int *bytes_per_char);
void setMode(int mode);
void writeString(int col, int row,char *str,
     int color);

struct REGPACK reg;
char string[80] = {"This is the hour of destiny..."};
unsigned char far *char_table;
int lines, bytes per_char;

void main (void)
{
    setMode(16);
    char_table = findChar (2, &lines, &bytes_per_char);
    writeString(2,4,string,31);
    printf("\nlines: %d   bytes per character: %d   ",
        lines,bytes_per_char);
    getch();
}
```

```
/*
    findchar() = Returns the address of a character table
         and bytes per character and rows on screen
*/

unsigned char far *findChar (int type, int *lines,
    int bytes_per_char)
{
    unsigned char far *address;
    reg.r_bx = type << 8;
    reg.r_ax = 0x1130;
    intr(0x10, &reg);
    address = (unsigned char far *)(reg.r_es*0x10000 +
        reg.r_bp);
    *lines = reg.r_dx;
    *bytes_per_char = reg.r_cx;
    return (address);
}

/*
    writeString() = Writes a string of characters to the
                         screen
*/

void writeString(int col, int row,char *str, int
    color)
{
    int i = 0, j, k, mask1, mask2;
    unsigned int offset;
    char far * mem_address;
    int char_offset, foreground, background, width,
        point_color, dummy;
    unsigned char char_test;
    while (str[i])
    {
        char_offset = str[i] * 14;
        for (k=0; k<14; k++)
        {
            offset = (long)(row*14+k) * 80L + col;
            mask1 = 0x10;
            mask2 = 0x01;
            for (j=0; j<4; j++)
            {
                if (((mask1 & color)!=0) && ((mask2 &
                    color)!=0))
                    display(offset,j,0xFF);
                else
                {
                    if ((mask1 & color) != 0)
```

```
                        display(offset,j,
                        ~char_table[char_offset
                            +k]);
                    else
                    {
                        if ((mask2 & color) != 0)
                            display(offset,j,
                                char_table[char_offset + k]);
                    }
                }
                mask1 <<= 1;
                mask2 <<= 1;
            }
        }
        i++;
        col++;
    }
}

/*

        display() = Writes a byte to one display memory plane

*/

#define seq_out(index,val)  {outp(0x3C4,index);\
                             outp(0x3C5,val);}

void display(unsigned long int address, int
    color_plane, unsigned char ch)
{
    char far * mem_address;
    char dummy;
    mem_address = (char far *) 0xA0000000L + address;
    seq_out(2,(0x01 << color_plane));
    *mem_address = ch;
}

/*

                setMode() = Sets video mode

*/
void setMode(int mode)
{
    union REGS reg;

    reg.h.ah = 0;
    reg.h.al = mode;
    int86 (0x10,&reg,&reg);
}
```

Getting EGA/VGA Video Information (EGA/VGA Video Service 12H, Subservice 10H)

Register Inputs	Register Outputs
AH = 12H AL = 00H BL = 10H	BH = 0 = Current mode is color = 1 = Current mode is monochrome BL = 00H = EGA/VGA memory size is 64K bytes = 01H = EGA/VGA memory size is 128K bytes = 02H = EGA/VGA memory size is 192K bytes = 03H = EGA/VGA memory size is 256K bytes CH = Feature bits CL = Switch settings

This video service returns information on the configuration of the EGA/VGA and its current display mode. Most VGA and Super VGA cards have paged memory greater than 256K, but since 256K is the maximum that can be read with this service, that is all that can be returned. The memory size report doesn't have much use any more. The feature bits are reported for the EGA only. Feature boards attached to the two EGA feature connectors never became popular, so this is another report that has little use. Typically the EGA has four sense switches located on its rear panel. These switches determine the EGA configuration. Their positions are reported by this video service in register *CL*. This also reports the configuration information for the VGA, although this is stored in software rather than by physical switches. The computer can have two types of display adapter card present, with one designated as primary and the other as secondary. The configuration information indicates what combination is present. The following are the possible configurations:

Reg CL Hex	Switches				EGA/VGA	MGA	CGA
	1	2	3	4			
01	Off	Off	Off	On	Primary Color Display 80x25	Secondary	
02	Off	Off	On	Off	Primary Monochrome		Secondary
03	Off	Off	On	On	Secondary Enhanced Display Hi-Res Mode	Primary	
05	Off	On	Off	Off	Secondary Mono-chrome		Primary 80 x 25
06	Off	On	On	Off	Primary Enhanced Display Hi-Res Mode	Secondary	
07	Off	On	On	On	Secondary Color Dis-play 80x25	Primary	
09	On	Off	Off	On	Primary Color Display 40x25	Secondary	
0A	On	Off	On	Off	Primary Monochrome		Secondary 40x25
0B	On	Off	On	On	Secondary Enhanced Display Hi-Res Mode	Primary	
0D	On	On	Off	On	Secondary Mono-chrome		Primary 40x25
0E	On	On	On	Off	Primary Enhanced Display Emulation Mode	Secondary	
0F	On	On	On	On	Secondary Color Dis-play 80x25	Primary	

Revector Print Screen (EGA/VGA Video Service 12H, Subservice 20H)

Register Inputs	Register Outputs
AH = 12H AL = 00H BL = 20H	None

Selecting Number of Scan Lines for Text Modes (EGA/VGA Video Service 12H, Subservice 30H)

Register Inputs	Register Outputs
AH = 12H AL = 00H = 200 scan lines = 01H = 350 scan lines = 02H = 400 scan lines BL = 30H	AL = 12H indicates that this video service is supported

This video service works for the VGA in text modes only. It selects the number of scan lines and the default character set that are to be used in a text mode that is called for by the next mode set.

Specifying VGA Palette Loading (EGA/VGA Video Service 12H, Subservice 31H)

Register Inputs	Register Outputs
AH = 12H AL = 00H = Enable palette loading = 01H = Disable paletteloading BL = 31H	AL = 12H indicates that this video service is supported

This video service works with the VGA only. It determines whether the default palette will be loaded during a mode set. If this service is set for *Enable*, the default values for the palette and color registers will be restored upon mode set. If set for *Disabled*, the current palette and color register settings will be kept when mode set takes place.

Video Enable or Disable (EGA/VGA Video Service 12H, Subservice 32H)

Register Inputs	Register Outputs
AH = 12H AL = 00H = Enable video = 01H = Disable video BL = 32H	AL = 12H indicates that this video service is supported

This video service works with the VGA only. When it is run to disable the VGA, all input and output to the VGA registers are disabled and all reads and writes to display memory of this VGA are disabled. This effectively takes the VGA out of the system and enables you to substitute some other device that uses the same memory and port addresses if you have the means for enabling it.

Summing Colors to a Gray-Scale (EGA/VGA Video Service 12H, Subservice 33H)

Register Inputs	Register Outputs
AH = 12H AL = 00H = Enable summing = 01H = Disable summing BL = 33H	AL = 12H indicates that this video service is supported

This video service works only with the VGA. It sums the color values of each color register that is operated upon to a gray value by the equation:

$$\text{gray-scale} = (0.30 \times \text{red}) + (0.59 \times \text{green}) + (0.11 \times \text{blue})$$

Unlike video service 10H subservice 1BH, this service does not replace the color register contents with the gray intensity values that are obtained. Instead, it causes the gray value to be output to the screen instead of the color values when each register is designated in displaying a screen. This will result in a realistic black-and-white reproduction. A C function to use this video service follows:

```
/*
    displayGrayScale() = Displays a picture in monochrome
*/

void displayGrayScale(char enable)
{
    union REGS regs;

    regs.h.ah = 0x12;
    regs.h.al = enable;
    regs.h.bl = 0x33;
    int86(0x10,&regs,&regs);
}
```

Emulating the Cursor (EGA/VGA Video Service 12H, Subservice 34H)

Register Inputs	Register Outputs
AH = 12H AL = 00H = Enable emulation = 01H = Disable emulation BL = 34H	AL = 12H indicates that this video service is supported

This video service works with the VGA only. When emulation is disabled, the cursor is defined by the values passed in video service 01H. When emulation is enabled, it assigns a different meaning to the cursor definition in video service 01H. The new definitions are as follows:

Video Service 01H Parameter Values	Cursor Type
Start line bit 5 = 1	No cursor
Start line < End line and <= 3	Overbar cursor
Start line + 2 >= End line	Underline cursor
Start line >= 2	Half-block cursor
Start line <= 2 or end line < start line	Full-block cursor

Switching the Display Adapter (EGA/VGA Video Service 12H, Subservice 35H)

Register Inputs	Register Outputs
AH = 12H AL = 00H = Initial switch off adapter video = 01H = Initial switch on planar video = 02H = Switch off active display = 03H = Switch on inactive display BL = 35H ES:DX = Pointer to 128-byte buffer for adapter or planar status	AL = 12H indicates that this video service is supported

This video service permits switching between a display adapter device on the motherboard (planar) and one on a plug-in card (adapter). If both types of display support are available, the system will try to initialize both upon power-up. Should there be a conflict between port or memory addresses, only one device can be active at a time, so the system will (by default) disable the planar device and enable the adapter. To use this service, it should first be called with $AL = 0$, which switches off the adapter and stores its status in the designated buffer. The service should then be run with $AL = 1$ to turn on the planar video and store its status in the designated buffer. This reverses the default condition. After this, you can switch at will between the two devices by setting AL to 2 to turn off the active video and then to 3 to turn on the inactive video.

Turning off the Video Screen (EGA/VGA Video Service 12H, Sub-service 36H)

Register Inputs	Register Outputs
AH = 12H AL = 00H = Enable video output = 01H = Disable video output BL = 36H	AL = 12H indicates that this video service is supported

This output prevents all reads of the display memory by circuits that transfer memory information to the screen, thereby disabling output to the video screen, leaving the screen black. Normally, the computer can only refresh display memory when it is not being accessed by the display circuits. Therefore, when this service disables display circuit to display memory, more time is available for computer access, resulting in a substantial decrease in the time it takes to write a screenful of data to display memory. Whether you want to use this depends upon whether you would rather see a new display build up on the screen or gain speed by having the display black for a while and then having the full display pop up. A C function to utilize this video service follows:

```
/*

        screen_enable() = Enables or disables the display
                                screen

*/

void screen_enable (char enable)
{
    union REGS regs;

    regs.h.ah = 0x12;
    regs.h.bl = 0x36;
    regs.h.al = enable;
    int86 (0x10,&regs,&regs);
}
```

Writing a Character String on the Video Screen (EGA/VGA Video Service 13H)

Register Inputs	Register Outputs
AH = 13H AL = 00H = Fixed attribute; cursor returns to starting position BL = Attribute = 01H = Fixed attribute; cursor stays at ending position BL = Attribute = 02H = String includes attributes; cursor returns to starting position = 03H = String includes attributes; cursor stays at ending position BH = Page number CX = Number of characters in string DH = Character row DL = Character column	AL = 12H indicates that this video service is supported

This video service, which works with the VGA only, makes use of the TTY character-writing service (video service 0EH) to write a string of characters. See the description of that service for the way in which special characters are intercepted and used for display positioning, etc. This service gives you four options. The first pair of options (AL = 0 or 1) let you write the string with a fixed specified attribute and end with the cursor back at the beginning of the string or at the end, respectively. The second pair of (AL = 2 or 3) give you the same choices for the cursor, but include an attribute for each character in the string, so that the string bytes are actually character, attribute, character, attribute, etc. The following is a C function that makes use of this video service. It uses only option 2, to write the string with a fixed attribute and leave the cursor at the end of the string. It doesn't allow you to set the string length; instead, it uses the C *strlen* function to determine the length of a standard C string. It uses a fixed value for page 0.

```
/*
    write_s() = Writes a string to the screen in TTY mode
*/

void write_s(int x, int y, char *string, char color)
{
    struct REGPACK regs;
    struct SREGS segregs;

    segread(&segregs);
    regs.r_es = segregs.ds;
    regs.r_bp = (int) string;
    regs.r_ax = 0x1301;
    regs.r_bx = color;
    regs.r_cx = strlen(string);
    regs.r_dx = (y<<8) | x;
    intr(0x10,&regs);
}
```

Read/Write the Display Combination Code (EGA/VGA Video Service 1AH)

Register Inputs	Register Outputs
AH = 1AH AL = 00H = Read the display combination code = 01H = Write the display combination code BH = Inactive video system display combination code BL = Active video system display combination code	AL = 1AH indicates that this video service is supported BH = Inactive video system display combination code BL = Active video system display combination code

This service reads or writes the display combination code into low memory. It is used when the computer is powered up. It is not normally used by the programmer. The display combination codes are:

Display Combination Code	Display
00H	No display
01H	Monochrome display Adapter (MGA)
02H	Color Graphics Adapter (CGA)
04H	Enhanced Graphics Adapter (EGA) monochrome monitor
05H	Enhanced Graphics Adapter (EGA) color monitor
06H	Professional Graphics Adapter (PGA)
07H	Video Graphics Array (VGA) monochrome monitor
08H	Video Graphics Array (VGA) color monitor
0BH	Multi-Color Graphics Array (MCGA) monochrome monitor
0CH	Multi-Color Graphics Array (MCGA) color monitor

Reading VGA State Information (EGA/VGA Video Service 1BH)

Register Inputs	Register Outputs
AH = 1BH ES:DI Pointer to state information buffer	AL = 1BH indicates that this video service is supported ES:DI Pointer to state information buffer

This video service reads the EGA/VGA functionality/state information into a 40H-byte buffer whose address must be specified by the programmer. After executing this video service, the buffer contents will be as follows:

Buffer Address	Size	Description
00H	word	Offset to static functionality information
02H	word	Segment to static functionality information
04H	byte	Video mode
05H	word	Number of columns on screen
07H	word	Length of regenerator buffer
09H	word	Start address of regenerator buffer
0BH	8 × word	Cursor position (row,column) for 8 pages
1BH	word	Cursor type setting (start, end, value)
1DH	byte	Active display page
1EH	word	CRT controller address 3BX—monochrome 3DX—color
20H	byte	Current setting of 3x8 register (mode)
21H	byte	Current setting of 3x9 register
22H	byte	Rows on screen (character lines)

Buffer Address	Size	Description
23H	word	Character height
25H	byte	Active display combination code
26H	byte	Alternate display combination code
27H	word	Colors supported by current video mode
29H	byte	Display pages supported by current video mode
2AH	byte	Scan lines in current video mode
2BH	byte	Primary character block
2CH	byte	Secondary character block
2DH	byte	Miscellaneous state information
2EH	byte	Reserved
2FH	byte	Reserved
30H	byte	Reserved
31H	byte	Video memory available
32H	byte	Save pointer state information
33H–3FH	byte	Reserved

Saving or Restoring the Video State (EGA/VGA Video Service 1CH)

Register Inputs	Register Outputs
AH = 1CH AL = 00H = Return size of save/restore buffer = 01H = Save video state = 02H = Restore video state CX = 01H = Video hardware state = 02H = Video data areas = 04H = Video DAC state and color registers ES:BP = Pointer to save/restore buffer	AL = 1CH = Indicates that this video service is supported BH = Inactive video system Display Combination Code BL = Active video system Display Combination Code

This service permits saving video state data to a host buffer and then restoring it to the video device. Three types of video data can be saved, depending upon the setting of the *CX* register. When utilizing this service, you should select the type of data that you want to save and then run the service with *AL* set to 0. This will return the size of the buffer needed to store the video data. Use this to set up the appropriate buffer and then run the service again to save the video data.

8

The VESA Standard for Super VGA Cards

If you upgraded your display adapter card at just the wrong time (between the time when the first Super VGA cards were released and the time when all Super VGA cards began complying with the VESA standards), you'll find that your particular brand of card has many additional internal registers that are used to set up the Super VGA modes and write to and read from the screen in these modes. Usually documentation on these modes does not come with the card, and it is often quite a job to extract it from the card manufacturer, especially now that the card is a few years old. Unless you want to spend many hours digging into the intricacies of your card's hardware, you'd be well advised to junk that card and get a new, modern Super VGA card. Chances are, anyway, that your old card won't support the high-resolution true color modes that produce breath-taking photographic reproduction on the screen. This book is going to make the assumption that you have a Super VGA card that is fully VESA compliant. This will reduce your work in programming to a minimum and will get the most from your card.

The VESA Super VGA [illegible] es high resolution multicolor modes and extended ROM BIO[illegible] s to support them. You can get a copy of the standard from:

Video El[illegible] rds Association
2150 No[illegible], Suite 360
San Jos[illegible] 0

Phone ([illegible]

VESA Display Modes

Tables 8-1 and 8-2 list the VESA display modes. You will note that both high-resolution text and graphics modes are included. Each of these modes requires more than the 64K of memory space allocated as display memory. The Super VGA card may contain from 256K bytes to 4 megabytes of memory to support these modes. As far as your computer is concerned, this memory is paged so that only a 64K window can be accessed at any one time. A page register determines which 64K of memory is accessible to the computer. On the other hand, when the Super VGA card transfers data from its memory to the monitor, the 64K constraint doesn't exist; the board internally handles the procedure for continually rescanning whatever amount of memory is required by the resolution of the display mode.

Table 8-1. VESA Text Display Modes

Mode No. (Hex)	Colors	Columns	Rows
108	16/256K	80	60
109	16/256K	132	25
10A	16/256K	132	43
10B	16/256K	132	50
10C	16/256K	132	60

VESA Video BIOS Extensions

The VESA standard defines nine extensions to the ROM BIOS video services supported by DOS. These extensions provide all of the actions needed to work with the VESA display modes, except for writing pixels to the screen. This latter action needs to be faster than the speed that can be achieved by using the BIOS video service interrupt-driven procedure, so it requires direct-writing to display memory and Super VGA registers. How to do this has already been described in Chapter 6.

Table 8-2. VESA Graphics Display Modes

Mode No. (Hex)	Colors (Displayed/Available)	Display Resolution (Pixels)
100	256/256K	640 × 400
101	256/256K	640 × 480
102 or 6A	16/256K	800 × 600
103	256/256K	800 × 600
104	16/256K	1024 × 768
105	256/256K	1024 × 768
106	16/256K	1280 × 1024
107	256/256K	1280 × 1024
10D	32K/32K	320 × 200
10E	64K/64K	320 × 200
10F	16.8M/16.8M	320 × 200
110	32K/32K	640× 480
111	64K/64K	640 × 480
112	16.8M/16.8M	640 × 480
113	32K/32K	800 × 600
114	64K/64K	800 × 600
115	16.8M/16.8M	800 × 600
116	32K/32K	1024 × 768
117	64K/64K	1024 × 768
118	16.8M/16.8M	1024 × 768
119	32K/32K	1280 × 1024
11A	64K/64K	1280 × 1024
11B	16.8M/16.8M	1280 × 1024

All extended Super VGA BIOS calls are grouped as sub-services under a single Super VGA extended function number, 4FH. Before calling the video interrupt 01H, this function number is placed in the *AH* register and the sub-service number is placed in register *AL*. If this function is called when you are using a standard VGA card, nothing happens. Currently, sub-services 00H through 07H have been defined. We will show you how to use these sub-services in the sections that follow.

VESA Sub-Service 00H–Return Super VGA Information

It would make life a lot easier if every Super VGA card and monitor combination supported the same VESA video modes and extended BIOS services. Unfortunately, this is not the case. It therefore becomes the responsibility of the programmer to produce software that determines whether the Super VGA card supports the modes and capabilities that he wishes to use. The first VESA BIOS extension, sub-service 00H, provides information about the Super VGA card that the programmer may need to determine its capabilities. The registers are set as follows:

Register	Value	Description
AL	4FH	VESA Super VGA Extension Function
AH	00H	Sub-service Number
E:DI		Pointer to buffer where returned Super VGA information will be stored

The following C language structure can be set up to hold the returned Super VGA information and its address passed in registers E and DI:

```
struct
{
      char signature[4];
      int version;
      long int far *OEM_string;
      char capabilities[4];
      long int far *Modes;
      int memory_size;
      char reserved[236];
}
```

The *signature* field contains the characters 'VESA', indicating that the Super VGA board supports VESA capabilities.

The *version* field specifies the level of the VESA standard to which the Super VGA board conforms. An earlier board may not support all of the features of later versions of the VESA specification.

The *OEM_string* points to the location of an alphanumeric string giving information as to the manufacturer and name of the Super VGA board or chip set used. This data is totally at the discretion of the board manufacturer.

The *capabilities* field describes what general features are supported by the Super VGA board. Currently, only the least significant bit (D0) has meaning. The other bits are reserved for possible future upgrades. If the least significant bit is 0, the digital-to-analog converter (DAC) is fixed width, with 6 bits for each primary color. If it is 1, the DAC width is switchable.

The *Modes* field is a pointer to a list of mode numbers supported by the Super VGA. Each mode number occupies one word (16 bits). The list is terminated by a 1 (FFFFH). This list is not required to include regular VGA modes, but some manufacturers do. Also, some of the returned modes may not actually be available because the Super VGA does not have enough memory to support them or because they cannot be run on the monitor currently on the system.

The *memory_size* field is the number of 64K byte blocks of memory installed on the VGA board when you buy it. If your board can be upgraded by adding more memory, this field will not be changed to the new memory size unless you also upgrade the Super VGA card's BIOS chip.

VESA Sub-Service 01H–Return Super VGA Mode Information

The second VESA BIOS extension, sub-service 01H, returns information on a specific Super VGA mode. The registers are set as follows:

Register	Value	Description
AL	4FH	VESA Super VGA Extension Function
AH	01H	Sub-service Number
CX		Super VGA Mode (must be one returned by sub-service 00H)
E:DI		Pointer to buffer 256 byte where returned Super VGA mode information will be stored

The following C language structure can be used to hold the returned Super VGA mode information (for the single Super VGA mode specified):

```
struct
{
      int ModeAttributes;
      char WinAAttributes;
      char WinBAttributes;
      int WinGranularity;
      int WinSize;
      int WinASegment;
      int WinBSegment;
      long int WinFuncPtr;
      int BytesPerScanLine;
      int XResolution;
      int YResolution;
      char XCharSize;
      char YCharSize;
      char NumberOfPlanes;
      char BitsPerPixel;
      char NumberOfBanks;
      char MemoryModel;
      char BankSize;
      char NumberOfImagePages;
      char Reserved;
      char RedMaskSize;
      char RedFieldPosition;
      char GreenMaskSize;
      char GreenFieldPosition;
      char BlueMaskSize;
      char BlueFieldPosition;
      char RsvdMaskSize;
      char RsvdFieldPosition;
      char DirectColorModeInfo;
      char Filler[216];
}
```

The *ModeAttributes* field describes important characteristics of the selected video mode. The field is defined as follows:

D0=Mode supported in hardware
    0=Mode not supported in hardware
    1=Mode supported in hardware

D1=1 (Reserved) Previously used to indicate whether all fields of mode information were supported. Now support is mandatory.

D2=Output functions supported by BIOS
    0=Output functions not supported by BIOS
    1=Output functions supported by BIOS

D3=Monochrome/color mode (Monochrome modes are address-ed at 3B4H and have attributes of off, video, high intensity, and blink. Color modes are addressed at 3D4H and display pixel data.)
    0=Monochrome mode
    1=Color mode

D4=Mode type
    0=Text mode
    1=Graphics mode

D5-D15=Reserved

We will most often be examining bit D0. If it returns a 1 after we call the subservice for the VESA display mode we're interested in using, then the mode is supported by this Super VGA and we can go ahead and use it. Some of the newer Super VGA cards, such as the ATI Xpression card, allow you to initialize the card, indicating which graphics modes can be supported by your monitor when initializing the card. For such cards, modes not supported by the monitor return a 0 in bit D0, even if the Super VGA card is capable of supporting the mode. If you have one of these cards, any mode for which D0 returns a 1 can be used for display. If you have a card such as the STB Powergraph 64 which returns a 1 in D0 for every mode supported by the Super VGA card regardless of whether it will work on the monitor, just using D0 as a test will sometimes give you a display that cannot be synchronized by the monitor. In this case, you'll need to provide some way to tell your software not to use such a mode.

The *BytesPerScanLine* field is the number of bytes in a scan line in the selected display mode. Using this, you can compute the place in display memory where a pixel is stored. It is safest to use this parameter in your calculations, since some Super VGA boards include some empty bytes in each scan line.

The *XResolution* field is the number of pixels in a horizontal row in the selected display mode.

The *YResolution* field is the number of rows in the selected display mode (the number of pixels in a vertical column).

You probably won't be using the other mode information very often. If you do need it for some special application, get a copy of the VESA specification and study the detailed information given there.

VESA Sub-Service 02H Set Super VGA Video Mode

The Set Super VGA video mode sub-service is VESA BIOS extension sub-function 02H. We've already described how to use it in Chapter 5. The registers are set as follows:

Register	Value	Description
AL	4FH	VESA Super VGA Extension Function
AH	02H	Sub-service Number
BX		Video mode D0-D14=Video mode D15=Clear memory flag 0=Clear video memory 1= Don't clear video memory)

VESA Sub-Service 03H–Return Current Video Mode

VESA BIOS extension sub-service 03H returns the current video mode in register *BX*. The registers are set as follows:

Input

Register	Value	Description
AL	4FH	VESA Super VGA Extension Function
AH	03H	Sub-service Number

Output

Register	Value	Description
AX		Status
BX		Current video mode

VESA Sub-Service 04H–Save/Restore Super VGA Video State

This sub-service enables you to save all of the information needed to define the current state of the video, except for the contents of display memory, and to use this information to restore the video to the same state. The first thing you must do is run the sub-service with the following register settings:

Input

Register	Value	Description
AL	4FH	VESA Super VGA extension function
AH	04H	Sub-service number
DL	00H	Return save/restore state buffer size
CX		Requested states D0=Save/restore video hardware state D1=Save/restore video BIOS data state D2=Save/restore video DAC state D3=Save/restore Super VGA state

Output

Register	Value	Description
BX		Number of 64-byte blocks needed to hold the state buffer

You next have to create a buffer area having the size specified by register *BX*. Then, to save the video state in this buffer, you run the sub-service with the following settings:

Register	Value	Description
AL	4FH	VESA Super VGA extension function
AH	04H	Sub-service number
DL	01H	Save Super VGA video state
CX		Requested states (see above)

The requested video data is now stored in the buffer. To restore the video, you run the sub-service with the following register settings:

Register	Value	Description
AL	4FH	VESA Super VGA extension function
AH	04H	Sub-service number
DL	02H	Restore Super VGA video state
CX		Requested states (see above)
ES:BX		Pointer to buffer

This will restore the video to the previously saved state.

VESA Sub-Service 05H–CPU Memory Window Control

Sub-service 05H is called the CPU Video memory window control sub-service, because VESA likes to talk about windows when others are referring to memory banks or pages. This is the function we use to change memory banks (which 64K of the large internal Super VGA board memory appears in the CPU 64K-memory window, where it is possible to write graphics data to it). To set a desired bank in the memory window, the registers are set as follows:

Register	Value	Description
AL	4FH	VESA Super VGA extension function
AH	05H	Sub-service number
BH	00H	Select Super VGA memory window (page)
BL		Window number 0=Window A 1=Window B
DX		Window position in video memory (in window granularity units)

The *window granularity unit* is one of the parameters we obtained from the Super VGA board when using sub-service 01H. For most video modes and Super VGA boards, it is 64K bytes; thus the number to set in *DX* is the calculated video display memory offset from the base address divided by 64K bytes. To find which memory bank should be in the window at a given time, we calculate the offset of the pixel that we are working with from the base video memory address without limiting ourselves to the 64K maximum window size. Then, we divide this offset by 64K (or shift left 16 places) to obtain the number of the memory bank.

If we need to know what the current window setting or page number is, we may find it by using this same sub-service. Instead of setting *BH* to 00H, we set it to 01H. We don't need to insert anything in register *DX*; instead *DX* returns the current page number.

If your Super VGA card supports two separate windows, you can write to one window while displaying the other and then instantaneously switch to display the new window. The parameters *WinAAttributes* and *WinBAttributes* obtained by using sub-service 01H will tell you whether each window is available for reading or writing. If the windows are available, their base memory addresses are given in *WinASegment* and *WinBSegment*.

Here is a function you can use to make sure that your memory is set to the proper page before you write a pixel:

```
/*
        setPage() = sets the display memory page and
          read/write if different from stored page.
*/

1       void Graphics::setPage(unsigned long int offset, char
2             read_write)
3       {
4             static int old_bank, old_mode;
5             union REGS reg;
6             reg.x.dx = int(offset >> 16);
7             if ((reg.x.dx != old_bank) || (read_write !=
8             old_mode))
9             {
10                old_bank = int(offset>>16);
11                old_mode = read_write;
12                reg.x.ax = 0x4F05;
13                reg.x.bx = read_write;
14                int86(0x10, &reg, &reg);
15            }
16      }
```

The parameters passed to this function are *offset*, which is the amount the pixel is to be offset from the base display memory address, and *read_write*, which indicates whether a read or write operation is to be performed on the display memory. The *offset* parameter is shifted 16 binary places to the right and converted to an integer to give the memory bank number in line 6. The *read_write* parameter is set to 0 if you want to write a pixel to display memory, or a 1 if you want to read from display memory. Some Super VGA boards require that you are set to Window A in order to write and Window B in order to read. Setting register B this way in line 13 takes care of that situation; if your board has just one window, the setting of register B doesn't matter. If you just went ahead from here and rewrote the bank number on each pass through the function, your graphics writing routines would really be slow. Consequently, lines 7 and 8 test to see whether the bank and read/write mode are the same as they were on the previous pass through the function. If they are, simply return without any changes. The old bank and mode are stored in the parameters *old_bank* and *old_mode* by lines 10 and 11, and because they are of type static, will retain their values between calls to the function. If either parameter indicates a change, we go ahead and set the registers and call the interrupt to activate the VESA extended ROM BIOS video service.

This function will work for almost all Super VGA cards, but if you have a weird one, you'll need to write a function especially for it. If you want to make a truly universal function, you'll have to call VESA BIOS extension 00H to get the detailed card information and then use the window granularity data and the information on Windows A and B to properly set up your function. This would all become part of the *setMode* function and you might then have several overloaded versions of *setPage* to cover all situations. Another thing to watch out for is that if the memory bank is changed by some other function than *setPage*, for example by calling *printf*, then *setPage* won't know about it and won't restore to the right memory bank, since it thinks it's already there.

VESA Sub-Service 06H–Set/Get Logical Scan Line Length

Through the use of sub-service 06H, you can store in display memory a display that has longer line lengths than the resolution of the display mode you're using. Suppose that you are using a display mode where the length of each line is 800 pixels. You have a graphics file where each line of the graphic is 840 pixels. You could write some software to transfer 800 pixels of each line to the display and then throw away the remaining 40 pixels. However, using this sub-service, you can set the logical line length to 840 pixels. Then your entire line is saved in display memory, even though only 800 pixels are displayed. The only limitation is that you must have enough memory on your Super VGA card to store the graphic that you want to display. Besides being simpler to program, this method of setting up the display allows you to make use of sub-service 07H to change the starting point of the display. In this way, you can display whatever 800-pixel section of the 840-pixel line you desire. To set the logical scan line length, the registers are set as follows:

Input

Register	Value	Description
AH	4FH	VESA Super VGA extension function
AL	06H	Logical scan line length
BL	00H	Select scan line length
CX		Desired width in pixels

Output

Register	Value	Description
AX		Status
BX		Bytes per scan line
CX		Actual pixels per scan line
DX		Maximum number of scan lines

Once you have set up the desired number of pixels per scan line, you can get back the pertinent information by running the sub-service with the following settings:

Input

Register	Value	Description
AH	4FH	VESA Super VGA extension function
AL	06H	Logical scan line length
BL	01H	Return scan line length

Output

Register	Value	Description
AX		Status
BX		Bytes per scan line
CX		Actual pixels per scan line
DX		Maximum number of scan lines

There may be hardware limitations that prevent the number of pixels per line that you specify from being physically achievable. If so, the actual number of pixels in the scan line will be increased to the next achievable number, which will be returned in register CX. Thus, you may find that a little more display memory is required than you anticipated. Register DX returns the maximum number of scan lines that can be achieved using the total amount of display memory available. If this isn't enough, you won't be able to store your entire graphic.

VESA Sub-Service 07H–Set/Get Display Start

VESA BIOS extension sub-service 07H allows you to pan around a display whose logical screen is larger than the display screen by setting the top left corner of the display on the logical screen. This setting is made by setting the registers as follows:

Register	Value	Description
AH	4FH	VESA Super VGA extension function
AL	07H	Display sart cntrol
BH	00H	Reserved - mst be 0
BL	00H	Select display start
CX		First displayed pixel in scan line
DX		First displayed scan line

When you use this sub-service in a program, you need to be careful in how you set up the top left corner. If you add the display-column resolution in pixels to the column number you select for the top left corner, the result should not be greater than the size of the logical display line; if it is, your display will have some of the beginning of the logical display tacked onto the end of the actual display. Similarly, if you add the row resolution to the row number you select, it should not be greater than the end row of the logical display. If it is, funny things will happen to the bottom of the display.

This same sub-service may be used to find the current location of the top left corner as follows:

Input

Register	Value	Description
AH	4FH	VESA Super VGA extension function
AL	07H	Display start control
BL	01H	Return display start

Output

Register	Value	Description
AX		Status
BH	00H	Reserved - will always be 0
CX		First displayed pixel in scan line
DX		First displayed scan line

VESA Sub-Service 08H–Set/Get DAC Palette Control

VESA BIOS extension sub-service 08H allows setting the digital-to-analog converter (DAC) to operate with other than the 6-bit per color information that is standard for the VGA, providing your Super VGA card has this capability. When sub-function 02H sets the display mode, the DAC is set for 6-bit per color operation by default. To change to another type of DAC operation, you must then run sub-service 08H. The register settings are:

Input

Register	Value	Description
AH	4FH	VESA Super VGA extension function
AL	08H	Set/Get DAC palette control
BL	00H	Set DAC palette width
BH		Desired number of bits of color per primary

Output

Register	Value	Description
AX		Status
BH		Current number of bits of color per primary

This sub-service may also be used to find the number of bits of color per primary currently being used. The register settings are:

Input

Register	Value	Description
AH	4FH	VESA Super VGA extension function
AL	08H	Set/Get DAC palette control
BL	01H	Get DAC palette width

Output

Register	Value	Description
AX		Status
BH		Current number of bits of color per primary

Part 3

Positioning Graphics

9

System and Display Coordinates and How They Interact

If you want the very fastest graphics functions, you can write each one specifically for the display mode you will be using. However, if you decide to change display modes (you decide you need more resolution, for example, or you buy a new and better display board and monitor), you will have to rewrite all of the graphics functions to work with the new mode. If this doesn't appeal to you, you can sacrifice a little speed and set up a set of universal system coordinates that will work with every display mode. Then when you use the *setMode* function to select a new display mode, the graphic will automatically be displayed on the new screen at its proper resolution without your having to change anything else. In *The C Graphics Handbook*, some of the programs used system coordinates and some used display coordinates. I can assure you that it's no fun to go through a program with a calculator to change each pair of coordinates from one system to another.

The screen coordinate system must have been designed by an English teacher. It reads like a book, with the coordinate pair (0,0) at the top lefthand corner of the screen. The *x* coordinates increase as we move toward the right, as if we were counting letters of a line of type, and the y coordinates increase as we move to the bottom of the screen, as if we were counting lines of text. This booklike system is totally unlike most mathematical and geometrical coordinate systems. For a geometric system, you usually want to have the coordinate pair (0,0) at the center of the page, with positive values of *x* going toward the right and negative values toward the left, and positive values of y going upward, and negative values downward. In some cases, where you are going to be handling only positive numbers, you might want (0,0) to be at the bottom left corner of the page, with increasingly positive values of x going toward the right and increasingly positive values of y going upward. The fact that the screen coordinate system does not correspond with any coordinate system usually used in mathematical and geometric work is one good reason why you may not be satisfied with using the screen coordinate system and may want to create a coordinate system of your own.

The scale of the screen coordinate system depends upon the resolution of the display mode that you are using. For example, if you are using a display mode that has a resolution of 320 × 200 pixels, then you have 320 pixels across the screen in the x direction and 200 pixels down the screen in the y direction. Similarly a 640 × 350 pixel display mode has 640 pixels in the x direction and 350 in the y direction. It would be ideal if all display modes resulted in square pixels (pixels whose x and y dimensions were the same), but this is often not the case. Remembering that the aspect ratio of the display screen is 4:3 (in other words the height is 3/4 of the width), a display mode having square pixels would be 640 × 480 pixels. Thus the 640 × 350 pixel display mode would have pixels whose x dimension is only 0.7129166 of their y dimension. The unfortunate thing about this is that if you are drawing curves that are described by algebraic equations (circles, for example), their shape is only correct if you have square pixels. Thus, you can draw a circle without problems in the 640 × 480 pixel mode, but if you use the same technique in the 640 × 350 display mode, you will get an ellipse. This is another excellent reason for abandoning the screen coordinate system in favor of a coordinate system of your own.

Choosing System Coordinates

We are going to set up the system coordinates with the origin (coordinate pair (0,0)) at the middle of the screen. We want its resolution to be capable of showing all of the detail of the best VESA-supported display mode. Unfortunately, this mode is 1280 × 1024 pixels, which does not result in square pixels; the pixels have a height that is only 0.9375 of their width. So we've chosen the 1280-pixel width as the standard of resolution and will have to modify the pixel height to obtain square pixels. This results in our reference system having a minimum horizontal value of minus 640 pixels, a maximum horizontal value of 639 pixels, a minimum vertical value of minus

480 pixels, and a maximum vertical value 479 pixels. (The reason for the slight dissymetry is that we have to allow 1 pixel for zero; thus 1280 resolution allows a pixel for zero and 640 on one side and 639 on the other.)

The time required to write a pixel to the screen is usually a lot greater than that used for all the mathematical operations that determine where the pixel is located. Therefore, it won't cost you much more time to compute in the system coordinate system as long as you do your conversions before you plot to the screen. If you want maximum speed while using display coordinates, you'll want to avoid methods that end up, after conversion to display coordinates, writing the same screen pixel more than once.

Conversion Functions

If you're using system coordinates, each time you write a pixel to the screen you'll have to convert its coordinate pair from system coordinates to display coordinates. That can be a big bottleneck if you're using mathematical operations that consume a lot of computer time. Floating-point operations are definitely out. In the best of all possible worlds, you should make all your conversions using integer addition, subtraction, and shifting operations. Usually, this is not possible. An occasional multiplication won't hurt you. For some conversions, a division is absolutely necessary, but you should be aware that it's going to slow things up. With these opening remarks, lets take a look at the conversion routines that will be used for all the graphics programs in this book. They are shown in Listing 9-1.

Observe that we are using separate conversion functions for the x and y conversions. We do this because we may sometimes have a situation such as a horizontal line, which is defined by $x1$, $x2$, and y, where $x1$ is the beginning horizontal coordinate of the line, $x2$ is its end, and y is its vertical coordinate. If we were using a single conversion function for a coordinate pair, we would have a problem. Converting $(x1,y)$ would be all right, but what do we do for $x2$? If we convert it and y together, then y will have been converted twice and will have the wrong value. Of course, we could set up separate $y1$ and $y2$ and make them equal to y before the conversion and then use them from then on, but this is a waste of computer power and memory. Using separate conversion functions solves such problems in the easiest possible way. First, let's take a look at the *convert_x* function. It requires one passed parameter (the value of x) and one external parameter (*mode*, the number of the display mode). In line 8, we begin by adding 640 to the x value. This changes from a range for x of minus 640 to +639 to a range of 0 to 1279. We next have to scale this to match the resolution of the current display mode. The *switch* statement that starts on line 9 selects the proper procedure, based upon the display mode. The modes listed in the case statements from line 11 through line 15 have a horizontal resolution (range of values) of 320. This requires that the coordinate that enters the switch statement be divided by four. This is accomplished in line 17 by a binary right shift of two places. The cases in lines 18 through 27 have a horizontal resolution of 640 so that the entering coordinate must be divided by 2. This is accomplished in line 28 by a binary right shift of one place. The above sets of cases are very fast. The cases in lines 30 through 34 have a horizontal resolution of 800. There is no very fast way of transforming from 1280 to 800 pixels; the best we can do is use an integer multiplication and division, which is pretty slow compared with the previous cases. The remaining cases in lines 37 through 42 have a horizontal resolution of 1024; we can achieve the desired scaling by one left shift of two places followed by an integer divide. This is a little faster than the multiply and divide procedure discussed just before this. the remaining cases we're interested in have a horizontal resolution of 1280, which is the same range of values as our original system coordinates, so we don't have to consider these at all in our switch statement.

Listing 9-1. Coordinate Conversion Functions

```
        /*

                Coordinate Conversion Functions

        */


1       /*

          convert_x() = converts an x in system coordinates to
               an x in display coordinates.

4       */

5       int Graphics::convert_x(int x)
6       {
7            extern int mode;
```

```
        x += 640;
        switch(mode)
        {
            case 0x0D:
            case 0x13:
            case 0x10D:
            case 0x10E:
            case 0x10F:
                x >>= 2;
                break;
            case 0x0E:
            case 0x0F:
            case 0x10:
            case 0x11:
            case 0x12:
            case 0x100;
            case 0x101:
            case 0x110:
            case 0x111:
            case 0x112:
                x >>= 1;
                break;
            case 0x102:
            case 0x103:
            case 0x113:
            case 0x114:
            case 0x115:
                x = (3 * x)/5;
                break;
            case 0x104:
            case 0x105:
            case 0x116:
            case 0x117:
            case 0x118:
                x = (x << 2)/5;
                break;
        }
        return(x);
}
/*

    convert_y() = converts a y in system coordinates to
        a y in display coordinates.

*/
int Graphics::convert_y(int y)
{
        extern mode;

        y = 479 - y;
        switch(mode)
        {
```

```
57              case 100:
58                 y <<= 1;
59              case 0x0D:
60              case 0x0E:
61              case 0x13:
62              case 0x10D:
63              case 0x10E:
64              case 0x10F:
65                 y = int((y * 27L) >> 7);
66                 break;
67              case 0x0F:
68              case 0x10:
69                 y =int((y * 93L) >> 8);
70                 break;
71              case 0x11:
72              case 0x12:
73              case 0x101:
74              case 0x110:
75              case 0x111:
76              case 0x112:
77                 y >>= 1;
78                 break;
79              case 0x102:
80              case 0x103:
81              case 0x113:
82              case 0x114:
83              case 0x115:
84                 y = (3 * y)/5;
85                 break;
86              case 0x104:
87              case 0x105:
88              case 0x116:
89              case 0x117:
90              case 0x118:
91                 y = (y << 2)/5;
92                 break;
93              case 0x106:
94              case 0x107:
95              case 0x119:
96              case 0x11A:
97              case 0x11B:
98                 y = (y << 4)/15;

99          }
100         return(y);
101    }
```

The conversion in the *y* direction is accomplished by the *convert_y* function. It requires one passed parameter (the value of *y*) and one external parameter (*mode*, the number of the display mode). In line 54, we begin by subtracting the *y* coordinate from 479. This inverts the *y*'s and also changes the range so that instead of going from minus 480 to +479, the new *y*'s range from 959 to 0. We next have to scale this to match the resolution of the current display mode. The *switch* statement that starts on line 55 selects the proper procedure, based upon the display mode. The modes listed in the case statements from line 59 through line 64 have a vertical resolution (range of values) of 200. The best we can do to approximate the scaling is to multiply by 27 and then divide by 128 (a right binary shift of seven places). This is done in line 65. Display mode 100H (the case in line 57) has a vertical resolution of 400. To achieve this, we first binary shift one place to the left (doubling the number); then, because there is no break, it follows the same conversion as lines 59 through 64. The cases in lines 67 and 68 have a vertical resolution of 350. Again, the best integer approximation of the scaling factor is accomplished by a multiplication (by 93) and a binary right shift (of eight places). The cases in lines 71 through 76 have a vertical resolution of 480. The scaling can be accomplished very rapidly through a single right binary shift. The cases in lines 79 through 83 have a resolution of 600. The scaling is achieved quite slowly by a multiplication and a divide. The cases in lines 86 through 90 are also performed by a slow multiply and divide. The cases in lines 93 through 97 have a resolution of 1024, which is greater than our 960 pixel system coordinate resolution. The scaling is accomplished in line 98 by a four-place binary left shift followed by a division (by 15).

10

Clipping Techniques

Many of the functions that have been described in this book involve plotting points to the display screen, but do not place any limits on the values that may be specified for the *x* and *y* coordinates of each point. It is up to the programmer to make sure that these values are such that the point will actually be at the proper place on the screen. The graphics package listed in Chapter 11 checks each point that is written to the screen to make sure it is actually within the screen display area; if not, the point is not written to the display memory. This is important because it can be rather embarrassing if we try to write a point outside the assigned display memory. If you refer back to Chapter 6, you'll see that the plotting functions convert the *x* and *y* coordinates that you specify for a point location into an address in display screen memory. If you exceed the limit for the *x* coordinate, you usually end up with a point that moves down one or more lines on the screen and is displaced to the left or right of the desired position. You may have thought that since the point was located to the right of the displayed area it just wouldn't show up, so you didn't need to worry about it, but actually, it appears in some undesired position on top of part of the display that you wanted to see. If you exceed the limit for the *y* coordinate, you are likely to write to a different memory page, which you may never notice if you don't switch pages. If you do switch to another page, however, you may be unpleasantly surprised to discover that you have inadvertently already written something to a page that you thought was blank, or you may have overwritten something on the new page that you thought you were saving. One other unfortunate possibility is that you may send negative numbers to the coordinates, or numbers so big as to cause you to exceed the bounds of display memory. In either case, you may attempt to write sections of memory that are not reserved for the display, which can result in a number of strange effects, including changing of some of your program variables or the total crashing of the program.

The graphics package takes care of this problem, but there may be cases where you want to clip everything outside a smaller rectangular window located within your display. One way of doing this is used in the graphics package, but it requires that every pixel be calculated and a decision made as to whether to plot it. For straight lines, there are faster ways of clipping, which we will describe in this chapter.

A Simple Clipping Method

The simplest clipping method is to go directly to the plot function and enclose its whole body within an *if* statement similar to the following:

```
if (( x>= xstart) && (x < xend) && (y >= ystart) &&
    (y < yend))
{
    /*  body of plotting function */
}
```

This ensures that a pixel will be plotted to the screen only if it is within the rectangle whose top left corner is (*xstart*, *ystart*) and whose bottom right corner is *(xend-1*, *yend-1*). The graphics package uses this technique, with the bounds representing the whole screen area. However, you can use the same technique to specify any size rectangle you desire within the screen area. You can do this for a particular situation by using the statement above before each call to the point-plotting function, or you can have a more complex point-plotting function that has the clipping rectangle bounds passed to it and only plots points within the specified bounds. Since this four-way test must be made for each pixel, this is usually the slowest possible method of clipping. However, for such things as circles, ellipses, and arcs, as described in following chapters, this primitive method is the only practical way that clipping can be achieved.

Clipping Straight Lines

If a line extends beyond the boundaries of a specified clipping rectangle, it may make sense to compute new beginning and/or ending points for the line that make it wholly within the clipping rectangle, and then plot this new line pixel by pixel, rather than perform the four-way clipping test on each pixel.

Whether this will reduce plotting time depends largely on how long a line you are going to draw. Determining the new line endpoints usually takes several times as long as would be required to use the primitive four-way test on the beginning and ending pixels of the line, so if you are drawing lines that are just a few pixels long, you had better stick to the primitive method. On the other hand, if you are working with long lines, you can save a considerable amount of time by recomputing the endpoints. (The savings come about in two ways. First, the computer time to compute the new endpoints is much less than would be required to make the primitive four-way test on each pixel in the line. Second, once the new endpoints are computed, you don't have to do anything for the parts of the original line that are outside the bounding rectangle.) Listing 10-1 lists a program called *cliptest.cpp* that tests the clipping of straight lines. This program makes use of the graphics package that we'll describe in the next chapter. The main program begins by setting the display mode in line 22 and then defining the limits of the bounding rectangle in lines 23 through 26. Next, the first display is created in lines 27 through 38. This consists of a *for* loop that iterates to generate 2500 lines. Within this loop, we first find random pairs of starting and ending coordinates for the line. In line 33 the line is drawn, using one of the darker colors. Next *clipline1* is called in line 34. This is the clipping function that uses line geometry. The function sets the starting x coordinate to 999 if the line is entirely outside the clipping rectangle. Otherwise, if the starting or ending coordinates are outside the clipping rectangle, it creates a new set of coordinates at the boundary edge. In line 35, we test whether the line is inside or outside the clipping rectangle; if it's inside, we draw it in line 36, using the same color that the whole line was drawn in but the brighter shade of the color. When this display is complete, the bright rectangle is easy to observe within the varicolored background. Also if there is anything wrong that causes supposedly clipped lines to extend outside the rectangle, the bright slashes of color are fairly obvious. The code for the second display is listed in lines 44 through 63. We begin by clearing the screen in line 44. As with the previous display, we have a *for* loop (beginning in line 45) but this loop only generates 250 lines. Again, as in the previous display, within the loop we first set up the random coordinates for the beginning and end of each line. The *clipline1* function is then called to clip the line, in line 51, and if the clipped line is within the clipping rectangle, it is drawn to the screen in a bright color in line 53. Lines 55 through 62 then draw a six-pixel-wide white rectangle at the clipping boundaries.

Now let's look at the function called *clipline1*, which uses a straightforward mathematical approach to determining the new line endpoints. The generalized equation for a line is:

$$y = mx + b$$

(Equation 12-1)

where m is the slope of the line and b represents an offset. The slope may also be written as:

$$m = \frac{y_2 - y_1}{x_2 - x_1}$$

(Equation 12-2)

If we are looking for a new point on the line, we can put together the information in the two preceding equations to obtain the following equations:

$$y_3 = \frac{(x_3 - x_1)(y_2 - y_1)}{x_2 - x_1} + y_1$$

(Equation 12-3)

$$x_3 = \frac{(y_3 - y_1)(x_2 - x_1)}{y_2 - y_1} + x_1$$

(Equation 12-4)

For a line that passes through any one of the four boundaries that make up the clipping rectangle, we can obtain the new line ending by setting the appropriate coordinate equal to the boundary value and then solving Equation 12-3 if a new y value is required or Equation 12-4 if a new x value is required. The function to do this is listed beginning in line 115. Ordinarily, we would have to make eight tests, one for the line beginning at each of the four boundaries and one for the line end at each of the four boundaries.

However, we begin the function by swapping coordinates, if necessary, in lines 121 through 126, so that the starting coordinate set, (*xs*,*ys*), is such that *xs* is always smaller than (to the left of) *xe*, which reduces the number of required tests to six. Before performing these six tests, however, in lines 128 and 129 we perform a simple test that discards all lines that are totally to the left or right of the bounds of the clipping rectangle. This gets rid of all cases where *xe* is less than the lefthand boundary, where *xs* is greater than the righthand boundary, where *ys* is greater than the top boundary, or where *ye* is less than the bottom boundary. If the line has not been rejected, it cuts through the clipping rectangle, so we need to test only six more conditions. First, however, we have to treat separately the case of horizontal and vertical lines, since either of these would cause a divide-by-zero error in one of the six conditional boundary tests. This takes place in lines 134 through 147. For vertical lines, we don't know whether *ye* is greater than *ys* or vice versa, so we have to do four tests to ensure that both ends of the line are limited to within the clipping rectangle boundaries. For horizontal lines we only need to make two tests since we already know that *xs* is smaller than *xe*. Next, in lines 148 and 149, we compute the slopes that are needed to calculate the new line endpoints in the following six tests. In lines 150 through 179, the function has a series of six *if* statements that check the six remaining boundary conditions and use the boundary conditions and the equations described earlier to compute a new line ending for each condition that applies. Once in a while, there is a pathological case in which truncation errors in computing new endpoints result in a new line segment being found outside the clipping boundary. Such lines are removed by lines 180 and 181, which perform the same test originally done in lines 128 and 129.

Clipping with the Cohen-Sutherland Algorithm

Lines 71 through 110 of the *main* program create the same two displays as the first two displays described above, except that the Cohen-Sutherland algorithm is used to do the clipping. Cohen and Sutherland developed a clipping algorithm based upon dividing the world into nine regions, one being within the clipping window and the others above, below, to the right, and to the left of the window and combinations of these. Each region is then assigned a unique four-bit identifying number. This scheme for dividing the world is shown in Figure 10-1. An identifying code is assigned to each endpoint of the line, depending upon which of the nine regions it lies in. The method of assigning codes has several nice features. First, it is very easy to generate the code that is assigned to each endpoint of the line. This is demonstrated in the macro at the beginning of the *clipline2* function. The code is first set to 0; then a check is made against the left boundary and the code ORed with 1 if the x coordinate is to the left. If this is the case, nothing further needs to be done with x. Otherwise, x is checked to see if it is to the right, and if so, the code is ORed with 2. In a similar manner, an 8 is ORed into the code if y is above the window and a 4 ORed in if y is below the window. That's all that needs to be done to generate the code for a coordinate pair. Another nice feature comes about in testing. If the both endpoints of the line are within the window, both codes are 0. If these codes are ORed together, the result is then 0, which indicates the function should return the line value, since it is in the window. If the codes for the endpoint have the same bit set to 1 in both, this indicates that the entire line is outside the window, which means that the line can be disregarded. This situation can be identified by the fact that ANDing the two codes yields a 1 if two corresponding bits are 1 and a 0 otherwise. For this situation, the function first changes the value of *xs* to -999. Since this value can never occur naturally, it is a signal to the calling function that the line is entirely outside the clipping boundaries and therefore should not be printed. Another way that you might want to handle this situation is to include a Boolean variable in the line structure that tells whether or not the line should be printed. This Boolean value would be set within the *clipline* function and would be automatically passed to the function used to draw the line to determine whether the line should be displayed or not.

Figure 10-1. Cohen-Sutherland Method of Dividing Space Around a Clipping Rectangle (Window)

Above Left (1001)	Above (1000)	Above Right (1010)
Left (0001)	Within (0000)	Right (0010)
Below Left (0101)	Below (0100)	Below Right (0110)

Listing 10-1. Listing of the cliptest.cpp Program

```
/*

        CLIPTEST = Test of functions for clipping lines
                 By Roger T. Stevens  2-11-96

*/

#include "c:\cpphbook\program\graphics.cpp"

Graphics graphic;
Line line;

typedef struct
{
    int xs, ys, xe, ye;
} Bounds;
Bounds bounds;

void clipLine1(int *xs, int *ys, int *xe, int *ye, Bounds
    bounds);
void clipLine2(int *xs, int *ys, int *xe, int *ye, Bounds
```

```
bounds);

void main()
{
    int i, xs, ys, xe, ye;

/*
                         Display 1
         2500 lines clipped by line geometry displayed
           in bright colors; same lines unclipped
                displayed in darker colors.
*/

    graphic.setMode(16);
    bounds.xs = -440;
    bounds.ys = -100;
    bounds.xe = 440;
    bounds.ye = 360;
    for (i=0; i<2500; i++)
    {
        xs = rand()/26 - 640;
        ys = 480 - rand()/34;
        xe = rand()/26 -640;
        ye = 480 - rand()/34;
        line.draw(xs,ys,xe,ye,(i %6) + 1);
        clipLine1(&xs, &ys, &xe, &ye, bounds);
        if (xs != -999)
            line.draw(xs, ys, xe, ye, (i % 6) + 9);
    }
    getch();

/*
                         Display 2
         250 lines clipped by line geometry displayed
                  with clipping boundary.
*/

    graphic.cls(0);
    for (i=0; i<250; i++)
    {
        xs = rand()/26 - 640;
        ys = 480 - rand()/34;
        xe = rand()/26 -640;
        ye = 480 - rand()/34;
        clipLine1(&xs, &ys, &xe, &ye, bounds);
        if (xs != -999)
            line.draw(xs, ys, xe, ye, (i % 6) + 9);
    }
```

```
        line.draw(bounds.xs, bounds.ys, bounds.xe,
        bounds.ys,15,6);
        line.draw(bounds.xe, bounds.ys, bounds.xe,
        bounds.ye,15,6);
        line.draw(bounds.xe, bounds.ye, bounds.xs,
        bounds.ye,15,6);
        line.draw(bounds.xs, bounds.ye, bounds.xs,
            bounds.ys,15,6);
        getch();

    /*

                        Display 3

        2500 lines clipped by Cohen-Sutherland
        algorithm displayed in bright colors;
            same lines unclipped displayed
                  in darker colors.

    */

        graphic.cls(0);
        for (i=0; i<2500; i++)
        {
            xs = rand()/26 - 640;
            ys = 480 - rand()/34;
            xe = rand()/26 -640;
            ye = 480 - rand()/34;
            line.draw(xs,ys,xe,ye,(i %6) + 1);
            clipLine2(&xs, &ys, &xe, &ye, bounds);
            if (xs != -999)
                line.draw(xs, ys, xe, ye, (i % 6) + 9);
        }
        getch();

    /*

                        Display 4

        250 lines clipped by Cohen-Sutherland
              algorithm displayed with
                 clipping boundary.

    */

        graphic.cls(0);
        for (i=0; i<250; i++)
        {
            xs = rand()/26 - 640;
            ys = 480 - rand()/34;
            xe = rand()/26 -640;
```

```
            ye = 480 - rand()/34;
            clipLine2(&xs, &ys, &xe, &ye, bounds);
            if (xs != -999)
                line.draw(xs, ys, xe, ye, (i % 6) + 9);
        }
        line.draw(bounds.xs, bounds.ys, bounds.xe,
        bounds.ys,15,6);
        line.draw(bounds.xe, bounds.ys, bounds.xe,
        bounds.ye,15,6);
        line.draw(bounds.xe, bounds.ye, bounds.xs,
        bounds.ye,15,6);
        line.draw(bounds.xs, bounds.ye, bounds.xs,
        bounds.ys,15,6);
        getch();
    }

    /*

        clipLine1() = Changes line coordinates so that line
                will be within a designated window.

    */

    void clipLine1(int *xs, int *ys, int *xe, int *ye, Bounds
            bounds)
    {
        int dx, dy, temp;

        if (*xs > *xe)
        {
            temp = *xe;
            *xe = *xs;
            *xs = temp;
            temp = *ye;
            *ye = *ys;
            *ys = temp;
        }
        if ((*xs >= bounds.xe) || (*xe <= bounds.xs) || (*ys
            >= bounds.ye) || (*ye <= bounds.ys))
        {
            *xs = -999;
            return;
        }
        if (*xs == *xe)
        {
            *ys = min(bounds.ye, *ys);
            *ys = max(bounds.ys, *ys);
            *ye = min(bounds.ye, *ye);
            *ye = max(bounds.ys, *ye);
            return;
        }
        if (*ys == *ye)
```

```
    {
        *xs = max(bounds.xs, *xs);
        *xe = min(bounds.xe, *xe);
        return;
    }
    dy = *ye - *ys;
    dx = *xe - *xs;
    if (*xs < bounds.xs)
    {
        *ys = *ys + (long)(bounds.xs - *xs)*dy/dx;
        *xs = bounds.xs;
    }
    if (*ys < bounds.ys)
    {
        *xs = *xs + (long)(bounds.ys - *ys)*dx/dy;
        *ys = bounds.ys;
    }
    if (*ys > bounds.ye)
    {
        *xs = *xs + (long)(bounds.ye - *ys)*dx/dy;
        *ys = bounds.ye;
    }
    if (*xe > bounds.xe)
    {
        *ye = *ys + (long)(bounds.xe - *xs)*dy/dx;
        *xe = bounds.xe;
    }
    if (*ye < bounds.ys)
    {
        *xe = *xs + (long)(bounds.ys - *ys)*dx/dy;
        *ye = bounds.ys;
    }
    if (*ye > bounds.ye)
    {
        *xe = *xs + (long)(bounds.ye - *ys)*dx/dy;
        *ye = bounds.ye;
    }
    if ((*xs >= bounds.xe) || (*xe <= bounds.xs) || (*ys
        >= bounds.ye) || (*ye <= bounds.ys))
    {
        *xs = -999;
        return;
    }
}

/*

    clipLine2() = Changes line coordinates so that line
            will be within a designated window.

*/

#define outcodes(x, y, bounds, outcode) { outcode = 0; \
    if (x < bounds.xs)                          \
```

```
            outcode |= 1;              \
        else                           \
            if (x > bounds.xe)         \
                outcode |= 2;          \
        if (y < bounds.ys)             \
            outcode |= 8;              \
        else                           \
            if (y > bounds.ye)         \
                outcode |= 4;}         \

        #define test {if (outcode1 & outcode2)  {  \
                            *xs = -999;            \
                            return;}       \
                    if (! (outcode1 | outcode2)) \
                            return; }              \

    void clipLine2(int *xs, int *ys, int *xe, int *ye, Bounds
        bounds)
    {
        int outcode1, outcode2, temp, dx, dy;

        if (*xs > *xe)
        {
            temp = *xe;
            *xe = *xs;
            *xs = temp;
            temp = *ye;
            *ye = *ys;
            *ys = temp;
        }
        outcodes(*xs, *ys, bounds, outcode1);
        outcodes(*xe, *ye, bounds, outcode2);
        test;
        dx = *xe - *xs;
        dy = *ye - *ys;
        while (1)
        {
            if (outcode1 & 1)
            {
                *ys += (long)(bounds.xs - *xs) *dy/dx;
                *xs = bounds.xs;
                outcode1 = (*ys > bounds.ye) ? 4 :
                    ((*ys < bounds.ys) ? 8: 0);
                test;
            }
            if (outcode1 & 8)
            {
                *xs += (long)(bounds.ys - *ys)*dx/dy;
                *ys = bounds.ys;
                outcode1 = (*xs > bounds.xe) ? 2 :
                    ((*xs < bounds.xs) ? 1: 0);
                test;
            }
            if (outcode1 & 4)
            {
```

```
245                 *xs += (long)(bounds.ye - *ys)*dx/dy;
246                 *ys = bounds.ye;
247                 outcode1 = (*xs > bounds.xe) ? 2 :
248                     ((*xs < bounds.xs) ? 1: 0);
249                 test;
250             }
251             if (outcode2 & 2)
252             {
253                 *ye = *ys + (long)(bounds.xe -
254                 *xs)*dy/dx;
255                 *xe = bounds.xe;
256                 outcode2 = (*ye > bounds.ye) ? 4 :
257                     ((*ye < bounds.ys) ? 8: 0);
258                 test;
259              }
260             if (outcode2 & 8)
261             {
262                 *xe = *xs + (long)(bounds.ys -
263                 *ys)*dx/dy;
264                 *ye = bounds.ys;
265                 outcode2 = (*xe > bounds.xe) ? 2 :
266                     ((*xe < bounds.xs) ? 1: 0);
267                 test;
268             }
269             if (outcode2 & 4)
270             {
271                 *xe = *xs + (long)(bounds.ye -
272                 *ys)*dx/dy;
273                 *ye = bounds.ye;
274                 outcode2 = (*xe > bounds.xe) ? 2 :
275                     ((*xe < bounds.xs) ? 1: 0);
276                 test;
277             }
278         }
279     }
```

Now let's look at the Cohen-Sutherland clipping function in a little more detail. As with the previous clipping function, it begins in lines 211 through 219 by swapping coordinate pairs, if necessary, so that *xs* is always less than *xe*. Then the *outcodes* macro is called to generate the *outcode* for each of the line endpoints. This macro is listed in lines 191 through 201. The macro *test* (lines 202 through 206) is then run to check whether we have a line totally outside the clipping rectangle or one totally inside it. In either of these two special cases, the function terminates, returning a set of line endpoint values. If neither of these trivial cases is true, the function begins a *while* loop at line 225, which executes until one of the subsequent calls to *test* causes the function to return to the calling program. In this *while* loop are the six boundary conditions that we described for the previous clipping function. Once a condition is found true and the new endpoint coordinates are computed, the *outcode* is modified appropriately. If you're not familiar with the *?* operator in C, this may seem a little obscure to you. A typical *outcode* modifying expression is

```
outcode1 = (line.ys > bounds.ye) ? 4:
((line.ys < bounds.ys) ? 8: 0);
```

This is equivalent to the following code:

```
if (line.ys > bounds.ye)
    outcode1 = 4;
else
    if (line.ys < bounds.ys)
        outcode = 8;
    else
            outcode = 0;
```

Then *test* is called to check whether the new line coordinates are both inside or outside of the clipping rectangle, thereby indicating that it is time to terminate. The loop continues to iterate until one of these conditions is met. We need to point out two things about this loop. First, one pass through the loop should be sufficient to determine the new endpoints for any line. Unfortunately, however, there is an occasional pathological line where truncation errors during computation cause one pass through the loop to be insufficient. This occurs very rarely, but when it does a second pass through the loop resolves the situation. Second, you might ask why after each coordinate change the whole *test* macro should be run, since it seems obvious that if a line is not totally outside the clipping rectangle to begin with, it will not become so after alteration. This is mathematically true, but when truncation errors creep in, a line right at the edge of the clipping rectangle can occasionally creep outside. Without some provision for this case, such a situation will cause the function to remain in the *while* loop forever, thereby locking up the computer. Color Plate 1 shows a display of the clipping boundary and a lot of random lines that are clipped by it. You can easily see that none of the lines extend beyond the boundary.

Clipping Filled Shapes

In the next four chapters, we are going to encounter functions for filling a wide variety of shapes such as circles, ellipses, irregular polygons, and rounded rectangles. In most cases, such shapes are filled with horizontal lines. At some point in each function, the function has determined the top and bottom values of y for which the horizontal lines are to be drawn. You need to modify these values so that they are not beyond the top and bottom of the clipping rectangle. Then, for each horizontal line that is to be drawn, you need to modify the starting and ending values of x, if necessary, to be within the clipping rectangle. The one exception to this neat operation is the flood-filling function. This function keeps changing the colors of points until it encounters the boundaries of a closed curve. If any part of a boundary is outside the screen limits, the function goes berserk and is likely to fill the whole screen. In using this function, then, you as the programmer must ensure that the figure being operated upon never extends beyond the screen boundaries.

Part 4

Drawing Primitive Graphic Figures

11

Classes and Functions for Primitive Graphics

The primitive figures that we're going to develop for use in drawing more complicated graphics include lines, circles, ellipses, arcs, polygons, triangles, quadralaterals, and Bezier and B-Spline curves. In this chapter, we're going to show you a *graphics* module that defines classes and functions for all of these graphics figures. The functions will permit drawing the curves with every VGA and VESA Super VGA mode except the true color (16.8 million-color modes). The true color modes give breath-taking realism when used to reproduce photographs, but they are really overkill for graphics created by you with the aid of a computer. Your eye can't distinguish 16.8 million different shades of color, so why try to specify them. The code given here will have to be used with every demonstration program given in the following chapters.

Using the *graphics* Module

The easiest way to use the *graphics* module is to reference it by an *include* statement at the beginning of each program where you are going to use it. If you look at a typical demonstration program, such as the *linetest* program in the next chapter, you'll see near the beginning a statement like this:

```
#include "c:\cpphbook\program\graphics.cpp"
```

You'll note that this *include* statement differs from other *include* statements in that its body is enclosed in quotation marks rather than carets. The carets are used to designate files that are found in the compiler *include* library. The *include* statement for the graphics module gives the full path for the file as it appears on my hard drive; for each program you'll need to modify this statement to reflect the directory and drive or CD-ROM where your *graphics* module is stored. Using such an *include* statement is the easiest way to include the *graphics* module in your program, but if you have a version of C++ that requires project files, you may simply want to include *graphics.cpp* as one of the files in your project. The advantage is that if you change the main program but not the *graphics.cpp* module, only the former needs to be recompiled. The *graphics.cpp* module contains all of the *includes*, *defines*, and global variables needed by the module. The entire module is given in Listing 11-1. In this chapter, we'll just describe those generic functions that are included in the base *Graphics* class. The derived classes for the primitive graphics figures will be described in one of Chapters 12, 13, 14, 15, 16, 17, or 18.

Considerations in Using the *graphics* Module

The *graphics* module is designed to work with all EGA, VGA, and VESA Super VGA display modes to create a lot of different primitive graphics shapes. The penalty you pay for this is that the module runs much slower than if it were optimized for your own specific computer configuration and applications. If you're using a 486 or newer computer, most of your displays will appear almost instantaneously, so any loss of speed won't bother you. But if you do want to optimize for speed, you should be able to do so after reading this book. One further tip: Many of the operations in the *graphics* module run much faster when compiled with a Borland C++ compiler than when compiled with a MicroSoft C++ compiler.

The *Graphics* Class

The *Graphics* class is the base class upon which all of the *graphics* module is built. Table 11-1 shows the protected functions defined for the Graphics class and gives a description of each. Protected functions are available to any function dervived from the base function, but are not available for general public use. Functions are likely to be declared as protected when they are used internally by several public functions in a derived class, but we don't want them to be generally available. In this way we have full control of where each protected function is used, so that if we have to modify it in any way, we'll know exactly where it is used.

Table 11-1. Graphics Class Protected Functions

Function Name	Transferred Parameters	Description
fillLine	int x1, int x2, int y, int color	Draws a horizontal line from x1 to x2 at y in selected color using display coordinates.
fillsLine	int x1, int x2, int y, int color	Draws a horizontal line from x1 to x2 at y in selected color using system coordinates.
plot	int x, int y, int color	Plots a point at coordinate pair (x,y) in display coordinates in selected color.
plots	int x, int y, int color	Plots a point at coordinate pair (x,y) in system coordinates in selected color.
setPage	unsigned long int offset	Sets the proper display memory bank.
compare_color	int x, int y, int color	Compares the color at (x,y) with *color*. Returns 1 for a match or 0 for non-match.

Listing 11-1. The graphics Module.

```
/*

        graphics.cpp = Classes and function for primitive
                       graphic figures.

                  By Roger T. Stevens  2-10-96

*/
#include <bios.h>
#include <conio.h>
```

```
#include <ctype.h>
#include <dos.h>
#include <math.h>
#include <memory.h>
#include <stdlib.h>
#include <stdio.h>
#include <stdarg.h>
#include <float.h>
#define compare(a,b,c)  {if (a<b) b = a; if (a>c) c = a;}
#define max(a,b)     (((a) > (b)) ? (a) : (b))
#define min(a,b)     (((a) < (b)) ? (a) : (b))

/*

                    Graphics class

*/

class Graphics
{
    protected:
        void fillLine(int x1, int x2, int y, int color);
        void fillsLine(int x1, int x2, int y, int color);
        void plots(int x, int y, int color);
        void plot(int x, int y, int color);
        char compare_color(int x, int y, int color);
    public:
        void cls(int color);
        int convert_x(int x);
        int convert_y(int y);
        void floodfill (int x, int y, int color);
        void setEGApalette(int palette, int color);
        void setVGApalette(int first_color, int no_colors,
            unsigned char *buffer);
        void setMode(int vmode);
        void setPage(unsigned long int offset, char
        read_write);
        void set_screen(int top_color, int bottom_color,
            int boundary);
};

/*

    cls() = Clears the Screen to a specified color.

*/
void Graphics::cls(int color)
{
    union REGS reg;

    extern mode, xres, yres;
```

```
    if(mode > 0x107)
        return;
    reg.h.dh = yres>>3;
    reg.h.dl = xres>>3;
    reg.h.bh = color;
    reg.x.ax = 0x0600;
    reg.x.cx = 0;
    int86(0x10,&reg,&reg);
}

/*

      compare_color() = Read a pixel from the screen.

*/

char Graphics::compare_color(int x, int y, int test_color)
{
    char far *address;
    char ch, mask;
    int k,color;
    unsigned long int offset;
    extern int mode;
    extern int xres, yres;
    if ((x<0) || (x>xres-1) || (y<0) || (y>yres-1))
        return(1);
    switch(mode)
    {
        case 0x0D:
        case 0x0E:
        case 0x0F:
        case 0x10:
        case 0x12:
            FP_SEG(address) = 0xA000;
            FP_OFF(address) =((long)y * xres + x) >> 3;
            outpw(0x3CE, 0x0805);
            outpw(0x3CE, (test_color << 8) | 0x02);
            mask = 0x80 >> (x & 0x07);
            ch = *address & mask;
            outpw(0x3CE, 0x0005);
            outpw(0x3CE, 0x0002);
            for (k=0; k<1; k++)
            if (!ch)
                return(0);
            break;
        case 0x102:
        case 0x104:
        case 0x106:
            offset = ((long)y * xres + x) >> 3;
            setPage(offset,0);
            outpw(0x3CE, 0x0805);
            outpw(0x3CE, (test_color << 8) | 0x02);
            mask = 0x08 >> (x & 0x07);
            ch = *address & mask;
```

```
            outpw(0x3CE, 0x0002);
            outpw(0x3CE, 0x0005);
            if (!ch)
                  return(0);
            break;
        case 0x13:
            offset = (long)y * xres + (long)x;
            address = (char far *) 0xA0000000L + (unsigned
                int) offset;
            if (test_color != *address)
                return(0);
            break;
        case 0x100:
        case 0x101:
        case 0x103:
        case 0x105:
        case 0x107:
            offset = (long)y * xres + (long)x;
            setPage(offset,1);
            address = (char far *) 0xA0000000L + (unsigned
                int) offset;
            color = *address;
            setPage(offset,0);
            if (test_color != color)
                return(0);
            break;
        case 0x10D:
        case 0x10E:
        case 0x110:
        case 0x111:
        case 0x113:
        case 0x114:
        case 0x116:
        case 0x117:
        case 0x119:
        case 0x11A:
            offset = ((long)y * xres + (long)x)*2L;
            setPage(offset,1);
            address = (char far *) 0xA0000000L + (unsigned
                int) offset;
            color = (*address + (int)((*address+1)<<8));
            setPage(offset,0);
            if (test_color != color)
                return(0);
            break;
    }
    return(1);
}
```

```
/*
    convert_x() = converts an x in system coordinates
                  to an x in display coordinates.
*/

int Graphics::convert_x(int x)
{
    extern mode;

    x += 640;
    switch(mode)
    {
        case 0x0D:
        case 0x13:
        case 0x10D:
        case 0x10E:
        case 0x10F:
            x >>= 2;
            break;
        case 0x0E:
        case 0x0F:
        case 0x10:
        case 0x11:
        case 0x12:
        case 0x101:
        case 0x110:
        case 0x111:
        case 0x112:
        case 0x100:
            x >>= 1;
            break;
        case 0x102:
        case 0x103:
        case 0x113:
        case 0x114:
        case 0x115:
            x - (5 * x) >> 3;
            break;
        case 0x104:
        case 0x105:
        case 0x116:
        case 0x117:
        case 0x118:
            x = (x << 2)/5;
            break;
    }
    return(x);
}
```

```
/*
        convert_y() = converts a y in system coordinates
                      to a y in display coordinates.
*/

int Graphics::convert_y(int y)
{
    extern int mode;

    y = 479 - y;
    switch(mode)
    {
        case 0x0D:
        case 0x13:
        case 0x10D:
        case 0x10E:
        case 0x10F:
            y /= 5;
            break;
        case 0x0E:
            y = int(y * 27L >> 7);
            break;
        case 0x0F:
        case 0x10:
            y =int((y * 93L) >> 8);
            break;
        case 0x11:
        case 0x12:
        case 0x101:
        case 0x110:
        case 0x111:
        case 0x112:
            y >>= 1;
            break;
        case 0x100:
            y = int(y * 54L >> 7);
            break;
        case 0x102:
        case 0x103:
        case 0x113:
        case 0x114:
        case 0x115:
            y = (3 * y)/5;
            break;
        case 0x104:
        case 0x105:
        case 0x116:
        case 0x117:
        case 0x118:
            y = (y << 2)/5;
            break;
        case 0x106:
        case 0x107:
```

```
            case 0x119:
            case 0x11A:
            case 0x11B:
                y = (y << 4)/15;
        }
        return(y);
}

/*

    fillsLine() = draws a horizontal line using system
                        coordinates.

*/

void Graphics::fillsLine(int x1, int x2, int y, int color)
{
    x1 = convert_x(x1);
    x2 = convert_x(x2);
    y = convert_y(y);
    fillLine(x1,x2,y,color);
}

/*

    fillLine() = draws a horizontal line using system
                    display coordinates.

*/

#define graph_out(index,val)  {outp(0x3CE,index);\
                               outp(0x3CF,val);}

void Graphics::fillLine(int x1, int x2, int y, int color)
{

    extern xres, yres, mode;
    int i, temp;
    unsigned long int offset;
    char far *address;

    if (x1 > x2)
    {
        temp = x1;
        x1 = x2;
        x2 = temp;
    }
    if (x1 < 0)
        x1 = 0;
    if (x1 >= xres)
```

```
        return;
    if (x2 >= xres)
        x2 = xres - 1;
    if (x2 < 0)
        return;
    if ((y<0) || (y>(yres-1)))
        return;
    switch(mode)
    {
        case 0x0D:
        case 0x0E:
        case 0x0F:
        case 0x10:
        case 0x12:
        case 0x102:
        case 0x104:
        case 0x106:
            i = x1;
            while (i<=x2)
            {
                if ((i%8) || (i+8 > x2))
                    plot(i++,y,color);
                else
                {
                    outpw(0x3CE, 0x0F01);
                    outpw(0x3CE, (color << 8) | 0);
                    offset = ((long int)y*xres + i) >> 3;
                    setPage(offset,0);
                    FP_SEG(address) = 0xA000;
                    FP_OFF(address) = offset;
                    *address |= 0xFE;
                    outpw(0x3CE, 0x0001);
                    i+= 8;
                }
            }
            break;
        case 0x13:
            for (i=x1; i<=x2; i++)
            {
                offset = (long int)y * xres + (long)i;
                address = (char far *)(0xA0000000L +
                (unsigned int)offset);
                *address = color;
            }
            break;
        case 0x100:
        case 0x101:
        case 0x103:
        case 0x105:
        case 0x107:
            for (i=x1; i<=x2; i++)
            {
                offset = (long int)y * xres + (long)i;
                setPage(offset,0);
                address = (char far *)(0xA0000000L +
```

```
                    (unsigned int)offset);
                    *address = color;
                }
                break;
            case 0x10D:
            case 0x10E:
            case 0x110:
            case 0x111:
            case 0x113:
            case 0x114:
            case 0x116:
            case 0x117:
            case 0x119:
            case 0x11A:
                for (i=x1; i<=x2; i++)
                {
                    offset = ((long int)y*xres+(long int)i)*2;
                    setPage(offset,0);
                    address = (char far *)(0xA0000000L +
                    (unsigned int)offset);
                    *address++ = color & 0xFF;
                    *address = color >> 8;
                }
        }
}

/*

    floodfill() = fills an area bounded by a designated
        color when a point within the area is specified.

*/

#define Push(Y, XL, XR, dY) \
    {if (sp < 2000) buffer[sp].y = Y; buffer[sp].xl =\
        XL; buffer[sp].xr = XR; buffer[sp++].dy = dY;}
#define Pop(Y, XL, XR, dY) \
    {if(sp--) Y = buffer[sp].y+(dY=buffer[sp].dy); XL\
        - buffer[sp].xl; XR = buffer[sp].xr;}

void Graphics::floodfill (int x, int y, int color)
{

    extern xres, yres;

    int dy, sp=0, left, x1, x2;
    struct
    {
        int y, xl, xr, dy;
    } buffer[2000];

    x = convert_x(x);
```

```
        y = convert_y(y);
        if ((x<0) || (x>xres-1) || (y<0) || (y>yres-1))
            return;
        Push(y,x,x,1);
        Push(y+1,x,x,-1);
        while (sp)
        {
            Pop(y,x1,x2,dy);
            x = x1;
            while ((x>=0) && !(compare_color(x,y,color)))
                 plot(x--,y,color);
            if (x == x1)
            {
                while ((++x <= x2) &&
        (compare_color(x,y,color)));
                    left = x;
                if (x > x2)
                    continue;
            }
            else
            {
                left = x + 1;
                if (left < x1)
                    Push(y,left,x1-1,-dy);
                x = x1 + 1;
            }
            do
            {
                while ((x < xres) &&
                    !(compare_color(x,y,color)))
                plot(x++,y,color);
                Push(y,left,x-1,dy);
                if (x > (x2 + 1))
                    Push(y,x2+1,x-1,-dy);
                while ((++x <= x2) &&
        (compare_color(x,y,color)));
                    left = x;
            } while (x <= x2);
        }
    }

    /*

        plots() = plots a point on the screen at designated
                  system coordinates using selected color.

    */

    void Graphics::plots(int x, int y, int color)
    {
        x = convert_x(x);
        y = convert_y(y);
        plot(x,y,color);
```

```
}

/*

    plot() = plots a point on the screen at designated
             screen coordinates using selected color.

          */

void Graphics::plot(int x, int y, int color)
{
    unsigned long int offset;
    unsigned char far *address, mask;
    extern mode, xres, yres;

    if ((x >= xres) || (x < 0) || (y >= yres) || (y < 0))
        return;
    switch(mode)
    {
        case 0x0D:
        case 0x0E:
        case 0x0F:
        case 0x10:
        case 0x12:
            outpw(0x3CE, 0x0F01);
            outpw(0x3CE, (color << 8) | 0);
            outp(0x3CE, 8);
            FP_SEG(address) = 0xA000;
            FP_OFF(address) =((long int)y*xres + x) >> 3;
            mask = 0x80 >> (x & 0x07);
            outp(0x3CF, mask);
            *address |= 0xFE;
            outp(0x3CF, 0xFF);
            outpw(0x3CE, 0x0001);
            break;
        case 0x102:
        case 0x104:
        case 0x106:
            offset = ((long int)y * xres + x) >> 3;
            setPage(offset,0);
            outpw(0x3CE, 0x0F01);
            outpw(0x3CE, (color << 8) | 0);
            outp(0x3CE, 8);
            FP_SEG(address) = 0xA000;
            FP_OFF(address) =(offset);
            mask = 0x80 >> (x & 0x07);
            outp(0x3CF, mask);
            *address |= 0xFE;
            outp(0x3CF, 0xFF);
            outpw(0x3CE, 0x0001);
            break;
        case 0x13:
            offset = (long int)y * xres + (long int)x;
            address = (unsigned char far *) 0xA0000000L +
                (unsigned int) offset;
```

```
                *address = color;
                break;
            case 0x100:
            case 0x101:
            case 0x103:
            case 0x105:
            case 0x107:
                offset = (long int)y * xres + (long int)x;
                setPage(offset,0);
                address = (unsigned char far *) 0xA0000000L +
                    (unsigned int) offset;
                *address = color;
                break;
            case 0x10D:
            case 0x10E:
            case 0x110:
            case 0x111:
            case 0x113:
            case 0x114:
            case 0x116:
            case 0x117:
            case 0x119:
            case 0x11A:
                offset = ((long int)y*xres + (long int)x)*2L;
                setPage(offset,0);
                address = (unsigned char far *) 0xA0000000L +
                    (unsigned int) offset;
                *address++ = color & 0xFF;
                *address = color >> 8;
                break;
        }
}

/*

    setEGApalette() = sets the color for an EGA palette
                              number.

*/

void Graphics:: setEGApalette(int palette, int color)
{
    union REGS reg;

    reg.h.ah = 0x10;
    reg.h.al = 0;
    reg.h.bh = color;
    reg.h.bl = palette;
    int86(0x10,&reg,&reg);
}
```

```
/*
        setVGApalette() = Function to set VGA color
                          registers.
*/

void Graphics::setVGApalette(int first_color, int
no_colors, unsigned char *buffer)
{
    struct SREGS inreg;
    union REGS reg;

    reg.x.ax = 0x1012;
    segread(&inreg);
    inreg.es = inreg.ds;
    reg.x.bx = first_color;
    reg.x.cx = no_colors;
    reg.x.dx = (int)&buffer[0];
    int86x(0x10,&reg,&reg,&inreg);
}

/*
            setMode() = Sets Video Mode.
*/

void Graphics::setMode(int vmode)
{
    union REGS reg;
    extern int mode, xres, yres;
    mode = vmode;
    switch(mode)
    {
        case 0x0D:
        case 0x13:
        case 0x10D:
        case 0x10E:
        case 0x10F:
            xres = 320;
            yres = 200;
            break;
        case 0x0E:
            xres = 640;
            yres = 200;
            break;
        case 0x0F:
        case 0x10:
            xres = 640;
            yres = 350;
            break;
        case 0x11:
```

```
        case 0x12:
        case 0x101:
        case 0x110:
        case 0x111:
        case 0x112:
            xres = 640;
            yres = 480;
            break;
        case 0x100:
            xres = 640;
            yres = 400;
            break;
        case 0x102:
        case 0x103:
        case 0x113:
        case 0x114:
        case 0x115:
            xres = 800;
            yres = 600;
            break;
        case 0x104:
        case 0x105:
        case 0x116:
        case 0x117:
        case 0x118:
            xres = 1024;
            yres = 768;
            break;
        case 0x106:
        case 0x107:
        case 0x119:
        case 0x11A:
        case 0x11B:
            xres = 1280;
            yres = 1024;
    }
    if (vmode >= 0x100)
    {
        reg.x.ax = 0x4F02;
        reg.x.bx = mode;
    }
    else
        reg.x.ax = mode;
    int86 (0x10,&reg,&reg);
}

/*

        setPage() = sets the display memory page.

*/

void Graphics::setPage(unsigned long int offset, char
read_write)
```

```
{
    static int old_bank, old_mode;

    union REGS reg;

    reg.x.dx = int(offset >> 16);
    if ((reg.x.dx != old_bank) || (read_write !=
old_mode))
    {
        old_bank = int(offset>>16);
        old_mode = read_write;
        reg.x.ax = 0x4F05;
        reg.x.bx = read_write;
        int86(0x10, &reg, &reg);
    }
}

/*

    set_screen() = Sets the screen background colors.

*/

void Graphics::set_screen(int top_color, int bottom_color,
    int boundary)
{
    union REGS reg;

    reg.h.ah = 0x06;
    reg.h.al = boundary;
    reg.x.cx = 0;
    reg.x.dx = 0x1E4F;
    reg.h.bh = top_color;
    int86(0x10,&reg,&reg);
    reg.h.al = 31 - boundary;
    reg.x.cx = 0;
    reg.x.dx = 0x1E4F;
    reg.h.bh = bottom_color;
    int86(0x10,&reg,&reg);
}

/*

                    Edge class.

*/

class Edge
{
    public:
        Edge *NextEdge;
```

```
                int x;
                int y;
                int move_x;
                int xdir;
                int decision;
                int decisionUp;
                int decisionDown;
                int Count;
                Edge(int x1, int y1, int dx, int dy);
};

/*
                    Edge Constructor.
*/

Edge::Edge(int x1, int y1, int dx, int dy)
{
    int width;

    x = x1;
    y = y1;
    width = abs(dx);
    xdir = (dx > 0) ? 1 : -1;
    Count = dy;
    decisionDown = dy;
    if (dx >= 0)
        decision = 0;
    else
        decision = -dy + 1;
    if (dy >= width)
    {
        move_x = 0;
        decisionUp = width;
    }
    else
    {
        move_x = (width / dy) * xdir;
        decisionUp = width % dy;
    }
}

/*
                    Line class.
*/

class Line : public Graphics
{
    int xstart, ystart, xend, yend, width, color;
```

```
    int dx, dy, i, j, x, y, x_sign, y_sign, decision;
    protected:
        int xs,ys,xe,ye;
        unsigned long int mask;
    public:
        void draw(int xend, int yend, int color);
        void draw(int xend, int yend, int color, int
        width);
        void draw(int xstart, int ystart, int xend, int
            yend, int color);
        void draw(int xstart, int ystart, int length,
        float angle, int color);
        void draw(int xstart, int ystart, int xend, int
            yend, int color, int width);
        void draw(int xstart, int ystart, int length,
        float angle, int color, int width);
};

/*

    Draws a line from internal starting coordinates
    to specified end coordinates in specified color.

*/

void Line::draw(int xend, int yend, int color)
{
    extern unsigned long int PATTERN;

    mask = 0x80000000L;
    dx = abs(xend - xs);
    dy = abs(yend - ys);
    if (((dx >= dy) && (xs > xend)) ||
        ((dy > dx) && (ys > yend)))
    {
        xe = xs;
        xs = xend;
        ye = ys;
        ys = yend;
    }
    else
    {
        xe = xend;
        ye = yend;
    }
    if (dx == 0)
    {
        for (i=ys; i<=ye; i++)
        {
            mask = mask !=1 ? mask >> 1 : 0x80000000L;
            if (PATTERN & mask)
                plots(xe,i,color);
```

```
          }
          ys = yend;
          return;
     }
     if (dy == 0)
     {
          for (i=xs; i<=xe; i++)
          {
               mask = mask !=1 ? mask >> 1 : 0x80000000L;
               if (PATTERN & mask)
                    plots(i,ye,color);
          }
          xs=xend;
          return;
     }
     y_sign = (ye - ys)/dy;
     x_sign = (xe - xs)/dx;
     if (dx >= dy)
     {
          for (x=xs,y=ys,decision=0; x<=xe;
x++,decision+=dy)
          {
               mask = mask !=1 ? mask >> 1 : 0x80000000L;
               if (decision>=dx)
               {
                    decision -= dx;
                    y+= y_sign;
               }
               if (PATTERN & mask)
                         plots(x,y,color);
          }
     }
     else
     {
          for (x=xs,y=ys,decision=0; y<=ye;
y++,decision+=dx)
          {
               mask = mask !=1 ? mask >> 1 : 0x80000000L;
               if (decision>=dy)
               {
                    decision -= dy;
                    x += x_sign;
               }
               if (PATTERN & mask)
                    plots(x,y,color);
          }
     }
     xs = xend;
     ys = yend;
}
```

```
/*
        Draws a line from specified starting coordinates
        to specified end coordinates in specified color.
*/

void Line::draw(int xstart, int ystart, int xend, int
yend, int color)
{
    xs = xstart;
    ys = ystart;
    Line::draw(xend, yend, color);
}

/*
     Draws a single-pixel-wide line from specified starting
    coordinates for specified length in specified direction
                  (angle) in specified color.
*/

void Line::draw(int xstart, int ystart, int length, float
    angle, int color)
{
    xs = xstart;
    ys = ystart;
    xe = xs + int(length * (cos(0.017453292 * angle)));
    ye = ys - int(length * (-sin(0.017453292 * angle)));
    Line::draw(xs,ys,xe,ye,color);
}

/*
        Draws a line of specified width from internal
            starting coordinates to specified end
               coordinates in specified color.
*/

void Line::draw(int xend, int yend, int color, int width)
{
    extern unsigned long int PATTERN;

    mask = 0x00000001L;
    dx = abs(xend - xs);
    dy = abs(yend - ys);
    if (((dx >= dy) && (xs > xend)) ||
        ((dy > dx) && (ys > yend)))
```

```
    {
        xe = xs;
        xs = xend;
        ye = ys;
        ys = yend;
    }
    else
    {
        xe = xend;
        ye = yend;
    }
    if (dx == 0)
    {
        for (i=ys; i<=ye; i++)
        {
            mask = mask !=1 ? mask >> 1 : 0x80000000L;
            for (j=xe-width/2; j<=xe+width/2; j++)
            {
                if (PATTERN & mask)
                        plots(j,i,color);
            }
        }
        ys = yend;
        return;
    }
    if (dy == 0)
    {
        for (i=xs; i<=xe; i++)
        {
            mask = mask !=1 ? mask >> 1 : 0x80000000L;
            for (j=ye-width/2; j<=ye+width/2; j++)
            {
                if (PATTERN & mask)
                        plots(i,j,color);
            }
        }
        xs=xend;
        return;
    }
    y_sign = (ye - ys)/dy;
    x_sign = (xe - xs)/dx;
    for(j=0; j<=width/2; j++)
        for (i=width/2-j; i>=0; i--)
        {
                plots(xend+i*x_sign,yend-j*y_sign,color);
        }
        for (i=0; i<=width/2; i++)
            for (j=width/2-i; j>=0; j--)
        {
                plots(xend+i*x_sign,yend+j*y_sign,color);
        }
    if (dx >= dy)
    {
        for (x=xs,y=ys,decision=0; x<=xe;
x++,decision+=dy)
```

```
        {
            mask = mask !=1 ? mask >> 1 : 0x80000000L;
            if (decision>=dx)
            {
                decision -= dx;
                y+= y_sign;
            }
            if (PATTERN & mask)
            {
                for (j=y-width/2; j<=y+width/2; j++)
                {
                        plots(x,j,color);
                }
            }
        }
    }
    else
    {
        for (x=xs,y=ys,decision=0; y<=ye;
y++,decision+=dx)
        {
            mask = mask !=1 ? mask >> 1 : 0x80000000L;
            if (decision>=dy)
            {
                decision -= dy;
                x += x_sign;
            }
            if (PATTERN & mask)
                for (j=x-width/2; j<=x+width/2; j++)
                {
                        plots(j,y,color);
                }
        }
    }
    xs = xend;
    ys = yend;
}

/*

        Draws a line of specified width from specified
            starting coordinates to specified end
               coordinates in specified color.

*/

void Line::draw(int xstart, int ystart, int xend, int
yend, int color, int width)
{
    xs = xstart;
    ys = ystart;
    Line::draw(xend, yend, color, width);
}
```

```
/*

    Draws a line from specified starting coordinates for
    specified length in specified direction (angle) in
    specified color and specified width.

*/

void Line::draw(int xstart, int ystart, int length, float
    angle, int color, int width)
{
    xs = xstart;
    ys = ystart;
    xe = xs + int(length * (cos(0.0017453292 * angle)));
    ye = ys - int(length * (-sin(0.0017453292 * angle)));
    Line::draw(xs,ys,xe,ye,color,width);
}

/*

                    Circle class.

*/

class Circle : public Graphics
{
    int xstart, ystart, xend, yend, width, color;
    int dx, dy, i, j, x, y, x_sign, y_sign, decision;
    unsigned long int mask;

    public:
        int xs, ys, xe, ye, wid;
        void draw(int x, int y, int r, int color);
        void draw(int x, int y, long int r, int color);
        void draw(int x, int y, int r, int color, int
        width);
        void fill(int x, int y, int r, int color);
};

/*

    draw() = Draws a single pixel wide circle using
              Bresenham's algorithm.

*/
void Circle::draw(int x, int y, int r, int color)
{

    int row, col, px, py;
```

```
    long int sum;

    py = r;
    px = 0;
    sum = -r;
    while (px <= py)
    {
        col = x + px;
        row = y + py;
        plots(col,row,color);
        row = y - py;
        plots(col,row,color);
        col = x - px;
        plots(col,row,color);
        row = y + py;
        plots(col,row,color);
        col = x + py;
        row = y + px;
        plots(col,row,color);
        row = y - px;
        plots(col,row,color);
        col = x - py;
        plots(col,row,color);
        row = y + px;
        plots(col,row,color);
        sum +=px++;
        if (sum >= 0)
        {
            sum-=py--;
        }
    }
}

/*

        draw() = Draws a single pixel wide improved
                     accuracy circle.

*/

void Circle::draw(int x, int y, long int r, int color)
{

    int row, col, px, py;
    long int sum;

    py = int(r<<1);
    px = 0;
    sum = -(r<<1);
    while (px <= py)
    {
        if ( !(px & 1))
        {
            col = x + (px>>1);
```

```
                row = y + (py>>1);
                plots(col,row,color);
                row = y - (py>>1);
                plots(col,row,color);
                col = x - (px>>1);
                plots(col,row,color);
                row = y + (py>>1);
                plots(col,row,color);
                col = x + (py>>1);
                row = y + (px>>1);
                plots(col,row,color);
                row = y - (px>>1);
                plots(col,row,color);
                col = x - (py>>1);
                plots(col,row,color);
                row = y + (px>>1);
                plots(col,row,color);
            }
            sum +=px++;
            sum += px;
            if (sum >= 0)
            {
                sum -=py--;
                sum -=py;
            }
        }
}

/*

    draw() = Draws a wide line circle using Bresenham's
                        algorithm.

*/

void Circle::draw(int x, int y, int r, int color, int
    width)
{
    int i, row, col, px, py;
    long int sum;

    r += width /2;
    py = r<<1;
    px = 0;
    sum = -(r<<1);
    while (px <= py)
    {
        col = x + (px>>1);
        row = y + (py>>1);
        for (i=0; i<width; i++)
            plots(col,row-i,color);
        row = y - (py>>1);
        for (i=0; i<width; i++)
            plots(col,row+i,color);
```

```
        col = x - (px>>1);
        for (i=0; i<width; i++)
            plots(col,row+i,color);
        row = y + (py>>1);
        for (i=0; i<width; i++)
            plots(col,row-i,color);
        col = x + (py>>1);
        row = y + (px>>1);
        for (i=0; i<width; i++)
            plots(col-i,row,color);
        row = y - (px>>1);
        for (i=0; i<width; i++)
            plots(col-i,row,color);
        col = x - (py>>1);
        for (i=0; i<width; i++)
            plots(col+i,row,color);
        row = y + (px>>1);
        for (i=0; i<width; i++)
            plots(col+i,row,color);
        sum +=px++;
        if (sum >= 0)
            sum-=py--;
    }
}
```

fill() = Fills a circle with a designated color.

```
void Circle::fill(int x, int y, int r, int color)
{
    int col_start, col_end, row, px, py;
    long int sum;

    py = r<<1;
    px = 0;
    sum = -(r<<1);
    while (px <= py)
    {
        if ( !(px & 1))
        {
            col_start = x - (px>>1);
            col_end = x + (px>>1);
            col_start = convert_x(col_start);
            col_end = convert_x(col_end);
            row = convert_y(y+(py>>1));
            fillLine(col_start, col_end, row, color);
            row = convert_y(y-(py>>1));
            fillLine(col_start, col_end, row, color);
            col_start = x - (py>>1);
            col_end = x + (py>>1);
            col_start = convert_x(col_start);
            col_end = convert_x(col_end);
            row = convert_y(y+(px>>1));
```

```
            fillLine(col_start, col_end, row, color);
            row = convert_y(y-(px>>1));
            fillLine(col_start, col_end, row, color);
        }
        sum +=px++;
        if (sum >= 0)
            sum-=py--;
    }
}

/*
                    Ellipse class.
*/

class Ellipse : public Circle
{
    public:
        void draw(int xl, int yt, int xr, int yb, int
            color, int width);
        void draw(int xl, int yt, int xr, int yb, int
            color, char width);
        void draw(int xl, int yt, int xr, int yb, float
            angle, int color);
        void draw(int x, int y, int x_axis, int y_axis,
            float angle, long int color);
        void fill(int x, int y, int x_axis, int y_axis,
            float angle, long int color);
};

/*
    Draw wide ellipses by drawing a series of 1 pixel wide
                        ellipses.
*/

void Ellipse::draw(int xl, int yt, int xr, int yb, int
color, int width)
{
    int i, a, b, row, col, t_row, t_col, px, py, x, y;
        long int sum, asq, bsq;

    a = max((yt - yb + width) >> 1,1);
    b = max((xr - xl + width) >> 1,1);
    x = (xl + xr)>>1;
    y = (yb + yt) >> 1;
    for (i=1; i<=width; i++)
    {
        asq = (long)a*a;
```

```
        bsq = (long)b*b;
        py = a << 1;
        px = 0;
        sum = 0;
        while (asq*px <= bsq*py)
        {
            t_row = (py + 1) >> 1;
            t_col = px >> 1;
            col = x + t_col;
            row = y + t_row;
            plots(col,row,color);
            row = y - t_row;
            plots(col,row,color);
            col = x - t_col;
            plots(col,row,color);
            row = y + t_row;
            plots(col,row,color);
            sum += asq*px++;
            sum += asq*px;
            if (sum > 0)
            {
                sum -= bsq*py--;
                sum -= bsq*py;
            }
        }
        sum = 0;
        py = 0;
        px = b << 1;
        while (asq*px >= bsq*py)
        {
            if ((!(py & 1)) || ((i>1) && (i < width)))
            {
                t_row = (py + 1) >> 1;
                t_col = px >> 1;
                col = x + t_col;
                row = y + t_row;
                plots(col,row,color);
                row = y - t_row;
                plots(col,row,color);
                col = x - t_col;
                plots(col,row,color);
                row = y + t_row;
                plots(col,row,color);
            }
            sum += bsq*py++;
            sum += bsq*py;
            if (sum > 0)
            {
                sum -= asq*px--;
                sum -= asq*px;
            }
        }
        a--;
        b--;
    }
}
```

```
/*

    Draw wide ellipses in one pass by drawing wide lines.

*/

void Ellipse::draw(int xl, int yt, int xr, int yb, int
color,char width)
{
    int i, a, b, row, col, t_row, t_col, px, py, x, y;
        long int sum, asq, bsq;

    a = max((yt - yb + (width) >> 1),1);
    b = max((xr - xl + (width) >> 1),1);
    x = (xl + xr) >> 1;
    y = (yb + yt) >> 1;
    asq = (long)a*a;
    bsq = (long)b*b;
    py = a << 1;
    px = 0;
    sum = -bsq*py;
    while (asq*px <= bsq*py)
    {
        col = x + (px>>1);
        row = y + (py>>1);
        for (i=0; i<width; i++)
            plots(col,row-i,color);
        row = y - (py>>1);
        for (i=0; i<width; i++)
            plots(col,row+i,color);
        col = x - (px>>1);
        for (i=0; i<width; i++)
            plots(col,row+i,color);
        row = y + (py>>1);
        for (i=0; i<width; i++)
            plots(col,row-i,color);
        sum += asq*px++;
        sum += asq*px;
        if (sum > 0)
        {
            sum -= bsq*py--;
            sum -= bsq*py;
        }
    }
    py = 0;
    px = b << 1;
    sum = -asq*px;
    while (asq*px >= bsq*py)
    {
        if (!(py & 1))
        {
            col = x + (px>>1);
            row = y + (py>>1);
```

```
            for (i=0; i<width; i++)
                plots(col-i,row,color);
            row = y - (py>>1);
            for (i=0; i<width; i++)
                plots(col-i,row,color);
            col = x - (px>>1);
            for (i=0; i<width; i++)
                plots(col+i,row,color);
            row = y + (py>>1);
            for (i=0; i<width; i++)
                plots(col+i,row,color);
        }
        sum += bsq*py++;
        sum += bsq*py;
        if (sum > 0)
        {
            sum -= asq*px--;
            sum -= asq*px;
        }
    }
}

/*
     Draws an ellipse bounded by a box, with designated
       angle and color using single pixel wide lines.
*/

void Ellipse:: draw(int xl, int yt, int xr, int yb, float
    angle, int color)
{
    int i, a, b, row, col, t_row, t_col, px, py, x, y, ca,
        sa, tx, ty, tix, tiy;
    long int sum, asq, bsq;

    ca = int(cos(angle * 0.017453292) * 512);
    sa = int(sin(angle * 0.017453292) * 512);
    a = max((yt - yb) >> 1,1);
    b = max((xr - xl) >> 1,1);
    x = xl + b;
    y = yb + a;
    asq = (long)a*a;
    bsq = (long)b*b;
    py = a << 1;
    px = 0;
    sum = -bsq*py;
    while (asq*px <= bsq*py)
    {
        if (!(px & 1))
        {
            t_row = (py + 1) >> 1;
```

```
            t_col = px >> 1;
            tx =  (((long)t_col * ca) >> 9) -
                (((long)t_row * sa) >> 9);
            ty = (((long)t_col * sa) >> 9) +
                (((long)t_row * ca) >> 9);
            tix =  (((long)t_col * ca) >> 9) +
                (((long)t_row * sa) >> 9);
            tiy = (((long)t_col * sa) >> 9) -
                (((long)t_row * ca) >> 9);
            col = x + tx;
            row = y + ty;
            plots(col,row,color);
            col = x - tix;
            row = y - tiy;
            plots(col,row,color);
            col = x + tix;
            row = y + tiy;
            plots(col,row,color);
            col = x - tx;
            row = y - ty;
            plots(col,row,color);
        }
        sum += asq*px++;
        sum += asq*px;
        if (sum > 0)
        {
            sum -= bsq*py--;
            sum -= bsq*py;
        }
    }
    py = 0;
    px = b << 1;
    sum = -asq*px;
    while (asq*px >= bsq*py)
    {
        if (!(py & 1))
        {
            t_row = (py + 1) >> 1;
            t_col = px >> 1;
            tx =  (((long)t_col * ca) >> 9) -
                (((long)t_row * sa) >> 9);
            ty = (((long)t_col * sa) >> 9) +
                (((long)t_row * ca) >> 9);
            tix =  (((long)t_col * ca) >> 9) +
                (((long)t_row * sa) >> 9);
            tiy = (((long)t_col * sa) >> 9) -
                (((long)t_row * ca) >> 9);
            col = x + tx;
            row = y + ty;
            plots(col,row,color);
            col = x - tix;
            row = y - tiy;
            plots(col,row,color);
            col = x + tix;
            row = y + tiy;
            plots(col,row,color);
```

```
            col = x - tx;
            row = y - ty;
            plots(col,row,color);
        }
        sum += bsq*py++;
        sum += bsq*py;
        if (sum > 0)
        {
            sum -= asq*px--;
            sum -= asq*px;
        }
    }
}

/*

        Draws an ellipse which has the following
                   characteristics:
   (x,y) = point on y axis at left end of x axis,
            x_axis = length of x axis,
            y_axis = length of y axis,
            angle = tilt angle of oval,
              color = color of oval.

*/

void Ellipse::draw(int x, int y, int x_axis, int y_axis,
    float angle, long int color)
{
    int i, a, b, row, col, t_row, t_col, px, py, ca, sa;
    long int sum, asq, bsq;

    ca = int(cos(angle * 0.017453292) * 512);
    sa = int(sin(angle * 0.017453292) * 512);
    a = max((y_axis) >> 1,1);
    b = max((x_axis) >> 1,1);
    asq = 4L*a*a;
    bsq = 4L*b*b;
    py = a << 1;
    px = 0;
    sum = -bsq*py;
    while (asq*px <= bsq*py)
    {
        if (!(px & 1))
        {
            t_row = (py + 1) >> 1;
            t_col = px >> 1;
            col = x + (((long)(t_col + b)* ca) >> 9) -
                (((long)t_row * sa) >> 9);
            row = y + (((long)(t_col + b)* sa) >> 9) +
                (((long)t_row * ca) >> 9);
            plots(col,row,color);
            col = x - (((long)(t_col - b) * ca) >> 9) -
                (((long)t_row * sa) >> 9);
```

```
            row = y - (((long)(t_col - b)* sa) >> 9) +
                (((long)t_row * ca) >> 9);
            plots(col,row,color);
            col = x + (((long)(t_col + b) * ca) >> 9) +
                (((long)t_row * sa) >> 9);
            row = y + (((long)(t_col + b)* sa) >> 9) -
                (((long)t_row * ca) >> 9);
            plots(col,row,color);
            col = x - (((long)(t_col - b) * ca) >> 9) +
                (((long)t_row * sa) >> 9);
            row = y - (((long)(t_col - b) * sa) >> 9) -
                (((long)t_row * ca) >> 9);
            plots(col,row,color);
        }
        sum += asq*px++;
        sum += asq*px;
        if (sum > 0)
        {
            sum -= bsq*py--;
            sum -= bsq*py;
        }
    }
    py = 0;
    px = b << 1;
    sum = -asq*px;
    while (asq*px >= bsq*py)
    {
        if (!(py & 1))
        {
            t_row = (py + 1) >> 1;
            t_col = px >> 1;
            col = x + (((long)(t_col + b) * ca) >> 9) -
                (((long)t_row * sa) >> 9);
            row = y + (((long)(t_col + b) * sa) >> 9) +
                (((long)t_row * ca) >> 9);
            plots(col,row,color);
            col = x - (((long)(t_col - b) * ca) >> 9) -
                (((long)t_row * sa) >> 9);
            row = y - (((long)(t_col - b) * sa) >> 9) +
                (((long)t_row * ca) >> 9);
            plots(col,row,color);
            col = x + (((long)(t_col + b) * ca) >> 9) +
                (((long)t_row * sa) >> 9);
            row = y + (((long)(t_col + b) * sa) >> 9) -
                (((long)t_row * ca) >> 9);
            plots(col,row,color);
            col = x - (((long)(t_col - b) * ca) >> 9) +
                (((long)t_row * sa) >> 9);
            row = y - (((long)(t_col - b) * sa) >> 9) -
                (((long)t_row * ca) >> 9);
            plots(col,row,color);
        }
        sum += bsq*py++;
        sum += bsq*py;
        if (sum > 0)
        {
```

```
                sum -= asq*px--;
                sum -= asq*px;
            }
        }
}

/*
              Fills an ellipse. The ellipse has the
                has the following characteristics:
        (x,y) = point on y axis at left end of x axis,
                   x_axis = length of x axis,
                 angle = tilt angle of ellipse,
                    color = color of ellipse.
*/

void Ellipse::fill(int x, int y, int x_axis, int y_axis,
    float angle, long int color)
{
    extern xres, yres;

    int i, a, b, tx, ty, px, py, ca, sa, row, col,
        minrow=512, maxrow=-512;
    int coord[2][1024];
    long int sum, asq, bsq;

    for (i=0; i<1024; i++)
    {
        coord[0][i] = 1000;
        coord[1][i] = -1000;
    }
    ca = int(cos(angle * 0.017453292) * 2048);
    sa = int(sin(angle * 0.017453292) * 2048);
    a = max (y_axis >> 1,1);
    b = max (x_axis >> 1,1);
    asq = (long)a*a;
    bsq = (long)b*b;
    py = a << 1;
    px = 0;
    sum = -bsq*py;
    while (asq*px <= bsq*py)
    {
        col = x + ((((long)(px + (b<<1)) * ca) -
            ((long)(py + 1) * sa)) >> 12);
        row = y + ((((long)(px + (b<<1)) * sa) +
            ((long)(py + 1) * ca)) >> 12);
        compare(col,coord[0][row+512],coord[1][row+512]);
        compare(row,minrow,maxrow);
        col = x - ((((long)(px - (b<<1)) * ca) -
            ((long)(py + 1) * sa)) >> 12);
        row = y - ((((long)(px - (b<<1)) * sa) +
            ((long)(py + 1) * ca)) >> 12);
        compare(col,coord[0][row+512],coord[1][row+512]);
```

```
        compare(row,minrow,maxrow);
        col = x + ((((long)(px + (b<<1)) * ca) +
            ((long)(py + 1) * sa)) >> 12);
        row = y + ((((long)(px + (b<<1)) * sa) -
            ((long)(py + 1) * ca)) >> 12);
        compare(col,coord[0][row+512],coord[1][row+512]);
        compare(row,minrow,maxrow);
        col = x - ((((long)(px - (b<<1)) * ca) +
            ((long)(py + 1) * sa)) >> 12);
        row = y - ((((long)(px - (b<<1)) * sa) -
            ((long)(py + 1) * ca)) >> 12);
        compare(col,coord[0][row+512],coord[1][row+512]);
        compare(row,minrow,maxrow);
        sum += asq*px++;
        sum += asq*px;
        if (sum > 0)
        {
            sum -= bsq*py--;
            sum -= bsq*py;
        }
    }
    py = 0;
    px = b << 1;
    sum = -asq*px;
    while (asq*px >= bsq*py)
    {
        col = x + ((((long)(px + (b<<1)) * ca) -
            ((long)(py + 1) * sa)) >> 12);
        row = y + ((((long)(px + (b<<1)) * sa) +
            ((long)(py + 1) * ca)) >> 12);
        compare(col,coord[0][row+512],coord[1][row+512]);
        compare(row,minrow,maxrow);
        col = x - ((((long)(px - (b<<1)) * ca) -
            ((long)(py + 1) * sa)) >> 12);
        row = y - ((((long)(px - (b<<1)) * sa) +
            ((long)(py + 1) * ca)) >> 12);
        compare(col,coord[0][row+512],coord[1][row+512]);
        compare(row,minrow,maxrow);
        col = x + ((((long)(px + (b<<1)) * ca) +
            ((long)(py + 1) * sa)) >> 12);
        row = y + ((((long)(px + (b<<1)) * sa) -
            ((long)(py + 1) * ca)) >> 12);
        compare(col,coord[0][row+512],coord[1][row+512]);
        compare(row,minrow,maxrow);
        col = x - ((((long)(px - (b<<1)) * ca) +
            ((long)(py + 1) * sa)) >> 12);
        row = y - ((((long)(px - (b<<1)) * sa) -
            ((long)(py + 1) * ca)) >> 12);
        compare(col,coord[0][row+512],coord[1][row+512]);
        compare(row,minrow,maxrow);
        sum += bsq*py++;
        sum += bsq*py;
        if (sum > 0)
        {
            sum -= asq*px--;
            sum -= asq*px;
```

```
        }
    }
    for (i=minrow; i<=maxrow; i++)
    {
        fillsLine(coord[0][i+512],coord[1][i+512], i,
        color);
    }
}

/*
                         Arc class.
*/

class Arc : public Circle
{
    void data (int x, int y, int test_var, int type,
        int start_test, int end_test);
    void dLine(int xs, int ys, int xe, int ye);
    void plot (int x, int y, int test_var, int type, int
        color, int x_start_test, int x_end_test);
    public:
    void draw (int xc, int yc, int radius, float
start_angle, float end_angle, int color);
    void draw (int xc, int yc, int radius, float
start_angle, float end_angle, int color, int
        width);
    void fill(int xc, int yc, int radius, float
        start_angle, float end_angle, int color);
};

/*
   Determines whether point on a circle should be saved.
*/

void Arc::data (int x, int y, int test_var, int type,
    int start_test, int end_test)
{
    extern int coord[2][960], minrow, maxrow;

    if((y<-480) || (y>479))
        return;
    if (x<-640)
        x = -640;
    if (x>639)
        x = 639;
    x = convert_x(x);
    y = convert_y(y);
```

```
    switch(type)
    {
        case 1:
            if (test_var<start_test)
                return;
        case 2:
            break;
        case 3:
            if (test_var>end_test)
                return;
            break;
        case 4:
            if ((test_var<start_test) ||
    (test_var>end_test))
                return;
            break;
        case 5:
            if ((test_var>end_test) ||
    (test_var<start_test))
                return;
            break;
        default:
            return;
    }
    compare(x,coord[0][y],coord[1][y]);
    compare(y,minrow,maxrow);
}

/*

        Rejects points beyond arc limit boundaries.

*/

void Arc::dLine(int xs, int ys, int xe, int ye)
{
    extern int coord[2][960], minrow, maxrow;
    int temp, dx, dy, y_sign, x, y, decision;

    xs = convert_x(xs);
    xe = convert_x(xe);
    ys = convert_y(ys);
    ye = convert_y(ye);
    if (xs > xe)
    {
        temp = xs;
        xs = xe;
        xe = temp;
        temp = ys;
        ys = ye;
        ye = temp;
    }
    dx = abs(xe - xs);
```

```
    dy = abs(ye - ys);
    y_sign = 1;
    if ((ye - ys) < 0)
        y_sign = -1;
    if (dx > dy)
    {
        for (x=xs,y=ys,decision=0; x<=xe;
            x++,decision+=dy)
        {
            if (decision>=dx)
            {
                decision -= dx;
                y+= y_sign;
            }
            compare(x,coord[0][y], coord[1][y]);
            compare(y,minrow,maxrow);
        }
    }
    else
    {
        for (x=xs,y=ys,decision=0; y!=ye;
y+=y_sign,decision+=dx)
        {
            if (decision>=dy)
            {
                decision -= dy;
                x++;
            }
            compare(x,coord[0][y], coord[1][y]);
            compare(y,minrow,maxrow);
        }
    }
}

/*

      Draws an arc centered at (xc,yc) with radius 'b'
            in y direction from starting angle
            'start_angle' in degrees to ending
               angle 'end_angle' in degrees
                with aspect ratio 'aspect'
                  and in color 'color'.

*/

void Arc::draw (int xc, int yc, int radius, float
start_angle, float end_angle, int color)
{
    int arcs[8], i, j, px, py, start_sector,
        end_sector, x_start_test, x_end_test,
        y_start_test, y_end_test;
    long int sum;
```

```
    while (start_angle >= 360)
        start_angle -= 360;
    while (end_angle >= 360)
        end_angle -= 360;
    radius = max(radius,1);
    for (j=0; j<8; j++)
        arcs[j] = 0;
    start_sector = (int)(start_angle/45) % 8;
    end_sector = (int)(end_angle/45) % 8;
    x_start_test = int(xc + radius *
        cos(start_angle*.017453));
    x_end_test = int(xc+radius*cos(end_angle*.017453));
    y_start_test = int(yc + radius *
        sin(start_angle*.017453));
    y_end_test = int(yc+radius*sin(end_angle*.017453));
    if (start_sector == end_sector)
    {
        if (end_angle < start_angle)
        {
            arcs[start_sector] = 5;
            for (i=0; i<8; i++)
            {
                if (i != start_sector)
                    arcs[i] = 2;
            }
        }
        else
            arcs[start_sector] = 4;
    }
    else
    {
        arcs[start_sector] = 1;
        arcs[end_sector] = 3;
        for (i=(start_sector+1)%8; i!=end_sector; i=
        (i+1)%8)
            arcs[i] = 2;
    }
    py = radius << 1;
    px = 0;
    sum = -py;
    while (px <= py)
    {
        plot (xc+(px>>1), yc+(py>>1), -xc-(px>>1),
            arcs[1], color, -x_start_test, -x_end_test);
        plot (xc+(px>>1), yc-(py>>1), xc+(px>>1), arcs[6],
            color, x_start_test, x_end_test);
        plot (xc-(px>>1), yc+(py>>1), -xc+(px>>1),
            arcs[2], color, -x_start_test, -x_end_test);
        plot (xc-(px>>1), yc-(py>>1), xc-(px>>1), arcs[5],
            color, x_start_test, x_end_test);
        plot (xc+(py>>1), yc+(px>>1), yc+(px>>1), arcs[0],
            color, y_start_test, y_end_test);
        plot (xc+(py>>1), yc-(px>>1), yc-(px>>1), arcs[7],
            color, y_start_test, y_end_test);
        plot (xc-(py>>1), yc+(px>>1), -yc-(px>>1),
```

```
            arcs[3], color, -y_start_test, -y_end_test);
        plot (xc-(py>>1), yc-(px>>1), -yc+(px>>1),
            arcs[4], color, -y_start_test, -y_end_test);
        sum += px++;
        sum += px;
        if (sum > 0)
        {
            sum -= py--;
            sum -= py;
        }
    }
}

/*

   Draws an arc centered at (xc,yc) with radius 'b' in y
     direction from starting angle  'start_angle' in
        degrees to ending angle 'end_angle' in
         degrees with aspect ratio 'aspect',
          color 'color' and width 'width'.

*/

void Arc::draw (int xc, int yc, int radius, float
start_angle, float end_angle, int color, int width)
{
    int arcs[8], i, j, px, py, start_sector,
        end_sector, x_start_test, x_end_test,
        y_start_test, y_end_test;
    long int sum;

    while (start_angle >= 360)
        start_angle -= 360;
    while (end_angle >= 360)
        end_angle -= 360;
    radius = max(radius - (width>>1),1);
    for (j=0; j<8; j++)
        arcs[j] = 0;
    start_sector = (int)(start_angle/45) % 8;
    end_sector = (int)(end_angle/45) % 8;
    x_start_test = int(xc + radius * cos(start_angle *
    0.017453));
    x_end_test = int(xc+radius*cos(end_angle*.017453));
    y_start_test = int(yc + radius * sin(start_angle *
    0.017453));
    y_end_test = int(yc+radius*sin(end_angle*.017453));
    if (start_sector == end_sector)
    {
        if (end_angle < start_angle)
        {
            arcs[start_sector] = 5;
            for (i=0; i<8; i++)
            {
```

```
                if (i != start_sector)
                    arcs[i] = 2;
            }
        }
        else
            arcs[start_sector] = 4;
    }
    else
    {
        arcs[start_sector] = 1;
        arcs[end_sector] = 3;
        for (i=(start_sector+1)%8; i!=end_sector; i=
        (i+1)%8)
            arcs[i] = 2;
    }
    for (j=0; j<width; j++)
    {
        py = radius << 1;
        px = 0;
        sum = -py;
        while (px <= py)
        {
            plot (xc+(px>>1), yc+(py>>1), -xc-(px>>1),
            arcs[1], color, -x_start_test,
                -x_end_test);
            plot (xc+(px>>1), yc-(py>>1), xc+(px>>1),
            arcs[6], color, x_start_test, x_end_test);
            plot (xc-(px>>1), yc+(py>>1), -xc+(px>>1),
            arcs[2], color, -x_start_test,
                -x_end_test);
            plot (xc-(px>>1), yc-(py>>1), xc-(px>>1),
            arcs[5], color, x_start_test, x_end_test);
            plot (xc+(py>>1), yc+(px>>1), yc+(px>>1),
            arcs[0], color, y_start_test, y_end_test);
            plot (xc+(py>>1), yc-(px>>1), yc-(px>>1),
            arcs[7], color, y_start_test, y_end_test);
            plot (xc-(py>>1), yc+(px>>1), -yc-(px>>1),
            arcs[3], color, -y_start_test,
                -y_end_test);
            plot (xc-(py>>1), yc-(px>>1), -yc+(px>>1),
            arcs[4], color, -y_start_test,
                -y_end_test);
            sum += px++;
            sum += px;
            if (sum > 0)
            {
                sum -= py--;
                sum -= py;
            }
        }
        radius++;
    }
}
```

```
/*
    Determines which points should be plotted on the
    screen.
*/
void Arc::plot (int x, int y, int test_var, int type, int
    color, int start_test, int end_test)
{
    switch(type)
    {
        case 1:
            if (test_var>=start_test)
                plots(x,y,color);
            break;
        case 2:
            plots(x,y,color);
            break;
        case 3:
            if (test_var<=end_test)
                plots(x,y,color);
            break;
        case 4:
            if ((test_var>=start_test) &&
(test_var<=end_test))
                plots(x,y,color);
            break;
        case 5:
            if ((test_var<=end_test) ||
(test_var>=start_test))
                plots(x,y,color);
            break;
    }
}

/*
    fills an arc centered at (x,y) with radius 'radius'
    from starting angle 'start_angle' in tenths of
    a degree to ending angle 'end_angle' in
    tenths of a degree in color 'color'.
*/

void Arc::fill(int xc, int yc, int radius, float
start_angle, float end_angle, int color)
{
    extern int coord[2][960], minrow, maxrow;
    long int sum;
    int arc[8], i, j, px, py, start_sector, end_sector,
```

```
        x_start_test, x_end_test, y_start_test,
        y_end_test, flag=1;
    float temp_angle;

    start_angle = fmod(start_angle, 360);
    end_angle = fmod(end_angle, 360);
    temp_angle = end_angle - start_angle;
    if (temp_angle < 0)
        temp_angle+= 360;
    if (temp_angle > 180)
    {
        flag++;
        temp_angle = end_angle;
        end_angle = (start_angle + 180);
        end_angle = fmod(end_angle, 360);
    }
    radius = max(radius,1);
    while (flag > 0)
    {
        minrow = 960;
        maxrow = 0;
        for (i=0; i<960; i++)
        {
            coord[0][i] = 640;
            coord[1][i] = -640;
        }
        for (j=0; j<8; j++)
            arc[j] = 0;
        start_sector = (int)(start_angle/45) % 8;
        end_sector = (int)(end_angle/45) % 8;
        x_start_test = int(xc + radius * cos(start_angle *
            0.017453));
        x_end_test = int(xc + radius *
            cos(end_angle*.017453));
        y_start_test = int(yc + radius * sin(start_angle *
            0.017453));
        y_end_test = int(yc + radius *
            sin(end_angle*.017453));
        if (start_sector == end_sector)
        {
            if (end_angle < start_angle)
            {
                arc[start_sector] = 5;
                for (i=0; i<8; i++)
                {
                    if (i != start_sector)
                        arc[i] = 2;
                }
            }
            else
                arc[start_sector] = 4;
        }
        else
        {
            arc[start_sector] = 1;
```

```
            arc[end_sector] = 3;
            for (i=(start_sector+1)%8; i!=end_sector; i=
                (i+1)%8)
                arc[i] = 2;
        }
        py = radius << 1;
        px = 0;
        sum = -py;
        while (px <= py)
        {
            if (!(px & 1))
            {
                data (xc+(px>>1), yc+(py>>1), -xc-(px>>1),
                    arc[1], -x_start_test, -x_end_test);
                data (xc+(px>>1), yc-(py>>1), xc+(px>>1),
                    arc[6], x_start_test, x_end_test);
                data (xc-(px>>1), yc+(py>>1), -xc+(px>>1),
                    arc[2], -x_start_test, -x_end_test);
                data (xc-(px>>1), yc-(py>>1), xc-(px>>1),
                    arc[5], x_start_test, x_end_test);
                data (xc+(py>>1), yc+(px>>1), yc+(px>>1),
                    arc[0], y_start_test, y_end_test);
                data (xc+(py>>1), yc-(px>>1), yc-(px>>1),
                    arc[7], y_start_test, y_end_test);
                data (xc-(py>>1), yc+(px>>1), -yc-(px>>1),
                    arc[3], -y_start_test, -y_end_test);
                data (xc-(py>>1), yc-(px>>1), -yc+(px>>1),
                    arc[4], -y_start_test, -y_end_test);
            }
            sum += px++;
            sum += px;
            if (sum > 0)
            {
                sum -= py--;
                sum -= py;
            }
        }
        dLine(xc, yc, x_end_test, y_end_test);
        dLine(xc, yc, x_start_test,y_start_test);
        for (i=minrow; i<=maxrow; i++)
        {
            if (coord[0][i] == coord[1][i+1])
                if ((i != minrow) && (i != maxrow))
                {
                    coord[0][i] = (coord[0][i-1] +
                        coord[0][i+1])/2;
                    coord[1][i] = (coord[1][i-1] +
                        coord[1][i+1])/2;
                }
            fillLine(coord[0][i],coord[1][i], i, color);
        }
        for (i=0; i<8; i++)
```

```
            arc[i] = 0;
        flag--;
        start_angle = end_angle;
        end_angle = temp_angle;
    }
}

/*
                          Polygon class.
*/

class Polygon : public Line
{
    public:
        void draw(int color, int * point);
        void draw(int color, ...);
        void fill(int color,int *point);
        void fill(int color, ...);
};

/*
    draw() = Draws a polygon in a designated color by
         drawing lines between sets of coordinates
          specified and then drawing a line from
          last coordinates to first. Coordinates
                     are in an array.
*/

void Polygon::draw(int color,int *point)
{
    int i=0, j;

    while (point[i++] > -5000);
    if (i<6) return;
    Line::draw(point[0], point[1], point[2], point[3],color);
    for (j=2; j<i-1; j+=2)
        Line::draw(point[j], point[j+1],color);
    Line::draw(point[0], point[1],color);
}
```

```
/*
        draw() = Draws a polygon in a designated color by
             drawing lines between sets of coordinates
               specified and then drawing a line from
                     last coordinates to first.
*/

void Polygon::draw(int color,...)
{
    va_list coord;
    int i=0, j, xpoint[150],ypoint[150];
    va_start(coord,color);
    while (((xpoint[i]=va_arg(coord,int)) >= -5000) &&
        ((ypoint[i]=va_arg(coord,int)) >= -5000) &&
        ((i++)<150));
    va_end(coord);
    if (i<3) return;
    xpoint[i] = xpoint[0];
    ypoint[i++] = ypoint[0];
    Line::draw(xpoint[0], ypoint[0],xpoint[1],
ypoint[1],color);
    for (j=2; j<i; j++)
        Line::draw(xpoint[j],ypoint[j],color);
}

/*
        fill() = Fills a polygon in a designated color.
             Coordinates passed as parameter list.
*/

void Polygon::fill(int color,...)
{
    va_list coord;
    int i=0, point[1500];

    va_start(coord,color);
    while (((point[i++]=va_arg(coord,int)) >= -5000) &&
        ((point[i]=va_arg(coord,int)) >= -5000) &&
    ((i++)<750));
    va_end(coord);
    fill(color,point);
}
```

```
/*

        fill() = fills a polygon in specified color by
             filling in boundaries resulting from
              connecting specified points in the
                order given and then connecting
                 last point to first.  Uses an
                  array to store coordinates.

*/

void Polygon::fill(int color,int *point)
{
    Edge *global_edge_tablePtr, *active_edge_tablePtr,
        *active_edge_tableEdge,
        **active_edge_tableEdgePtr, *TempEdge,
        *PresentEdge, **PresentEdgePtr, *NewEdgePtr,
        *NextEdge, **NextEdgeLink;
    int i, xs, ys, xe, ye, dy, dx, width, temp, x, y,
        length=0, LeftX, swapped;

    while(point[length++] > -5000);
    if (--length < 6)
        return;
    global_edge_tablePtr = NULL;
    xs = convert_x(point[length-2]);
    ys = convert_y(point[length-1]);
    for (i = 0; i < length; i+=2)
    {
        xe = convert_x(point[i]);
        ye = convert_y(point[i+1]);
        if (ys > ye)
        {
            temp = xs;
            xs = xe;
            xe = temp;
            temp = ys;
            ys = ye;
            ye = temp;
        }
        if ((dy = ye - ys) != 0)
        {
            dx = xe - xs;
            if ((NewEdgePtr = new Edge(xs, ys, dx, dy)) ==
                NULL)
                return;
            NextEdgeLink = &global_edge_tablePtr;
            while (((NextEdge = *NextEdgeLink) != NULL) &&
                (NextEdge->y <= ys) && ((NextEdge->y !=
                    ys) ||
                (NextEdge->x < xs)))
                NextEdgeLink = &NextEdge->NextEdge;
            NewEdgePtr->NextEdge = NextEdge;
```

```
            *NextEdgeLink = NewEdgePtr;
        }
        xs = convert_x(point[i]);
        ys = convert_y(point[i+1]);

    }
    active_edge_tablePtr = NULL;
    y = global_edge_tablePtr->y;
    while ((global_edge_tablePtr != NULL) ||
(active_edge_tablePtr != NULL))
    {
        active_edge_tableEdgePtr = &active_edge_tablePtr;
        while ((global_edge_tablePtr != NULL) &&
    (global_edge_tablePtr->y == y))
        {
            x = global_edge_tablePtr->x;
            for (;;)
            {
                active_edge_tableEdge =
    *active_edge_tableEdgePtr;
                if ((active_edge_tableEdge == NULL) ||
                (active_edge_tableEdge->x >= x))
                {
                    TempEdge =
    global_edge_tablePtr->NextEdge;
                    *active_edge_tableEdgePtr =
                global_edge_tablePtr;
                    global_edge_tablePtr->NextEdge =
                    active_edge_tableEdge;
                    active_edge_tableEdgePtr =
            &global_edge_tablePtr->NextEdge;
                    global_edge_tablePtr = TempEdge;
                    break;
                }
                else
                    active_edge_tableEdgePtr =
            &active_edge_tableEdge->NextEdge;
            }
        }
        PresentEdge = active_edge_tablePtr;
        while (PresentEdge != NULL)
        {
            LeftX = PresentEdge->x;
            PresentEdge = PresentEdge->NextEdge;
            fillLine(LeftX,PresentEdge->x-1,y, color);
            PresentEdge = PresentEdge->NextEdge;
        }
        PresentEdgePtr = &active_edge_tablePtr;
        while ((PresentEdge = *PresentEdgePtr) != NULL)
        {
            if ((--(PresentEdge->Count)) == 0)
            {
                *PresentEdgePtr = PresentEdge->NextEdge;
```

```
                delete(PresentEdge);
            }
            else
            {
                PresentEdge->x += PresentEdge->move_x;
                if ((PresentEdge->decision +=
                    PresentEdge->decisionUp) > 0)
                    {
                        PresentEdge->x +=
            PresentEdge->xdir;
                        PresentEdge->decision -=
                            PresentEdge->decisionDown;
                    }
                    PresentEdgePtr =
                &PresentEdge->NextEdge;
            }
        }
        if (active_edge_tablePtr != NULL)
        {
            do
            {
                swapped = 0;
                PresentEdgePtr = &active_edge_tablePtr;
                while ((PresentEdge =
    *PresentEdgePtr)->NextEdge != NULL)
                {
                    if (PresentEdge->x >
        PresentEdge->NextEdge->x)
                    {
                        TempEdge =
                        PresentEdge->NextEdge->NextEdge;
                        *PresentEdgePtr =
            PresentEdge->NextEdge;
                        PresentEdge->NextEdge->NextEdge =
                            PresentEdge;
                        PresentEdge->NextEdge = TempEdge;
                        swapped = 1;
                    }
                    PresentEdgePtr =
    &(*PresentEdgePtr)->NextEdge;
                }
            } while (swapped != 0);
        }
        y++;
    }
}

/*
        Triangle class.
*/
```

```
class Triangle : public Polygon
{
    public:
        void fill (int xa, int ya, int xb, int yb, int xc,
            int yc,int color);
};

/*
        fill() = Fills a triangle in specified color.
*/

void Triangle::fill (int xa, int ya, int xb, int yb, int
xc, int yc, int color)
{
    int point[7];
    point[0] = xa;
    point[1] = ya;
    point[2] = xb;
    point[3] = yb;
    point[4] = xc;
    point[5] = yc;
    point[6] = -9999;
    Polygon::fill(color,point);
}


/*
                    Quadralateral class.
*/

class Quadralateral : public Triangle
{
    public:
        void fill (int xa, int ya, int xb, int yb, int xc,
            int yc,int xd, int yd, int color);
};

/*
      fill() = Fills a quadralateral in specified color.
*/

void Quadralateral::fill (int xa, int ya, int xb, int yb,
    int xc, int yc, int xd, int yd, int color)
```

```
{
    Triangle::fill (xa,ya,xb,yb,xc,yc, color);
    Triangle::fill (xc,yc,xd,yd,xa,ya,color);
}

/*

                        Bezier class.

*/

class Bezier : public Line
{
    public:
        void drawLit(int bcurve[], int color);
        void drawdeC(int bcurve[], int color);
        void drawBer(int bcurve[], int color);
        void draw(int color,...);
};

/*

  drawLit() = Draws Bezier curve using literal method.

*/

void Bezier::drawLit(int bcurve[], int color)
{
    float x,y;
    int xc,yc;
    float t;

    xs = bcurve[0];
    ys = bcurve[1];
    if ((bcurve[0] == bcurve[6]) && (bcurve[1] ==
        bcurve[7]) && (bcurve[2] == bcurve[4]) &&
        (bcurve[3] == bcurve[5]))
    {
        Line::draw((int)bcurve[2], (int)bcurve[3],color);
        return;
    }
    for (t=0.0; t<=1.0; t+= 0.01)
    {
        x=(1-t) * (1-t) * (1-t) * bcurve[0] + 3. * t *
            (t-1) * (t-1) * bcurve[2] + 3 *t *t * (1-t) *
            bcurve[4] + t * t * t * bcurve[6];
        y=(1-t) * (1-t) * (1-t) * bcurve[1] + 3 * t *
            (t-1) * (t-1) * bcurve[3] + 3 *t *t * (1-t) *
            bcurve[5] + t * t * t * bcurve[7];
        xc=(int)x;
        yc=(int)y;
        Line::draw(xc,yc,color);
```

```
    }
}

/*
     drawdeC() = Draws Bezier curve using deCasteljau
                         method.
*/

void Bezier::drawdeC(int bcurve[], int color)
{
    static int B_level;
    int curve1[8], curve2[8], x, y;

    if ((bcurve[0] == bcurve[6]) && (bcurve[1] ==
        bcurve[7]) && (bcurve[2] == bcurve[4]) &&
        (bcurve[3] == bcurve[5]))
    {
        Line::draw(bcurve[6], bcurve[7], bcurve[2],
        bcurve[3],color);
        return;
    }
    if (B_level > 2)
    {
        Line::draw(bcurve[0], bcurve[1],
        bcurve[2],bcurve[3], color);
        Line::draw(bcurve[4],bcurve[5], color);
        Line::draw(bcurve[6],bcurve[7], color);
        return;
    }
    B_level++;
    curve1[0] = bcurve[0];
    curve1[1] = bcurve[1];
    curve2[6] = bcurve[6];
    curve2[7] = bcurve[7];
    curve1[2] = (curve1[0] + bcurve[2]) >> 1;
    curve1[3] = (curve1[1] + bcurve[3]) >> 1;
    curve2[4] = (bcurve[4] + bcurve[6]) >> 1;
    curve2[5] = (bcurve[5] + bcurve[7]) >> 1;
    curve1[4] = (curve1[2] + ((bcurve[2] + bcurve[4]) >>
        1)) >> 1;
    curve1[5] = (curve1[3] + ((bcurve[3] + bcurve[5]) >>
        1)) >> 1;
    curve2[2] = (((bcurve[2] + bcurve[4]) >> 1) +
        curve2[4]) >> 1;
    curve2[3] = (((bcurve[3] + bcurve[5]) >> 1) +
        curve2[5]) >> 1;
    curve1[6] = (curve1[4] + curve2[2]) >> 1;
    curve1[7] = (curve1[5] + curve2[3]) >> 1;
    curve2[0] = curve1[6];
    curve2[1] = curve1[7];
    drawdeC(curve1,color);
    drawdeC(curve2,color);
```

```
    B_level--;
}

/*
        draw() = Draws Bezier curve using Bernstein
                        polynomials.
*/

void Bezier::drawBer(int bcurve[], int color)
{
    int i,j,k;
    float x,y,b,t;

    xs = (int)bcurve[0];
    ys = (int)bcurve[1];
    if ((bcurve[0] == bcurve[6]) && (bcurve[1] ==
        bcurve[7]) && (bcurve[2] == bcurve[4]) &&
        (bcurve[3] == bcurve[5]))
    {
        Line::draw((int)bcurve[2], (int)bcurve[3],color);
        return;
    }
    for (t=0.01; t<1.0; t+=0.01)
    {
        x = 0;
        y = 0;
        for (j=0; j<4; j++)
        {
            b = 1.0;
            for (k=3; k>j; k--)
                b *= k;
            for (k=3-j; k>1; k--)
                b /= k;
            for (i=1; i<=j; i++)
                b *= t;
            for (i=1; i<=3-j; i++)
                b *= (1-t);
            x += bcurve[j*2]*b;
            y += bcurve[j*2 + 1]*b;
        }
            Line::draw((int)x,(int)y,color);
    }
}

/*
        draw() = Draws Bezier curve using Bernstein
            polynomials with multipoint input.
*/
```

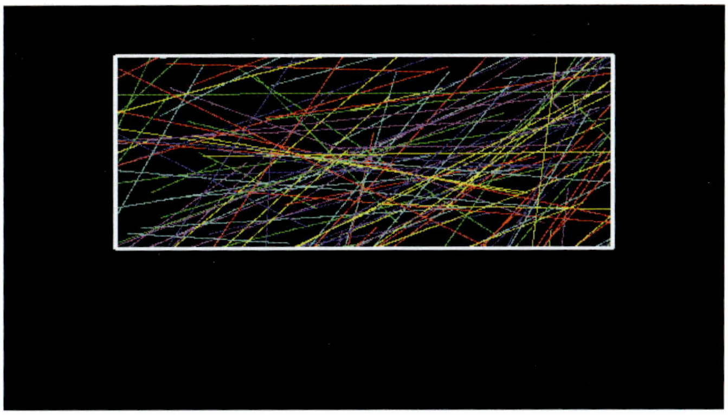

Plate 1: Test of Line Clipping

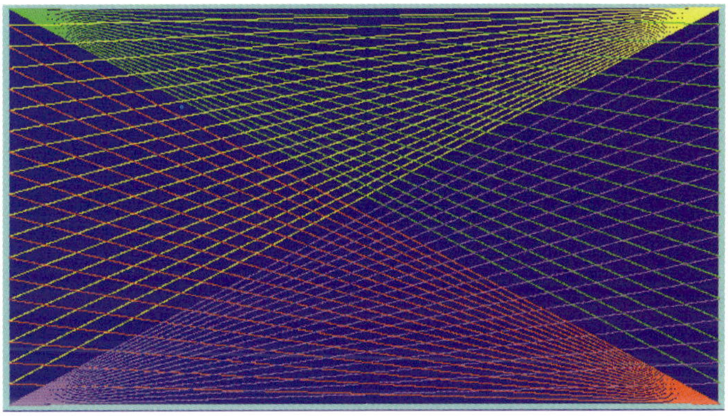

Plate 2: Straight Line Pattern

Plate 3: Random Starbursts of Straight Lines

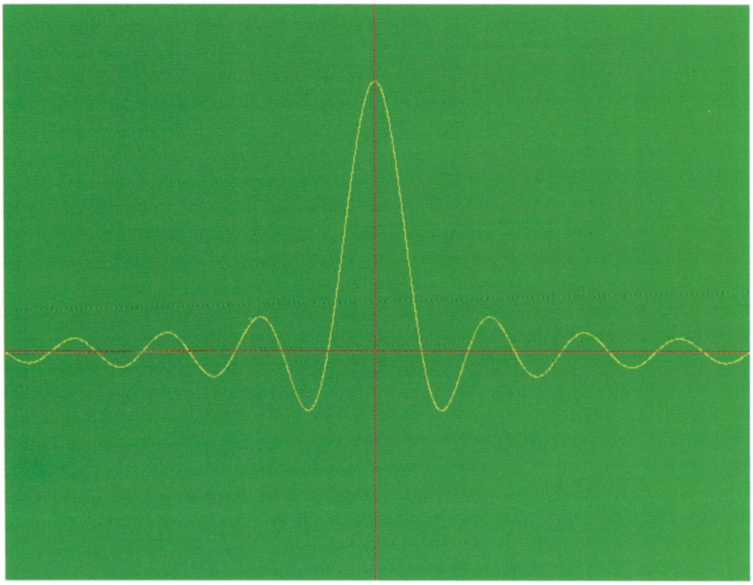

Plate 4: The sinc ((six x)/x) Function

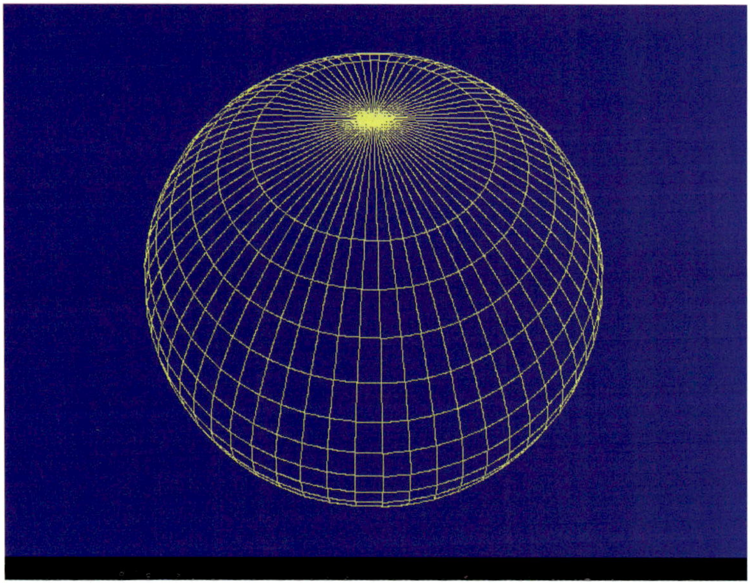

Plate 5: Sphere Drawn with Straight Lines

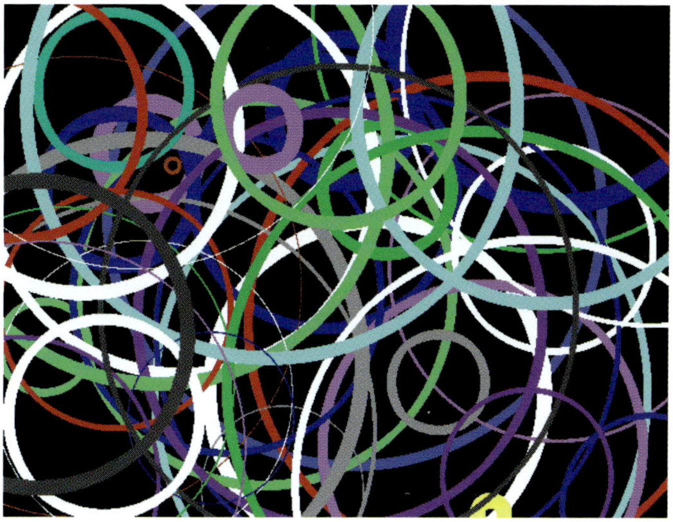

Plate 6: Randomly Located Circles of Random Width and Diameter

Plate 7: Randomly Located and Sized Filled Circles

Plate 8: Sunflower Seeds at Golden Angle (225.5 Degrees)

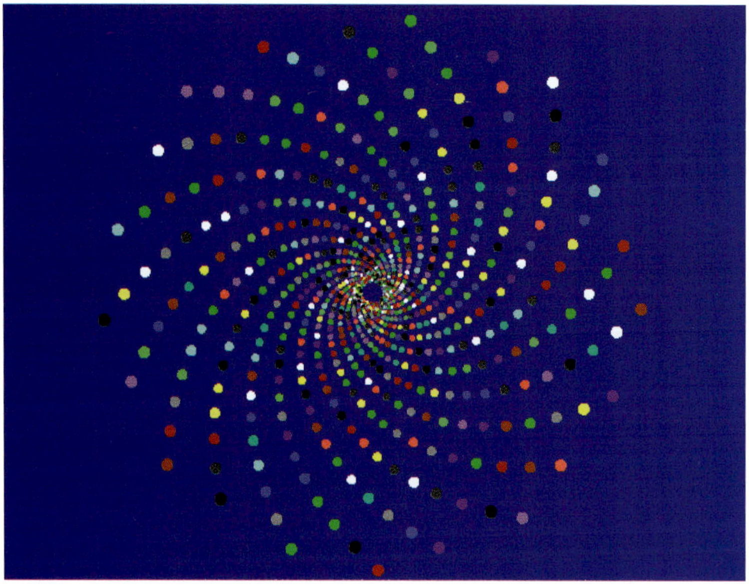

Plate 9: Sunflower Seeds at 225.6 Degrees

Plate 10: Apollonian Packing of Circles

Plate 11: "He Loves Me, He Loves Me Not"
(Daisy with Plucked Petals)

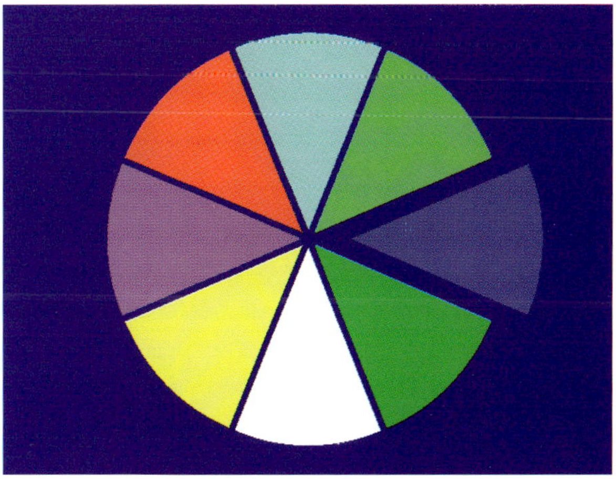

Plate 12: Pie Chart Made with Filled Arc Function

Plate 13: Arcs of Random Diameter, Width, Location and Extent

Plate 14: Rainbow Made with Arc Function

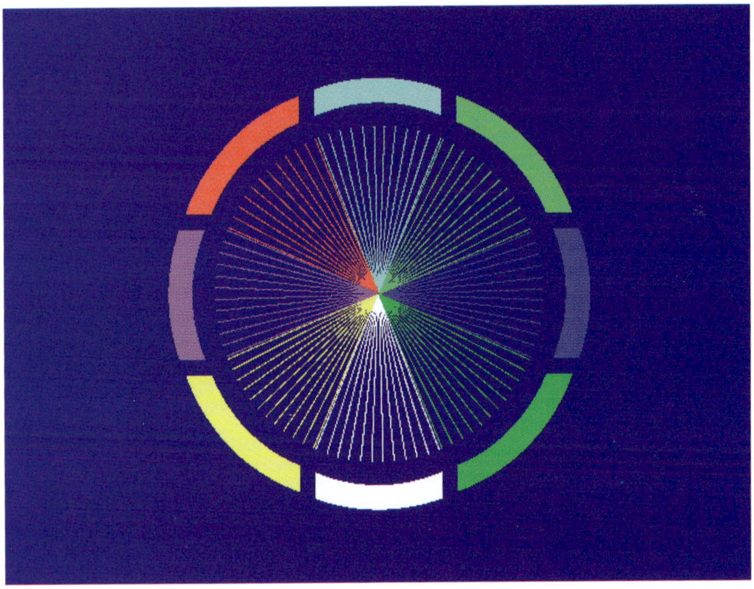

Plate 15: Arcs with Angled Lines

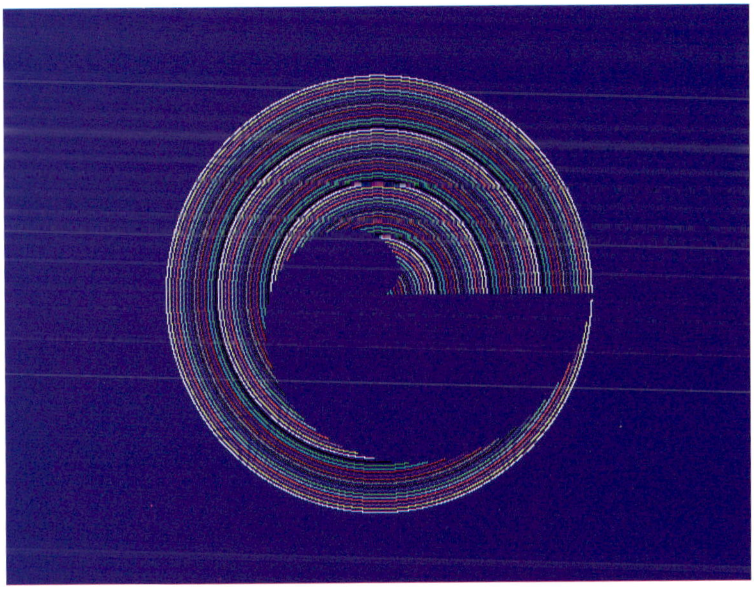

Plate 16: Testing of Arc Function

Plate 17: Filled Irregular Polygons

Plate 18: The New Jerusalem Diagram

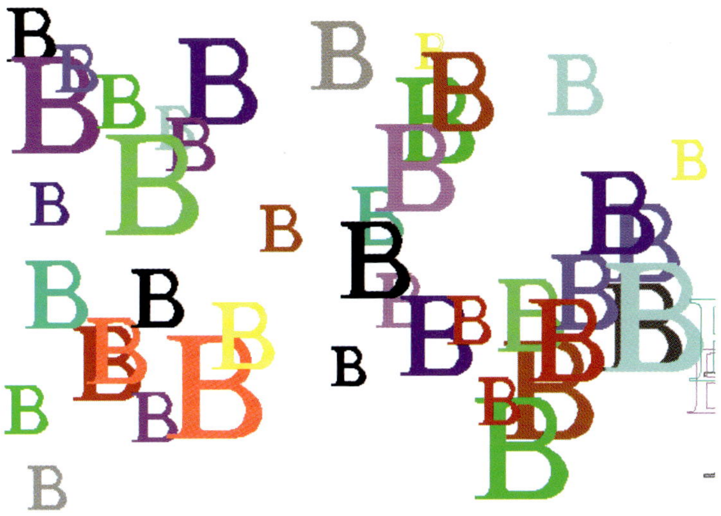

Plate 19: B's Generated with Filled Bezier Curves

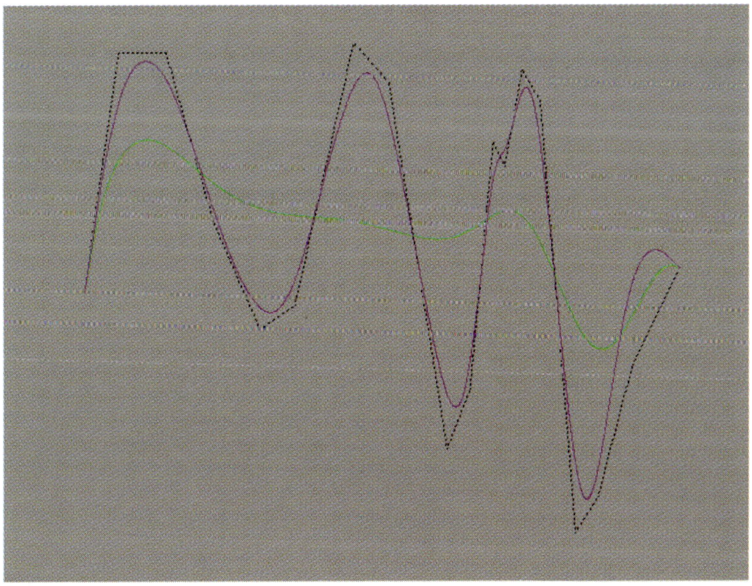

Plate 20: Bezier Curve and B-Spine Curve Approximations to the Same Control Points

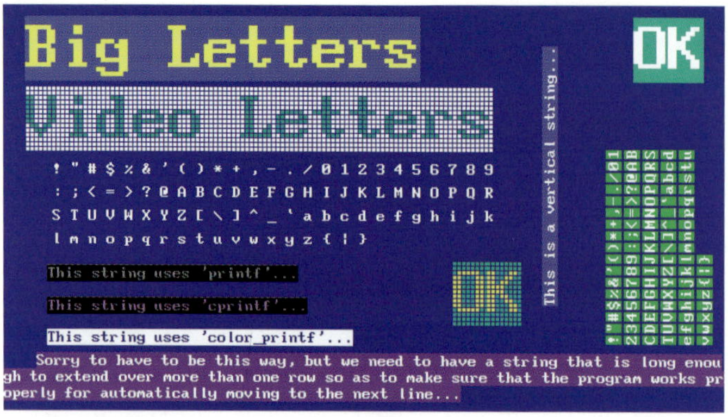

Plate 21: Functions for Generating Alphanumerics on a Graphic Display

Plate 22: Rotated Triangles

Plate 23: Solid Modeled Cones and Sphere

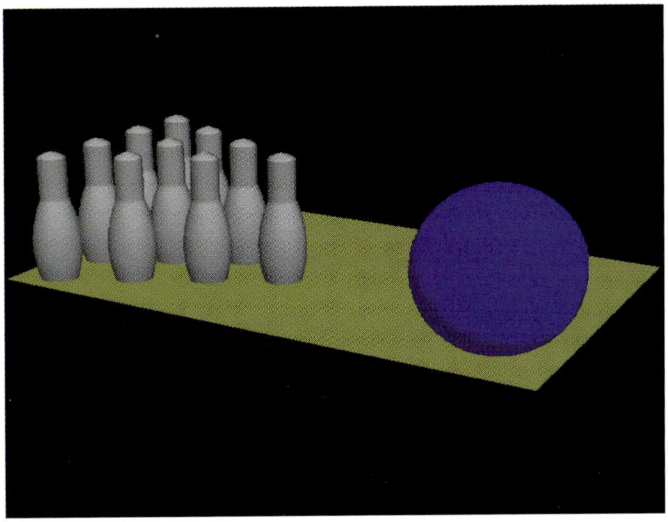

Plate 24: Bowling Using Solid Modeled Solids of Revolution and Sphere

Plate 25: Chessboard Using Solid Modeled Solids of Revolution

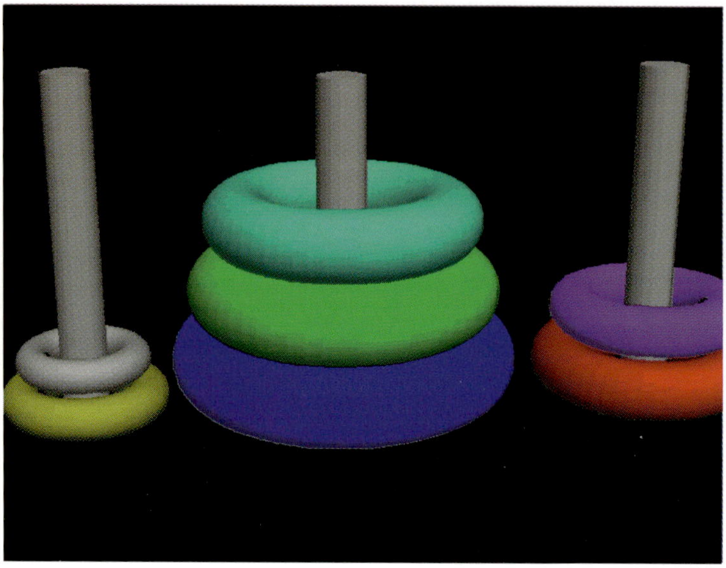

Plate 26: Towers of Hanoi Puzzle Using Solid Modeled Toroids

Plate 27: Ray Traced Bowl and Ball

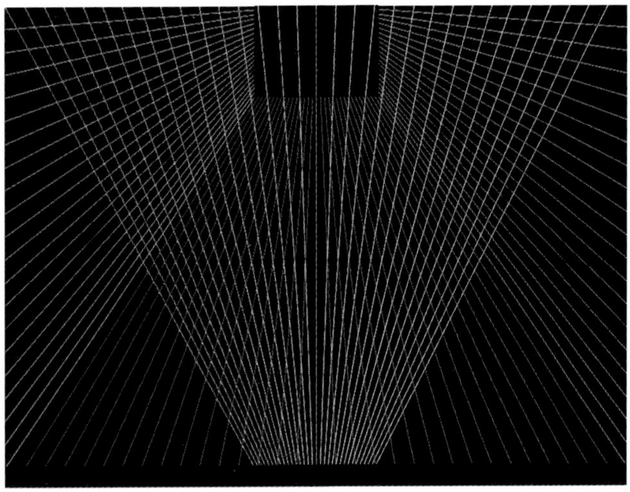

Plate 28: Wu Anti-Aliased Line Pattern

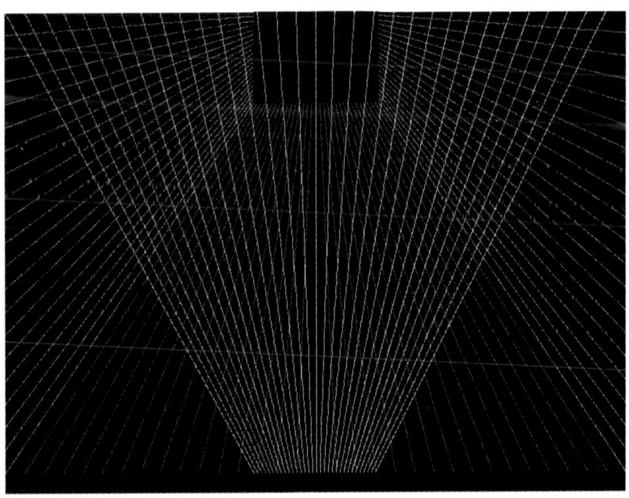

Plate 29: Same Line Pattern with Aliasing

Plate 30: A Complex Display: The Tennessee State Flag

Plate 31: The Flag of Wales

Plate 32: Distortion in an Uncorrected Photograph

Plate 33: Photo of Plate 32 After Warping to Correct Distortion

Plate 34: Photograph Scanned to a PCX File

Plate 35: Photograph Scanned to a BMP File

Plate 36: Photograph Scanned to a TGA File

```
void Bezier::draw(int color,...)
{
    va_list coord;
    int xpoint[20],ypoint[20],i=0,j,k,end;
    float b,t,x,y;
    va_start(coord,color);
    while (((xpoint[i]=va_arg(coord,int)) >= -640) &&
        ((ypoint[i]=va_arg(coord,int)) >= -480) &&
(i++<=20));
    va_end(coord);
    end = --i;
    xs = xpoint[0];
    ys = ypoint[0];
    for (t=0.01; t<1.0; t+=0.01)
    {
        x = 0;
        y = 0;
        for (j=0; j<=end; j++)
        {
            b = 1.0;
            for (k=end; k>j; k--)
                b *= k;
            for (k=end-j; k>1; k--)
                b /= k;
            for (i=1; i<=j; i++)
                b *= t;
            for (i=1; i<=end-j; i++)
                b *= (1-t);
            x += xpoint[j]*b;
            y += ypoint[j]*b;
        }
            Line::draw((int)x,(int)y,color);
    }
}

/*
                    BSpline class.
*/

class BSpline : public Line
{
    public:
        void draw(int bcurve[], int color);
        void draw(int color,...);
};
```

```
/*
                draw() = Draws B-Spline curve.
*/

void BSpline::draw(int bcurve[], int color)
{
    float x,y;
    float nc1, nc2, nc3, nc4, t;
    int xpoint[8], ypoint[8], i, last;

    xs = bcurve[0];
    ys = bcurve[1];
    if ((bcurve[0] == bcurve[6]) && (bcurve[1] ==
        bcurve[7]) && (bcurve[2] == bcurve[4]) &&
        (bcurve[3] == bcurve[5]))
    {
        Line::draw((int)bcurve[2], (int)bcurve[3],color);
        return;
    }
    for (i=0; i<4; i++)
    {
        xpoint[i+1] = bcurve[i*2];
        ypoint[i+1] = bcurve[i*2+1];
    }
    xpoint[0] = xpoint[1];
    ypoint[0] = ypoint[1];
    xpoint[5] = xpoint[4];
    ypoint[5] = ypoint[4];
    xpoint[6] = xpoint[4];
    ypoint[6] = ypoint[4];

    last = 4;
    for(i=0; i<last; i++)
    {
        for (t=0.0; t<=1.0; t+=0.01)
        {
            nc1=-(t*t*t/6)+t*t/2-t/2+1.0/6;
            nc2=t*t*t/2-t*t+2.0/3;
            nc3=(-t*t*t+t*t+t)/2 + 1.0/6;
            nc4=t*t*t/6;
            x = (nc1*xpoint[i] + nc2 * xpoint[i+1] +
            nc3*xpoint[i+2] + nc4*xpoint[i+3]);
            y = (nc1 * ypoint[i] + nc2*ypoint[i+1] +
            nc3*ypoint[i+2] + nc4*ypoint[i+3]);
            Line::draw((int)x,(int)y,color);
        }
    }
}
```

```
/*
    draw() = Draws a B-Spline curve with multi-point
                  inputs.
*/

void BSpline::draw(int color,...)
{

    va_list coord;
    int xpoint[24],ypoint[24],j=1,i,x,y;
    float t,nc1,nc2,nc3,nc4;

    va_start(coord,color);
    while (((xpoint[j]=va_arg(coord,int)) >= -640) &&
        ((ypoint[j]=va_arg(coord,int)) >= -480) &&
 (j++<=20));
    va_end(coord);
    xpoint[0]=xpoint[1];
    ypoint[0]=ypoint[1];
    for(i=j; i<j+3; i++)
    {
        xpoint[i]=xpoint[i-1];
        ypoint[i]=ypoint[i-1];
    }
    for(i=0; i<j; i++)
    {
        for (t=0.0; t<=1.0; t+=0.01)
        {
            nc1=-(t*t*t/6)+t*t/2-t/2+1.0/6;
            nc2=t*t*t/2-t*t+2.0/3;
            nc3=(-t*t*t+t*t+t)/2 + 1.0/6;
            nc4=t*t*t/6;
            x = int(nc1 * xpoint[i] + nc2 * xpoint[i+1] +
                  nc3*xpoint[i+2] + nc4*xpoint[i+3]);
            y = int(nc1 * ypoint[i] + nc2 * ypoint[i+1] +
                  nc3 * ypoint[i+2] + nc4*ypoint[i+3]);
            if ((i==0) && (t==0.0))
                Line::draw(xpoint[0], ypoint[0],
                    (int)x,(int)y, color);
            else
                Line::draw((int)x,(int)y,color);
        }
    }
}

#define compare(a,b,c)  {if (a<b) b = a; if (a>c) c = a;}
#define max(a,b)     (((a) > (b)) ? (a) : (b))
#define min(a,b)     (((a) < (b)) ? (a) : (b))

int coord[2][960], minrow, maxrow;
int color, mode, xres, yres;
unsigned long int PATTERN = 0xFFFFFFFFL;
```

The *plots* and *plot* Functions

The *plots* function is used to plot points that are specified in system coordinates to the screen. It begins in lines 417 and 418 by calling *convert_x* and *convert_y* to convert the passed coordinates to their corresponding display coordinate values. Then, in line 419, it calls *plot* to plot the point to the screen. The *plot* function first defines needed internal variables in lines 426 through 428. Lines 429 and 430 cause the function to return without plotting a point if the specified point is outside the display screen. The function then enters a *switch* statement in line 431, which causes the right operations to be performed to plot a point to the screen in the current display mode. Lines 433 through 437 are the 16-color unpaged modes. Chapter 6 shows a number of different ways to plot a point to the screen. All of these methods work well with Borland C++, but not all of them work with MicroSoft C++. The method used here works with either C++ compiler. It sets graphics register 01 to 0FH in line 438 and graphics register 00H to the desired color in line 439. Line 440 selects the mask register. In lines 441 and 442 the correct pixel address is computed. Line 443 computes the pixel mask, which is sent to the register in line 444. The OR statement in line 445 both reads the existing memory data to the latches and changes the color of the masked pixel. Finally, in lines 446 and 447, the registers are returned to their default values.

Lines 449 through 451 are the 16-color paged memory modes. The code is the same as that just described, except that for each pixel *setPage* is called to ensure that the proper memory page is selected.

Line 465 is the unpaged 256-color display mode. All that needs to be done here is to set up the correct pixel address in display memory and send the designated color to it.

Lines 471 through 475 are the paged 256-color modes. They do the same as just described except that *setPage* is called first to set up the correct display memory page.

Lines 482 through 491 are the 32K-color and 64K-color paged display modes. These modes use two bytes per pixel to store color information. After *setPage* is called and the display memory address is calculated, the color integer is broken up into two bytes, which are transferred to adjacent display memory addresses in lines 496 and 497.

The *fillsLine* and *fillLine* Functions

These functions draw a horizontal line on the display. The *fillsLine* function simply calls *convert_x* and *convert_y* in lines 254 through 256 to convert from system coordinates to display coordinates. Then, in line 257 the *fillLine* function is called to actually draw the line.

The *fillLine* function begins in lines 271 through 276 by swapping *x1* and *x2*, if necessary, so that *x1* has the smaller value. Then the function tests whether the entire line is off the display screen. If so, the function returns without drawing anything. The tests occur in lines 279 and 280, lines 283 and 284, and lines 285 and 286. Next, if *x1* is less than 0, it is set to zero by lines 277 and 278, and if *x2* exceeds the value of the right edge of the display, it is truncated to this value in lines 281 and 282. The function next enters a *switch* statement on line 287 that selects the code to actually draw the line, depending upon the display mode currently in use. Lines 289 through 296 are the 16-color display mode cases. In line 297, the index is set to the beginning of the line to be drawn. Next, in line 298, the function enters a *while* loop that iterates until the end of the line is reached. The *if* statement in line 300 causes a pixel to be plotted by the *plot* function and the index incremented if the pixel is not at the beginning of a byte boundary or if less than eight pixels remain before the end of the line. All of the rest of the line consists of full bytes of the line color. The *else* case in lines 302 through 313 uses the same code used to write a pixel, except that no masking is done so that the color is written to all eight pixels of the byte. This is at least eight times as fast as writing one pixel at a time. In line 312 the index is increased by 8 and the next iteration of the *while* loop then takes place. The remaining cases in the switch statement (for 256-color, 32K-color, and 64K-color display modes) simply use *for* loops to draw the horizontal line a pixel at a time using the same code used for the *plot* function.

The *setPage* function is listed in lines 607 through 622. This function takes the calculated memory address offset and shifts it 16 places to the right to obtain a memory page number (line 612). In line 613, the function checks whether the memory page is the same as the previous one (*old_mode*) and whether the mode (read or write) is the same as the old one (*old_mode*). If neither has changed, the function returns without doing anything further. If there is a difference, the new page number is put into *old_bank*, the new mode (write or read; or Window A or Window B) is put in *old_mode*, the registers are properly set, and the VESA extended ROM BIOS video service is called to set the new page number and window.

The *compare_color* function is listed in lines 58 through 143. The function begins in line 66 by testing to see whether the specified pixel is within the screen boundaries. If not, the function returns an indication of a color match, thus stopping the calling function from writing a new pixel. Next, the function enters a *switch* statement on line 68. Lines 70 through 74 are the unpaged 16-color display modes. In lines 75 and 76 the address of the byte in display memory is computed. Lines 77 and 78 set up graphics registers 5 and 2 for the color comparison test. Line 79 creates a mask for only the desired pixel. Line 80 reads and masks display memory byte contents. The memory contains a 1 for each pixel position where the color of the pixel matches the test color. All but the selected pixel are masked out. The meaningless statement in line 83 was inserted because MicroSoft C++ version 7.0 had some sort of timing problem such that the function wouldn't work without a little additional delay at this point. Lines 81 and 82 return the graphics registers to their default state. Lines 84 and 85 return a 0 for no match if *ch* is empty. Otherwise the function breaks to the end of the *switch* statement, where in line 142 a 1 is returned to indicate a match. Lines 87 through 89 are the 16-color paged video modes. The code is the same as for the cases just described except that *setPage* is called to select the correct display memory page. For the remaining cases, the function simply reads the pixel color from the proper address, compares it with the test color, and returns a zero if there is no match or breaks from the *switch* statement if there is a match.

Public *Graphics* Class Functions

Table 11-2 shows the public functions that are available for external use from the *Graphics* class and gives a description of each. All of these except the *floodfill* function have been described in previous chapters.

The *floodfill* Function

The *floodfill* function is listed in lines 364 through 409. This function starts at a specified point within an area on the screen that is bounded with a given color and fills the entire area with that color. It can be used not only for filling regular polygons, but also for filling circles and many other types of closed curves. This function is rather slow, so if there is a faster way to fill a figure, use it. However, there are figures that can only be successfully filled by this function. In particular, we may have several crossing lines that define a bounded area we want to fill, but we don't know the exact coordinates of the crossing points, so we can't define an irregular polygon to which we can apply the fast-filling functions. However, the flood-filling technique will fill such an area just fine. Flood filling is difficult, because an irregular polygon may have a strange shape that makes it easy for one or more sections not to get filled. The algorithm used for this function is based on one in Andrew Glassner's book *Graphics Gems*. It works just fine as long as you choose a starting point that isactually within the bounded area and as long as you make sure there are no gaps in the bounding line. After converting to display coordinates in lines 374 and 375, the function begins in lines 378 and 379 by putting the beginning point and one point on the next line onto a stack. It then begins processing the stack in line 380, comparing the color of pixels from the screen to the right of the selected point in line 384 and replotting them in the designated color in line 385 until a pixel matching the designated color is found, indicating that the boundary has been reached. Lines 386 through 393 take care of the case where popped pixel was already at the lefthand boundary. Otherwise, in lines 394 through 400, we check and push any additionally needed pixels to the stack. Then in lines 401 through 412 the comparing and plotting process is repeated for points to the right of the one read off the stack. In lines 404 and 405, points to the right are checked for color and plotted until a color matching the designated color is encountered. When the line is finished, the function then puts whatever points are necessary on the stack. Lines 409 and 410 skip

Table 11-2. Graphics Class Public Functions

Function Name	Transferred Parameters	Description
cls	int color	Clears the screen to the specified background color for 16- and 256-color modes.
convert_x	int x	Converts *x* from system coordinates to display coordinates.
convert_y	int y	Converts *y* from system coordinates to display coordinates.

Table 11-2. Graphics Class Public Functions (continued)

Function Name	Transferred Parameters	Description
floodfill	int x, int y, int color	Fills an enclosed figure with the designated color, beginning at seed point (x,y).
setEGApalette	int palette, int color	Sets the designated EGA palette number to the specified color. Works with EGA and VGA 16- and 256- color modes.
setVGApalette	unsigned char *buffer	Fills a specified number of VGA color registers with the colors specified in the buffer.
setMode	int vmode	Sets the screen to an EGA, VGA, or VESA display mode.
set_screen	int top_color, int bottom_color, int boundary	Clears the screen and sets lines from the top to the boundary to top_color and lines from there to the bottom of the screen to bottom_color.

to the right over any points in the designated color. The *do while* loop of line 401 then repeats this process until the stack is empty. If all has gone well, the enclosed figure is now filled with the specified color.

This version of the *floodfill* function fills an entire area that is bounded by a specified color with that color. You might want to write your own version of the function in which the boundary color and the filling color are not the same.

12

Lines and Rectangles

The *Line* class is derived from the *Graphics* base class. Its definition begins at line 689 of the *graphics* module listed in Chapter 11. Through the C++ concept of inheritance, the *Line* class now has access to all of the *Graphics* variables and functions as if they were its own. This enables *Line* to access such functions as *plot* and *plots* to draw pixels to the screen. The *Line* class also has a number of functions of its own, which are used to draw various kinds of straight lines. Prototypes for these are listed in lines 697 through 712. To create these functions, we make use of another C++ capability, namely, function overloading. Function overloading enables us to have many different functions that share a common name; all that is required is for each function to have its own distinct selection of parameters. Table 12-1 gives the characteristics of the *Line* class functions. Observe that all the functions are called *draw*; which one is used depends upon the parameters that are passed to the *draw* function. The *Line* class also has a number of internal private parameters that are listed in lines 691 and 692.

Drawing a Single-Pixel Line from an Internal Starting Point

The first version of the *draw* function is listed in lines 718 through 793. The first thing this function does is set up a value for *mask* as a long integer (32-bit) value having a single bit in the most significant position. This is used to create line styles,—dotted lines, dashed lines, etc. Each time a pixel in the line is generated, the *mask* is compared against the *PATTERN* variable and if the result is not zero, the pixel is drawn on the display. The mask is then shifted one bit to the right.

Table 12-1. Line Class Public Functions.

Function Name	Transferred Parameters	Description
draw	int xend, int yend, int color	Draws a single-pixel-wide line from internal coordinates (xs,ys) to (xend,yend) in selected color and leaves (xend,yend) in (xs,ys).
draw	int xstart, int ystart, int xend, int yend, int color	Draws a single-pixel-wide line line from (xstart,ystart) to (xend, yend) in selected color and leaves (xend,yend) in (xs,ys).
draw	int xstart, int ystart, int length, float angle, int color	Draws a single-pixel-wide line from (xstart, ystart) at specified angle to horizontal for specified length in specified color.
draw	int xend, int yend, int color, int width	Draws a line of specified width from internal coordinates (xs,ys) to (xend,yend) in selected color and leaves (xend,yend) in (xs,ys).
draw	int xstart, int ystart, int xend, int yend, int color, int width	Draws a line of specified width from (xstart,ystart) to (xend, yend) in selected color and leaves (xend,yend) in (xs,ys).
draw	int xstart, int ystart, int length, float angle, int color, int width	Draws a line of specified width from (xstart, ystart) at specified angle to horizontal for specified length in specified color.

When it drops off the right end, it is restored to the most significant bit position. Any time *mask* corresponds to a zero in *PATTERN*, no pixel is drawn and the line contains a gap. Line 741 is an example of *mask* being advanced one position; lines 742 and 743 show how the test works to draw or not draw a pixel. Similar code occurs at several places in the line-drawing loops. *PATTERN* may be chosen externally from any of an array of eight long integers called *style*, which define other line styles. The first of these is the solid line style. The next is 0xC0C0C0C0, which is the binary pattern 11001100110011001100110011001100. The resulting line consists of two pixels followed by two blanks followed by two pixels. Before calling the line-drawing function, you transfer one of these styles (or any style of your own) to the global variable *PATTERN*. The various *style* values are all 32 bits long and therefore recycle at least every 32 pixels and, depending upon the pattern, may recycle with a shorter repetition frequency. As long as you are drawing lines that are longer than the recycle period, this system works well; if you are drawing a number of very small line segments to reproduce a complex curve, the line styles may reproduce only a part of the pattern for each line segment. If this happens to be a part of the pattern that is zeroes, nothing will appear on the screen. Therefore take considerable care in using line styles with small line segments.

Since creating a patterned line uses an additional calculation and test for each pixel of the line, you can speed up your line-drawing function by eliminating this altogether if you have no intention of ever drawing anything other than solid lines.

As we enter the function, the beginning coordinates of the line are the coordinates of the end of the line previously drawn (*xs,ys*), which are stored within the class. The end coordinates of the line are the coordinates (*xend,yend*), which are passed to the function. We are first going to find the distance *dx* between the beginning and ending *x* coordinates (line 722) and then the distance *dy* between the beginning and ending *y* coordinates (line 723). We are going to draw the line from (*xs,ys*) to (*xe,ye*). To simplify the drawing process, we want to start at the left end of the line if the *x* distance is greater than or equal to the *y* distance ($dx>=dy$), and at the top end of the line otherwise ($dx<dy$). This may require swapping the beginning and ending sets of coordinates. Lines 724 through 731 perform the necessary tests and end up with the proper sets of coordinates in (*xs,ys*) and (*xe,ye*). Lines 737 through 747 take care of the special case where $dx=0$ (a vertical line). Line 739 begins a *for* loop that draws pixels at coordinate *xe* for coordinates *ys* to *ye*, incrementing the *y* at each iteration. Line 745 sets *ys* to the original *y* ending coordinate (*yend*); *xs* has not changed. We are now ready for the next call of the function. The function then returns to the calling program.

Lines 748 through 758 take care of the special case where $dy=0$ (a horizontal line). Line 750 begins a *for* loop that draws pixels at coordinate *ye* for coordinates *xs* to *xe*, incrementing the *x* at each iteration. Line 756 sets *xs* to the original *x* ending coordinate (*xend*); *ys* remains unchanged. We are now ready for the next call of the function. The function then returns to the calling program.

Drawing Slanting Lines

Since the computer display screen is composed of discrete pixels, we can never draw a perfect slanting line on the screen. Given a starting point, the best we can do is step to the nearest pixel to the line's true position and then continue this process until we reach the end of the line. A typical result of this process is shown in Figure 12-2. The resulting line has steps, which are particularly objectionable for low-resolution displays. These are the so-called jaggies that plague computer display line drawings. In Chapter 23, we'll talk about how to use color shading to minimize the effect of these steps. For now, however, the best we can do is find how to select the pixels to be displayed so as to get the best approximation to the slanting line we'd like to draw. First let's take an overview of the situation. For the line shown in the figure, x increases more rapidly than y. Therefore, for each pixel step on the line we know that x is going to increase by one. The only question that remains is whether will remain the same or increase. This will be determined through the use of a decision function. To obtain this decision function, we are going to use a method called Bresenham's algorithm. This method makes use of the derivative of the function, which is the change in y, given a small change in x. The equation of a line is:

$$y = \frac{y_2 - y_1}{x_2 - x_1}x + b$$

(Equation 9-1)

The derivative for a line is:

$$dy = \frac{y_2 - y_1}{x_2 - x_1}dx$$

(Equation 9-2)

Figure 12-2. Drawing a Line with Discrete Pixels

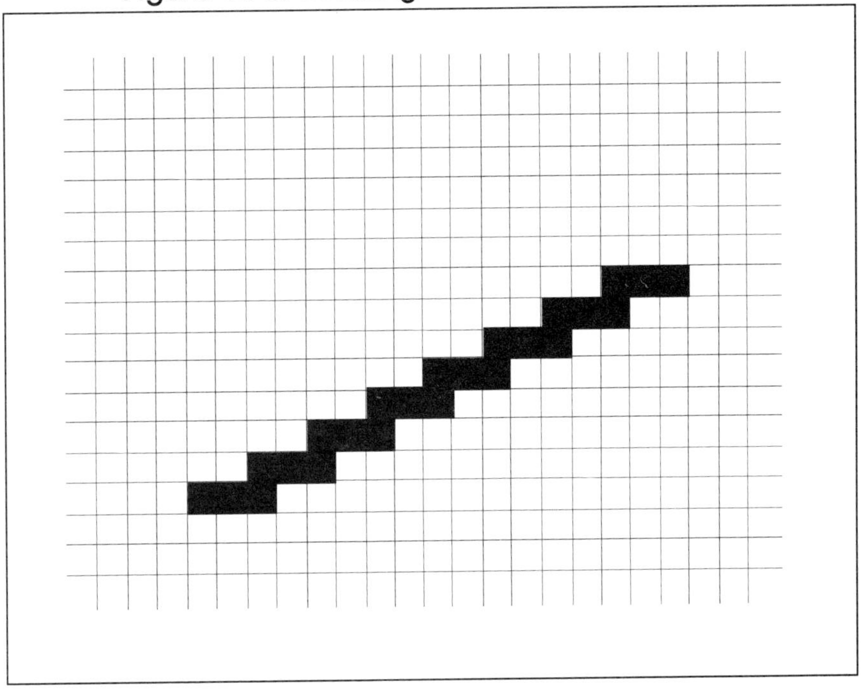

To use the derivative directly, we let dx be equal to 1, since we are going to increase x by one pixel for each step. We then increase y by the fractional part of the equation. However, we can actually only increase y in steps of 1, so we keep track of the actual value of y but do not actually increment y on the screen until the actual value of y has increased by 1. This is the first part of Bresenham's algorithm. It is not limited to straight lines, but can be applied to any curve for which we can take the derivative. The second part of Bresenham's algorithm modifies the decision function to speed up operation by eliminating any divisions. To do this, we multiply both sides of the derivative equation by $x_2 - x_1$. We then set up the decision function so that it starts at 0. Each time we increment x, we increase the decision function by $y_2 - y_1$. When the decision function exceeds $x_2 - x_1$, we increment y and decrease the decision function by $x_2 - x_1$. Mathematically, this is just the same as using the derivative, but it avoids all of the time consuming divisions. Finally, for Bresenham's algorithm to be complete, we need to consider a few other possibilities that have not yet been mentioned. First, the line in the figure is moving upward as it goes from right to left. If it were moving downward, although the derivative would then be negative, we could still use the same values in the decision function, but we would have to decrement the y value instead of increment it each time a change in its value was called for. Next, suppose that we have a line with a slope of more than 45 degrees, so that at each step the y value increases but the x value doesn't necessarily do so. If we use the algorithm as given previously, we will plot only the points where x increases, so although these points will be placed correctly, a lot of points will be left out. We can overcome this situation by interchanging x and y in the procedure.

Now we are ready to continue with the *draw* function we were looking at earlier. Lines 759 and 760 compute *x_sign* and *y_sign*, which determine the direction in which the second coordinate is to move for each of the loops that draw the line. If the line is increasing faster in the x direction than in the y direction, as determined by the *if* test in line 761, we enter a *for* loop (lines 763 and 764) that begins at the starting line coordinates, with the decision function zero, and continues until the ending x coordinate is reached. At each iteration, the x coordinate is incremented and the decision variable is increased by the y length. Within the loop, if the decision variable exceeds the x length (as determined by the test in line 767), we reduce it by the x length (line 769) and move y one unit in the appropriate direction (line 770). If the line pattern requires it (as determined in line 772), a point is then plotted to the screen at the current coordinates. For the case where the line is increasing faster in the y direction than in the x direction, the function jumps from the test at line 761 to line 778, where there is another *for* loop that is exactly the same in structure as lines 763 and 764, except that the operations on x and y are interchanged.

When the slant line has been drawn, the internal starting coordinates (*xs,ys*) are set to the original end coordinates of the line (*xend,yend*) to be ready for the next time the function is called (lines 791 and 792). If you're drawing a series of lines, each beginning at the end of the previous one, this is the function to use since you don't need to specify the starting coordinates; they are already stored in the function. Note, however, that you can't use this for your very first line call, because (*xs,ys*) will initially be (0,0) and will start the line from there.

Drawing a Line with Beginning and End Specified

Suppose we need to specify both the starting and ending coordinates of a line. The *draw* function listed in lines 798 through 804 performs this task. In lines 801 and 802, the internal parameters (*xs,ys*) are set to the starting values passed to the function (*xstart,ystart*). In line 803, the previously described *draw* function is called, passing only the line end parameters (*xend,yend*) and *color*. We've already loaded the proper values into (*xs,ys*) in the two previous lines, so the line is drawn exactly as we specified.

Drawing a Line in a Given Direction

The function listed in lines 810 through 818 draws a line when the starting point, length, direction angle, and color are specified. Lines 813 and 814 put the specified starting coordinates (*xstart,ystart*) into (*xs,ys*). Line 815 uses the *x* starting point, the length, and the direction angle to compute the location of the *x* ending point *xe*. Line 816 performs a corresponding computation to determine *ye*. Then line 817 calls the *draw* function described in the section above to draw the desired line.

Drawing Wide Lines

Thus far, we've only drawn single-pixel-wide lines. The function listed in lines 824 through 923 is quite similar to the first *draw* function we described (lines 718 through 793) except that it permits us to draw wide lines. This function takes over when a *width* is passed to the *draw* function together with the other parameters. When we're drawing vertical lines, the only difference from the original function is that an additional *for* loop is added (line 848) that draws additional pixels to the left and right of the one-pixel-wide line drawn by the original function to create a line of the specified width. The number of pixels drawn to the left of the original line must be equal to the number of pixels drawn to the right, so that the actual width of the line is always an odd number of pixels. If you specify an even width, it will be truncated to the next lower odd number.

The same holds true for horizontal lines (as listed in lines 857 through 870). In this case, the additional pixels are drawn above and below the original pixel by the *for* loop of line 862.

When we are drawing slant lines, a really correct wide line will have the additional pixels drawn at right angles to the slope of the line. The mathematics of this are quite complicated and will considerably slow down the line-drawing process. So we're going to compromise and only add pixels vertically above and below or horizontally to the left and right of the original pixel. You might think at first that this is dangerous. Suppose we have a line that is almost horizontal and add pixels to the left and right of each original pixel. No matter what line width is specified, the actual width will hardly be increased. Remember, however, that in the original function, we have two ways of drawing the line; one is used when the horizontal distance is greater than or equal to the vertical distance and the other when the vertical distance is greater than the horizontal distance. If we add pixels vertically in the first case and horizontally in the second, the worst case we will encounter is for a 45-degree line, when the actual width will be 0.707 times the desired width. In many cases, this will be within the one-pixel accuracy that is all we can obtain anyway. The only thing you need to worry about in using this simplification is that the line ends will not be at right angles to the line itself, which causes difficulties in joining wide line segments. More about this later.

The *draw* function listed in lines 929 through 935 draws wide lines when both the starting and ending coordinates are specified. It works in the same way as its corresponding narrow-line function, except that it calls the appropriate wide line function to draw the line.

The *draw* function listed in lines 941 through 949 draws wide lines when both the starting coordinates and the length, angle, color, and width are specified. It works in the same way as its corresponding narrow-line function, except that it calls the appropriate wide-line function to draw the line.

The *LINETEST.CPP* Program

Listing 12-1 is a listing of *LINETEST.CPP*, a demonstration program to show the various line drawing capabilities. The section of code from line 35 through line 39 draws the first display. The *setMode* function is called in line 35 to set the display to the 320 × 200 pixel × 256-color mode. In line 36, the color of the first line is set to dark gray (8). Lines 37 and 38 comprise a *for* loop that starts with the horizontal coordinate of a line at 0 and increases 45 pixels for each line drawn until the horizontal coordinate exceeds 320. At each iteration, the *line.draw* function is called to draw a line whose beginning and ending horizontal coordinates are the same, whose beginning vertical coordinate is 0, and whose ending coordinate is 199. After each *line.draw* call, the color is incremented so that the next line will be in the next color. Note that although we are in the 256-color mode, the first 16 colors of that mode are, by default, the same as the first 16 colors of the 16-color mode. Since this display never gets beyond color 15, you won't see any difference from the colors used in a 16 color display mode. The *draw* function is called with starting and ending coordinates; since the beginning and ending *x* coordinates are the same, the function will use the vertical-line drawing technique.

Listing 12-1. LINETEST.CPP Program for Demonstrating Line-Drawing Capabilities.

```
/*
 ┌──────────────────────────────────────────────────────┐
 │                                                      │
 │      LINETEST = Test of line drawing function        │
 │                                                      │
 │          By Roger T. Stevens   2/7/96                │
 │                                                      │
 └──────────────────────────────────────────────────────┘
*/

#include "c:\cpphbook\program\graphics.cpp"

void perspective(int no_of_points,float rot_pts[][3],float
    pt[][3],int vx[], int vy[]);
float surface_test(float x1, float y1, float z1, float x2,
    float y2, float z2, float x3, float y3, float z3);

Graphics graphic;
Line line;
unsigned long int style[8] = { 0xFFFFFFFFL, 0xC0C0C0C0L,
    0xFF00FF00L, 0xFFF0FFF0L, 0xF000F000L, 0xFFFF0000L,
    0xFFFFF0F0L, 0xFFF0F0F0L};
typedef struct
{
    unsigned char red;
    unsigned char green;
    unsigned char blue;
} RGB;

RGB palette[256];
int hue, length, xs, ys, xe, ye;
float sp, pt1[73][3], pt2[73][3], rot_pts1[73][3],
rot_pts2[73][3];
float yaw, roll, pitch, latitude, longitude, CP, SP, CY,
    SY, CR, SR;
```

```
int d=375, mx=0, my=0, mz=-200, off_x,off_y,sx, sy;
int vx1[73],vy1[73],vx2[73],vy2[73];

void main()
{
    int i,j, k, iter, denom, xlength=260, ylength=180, r,
        radius, xb, yb;
    char ch=0;

/*
                    Display 1
    320 x 200 Pixel x 256 Color Mode 13H
                  Vertical Lines
*/

    graphic.setMode(0x13);
    color = 8;
    for (i=-640; i<640; i+=180)
        line.draw(i,-480,i,479,color++);
    getch();

/*
                    Display 2
    640 x 350 Pixel x 16 Color Mode 10H
                  Vertical Lines
*/

    graphic.setMode(0x10);
    color = 8;
    for (i=-640; i<640; i+=180)
        line.draw(i,-480,i,479,color++);
    getch();

/*
                    Display 3
    320 x 200 Pixel x 256 Color Mode 13H
               Wide Vertical Lines
*/
```

```
        graphic.setMode(0x13);
        color = 8;
        for (i=0; i<8; i++)
        {
            PATTERN = style[i];
            line.draw(i*176 - 640,-480,i*176 -
                640,479,color++,4*i+1);
        }
        PATTERN = style[0];
        getch();

    /*
                               Display 4

                  640 x 350 Pixel x 16 Color Mode 10H
                                                          Wide
                            Vertical Lines
    */

        graphic.setMode(0x10);
        graphic.cls(0);
        color = 8;
        for (i=0; i<8; i++)
        {
            PATTERN = style[i];
            line.draw(i*176 - 640, -480, i*176 - 640,
        479,color++, 2*i+1);
        }
        PATTERN = style[0];
        getch();

    /*
                               Display 5

                  320 x 200 Pixel x 256 Color Mode 13H

                        Wide Horizontal Lines
    */

        graphic.setMode(0x13);
        color = 8;
        for (i=0; i<8; i++)
        {
```

```
            PATTERN = style[i];
            line.draw(-630,i*120-450,630,i*120 -
450,color++,4*i+1);
        }
        PATTERN = style[0];
        getch();

/*
                              Display 6

            640 x 350 Pixel x 16 Color Mode 10H

                       Wide Horizontal Lines
*/

        graphic.setMode(0x10);
        graphic.cls(0);
        color = 8;
        for (i=0; i<8; i++)
        {
            PATTERN = style[i];
            line.draw(-630,i*120-450,630,i*120 -
450,color++,4*i+1);
        }
        PATTERN = style[0];
        getch();

/*
                              Display 7

            640 x 350 Pixel x 16 Color Mode 10H

                  Horizontal and Vertical Lines
*/

        graphic.cls(1);
        color = 0;
        for (i=-630; i<630; i += 60)
        {
            line.draw(i,-470,i,470,color++);
            color %= 16;
            if (color == 1)
                color++;
```

```
    }
    for (i=-475; i<480; i+=60)
    {
        line.draw(-630,i,630,i,color++);
        color %= 16;
        if (color == 1)
            color++;
    }
    getch();

/*
                    Display 8

      320 x 200 Pixel x 256 Color Mode 13H

                 Wide Rectangle
*/

    graphic.setMode(0x13);
    graphic.cls(1);
    line.draw(-640,-474,639,-474,14,12);
    line.draw(-640,473,639,473,14,12);
    line.draw(-634,-474,-634,474,14,12);
    line.draw(633,-474,633,474,14,12);
    getch();

/*
                    Display 9

      640 x 350 Pixel x 16 Color Mode 10H

                 Wide Rectangle
*/

    graphic.setMode(0x10);
    graphic.cls(12);
    line.draw(-640,-474,639,-474,14,12);
    line.draw(-640,473,639,473,14,12);
    line.draw(-634,-474,-634,474,14,12);
    line.draw(633,-474,633,474,14,12);
    getch();
```

```
/*
                        Display 10
        640 x 350 Pixel x 16 Color Mode 10H
                       Line Pattern
*/

    graphic.cls(1);
    line.draw(-640,-474,639,-474,11,10);
    line.draw(-640,473,639,473,11,10);
    line.draw(-634,-474,-634,474,11,10);
    line.draw(633,-474,633,474,11,10);
    for (i=-420; i< 470; i+=50)
    {
        line.draw(-630,-470,630,i,13);
        line.draw(630,470,-630,i,14);
        line.draw(-630,470,630,i,10);
        line.draw(630,-470,-630,i,12);
    }
    getch();
/*
                        Display 11
        320 x 200 Pixel x 256 Color Mode 13H
                       Line Pattern
*/

    graphic.setMode(0x13);
    line.draw(-640,-474,639,-474,42,10);
    line.draw(-640,473,639,473,42,10);
    line.draw(-634,-474,-634,474,42,10);
    line.draw(633,-474,633,474,42,10);
    hue = 1;
    for (i=-420; i< 470; i+=50)
    {
        line.draw(-630,-470,630,i,hue++);
        line.draw(630,470,-630,i,hue++);
        line.draw(-630,470,630,i,hue++);
        line.draw(630,-470,-630,i,hue++);
    }
    getch();
```

```
/*

                    Display 12

     1024 x 768 Pixel x 256 Color Mode 105H
                  Line Pattern

*/

    graphic.setMode(0x105);
    line.draw(-640,-474,639,-474,42,10);
    line.draw(-640,473,639,473,42,10);
    line.draw(-634,-474,-634,474,42,10);
    line.draw(633,-474,633,474,42,10);
    hue = 1;
    for (i=-420; i< 470; i+=50)
    {
        line.draw(-630,-470,630,i,hue++);
        line.draw(630,470,-630,i,hue++);
        line.draw(-630,470,630,i,hue++);
        line.draw(630,-470,-630,i,hue++);
    }
    getch();

/*

                    Display 13

       640 x 350 Pixel x 16 Color Mode 10H

                Lines at an angle

*/

    graphic.setMode(0x10);
    while (ch != 0x0D)
    {
        graphic.cls(1);
        for (i=0; i<80; i++)
        {
            length = rand()/205 + 40;
            color = rand() & 0x0F;
            if (color == 1)
                color = 0;
            xs = rand()/26 - 640;
            ys = rand()/34 - 480;
            for (j=0; j<3600; j+=150,length/=1.02)
                line.draw(xs, ys, length, (float)j,
```

```
                    color);
        }
        ch = getch();
    }

/*
                    Display 14

        640 x 350 Pixel x 16 Color Mode 16

              Joining line segments
*/

    graphic.cls(0);
    line.draw(-560,400,560,400,13,16);
    line.draw(560,-400,13,16);
    line.draw(-560,-400,13,16);
    line.draw(-560,400,13,16);
    line.draw(-560,-60,140,-400,12,16);
    line.draw(-160,20,10,16);
    line.draw(40,350,12,16);
    line.draw(240,390,10,16);
    line.draw(550,60,12,16);
    getch();

/*
                    Display 15

        640 x 480 Pixel x 16 Color Mode 12H

               Wide Line End Test
*/

    int width=1;

    xres = 640;
    yres = 480;
    graphic.setMode(0x12);
    color = 1;
    for(j=-420; j<440; j+=240)
    {
```

```
        for(i=-630; i<460  ; i+=320)
        {
            line.draw(i, j, i + xlength, j + ylength,
                color, width);
            line.draw(i, j + ylength, i + xlength, j,
                color, width);
            line.draw(i,j,i+xlength,j,color,width);
            line.draw(i, j + ylength, i + xlength, j +
            ylength, color, width);
            line.draw(i,j,i,j+ylength,color,width);
            line.draw(i + xlength, j, i + xlength, j +
            ylength, color, width++);
            color++;
            if (color == 0)
                color++;
         }
    }

    getch();

  /*

                        Display 16

          640 x 480 Pixel x 16 Color Mode 12H

               sinc (sine x / x) Waveform

  */

    graphic.setMode(0x12);
    graphic.cls(2);
    for (i=1; i<=256; i++)
    {
            ye = int((4600 * sin(6.283 * ((double)i)/64))
                /((double)i)-100);
            xe = int(1280 * (double)i/512);
            if (i==1)
            {
                xs = 0;
                ys = ye;
            }
            line.draw (xs, ys, xe, ye, 14);
            line.draw (-xs, ys, -xe, ye, 14);
            xs = xe;
            ys = ye;
    }
    line.draw(-640,-100,640,-100,12);
    line.draw(0,-480,0,479,12);
```

```
    getch();
/*
                    Display 17

          640 x 480 Pixel x 16 Color Mode 12H

                   Random Spirals
*/
    color = 1;
    graphic.setMode(0x12);
    for (k=0; k<75; k++)
    {
        denom = rand()/1638 + 4;
        xs = rand()/26 - 640;
        ys = rand()/34 - 480;
        r = 2;
        iter = rand() & 0x07 + 6;
        line.draw(xs,ys,xs,ys,color);
        for (i=1; i<iter; i++)
        {
            for (j=0; j<360; j+=2)
            {
                xb = xs + int(r*(cos(0.017453292 *
            j))/denom);
                yb = ys + int(r*(sin(0.017453292 *
            j))/denom);
                line.draw(xb, yb, color);
                r++;
            }
        }
        color++;
        if (color == 16)
            color = 1;
    }
    getch();

/*
                    Display 18

          800 x 600 Pixel x 256 Color Mode 103H

                  Wire Frame Sphere
*/
```

```
    graphic.setMode(0x103);
    graphic.cls(1);
    radius = 145;
    color = 14;
    yaw = 45;
    pitch = 115;
    CP = cos(0.017453292*pitch);
    SP = sin(0.017453292*pitch);
    CR = cos(0.017453292*roll);
    SR = sin(0.017453292*roll);
    CY = cos(0.017453292*yaw);
    SY = sin(0.017453292*yaw);
    pt1[0][0] = 0;
    pt1[0][1] = radius;
    pt1[0][2] = 0;
    perspective(1,rot_pts1,pt1,vx1,vy1);
    longitude = .087266462;
    for (latitude=0,i=0; i<72; i++,latitude+=0.087266462)
    {
        pt2[i][0] = cos(latitude)*sin(longitude)*radius;
        pt2[i][1] = cos(longitude)*radius;
        pt2[i][2] = sin(latitude)*sin(longitude)*radius;
    }
    pt2[72][0] = pt2[0][0];
    pt2[72][1] = pt2[0][1];
    pt2[72][2] = pt2[0][2];
    perspective(73,rot_pts2,pt2,vx2,vy2);
    for (i=0; i<72; i++)
    {
        sp = surface_test(rot_pts2[i+1][0],
rot_pts2[i+1][1], rot_pts2[i+1][2],
rot_pts2[i][0], rot_pts2[i][1],
rot_pts2[i][2], rot_pts1[0][0],
rot_pts1[0][1], rot_pts1[0][2]);
        if (sp<=0)
        {
            line.draw(vx2[i+1],vy2[i+1],vx1[0],
        vy1[0],color);
            line.draw(vx2[i],vy2[i],color);
            line.draw(vx2[i+1], vy2[i+1], color);
        }
    }
    for (j=0; j<32; j++)
    {
        longitude += 0.087266462;
        for (latitude=0,i=0; i<72;
i++,latitude+=0.087266462)
        {
            pt2[i][0] = cos(latitude) *
sin(longitude)*radius;
```

```
                pt2[i][1] = cos(longitude)*radius;
                pt2[i][2] = sin(latitude) *
    sin(longitude)*radius;
            }
            pt2[72][0] = pt2[0][0];
            pt2[72][1] = pt2[0][1];
            pt2[72][2] = pt2[0][2];
            for (i=0; i<73; i++)
            {
                for (k=0; k<3; k++)
                    rot_pts1[i][k] = rot_pts2[i][k];
                vx1[i] = vx2[i];
                vy1[i] = vy2[i];
            }
            perspective(73,rot_pts2,pt2,vx2,vy2);
            for (i=0; i<72; i++)
            {
                sp = surface_test(rot_pts1[i][0],
        rot_pts1[i][1], rot_pts1[i][2],
    rot_pts1[i+1][0], rot_pts1[i+1][1],
                    rot_pts1[i+1][2], rot_pts2[i+1][0],
                rot_pts2[i+1][1], rot_pts2[i+1][2]);
                if (sp<=0)
                {
                    line.draw(vx1[i], vy1[i], vx2[i], vy2[i],
                        color);
                    line.draw(vx2[i+1], vy2[i+1], color);
                    line.draw(vx1[i+1], vy1[i+1], color);
                    line.draw(vx1[i], vy1[i], color);
                }
            }
        }
        pt1[0][0] = 0;
        pt1[0][1] = -radius;
        pt1[0][2] = 0;
        perspective(1,rot_pts1,pt1,vx1,vy1);
        for (i=0; i<72; i++)
        {
            sp = surface_test(rot_pts2[i][0], rot_pts2[i][1],
                rot_pts2[i][2], rot_pts2[i+1][0],
    rot_pts2[i+1][1], rot_pts2[i+1][2],
    rot_pts1[0][0], rot_pts1[0][1],
                rot_pts1[0][2]);
            if (sp<=0)
            {
                line.draw(vx2[i], vy2[i], vx1[0], vy1[0],
                color);
                line.draw(vx2[i+1], vy2[i+1], color);
                line.draw(vx2[i], vy2[i], color);
            }
```

```
    }
    getch();
    graphic.setMode(3);
}

/*
        perspective() = Changes perspective of
    three-dimensional figure and changes it to two
                    dimensions.
*/

void perspective(int no_of_points, float rot_pts[][3],
float pt[][3], int vx[], int vy[])
{
    int i,j;
    float xa,ya,za,x,y,z;

    for (i=0; i<no_of_points; i++)
    {
        xa = - cos(yaw)*pt[i][0] - sin(yaw)*pt[i][2];
        za = - sin(yaw)*pt[i][0] + cos(yaw)*pt[i][2];
        rot_pts[i][0] = cos(roll)*xa + sin(roll)*pt[i][1]
            + mx;
        ya = cos(roll)*pt[i][1] - sin(roll)*xa;
        rot_pts[i][2] = cos(pitch)*za - sin(pitch)*ya +
            mz;
        rot_pts[i][1] = sin(pitch)*za + cos(pitch)*ya +
            my;
        vx[i] = d*rot_pts[i][0]/rot_pts[i][2]+off_x;
        vy[i] = -d*rot_pts[i][1]/rot_pts[i][2]+off_y;
    }
}

/*
    surface_test() = Tests whether surface is visible.
*/

float surface_test(float x1, float y1, float z1, float x2,
    float y2, float z2, float x3, float y3, float z3)
{
    float stest;
```

```
482       stest = x1*(y3*z2-y2*z3) - x2*(y3*z1 - y1*z3)
483           -x3*(y1*z2-y2*z1);
484       return (stest);
485   }
```

The section of code from line 45 through line 49 creates the second display. The *setMode* function is called in line 45 to set the display to the 640 × 350 pixel × 16-color mode. In line 46, the color of the first line is set to dark gray (8). Lines 47 and 48 comprise a *for* loop that starts with the horizontal coordinate of a line at 0 and increases 91 pixels for each line drawn until the horizontal coordinate exceeds 640. At each iteration, the *line.draw* function is called to draw a line whose beginning and ending horizontal coordinates are the same, whose beginning vertical coordinate is 0, and whose ending coordinate is 349. After each *line.draw* call, the color is incremented so that the next line will be in the next color in the 16-color palette. The *draw* function is called with starting and ending coordinates; since the beginning and ending *x* coordinates are the same, the function will use the vertical line-drawing technique.

The section of code from line 55 through line 64 draws the third display. The *setMode* function is called in line 55 to set the display to the 320 × 200 pixel × 256-color mode. In line 56, the color of the first line is set to dark gray (8). Lines 57 through 62 comprise a *for* loop that starts with the horizontal coordinate of a line at 0 and increases 44 pixels for each of eight lines drawn. At each iteration, line 59 sets *PATTERN* to create a new line style. The *line.draw* function is then called to draw a line whose beginning and ending horizontal coordinates are the same, whose beginning vertical coordinate is 0 and whose ending coordinate is 199, and whose width is *i+1* pixels. Because the call to *line.draw* specifies a width parameter as well as the beginning and ending coordinates and the color, the version of *draw* that makes wide lines is used. After each *line.draw* call, the color is incremented so that the next line will be in the next color; since only colors 8 through 15 are used they will be the same as for 16-color modes. The *draw* function is called with starting and ending coordinates; since the beginning and ending *x* coordinates are the same, the function will use the vertical-line drawing technique. The final display has each line a different width, color, and style.

The code for the fourth display is listed in lines 71 through 81. The *setMode* function is called in line 71 to set the display to the 640 × 350 pixel × 16-

color mode. In line 73, the color of the first line is set to dark gray (8). Lines 74 through 79 comprise a *for* loop that starts with the horizontal coordinate of a line at 0 and increases 88 pixels for each of eight lines drawn. At each iteration, line 76 sets *PATTERN* to create a new line style. The *line.draw* function is then called to draw a line whose beginning and ending horizontal coordinates are the same, whose beginning vertical coordinate is 0 and ending coordinate is 349, and whose width is $i+1$ pixels. Because the call to *line.draw* specifies a width parameter as well as the beginning and ending coordinates and the color, the version of *draw* that makes wide lines is used. After each *line.draw* call, the color is incremented so that the next line will be in the next color in the 16-color palette. The *draw* function is called with starting and ending coordinates; since the beginning and ending x coordinates are the same, the function will use the vertical-line drawing technique. The final display has each line a different width, color, and style.

The code for fifth display is listed in lines 87 through 96. It is just the same as the code for the third display, except that each line is drawn with the beginning and ending y coordinates the same and the x coordinate changing, so that a set of wide horizontal lines is drawn using the 320 × 200 pixel × 256-color mode, with the width increasing for each line drawn.

The code for sixth display is listed in lines 102 through 112. It is just the same as the code for the fourth display, except that each line is drawn with the beginning and ending y coordinates the same and the x coordinate changing, so that a set of wide horizontal lines is drawn using the 640 × 350 pixel × 16-color mode with the width increasing for each line drawn.

The code for the seventh display is listed in lines 118 through 134. We're still using the same 640 × 350 pixel × 16-color mode used in the previous display, so we don't have to change the display mode. In line 118, the *cls* function is used to clear the screen to a blue backgound (color 1). Line 119 sets the initial line color to 0 (black). Lines 120 through 126 comprise a *for* loop that draws a series of vertical lines, cycling through the 16 colors. Each call of *line.draw* in line 122 causes the color value to increment. Line 123 takes the color modulo 16, so that when color reaches 16, it resets to 0. Lines 124 and 125 make sure the line color is never the same as the blue background color. In a similar manner, lines 127 through 133 comprise a *for* loop that draws a set of horizontal lines, each a different color. The result is a grid display.

Display 8 (code listed in lines 140 through 146) uses the wide version of the *draw* function to draw a 12-pixel-wide rectangle filling nearly the full screen. Line 140 sets the display to the 320 × 200 pixel × 256-color mode. Line 141 then clears the screen to a blue background. Lines 142 through 145 each draw one of the four lines that make up the rectangle. Note how the *x* and *y* coordinates of the lines are adjusted so that the rectangle will have square corners without any gaps.

Display 9 (code listed in lines 152 through 158) uses the wide version of the *draw* function to draw a 12-pixel-wide rectangle filling nearly the full screen. Line 152 sets the display to the 640 × 350 pixel × 16-color mode. Line 153 then clears the screen to a bright red background. Lines 154 through 157 each draw one of the four lines that make up the rectangle. Note how the *x* and *y* coordinates of the lines are adjusted so that the rectangle will have square corners without any gaps.

Display 10 (code listed in lines 164 through 176) uses the same display mode as the previous display. Line 164 clears the screen to a blue background. Lines 165 through 168 then draw a 10-pixel-wide bright cyan rectangle around the screen. Lines 169 through 175 comprise a *for* loop that includes line 171, which draws lines that start at the top left corner of the inside of the rectangle and extend to the right side of the rectangle at vertical positions from 30 pixels from the top to the bottom of the rectangle in steps of 20 pixels in color 13 (bright magenta). Line 172 draws lines that start at the bottom right corner of the inside of the rectangle and extend to the left side of the rectangle at vertical positions from 30 pixels from the top to the bottom of the rectangle in steps of 20 pixels in color 14 (yellow). Line 173 draws lines that start at the bottom right corner of the inside of the rectangle and extend to the left side of the rectangle at vertical positions from 30 pixels from the top to the bottom of the rectangle in steps of 20 pixels in color 10 (bright green). Lines 174 draws lines that start at the top right corner of the inside of the rectangle and extend to the left side of the rectangle at vertical positions from 30 pixels from the top to the bottom of the rectangle in steps of 20 pixels in color 12 (bright red). The resulting display is shown in Plate 2.

Display 11 (code listed in lines 182 through 195) creates a similar display using the 320 × 200 pixel × 256-color mode. The mode is set in line 182. Line 187 sets the initial value of *hue* (the line color) to 1 (dark blue). Lines 188 through 194 draw lines in the same way as was done in the previous display.

Instead of all lines from a given corner being drawn in the same color, the initial value of *hue* is incremented each time a line is drawn.

Display 12 (code listed in lines 201 through 214) uses the 640 × 480 pixel × 16-color mode 105H. Otherwise, it is just the same as Display 11.

Display 13 (code listed in lines 220 through 237) shows one way of using the *line.draw* function where the specified parameters are four integers (the starting *x* and *y* coordinates, the line length, and the color) and one floating-point number (the direction angle of the line). Line 220 sets the display to the 640 × 350 pixel × 16-color display mode. Line 221 begins a *while* loop that creates a new display whenever *ch* is not the Enter key. The loop begins by clearing the screen to a blue background in line 223. Line 224 begins a *for* loop that draws 80 figures to the screen. In line 226 the initial line length for the figure is randomly selected to be a value between 20 and 100. In lines 227 through 229 the color is selected to be a value from 0 to 15, excluding 1 (the background color). In line 230, the starting *x* coordinate is set to be somewhere on the screen, and in line 231 the starting *y* coordinate is similarly set. Line 232 begins a *for* loop that first draws a horizontal line from the starting point for the selected length. It then draws additional lines, each one having its direction angle increased by 15 degrees and its length decreased by 1/1.02, until the angle has moved through one revolution. The actual drawing of each line takes place in lines 233 and 234. When the two *for* loops are done, there is a display of 80 starburst figures. This display is shown in Plate 3. The program then waits for a character to be typed on the keyboard. If the key struck is the Enter key, the program continues to the next display; otherwise, another version of the current display is created.

Joining Wide-Line Segments

As long as we are connecting line segments that are one pixel wide, we have no problems. When we start joining wide lines, however, the process which seems intuitively so simple when we are creating joined line segments with a paint brush, becomes exceedingly difficult with a computer. Depending upon the angle at which two lines are joined, there is a gap or an overlap if we simply give the ending coordinates of one line segment as the beginning coordinates for the next one. Display 14 (code in lines 243 through 253) is an example of the kind of difficulties we encounter. All the line segments are 16 pixels wide and all except the first are drawn using the version of *line.draw* that makes use of the internally stored beginning coordinates (which are the end coordinates of the previous line) and specifies only the end coordinates, color, and width. There are various ways that we could modify the wide-line drawing algorithm to change the way the end and beginning of a wide line are created depending upon the angle between the line and the adjacent line segment, but they are very complicated. In most cases, you will find the best solution is to specify both the beginning and ending points for each line segment and modify them by trial and error to get a good fit.

In display 15 (code in lines 259 through 283), we draw a series of rectangles and their diagonals, beginning with one having single-pixel-width lines and going on up in steps of 1 pixel (remember however that only widths of an odd number of pixels are actually drawn) to 12 pixels. This display is typical of the problems that occur with joining wide lines without some form of adjustment. Incidently, with these particular figures it is very easy to adjust so that they look just fine.

The *sinc* ((sine x) / x) Function

The code in lines 289 through 308 shows the sixteenth display, an example of using short line segments to create a complex figure. Line 289 sets the 640 × 480 pixel × 16-color display mode. Line 290 clears the screen to a green background. Lines 291 through 305 comprise a *for* loop that generates 512 line segments. For each iteration of the loop, the end coordinates of the line segment are generated. The *xe* coordinate moves across the display horizontally in steps of 1/512 of the display width. The *ye* coordinate is found by multiplying the sine of the angle represented by *x* by a scale factor and dividing by *x*. For the first line segment only, the beginning coordinates are *(0,xe)*, which must be inserted after the first *xe* and *ye* are computed. For the remainder of the loop, the end coordinates are stored as the starting coordinates for the next line segment after each pair of line segments are drawn (lines 303 and 304). Since the function is symmetrical about the *y* axis, two calls to the line drawing function are made (one for *xs* and one for - *xs*) for each line-segment to be drawn (lines 301 and 302). After the loop is finished, the *x* and *y* axes are drawn in lines 306 and 307. The resulting graphic is shown in Plate 4.

Random Spirals

Display 17 (code in lines 314 through 340) is another example of using small line segments to create complex waveforms. The 640 × 480 pixel × 16-color mode is set in line 315, and *color* set to 1 in line 314. Then, a *for* loop begins in line 316 that creates 75 spirals. For each one, the size (computed from *denom*) and starting coordinates are found randomly as is *iter*, which determines how many revolutions of the spiral will be generated. In line 323, a line is drawn with the same starting and ending coordinates (so it is just a point) to establish the inner starting coordinates. The *for* loop that starts at line 324 then iterates for the specified number of revolutions (*iter*), and within this the *for* loop that begins at line 326 iterates once for each degree from 0 to 359. Within this loop, the endpoints for the line segment are computed. The *line.draw* function is then called in line 332 to draw the line segment. After the pair of inner *for* loops have finished with a spiral the color is incremented (or reset to 1 if it is 16 or greater) and the program returns to the beginning of the outer *for* loop (line 316) to determine the initial values for a new spiral. When the outer *for* loop is complete, we have a display of 75 spirals.

Wire Frame Sphere

Display 18 lists the code to draw a wire frame sphere (lines 346 through 446). Line 346 sets the mode to 800 × 600 pixels × 256 colors. Line 347 clears the screen to dark blue. The color, sphere radius, and viewing angles are then set. Next, in lines 352 through 357, the sines and cosines of the viewing angles are computed. From line 358 through line 446, the program goes through the process of computing triangles and quadralaterals that make up the sphere. We won't get into detail here, since Chapter 23 will describe solid-state modeling in detail. We are mainly trying to show here that a good representation of a sphere can be created with line segments. Two other functions are used. The first, *perspective*, rotates each point on the the sphere in accordance with the specified roll, yaw, and pitch angles and then converts from three dimensions into a two-dimensional perspective view. The second function, *surface_test*, takes one of the triangles or quadralaterals that make up the sphere and tests whether it is visible to the viewer. If so, its bounding lines are drawn to the screen; if the surface test fails, the figure is not drawn. You might want to put the statement:

```
sp = -1;
```

before each of the three *if* tests of the *sp* parameter, thereby forcing all the hidden lines to be drawn. This will give you an idea of how they all look and will give you a clue as to why the program works so long before anything is drawn to the screen (it is computing hidden lines). The resulting wire frame sphere is shown in Plate 5.

Display Modes

As you look at the listing of the *LINETEST.CPP* program, you'll note that some of the displays make use of VESA modes that are not supported by earlier VGA cards. Because of the way the *graphics* module is designed, this doesn't pose a problem. Simply change any display mode that your equipment doesn't support to one that it does. The graphics will work just fine with the new mode.

13

Drawing and Filling Circles

Circles and ellipses are the most commonly used curves in graphics applications. In this chapter we are going to look at the theory involved in producing circles and develop some functions that produce fast and accurate figures. These functions compare favorably in speed with commercial drawing packages, but offer the flexibility to design functions exactly the way you want them instead of being constrained by the preferences of the program designers.

The circle functions are all part of the *graphics.cpp* module that was listed in Chapter 11 and thus will work with any display mode except the 24-bit color modes. The circle-drawing algorithm will work with these display modes too, but you'll have to write your own functions to pass three color bytes to the display. The *Circle* class and its functions are listed in line 953 through 1126 of Listing 11-1. You'll note that the circle-drawing algorithms are performed using the system coordinates; conversion to screen coordinates doesn't occur until we are ready to plot a pixel to the screen. This means that we may calculate the coordinates of several points that end up being plotted to the same pixel location, which slows down the circle drawing somewhat. However, this does handle the problem of pixels that are not square. Remember that the display screen is a rectangle having the aspect of 4 to 3. Thus, if the screen is divided into squares, a screen that has 640 pixels in the horizontal direction should have 480 pixels in the vertical direction. Unfortunately, not all display modes preserve this ratio; thus, for example, if we tried to use the circle algorithm on a screen having a resolution of 640 × 350 pixels (mode 10H), the circles would come out to be egg-shaped instead of round.

Table 13-1 shows the functions that are available in the *grqaphics.cpp* module for drawing circles.

Table 13-1. Circle Drawing Functions

Function Name	Transferred Parameters	Description
draw	int x, int y, int r, int color	Draws a circle using Bresenham's algorithm
draw	int x, int y, long int r, int color	Draws an improved- accuracy circle
draw	int x, int y, int r, int color, int width	Draws a circle of a specified width
fill	int x, int y, int r, int color	Fills a circle

Drawing Circles with Bresenham's Algorithm

Lines 970 through 1003 of Listing 11-1 draw a single-pixel-wide circle using Bresenham's algorithm, which was first described for drawing slanting lines in Chapter 12. The equation for a circle (assuming that the center is at the origin) is:

$$x^2 + y^2 = r^2$$

(Equation 13-1)

where x and y indicate the coordinates and r is the radius of the circle. Bresenham's algorithm requires the derivative of this equation, which can be expressed as:

$$dy = \frac{x}{y}dx$$

(Equation 13-2)

We are going to begin Bresenham's algorithm with a point on the circumference of the circle at *(0,r)*, as set up by lines 974 and 975. If we increase *px* by one pixel, then *py* decreases by *px/py* pixels. We are working with discrete values, so we need to set up a decision function (*sum* in line 976) in which we store decreases in *py* until we have accumulated one whole pixel, at which point we actually change the *py* value. The second part of Bresenham's algorithm involves modifying the decision function so that we don't have to worry about floating-point operations or divisions. We accomplish this by multiplying both sides of equation 13-2 by *-y*. We now have a decision function which we increase by *px* each time we increase *px* one pixel. When the decision function is greater than 0, we decrease *py* by one pixel and decrease the decision function by *py*. We do this in a *while* loop that encompasses lines 977 through 1002. From our starting point, the loop computes points for one octant of the circle. The whole of Bresenham's algorithm is included in lines 997 through 1001. Line 997 increases *sum* by *px* and then increments *px*. Line 998 checks *sum* to see if it exceeds 0; if so, *sum* is decreased by *py* and *py* is decremented in line 1000. The *while* loop only computes one octant of the circle. If we went further than the point where *px = py*, we would have to consider changes in the direction of *px* and *py* and of the decision function. Fortunately we can use the symmetry of a circle to plot eight octants of the circle while calculating the values of only one. Because this octant (from the radius making a 90-degree angle with the *x* axis to a 45-degree angle) is always increasing, *y* is always decreasing, and the decision function always changes in the same direction. All of the earlier part of the *while* loop is devoted to using the symmetry of a circle to combine *px* and *py* with the circle center coordinates *x* and *y* so as to obtain a location on the circumference for the corresponding point in each of the octants and to plot each point to the display. Note that the decision function, *sum*, starts with a value of *-r*. This ensures that we don't get an objectionable pip sticking out of the top of the circle due to the *y* coordinate being increased by one pixel on the very first iteration, even though it was too early for this to occur.

You may find that this *draw* function is perfectly adequate for all of your circle-drawing needs. However, there is a subtle problem with this implementation of the algorithm. When we decide to change the value of *y*, the decision function is almost always larger than 0, which means we are just a little late making the change. This means that our *y* values are always on or just inside the circle circumference, whereas we would like them to be half on each side of the line to give a correct average value. For large circles, you'll never notice the difference, but for very small circles, you will observe a rather objectionable squarish shape with the function just described.

Drawing Circles More Accurately

The function shown in lines 1008 through 1046 of Listing 11-1 provides a way of drawing a more accurate circle. We use the overloading of functions so that this function is automatically called if you specify the radius *r* as a long integer rather than a regular integer. The function begins in line 1012 by doubling the radius, and we then compute an octant of a circle that is twice the specified radius. Each time we change the decision function, we increase (or decrease) it once by the current coordinate value (line 1038), then increment the *px* coordinate (line 1038) and increase (or decrease) the decision function using the new coordinate value (line 1039). Effectively, the result is that of using the derivative at an average of the values it assumes at the two points. When we plot points to the circle, we use only half of the coordinate values (line 1017 activates lines 1018 through 1037 only for even values of *px*), so that the resulting octant has the actual radius initially specified. The coordinate values are plotted only when the most rapidly changing coordinate value is even, since these are the ones that represent the most accurate path for the circumference. When you run the test program, some examples, which will be described later, show you the difference between circles drawn with the two circle-drawing algorithms. If you decide you want to change from one to the other, it's a simple matter of casting the value of *r* to the proper type.

Drawing Wide-Line Circles

The preceding functions are fine for drawing circles that are one pixel wide, but they don't provide much help if you want to draw circles with wide lines. The function listed in lines 1051 through 1092 of Listing 11-1 will enable you to draw circles with any line width that you desire. One way of doing this is to provide a *for* loop that begins with the smallest-radius circle represented by the inside of the wide line and then draws a circle for each radius from this to the radius representing the outer edge of the wide line. Unfortunately, this does not result in a completely filled-in line, since drawing concentric circles with a one pixel difference in their radii doesn't guarantee that all pixels within the inner and outer boundary will be included. If you want to use this technique, you need to remove the *if* statement that permits only the correct even-valued coordinate sets from being plotted and use the second *draw* function so that there will be a lot of extra points plotted to fill in the gaps in the wide line. For best accuracy, however, this should not apply for the inner and outer boundary circles.

There is a better and faster way to accomplish the same result, however. You'll remember that we drew straight lines by drawing pixels on either side of the one-pixel line for cases where y was increasing faster than x and by drawing pixels above and below the one-pixel line for the opposite case. Fortunately, it is easy to identify which case is true for each octant of the circle and perform the proper operation. The only concern is whether the peculiar ends of each octant will meet properly or leave gaps. It turns out that in every case they overlap, so that the resulting circle is perfect. This technique doesn't leave any gaps inside the line, either. Again, we use function overloading so that this function is called automatically if you add a width parameter at the end of the parameters you are passing to the *draw* function.

Filling Circles

The function to produce filled-in circles is *fill*. It is listed in lines 1094 through 1126 of Listing 11-1. You'll observe that this is very similar to the second *draw* function, except that instead of plotting eight pixels at each iteration, (one for each of the eight octants that make up the circle) for four pairs of points, we determine the pair of points that are opposite each other on the same row of the circle and call *fillLine* to draw a fast horizontal line between them.

The *circle.cpp* Program

The program to test the circle-drawing and -filling functions is *circle.cpp*. It is given in Listing 13-1. I designed this program to use every display mode (except 24-bit color modes) of which my computer was capable. Before compiling it, you should look over the display modes and change any that your computer won't handle to ones that it will. If you're just going to run the executable version of the program, you are most likely to find that a display using a mode that your computer is to capable of handling will produce either a blank screen on the computer or an unsynched display. Modern monitors don't self-destruct when fed incorrect signals, but if an unsynched display does come up, hit a key quickly to go on to the next display with minimum strain to your computer.

Listing 13-1. The circle.cpp Program.

```
/*

        circle.cpp = Program to test circle drawing
                   using VGA and VESA modes

              By Roger T. Stevens  1-16-96

*/

#include "c:\cpphbook\program\graphics.cpp"

Graphics graphic;
Circle circle;

/*

                    MAIN PROGRAM

*/

void main(void)
{
    int i,j,x_cen, y_cen, radius,ran_param;
    unsigned int red, green, blue;

    double angle= 222.5, r, phi, rad;

/*

                    Display 1

        320 x 200 Pixel x 16 Color Mode 0DH

                 Draws a circle

*/

    graphic.setMode(0x0D);
    circle.draw(-40,20,400,11);
    getch();
```

```
/*
                     Display 2
       640 x 200 Pixel x 16 Color Mode 0EH
      Draws a circle with improved accuracy
*/
   graphic.setMode(0x0E);
   circle.draw(-40,20,400L,13);
   getch();

/*
                     Display 3
       640 x 350 Pixel x 2 Color Mode 0FH
      Draws a circle with improved accuracy
*/

   graphic.setMode(0x0F);
   circle.draw(-40,20,400L,13);
   getch();

/*
                     Display 4
       640 x 350 Pixel x 16 Color Mode 10H
 Superimposes an improved accuracy circle on a regular
                      circle.
*/

   graphic.setMode(0x10);
   circle.draw(-40,20,400,14);
   circle.draw(-40,20,400L,10);
   getch();
```

```
/*
                  Display 5
    640 x 480 Pixel x 16 Color Mode 12H
         Draws 50 concentric circles.
*/

    graphic.setMode(0x12);
    for (i=4; i<400; i+=8)
        circle.draw(-40,20,i,i%15+1);
    getch();

/*
                  Display 6
    320 x 200 Pixel x 256 Color Mode 13H
    Draws a circle with improved accuracy
*/

    graphic.setMode(0x13);
    circle.draw(-40,20,400L,13);
    getch();

/*
                  Display 7
    640 x 400 Pixel x 256 Color Mode 100H
 Draws 50 improved accuracy concentric circles
*/

    graphic.setMode(0x100);
    for (i=4; i<400; i+=8)
        circle.draw(-40,20,(long)i,(i%15)+1);
    getch();
```

```
/*
                         Display 8
         640 x 480 Pixel x 256 Color Mode 101H
               Draws two very small circles
*/
    graphic.setMode(0x101);
    circle.draw(40,20,12,10);
    circle.draw(-40,20,12L,14);
    getch();

/*
                         Display 9
         800 x 600 Pixel x 256 Color Mode 103H
          Draws 17 concentric 10 wide circles
*/
    graphic.setMode(0x103);
    for (i=0; i<17; i++)
    {
       circle.draw(0,0,28*i + 20,i,10);
    }
    getch();

/*
                         Display 10
        1024 x 768 Pixel x 256 Color Mode 105H
  Draws 100 Circles with Random Center, Random Radius,
                   and Varying Colors.
*/
    graphic.setMode(0x105);
    for (i=0; i<100; i++)
    {
       circle.draw(rand()/26 - 640, rand()/34 -480,
```

```
            (long)rand()/68, i%15 + 1);
    }
    getch();

/*
                     Display 11
     640 x 480 Pixel x 32K Color Mode 110H
        Random sets of Concentric Circles.
*/

    graphic.setMode(0x110);
    for (i=0; i<30; i++)
    {
        x_cen = rand()/26 - 640;
        y_cen = rand()/34 - 480;
        radius = (rand() & 0x0F) + 10;
        color = rand();
        if (color == 0)
         color = 31;
        for (j=1; j<10; j++)
        {
            circle.draw(x_cen, y_cen, long((radius *
                j)), color);
        }
    }
    getch();

/*
                     Display 12
     800 x 600 Pixel x 32K Color Mode 113H
              Draws a Filled Circle.
*/

    graphic.setMode(0x113);
    circle.fill(-40,20,400,0x3FF);
    getch();
```

```
/*
        Display 13

  1024 x 768 Pixel x 32K Color Mode 116H

     Draws a Filled Circle.
*/

    graphic.setMode(0x116);
    circle.fill(-40,20,400,0xF114);
    getch();
/*
        Display 14

  640 x 480 Pixel x 64K Color Mode 111H

Draws 50 Circles with Random Center, Radius and color
*/

    graphic.setMode(0x111);
    for (i=0; i<50; i++)
    {
        red = rand() & 0x1F;
        green = rand() & 0x3F;
        blue = rand() & 0x1F;
        color = (red << 11) | (green << 5) | blue;

        circle.draw(rand()/26 - 640,
rand()/34 - 480,rand()/68,
            color,rand()/820);
    }
    getch();


/*
        Display 15

  800 x 600 Pixel x 64K Color Mode 114H

Draws 50 Circles with Random Center, Radius and
       Width and Varying Colors.
```

```
*/

    graphic.setMode(0x114);

    for (i=0; i<50; i++)
    {
        red = rand() & 0x1F;
        green = rand() & 0x3F;
        blue = rand() & 0x1F;
        color = (red<<11) | (green<<5) | blue;
        circle.draw(rand()/26 - 640,
rand()/34-480,rand()/68,
            color,rand()/820);
    }
    getch();

/*
                        Display 16

          1024 x 768 Pixel x 64K color Mode 117H

        Draws 70 Filled Circles with Random Center,
                 Radius and Varying Color.
*/

    graphic.setMode(0x117);
    for (i=0; i<70; i++)
    {
        red = rand() & 0x1F;
        green = rand() & 0x3F;
        blue = rand() & 0x1F;
        color = (red<<11) | (green<<5) | blue;
        circle.fill(rand()/26 - 640,
rand()/34-480,rand() & 0x7F,
            color);
    }
    getch();
```

```
195    /*
                    Display 17

         640 x 480 Pixel x 16 Color Mode 12H

                Draws a Filled Circle.
199    */
200        graphic.setMode(0x12);
201        circle.fill(-40,20,400,0x11);
202        getch();
203    /*
                    Display 18

         800 x 600 Pixel x 256 Color Mode 103H

                Draws Sunflower seeds.
207    */
208        graphic.setMode(0x103);
209        for (j=0; j<2; j++)
210        {
211            graphic.cls(1);
212            for (r=20.,phi=0.0, rad=2; r<470;
213        r*=1.004,phi+=angle,rad*=1.002)
214            {
215                x_cen = r*cos(0.017453292*phi);
216                y_cen = -r*sin(0.017453292*phi);
217                color = rand() & 0x0F;
218                if (color == 1)
219                    color++;
220                circle.fill(x_cen,y_cen,rad,color);
221            }
222            getch();
223            angle+= 0.1;
224        }
225        graphic.setMode(3);
226    }
```

Drawing Circles

Display 1 (lines 17 through 19, simply draws a large circle on the screen using the 320 × 200 pixel × 16-color display mode 0DH using the first *draw* function. Display 2 (lines 25 through 27) uses the improved-accuracy *draw* function to draw the same sized circle using 640 × 200 pixel × 16-color display mode 0EH. This same circle is drawn in the 640 × 350 pixel × 2-color (black-and-white) display mode 0FH in Display 3 (lines 33 through 35). Display 4 (lines 42 through 45) uses the 640 × 350 pixel × 16-color mode to draw two circles. First, the first *draw* function is used to draw a circle in yellow. Then the same circle is drawn using the improved-accuracy *draw* function and superimposed on the other circle in green. You should be able to examine the differences and see which method you prefer to use for your circle-drawing projects. Display 5 (lines 51 through 54) uses a *for* loop and the first *draw* function to draw 50 concentric circles, each having a different color and a radius 8 units larger than the previous one. Display mode 12H, 640 × 480 pixels × 16-colors, is used. Display 6 (lines 60 through 62) uses display mode 13H, 320 × 200 pixels × 256 colors, to draw an improved accuracy circle. Display 7 (lines 68 through 71) uses a *for* loop and the improved-accuracy *draw* function to draw 50 concentric circles. Display 8 (lines 77 through 80) draws two very small circles using the 640 × 480 pixel × 256-color mode (mode 101H). The green circle is drawn using the first *draw* function and the yellow circle is drawn using the improved-accuracy *draw* function. At this point, we might well be leaning toward drawing all our circles with the first function, which is much simpler. After looking at a number of circles drawn with each method, it should be evident that for small circles, there is an objectionable squareness to circles drawn with first *draw* function. You'll note that as the circles become large, there isn't very much difference between the two functions. Display 9 (lines 86 through 91) draws a set of 16 concentric circles having a line width of ten, using display mode 103H, 800 pixels × 600 pixels × 256 colors.

Display 10 (lines 98 through 104) uses a *for* loop to draw 100 circles using the first *draw* function. The center coordinates and radius of each circle are set randomly. The color is cycled from 1 through 15. Display mode 105H, 1024 pixels × 768 pixels × 256 colors, is used. Display 11 (lines 110 through 125) makes use of the first *draw* function and two nested *for* loops to draw randomly located and sized sets of 10 concentric circles, all members of each set having the same color but the color changing randomly from set to set. Display mode 110H, 640 pixels × 480 pixels × 32K-colors, is used. Display 12 (lines 131 through 133) draws a filled circle using the *fill* function and display mode 113H, 800 pixels × 600 pixels × 32K-colors. Display 13 (lines 139 through 141) draws a filled circle using the *fill* function and display mode 116H, 1024 pixels × 768 pixels × 32K-colors. Display 14 (lines 148 through 159) draws 50 randomly centered and sized circles using display mode 111H,

640 pixels × 480 pixels × 64K colors. The red, green, and blue components of each color are selected randomly and combined to form the color variable. Note that in the 64-color modes, red and blue have a range of 32 colors while green has a range of 64 colors. The random values are limited to the proper range by an AND operation to eliminate the higher-order bits. (A well-behaved random number has each bit occurring randomly, so that by chopping off the higher bits, a random number over a lower range is obtained.)

Display 15 (lines 166 through 177) uses the 800 pixel × 600 pixel × 64K-color mode 114H to display 50 circles having random center, radius, and width. The colors are formed randomly using the same technique described for display 14. This display is shown in Plate 6. Display 16 uses the *fill* function to display 70 filled circles using display mode 117H, 1024 pixels × 768 pixels × 64K-colors. This display is shown in Plate 7. Display 17 just draws a filled circle using the *fill* function and display mode 12H, 640 pixels × 480 pixels × 16-colors.

Display 18 is a very interesting one. We start with a small circle whose center is defined in polar coordinates. We then draw another circle at a slightly larger distance and of slightly larger radius and displaced from the previous circle location by 222.5 degrees. This is the *golden angle*. It is found by taking the golden mean:

$$\frac{\sqrt{5}-1}{2}$$

and multiplying it by 360 degrees. The resulting picture is shown in Plate 8. It is similar to the structure of seeds in a sunflower. To the eye, it appears somewhat random. We now run the same code again, but change the angle to 222.6 degrees. The eye now sees a pronounced spiral structure, as shown in Plate 9.

Apollonian Packing of Circles

An interesting fractal, known as the Apollonian packing of circles, provides an excellent test of the circle-filling function. In fact, using this program for testing, a major error in the first version of the circle-filling function was discovered. This test program is given in Listing 13-2. One must start out with defining three circles that are tangental to each other. The method I used was to set up a small program to draw and fill the three circles and experiment with their placing until they were somewhat of the size and in the proper locations that I desired. I then froze the values for the center coordinates of the first circle and the radii of the three circles and then calculated where the centers of the second and third circles had to be for all three circles to be tangental. You don't need to go through this, since the proper locations for the three initial circles have already been calculated and are in the program. The result after drawing the first three circles is that a curvilinear triangle is found to be formed by the meeting of the three circles. The program then finds the largest circle that can be drawn within this triangle, making it tangental to each of the three original circles. The math for this is a little complex. It makes use of a relationship called Soddy's formula, which states:

$$2\left(\frac{1}{a^2}+\frac{1}{b^2}+\frac{1}{c^2}+\frac{1}{r^2}\right)=\frac{1}{a}+\frac{1}{b}+\frac{1}{c}+\frac{1}{r}$$

(Equation 13-3)

You'll find all of the mathematical equations in the program listing if you are interested in pursuing the matter. At any rate, creating this new circle produces three more curvilinear triangles. We then fill each one with the largest possible circle, creating three new curvilinear triangles in each, and continue doing this for as long as we want to (in this program we do it eight times). Each circle is filled with a different color. The result is the interesting display shown in Plate 10.

Listing 13-2. apollon.cpp *Program for Apollonian Packing of Circles*

```
/*
 ┌──────────────────────────────────────────────────────────────┐
 │                                                              │
 │          apollon = APOLLONIAN PACKING OF CIRCLES             │
 │                                                              │
 │              By Roger T. Stevens   2-20-96                   │
 │                                                              │
 └──────────────────────────────────────────────────────────────┘
*/
```

```
#include "c:\cpphbook\program\graphics.cpp"

Graphics graphic;
Circle circle;

void rep_circle(float xa,float ya,float a,float xb,float
    yb, float b,float xc,float yc,float c, int level);

int level = 9;


main()
{
    float a=1250, b=1000, c=2090, xa=-1360, xb=890,
    xc=120, ya=554, yb=552, yc=-2440, temp;
    color = 14;
    graphic.setMode(0x12);
    circle.fill(xa,ya,a,color--);
    circle.fill(xb,yb,b,color--);
    circle.fill(xc,yc,c,color--);
    rep_circle(xa,ya,a,xb,yb,b,xc,yc,c,level);
    getch();
}

void rep_circle(float xa,float ya,float a,float xb,float
    yb, float b,float xc,float yc,float c, int level)
{
    float s, xs, ys, mult;

    level--;
    s = 1/(1/a + 1/b + 1/c + 2*(sqrt(1/(b*c) + 1/(c*a) +
        1/(a*b))));
    mult = (s+a)*(s+a) - (s+b)*(s+b) - xa*xa + xb*xb -
    ya*ya + yb*yb;
    ys = (mult*(xc-xa) - (xb - xa)*((s+a)*(s+a) -
(s+c)*(s+c) - xa*xa + xc*xc - ya*ya +
yc*yc))/(2*((yb-ya)*(xc-xa) - (yc-ya)*
        (xb - xa)));
    xs = (mult - 2*ys*(yb - ya))/(2*(xb - xa));
    color--;
    if (color == 0)
        color = 15;
    circle.fill(xs,ys,s,color);
    color--;
    if (color == 0)
        color = 15;
    if (level > 0)
    {
        rep_circle(xa,ya,a,xb,yb,b,xs,ys,s,level);
        rep_circle(xb,yb,b,xc,yc,c,xs,ys,s,level);
        rep_circle(xa,ya,a,xc,yc,c,xs,ys,s,level);
    }
}
```

14

Drawing and Filling Ellipses

Specifying the parameters for drawing a circle is easy. All you have to do is identify the coordinates for the circle's center and specify the radius. When we attempt to define an ellipse, things become much more complicated. Unlike the circle, which is symmetrical, the ellipse has a shape. It is long in one direction and short in the other. There are several ways in which we can specify this. One is to define an x-axis value, which is the distance from the center of the ellipse to its circumference along the x axis, and a y-axis value, which is the distance from the center of the ellipse to its circumference along the y axis. These values, along with the coordinates of the center of the ellipse, are sufficient to completely define the ellipse. Another way to define the ellipse is to define the coordinates of the upper left corner and lower right corner of a rectangle, with the ellipse being tangent to all four sides of the rectangle. These techniques define a well-behaved ellipse whose focii are on one of the two coordinate systems axes. Unlike the circle, however, the ellipse can be rotated and appears different at each orientation. If we are going to allow rotation, the generation of the ellipse becomes much more complex, and we also have to specify the orientation angle. Finally, we may not want to use either of these methods for describing the ellipse, but may want to specify a point on the circumference of the ellipse at the end of one axis along with the two axis values. All of these techniques for defining an ellipse are included in the function definitions for the *Ellipse* class, which are given in Listing 11-1, lines 1130 through 1584. If you're creating you own *Ellipse* class, you don't need to use all these functions; you can include only those functions you need for your particular application. Table 14-1 shows the functions included in the *Ellipse* class.

Table 14-1. Ellipse Drawing Functions

Function Name	Transferred Parameters	Description
draw	int xl, int yt, int xr, int yb, int color, int width	Draws an ellipse of specified width in specified color by drawing a series of 1-pixel-wide ellipses. Ellipse is in a box specified by (xl,yt) and (xr, yb).
draw	int xl, int yt, int xr, int yb, int color, char width	Draws an ellipse of specified width in specified color by drawing wide lines. Ellipse is in a box specified by (xl,yt) and (xr, yb).
draw	int xl, int yt, int xr, int yb, float angle, int color	Draws an ellipse at specified angle in specified color. Ellipse is in a box specified by (xl,yt) and (xr, yb).
draw	int x, int y, int x_axis, int y_axis, float angle, long int color	Draws an ellipse having the following characteristics: (x,y) = point on y axis at end of x axis; x_axis = length of x axis; y_axis = length of y axis; angle = tilt angle of ellipse; color = color of ellipse
fill	int x, int y, int x_axis, int y_axis, float angle, int color	Fills an ellipse having the following characteristics: (x,y) = point on y axis at end of x axis; x_axis = length of x axis; y_axis = length of y axis; angle = tilt angle of ellipse; color = color of ellipse

Drawing Ellipses with Bresenham's Algorithm

The version of Bresnham's algorithm that we used for drawing circles is almost the same as the one needed for drawing ellipses. The equation for an ellipse (assuming that the center is at the origin) is:

$$\left(\frac{x}{a}\right)^2 + \left(\frac{y}{b}\right)^2 = 1$$

(Equation 14-1)

where x and y indicate the coordinates, a is the semi-major axis and b the semi-minor axis of the ellipse. Bresenham's algorithm requires the derivative of this equation, which can be expressed as:

$$dy = \frac{b^2 x}{a^2 y} dy$$

(Equation 14-2)

Comparing Equation 14-2 with Equation 13-2, we see that we can use the very same algorithm for drawing ellipses that we used for drawing circles, except that there is a different multiplication factor each time we increase the *sum* decision variable.

Drawing a Wide-Line Ellipse in a Box

The first *draw* function for ellipses consists of lines 1148 through 1215 of Listing 11-1. It draws a wide line oval when the bounding rectangle is specified. The parameters that are sent to this function are the coordinates of the top left and bottom right corners of the bounding rectangle and the color. Lines 1153 and 1154 compute double the semi-major and semi-minor axes of the ellipse, compensating for line width, so that the ellipse that will be drawn first is that of the inside of the line width. Then the coordinates of the center of the ellipse (x,y) are computed from the rectangle definition coordinates in lines 1155 and 1156. Line 1157 begins a *for* loop that draws one-pixel-wide ellipses, increasing the axes of the ellipse by one pixel at each iteration until the desired width is achieved. Lines 1159 and 1160 find the squares of the double semi-major and semi-minor axes, as these will be needed repeatedly in computing the decision function. Except for the use of these as multipliers, the rest of the function proceeds exactly like the function for drawing an improved accuracy circle, except that the *while* loop of line 1164 iterates over a quarter of the ellipse rather than an eighth as was the case with the circle.

The *draw* function listed in lines 1219 through 1285 of Listing 11-1 is very similar to the function just described, except that it makes a single pass through the code, drawing wide lines instead of single pixels. This function, like the corresponding one for the circle, determines from the slope of the figure at any given point whether the wide line should be created by drawing additional pixels at either side of the current pixel on the screen or drawing additional pixels above and below the current pixel on the screen. You'll remember that in Chapter 12, when we discussed making wide straight lines, we commented on the difficulties of having wide-line ends terminate properly. This didn't give us any problems in drawing circles, since the overlap between the line segments that are drawn to make up the circle does not usually extend beyond the boundaries of the next line segment. (You may note, however, that if we draw a very small circle with a very wide line width, the inside of the circle appears a little more squarish than it should be.) The problem gets much worse when we are drawing ellipses. When using a wide line to draw an ellipse that is long in one direction and very narrow in the other, the line ends of the wide line extend beyond where they should be, resulting in some funny tails on the ellipse. If you want to use this function, you'll need to experiment with the types of ellipses that you want to draw and the desired line widths to determine if the results are acceptable. Most normal ellipses will be all right, so you may well decide that this is the function for you. If this function will not do, you can use instead the first *draw* function instead. It is a lot slower, but it draws a more accurate ellipse.

Drawing an Ellipse at an Angle

The function listed in lines 1290 through 1380 of Listing 11-1 draws an ellipse at any desired angle orientation. This is very useful, but unfortunately it can be done only with single-pixel-wide ellipses, because for wide lines, the transformations used to perform the rotation produce many unfilled holes within the wide line that cannot be eliminated easily. The parameters passed to the function are the bounding rectangle coordinates, the rotation angle, and the color. We are going to consider zero degrees of rotation as the position of the unrotated ellipse that is drawn by the two functions previously described. We then rotate around the center of the ellipse in a counterclockwise direction. To do this, we have to transform every point that we plot using a standard coordinate rotation transformation that requires a sine and cosine. We need to do this in the most efficient manner possible to minimize the amount of time required to draw the ellipse. Essentially, this means that we need to use integer arithmetic and avoid any divisions, since division is a lengthy process, even with integers. We also need to observe that we require only enough accuracy in the sine and cosine functions to obtain the right coordinate value to the nearest pixel. All of this is accomplished by first obtaining the sine and cosine of the angle and creating from each an integer that is 512 times the actual value. This is accomplished in lines 1296 and 1297. Note that we can't use a shift rather than a multiplication because we are working with a fractional floating-point number. After we compute each point on the standard ellipse (lines 1311 and 1312), we use the sine and cosine of the rotation angle to perform the proper transformation to obtain the new set of coordinates after the ellipse is rotated. We do this by multiplying by the integer functions that we computed earlier and then shifting the result to the right by nine bit positions, which is effectively a division by 512. This takes place in lines 1313 through 1320. It gives us the same result as if we had done a floating-point operation using the sine or cosine. However, this technique is much faster and produces a complete tilted ellipse in a reasonable amount of time.

Ellipse Tilted from the End

he ellipse *draw* function just described rotates an ellipse around the center. Often, however, it is more convenient to specifiy an ellipse that is rotated around one end. The function listed in lines 1390 through 1477 of Listing 11-1 does this. If you compare the listing of this function with that of the one just described, you'll see that they are very similar in many ways. The main differences are that we pass to the new function the coordinates of a point at the left end of the x axis of the ellipse, instead of the center, and that we perform the rotation in such a way that the new coordinates for each point on the ellipse are computed in a coordinate system that has its origin at the position defined by this set of coordinates rather than having it at the center of the ellipse.

Filling a Tilted Ellipse

This function is very useful for creating such things as the petals of flowers. It is listed in lines 1486 through 1584. The function, like that just described, is passed the coordinates of a point at the left end of the x axis of the ellipse, the values of the x and y axes, a tilt angle, and the desired color. At the very beginning of the function, we have a new array that consists of 2 by 1024 elements (line 1492). This is adequate for the highest-resolution VESA Super VGA display, which has a maximum of 1024 lines. The $(0,n)$ element of the array represents the value of *x* for the lefthand boundary of the ellipse at the *y* value of *n*. The *(1,n)* element of the array represents the value of *x* for the right-hand boundary of the ellipse at the *y* value of *n*. The array is initialized with the left-hand boundaries all set to 1000 and the right-hand boundaries all set to -1000 (lines 1494 through 1498). The function then proceeds to compute the points on the circle boundary in the same way as the previous program, except that instead of plotting them to the screen, it performs a *compare* operation on each point. This operation, which is defined in the *graphics.cpp* module, compares the current point with *coord[0][y]* and *coord[1][y]*, where *y* indicates the vertical coordinate of the current point. If the *x* coordinate is smaller than the value for the lefthand boundary, it replaces that value; if it is larger than the value for the righthand boundary, it replaces that value. Another *compare* is then performed, which replaces *minrow* or *maxrow* with the *y* coordinate of the current point if it is smaller than the first or larger than the second. All this takes place in a *while* loop that begins at line 1508 and ends at line 1541 and another *while* loop that occupies lines 1545 through 1578. Note that we can't make use of the symmetry of the ellipse in this function, so we have to use Bresenham's algorithm for the whole thing. This requires two *while* loops; one is used when *asq*px* is greater than or equal to *bsq*py* and the other when it is less. At the end of this process, we have in *minrow* the smallest value of *y* for the ellipse and in *maxrow* the largest value of *y*. In all of the members of the *coord* array that are between these *y* values, we have the minimum value of *x* for the ellipse in *coord[0][y]* and the maximum value of *x* for the ellipse in *coord[1][y]*. Line 1579 begins a for loop that, for each row between *minrow* and *maxrow*, draws a horizontal line between the minimum and maximum values of *x* as specified by the appropriate members of the *coord* array in the designated color. The result is a filled oval.

The *ovalchk.cpp* Program

The program *ovalchk.cpp* is used to demonstrate various examples of drawing and filling ellipses. It is given in Listing 14-1. The program displays a number of screens that demonstrate the proper operation of the ellipse drawing and filling functions. Display 1 (lines 16 through 21) shows three interlocking circles drawn with the first ellipse *draw* function using display mode 10H, 640 pixels × 350 pixels × 16 colors. Display 2 (lines 27 through 35) shows three pairs of ellipses drawn with the second ellipse *draw* function using display mode 12H, 640 pixels × 480 pixels × 16 colors. One ellipse in each pair has the *x* axis the long axis and the *y* axis the short axis, while the other has the *x* axis the short axis and the *y* axis the long axis. Display 3 (lines 41 through 55) draws 80 single-pixel-wide ellipses with the second *draw* function, with the center coordinates and the two axes for each ellipse set randomly. This display uses display mode 103H, 800 pixels × 600 pixels × 256 colors. Display 4 (lines 61 through 76) draws 80 ellipses with the second *draw* function, using display mode 105H, 1024 pixels × 768 pixels × 256 colors. The center coordinates, the two axes for each ellipse, and the line width are set randomly. Display 5 (lines 83 through 87) compares two long narrow ellipses with wide lines using display mode 12H, 640 pixels × 480 pixels × 16 colors. The first ellipse (in magenta) uses the first *draw* function. The second ellipse (in red) uses the second *draw* function. You can see the objectionable tails produced by the second function. Display 6 (lines 93 through 96) uses the third (rotated) *draw* function to draw an unrotated ellipse using display mode 12H, 640 pixels × 480 pixels × 16 colors). Display 7 (lines 102 and 103) uses the same display mode and does not clear the screen from the previous display. Instead, the same ellipse is superimposed on the display using a different color and rotating it 90 degrees.

Listing 14-1. The ovalchk.cpp Program

```
    /*

    ovalchk = Program to check algorithms for drawing and
                  filling ovals.
              By Roger T. Stevens  2-20-96

    */
1   #include "c:\cpphbook\program\graphics.cpp"
2   Graphics graphic;
3   Ellipse ellipse;
4   Line line;
5   /*

                       MAIN PROGRAM

7   */
```

```
void main(void)
{
   int i, x, y, xc, yc, xa, ya, angle;

/*

                    Display 1

       640 x 350 Pixel x 16 Color Mode 10H

    Circles Drawn With Ellipse draw Function.

*/
   graphic.setMode(0x10);
   graphic.cls (1);
   ellipse.draw(-540,380,-60,-100,14,1);
   ellipse.draw(-240,100,240,-380,14,1);
   ellipse.draw(60,380,540,-100,14,1);
   getch();

*/

                    Display 2

       640 x 480 Pixel x 16 Color Mode 12H

               3 Pairs of Ellipses

/*

   graphic.setMode(0x12);
   graphic.cls(1);
   ellipse.draw(-420,380,-180,-100,14,(char)1);
   ellipse.draw(-120,100,120,-380,14,(char)1);
   ellipse.draw(180,380,420,-100,14,(char)1);
   ellipse.draw(-540,260,-60,20,14,(char)1);
   ellipse.draw(-240,-20,240,-260,14,(char)1);
   ellipse.draw(60,260,540,20,14,(char)1);
   getch();
```

```
/*
                    Display 3
      800 x 600 Pixel x 256 Color Mode 103H
                80 Random Ellipses.
*/
    graphic.setMode(0x103);
    graphic.cls(1);
    color = rand() & 0x0F;
    for (i=0; i<80; i++)
    {
        color = color%16;
        if (color == 1)
            color++;
        xc = rand()/26 - 640;
        yc = rand()/34- 480;
        xa = xc + 80 + rand()/52;
        ya = yc - 80 - rand()/68;
        ellipse.draw(xc, yc, xa, ya,color++,(char)1);
    }
    getch();
/*
                    Display 4
      1024 x 768 Pixel x 256 Color Mode 105H
      80 Random Ellipses with Random Widths
*/
    graphic.setMode(0x105);
    graphic.cls(1);
    color = rand() & 0x0F;
    for (i=0; i<80; i++)
    {
        color = color%16;
        if (color == 1)
            color++;
        xc = rand()/26 - 640;
        yc = rand()/34 - 480;
        xa = xc + 80 + rand()/52;
        ya = yc - 80 - rand()/68;
        ellipse.draw(xc, yc, xa, ya,color++,(char)(rand()
            & 0x1F));
    }
```

```
    getch();

/*
            Display 5
    640 x 480 Pixel x 16 Color Mode 12H
Comparing Wide Ellipses by Two Different Drawing
            Methods.
*/

    graphic.setMode(0x12);
    graphic.cls(1);
    ellipse.draw(-400,180,400,100,13,40);
    ellipse.draw(-400,-100,400,-180,12,(char)40);
    getch();

/*
            Display 6
    640 x 480 Pixel x 16 Color Mode 12H
  Draw ordinary ellipse with angle function.
*/

    graphic.cls(1);
    color = 3;
    ellipse.draw(-400,200,400,-200,(float)0.0,color++);
    getch();

/*
            Display 7
    640 x 480 Pixel x 16 Color Mode 12H
  Draw 90 degree ellipse with angle function.
*/

    ellipse.draw(-400,200,400,-200,(float)90.0,color++);
    getch();
```

```
/*
        Display 8
        1024 x 768 Pixel x 256 Color Mode 105H
        Big and Little Ellipses
*/
    graphic.setMode(0x105);
    color = 9;
    graphic.cls(1);
    ellipse.draw(-4,2,4,-2,color++,(char)1);
    ellipse.draw(-636,476,636,-476,color,(char)1);
    getch();
/*
        Display 9
        320 x 200 Pixel x 256 Color Mode 13H
        Two wide ellipses.
*/
    graphic.setMode(0x13);
    graphic.cls(1);
    ellipse.draw(-400,300,400,-300,12,(char)12);
    ellipse.draw(-616,456,616,-456,13,(char)12);
    getch();

/*
        Display 10
        800 x 600 Pixel x 256 Color Mode 103H
        Ellipses Rotated Around Center in 15 Degree Steps.
*/
    graphic.setMode(0x103);
    graphic.cls(1);
```

```
    color = 3;
    for (i=0; i<180; i+=15)
    {
        ellipse.draw(-400,200,400,-200,(float)i,color++);
    }
    getch();

/*
            Display 11

    640 x 480 Pixel x 16 Color Mode 12H

 Rotate Smaller Ellipses in 15 Degree Steps.
*/

    graphic.setMode(0x12);
    graphic.cls(1);
    color = 3;
    for (i=0; i<360; i+=15)
    {
        ellipse.draw(-240,100,240,-100,(float)i,color++);
        if (color == 1)
            color++;
    }
    getch();

/*
            Display 12

    640 x 480 Pixel x 16 Color Mode 12H

 Rotate Small Ellipses Centered at Upper Right.
*/

    graphic.cls(1);
    color = 3;
    for (i=0; i<360; i+=15)
    {
        ellipse.draw(-440,300,40,100,(float)i,color++);
        if (color == 1)
            color++;
    }
    getch();
```

```
/*
        Display 13

        640 x 350 Pixel x 16 Color Mode 10H

        Rotate Ellipses in 15 Degree Steps Around One End.
*/

    graphic.setMode(0x10);
    graphic.cls(1);
    color = 3;
    for (i=0; i<360; i+=15)
        ellipse.draw(0,0,400,200,(float)i,(long
            int)color++);
    getch();


/*
        Display 14

        640 x 480 Pixel x 16 Color Mode 12H

        Fills Ellipse and Outlines It.
*/

    graphic.setMode(0x12);
    graphic.cls(6);
    color = 13;
    ellipse.fill(-454,-300,910,496,45.0,(long)color);
    color = 15;
    ellipse.draw(-454,-300,910,496,45.0,(long int)color);
    getch();

/*
        Display 15

        640 x 480 Pixel x 16 Color Mode 12H

        "He loves me, he loves me not"
        Daisy with two petals plucked.
*/
```

```
        graphic.cls(1);
        line.draw(0,80,-40,-479,2,18);
        for (i=0,angle=0; angle < 360; i++,angle += 30)
        {
            if (angle == 210)
            {
                x = int(60. * cos(angle * 0.017453292) -150);
                y = int(160. + 60. * sin(angle * 0.017453292)
                    - 100);
            }
            else
            {
                if (angle == 240)
                {
                    x = int(60. * cos(angle * 0.017453292)
                    -120);
                    y = int(160. + 60. * sin(angle *
                0.017453292) - 140);
                }
                else
                {
                    x = int(60. * cos(angle * 0.017453292));
                    y = int(160. + 60. * sin(angle *
                0.017453292));
                }
            }
            if ((i%2) == 0)
                color = 14;
            else
                color = 15;
            ellipse.fill(x,y,200,100,angle,(long int)color);
        }
        ellipse.fill(-60,160,128,128,0.0,(long int)6);
        getch();

    */
```

Display 16

640 x 480 Pixel x 16 Color Mode 12H

Three Daisies.

```
    /*

        graphic.cls(1);
        line.draw(0,200,-80,-478,2,9);
        line.draw(-410,60,-76,-430,2,9);
```

```
239         line.draw(390,-70,-75,-390,2,9);
240         for (angle=0; angle < 360; angle += 60)
241         {
242             x = int(60. * cos(angle * 0.017453292));
243             y = int(200. + 60. * sin(angle * 0.017453292));
244             ellipse.fill(x,y,200,100,angle,(long int)14);
245             x = int(40. * cos(angle * 0.017453292));
246             y = int(200. + 40. * sin(angle * 0.017453292));
247             ellipse.fill(x-410,y-140,160,60,angle,(long
248             int)14);
249             ellipse.fill(x+390,y-270,160,60,angle,(long
250             int)14);
251         }
252         for (angle=30; angle < 360; angle += 60)
253         {
254             x = int(60. * cos(angle * 0.017453292));
255             y = int(200. + 60. * sin(angle * 0.017453292));
256             ellipse.fill(x,y,200,100,angle,(long int)15);
257             x = int(40. * cos(angle * 0.017453292));
258             y = int(200. + 40 * sin(angle * 0.017453292));
259             ellipse.fill(x-410,y-140,160,60,angle,(long
260                 int)15);
261             ellipse.fill(x+390,y-270,160,60,angle,(long
262             int)15);
263         }
264         ellipse.fill(-60,200,128,128,0.0,(long int)6);
265         ellipse.fill(-470,60,110,110,0.0,(long int)6);
266         ellipse.fill(330,-70,110,110,0.0,(long int)6);
267         getch();
268     }
```

Display 8 (lines 109 through 114) draws a very small and a very large ellipse using the second *draw* function and display mode 105H, 1024 pixels × 768 pixels × 256 colors. Display 9 (lines 120 through 124) draws two wide ellipses using the second *draw* function and display mode 13H, 320 pixels × 200 pixels × 256 colors. Display 10 (lines 130 through 137) uses display mode 103H, 800 pixels × 600 pixels × 256 colors, and the third (rotating) *draw* function to create a series of ellipses with angles of rotation in 15-degree increments. Display 11 (lines 143 through 152) does essentially the same thing except that display mode 12H, 640 pixel × 480 pixel × 16 colors, is used and the ellipses are smaller. Display 12 (lines 158 through 166) is just the same as display 11, except that the box for the ellipse is in the top left quadrant of the screen rather than the center. Display 13 (lines 172 through 178) uses the fourth *draw* function (rotating around the end of the ellipse) to draw a set of rotated ellipses at 15-degree intervals from 0 to 345 degrees. The lefthand end of the x axis is at the middle of the screen, and the ellipses are rotated around this point. The 640 pixel × 350 pixel × 16-color mode 10H is used. Display 14 uses the *fill* function to fill an ellipse in magenta and then uses the fourth *draw* function to outline it in white. This shows up any discepencies between the functions. Display mode 12H, 640 pixels × 480 pixels × 16 colors, is used. Display 15 (lines 197 through 230) uses the *fill* function to draw a daisy with two petals plucked in reminiscence of the childhood game "He loves me, he loves me not." This graphic is shown in Plate 11. Display mode 12H is used. Display 16 (lines 236 through 268) uses the same display mode and the *fill* function to draw three daisies.

15

Drawing and Filling Circular Arcs

Many functions for drawing and filling arcs make use of floating-point operations, using the sine and cosine to determine points on the arc as the angle moves in increments from the specified starting angle to the specified ending angle. This results in a function that is sluggish, to say the least. Furthermore, the angle increment needed to ensure that every pixel on the arc is obtained varies with the radius of the circle, which introduces an additional complication. The technique that we will use here uses exactly the same algorithm that we used to generate a circle in Chapter 13 to compute the points on an octant of the arc and then modify this data to extend all eight octants. However, instead of actually plotting all of these points, we test each one to determine whether it is in the specified arc or not and plot only those points that are within the proper range. It is a bit complicated to sort out all of the tests that are needed, but once this is done, the function produces fast arcs. Even in the case of a very small arc (one or two degrees), where the function is at a disadvantage because it still has to compute all of the points in an octant, it is still much faster than functions that use floating-point operations.

The *Arc* class and all of the functions associated with it are given in Listing 11-1 of the *graphics* module, lines 1588 through 2026. Table 15-1 lists the public functions of the *Arc* class. There are also three private functions used solely in the production of arcs. These functions are not available for use outside the *Arc* class. They will be discussed as we progress through the description of the public classes.

Table 15-1. Arc-Drawing Functions

Function Name	Transferred Parameters	Description
draw	int xc, int yc, int radius, float start_angle, float end_angle, int color	Draws a single-pixel-wide arc centered at (xc,yc) of specified radius and color from start angle to end angle.
draw	int xc, int yc, int radius, float start_angle, float end_angle, int color, int width	Draws an arc centered at (xc,yc) of specified width, radius, and color from start angle to end angle.
fill	int xc, int yc, int radius, float start_angle, float end_angle, int color	Fills the area bounded by an arc centered at (xc,yc) of specified radius from start angle to end angle and lines drawn from the ends of the arc to (xc,yc) in specified color.

Drawing an Arc

The *draw* function for drawing a single-pixel-wide arc is given in Listing 11-1, lines 1708 through 1781. First, just glance through the listing of this function and observe that the method for computing the points of the circle in lines 1752 through 1780 is just the same as that used for the improved-accuracy *draw* function for the *Circle* class. Before the circle is computed, two *while* loops are used in lines 1715 through 1618 to ensure that the start and end angles are between 0 and 360 degrees. They do this by repeatedly subtracting 360 degrees until the resulting angle falls within the desired range. This works just fine as long as you don't specify any negative angles. If you use this function and are worried about that possibility, you need to add a couple more loops to handle the negative cases. The program then clears the values in the array *arc* to 0 in lines 1670 and 1671. This array contains the status of each octant that makes up the circle. Next, the number of the octant in which the arc starts is found by dividing the starting angle by 45 degrees and taking the result modula 8 (line 1722). This gives us a starting octant from 0 to 7. The same procedure is then performed in line 1723 to find the ending octant. In lines 1724 through 1729 the function uses some simple geometry to find the x and y coordinates of the starting and ending points on the arc. Then, in lines 1730 through 1751, it proceeds to fill the *arc* array.

There are six possible values to represent the contents of each octant. They are:

> 0 — this octant does not contain any part of the arc.
>
> 1 — the arc starts in this octant but ends in another octant.
>
> 2 — this octant is entirely filled by a portion of the arc, which starts and ends in other octants.
>
> 3 — the arc starts in another octant and ends in this octant.
>
> 4 — the arc begins and ends in this octant and does not extend into any other octant.
>
> 5 — the arc starts and ends in this octant, but makes nearly a full revolution, filling all other octants.

The function first checks whether the starting and ending octants are the same. If so, it next checks whether the end angle is less than the start angle. If this is the case, we have an arc that fills all of the circle except the space between the end angle and the start angle in this octant. Hence we set this octant's value to 5 and set all of the other octants to a value of 2. If the end angle is larger than or equal to the start angle, we have an arc that extends from the start angle to the end angle in this octant and doesn't appear in any other octant. Consequently, we set this octant to 4 and do nothing to the other octants. If the starting and ending octants are not the same, we first set the value for the starting octant to 1 and then set the value of the ending octant to 3. We then enter a *for* loop that fills all of the octants from the one next to the starting octant around to the one next to the ending octant with a value of 2. We use modulus arithmetic to ensure that no problems are encountered if we pass from octant 7 to octant 0 during this loop. Finally, we are ready to compute the points on the circle. Although this algorithm looks just the same as that used to draw a circle, for a computed point we call the private function *plot* to determine what to do with the point in each of the octants. The *plot* function is listed in lines 1875 through 1902. The parameters that are passed to this are the *x* and *y* coordinates of the point to be plotted, a variable to be tested to determine what plotting action to take, the type of octant (0 to 5 as listed previously), and the starting and ending test values. The function consists of a *switch* statement (line 1878) that causes the function to perform a different action for each type of octant. Let's look at these actions first and later go into more detail about how the tests work. The simplest case is an octant of type 0 (no plotting within this octant). It isn't covered by the *switch* statement, so the function does nothing. The next simplest is an octant of type 2; for this case the entire octant is included in the arc, so the function just plots every point. For an octant of type 1, where the arc begins in the octant but ends elsewhere, the program begins plotting points when the test variable achieves the value of the *start_test* parameter and continues to the end of the octant. Similarly, for type 3, where the arc begins elsewhere but ends in this octant, the function plots points from the beginning of the octant until the value of the test variable reaches the value of the *end_test* parameter; after this it doesn't plot any more points. For type 4, where the arc is included only in this octant, the function starts plotting points when the test variable achieves the value of the *start_test* parameter and stops plotting points when the value of the test variable reaches the value of the *end_test* parameter. For type 5, where the arc begins and ends in this octant and extends through all the other octants (almost, but not quite, a complete circle), the program plots points from the beginning of the octant until the test variable reaches the value of the *end_test* parameter and then stops plotting points until the test variable reaches the value of the *start_test* parameter. It then begins plotting points again and continues to do so until the end of the octant is reached. (This description seems to imply that we are plotting points in some particular direction around the circle, but actually, the appropriate test is made for every point, to determine whether it should be plotted, and it doesn't really matter in what order the points are computed.)

This describes what the *arc_plot* function does, but sorting out what variable is to be tested against what is a little more complicated. The first thing to observe is that, in any octant, it is sufficient to test against either the x or the y coordinate of the starting or ending point, and for angles around multiples of 45 degrees it doesn't really matter which test is made. However, at angles that are multiples of 90 degrees, the situation is different. At 0 and 180 degrees, the y value is changing very rapidly, while the x value is changing very slowly. Therefore, octants that include these values should be tested for the y coordinate, since this gives the most precise test and stops or starts the arc at the closest point to the specified angle. For the case of 90 or 270 degrees, the reverse situation is true, so the most precise test is performed with the x variable. Once we have determined which octants are associated with x tests and which with y tests, we pass the parameters x, *x_start_test*, and *x_end_test* to *arc_plot* for the former cases and *y*, *y_start_test*, and *y_end_test* to *arc_plot* for the latter cases. Finally, we have to note that all of the tests, as just described, assume that the coordinate being tested is increasing toward the test parameter. However, in some octants the coordinate being tested starts at a higher value than the test parameter and decreases toward it. In these cases, the direction of the test inequality should be reversed (less than instead of greater than or vice versa). Since the inequalities are a part of the *arc_test* function, they cannot easily be switched, but we can accomplish the same result by passing the negative of the coordinate being tested and the start and end test parameters to the function. To sum up, we now have an arc-drawing function that computes all of the points on a circle and then determines for each point whether it is within the bounds of a specified arc. If it is, the point is plotted to the screen.

It happens that in duplicating names here, we have demonstrated an interesting characteristic of C++. Each time we call *plot* from one of the arc-drawing functions, it calls the version of *plot* defined in lines 1825 through 1852. Then, within this *plot* function we call *plots* several times. The *plots* function is inherited from the *Circle* class and by it from the *Graphics* class. The *plots* function has within it a call to the *plot* function, but this is not the same plot function we referred to above; instead it is the *plot* function defined for the *Graphics* class. The C++ compiler takes care of this automatically, and you don't even need to worry about the fact that the same name is used for two functions.

Drawing a Wide Arc

The *draw* function listed in lines 1739 through 1870 draws an arc whose width is specified. The only difference between this function and the one previously described is that the circle-computing and arc-drawing portions of the function (lines 1835 through 1867) are contained within a *for* loop that begins on line 1833. This *for* loop iterates once for each pixel of arc width. At each iteration a one-pixel-wide arc is drawn and then the radius is incremented. When the *for* loop is complete, a series of one-pixel-wide arcs has been drawn which sum up to an arc of the specified width.

Filling an Arc

We need to begin this section by defining what we mean by filling an arc. What we refer to is filling the area bounded by an arc that forms part of the circumference of a circle and by two straight lines that begin at the center of the circle and extend to the beginning and end of the arc, respectively. The *fill* function is listed in Lines 1909 through 2026 of Listing 11-1. You'll find this function much like that for drawing the arc in many ways, but there are some significant differences. You'll recall that we filled a circle by drawing horizontal lines between the beginning and ending x values for each vertical row that made up the circle, and that in the more complicated situation of the tilted ellipse we first let each x value be compared to the proper row values of two arrays, one of which contained minimum values of x for each row and the other maximum values of x for each row. The minimums and maximums were saved, and after the ellipse was completely calculated a horizontal line was drawn from the minimum x to the maximum x for each row of the ellipse. For the filled arc, we need to use this latter procedure to process all points in the arc and in each of the straight lines, and then we draw the appropriate filled lines. Unfortunately, if we have an arc that extends for an angle greater than 180 degrees, we may have a situation where a particular row contains two filled portions separated by a blank space. Our procedure for filling the ellipse would, in this case, result in a single horizontal line being drawn from the minimum x value to the maximum x value, which would include filling in that portion of each line that we really wanted to be empty. To avoid this problem, we first determine the difference between the starting and ending angle in line 1920. If it is greater than 180 degrees, we increment a flag in line 1925 that was initialized to 1 in line 1916 and then save the original ending angle and create a new ending angle 180 degrees greater than the starting angle. We then enter a *while* loop in line 1931 that executes the entire arc-filling process and then decrements the flag for as long as the flag is not 0. At the end of this loop, in lines 2023 and 2024, the starting angle is changed to the ending angle (starting angle + 180 degrees) and the ending angle is changed to the original ending angle. Thus if the original difference in arc starting and ending angles was 180 degrees or less, the original angles are preserved and the loop is executed once. However, if the angle difference was more than 180 degrees, a first pass is made through the loop to cover the section of the arc from the beginning angle to 180 degrees plus that angle, and a second pass is made through the loop to fill the rest of the arc. Since each pass through the loop fills an arc of 180 degrees or less, there are no ambiguities and the arc is filled perfectly.

The only other differences between this function and the function for drawing an arc are that we initialize two coordinate arrays at the beginning of the program (lines 1935 through 1939) and then, instead of calling *plot* to test whether a point should be plotted and plot it if it should, we call *data* (lines 1607 through 1645), which performs the same tests but, if the point is part of the arc, instead of plotting it, checks whether it should replace the appropriate member of one of the coordinate arrays and, if it should, performs the replacement. After the circle has been computed completely, we call the function *dLine* (lines 1649 through 1699) twice to compute the two straight lines that are needed to form the remaining boundaries of the figure to be filled. The *dLine* function is just like the line *draw* function described in Chapter 12, except that instead of plotting points, it computes entries into the *coord* array. At the same time, both for these lines and the arc, we keep track of the maximum and minimum row values that occur. When we are through, the arrays contain the values for the beginning and end of a straight line to be drawn at each of the rows that make up the figure. We then use a *for* loop (lines 2008 through 2019) to draw all of these lines, resulting in a filled arc. After this process has been repeated once or twice as needed, the full filled arc results.

Elliptical Arcs

If you need to draw and/or fill elliptical arcs, you can often achieve the desired result by using the functions just described but inserting the ellipse-drawing or -filling algorithms given in Chapter 14 instead of the circle-drawing or -filling algorithms of Chapter 13. These work well for most starting and ending angles, but there are a few angles for which the function breaks down. The problem is that we begin by defining eight octants as portions of the ellipse that cover a 45-degree angle. When we actually compute the points that make up the ellipse, we compute from 0, 90, 180, or 270 degrees until the point at which the x and y coordinates are equal. This point is exactly a multiple of 45 degrees for a circle, so that each octant is consistent from one definition to the other and we have no problems. For the ellipse, however, this point is not a multiple of 45 degrees; the actual angle differs, depending upon the shape of the ellipse. We have an ambiguous region at one boundary of each pair of octants, where the angular definition says that the start and end test coordinates are in one octant, but the algorithm for actually computing the points says they are in another. If your starting or ending angle is in this region, strange results occur. If you can live with these regions of uncertainty, you'll have no problem with elliptical arcs. I've created such a function and used it for making a lot of arcs without any difficulties. If you really need a perfect function, you'll have to create a lot more complex method of determining the octant boundaries at the beginning of the program. You should be able to calculate the angles at which the two coordinates are equal for each quadrant and from these determine what the actual angular boundaries of each octant are. Once you determine the proper type for each octant, based upon its actual boundaries, the algorithm should work perfectly for every case.

The arctest.cpp Program for Testing Arcs

The *arctest.cpp* program generates a lot of test screens that you can use to ensure that your arc functions are working properly. The program is given in Listing 15-1. All of the displays in this demonstration program use display mode 12H, the 640 pixel × 480 pixel × 16-color mode, but you can easily change any one of them simply by changing the *setMode* statement. Display 1 (lines 14 through 24) is a segmented pie chart with one section partially removed. It shows the capabilities of the arc *fill* function and is illustrated in Plate 12. Display 2 (lines 31 through 33) uses the *fill* function to fill an arc that extends from 45 degrees around counterclockwise to 22.5 degrees, to fill all of a circle except a 22.5-degree segment. Display 3 (lines 40 through 42) uses the same function to fill an arc that extends from 350 degrees counterclockwise to 340 degrees, filling all of the circle except a 10-degree segment. These two displays demonstrate the capability of the *fill* function to fill arcs greater than 180 degrees. Display 4 (lines 50 through 53) uses the *draw* function to draw a very small and a very large 358-degree arc. The small one is so small that it may look like a full circle. Display 5 (lines 60 through 74) uses the *draw* function to draw 100 arcs with random centers and random starting and ending angles. All of these arcs are drawn with single-pixel-wide lines. If your *draw* function is doing anything peculiar, it ought to turn up in one of these arcs. Display 6 (lines 81 through 96) draws 80 arcs with random centers, random starting and ending angles, and random line widths. This screen should show up any problems with creating wide-line arcs. The screen is illustrated in Plate 13. Display 7 (lines 104 through 110) uses the *draw* function to draw three arcs on one screen, one at a time. You have to hit a key after each one is drawn before you get the next one. The first arc is drawn from 0 to 179 degrees, the second from 91 to 270 degrees, and the third from 1 to 359 degrees. If your arc function is giving problems near the angles 0, 90, 180, or 270 degrees, they should show up in this screen. Display 8 (lines 116 through 129) uses the wide-line version of the *draw* function to draw a rainbow using wide-line arcs. First, we reset the EGA palette colors to give more proper rainbow colors (lines 116 through

122). This screen is shown in Plate 14. Display 9 (lines 135 through 161) shows segmented arcs (drawn with the wide-line version of the *draw* function) around a circle combined with the use of the *line.draw* function to produce matching spaced radials. This screen is shown in Plate 15. Display 10 (lines 168 through 183) uses the single-pixel-wide *draw* function to perform a full check of the function. It begins by drawing arcs that start at zero degrees and end in 4-degree increments from 4 to 356 degrees. It then pauses 2.5 seconds, erases the screen, and draws the set of arcs beginning at 6 degrees. It continues this process with the starting angle increasing in 6-degree steps until it reaches a starting angle of 354 degrees. This gives you a chance to see whether almost any arc that can be drawn is drawn correctly. Since this is a lengthy process, you can terminate it at any time. A typical screen is shown in Plate 16.

Listing 15-1. Program for Testing Arc Functions

```
/*
   arctest.cpp = Tests functions for drawing and filling
                            arcs.

              By Roger T. Stevens    1-22-96
*/

1    #include "c:\cpphbook\program\graphics.cpp"

2    Arc arc;
3    Line line;
4    Graphics graphic;
5    char ch;

6    void main(void)
7    {
8       int i, start, end, xc, yc, radius;

9    /*
                        Display 1

           640 x 480 pixel x 16 color mode 12H

              Pie chart using 'arc.fill()'.
```

```
      */

         graphic.setMode(0x12);
         graphic.cls(1);
         arc.fill(90,0,400,337.5,22.5,9);
         arc.fill(14,14,400,22.5,67.5,10);
         arc.fill(0,20,400,67.5,112.5,11);
         arc.fill(-14,14,400,112.5,157.5,12);
         arc.fill(-20,0,400,157.5,202.5,13);
         arc.fill(-14,-14,400,202.5,247.5,14);
         arc.fill(0,-20,400,247.5,292.5,15);
         arc.fill(14,-14,400,292.5,337.5,2);
         getch();

    /*

                            Display 2

              640 x 480 pixel x 16 color mode 12H

      Filled arc from 45 degrees around to 22.5 degrees
                        using 'fillarc().

    */

         graphic.cls(1);
         arc.fill(0,0,300,45.0,22.5,10);
         getch();

    /*

                            Display 3

              640 x 480 pixel x 16 color mode 12H

      Filled arc from 350 degrees around to 340 degrees
                        using 'fillarc().

      */

         graphic.cls(7);
         arc.fill(0,0,400,350.0,340.0,9);
         getch();
```

```
/*

                        Display 4

          640 x 480 pixel x 16 color mode 12H

   Draw very small and very large 358 degree arcs with
        arc.draw() and single pixel width lines.

*/
    graphic.setMode(0x12);

    graphic.cls(1);
    arc.draw(0,0,4,1,359,10);
    arc.draw(0,0,476,1,359,14);
    getch();

/*

                        Display 5

          640 x 480 pixel x 16 color mode 12H

   Draw 100 arcs with random angles and centers and
    single pixel wide lines using arc.drawarc().

*/

    graphic.cls(1);
    color = 0;
    for (i=0; i<100; i++)
    {
        color = color%16;
        if (color == 1)
            color++;
        start = rand()/22;
        end = rand()/22 + start;
        xc = rand()/32 - 640;
        yc = rand()/42 - 480;
        radius = 20 + rand()/80;
        arc.draw(xc, yc, radius, start, end,color++);
    }
    getch();
```

```
/*

                    Display 6

     640 x 480 pixel x 16 color mode 12H

  Draw 100 arcs with random angles, centers, and
        line widths using arc.draw().

*/

    graphic.cls(1);
    color = 0;
    for (i=0; i<80; i++)
    {
        color = color%16;
        if (color == 1)
            color++;
        start = rand()/22;
        end = rand()/22 + start;
        xc = rand()/32 - 640;
        yc = rand()/42 - 480;
        radius = 20 + rand()/80;
        arc.draw(xc, yc, radius, start, end,color++,rand()
            & 0x1F);
    }
    getch();

/*

                    Display 7

     640 x 480 pixel x 16 color mode 12H

  Draw single pixel wide arcs from 0 to 179 degrees,
 from 91 to 270 degrees, and from 1 to 359 degrees,
      with waits in between using arc.draw().

*/

    graphic.cls(1);
    arc.draw(0,0,476,0,179,11);
    getch();
    arc.draw(0,0,150,91,270,10);
    getch();
    arc.draw(0,0,300,1,359,10);
    getch();
```

```
/*
        Display 8

        640 x 480 pixel x 16 color mode 12H

        Draw rainbow using arc.draw().
*/

    graphic.set_screen(13,2,16);
    graphic.setEGApalette(9,44);
    graphic.setEGApalette(10,52);
    graphic.setEGApalette(11,62);
    graphic.setEGApalette(12,58);
    graphic.setEGApalette(13,57);
    graphic.setEGApalette(14,45);
    arc.draw(0,-32,470,0,180,9,40);
    arc.draw(0,-32,430,0,180,10,40);
    arc.draw(0,-32,390,0,180,11,40);
    arc.draw(0,-32,350,0,180,12,40);
    arc.draw(0,-32,310,0,180,1,40);
    arc.draw(0,-32,270,0,180,14,40);
    getch();

/*
        Display 9

        640 x 480 pixel x 16 color mode 12H

        Draw spaced octant arcs using arc.draw() .
*/

    graphic.setMode(0x12);
    graphic.cls(1);
    arc.draw(40,0,300,337.5,22.5,9,40);
    for (i=3375; i<3825; i+=40)
        line.draw (0,0,280,(float)i,9);
    arc.draw(28,28,300,22.5,67.5,10,40);
    for (i=225; i<675; i+=40)
        line.draw (0,0,280,(float)i,10);
    arc.draw(0,40,300,67.5,112.5,11,40);
    for (i=675; i<1125; i+=40)
        line.draw (0,0,280,(float)i,11);
    arc.draw(-28,28,300,112.5,157.5,12,40);
    for (i=1125; i<1575; i+=40)
```

```
            line.draw (0,0,280,(float)i,12);
        arc.draw(-40,0,300,157.5,202.5,13,40);
        for (i=1575; i<2025; i+=40)
            line.draw (0,0,280,(float)i,13);
        arc.draw(-28,-28,300,202.5,247.5,14,40);
        for (i=2025; i<2475; i+=40)
            line.draw (0,0,280,(float)i,14);
        arc.draw(0,-40,300,247.5,292.5,15,40);
        for (i=2475; i<2925; i+=40)
            line.draw (0,0,280,(float)i,15);
        arc.draw(28,-28,300,292.5,337.5,2,40);
        for (i=2925; i<3375; i+=40)
            line.draw (0,0,280,(float)i,2);
        getch();

    /*

                          Display 10

                640 x 480 pixel x 16 color mode 12H

           Test of arcs with 6 degree starting increments and
              4 degree lengths. Hit any key to terminate.

    */
        graphic.setMode(0x12);
        graphic.cls(1);
        for (start=0; start<360; start+=4)
        {
            color = 0;
            for (end=0; end<360; end+=6)
            {
                 arc.draw(0,0,10+end,start,end+start+4,color);
                if ((color = (color + 1) % 16) == 1)
                    color = 2;
            }
            ch = getch();
            if (ch == 0x0D)
                break;;
        }
    }
```

16

Drawing and Fast-Filling Polygons

There are many cases in which you will want to create some enclosed figure with a number of straight line segments. Of course, you could repeatedly call a *drawLine* function until every line segment was drawn, but this is a rather tedious process. It makes a lot more sense to have a function that will take a lot of sets of coordinates defining points and draw lines from one to the next, to the next, and so forth. The main decision that needs to be made is whether to pass all of the coordinates to the function in the calling statement or to have them stored in an array that the function references. We will show functions that use each of these techniques. You may also want to fill one of these enclosed figures with solid color. We'll show some very fast ways of doing this. You can also use the *floodfill* function described in Chapter 11. This is much slower, but is very effective if you know that you have a closed area, don't really know the locations of its boundary lines, but do know at least one point within the bounds. The class *Polygon* is given in Listing 11-1, lines 2030 through 2240. Table 16-1 gives a description of the public functions included in this class.

Drawing a Polygon

The first function for drawing a polygon is listed in lines 2045 through 2055 of Listing 11-1. The function is passed an integer color number and the address of an array of point coordinates. The array must con-

Table 16-1. Polygon Public Functions

Function Name	Transferred Parameters	Description
draw	int color, int * point	Draws a polygon in specified color connecting all points in *point* array in sequence.
draw	int color, ...	Draws a polygon in specified color connecting all points passed to the function in sequence. Passing 9999 terminates the input.
fill	int color, int * point	Fills a polygon in specified color created by connecting all points in *point* array in sequence.
fill	int color, ...	Fills a polygon in specified color created by connecting all points passed to the function in sequence. Passing 9999 terminates the input.

tain alternating values for *x* and *y*, and must end with a number more negative than -5000. The function begins in line 2048 with a *while* loop that scans through the *point* array until it encounters a number more negative than -5000. At this point the loop is terminated, leaving the index *i* containing the number in the array of this negative number. In line 2049, we check whether this number is less than 6; if so, we don't have enough points in the array to create a two-dimensional figure, so we return to the calling program. Next, in lines 2050 and 2051, we draw a line from the first coordinate in the array to the second one. Then, in lines 2052 and 2053, a *for* loop is used to draw from the previous ending line position to the next point specified by the *point* array, and so forth, until all of the points in the array have been used. Finally, in line 2054, a line is drawn from the last point in the array to the first point in the array.

Drawing a Polygon with Passed Parameters

The second function for drawing a polygon is given in lines 2062 through 2078 of Listing 11-1. This function passes up to 150 pairs of coordinate values in the call to the function. Since the number of coordinate pairs passed may vary, we have to make use of some C++ functions that are specifically designed for cases where the number of variables passed is not known in advance. The nonvariable parameters are passed to the function at the beginning of the parameter list. In this case, there is just one, the color. This is followed by a comma and then three dots, which indicate that there may follow any number of parameters. At the beginning of the function (in line 2066), we define a parameter array called *coord* to be of type *va_list*. This type is mandatory for receiving the variable-length parameter list. Next, to prepare for reading the list, we run *va_start*. This function has two parameters, first the parameter list that we just defined and second the name of the last fixed parameter that is passed to the function *drawPoly* before the variable-length parameter list begins. In order to get each member of the variable-length list transferred to the *drawPoly* function, we successively run the function *va_arg* for each parameter in the list in lines 2067 through 2069. Its two parameters are the name of the list (*coord*) and the type of the parameter passed (for this function, always an integer). You'll note that the procedure just described has no way of knowing when to stop getting parameter values. It's up to you to tell it when to stop; if it keeps on going, the results will be disastrous. For this function, we have set up a *while* loop in line 2067 that keeps reading coordinate pairs and storing them in the *xpoint* and *ypoint* arrays until either 150 pairs of coordinates have been stored (which is all we have room for) or until one of the coordinates has a value less than -5000. Since we are operating in the system coordinate space, which can have *x* values of -640 to +639 and *y* values of -480 to +479, there can never be a coordinate that has an actual value of less than 5000. Thus when we deliberately insert such a value into the list of parameters being passed, it is a sign to stop. Then, in line 2070, the function runs *va_end* to end the variable parameter list process. If this function isn't run, weird results can occur in the rest of your program. We now have a couple arrays with the coordinate values in them. To complete these arrays, we set the next member of the array to be the same as the first member in lines 2072 and 2073, so that the final line that is drawn will close the figure. Lines 2074 and 2075 draw the first line of the polygon. Next we are ready to begin a *for* loop that calls *draw* to draw a line between each successive pair of coordinates in the selected color. When this loop is complete, we have drawn our enclosed regular polygon.

Filling an Irregular Polygon with Passed Parameters

The function *fill* in Listing 11-1, lines 2083 through 2093, takes up to 750 pairs of coordinates that are passed to the function and uses the *va_list*, *va_start*, *va_arg*, and *va_end* functions just described to put these all into an array called *point*. When the array has been assembled, in line 2092 the version of the function *fill* that passes the address of the array is used to fill the polygon.

Filling an Irregular Polygon Using a Coordinate Array

The *fill* function in lines 2102 through 2240 of Listing 11-1 is passed the color and the address of an array of point coordinates. We're going to begin by assembling a linked list that contains parameters of each of the vertices that make up the polygon, in order of ascending *y* coordinates and then, for equal *y*'s, of ascending *x* coordinates. The class *Edge* that contains these parameters for a vertex is given in Listing 11-1, lines 642 through 685. Lines 645 through 658 define the class and its parameters. Lines 662 through 685 define a constructor for the class. Whenever a new member of the class is created, with the parameters *x1, y1, dx,* and *dy* passed to it, the constructor initializes the class with the values shown. Now, if you'll look at line 2111, you'll see that the function uses a *while* loop to determine the number of points in the passed array, which is left in *length*. Then, in lines 2112 and 2113, if there are not at least three pairs of coordinate points (which would create a triangle), the function returns without doing anything since there is no geometric figure that can be filled. In line 2114, the beginning member of the linked list is set to a NULL address. Lines 2115 through 2130 convert all the coordinates from system coordinates to display coordinates and reverse the two sets of coordinates that define a line if the starting *y* coordinate is greater than the ending *y* coordinate. Lines 2130 through 2144 start with an *if* statement that causes a new member of the *Edge* class to be created only if there is a change in *y* across the line. Lines 2133 through 2135 create the new member of the *Edge* class, if there is space available for it; otherwise, the function returns without filling the polygon. Lines 2136 through 2143 scan through the members of the linked list until the proper place for the new *Edge* to be inserted is found, and then the link addresses are modified to insert this entry into the list. When the *for* loop is finally complete, we have a global edge table consisting of information on all the vertices in order. In line 2148, we set the pointer for an active edge table to NULL and then in line 2149 set the value of *y* to the first *y* in the global edge table. Line 2150 begins a *while* loop that iterates until the global edge table is empty. In the *while* loop of line 2156 through line 2180 and the enclosed *for* loop from line 2158 through line 2179, all *Edge* members with *y* coordinates equal to the current *y* are transferred to the active edge table. Lines 2181 through 2188 cause *fillLine* to be called to color in a line from an odd-numbered intersection to an even-numbered intersection, but not visa versa. Line 2192 decrements the *Count* parameter of the present edge. If the count is zero, we are through with that member of the table, so it is removed from the chain and deleted from memory. Otherwise, new *x* and *y* values are computed for the edge and the process is repeated until all members of the global and active edge tables have been used.

Two additional classes have been derived from the *Polygon* class. They are the *Triangle* class (lines 2244 through 2265) and the *Quadrilateral* class (lines 2269 through 2283). Each of these has its own *fill* function. The *Triangle fill* function simply sets three pairs of coordinates into an array and then calls the *Polygon fill* function to fill the triangle. The *Quadrilateral fill* function accepts four coordinate pairs and divides them into two triangles, each of which is filled by the *Triangle fill* function.

The *polytest.cpp* Program

Listing 16-1 gives the *polytest.cpp* program, which includes displays that demonstrate all of the polygon-drawing and -filling functions. Display 1 (lines 94 through 96) creates an abstract pattern in black and white that is a good test of how well the *fill* algorithm works. Display 2 (lines 102 through 132) draws three irregular polygons in the shape of dinosaurs. Display 3 (lines 138 through 141) uses the *floodfill* function to fill these dinosaurs. Display 4 (lines 147 through 152) draws two wide lines and then two filled triangles to test the *Triangle fill* function. Display 5 (lines 158 through 163) fills two quadrilaterals to test the *Quadrilateral fill* function. Display 6 (lines 169 through 173) uses a parameter array to fill three dinosaurs. Display 7 (lines 179 through 183) draws three irregular polygons (dinosaurs). Display 8 (lines 189 through 219 uses passed parameters to create three filled dinosaurs. Plate 17 shows this display. Display 9 (lines 225 through 228) uses an array and the *fill* function to draw a map of Africa. Display 10 (lines 234 through 237) uses an array and the *fill* function to draw a map of the United States. Display 11 (lines 243 through 283) draws the New Jerusalem figure, which is illustrated in Plate 18. This curve is supposed to be associated with the New Jerusalem as described in the Bible in the book of Revelations, because it combines the mystical numbers 7 and 12 that are used in the Revelations descriptions. In particular, the New Jerusalem curve is a good example of how several different drawing and filling functions can be combined to produce interesting displays.

Listing 16-1. polytest.cpp *Program*

```
/*

      polytest = Program to demonstrate polygon and flood
                          fill functions

                    By Roger T. Stevens  2-7-96

*/

#include "c:\cpphbook\program\graphics.cpp"

Graphics graphic;
Polygon polygon;
Line line;
Triangle triangle;
Quadralateral quad;
Circle circle;

int xc[28], yc[28];
int poly1[] = {-600, -72, -520, -216, -408, -216, -328,
-168, -296, -216, -248, -216, -176, -136, -136, -24,
-152, 56, -200, -72, -216, -56, -184, 72, -88, 88, -88,
104, -40, 104, -56, 168, -152, 136, -152, 200, 8, 184,
-24, 216, 8, 248, -40, 328, -184, 344, -216, 296, -216,
200, -318, 136, -392, 72, -440, -24, -472, -132, -520,
-184, -536, -176, -578, -88, -9999};
int poly2[] = {100, 100, 116, 132, 164, 180, 228, 204,
356, 212, 404, 220, 452, 220, 484, 212, 524, 164, 540,
132, 596, 84, 540, 116, 548, 36, 532, -12, 500, -44,
484, -44, 468, -28, 460, -12, 468, -4, 476, -20, 484,
-20, 518, -4, 516, 36, 516, 68, 484, 100, 428, 100, 404,
76, 388, 52, 412, -76, 364, -76, 348, 36, 340, -76, 332,
-76, 300, 36, 228, 36, 228, -76, 196, -76, 188, 36,
140, 100, 116, 68, 116, 36, 124, 4, 100, 36, 100, 100,
-9999};

int poly3[] = {-200, -344, -164, -284, -116, -284, -80,
-296, -56, -272, -80, -248, -92, -224, -44, -224, -56,
-176, 4, -188, 28, -140, 64, -164, 112, -116,
136, -176, 184, -164, 196, -212, 232, -212, 220,
-248, 244, -248, 232, -296, 268, -284, 268, -308, 304,
-284, 316, -308, 340, -308, 328, -332, 304, -368, 232,
-380, 112, -368, 112, -416, 52, -416, 28, -380, -8,
```

```
-380, -20, -416, -92, -416, -68, -368, -140, -380, -164,
-368, -188, -392, -200, -392, -9999};

int africa[] = {-434, 230, -404, 292, -396, 292, -388,
306, -366, 322, -350, 336, -350, 352, -342, 374, -328,
382, -290, 406, -266, 398, -236, 412, -190,
   420, -130, 428, -122, 382, -138, 374, -100, 368,
-76, 368, -68, 352, -54, 352, -30, 344, -24, 352, -24,
 368, -16, 374, 6, 374, 96, 344, 112, 352, 126, 352,
 126, 322, 150, 260, 126, 246, 152, 246, 150, 238, 150,
 200, 164, 184, 172, 170, 188, 154, 240, 108, 248, 108,
324, 124, 316, 108, 264, 18, 218, -26, 172, -80, 188,
-118, 196, -124, 202, -178,
   180, -200, 158, -208, 134, -232, 152, -270, 112,
-284, 112, -322, 66, -390, -38, -406, -54, -384, -46,
-384, -84, -300, -84, -270, -114, -208, -114, -162, -106,
-156, -92, -132, -100, -102, -106, -72, -144, -10,
-138, 32, -152, 48, -176, 48, -182, 48, -190, 64,
-220, 64, -252, 56, -266, 48, -290, 56, -328, 48,
-380, 78, -426, 140, -418, 146, -426, 154, -418, 184,
-418, 200, -426, 208, -426, 222, -9999};

int usa[] = {-302, 222, -292, 214, -288,  192, -280,  192,
   -276, 206, -278, 222, -270, 224, -222, 206, -182,
   192, -130, 184, -78, 178, -26, 170, 26, 170, 88,
   164, 64, 142, 60, 136, 70, 136, 82, 144, 82,
136,  88, 136, 108, 162, 114, 162, 106, 148, 122, 144,  124,
140, 146, 150, 146, 144, 158, 142, 158, 140,  150, 134, 138,
132, 126, 122, 122, 96, 122, 68,  126, 54, 130, 54,
138, 76, 132, 96, 134, 110, 142,  120, 156, 132, 164,
132, 168, 122, 168, 118, 174,  112, 172, 98, 178, 110,
186, 90, 174, 68, 186,
   62, 228, 96, 226, 106, 254, 118, 260, 136, 304,
164, 312, 214, 316, 220, 324, 214, 324, 210, 330, 210,
348, 178, 320, 136, 320, 122, 330, 110, 334,  112, 294,
118, 316, 118, 316, 110, 320, 100, 298,  68, 298, 40,
294, 34, 286, 48, 280, 48, 294, 30,  288, 2, 294, -4,
298, -16, 298, -26, 290, -30, 290,  -38, 298, -38,
260, -78, 230, -110,  238, -122, 246,  -150, 246, -150,
260, -170, 264, -178, 268, -192, 270, -206, 268, -228,
260, -230, 246, -220, 230,  -192, 220, -158, 212, -144,
208, -142, 192,  -154,  175, -170, 150, -142, 148,
-148, 130, -148, 122,  -156, 130, -170, 104, -172, 90,
```

```
-164, 56, -166, 38,  -170, 26, -184, 10, -206, 10, -232,
4, -238, -2,  -238, -14, -232, -18, -228, -22, -222,
-24, -208,  -26, -200, -42, -180, -52, -166, -66,
-164, -84, 180, -114, -140, -130, -128, -154, -122,
-156, -132,  -196, -128, -248, -96, -274, -96, -278,
-90, -278,  -74, -292, -54, -318, -40, -322, -12, -330, 0,
-330, 8, -340, 40, -344, 54, -344, 82, -330,
110, -320, 156, -304, 192, -300, 206, -302, 222, -9999};

void main(void)
{
    int i,  j,  size;
    int Polygon8[] = {-640, 480, -240, -240, 640, 480,
        -640, -480, 240, 240, 640, -480, -9999};

/*
                Display 1
    640 x 480 pixels x 16 colors - Mode 12H
        Fill polygon with array reference.
 */

    graphic.setMode(0x12);
    polygon.fill(15,Polygon8);
    getch();

/*
                Display 2
    640 x 350 pixels x 16 colors - Mode 10H
  Draw irregular polygons with passed parameters.
*/

    graphic.setMode(0x10);
    graphic.set_screen(9,10,14);
    polygon.draw(12, -200, -344, -164, -284, -116, -284,
            -80, -296, -56, -272, -80, -248, -92,
            -224,-44,-224,-56,-176,4,-188, 28,-140,64, -164, 112,
            -116, 136, -176, 184, -164, 196, -212, 232, -212,
            220, -248, 244, -248, 232, -296, 268, -284, 268,
```

```
            -308, 304, -284, 316, -308, 340, -308, 328, -332,
            304, -368, 232, -380, 112, -368, 112, -416, 52,
            -416, 28, -380, -8, -380, -20, -416, -92, -416,
            -68, -368, -140, -380, -164, -368, -188, -392,
        -200, -392, -9999);
        polygon.draw(2, -600, -72, -520, -216, -408, -216,
            -328, -168, -296, -216, -248, -216, -176, -136,
            -136, -24, -152, 56, -200, -72, -216, -56, -184,
            72, -88, 88, -88, 104, -40, 104, -56, 168, -152,
            136, -152, 200, 8, 184, -24, 216, 8, 248, -40,
            328, -184, 344, -216, 296, -216, 200, -318, 136,
            -392, 72, -440, -24, -472, -132, -520, -184,
        -536, -176, -578, -88, -9999);
        polygon.draw(7, 100, 100, 116, 132, 164, 180, 228,
                204, 356, 212, 404, 220, 452, 220, 484, 212, 524,
                164, 540, 132, 596, 84, 540, 116, 548, 36, 532,
                -12, 500, -44, 484, -44, 468, -28, 460, -12, 468,
                -4, 476, -20, 484, -20, 518, -4, 516, 36, 516,
                68, 484, 100, 428, 100, 404, 76, 388, 52, 412,
            -76, 364, -76, 348, 36, 340, -76, 332, -76, 300,
        36, 228, 36, 228, -76, 196, -76, 188, 36, 140,
100, 116, 68, 116, 36, 124, 4, 100, 36, 100, 100,
-9999);
    getch();

/*
                          Display 3

            640 x 350 pixels x 16 colors - Mode 10H

               Flood fill the irregular polygons.
 */

    polygon.floodfill(-240, 0, 2);
    polygon.floodfill(280, 60, 7);
    polygon.floodfill(0, -200, 12);
    getch();
```

```
/*
                         Display 4
        640 x 350 pixels x 16 colors - Mode 10H
          Draw wide lines and filled triangles.
 */
    graphic.cls(1);
    line.draw(-600, 440, -600, -300, 14, 40);
    line.draw(600, 440, 600, -300, 14, 40);
    triangle.fill(-500, -300, 8, 440, 500, -300, 13);
    triangle.fill(-246, 70, 250, 70, 0, -300, 10);
    getch();
/*
                         Display 5
        640 x 350 pixels x 16 colors - Mode 10H
               Generate Quadrilaterals.
*/

    graphic.cls(10);
    quad.fill(-500, -300, -380, 440, 540, 400, -360,
    -360, 9);
    quad.fill(-440, 70, 80, 420, 90, 20, -430, -330,
    14);
    getch();
/*
                         Display 6
        640 x 350 pixels x 16 colors - Mode 10H
     Fill irregular polygons with parameter array.
*/
    graphic.cls(1);
    polygon.fill(11, poly1);
    polygon.fill(12, poly2);
    polygon.fill(14, poly3);
```

```
    getch();

/*
    ┌──────────────────────────────────────────────────────┐
    │                      Display 7                       │
    │       640 x 350 pixels x 16 colors - Mode 10H        │
    │     Draw irregular polygons with parameter array.    │
    └──────────────────────────────────────────────────────┘
*/

    graphic.cls(1);
    polygon.draw(11, poly1);
    polygon.draw(12, poly2);
    polygon.draw(14, poly3);
    getch();

/*
    ┌──────────────────────────────────────────────────────┐
    │                      Display 8                       │
    │       640 x 480 pixels x 16 colors - Mode 12H        │
    │    Fill irregular polygons with passed parameters.   │
    └──────────────────────────────────────────────────────┘
*/

    graphic.setMode(0x12);
    graphic.cls(1);
      polygon.fill(2, -600, -72, -520, -216, -408, -216,
          -328, -168, -296, -216, -248, -216, -176, -136,
          -136, 24, -152, 56, -200, -72, -216, -56, -184,
          72, -88, 88, -88, 104, -40, 104, -56, 168, -152,
          136, -152, 200, 8, 184, -24, 216, 8, 248, -40,
          328, -184, 344, -216, 296, -216, 200, -318, 136,
          -392, 72, -440, -24, -472, -132, -520, -184,
      -536, -176, -578, -88, -9999);

      polygon.fill(7, 100, 100, 116, 132, 164, 180, 228,
          204, 356, 212, 404, 220, 452, 220, 484, 212, 524,
          164, 540, 132, 596, 84, 540, 116, 548, 36, 532,
          -12, 500, -44, 484, -44, 468, -28, 460, -12, 468,
          -4, 476, -20, 484, -20, 518, -4, 516, 36, 516,
          68, 484, 100, 428, 100, 404, 76, 388, 52, 412,
```

```
            -76, 364, -76, 348, 36, 340, -76, 332, -76, 300,
            36, 228, 36, 228, -76, 196, -76, 188, 36, 140,
        100, 116, 68, 116, 36, 124, 4, 100, 36, 100, 100,
        -9999);

        polygon.fill(12, -200, -344, -164, -284, -116, -284,
            -80, -296, -56, -272, -80, -248, -92, -224, -44,
            -224, -56, -176, 4, -188, 28, -140, 64, -164,
        112, -116, 136, -176, 184, -164, 196, -212, 232,
        -212, 220, -248, 244, -248, 232, -296, 268, -284,
        268, -308, 304, -284, 316, -308, 340, -308, 328,
        -332, 304, -368, 232, -380, 112, -368, 112, -416,
        52, -416, 28, -380, -8, -380, -20, -416, -92,
            -416, -68, -368, -140, -380, -164, -368, -188,
        -392, -200, -392, -9999);
    getch();

/*
        Display 9

        640 x 480 pixels x 16 colors - Mode 12H

        Generate map of Africa.
*/
    graphic.setMode(0x12);
    graphic.cls(1);
    polygon.fill(10, africa);
    getch();

/*
        Display 10

        800 x 600 pixels x 256 colors - Mode 103H

        Generate map of USA.
*/
    graphic.setMode(0x103);
    graphic.cls(1);
    polygon.fill(10, usa);
    getch();
```

```
/*

                    Display 11

     800 x 600 pixels x 256 colors - Mode 103H

        Generate the New Jerusalem figure.

*/
    graphic.setMode(0x103);
    graphic.cls(1);
    circle.fill(0, 0, 350, 5);
    for (i=0; i<28; i++)
    {
        xc[i] = int(350. * cos(.22439947 * i));
        yc[i] = int(350. * sin(.22439947 * i));
    }
    circle.fill(xc[1], yc[1], 75, 6);
    circle.fill(xc[4], yc[4], 75, 2);
    circle.fill(xc[6], yc[6], 75, 3);
    circle.fill(xc[8], yc[8], 75, 4);
    circle.fill(xc[11], yc[11], 75, 7);
    circle.fill(xc[13], yc[13], 75, 10);
    circle.fill(xc[15], yc[15], 75, 9);
    circle.fill(xc[18], yc[18], 75, 8);
    circle.fill(xc[20], yc[20], 75, 13);
    circle.fill(xc[22], yc[22], 75, 14);
    circle.fill(xc[25], yc[25], 75, 11);
    circle.fill(xc[27], yc[27], 75, 12);
    circle.draw(0, 0, 350, 0);
    for (i=0; i<28; i+=4)
    {
        line.draw(xc[i], yc[i], xc[(i+12)%28],
yc[(i+12)%28], 15);
    }
    polygon.floodfill(0, 110, 15);
    graphic.floodfill(100, 0, 15);
    graphic.floodfill(100, 100, 15);
    graphic.floodfill(-100, 100, 15);
    graphic.floodfill(-60, -100, 15);
    graphic.floodfill(-100, -100, 15);
    graphic.floodfill(100, -100, 15);
    for (i=0; i<28; i++)
    {
        if ((i%4) != 0)
            line.draw(xc[i], yc[i], xc[(i+12)%28],
        yc[(i+12)%28], 0);
    }
    getch();
}
```

17

Drawing and Filling Rounded Rectangles

The rectangle with rounded corners makes a pleasing background on which to display menus or similar alphanumeric messages while in a graphics mode. By judicious combination of the functions that have already been developed in previous chapters, we can produce functions that will draw or fill rounded rectangles. The functions are given in Listing 11-1 and have already been described. Listing 17-1 is a program to create rounded rectangles. The main program consists of three displays that are created one at a time, on top of each other. The first (line 17) uses the function *fillRndRect* to create a filled rounded rectangle that takes up the whole screen in magenta. When a key is hit, the program then uses the function *drawRndRect* to draw a rounded rectangle 12 units wide in white, just inside the previous rectangle (line 19). When a key is hit again, the *fillRndRect* function is used three times to create three filled rounded rectangles inside the previous one, each using slightly less than one-third of the available horizontal space (lines 21 through 23). The first is drawn in blue, the second in green, and the third in yellow.

Drawing a Rounded Rectangle

The function *drawRndRect* draws a rounded rectangle whose lines have the line width specified by *width*. This function is listed in lines 32 through 46. The parameters passed to this function are the coordinates of the top lefthand corner of the unrounded rectangle, the coordinates of the bottom righthand corner, the color, and the radius of the rounding circle. The function first uses the line *draw* function four times to to draw the straight wide horizontal and vertical portions of the rounded rectangle (lines 38 through 41). It then calls the arc *draw* function four times (lines 42 through 45) to draw 90-degree-wide arcs properly displaced to fill in the corners of the rounded rectangle.

Listing 17.1. The rndrect.cpp *Program*

```
/*

        rndrect = Program to test drawing and filling of
                      rounded rectangles

                   By Roger T. Stevens   3/1/96

*/
1    #include "c:\cpphbook\program\graphics.cpp"

2    void fillRndRect(int xl, int yt, int xr, int yb, int r, int
3        color);
4    void drawRndRect(int xl, int yt, int xr, int yb, int r, int
5        color, int width);

6    Arc arc;
7    Line line;
8    Graphics graphic;
9    Circle circle;

10   void main(void)
11   {
12       int i,j,x_cen, y_cen, radius,ran_param;

13       graphic.setMode(0x12);
14       fillRndRect (-640,480,639,-479,60,13);
15       getch();
16       drawRndRect (-620,460,620,-460,60,15,12);
17       getch();
18       fillRndRect (-600,420,-240,-420,60,9);
19       fillRndRect (-180,420,180,-420,60,10);
20       fillRndRect (240,420,600,-420,60,14);
21       getch();
22   }
```

```
/*
    drawRndRect() = Draws a rounded rectangle with top
     left and bottom right corners, radius, and color,
      specified, using line width in pixels specified
                          by width.
*/

void drawRndRect(int xl, int yt, int xr, int yb, int r, int
color, int width)
{
    int i, row, col, px, py;
    long int sum;

    r += (width>>1);
    line.draw(xl,yt-r,xl,yb+r,color,width);
    line.draw(xr,yt-r,xr,yb+r,color,width);
    line.draw(xl+r,yt,xr-r,yt,color,width);
    line.draw(xl+r,yb,xr-r,yb,color,width);
    arc.draw(xl+r,yt-r,r,90.0,180.0,color,width);
    arc.draw(xr-r,yt-r,r,0.0,90.0,color,width);
    arc.draw(xl+r,yb+r,r,180.0,270.0,color,width);
    arc.draw(xr-r,yb+r,r,270.0,0.0,color,width);
}

/*
    fillRndRect() = Fills a rounded rectangle when top
     left, and bottom right corners, radius and color
                      are specified.
*/

void fillRndRect(int xl, int yt, int xr, int yb, int r, int
    color)
{
    int i;

    for (i=yb+r; i<=yt-r; i++)
        arc.fillsLine(xl, xr, i, color);
    for (i=yb; i<=yb+r; i++)
        arc.fillsLine(xl+r-3,xr-r+3,i,color);
    for (i=yt-r; i<=yt; i++)
        arc.fillsLine(xl+r-3,xr-r+3,i,color);
    arc.fill(xl+r,yt-r,r,90.0,180.0,color);
    arc.fill(xr-r,yt-r,r,0.0,90.0,color);
    arc.fill(xl+r,yb+r,r,180.0,270.0,color);
```

```
62          arc.fill(xr-r,yb+r,r,270.0,0.0,color);
63      }
```

Filling a Rounded Rectangle

The function *fillRndRect* creates a filled rounded rectangle. This function is listed in lines 52 through 66. The parameters passed to this function are the coordinates of the top lefthand corner of the unrounded rectangle, the coordinates of the bottom righthand corner, and the color and radius of the rounding circle. The function first runs through three *for* loops, beginning at line 56. The first loop uses the *fillLine* function to draw lines covering the part of the rectangle that does not include any rounded corners. The second *for* loop (line 58) draw lines at the bottom of the rectangle that only extend from the first nonrounded point on the left to the last nonrounded point on the right. The third *for* loop (line 60) does the same for the top of the rectangle. We now have a filled display that is a rectangle with its corners cut out. These are then filled with the rounded corners in lines 62 through 65 by calling the arc *fill* function to draw a 90-degree filled arc properly positioned and with proper angular coverage to fill each corner.

18

Smooth Curves with Bezier and B-Spline Functions

When you want to draw a smooth curve of some unusual shape that can't be represented by a circle or ellipse or a standard conic section, you may find yourself resorting to representing the curve by a large number of short, straight line segments. This is not a very good solution, however, because it requires specifying a large number of points for line beginnings and endings and because it is often difficult to get the curve to look as smooth as you would like to have it. Fortunately, there are some methods for specifying a smooth curve of a desired shape through the use of a limited number of control points. The resulting curves are called *Bezier* and *B-Spline* curves. The Bezier curve was developed in the early 1970s by Pierre Bezier, who was attempting to use computers to design automobiles. The B-Spline curve is similar, but uses a different weighting of the control points so that the shape of the curve is different. In this chapter we're only going to look at Bezier and B-Spline curves in two dimensions, but the same techniques can easily be extended to three dimensions to generate pleasingly curved three-dimensional shapes such as automobile hoods and fenders.

One of the primary uses of Bezier curves is in the design of type fonts for reproducing text on a computer printer. Adobe and other companies that sell a variety of type font software rely heavily on Bezier curves to define the shape of each character in each different typeface. One of our examples in this chapter will be a typical letter from a typeface. You shouldn't expect this simple example to be quite as polished as the typefaces from Adobe, but it will give you some idea of how the technique is used. A number of different functions for generating Bezier and B-Spline curves are going to be discussed. They are all included in a demonstration program called *Bezier.cpp*, which provides a lot of examples of how they are used. Plate 19 shows an example of a number of control points connected by straight lines and then used as control points to draw Bezier and B-Spline curves. This gives you a good idea of the differences between the Bezier curve and a B-Spline curve using the same controls. Color Plate 19 shows variations of the letter *B* produced with Bezier curves.

Mathematics of the Bezier Curve

The Bezier curve is represented by the general equation:

$$p(u) = \sum_{i=0}^{n} a_i C_{(n,i)} t^i (1-t)^{n-t}$$

(Equation 18-1)

The coefficient $C_{(n,i)}$ is the binomial coefficient, so Equation 18-1 can also be written in the form:

$$p(t) = \sum_{i=0}^{n} \frac{n!}{i!(n-i)!} a_i t^i (1-t)^{n-t}$$

(Equation 18-2)

These two equations give the Bezier curve for any desired value of n, where n is the number of control points that directly influence the shape of the Bezier curve. Once we have selected a value for n, it is possible to write the Bezier curve equation in a third form using matrix notation. For $n = 4$ the matrix form is:

$$p(t) = [t^3\ t^2\ t\ 1] \begin{bmatrix} -1 & 3 & -3 & 1 \\ 3 & -6 & 3 & 0 \\ -3 & 3 & 0 & 0 \\ 1 & 0 & 0 & 0 \end{bmatrix} \begin{bmatrix} q_1 \\ q_2 \\ q_3 \\ q_4 \end{bmatrix}$$

(Equation 18-3)

The most commonly used form of the Bezier curve is with four control points. Figure 18-1 shows a box along with the resulting Bezier and B-Spline curves. The Bezier curve is the one nearest the top of the figure; the B-Spline curve is closer to the bottom. The control points are the corners of the box in the order top left, bottom left, bottom right, and top right. Observe how the Bezier curve with four control points has its beginning at the first control points; is tangential with the line between the first and second control points; has its ending at the fourth control point, and is tangential to the line between the third and fourth control points. This gives you some idea of how each curve segment will be shaped if you are designing a curved figure out of Bezier curve segments. It's not quite so easy to determine where the center of the curve is located; a little trial and error is necessary.

Mathematics of the B-Spline Curve

Like the Bezier curve, the B-Spline curve can be controlled by a specified number, n, of points. For a given number of points, the curve can be defined in the same way as the matrix representation of the Bezier curve, except that the weightings of the control points are different. Since these weightings can be varied as desired, there can be a whole family of B-Spline curves. Just one of these, for four control points, is represented by the following equation:

$$p(t) = [t^3\ t^2\ t\ 1] \begin{bmatrix} -1 & 3 & -3 & 1 \\ 3 & -6 & 3 & 0 \\ -3 & 0 & 3 & 0 \\ 1 & 4 & 1 & 0 \end{bmatrix} \begin{bmatrix} q_1 \\ q_2 \\ q_3 \\ q_4 \end{bmatrix}$$

(Equation 18-4)

Figure 18-1. Bezier and B-Spline Curves with Four Control Points

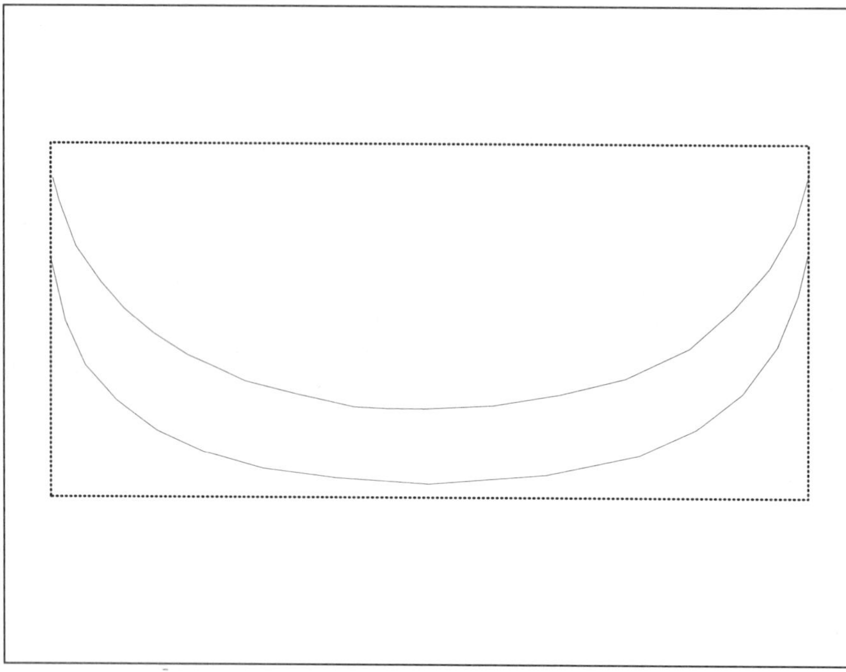

You will note from Figure 18-1 that the B-Spline curve tends to be closer to the control points than the Bezier curve. The first point of the B-Spline curve has to be designated twice if the curve is to progress smoothly from the starting point. Furthermore, it does not normally end at the fourth control point; to make this behavior occur, you have to redesignate the fourth control point at least three times.

The *Bezier* Class

The *Bezier* class is given in Listing 11-1, lines 2287 through 2449. It includes functions for drawing the Bezier curve with three different techniques. This gives you an opportunity to try each technique and make some judgments as to how fast each is and how well it works. You will observe that the results for the three methods are about equivalent, but the deCasteljau technique is much faster. So if you are going to incorporate the *graphics* module in your own graphics programs, you might want to include only this one technique for drawing Bezier curves.

The Literal Bezier Curve

The function *draw_Lit*, lines 2298 through 2324 of Listing 11-1, uses a literal rendering of Equation 18-1 to generate a Bezier curve in the box defined by four control points. The function begins in lines 2305 through 2310 by determining whether the bounding box for the Bezier curve is a straight line. If so, the function draws this line and then returns. If an actual box exists, the function uses Equation 17-1 to compute the x and y coordinates separately for increments of t of 0.01 over the range from 0 to 1 in the *for* loop comprising lines 2312 through 2323. After each increment is calculated, a line is drawn from the previous position to the new one in line 2322. Because of the very small steps, the line lengths are very short in most cases, so there is no point in trying to draw a line having a pattern (such as a dashed or dotted line), since even though the line-drawing function has this capability, each line segment is so short that the pattern just becomes a filled-in line. This is true of all of the Bezier and B-Spline drawing functions that follow. It is also possible that a line segment may be so short that it begins and ends on the same pixel. If this is true, you don't really have to draw it, so you may want to insert a test to throw out such line segments. You might also consider adjusting the step size so that you only have to plot a single pixel to the screen for each iteration of the *for* loop, which would make the function much faster.

Bezier Curves with the deCasteljau Method

The deCasteljau method is a geometric technique that gives the same results as the literal method but is much faster. It is given in lines 2329 through 2373 of Listing 11-1. It is by far the fastest of the three Bezier curve drawing methods described in this chapter. Figure 18-2 illustrates the technique that is used. The process is a recursive one; the figure shows the result after two iterations. One begins by finding the midpoints (a_1, b_1 and c_1) of the first three sides of the box defined by the four control points (a_0, b_0, c_0 and d_0). Next, a line is constructed from the first to the second midpoints and from the second to the third midpoints and the midpoints (a_2 and b_2) of these two lines are found. Then a line is constructed between these two midpoints and its midpoint (a_3) is found. This yields two new boxes, one defined by the points a_0, a_1, a_2, and a_3, and the other by the points a_3, b_2, c_1, and d_0.

We now perform exactly the same procedure for these two new boxes. We can repeat this procedure as many times as we want to achieve the resolution of the curve that we desire. At the last step, instead of further subdividing, we draw the curve along the set of line segments that define the newest set of boxes, as shown by the heavy line in the figure. The function to do all this is *drawdeC* in the listing. The function begins checking for a straight-line bounding box in lines 2333 through 2339, as with the previous function. Next, in line 2341 the function tests whether the recursion level has reached the point at which the figure is to be drawn. If so, three line segments are drawn to connect the corners of the current box, in lines 2343 through 2347. If the final level has not been reached, the level is incremented in line 2349, the four corners of each of two new boxes are computed in lines 2350 through 2369, and the function recursively calls itself twice, once for each of the two new boxes. The level is then decremented in line 2372 to make it correct for the previous level of the function before returning.

Figure 18-2. DeCasteljau Method for Generating Bezier Curves

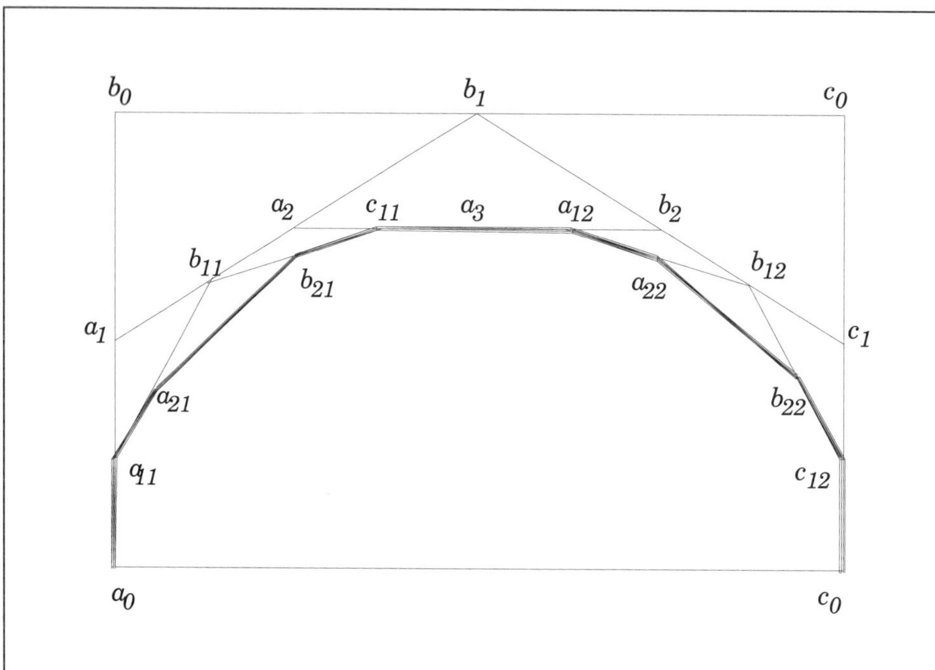

Drawing Bezier Curves with Bernstein Polynomials

The third technique for drawing Bezier curves makes use of what are called *Bernstein polynomials*. It is a little faster than the literal method but much slower than the deCasteljau method. It is included in Listing 11-1 *drawBer* in lines 2378 through 2411. Basically the math is the same as the literal method, but the function makes use of a series of *for* loops to perform the mathematical operations in sections. The beauty of this method is that not only does it work for the four-control-point version, by setting the upper limit of *j* to 3 in the second *for* loop, but it can be extended to any number of control points simply by increasing the upper limit of the second *for* loop without any other changes in the code.

Bezier Curves with Many Control Points

Thus far, we have restricted ourselves to the case where the Bezier curve is solely defined by four control points. There are two ways that we can extend the Bezier curve capability. The first is to create a more complex curve by combining individual Bezier curves that were generated using four control points. Since we know the direction that individual curves are taking at each endpoint and we also know exactly where each endpoint is, we can make sure that the ends of individual Bezier curves fit together well. The other option is to generate a complex Bezier curve by having many control points. The function *draw* in lines 2416 through 2449 of Listing 11-1 uses this option. We make use of the C++ functions *va_start*, *va_end* and *va_arg* together with a variable of the type *va_list* to extract parameters from a variable size list passed to the function. Any number of parameters may be passed by this technique, but we have limited ourselves to 20 pairs of coordinates by the size that we define in the function for the variables *xpoint* and *ypoint*. If you need more control points, simply increase the dimensions of these arrays. We've set things up in such a way that when the function encounters an *x* parameter that is less than -640 or a *y* parameter of less than -480, it stops reading in parameters. Thus the last value passed to the function must be less than -640 to stop the process. Once the parameters have all been loaded into the arrays, the function uses the same method of Bernstein polynomials that was used for *drawBer* above, except that in the second *for* loop of line 2433, we let the upper limit be the same as the number of control points that were passed to the function. The function is set up in such a way that the individual line segments that are drawn are very small. In fact, we could probably use the function for plotting a pixel to the screen instead of the line-drawing function and get faster but equally good results.

Drawing B-Spline Curves

The *BSpline* class is in Listing 11-1, lines 2453 through 2544, includes two versions of the *draw* function. The first, listed in lines 2462 through 2503, uses a literal rendering of Equation 18-4 to generate a B-Spline curve using four control points. The function begins in lines 2469 through 2475 by checking if the box is a straight line and, if so, drawing the line and returning. If a real box is present, lines 2476 through 2480 load the parameters from the structure of four points that is passed to the function into two point arrays. The point arrays consist of eight points. The first two points are duplicates of the starting point and the last four points are duplicates of the fourth point. The B-Spline math is repeated four times, for the first four points (points 0 through 3), then for points 1 through 4, for points 2 through 5, and finally for points 3 through 6.

Drawing a B-Spline Curve with Many Points

When dealing with many points, it might be better to use the same technique used with the Bezier curve and let all of the points influence the shape of the curve. To do so, however, would require a very large blending matrix. Since we don't have a good repetitive means of programming the process, the math can get very cumbersome. So instead we have produced a function that will use the B-Spline function already developed to draw a piece of the curve, using the four nearest control points, then draw the next piece with the four control points nearest it, and so forth. This version of the *draw* function is given in lines 2508 through 2544 of Listing 11-1. The function begins by assigning a variable number of passed parameters to point arrays in lines 2513 through 1517, just like the many-point Bezier function. It then enters a *for* loop, in line 2520, that is iterated for each set of four control points. Within this loop, the math is just the same as that for the B-Spline function described earlier.

The *bezier.cpp* Test Program

Listing 18-1 is a demonstration program used to show how the Bezier and B-Spline curve drawing functions work. The program begins by entering an infinite *for* loop in line 40. Each iteration of this loop starts in line 42 by setting the display mode for text and then (lines 43 through 53) displays a menu that allows you to select any of the three methods for generating a Bezier curve or the B-Spline curve or to quit. The program remains in a *while* loop (lines 48 through 53) until you make an acceptable selection. The *Quit* selection breaks out of the *for* loop begun in line 40 and allows you to go on to display 3; any of the other allowable selections produces displays 1 and 2 for the selected curve-generating technique. Display 1 is listed in lines 63 through 69. It generates six uppercase B's of different sizes, colors, and positions by calling the function *draw_alpha*. This function is listed in lines 194 through 223. The function is passed a pair of location coordinates *x* and *y*, a parameter *last* that represents the number of control boxes in the array describing the letter to be written, *letter*, which is the address of the array of control points, *scale*, which is the multiplication factor to establish the size of the letter to be drawn, and *color*, the color in which the character is to be painted. The function begins with a *for* loop in line 199 that iterates for each control box. Lines 201 through 205 form another *for* loop that sets up the properly scaled coordinates of the four points that establish a control box in the array *bline*. In line 206 the function enters a *switch* statement that calls the right Bezier drawing function as selected by the user previously. The *for* loop that started in line 199 ends in line 220. When it is complete, the outline of the character has been drawn. Lines 221 and 222 complete the function by flood-filling the character.

Display 2 is listed in lines 76 through 89. It draws 50 uppercase B's that are randomly positioned, sized, and colored. Both these displays create some variations of the letter *B* as an example of how typographical characters can be created with Bezier curves. They aren't quite as polished as those produced by a type font program, but they show clearly the nature of the process involved. The control points for making a *B* are in the array *upper_b* in lines 18 through 38. They were obtained by tracing a large B on graph paper, breaking it up into curve segments, determining the control points that would be the ends of each curve segment, and then placing the other two control points experimentally so that the curve will have the proper direction (tangential to the lines between control points 0 and 1 and between control points 3 and 4) and the curve will have the proper shape. A typical display of random B's is shown in Color Plate 19. An attempt has been made to ensure that the character is never too small and that it does not fall outside the screen boundaries. Either of these conditions confuses the floodfill function and will result in part of the character not being filled or, worse, in the function attempting to fill the entire screen with a solid color. One eccentricity of the floodfill function that you'll also observe is that if it attempts to fill a character outline that is partially superimposed on another character of the same color, the fill will be incomplete.

Listing 18-1. The bezier.cpp Test Program

```
/*

    bezier = Program to draw Bezier and B-Spline Curves

              By Roger T. Stevens   2/2/96

*/

#include "c:\cpphbook\program\graphics.cpp"

Arc arc;
Circle circle;
Line line;
Graphics graphic;
Bezier bezier;
BSpline bSpline;

void draw_alpha(int x,int y, int last, int letter[], float
scale, int color);

int x, y;
float size;
char type = NULL;
unsigned long int style[8] = {
0xFFFFFFFFL,0xC0C0C0C0L,0xFF00FF00L,0xFFF0FFF0L,
    0xF000F000L, 0xFFFF0000L, 0xFFFFF0F0L, 0xFFF0F0F0L};

void main(void)
{
    int upper_b[] = {
        -640,480,260,480,260,480,-640,480,
        -640,480,-640,440,-640,440,-640,480,
        -640,440,-480,440,-440,420,-440,320,
        -440,320,-440,-720,-440,-720,-440,320,
        -440,-720,-440,-800,-500,-820,-640,-820,
        -640,-820,-640,-860,-640,-860,-640,-820,
        -640,-860,260,-860,260,-860,-640,-860,
        160,-860,560,-860,560,-240,260,-240,
        260,-240,760,-80,760,480,160,480,
        -220,-160,160,-160,160,-160,-220,-160,
        -220,-160,-220,240,-220,240,-220,-160,
        -220,-280,60,-280,60,-280,-220,-280,
        -220,-280,-220,-620,-220,-620,-220,-280,
```

```
          160,-160,500,-160,500,380,120,380,
          40,-780,440,-780,440,-280,60,-280,
          160,380,-130,380,-130,380,160,380,
          60,-780,-140,-780,-140,-780,60,-780,
          -220,240,-220,360,-200,380,-20,380,
          -220,-620,-220,-760,-200,-780,-80,-780,
     };

     int i;

     for (;;)
     {
          graphic.setMode(3);
          printf("\nSelect one rendering method:");
          printf("\n    Literal (L)");
          printf("\n    Bernstein blend (B)");
          printf("\n    deCasteljau (D)\n    B spline (S)");
          printf("\n    Quit (Q)    ");
          while(type != 'D' && type != 'L' && type != 'B' && type != 'S' && type != 'Q')
          {
               scanf("%c",&type);
               type = toupper(type);
          }
          graphic.setMode(0x12);
          if (type == 'Q')
               break;

     /*

                         Display 1

          Draws upper case 'B' with selected method

          640 x 480 pixels x 16 colors - Mode 12H.

     */

          draw_alpha(-440,180,19,upper_b,0.2,13);
          draw_alpha(-140,120,19,upper_b,0.175,14);
          draw_alpha(210,60,19,upper_b,0.14,9);
          draw_alpha(400,-100,19,upper_b,0.095,15);
          draw_alpha(180,-180,19,upper_b,0.065,11);
          draw_alpha(0,-260,19,upper_b,0.048,12);
          getch();

     /*

                         Display 2

          Draws random upper case 'B's with selected method

          640 x 480 pixels x 16 colors - Mode 12H.
```

```
        */

            graphic.cls(15);
            color = 0;
            for (i=0; i<50; i++)
            {
                x = (rand()/25) - 544;
                y = 384 - rand() / 41;
                size = float(rand() / 300 + 30) * 0.001;
                draw_alpha(x,y,19,upper_b,size,color++);
                if (color == 15)
                    color = 0;
            }
            getch();
            type = 0;
        }
    /*

                        Display 3

        Draws a Bezier curve using Bernstein blend.

            640 x 480 pixel x 16 color mode 12H

    */

        graphic.setMode(0x12);
        graphic.cls(0);
        PATTERN = style[1];
        line.draw(-100, -40, -100,0,3);
        line.draw(0,0,3);
        line.draw(0,-240,3);
        line.draw(-320,-240,3);
        line.draw(-400,400,3);
        line.draw(180,300,3);
        line.draw(120,80,3);
        line.draw(400,-120,3);
        line.draw(520,60,3);
        getch();
        PATTERN = style[0];
        bezier.draw(14, -100, -40, -100, 0, 0, 0, 0, -240,
        -320, -240, -400, 400, 180, 300, 120, 80, 400,
    -120, 520, 60, -999);
        getch();

    /*

                        Display 4

    Draws two joined Bezier curves using Bernstein blend.

            640 x 480 pixel x 16 color mode 12H

```

```
    */
    graphic.cls(0);
    PATTERN = style[1];
    line.draw(-560,-50,-600,440,3);
    line.draw(-160,420,3);
    line.draw(-80,-50,3);
    line.draw(320,-50,3);
    line.draw(600,-50,5);
    line.draw(600,380,5);
    line.draw(80,420,5);
    line.draw(-340,-440,5);
    PATTERN = style[0];
    bezier.draw(10, -560, -50, -600, 440, -160, 420, -80,
        -50, 320, -50, -999);
    bezier.draw(12, 320, -50, 600, -50, 600, 380, 80, 420,
        -340, -440, -999);
    getch();
/*

                 Display 5

   Compares Bernstein blend Bezier and B-Spline Curves

      640 x 480 pixels x 16 colors - Mode 12H

*/
    graphic.cls(0);
    PATTERN = style[1];
    line.draw(-500,0,-440,400,3);
    line.draw(-360,400,3);
    line.draw(-280,120,3);
    line.draw(-200,-60,3);
    line.draw(-140,-20,3);
    line.draw(-40,416,3);
    line.draw(20,350,3);
    line.draw(120,-260,3);
    line.draw(160,-160,3);
    line.draw(200,250,3);
    line.draw(220,210,3);
    line.draw(250,370,3);
    line.draw(280,320,3);
    line.draw(340,-400,3);
    line.draw(380,-340,3);
    line.draw(440,-120,3);
    line.draw(520,40,3);
    PATTERN = style[0];
    bezier.draw(10, -500, 0, -440, 400, -360, 400, -280,
        120, -200, -60, -140, -20, -40, 416, 20, 350, 120,
        -260, 160, -160, 200, 250, 220, 210, 250, 370,
    280, 320, 340, -400, 380, -340, 440, 120, 520, 40,
    -999);
    bSpline.draw(13, -500, 0, -440, 400, -360, 400, -280,
        120, -200, -60, -140, -20, -40, 416, 20, 350, 120,
```

```
        -260, 160, -160, 200, 250, 220, 210, 250, 370,
    280, 320, 340, -400, 380, -340, 440, 120, 520, 40, -999);
    getch();

/*

                        Display 6

    Compares Bernstein blend Bezier and B-Spline Curves

            640 x 480 pixels x 16 colors - Mode 12H

*/

    graphic.cls(0);
    PATTERN = style[1];
    line.draw(-440,200,-440,-200,15);
    line.draw(440,-200,15);
    line.draw(440,200,15);
    line.draw(-440,200,15);
    PATTERN = style[0];
    bSpline.draw(14, -440, 200, -440, -200, 440, -200,
    440, 200, -999);
    getch();
    bezier.draw(13, -440, 200, -440, -200, 440, -200, 440,
    200, -999);
    getch();
    graphic.setMode(3);

}

/*

   draw_alpha() = Draws an alphanumeric character using
                  Bezier or B-Spline curves.

*/

void draw_alpha(int x, int y, int last, int letter[],
float scale, int color)
{
    int i,j;
    int bline[8];

    for (i=0; i<last; i++)
    {
        for (j=0; j<8; j++)
        {
               bline[j] = int(x + (letter[8*i+j] * scale));
               bline[++j] = int(y - (letter[8*i+j] * scale));
```

```
205             }
206             switch(type)
207             {
208                 case 'L':
209                     bezier.drawLit(bline, color);
210                     break;
211                 case 'D':
212                     bezier.drawdeC(bline, color);
213                 break;
214                 case 'B':
215                     bezier.drawBer(bline, color);
216                     break;
217                 case 'S':
218                     bSpline.draw(bline, color);
219             }
220         }
221         graphic.floodfill((int) (x + letter[3] * scale),
222             (int) (y - letter[4] * scale+4), color);
223     }
```

After you are tired of looking at different renditions of *B*, and select the *Quit* option, display 3 (lines 95 through 112) draws a curved line using the many-point Bernstein Bezier technique. The control points for this curve are connected with dashed lines so that you can see the shape of the hull which determines the curve. Display 4 (lines 118 through 133) draws two connected many-point Bezier curves in different colors, with their hulls also shown in different colors by dashed lines. Display 5 (lines 139 through 169) is a quite complex curve; its hull is shown in dashed lines and then the B-Spline and Bezier curves generated by these control points are drawn in different colors. This screen shows clearly how the B-Spline follows the points quite closely (while smoothing) whereas the Bezier curve is much smoother and looses a lot of detail in the original graph. This display is shown in Color Plate 20. Display 6 (lines 175 through 189) shows a rectangular hull (a single control box) together with the resulting Bezier and B-Spline curves. This shows how, for a simple curve, the B-Spline curve more closely approaches the intermediate control points and has a more boxy shape than the Bezier curve.

Part 5

More Complicated Displays

19

Displaying Text in the Graphics Modes

C programmers are all familiar with the C text-output function *printf*, and they know how to use it to produce all sorts of informative displays in the text display modes. You can also use *printf* in the regular EGA/VGA graphics display modes, but regardless of what colors you have on the screen, the data displayed by *printf* will be in white on a black background. I have seen some peculiar cases where *printf* produced totally garbage output on a graphics display, but I've never been able to isolate the exact conditions that cause this, and usually *printf* is pretty well behaved, even with graphics modes. However, VESA does not require that its extended display modes support the *printf* function, so you can't be sure when you're using one of these graphics functions exactly what you'll get if you use *printf*. It may be nothing; again, it may print okay but give very small characters if you're using a high-resolution display. There are also situations where you'll want to control the color of foreground and background in printing characters, which can't be done with *printf*. The C++ language has a function called *cout* that makes it easier to write to the screen but doesn't really address any of the problems with *printf* that we've just described. In this chapter, we're going to show you how to take charge of your own destiny by creating functions that give you control of color, size, and orientation of characters written to the screen in any display mode. You may want to create some additional classes to become part of the *Graphics* class, so that they can be used with all your graphics programs. We haven't done that here, because there are so many ways that you can define and use character routines that we don't want to force you into some limited mold. Instead, we've created the program *chartest.cpp*, which provides a good sampling of ways to work with graphics. Using these examples, you can decide just what you want to include for character generation in your *Graphics* class and find examples of how to do it. The *chartest.cpp* program is given in Listing 19-1.

The cprintf Function

Borland C++ and Turbo C++ have a function called *cprintf*, designed to be used with a global variable called *directvideo*. When this variable is set to 0, the console output uses the ROM BIOS video services to access the screen; when it is set to 1, direct-video RAM drivers are used to create the console output. The *cprintf* function only works with *directvideo* set to 0. When used in this way, *cprintf* is much like *printf* except that the foreground and background colors with which it prints characters can be specified by two functions called *textcolor* and *textbackground*, respectively. Setting of the foreground and background colors using these functions does not affect any characters already written on the screen; these functions affect only characters written after they are called. We could often use this flexibility in our programs, but unfortunately *cprintf* has two drawbacks. The first, and most serious, is that the background-setting function does not work for graphics modes, so that regardless of how hard you try, the background when using *cprintf* is always black. Second, even if you're in a text mode, the *textbackground* function can set only the eight low-intensity colors, so you cannot have high-intensity background colors using *cprintf*.

Using the Built-in Fonts

The functions described in the rest of this chapter make it possible for you to display characters on the screen that have various capabilities not available with *printf* and *cprintf*. In order for any of these functions to work, however, you need a table that defines the characteristics of each character in the font. For each character, we're going to be using an eight-pixel-wide character, but the lengths (number of character lines) may be 8, 14, or 16 lines. Therefore an array of 8, 14, or 16 bytes for each character is needed. If you want to, you can design each character on a sheet of grid paper and then convert the characters into array definitions, but it's a lot easier to make use of one of the character fonts that is already built into the ROM BIOS extensions that are part of your EGA or VGA card. To access one of these fonts, all you need to know is the address where the font array begins. To find this, we set up a pointer called *char_table* of type *unsigned char far ** in line 30 and then call the function *findChar* in line 40 to load this pointer with the font array address by means of the ROM BIOS video services. The function is listed in lines 408 through 421. It simply sets the registers properly and then calls *intr* in line 415 to access the ROM BIOS video service. The address for the character font we have selected is given in registers *reg.r_es* and *reg.r_bp*, which we transfer to *address* in lines 416 and 417. The number of lines per character is returned and set up in the global variable *lines* in line 418. The number of bytes per character is returned and set up in the global variable *bytes_per_char* in line 419. The *address* is then returned in line 420. The parameter type that is passed to this function determines which font's address will be returned; for cases 0, 1, 3, and 4 an 8-bit-high font is pointed to, for cases 2 and 5 a 14-bit-high font is pointed to, and for cases 6 and 7 a 16-bit-high font is pointed to.

Listing 19-1. Listing of chartest.cpp *Program*

```
/*

    chartest = Program to demonstrate display of characters
                        in graphics modes

                   By Roger T. Stevens  3/8/96

*/

1     #include <stdio.h>
2     #include <stdarg.h>
3     #include <math.h>
4     #include <dos.h>
5     #include <conio.h>

6     void cls(int color);
7     void color_printf (char *fmt,int color,...);
8     void display(unsigned long int address, int color_plane,
9     unsigned char ch);
10    unsigned char far *findChar (int type, int *lines, int
11    *bytes_per_char);
12    void setMode(int mode);
13    void setPage(unsigned long int offset);
14    void writeVchar(int x, int y, int ch, int color);
15    void writeHchar(int x, int y, char ch, int color);
16    void writeHstring(int x, int y, char *string, int color);
17    void writeString(int x, int y, char *string, int color);
18    void writeVstring(int x, int y, char *string, int color);
19    void writeBigChar(int x, int y, int ch, int color);
20    void writeBigString(int x, int y, char *string, int
```

```
color);
void writeHiResString(int x, int y, char *string, int
color);
void writeHiColString(int x, int y, char *string, int
back_color,int fore_color);
void writeVideoChar(int x, int y, int ch, int color);
void writeVideoString(int x, int y, char *string, int
color);

union REGS reg;

unsigned char far *char_table;
int color;
int xres = 640, yres = 350;
int lines,mode, old_bank,type;

void main(void)
{
    struct REGPACK reg;
    int k, x, y, bytes_per_char;

    directvideo = 0;
    type = 2;
    char_table = findChar (type, &lines, &bytes_per_char);

/*
╔══════════════════════════════════════════════════════════╗
║                                                          ║
║                        Display 1                         ║
║                                                          ║
║  Techniques for writing characters in display mode 12H   ║
║            640 pixels x 480 pixels x 16 colors           ║
║                                                          ║
╚══════════════════════════════════════════════════════════╝
*/

    setMode(0x10);
    cls(1);
    textbackground(3);
    textcolor(13);
    writeBigString(20,10,"Big Letters",158);
    writeVideoString(20,70,"Video Letters",243);
    writeBigChar(560,10,'O',63);
    writeBigChar(590,10,'K',63);
    writeVideoChar(400,220,'O',62);
    writeVideoChar(430,220,'K',62);
    x= 45;
    y= 115;
    for (k=0; k<93; k++)
```

```
        {
            if (!(k%25))
            {
                y+=20;
                x = 45;
            }
            writeHchar(x, y, k+33, 31);
            x += 16;
        }
        x= 520;
        y= 291;
        for (k=0; k<93; k++)
        {
            if (!(k%17))
            {
                x += 16;
                y = 291;
            }
            writeVchar(x, y, k+33, 47);
            y -= 10;
        }
        writeHstring(30,300,"Sorry to have to be this way,
        but we need to have a string that is long enough
        to extend over more than one row so as to make
sure that the program works properly for
automatically moving to the next line...",95);
        writeVstring(480,258, "This is a vertical
string...",159);
        gotoxy(6,17);
        printf("This string uses 'printf'...");
        gotoxy(6,19);
        cprintf("This string uses 'cprintf'...");
        gotoxy(6,21);
        color_printf("This string uses
'color_printf'...",241);
        getch();

/*

                        Display 2

        Displaying characeters in mode 70H
            320 x 400 pixels x 256 colors

*/

        setMode(0x70);
        xres = 320; yres = 400;
        type = 2;
```

```
    char_table = findChar (type, &lines,
&bytes_per_char);
    writeString(10,80,"These are the times that try
    men's souls. The summer soldier and the sunshine
    patriot...",31);
    getch();

/*

                    Display 3

      Displaying characters in mode 71H
        320 x 240 pixels x 256 colors

*/
    setMode(0x71);
    xres = 320; yres = 240;
    writeString(10,80,"These are the times that try
    men's souls. The summer soldier and the sunshine
    patriot...",31);
    getch();

/*

                    Display 4

      Displaying characters in mode 72H
        320 x 480 pixels x 256 colors

*/
    setMode(0x72);
    xres = 320; yres = 480;
    writeString(10,80,"These are the times that try
    men's souls. The summer soldier and the sunshine
    patriot...",31);
    getch();

/*

                    Display 5

      Displaying characters in mode 73H
        360 x 400 pixels x 256 colors

*/
```

```
    setMode(0x73);
    xres = 360; yres = 400;
    writeString(10,80,"These are the times that try
    men's souls. The summer soldier and the sunshine
    patriot...",31);
    getch();

/*
            Display 6

  Displaying characters in mode 74H
    360 x 480 pixels x 256 colors

*/
    setMode(0x74);
    xres = 360; yres = 480;
    writeString(10,80,"These are the times that try
    men's souls. The summer soldier and the sunshine
    patriot...",31);
    getch();

/*
            Display 7

  Displaying characters in mode 105H
   1024 x 768 pixels x 256 colors

*/

    setMode(0x105);
    printf("Now is the time for all good men");
    printf(" to come to the aid of their country");
    getch();
    writeHiResString(20,400,"Now is the time for all
    good men ",158);
    writeHiResString(548,400,"to come to the aid of
    their country",158);
    getch();
```

```
/*
                    Display 8

     Displaying characters in mode 116H
       1024 x 768 pixels x 32K colors
*/

    setMode(0x116);
    writeHiColString(20,400,"Now is the time for all
    good men ", 0x1F, 0x7F30);
    writeHiColString(548,400,"to come to the aid of
    their country", 0x1F,0x7F30);
    getch();
    setMode(0x03);
}

/*
   setMode() = Sets Video Mode (includes
         undocumented VGA modes)
*/

void setMode(int vmode)
{
    extern int old_bank, mode, xres, yres;
    char result;
    unsigned int params[17] = {0x6b00, 0x5901, 0x5a02,
    0x8e03, 0x5e04, 0x8a05,0x4009, 0x0014, 0xe317,
    0x0d06, 0x3e07, 0xea10, 0xac11, 0xdf12, 0xe715,
    0x0616, 0x4109};
    char far * address;
    long int i;

    mode = vmode;
    switch(mode)
    {
        case 0x70:  /* 320 x 400 pixel resolution */
            reg.h.al = 0x13;
            int86 (0x10,&reg,&reg);
            outport(0x3c4,0x0604);
            outportb(0x3d4,0x11);
            result = inportb(0x3d5);
            outportb(0x3d5,result & 0x7f);
            for (i=6; i<9; i++)
```

```
                outport(0x3d4,params[i]);
            break;

        case 0x71:  /* 320 x 240 pixels */
            reg.h.al = 0x13;
            int86 (0x10,&reg,&reg);
            outport(0x3c4,0x0604);
            outport(0x3c4,0x0100);
            outportb(0x3c2,0xc3);
            outport(0x3c4,0x300);
            outportb(0x3d4,0x11);
            result = inportb(0x3d5);
            outportb(0x3d5,result & 0x7f);
            for (i=7; i<17; i++)
                outport(0x3d4,params[i]);
            break;

        case 0x72:  /* 320 x 480 pixels */
            reg.h.al = 0x13;
            int86 (0x10,&reg,&reg);
            outport(0x3c4,0x0604);
            outport(0x3c4,0x0100);
            outportb(0x3c2,0xc3);
            outport(0x3c4,0x300);
            outportb(0x3d4,0x11);
            result = inportb(0x3d5);
            outportb(0x3d5,result & 0x7f);
            for (i=6; i<16; i++)
                outport(0x3d4,params[i]);
            outport(0x3d4,0x4009);
            break;

        case 0x73:  /* 360 x 400 pixels */
            reg.h.al = 0x13;
            int86 (0x10,&reg,&reg);
            outport(0x3c4,0x0604);
            outport(0x3c4,0x0100);
            outportb(0x3c2,0x67);
            outport(0x3c4,0x300);
            outportb(0x3d4,0x11);
            result = inportb(0x3d5);
            outportb(0x3d5,result & 0x7f);
            for (i=0; i<9; i++)
                outport(0x3d4,params[i]);
            outport(0x3d4,0x2d13);
            break;

        case 0x74:  /* 360 x 480 pixels */
            reg.h.al = 0x13;
            int86 (0x10,&reg,&reg);
            outport(0x3c4,0x0604);
            outport(0x3c4,0x0100);
```

```
           outportb(0x3c2,0xe7);
           outport(0x3c4,0x300);
           outportb(0x3d4,0x11);
           result = inportb(0x3d5);
           outportb(0x3d5,result & 0x7f);
           for (i=0; i<16; i++)
              outport(0x3d4,params[i]);
           outport(0x3d4,0x2d13);
           break;
        case 0x0D:
        case 0x13:
        case 0x10D:
        case 0x10E:
        case 0x10F:
           xres = 320;
           yres = 200;
           break;
        case 0x0E:
           xres = 640;
           yres = 200;
           break;
        case 0x0F:
        case 0x10:
           xres = 640;
           yres = 350;
           break;
        case 0x11:
        case 0x12:
        case 0x101:
        case 0x110:
        case 0x111:
        case 0x112:
           xres = 640;
           yres = 480;
           break;
        case 0x100:
           xres = 640;
           yres = 400;
           break;
        case 0x102:
        case 0x103:
        case 0x113:
        case 0x114:
        case 0x115:
           xres = 800;
           yres = 600;
           break;
        case 0x104:
        case 0x105:
        case 0x116:
        case 0x117:
        case 0x118:
```

```
                xres = 1024;
                yres = 768;
                break;
            case 0x106:
            case 0x107:
            case 0x119:
            case 0x11A:
            case 0x11B:
                xres = 1280;
                yres = 1024;
        }
        if ((mode >= 0x70) && (mode < 0x100))
        {
            outport(0x3c4,0x0f02);  // enable writes to all
                                    // four planes
            for(i=0; i<0xFFFF; i++)
            {
                address = (char far *) 0xA0000000L + i;
                *address = 0x00;
            }
        }
        else
        {
            if (vmode >= 0x100)
            {
                reg.x.ax = 0x4F02;
                reg.x.bx = mode;
            }
            else
                reg.x.ax = mode;
            int86 (0x10,&reg,&reg);
            old_bank = 0;
        }
}

/*
    writeString() - writes a string horizontally
*/

#define seq_out(index,val)   {outp(0x3C4,index);\
                             outp(0x3C5,val);}
#define graph_out(index,val)   {outp(0x3CE,index);\
                             outp(0x3CF,val);}

void writeString(int x, int y, char *string, int color)
{
    unsigned char char_test, exist_color;
    int i, j, k, foreground,background,point_color;
```

```
    unsigned long int offset;
    char far *address;
    unsigned int plane;
    int char_offset,p=0,lines;

    switch(type)
    {
        case 0:
        case 1:
        case 3:
        case 4:
            lines = 8;
            break;
        case 2:
        case 5:
            lines = 14;
            break;
        case 6:
        case 7:
            lines = 16;
    }
    foreground = color & 0x0F;
    background = (color & 0xF0) >> 4;
    while (string[p])
    {
        char_offset = (string[p]) * lines;
        for (i=0; i<lines; i++)
        {
            for (j=0; j<8; j++)
            {
                char_test = 0x80 >> j;
                if ((char_table[char_offset+i] &
            char_test) != 0)
                    point_color = foreground;
                else
                    point_color = background;
                offset = (long)xres * (y+i) + x + j;
                plane = (0x01 << (offset % 4));
                seq_out(2,plane);
                offset >>= 2;
                address = (char far *)(0xA0000000L +
                offset);
                *address = point_color;
            }

        }
        x += 8;
        if (x>xres-8)
        {
            x=0;
            y += lines;
        }
```

```
            p++;
        }
    }

    /*
        findChar() = Returns the address of a character table
    */

    unsigned char far *findChar (int type, int *lines, int
    *bytes_per_char)
    {
        struct REGPACK reg;
        unsigned char far *address;

        reg.r_bx = type << 8;
        reg.r_ax = 0x1130;
        intr(0x10,&reg);
        address = (unsigned char far*)(reg.r_es*0x10000 +
        reg.r_bp);
        *lines = reg.r_dx & 0xFF;
        *bytes_per_char = reg.r_cx;
        return(address);
    }

    /*
                    cls() = Clears the Screen
    */

    void cls(int color)
    {
         union REGS reg;

         reg.x.ax = 0x0600;
         reg.x.cx = 0;
         reg.x.dx = 0x184F;
         reg.h.bh = color;
         int86(0x10,&reg,&reg);
    }

    /*
         writeHchar() = writes a character horizontally
```

```
*/

#define seq_out(index,val)   {outp(0x3C4,index);\
                              outp(0x3C5,val);}
#define graph_out(index,val)  {outp(0x3CE,index);\
                              outp(0x3CF,val);}

void writeHchar(int x, int y, char ch, int color)
{
   char far * mem_address;
   unsigned char char_test, exist_color;
   int i, j, k, foreground,background, height, width,
      point_color,dummy,mask;

   int char_offset,lines;

   switch(type)
   {
      case 0:
      case 1:
      case 3:
      case 4:
         lines = 8;
         break;
      case 2:
      case 5:
         lines = 14;
         break;
      case 6:
      case 7:
         lines = 16;
   }
   char_offset = ch * lines;
   foreground = color & 0x0F;
   background = (color & 0xF0) >> 4;
   for (i=0; i<lines; i++)
   {
      height = y+i;
      for (j=0; j<8; j++)
      {
         width = x+j;
         char_test = 0x80 >> j;
         if ((char_table[char_offset+i] & char_test)
            != 0)
            point_color = foreground;
         else
            point_color = background;
         mem_address = (char far *)0xA0000000L +
         (long)(height) * 80L + ((long)(width) /
         8L);
```

```
                mask = 0x80 >> ((width) % 8);
                graph_out(8,mask);
                seq_out(2,0x0F);
                dummy = *mem_address;
                *mem_address = 0;
                seq_out(2,point_color);
                *mem_address = 0xFF;
            }
        }
        seq_out(2,0x0F);
        graph_out(8,0xFF);
    }

/*

        writeVchar() = writes a character vertically

*/

#define seq_out(index,val)   {outp(0x3C4,index);\
                              outp(0x3C5,val);}
#define graph_out(index,val)   {outp(0x3CE,index);\
                              outp(0x3CF,val);}

void writeVchar(int x, int y, int ch, int color)
{
    char far * mem_address;
    unsigned char char_test, exist_color;
    int i, j, k, foreground,background, height, width,
        point_color,dummy,mask;

    int char_offset,lines;

    switch(type)
    {
        case 0:
        case 1:
        case 3:
        case 4:
            lines = 8;
            break;
        case 2:
        case 5:
            lines = 14;
            break;
        case 6:
        case 7:
            lines = 16;
    }
    char_offset = ch * lines;
    foreground = color & 0x0F;
```

```
    background = (color & 0xF0) >> 4;
    for (i=0; i<lines; i++)
    {
        width = x+i;
        for (j=0; j<8; j++)
        {
            height = y-j;
            char_test = 0x80 >> j;
            if ((char_table[char_offset+i] & char_test)
                != 0)
                point_color = foreground;
            else
                point_color = background;
            mem_address = (char far *)0xA0000000L +
            (long)(height) * 80L + ((long)(width) /
            8L);
            mask = 0x80 >> ((width) % 8);
            graph_out(8,mask);
            seq_out(2,0x0F);
            dummy = *mem_address;
            *mem_address = 0;
            seq_out(2,point_color);
            *mem_address = 0xFF;
        }
    }
    seq_out(2,0x0F);
    graph_out(8,0xFF);
}

/*

        writeHstring() = writes a string horizontally

*/

#define seq_out(index,val)   {outp(0x3C4,index);\
                             outp(0x3C5,val);}
#define graph_out(index,val)  {outp(0x3CE,index);\
                             outp(0x3CF,val);}

void writeHstring(int x, int y, char *string, int color)
{
    char far * mem_address;
    unsigned char char_test, exist_color;
    int i, j, k, foreground,background, height, width,
        point_color,dummy,mask;

    int char_offset,p=0,lines;

    switch(type)
```

```
    {
        case 0:
        case 1:
        case 3:
        case 4:
            lines = 8;
            break;
        case 2:
        case 5:
            lines = 14;
            break;
        case 6:
        case 7:
            lines = 16;
    }
    while (string[p])
    {
        char_offset = (string[p]) * lines;
        foreground = color & 0x0F;
        background = (color & 0xF0) >> 4;
        for (i=0; i<lines; i++)
        {
            height = y+i;
            for (j=0; j<8; j++)
            {
                width = x+j;
                char_test = 0x80 >> j;
                if ((char_table[char_offset+i] &
            char_test) != 0)
                    point_color = foreground;
                else
                    point_color = background;
                mem_address = (char far *)0xA0000000L +
                    (long)(height) * 80L
                    + ((long)(width) / 8L);
                mask = 0x80 >> ((width) % 8);
                graph_out(8,mask);
                seq_out(2,0x0F);
                dummy = *mem_address;
                *mem_address = 0;
                seq_out(2,point_color);
                *mem_address = 0xFF;
            }
        }
        seq_out(2,0x0F);
        graph_out(8,0xFF);
        x += 8;
        if (x>xres-8)
        {
            x=0;
            y += lines;
        }
```

```
            p++;
        }
    }

    /*
            writeVstring() = writes a string vertically
    */

    #define seq_out(index,val)   {outp(0x3C4,index);\
                                 outp(0x3C5,val);}
    #define graph_out(index,val)   {outp(0x3CE,index);\
                                 outp(0x3CF,val);}

    void writeVstring(int x, int y, char *string, int color)
    {
        char far * mem_address;
        unsigned char char_test, exist_color;
        int i, j, k, foreground,background, height, width,
            point_color,dummy,mask;

        int char_offset,p=0,lines;

        switch(type)
        {
            case 0:
            case 1:
            case 3:
            case 4:
                lines = 8;
                break;
            case 2:
            case 5:
                lines = 14;
                break;
            case 6:
            case 7:
                lines = 16;
        }
        while (string[p])
        {
            char_offset = (string[p]) * lines;
            foreground = color & 0x0F;
            background = (color & 0xF0) >> 4;
            for (i=0; i<lines; i++)
            {
                width = x+i;
                for (j=0; j<8; j++)
                {
```

```
                  height = y-j;
                  char_test = 0x80 >> j;
                  if ((char_table[char_offset+i] &
              char_test) != 0)
                      point_color = foreground;
                  else
                      point_color = background;
                  mem_address = (char far *)0xA0000000L +
                      (long)(height) * 80L +
          ((long)(width) / 8L);
                  mask = 0x80 >> ((width) % 8);
                  graph_out(8,mask);
                  seq_out(2,0x0F);
                  dummy = *mem_address;
                  *mem_address = 0;
                  seq_out(2,point_color);
                  *mem_address = 0xFF;
              }
          }
          seq_out(2,0x0F);
          graph_out(8,0xFF);
          y -= 8;
          if (y<8)
          {
              y = yres - 8;
              x += lines;
          }
          p++;
      }
}

/*

        writeBigChar() = writes a big character

*/

#define seq_out(index,val)   {outp(0x3C4,index);\
                              outp(0x3C5,val);}
#define graph_out(index,val)   {outp(0x3CE,index);\
                              outp(0x3CF,val);}

void writeBigChar(int x, int y, int ch, int color)
{
    char far * mem_address;
    unsigned char char_test, exist_color;
    int i, j, k, m, foreground,background, height,
width, point_color,dummy,mask;
    int char_offset,lines;
```

```
        switch(type)
        {
            case 0:
            case 1:
            case 3:
            case 4:
                lines = 8;
                break;
            case 2:
            case 5:
                lines = 14;
                break;
            case 6:
            case 7:
                lines = 16;
        }
        char_offset = ch * lines;
        foreground = color & 0x0F;
        background = (color & 0xF0) >> 4;
        for (i=0; i<lines; i++)
        {
            for (j=0; j<8; j++)
            {
                for (m=0; m<4; m++)
                {
                    for (k=0; k<4; k++)
                    {
                        height = y+4*i+k;
                        width = x+4*j+m;
                        char_test = 0x80 >> j;
                        if ((char_table[char_offset+i] &
                        char_test) != 0)
                            point_color = foreground;
                        else
                            point_color = background;
                        mem_address = (char far
                *)0xA0000000L + (long)(height) *
                            80L + ((long)(width) / 8L);
                        mask = 0x80 >> ((width) % 8);
                        graph_out(8,mask);
                        seq_out(2,0x0F);
                        dummy = *mem_address;
                        *mem_address = 0;
                        seq_out(2,point_color);
                        *mem_address = 0xFF;
                    }
                }
            }
        }
        seq_out(2,0x0F);
        graph_out(8,0xFF);
    }
```

```
/*

    writeVideoChar() = writes a big video-type character

*/
#define seq_out(index,val)   {outp(0x3C4,index);\
                              outp(0x3C5,val);}
#define graph_out(index,val)  {outp(0x3CE,index);\
                              outp(0x3CF,val);}

void writeVideoChar(int x, int y, int ch, int color)
{
    char far * mem_address;
    unsigned char char_test, exist_color;
    int i, j, k, m, foreground,background, height,
width, point_color,dummy,mask;

    int char_offset,lines;

    switch(type)
    {
        case 0:
        case 1:
        case 3:
        case 4:
            lines = 8;
            break;
        case 2:
        case 5:
            lines = 14;
            break;
        case 6:
        case 7:
            lines = 16;
    }
    char_offset = ch * lines;
    foreground = color & 0x0F;
    background = (color & 0xF0) >> 4;
    for (i=0; i<lines; i++)
    {
        for (j=0; j<8; j++)
        {
            for (m=1; m<4; m++)
            {
                for (k=1; k<4; k++)
                {
                    height = y+4*i+k;
                    width = x+4*j+m;
```

```
                    char_test = 0x80 >> j;
                    if ((char_table[char_offset+i] &
                    char_test) != 0)
                       point_color = foreground;
                    else
                       point_color = background;
                    mem_address = (char far
              *)0xA0000000L + (long)(height)
                       * 80L +((long)(width) / 8L);
                    mask = 0x80 >> ((width) % 8);
                    graph_out(8,mask);
                    seq_out(2,0x0F);
                    dummy = *mem_address;
                    *mem_address = 0;
                    seq_out(2,point_color);
                    *mem_address = 0xFF;
                 }
              }
           }
        }
        seq_out(2,0x0F);
        graph_out(8,0xFF);
     }

     /*

        writeBigString() = writes a string of big characters

     */

     #define seq_out(index,val)   {outp(0x3C4,index);\
                                  outp(0x3C5,val);}
     #define graph_out(index,val)   {outp(0x3CE,index);\
                                  outp(0x3CF,val);}

     void writeBigString(int x, int y, char *string, int color)
     {
        char far * mem_address;
        unsigned char char_test, exist_color;
        int i, j, k, m, foreground,background, height,
     width, point_color,dummy,mask;
        int char_offset, p=0, lines[8]={8, 8, 14, 8, 8, 14,
           16, 16}, start,end;

        start = 0;
        end = 4;
        while (string[p])
        {
           char_offset = string[p] * lines[type];
           foreground = color & 0x0F;
```

```
        background = (color & 0xF0) >> 4;
        for (i=0; i<lines[type]; i++)
        {
            for (j=0; j<8; j++)
            {
                for (m=start; m<end; m++)
                {
                    for (k=start; k<end; k++)
                    {
                        height = y+4*i+k;
                        width = x+4*j+m;
                        char_test = 0x80 >> j;
                        if ((char_table[char_offset+i] &
                            char_test) != 0)
                            point_color = foreground;
                        else
                            point_color = background;
                        mem_address = (char far
                    *)0xA0000000L + (long)
                            (height) * 80L +
                ((long)(width)/ 8L);
                        mask = 0x80 >> ((width) % 8);
                        graph_out(8,mask);
                        seq_out(2,0x0F);
                        dummy = *mem_address;
                        *mem_address = 0;
                        seq_out(2,point_color);
                        *mem_address = 0xFF;
                    }
                }
            }
        }
        seq_out(2,0x0F);
        graph_out(8,0xFF);
        x += 32;
        if (x>607)
        {
            x=0;
            y += 56;
        }
        p++;
    }
}

/*

    writeHiResString() = writes a string of double sized
    characters in 1024 x 768 pixel x 256 color mode 105H.

*/
```

```
void writeHiResString(int x, int y, char *string, int
color)
{
    char far * mem_address;
    unsigned long int offset;
    unsigned char char_test, exist_color;
    int i, j, k, m, foreground,background, height,
width, point_color,dummy,mask;
    int char_offset, p=0, lines[8]={8, 8, 14, 8, 8, 14,
        16, 16}, start,end;

    start = 0;
    end = 2;
    while (string[p])
    {
        char_offset = string[p] * lines[type];
        foreground = color & 0x0F;
        background = (color & 0xF0) >> 4;
        for (i=0; i<lines[type]; i++)
        {
            for (j=0; j<8; j++)
            {
                for (m=start; m<end; m++)
                {
                    for (k=start; k<end; k++)
                    {
                        height = y+2*i+k;
                        width = x+2*j+m;
                        char_test = 0x80 >> j;
                        if ((char_table[char_offset+i] &
                            char_test) != 0)
                            point_color = foreground;
                        else
                            point_color = background;
                        offset = (long)height * 1024L +
                            width;
                        setPage(offset);
                        mem_address = (char far
                    *)(0xA0000000L +
                            (unsigned int) offset);
                        *mem_address = point_color;
                    }
                }
            }
        }
        x += 16;
        if (x>1008)
        {
            x=0;
            y += 28;
```

```
        }
        p++;
    }
}

/*
    writeHiColString() = writes a string of double sized
    characters in 1024 x 768 pixel x 32K color mode 116H
*/

void writeHiColString(int x, int y, char *string, int
back_color, int fore_color)
{
    char far * mem_address;
    unsigned long int offset;
    unsigned char char_test;
    int i, j, k, m, height, width,
point_color,dummy,mask;
    int char_offset, p=0, lines[8]={8, 8, 14, 8, 8, 14,
        16, 16}, start,end;

    start = 0;
    end = 2;
    while (string[p])
    {
        char_offset = string[p] * lines[type];
        for (i=0; i<lines[type]; i++)
        {
            for (j=0; j<8; j++)
            {
                for (m=start; m<end; m++)
                {
                    for (k=start; k<end; k++)
                    {
                        height = y+2*i+k;
                        width = x+2*j+m;
                        char_test = 0x80 >> j;
                        if ((char_table[char_offset+i] &
                            char_test) != 0)
                            point_color = fore_color;
                        else
                            point_color = back_color;
                        offset = (long)height * 2048L +
                            2*width;
                        setPage(offset);
                        mem_address = (char far
```

```
                        *)(0xA0000000L +
                             (unsigned int) offset);
                            *mem_address++ = point_color &
                            0xFF;
                            *mem_address = point_color >> 8;
                        }
                    }
                }
            }
            x += 16;
            if (x>1008)
            {
                x=0;
                y += 28;
            }
            p++;
        }
}

/*

    writeVideoString() = writes a big video-type string

*/

#define seq_out(index,val)  {outp(0x3C4,index);\
                             outp(0x3C5,val);}
#define graph_out(index,val)  {outp(0x3CE,index);\
                             outp(0x3CF,val);}

void writeVideoString(int x, int y, char *string, int
color)
{
    char far * mem_address;
    unsigned char char_test, exist_color;
    int i, j, k, m, foreground,background, height,
width, point_color,dummy,mask;

    int char_offset,p=0,lines,start,end;
    switch(type)
    {
        case 0:
        case 1:
        case 3:
        case 4:
            lines = 8;
            break;
        case 2:
        case 5:
```

```
                lines = 14;
                break;
            case 6:
            case 7:
                lines = 16;
        }
        start = 1;
        end = 4;
        while (string[p])
        {
            char_offset = string[p] * lines;
            foreground = color & 0x0F;
            background = (color & 0xF0) >> 4;
            for (i=0; i<lines; i++)
            {
                for (j=0; j<8; j++)
                {
                    for (m=start; m<end; m++)
                    {
                        for (k=start; k<end; k++)
                        {
                            height = y+4*i+k;
                            width = x+4*j+m;
                            char_test = 0x80 >> j;
                            if ((char_table[char_offset+i] &
                                char_test) != 0)
                                point_color = foreground;
                            else
                                point_color = background;
                            mem_address = (char far
                        *)0xA0000000L + (long)
                (height) * 80L +
((long)(width) / 8L);
                            mask = 0x80 >> ((width) % 8);
                            graph_out(8,mask);
                            seq_out(2,0x0F);
                            dummy = *mem_address;
                            *mem_address = 0;
                            seq_out(2,point_color);
                            *mem_address = 0xFF;
                        }
                    }
                }
            }
            seq_out(2,0x0F);
            graph_out(8,0xFF);
            x += 32;
            if (x>607)
            {
                x=0;
                y += 56;
```

```
        }
        p++;
    }
}

/*
    color_printf = printf with selected foreground and
                   background colors.
*/

#define seq_out(index,val)  {outp(0x3C4,index);\
                              outp(0x3C5,val);}

void color_printf (char *fmt,int color,...)
{
    union REGS reg;
    char ch, string[200];
    int i = 0 ,j, k, mask1, mask2;
    unsigned int offset;
    char far *address;
    int char_offset, foreground, background, width,
    point_color, dummy;
    unsigned char char_test;
    va_list ap;

    va_start (ap,color);
    vsprintf(string,fmt,ap);
    va_end(ap);
    while ((ch=string[i++]) != '\0')
    {
        if (ch == 0x0A)
        {
            reg.h.ah = 3;
            int86(0x10,&reg,&reg);
            reg.h.dl = 0;
            reg.h.dh++;
            reg.h.ah = 2;
            int86(0x10,&reg,&reg);
        }
        else
        {
            reg.h.ah = 3;
            reg.h.bh = 0;
            int86(0x10,&reg,&reg);
            char_offset = ch * 14;
            for (k=0; k<14; k++)
            {
                offset = (long)(reg.h.dh*14+k)*80L +
```

```
                    reg.h.dl;
                    mask1 = 0x10;
                    mask2 = 0x01;
                    address = (char far *) 0xA0000000L +
                    offset;
                    for (j=0; j<4; j++)
                    {
                        seq_out(2,(0x01 << j));
                        if ((mask1 & color) != 0) &&
                    ((mask2 & color) != 0))
                            *address = 0xFF;
                        else
                        {
                            if ((mask1 & color) != 0)
                                *address =
                    ~char_table[char_offset
                    + k];
                            if ((mask2 & color) != 0)
                                *address =
                char_table[char_offset +
                k];
                        }
                        mask1 <<= 1;
                        mask2 <<= 1;
                    }
                }
                reg.h.bh = 0;
                reg.x.dx++;
                reg.h.ah = 2;
                int86(0x10,&reg,&reg);
            }
        }
        seq_out(2,0x0F);
}

/*

        setPage() = sets the display memory page

*/

void setPage(unsigned long int offset)
{
    union REGS reg;

extern old_bank;
    reg.x.dx = (int)(offset >> 16);
    if (reg.x.dx != old_bank)
    {
        old_bank = reg.x.dx;
```

```
1169            reg.x.ax = 0x4F05;
1170            reg.x.bx = 0;
1171            int86(0x10, &reg, &reg);
1172        }
1173    }
```

The color_printf Function

The *color_printf* function is designed to do everything that *printf* does but also to give you both foreground and background control of individual characters It is listed in lines 1089 through 1158. This version of *color_printf* works only with 16-color graphics modes and the 8 × 14 pixel character set, but once you understand how it operates, you can easily make a comparable function that will work with 256-color graphics modes, with undocumented or extended modes, or with text modes. The function begins by using the C functions and variables *va_start*, *va_end*, *va_list*, and *vsprintf* to produce the exact ASCII string that *printf* would normally output to the screen; instead of sending it to the screen, however, the function places it in an array *string* (lines 1101 through 1104). We've set *string* to be 200 bytes in size, which gives you about two and a half lines of text. If you think you're going to need more than this for a single *color_printf* call, you can increase the size of the array. The function then enters a *while* loop (line 1105) that gets the first character from *string* and then on each iteration gets the next character until a NULL is encountered, indicating that the string is exhausted. At each iteration, the function first checks to see if the character is a line feed (line 1107). If it is, a ROM BIOS video service is called to get the current cursor position, the row value of this position is incremented, and another ROM BIOS video service is used to store the new cursor position (lines 1109 through 1114). If the character was not a line feed, the function continues by getting the cursor position (lines 1117 through 1120). It then computes the offset into the character table for the character just read from the string (line 1121). The function then enters a *for* loop (line 1122) that is iterated once for each of the 14 lines of the character. Within this loop, the function first computes the offset from the base display memory address where the first line of the character is to be placed (lines 1124 and 1125). In lines 1126 and 1127, the function initializes two masks for use with the background and foreground color determination. Lines 1128 and 1129 compute the display memory address. Then another *for* loop is entered (line 1130), which iterates once for each of the four color planes. Sequencer register 2 is first set to activate only the color plane indicated by the loop index (line 1132). At each iteration of the loop, the function then checks whether the background and foreground colors for this color plane are both unequal to 0 (lines 1133 and 1134). If this is the case, both foreground and background colors require each memory bit to be set to 1, so the display memory location is sent an 0xFF to set these bits to 1 (line 1135). If both colors weren't set for this character line, the function next checks whether the background color is to be set for this color plane. If so, it sends the inverse of the contents of the character table for this character line to display memory, causing all background bits to be set to 1 (lines 1138 through 1141). The function next checks whether the foreground color is to be set for this color plane. If so, it sends the contents of the character table for this character line to display memory, causing all foreground bits to be set to 1 (lines 1142 through 1145). You'll notice that if both these *if* statements were found to be true, the second addressing of display memory would override the first, causing an incorrect memory setting. However, this can never occur, since the case of both foreground and background colors being set in this plane was already handled by the previous conditional test, so that this section occurs only if one of the two colors was 0 for this color plane. After sending data to memory, the function shifts the location of the mask bits (lines 1147 and 1148) and performs another iteration of the loop. Once all four color planes have been processed, the function loops to the next character line, until all 14 character lines have been written to display memory. The function then increments the column position of the cursor position data and stores this through the ROM BIOS video service.

Writing a Horizontal Character

The *color_printf* function given previously is fast and efficient and gives you complete color control. So why not use it for every application? There are two situations where it just isn't satisfactory. The first situation is when you are going to move the beginning of the screen to some line partway down the screen. The cursor positions used by *color_printf* cover only rows and columns on the normal display screen. If you want to write characters on a screen that has been shifted upward, you just can't do it with that function. Second, *color_printf* can select character positions using only text character coordinates. Thus, for example, a mode-16 graphics screen has 80 × 25 character positions, but it also has 640 × 350 pixel positions. If you are willing to satisfy yourself with locating a character at one of the 80 × 25 character positions, *color_printf* will do just fine, but it always starts a character at a character position boundary in display memory. If you want to position characters with higher resolution between two rows (for example), *color_printf* just won't do the job. For such unusual situations, we have created the function *writeHchar*. This function writes a single character horizontally, beginning at the position specified in pixel coordinates by the parameters x and y passed to the function. The function is listed in lines 438 through 493. It works only with the 16-color graphics modes. The function begins in lines 448 through 463 by using the global parameter *type* to determine whether the character is to have 8, 14, or 16 lines. (Thus this function can handle any eight-pixel-wide type font.) Then it computes the offset into the character table for each character in line 464. It determines the foreground and background colors from the color parameter that was passed to it in lines 465 and 466. The function then enters a pair of *for* loops. The outer loop (line 467) iterates once for each line of the character. The inner loop (line 470) iterates once for each pixel of character width (eight in all). Each loop iteration begins by determining the position of the current pixel of the character being drawn (lines 469 and 472). The *char_test* mask is then set in line 473 to mask the bit corresponding to the current pixel of character width that is being processed. The appropriate bit in the character table is masked out and, if it is a 0, the variable *point_color* is set to the background color, whereas if it is a 1, the variable is set to the foreground color (lines 474 through 478). Next the display memory address for the current pixel is determined in lines 479 through 481. A mask is set in line 482 and output to graphics control register 8 in line 483 to ensure that only the currently selected pixel will be modified. Sequencer register 2 is then set for all color planes (line 484), and a dummy read of the appropriate memory address is performed in line 485 to get the data from the color planes into the proper EGA/VGA registers. Then in line 486 a 0 is sent to the memory address to zero out the selected bit in all color planes. Sequencer register 2 is set in line 487 to activate only those color planes corresponding to the desired pixel color. An *FFH* is sent to the memory address in line 488 to turn on the pixel bit in the proper color planes. When the two loops are complete, this process has been performed for eight pixels in a row for each line that makes up the desired character. Finally, the registers are reset to their nominal values and the function is complete.

Writing a Vertical Character to the Screen

None of the C compilers, either in their normal or graphics modes of operation, is capable of writing characters to the screen vertically. Yet this is often a desired option in creating graphics displays. The function *writeVchar* listed in lines 497 through 553 will write a character to the screen vertically, in any specified foreground and background colors, at a designated pixel position. The function works for any 16-color graphics mode. If you look at the listing for this function, you'll see that it is nearly identical to the *writeHchar* function, the only difference being that the addressing of the *x* and *y* coordinates is interchanged. If you use a mode having square pixels (such as mode 18, which is 640 × 480 pixels), the vertical characters will look exactly the same as horizontal characters, except that they are rotated 90 degrees. If you use a mode that doesn't have square pixels, then the characters appear a little distorted as compared with the horizontal characters, but they are still readable. This function causes characters to be written from the top to bottom of the screen. Once you understand how this one works, it should be a simple matter to write a similar function that writes characters from top to bottom.

Writing a Horizontal String to the Screen

Suppose that we want to write a whole string of characters horizontally to the screen. Of course, we could use the *writeHchar* string once for each character, being careful to supply the correct position coordinates each time the function was called. However, we have chosen to create a function called *writeHstring* that will do the whole job in one simple operation. It is listed in lines 557 through 622. The heart of this function is a *while* loop (line 584) that keeps reading characters from the string and processing them until a NULL is encountered to indicate that the string is complete. Within this loop, the function operates pretty much like *writeHchar*. There are a few extra things that we have to take care of, however. After each character has been written to the screen, we have to increase the *x* position coordinate by 8 (the character width) to position it properly to write the next character (line 615). Next, we have to check whether we have reached the end of the row. If so, we set the *x* position coordinate to 0 and increase the *y* position coordinate by the character height in pixels to properly position for the next character (lines 616 through 620). Finally, we have to increment the pointer that is pointing at the current string character (line 621).

Writing a Vertical String to the Screen

The function *writeVstring* (listed in lines 627 through 693) uses the same techniques that were used to write a horizontal string to the screen but interchanges the x and y values to cause the string to be written vertically up the screen.

Writing Big Horizontal Characters

If you want some really nice big horizontal characters, you need to design each character on a large grid and convert the resulting information into a character table. Then you can use a version of *writeHchar* or *writeHstring* to display these large characters. If you don't want to go to all of this trouble, the function *writeBigChar* (listed in lines 697 through 759) will use one of the existing character fonts and enlarge each pixel to a 4 × 4 pixel block. The result is a little chunky, but not at all bad. If you look at the listing for this function, you'll see that it is very much like the function for writing an ordinary horizontal character, except that the information for each pixel of the character is written in a 4 × 4 block of pixels instead of a single pixel. You can use this same technique to write a function for displaying vertical characters now that you understand how to do it.

Writing a String of Big Characters

The function *writeBigString* (listed in lines 829 through 899) is very similar to those already described. It is used to write a string of big characters to the screen horizontally.

Writing Video Characters

If we take the function for writing big characters and write only a 3 × 3 pixel square for each character pixel, within a 4 × 4 pixel space, we have a very interesting effect, similar to lighted signs on a theater marque. The function *writeVideoChar* (listed in lines 763 through 825) does this job.

Writing a String of Video Characters

The function *writeVideoString* (listed in lines 1008 through 1084) is very similar to those already described. It is used to write a string of video characters to the screen horizontally.

Writing a String in the Undocumented Modes

The undocumented 256-color display modes described in Chapter 5 are another place where the normal methods of displaying text will not work. You need to create your own function for displaying text in these modes. The function *writeString* (listed in lines 344 through 404) will do this for you. As with similar functions, you have to get the address of the desired font table before you use it. You can then use the function with either 8, 14, or 16-pixel-long characters, in whichever font you have selected. The function is just the same as the *writeHstring* function except for the part that writes the pixels out to display memory. That section is the same as the technique described for writing a pixel in Chapter 5. The mode numbers used in this part of the program are different from those used in Chapter 5, demonstrating the fact that for undocumented modes, the mode number selection is arbitrary as long as it doesn't overlap those modes assigned by IBM.

Writing Characters to VESA Display Modes

The function *WriteHiResString* (listed in lines 895 through 947) is a modification of *WriteBigString* to write characters consisting of 4 × 4 pixel blocks to VESA mode 105H, the 1024 × 768 pixel × 256-color mode. Because of the high resolution of the screen, the characters appear to be about normal size. The function *WriteHiColString* (listed in lines 952 through 1004) is a modification of *WriteBigString* to write characters consisting of 4 × 4 pixel blocks to VESA mode 116H, the 1024 × 768 pixel × 32K-color mode. Because of the high resolution of the screen, the characters appear to be about normal size.

The chartest.cpp Program

The program *chartest.cpp* demonstrates the various character-drawing techniques described in this chapter. The program begins by setting the display mode to mode 16 (640 × 350 pixels × 16 colors). It next finds the address of the 8 × 14 pixel font. Display 1 (lines 47 through 95) shows a variety of character display techniques. It displays "Big Letters" using the *writeBigString* function, "Video Letters" using the *writeVideoString* function, and "OK" using the *writeBigChar* and *writeVideoChar* functions. Next the program uses the *writeHchar* function to write the font of ASCII characters from 33 to 125. It then uses the function *writeVchar* to write these same characters. The program uses the function *writeHstring* to write a very long horizontal string, to demonstrate that carrying over from the end of one row to the beginning of the next works properly. It writes a vertical string using the function *writeVstring*, and then writes strings using *printf*, *cprintf*, and *color_printf*. Displays 2 through 6 show a typical character string display in each of the undocumented modes using the function *writeString* to display each string on the screen. Display 7 first uses *printf* to display a string on the screen and then uses *writeHiResString* to display the same string in 4-pixel-block characters in the VESA 1024 × 768 pixel × 256-color mode 105H. Depending upon your Super VGA card, you may or may not see the string printed by *printf*. If you do, you'll note that the characters are very small. The characters displayed by *writeHiResString* are of a more reasonable size. Display 8 uses *writeHiColString* to display the same string in the VESA 1024 × 768 pixel × 32K-color mode.

20

Rotating Geometric Figures

In Chapter 14 we had a brief introduction to figure rotation with one of the ellipse-drawing functions, which permitted the orientation of the ellipse to be specified. However, at that point, there wasn't much discussion of the principle involved. In this chapter, we'll look at the mathematics of coordinate rotation and come up with some techniques that can be used to rotate triangles and rectangles and that can easily be extended to just about any other type of geometric figure. The functions and a test program are all included in the file *testrot.cpp*, which is given in Listing 20-1.

Rotation Geometry

Figure 20-1 shows the geometry that is involved in a rotation. The coordinate system is rotated through an angle θ. One pair of rectangles shows what happens when a rectangle at the origin is rotated and another pair shows what happens when rotation occurs for a rectangle that is not centered at the origin. The dotted triangle is similar to the one formed by the original and rotated x coordinates, from which the distance expressions given in the diagram can be computed. From these, it can be seen that the new coordinates of a point $(x1,y1)$ are related to the original coordinates (x,y) as follows:

Figure 20-1. Coordinate Rotation Geometry

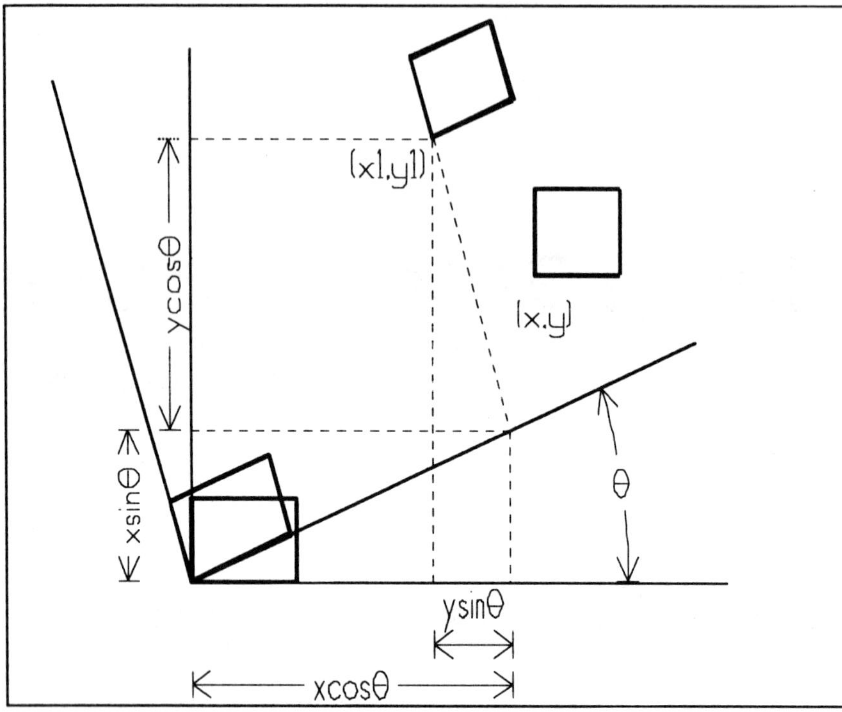

$$x1 = x\cos\theta - y\sin\theta$$

(Equation 20-1)

$$y1 = x\sin\theta - y\cos\theta$$

(Equation 20-2)

Before actually using these expressions in a function, we need to decide the location of the origin about which we want to rotate our geometric figures. Often, we want to rotate each geometric shape independently rather than the whole display. This requires that we temporarily shift the coordinate system so that its origin is at the point about which we wish to rotate a shape, perform the mathematics of rotation, and then shift the coordinate system back to where it was originally. In our rotation program, we have two geometric shapes, a rectangle and a triangle. The function for the rectangle is set up to rotate it about its top lefthand corner. The function for the triangle is set up to rotate it about the first of the three vertices that are passed to the function to specify the triangle. Once you get the feel for how this is done, you should be able to extend the process to any other geometric shape and to change the point about which you are rotating each shape to meet your particular requirements. Some of the functions you will need are given in Listing 20-1.

Rotating a Rectangle

The *rotate_rect* function is listed in lines 65 through 81. It is passed the coordinates of the bottom left *(xs,ys)* and top right *(xe, ye)* corners of a rectangle, the angle through which the rectangle is to be rotated, and the color in which the rectangle is to be drawn. With 0 rotation, the first line to be drawn would be to the right along the x axis. Since the rectangle is rotated around the bottom left vertex, the starting coordinates of the first line are unchanged, but the ending coordinates must be transformed to account for the rotation. Lines 69 and 71 compute the new location of the line end coordinates. Each set of coordinates needed is computed using the mathematics of Equations 20-1 and 20-2, with the endpoint of each line segment corresponding to the starting point of the next, and the endpoint of the fourth and final end segment corresponding to the starting point of the first line segment. Using floating-point calculations is pretty slow, but since we only have to compute three sets of coordinates for the rectangle, as opposed to drawing a whole lot of points to the screen, this doesn't slow down the overall function very much. Then line 71 uses the line *draw* function to draw the newly positioned line. Lines 72 through 75 compute the location of the next vertex of the rectangle (the one diagonal to the starting vertex) and the Line *draw* function is then used in line 76 to draw a line from the end of the first line to the new set of coordinates for the diagonal vertex. Next, lines 77 and 78 compute the location of the fourth vertex and line 79 draws a line from the end of the previous line to this vertex. Finally, line 80 draws a line from the end of the line just drawn back to the beginning of the rectangle.

Listing 20-1. The testrot.cpp Program for Testing Object Rotation

```
/*

    testrot = Program to test rotating of rectangles and
                         triangle.

               By Roger T. Stevens   3-8-96

*/

#include "c:\cpphbook\program\graphics.cpp"

Graphics graphic;
Line line;

void rotate_rect(int xs, int ys, int xe, int ye, float angle,
int color);
void rotate_tri(int x1, int y1, int x2, int y2, int x3, int
    y3, float angle, int color);

int angle;

/*

                    MAIN PROGRAM

*/

void main(void)
{
    int i, j, angle, xa, ya;

    graphic.setMode(0x10);
    graphic.cls (1);
    color = 3;
    for (i=0; i<360; i+=15)
        rotate_rect(0,0,400,200,i,color++);
    getch();
    graphic.cls (1);
    color = 2;
    for (i=0; i<360; i+=15)
    {
        rotate_tri(0, 0, 300, 200, 200, 0, i, color);
        color = (color + 1)% 16;
        if (color==1)
            color++;
```

```
        }
        getch();
        graphic.cls(4);
        color = 0;
        for (i=0; i<60; i++)
        {
            color = (++color)%16;
            if (color == 4)
                color++;
            if ((rand() & 0x11) == 0)
            {
                    rotate_rect((rand() & 0x3FF) - 640,
                (rand() & 0x1FF) - 480, (rand() &
            0x7FF) - 640, (rand() & 0x3FF)
                                - 480,float(rand() & 0xFF), color);
            }
            else
            {
                xa =  (rand() & 0x3FF) - 640;
                ya = (rand() & 0x1FF) - 480;
                rotate_tri(xa, ya, xa+(rand() & 0x1FF), ya +
                (rand() & 0x1FF), xa+(rand() & 0x1FF), ya +
                    (rand() & 0x1FF),
                    float(rand() & 0xFF), color);
            }
        }
        getch();
    }



    /*

          rotate_rect() = draws a rectangle which has the
                    following characteristics:

            line = top left hand corner and bottom right
                     hand corner of rectangle
      angle = tilt angle of rectangle (around top left corner
                    color = color of rectangle

    */

    void rotate_rect(int xs, int ys, int xe, int ye, float angle,
        int color)
    {
```

```
68        int xtemp, ytemp;

69        xtemp = xs + (xe - xs) * cos(0.017453292*angle);
70        ytemp = ys + (xe - xs) * sin(0.017453292*angle);
71        line.draw(xs,ys,xtemp,ytemp,color);
72        xtemp = xs + (xe - xs) * cos(0.017453292*angle) -
73            (ye - ys) * sin(0.017453292*angle);
74        ytemp = ys + (xe - xs) * sin(0.017453292*angle) +
75            (ye - ys) * cos(0.017453292*angle);
76        line.draw(xtemp,ytemp,color);
77        xtemp = xs - (ye - ys) * sin(0.017453292*angle);
78        ytemp = ys + (ye - ys) * cos(0.017453292*angle);
79        line.draw(xtemp,ytemp,color);
80        line.draw(xs,ys,color);
81    }

82    /*

          rotate_tri() = draws a rectangle which has the
                   following characteristics:
        (xa,ya), (xb,yb), (xc,yc) = vertices of triangle
                 angle = tilt angle of triangle
                   color = color of triangle

88    */
89    void rotate_tri(int x1, int y1, int x2, int y2, int x3, int
90        y3, float angle, int color)
91    {
92        int xtemp, ytemp;

93        xtemp = x1 + (x2 - x1) * cos(0.017453292*angle) -
94            (y2 - y1) * sin(0.017453292*angle);
95        ytemp = y1 + (x2 - x1) * sin(0.017453292*angle) +
96            (y2 - y1) * cos(0.017453292*angle);
97        line.draw(x1, y1, xtemp, ytemp, color);
98        xtemp = x1 + (x3 - x1) * cos(0.017453292*angle) -
99            (y3 - y1) * sin(0.017453292*angle);
100       ytemp = y1 + (x3 - x1) * sin(0.017453292*angle) +
101           (y3 - y1) * cos(0.017453292*angle);
102       line.draw(xtemp, ytemp, color);
103       line.draw(x1, y1, color);
104   }
```

Rotating a Triangle

The *rotate_tri* function is listed in lines 89 through 104. It is passed three pairs of coordinates, each of which represents one vertex of the desired triangle, a rotation angle for the triangle, and the color in which the triangle is to be drawn. The function works much like the one for rotating a rectangle, calculating the rotated values for the endpoints of the three line segments that make up the triangle and then drawing the sides of the rotated triangle. Observe that the first vertex specified for the triangle is the point around which the triangle is rotated.

The testrot.cpp Program

The *testrot.cpp* program begins by setting the display mode to 10H, 640 × 350 pixels × 16 colors (line 15) and then clearing the screen to a blue background (line 16). The first display (lines 18 through 20) shows a set of rectangles that represent rotations of the basic rec-tangle in 15-degree steps from 0 to 345 degrees, with each rectangle in a different color. The second display (lines 21 through 30) produces the same kind of display using a triangle as the basic element. The third display, lines 31 through 56, generates 60 geometric figures that are randomly either rectangles or triangles, with the shapes of each, its starting location, its rotation, and its color all computed randomly.

Part 6

Advanced Graphics Topics

21

The Mathematics of Modeling Solids

In order to make a picture of solid objects, we first have to define the position and shape of each object in three dimensions. Then the object is projected onto a two-dimensional viewing screen. The result is a two-dimensional picture of three-dimensional objects. The mathe-matics involves use of two- and three-dimensional vectors to represent positions and four-dimensional matrices to perform such operations as rotation, translation and scaling. One of the beauties of C++ is that we can create vector and matrix classes and overload operators so that we can use vectors and matrices just as we would integers and floating-point numbers in C. To define vectors and to move, scale, and reorient them, we'll need a lot of mathematical tools. Some of them are the simple tools of vector and matrix manipulation that you learned in school, but since they aren't a part of the mathematical repertory of the C libraries, we will have to create them for ourselves. Other functions are oriented more to the solid modeling task, but still need to be generalized for use in many operations. Before we get into the modeling itself, we will use this chapter to describe all of these mathematical techniques and how they are used. All of the vector, matrix, and mathematical functions are contained in a module called *vector.cpp*, which you can reference in an *include* program at the beginning of your program. This module is given in Listing 21-1.

Listing 21-1. Vector and Matrix Classes

```
/*

VECTOR.CPP = Classes for vector and Matrix manipulation

             By Roger T. Stevens  2-18-96

*/

#include <stdio.h>
#include <dos.h>
#include <conio.h>
#include <math.h>

/*

                  Vector and Matrix classes

*/

class Vector {
   public:
   float x, y, z;

   Vector();
   Vector(float x1, float y1, float z1);
   Vector (Vector &);
   Vector operator+(Vector &);
   Vector operator-(Vector &);
   Vector operator-();
   Vector operator=(Vector &);
   Vector operator*(Vector &);
   Vector operator*(float);
   Vector operator/(float);
   float operator%(Vector &);// dot product
   Vector operator^(Vector &);// cross product;
   Vector operator~();// normalize vector;
   float length();
};
class Matrix {
   public:
   float elem[4][4];

   Matrix();
   Vector operator*(Vector &);
   Matrix operator*(Matrix &);
};
```

```
Vector observer, perspective, surf_norm, light, tr,sc,ro;

/*
                Vector constructors
*/

Vector::Vector()
{
    x = 0;
    y = 0;
    z = 0;
}

Vector::Vector(float x1, float y1, float z1)
{
    x = x1;
    y = y1;
    z = z1;
}

Vector::Vector(Vector & otherVector)
{
    x = otherVector.x;
    y = otherVector.y;
    z = otherVector.z;
}



/*
            Vector overload of + operator
*/

Vector Vector::operator+(Vector & b)
{
    Vector c;

    c.x = x + b.x;
    c.y = y + b.y;
    c.z = z + b.z;
    return(c);
}
```

```
/*
        Vector overload of - operator (a - b)
*/

Vector Vector::operator-(Vector & b)
{
    Vector c;

    c.x = x - b.x;
    c.y = y - b.y;
    c.z = z - b.z;
    return(c);
}

/*
        Vector overload of - operator (-a)
*/

Vector Vector::operator-()
{
    Vector c;

    c.x = -x;
    c.y = -y;
    c.z = -z;
    return(c);
}

/*
        Vector overload of * operator (Vector x Vector)
*/

Vector Vector::operator*(Vector & b)
{
    Vector c;

    c.x = x*b.x;
    c.y = y*b.y;
    c.z = z*b.z;
    return(c);
}
```

```
/*
        Vector overload of * operator (Vector x float)
*/

Vector Vector::operator*(float b)
{
    Vector c;

    c.x = x*b;
    c.y = y*b;
    c.z = z*b;
    return(c);
}

/*
        Vector overload of / operator (Vector / float)
*/

Vector Vector::operator/(float b)
{
    Vector c;

    c.x = x/b;
    c.y = y/b;
    c.z = z/b;
    return(c);
}

/*
                Vector overload of = operator
*/

Vector Vector::operator=(Vector &b)
{
    x = b.x;
    y = b.y;
    z = b.z;
    return *this;
}
```

```
/*
        Vector overload of % operator (dot product)
*/

float Vector::operator%(Vector &b)
{
    float c;

    c = x*b.x + y*b.y + z*b.z;
    return c;
}

/*
        Vector overload of ^ operator (cross product)
*/

Vector Vector::operator^(Vector &b)
{
    Vector c;

    c.x = y*b.z - z*b.y;
    c.y = z*b.x - x*b.z;
    c.z = x*b.y - y*b.x;
    return c;
}

/*
        Vector overload of ~ operator (normalize)
*/

Vector Vector::operator~()
{
    Vector c;
    float length;

    length = *this % *this;
    length = sqrt(length);
    c.x = x/length;
    c.y = y/length;
    c.z = z/length;
    return c;
}
```

```
/*
        length() = Finds the length of a Vector
*/

float Vector::length()
{
    return(sqrt(x*x + y*y + z*z));
}

/*
                Matrix constructor
*/

Matrix::Matrix()
{
    int i,j;

    for (i=0; i<4; i++)
        for (j=0; j<4; j++)
            elem[i][j] = 0;
}

/*
    Matrix overload of * operator (Matrix x Matrix)
*/

Matrix Matrix::operator*(Matrix &b)
{
    int i,j,k;
    Matrix c;
    c = Matrix();
    for (i=0; i<4; i++)
    {
        for (j=0; j<4; j++)
        {
            for (k=0; k<4; k++)
                c.elem[i][j] += elem[i][k]*b.elem[k][j];
        }
    }
    return(c);
}
```

```
/*
    Matrix overload of * operator (Matrix x Vector)
*/

Vector Matrix::operator*(Vector &a)
{
    Vector b;
    b.x = elem[0][0]*a.x + elem[0][1]*a.y + elem[0][2]*a.z
        + elem[0][3];
    b.y = elem[1][0]*a.x + elem[1][1]*a.y + elem[1][2]*a.z
        + elem[1][3];
    b.z = elem[2][0]*a.x + elem[2][1]*a.y + elem[2][2]*a.z
        + elem[2][3];
    return(b);
}

Matrix transform(Vector tr, Vector sc, Vector ro);
Matrix scale(Vector &);
Matrix rotate(int axis, float angle);
Matrix translate(Vector &);

/*
    translate() = Creates a matrix to translate vectors
*/
Matrix translate(Vector &a)
{
    Matrix b;
    int i;

    b = Matrix();
    for (i=0; i<4; i++)
        b.elem[i][i] = 1.0;
    b.elem[0][3] = -a.x;
    b.elem[1][3] = -a.y;
    b.elem[2][3] = -a.z;
    return(b);
}

/*
    scale() = Creates a matrix to scale vectors
*/
```

```
Matrix scale(Vector &a)
{
    Matrix b;

    b = Matrix();
    b.elem[0][0] = a.x;
    b.elem[1][1] = a.y;
    b.elem[2][2] = a.z;
    b.elem[3][3] = 1.0;
    return(b);
}

/*

        rotate() = Creates a matrix to rotate vectors

*/

Matrix rotate(int axis, float angle)
{
    int i,j;
    Matrix a;
    float c,s;

    a = Matrix();
    a.elem[axis-1][axis-1] = 1.0;
    a.elem[3][3] = 1.0;
    i = (axis % 3) + 1;
    j = i %3;
    i -= 1;
    c = cos(angle * 0.017453292);
    s = sin(angle * 0.017453292);
    a.elem[i][i] = c;
    a.elem[i][j] = s;
    a.elem[j][j] = c;
    a.elem[j][i] = -s;
    return(a);
}

/*

    transform() = Creates a Vector transformation matrix

*/

Matrix transform(Vector tr, Vector sc, Vector ro)
{
    Matrix a1,a2,a3,a4,a5,temp;
```

```
274        a1 = scale(sc);
275        a2 = rotate(1,ro.x);
276        a3 = rotate(2,ro.y);
277        a4 = rotate(3,ro.z);
278        a5 = translate(tr);
279        temp = a2*a1;
280        temp = a3*temp;
281        temp = a4*temp;
282        temp = a5*temp;
283        return(temp);
284    }
```

Vector Constructors

The *Vector* class is defined in lines 8 through 25. A vector, as defined here, consists of three floating-point numbers, each representing the position in one dimension of three-dimensional space. In some applications, you might want to have vectors composed of integers or characters; if this is the case, you have to define these also, but for our solid-modeling purposes, floating-point vectors are sufficient. Lines 37 through 54 define the *Vector* class constructors. When you define a vector, the constructors determine what that vector will contain. Looking at lines 37 through 42, if you define a vector by:

```
vec = Vector();
```

where *vec* is of type *Vector*, then each of the three members of the vector will be 0. From lines 43 through 48, if you define the vector by:

```
vec = Vector(3.0, 4.0, 5.0);
```

then the three members of *vec* will be 3.0, 4.0, and 5.0, respectively. From lines 49 through 54, if you define the vector by:

```
vec = Vector(vec2);
```

where *vec2* is also of type *Vector*, then *vec* will be the same as *vec2*.

Adding, Subtracting, Multiplying, and Dividing Vectors

Using C++, we can overload various mathematical operators so that mathematical operations on vectors will be as much as possible like the same operations with numbers. For example,

$$c = a + b$$

(Equation 21-1)

can be a legitimate operation when *a, b,* and *c* are all vectors, as well as when they are numbers. Vector addition and subtraction are pretty simple; we simply add or subtract each pair of corresponding elements to obtain a new vector. Lines 58 through 65 define the + operator for vector addition, and lines 69 through 76 define the - operator for vector subtraction. Note that just taking the negative of a vector is a little different from subtracting one vector from another; we need the special case of lines 80 through 87 to handle this. Vector multiplication is a little more complicated. We have chosen to implement the overload of the * operator to multiply each element of a vector by the corresponding element of another vector (lines 91 through 98). This isn't really a legitimate vector multiplication operation, but it can be useful in computations. Lines 102 through 108 perform multiplication of a vector by a floating-point number. Each element of the vector is simply multiplied by the floating-point number. The dot product is a legitimate form of vector multiplication. This is a number obtained by multiplying together each pair of corresponding vector elements and then adding together the results. In lines 134 through 139, we overload the % operator to perform this function. The dot product can also be expressed as:

$$a \cdot b = AB \cos\theta$$

(Equation 21-2)

where a and b are the two vectors, A and B are the vector lengths respectively, and θ is the angle between the two vectors.

The vector cross product is another legitimate vector multiplication function. It is a combination of vector element products. You can plainly see the math involved in lines 143 through 150, where the ^ operator is overloaded to perform the operation. The result is a vector that is at right angles to the two input vectors and that has a length:

$$|a \times b| = AB \sin\theta$$

(Equation 21-3)

Vector Division

Lines 113 through 120 overload the / function to divide a vector by a floating-point number. Each element of the vector is simply divided by the same floating-point number.

Overloading the = Operator

Lines 124 through 130 show how the = operator is overloaded so that when we set a vector equal to another vector, the value of each of the three elements of the second vector is transferred to the corresponding element of the first vector.

Normalizing a Vector

A vector is normalized when it is converted to a unit vector having the same direction. The ~ operator is overloaded to perform this function in lines 154 through 164. We find the length of the vector by taking the square root of its dot product with itself. Each element of the vector is then divided by this length. You can check the math to satisfy yourself that this gives a vector of unit length in the same direction as the original vector.

Length of a Vector

Lines 168 through 171 define the function *length*, which computes and returns the length of the vector input to it. The math is simple: The length is the square root of the sum of the squares of each of the vector elements.

Matrix Constructor

Lines 175 through 181 list the matrix constructor, which simply fills a newly generated matrix with zeroes.

Multiplying a Vector by a Matrix

When a three-dimensional vector is multiplied by a 4×4 matrix, the result is a new vector that can represent a translation, rotation, or scaling of the old vector or a combination of all three, depending upon the values of the matrix elements. The actual multiplication process is quite similar to that used in obtaining the cross product of two vectors. You can see how the math is done by examining the overloading of the * operator given in lines 203 through 213.

Translating a Vector

The matrix for translating a vector by t_x in the x direction, t_y in the y direction, and t_z in the z direction is as follows:

$$T = \begin{bmatrix} 1 & 0 & 0 & 0 \\ -t_x & 1 & 0 & 0 \\ -t_y & 0 & 1 & 0 \\ -t_z & 0 & 0 & 1 \end{bmatrix}$$

(Equation 21-4)

Creating this matrix is accomplished by the function *translate* listed in lines 221 through 232. This function is passed a vector that consists of the three translation parameters and then generates the appropriate translation matrix. When the matrix operates upon a vector, the length and direction of the vector are unchanged but its position is changed as specified by the three parameters.

Scaling a Vector

The matrix for scaling a vector by s_x in the x direction, s_y in the y direction, and s_z in the z direction is as follows:

$$S = \begin{bmatrix} s_x & 0 & 0 & 0 \\ 0 & s_y & 0 & 0 \\ 0 & 0 & s_z & 0 \\ 0 & 0 & 0 & 1 \end{bmatrix}$$

(Equation 21-5)

Creating this matrix is accomplished by the function *scale* listed in lines 236 through 245. This function is passed a vector that consists of the three scaling parameters. It then generates the appropriate scaling matrix. When the matrix operates upon a vector, the position of the vector is unchanged but its length in each of the three axis directions is modified by the corresponding scaling parameter. Note that the scaling can differ for each axis direction, so that a cube could be scaled to become a rectangular parallelepiped or a sphere could be scaled to become an ellipsoid.

Rotating a Vector

A simple rotation matrix can be applied to a vector to rotate it about one of the three coordinate axes. One function, called *rotate*, is used for these operations. It is listed in lines 249 through 267. The first parameter passed to it represents the axis about which rotation is to take place; the second parameter is the angle of rotation in degrees. The matrix for scaling a vector around the x axis is:

$$R_x = \begin{bmatrix} 1 & 0 & 0 & 0 \\ 0 & \cos\theta & \sin\theta & 0 \\ 0 & -\sin\theta & \cos\theta & 0 \\ 0 & 0 & 0 & 1 \end{bmatrix}$$

(Equation 21-6)

The matrix for scaling a vector around the y axis is:

$$R_y = \begin{bmatrix} \cos\theta & 0 & -\sin\theta & 0 \\ 0 & 1 & 0 & 0 \\ -\sin\theta & 0 & \cos\theta & 0 \\ 0 & 0 & 0 & 1 \end{bmatrix}$$

(Equation 21-7)

The matrix for scaling a vector around the z axis is:

$$R_z = \begin{bmatrix} \cos\theta & \sin\theta & 0 & 0 \\ -\sin\theta & \cos\theta & 0 & 0 \\ 0 & 0 & 1 & 0 \\ 0 & 0 & 0 & 1 \end{bmatrix}$$

(Equation 21-8)

The function begins in line 254 by zeroing all elements of the new matrix. Next, in lines 255 through 259, it sets all of the matrix elements that are to be 1 or -1. Then, in lines 260 and 261, it computes the sine and cosine of the rotation angle and places them (lines 262 through 265) in the proper elements (with the proper sign) for the rotation axis selected. The effect of this matrix on a vector is that the vector retains the same length and the same orientation on the plane defined by the two axes not selected, but is rotated by the specified angle around the selected axis.

The *transform* Matrix

The function *transform* combines scaling, rotation about each of the three axes, and translation into one overall transformation matrix by multiplying the individual matrices together. It is listed in lines 274 through 284.

22

Solid-Modeling Techniques

Now that we've set up a module that includes the basic mathematical operations that are needed for creating solid objects, we can proceed with the actual mechanics of creating a program to perform the solid-modeling process. Such a program needs to perform the following basic steps. First, we have to define each solid that we want to model as a collection of facets, each of which is a small quadrilateral. Together, these quadrilaterals approximate the surface of the solid. We are going to define each generic solid as a collection of quadri-laterals that are centered at the origin and fit within a box that is + or -1 unit in each direction. Next we need the math that translates, scales, and rotates each generic object to make it into an object of the size we desire and in the position we desire it to be in the scene that we are creating. We then operate upon each facet of the object. Using information that has been stored for the position of the light source illuminating the scene, we determine the surface normal to the light projected upon the facet and from this compute the intensity of the light reflected from this facet back to the viewer. Finally, we determine the projection of the facet upon the two-dimensional screen and paint it on the screen in the appropriate color and brightness. Two things need to be noted here. First, as a rule we have tried to define each object in such a way that the back of the object is painted on the screen first, followed by the front of the object. This ensures that the front parts of the object will overdraw the back parts, which gives the effect that you would normally see in a scene. A test is also included that prevents painting a facet at all if the surface normal is pointed away from the viewer, indicating that it is a facet that cannot be seen. However, if you radically change the viewing angle, you may have to modify the order in which the facets of an object are painted to the screen to ensure that the front parts of the object are drawn last. Also, there are some cases where all of this is just not enough. For example, in the Tower of Hanoi scene, we want to have a cylinder go down through the middle of several tori. The only way that this can be done is to paint the back half of each torus to the screen, then paint each cylinder, and finally paint the front half of each torus. To make this possible, we've set up the torus drawing function so that it can be called to draw each half of a torus separately. The second thing to note is that no provision has been made for properly ordering the painting of solids in the scene. For the scene to appear natural, you must paint the object that is farthest from the viewer first, followed by the next farthest, and so forth, until the nearest object is painted last. It is up to you to determine the placement of the objects and place them in the proper order in your program. If you paint some of the nearer objects before the farther ones, you will get a very strange-looking scene. By just looking, it is sometimes hard to determine just what's wrong, but you'll surely know that something is wrong. We've designed the program to work with any 256-color mode. Currently, each graphic is displayed in mode 103H, 800 pixels × 600 pixels × 256 colors. However, you can easily change it just by changing the *setMode* functions to set up a different display mode. Just make sure it's a 256-color mode and that it is supported by the VESA extensions to your Super VGA card. If you don't have a Super VGA card, just use mode 13H, which is available on all VGA cards. The entire program for modeling solids, and displaying some typical scenes, is given in Listing 22-1.

Modeling Solids

The raw material that we're going to operate upon consists of a number of functions that create primitive solids. These include a cone, a pyramid (a cone that has only four facets), a sphere, a torus, a cylinder, a cube, a surface (a single facet), and a solid of revolution. This last allows you to specify a profile of 60 points, which is then rotated around the z axis. It comes with three types of profile: a chess pawn, a chess bishop, and a bowling pin. The functions are quite similar in the way they work, but we'll describe each on in detail. For each object, the surface is defined as a number of facets, each comprised of a quadrilateral.

Listing 22-1. The solid.cpp Program to Generate Scenes Made up of Solid Objects

```
/*

        SOLID.CPP = Program to model 3D Objects

            By Roger T. Stevens   3-12-96

*/

#include <iostream.h>
#include "c:\cpphbook\program\graphics.cpp"
#include "c:\cpphbook\program\vector.cpp"

#define LINES  0
#define SOLIDS 1
void save_screen(char filename[13]);

Graphics graphic;
Quadralateral quad;
Polygon polygon;

typedef struct
{
    int col, row;
} plane;

unsigned char palette[768];

#define light_phi 45
#define light_theta 45
#define light_max 35
#define compare(a,b,c)  {if (a<b) b = a; if (a>c) c = a;}

int angle=240, tilt=18;
int dmode=SOLIDS;
float CA,SA,CT,ST;
Matrix move;


/*

                FUNCTION PROTOTYPES

*/

void cone(int no_facets, int color);
```

```
void cylinder(int no_facets, int color);
void cube(int color);
void cube_face(Vector facet3D[], int color);
void display_facet(Vector facet3D[], int Color);
plane map(Vector a);
void solid_rev(int type, int color);
void surface(int color);
Vector surface_normal(Vector facet3D[]);
void sphere(int color);
void toroid(int type, int no_facets, float r1, float r2,
    int color);

/*
                        Main Program
*/

void main(void)
{
    Vector toroid_vecs[8];
    int i,j;
    Vector trans[10], facet3D[4];
    float phi, theta;
    float x, y, z;

    for(i=0; i<252; i++)
    {
        if (i>107)
            palette[3*i] = 1.8*(i%36);
        else
            palette[3*i] = 0.;
        if ((i>35 && i<108) || (i>179))

            palette[3*i+1] = 1.8*(i%36);
        else
            palette[3*i+1] = 0.;
        if((i<36) || (i>71 && i<108) || (i>143 && i<180)
            || (i>215))
            palette[3*i+2] = 1.8*(i%36);
        else
            palette[3*i+2] = 0.;
    }
    graphic.setMode(3);
    textcolor(YELLOW);
    textbackground(BLUE);
    clrscr();
    printf("Three-dimensional modeling of solids\n\n");
    printf("View Direction is %d around the z-Axis\n",
    angle);
```

```
    printf("                %d off the z-Axis and\n", tilt);
    printf("Light Direction is %d around the z-Axis",
        light_phi);
    printf("                %d off the z-Axis\n",
light_theta);
    getch();
    graphic.setMode(19);
    CA=cos(0.017453292*angle);
    SA=sin(0.017453292*angle);
    CT=cos(0.017453292*tilt);
    ST=sin(0.017453292*tilt);
    observer = Vector(sin(0.017453292*(90.0 - tilt)) *
    cos(0.017453292 * (270.0 - angle)),
sin(0.017453292 * (90.0-tilt)) * sin(0.017453292 *
(270.0 - angle)), cos(0.017453292 * (90.0-tilt)));
    phi=0.017453292*light_phi;
    theta=0.017453292*light_theta;
    light = Vector(sin(theta) * cos(phi), sin(theta) *
    sin(phi), cos(theta));

/*
                               Cube
*/

    graphic.setMode(0x103);
    graphic.setVGApalette(0,256,palette);
    sc = Vector(32.0,32.0,32.0);
    ro = Vector();
    tr = Vector();
    cube(5);
    getch();

/*
                           Cylinders
*/

    graphic.setMode(0x103);
    graphic.setVGApalette(0,256,palette);
    trans[6] = Vector(32.0, 10.0, -67.2);
    trans[7] = Vector(64.0, 10.0, -32.0);
    trans[8] = Vector(0.0, -48.0, -3.2);
    sc = Vector(32.0,32.0,32.0);
    ro = Vector();
    tr = trans[6];
```

```
    cylinder(60,1);
    tr = trans[7];
    cylinder(60,7);
    tr = trans[8];
    cylinder(60,3);
    getch();

/*
            Sphere and three cones
*/

    graphic.setMode(0x103);
    graphic.setVGApalette(0,256,palette);
    trans[6] = Vector(32.0, 10.0, -3.2);
    trans[7] = Vector(-32.0, 10.0, -3.2);
    trans[8] = Vector(0.0, -48.0, -3.2);
    trans[9] = Vector(0.0, -10.9, -57.6);
    sc = Vector(32.0,32.0,32.0);
    ro = Vector();
    tr = trans[6];
    cone(60,1);
    tr = trans[7];
    cone(60,4);
    tr = trans[8];
    cone(60,3);
    sc = Vector(41.6,41.6,41.6);
    ro = Vector();
    tr = trans[9];;
    sphere(2);
    getch();

/*
            Stacked cones
*/

    trans[0] = Vector(32.0, 16.0, -32.0);
    trans[1] = Vector(0.0, 16.0, -32.0);
    trans[2] = Vector(-32.0, 16.0, -32.0);
    trans[3] = Vector(16.0, -11.7, -32.0);
    trans[4] = Vector(-16.0, -11.7, -32.0);
    trans[5] = Vector(0.0, -39.4, -32.0);
    trans[6] = Vector(16.0, 6.8, -60);
    trans[7] = Vector(-16.0, 6.8, -60);
    trans[8] = Vector(0.0, -24.0, -60);
    trans[9] = Vector(-8.0, -9.2, -92);
```

```
    graphic.setMode(0x103);
    graphic.setVGApalette(0,256,palette);
    sc = Vector(16.0,16.0,16.0);
    ro = Vector();
    for(i=0; i<10; i++)
    {
        tr = trans[i];
        cone(60,(i%7) + 1);
    }
    getch();

/*
                    Stacked spheres
*/

    graphic.setMode(0x103);
    graphic.setVGApalette(0,256,palette);
    sc = Vector(16.0,16.0,16.0);
    ro = Vector();
    for(i=0; i<10; i++)
    {
        tr = trans[i];
        sphere((i%7) + 1);
    }
    getch();

/*
                    Stacked pyramids
*/

    graphic.setMode(0x103);
    graphic.setVGApalette(0,256,palette);
    for(i=0; i<10; i++)
    {
        sc = Vector(16.0,16.0,16.0);
        ro = Vector();
        tr = trans[i];
        cone(4,(i%7) + 1);
    }
    getch();
```

```
/*
                              Bowling
*/

    graphic.setMode(0x103);
    graphic.setVGApalette(0,256,palette);
    sc = Vector(70,112,1);
    ro = Vector();
    tr = Vector(45,25,0);
    move = transform(tr, sc, ro);
    facet3D[0] = Vector(1,1,0),
    facet3D[0] = move *facet3D[0];
    facet3D[1] = Vector(-1,1,0);
    facet3D[1] = move * facet3D[1];
    facet3D[2] = Vector(-1,-1,0);
    facet3D[2] = move * facet3D[2];
    facet3D[3] = Vector(1,-1,0);
    facet3D[3] = move * facet3D[3];
    display_facet(facet3D,6);
    sc = Vector(32.0,32.0,32.0);
    ro = Vector();
    trans[0] = Vector(152,184,0);
    trans[1] = Vector(120,184,0);
    trans[2] = Vector(88,184,0);
    trans[3] = Vector(56,184,0);
    trans[4] = Vector(136,152,0);
    trans[5] = Vector(104,152,0);
    trans[6] = Vector(72,152,0);
    trans[7] = Vector(120,120,0);
    trans[8] = Vector(88,120,0);
    trans[9] = Vector(104,88,0);
    for (i=0; i<10; i++)
    {
        tr = trans[i];
        solid_rev(2,7);
    }
    sc = Vector(36.0,36.0,36.0);
    tr = Vector(80,-30,0);
    sphere(1);
    getch();

/*
                              Chessboard
*/

    graphic.setMode(0x103);
```

```
    graphic.setVGApalette(0,256,palette);
    ro = Vector();
    sc = Vector(20,20,0);
    for (j=-40; j<250; j+=80)
        for (i=-40; i<250; i+=80)
        {
            tr = Vector(j,i,0);
            surface(4);
        }
    for (j=0; j<250; j+=80)
        for (i=0; i<250; i+=80)
        {
            tr = Vector(j,i,0);
            surface(4);
        }
    sc = Vector(22,22,20);
    tr = Vector(90,70,0);
    solid_rev(0,7);
    tr = Vector(178,202,0);
    solid_rev(0,7);
    tr = Vector(225,25,0);
    solid_rev(0,3);
    sc = Vector(22,22,26);
    tr = Vector(55,125,0);
    solid_rev(1,7);
    tr = Vector(12,-12,0);
    solid_rev(1,3);
    getch();

/*
             Towers of Hanoi
*/

    graphic.setMode(0x103);
    graphic.setVGApalette(0,256,palette);
    ro = Vector();
    toroid_vecs[0] = Vector(-45, 20,-17);
    toroid_vecs[1] = Vector(-45,-20,-38);
    toroid_vecs[2] = Vector(-45,-20,-59);
    toroid_vecs[3] = Vector(20,-90,-7);
    toroid_vecs[4] = Vector(20,-90,-24);
    toroid_vecs[5] = Vector(-80,50,-1);
    toroid_vecs[6] = Vector(-80,50,-13);
    for (i=0; i<7;i++)
    {
        sc = Vector(50-5*i,50-5*i,50-5*i);
        tr = toroid_vecs[i];
        toroid(1,60,.75,.25,i+1);
    }
```

```
    sc = Vector(7,7,55);
    tr = Vector(20,-90,-45);
    cylinder(90,7);
    tr = Vector(-45,-20,-45);
    cylinder(90,7);
    tr = Vector(-80,50,-45);
    cylinder(90,7);
    for (i=0; i<7;i++)
    {
        sc = Vector(50-5*i,50-5*i,50-5*i);
        tr = toroid_vecs[i];
        toroid(0,60,.75,.25,i+1);
    }
    getch();
    graphic.setMode(3);
}

/*
    display_facet() = Displays and shades a facet on screen
*/

void display_facet(Vector facet3D[],int Color)
{
    float ambient=0.30;
    float diffuse=0.50;
    float specular=0.20;
    float glossiness=5.0;
    float cos_theta, cos_alpha, cos_beta;
    Vector temp;
    int intensity;
    int i, row1,row2,col1,col2;
    plane facet2D[4], temp2;

    surf_norm = surface_normal(facet3D);
    temp = observer * surf_norm;
    cos_beta=temp.x + temp.y + temp.z;
    if (cos_beta > 0.0)
    {
        cos_theta = surf_norm % light;
        if(cos_theta<=0.0)
            intensity = light_max * ambient;
        else
        {
            temp = surf_norm * cos_theta;
            temp = ~temp;
            temp = temp - light;
            temp = ~ temp;
            cos_alpha = observer % temp;
            intensity = light_max * (ambient + diffuse *
```

```
                    cos_theta + specular * pow(cos_alpha,
                glossiness));
            }
            if(intensity>0)
            {
                for(i=0; i<4; i++)
                    facet2D[i] = map(facet3D[i]);
                if (intensity > light_max)
                    intensity = light_max;
                if(intensity>=1)
                {
                    if(dmode == LINES)
                    {
                        quad.draw(light_max * Color,
                    facet2D[0].col,facet2D[0].row,
                            facet2D[1].col,facet2D[1].row,
                            facet2D[2].col, facet2D[2].row,
                            facet2D[3].col, facet2D[3].row,
                            -9999);
                    }
                    if(dmode == SOLIDS)
                        quad.fill(facet2D[0].col,
                            facet2D[0].row, facet2D[1].col,
                            facet2D[1].row, facet2D[2].col,
                            facet2D[2].row, facet2D[3].col,
                            facet2D[3].row, ((light_max+1)*
                            (Color-1) + intensity) & 255);
                }
            }
        }
}

/*

    map() = Maps a three dimensional vector to a two-
                  dimensional surface

*/

plane map(Vector a)
{
    Vector t;
    plane b;

    t.x = 0.0 + a.x*CA - a.y*SA;
    t.y = -25 + a.x*SA*ST + a.y*CA*ST + a.z*CT;
    t.z = 450 + a.x*SA*CT + a.y*CA*CT - a.z*ST;
    b.col = 2400.*t.x/t.z;
    b.row = 2400.*t.y/t.z;
    return(b);
}
```

```
/*

    surface_normal() = Computes the surface normal vector
                       to a facet surface

*/

Vector surface_normal(Vector facet3D[])
{
    float length1, length2;
    Vector dir1, dir2, srf_normal1, srf_normal2;

    dir1 = facet3D[1] - facet3D[0];
    dir2 = facet3D[3] - facet3D[0];
    srf_normal1 = dir1 ^ dir2;
    length1 = srf_normal1.length();
    dir1 = facet3D[3] - facet3D[2];
    dir2 = facet3D[1] - facet3D[2];
    srf_normal2 = dir1 ^ dir2;
    length2 = srf_normal2.length();
    if(length1 == 0.0)
        srf_normal1 =  ~srf_normal2;
    else
    {
        srf_normal1 =  ~srf_normal1;
        if(length2 != 0.0)
        {
            srf_normal2 =  ~srf_normal2;
            srf_normal1= srf_normal1 + srf_normal2;
            srf_normal1 = srf_normal1 * 0.5;
        }
    }
    return(srf_normal1);
}

/*

          sphere() = Displays a sphere on screen

*/

void sphere(int color)
{
    int horizontal=60, vertical=45, theta, d_theta, phi,
        d_phi,i,j;
    float sp, cp;
    Matrix trans;
    Vector facet3D[4];
```

```
    trans = transform(tr, sc, ro);
    d_theta=180/horizontal;
    theta=d_theta;
    d_phi=90/vertical;
    phi=d_phi;
    for (i=0; i<vertical; i++)
    {
        for (j=0; j<horizontal; j++)
        {
            sp=sin((phi+d_phi)*0.017453292);
            cp=cos((phi+d_phi)*0.017453292);
            facet3D[0] = Vector((sp * cos((theta -
        d_theta) * 0.017453292)), (sp * sin((theta
        - d_theta) * 0.017453292)), cp);
            facet3D[0] = trans * facet3D[0];
            facet3D[1] = Vector((sp * cos((theta +
        d_theta) * 0.017453292)), (sp * sin((theta
        + d_theta) * 0.017453292)), cp);
            facet3D[1] = trans * facet3D[1];
            sp=sin((phi-d_phi)*0.017453292);
            cp=cos((phi-d_phi)*0.017453292);
            facet3D[2] = Vector((sp * cos((theta +
        d_theta) * 0.017453292)), (sp * sin((theta
        + d_theta) * 0.017453292)), cp);
            facet3D[2] = trans * facet3D[2];
            facet3D[3] = Vector((sp * cos((theta -
        d_theta) * 0.017453292)), (sp * sin((theta
        - d_theta) * 0.017453292)), cp);
            facet3D[3] = trans * facet3D[3];
            display_facet(facet3D,color);
            theta += 2*d_theta;
        }
        theta = d_theta;
        phi += 2*d_phi;
    }
}

/*
        cone() = Displays a conc on the screen
*/

void cone(int no_facets, int color)
{
    int theta, d_theta, phi, d_phi,i;
    Vector facet3D[4];
    Matrix trans;
```

```
    d_theta = 180/no_facets;
    theta = d_theta;
    trans = transform(tr,sc,ro);
    for (i=0; i<no_facets; i++)
    {
        facet3D[0] = Vector((cos((theta -
d_theta)*0.017453292)),(sin((theta - d_theta)*
0.017453292)), -1.0);
        facet3D[0] = trans * facet3D[0];
        facet3D[1] = Vector((cos((theta + d_theta) *
        0.017453292)), (sin((theta + d_theta) *
    0.017453292)), -1.0);
        facet3D[1] = trans * facet3D[1];
        facet3D[2] = Vector(0.0,0.0,1.0);
        facet3D[2] = trans * facet3D[2];
        facet3D[3] = Vector(0.0, 0.0, 1.0);
        facet3D[3] = trans * facet3D[3];
        display_facet(facet3D,color);
        theta += 2*d_theta;
    }
}

/*

    cylinder() = Displays a cylinder on the screen

*/

void cylinder(int no_facets, int color)
{
    int theta, d_theta, phi, d_phi,i, no_cap_facets;
    Vector facet3D[4];
    Matrix trans;

    no_cap_facets = no_facets/2 - 1;
    d_theta = 180/no_cap_facets;
    if ((no_cap_facets & 1) == 1)
        theta = 90 + d_theta;
    else
        theta = 90 + 2*d_theta;
    trans = transform(tr,sc,ro);
    for (i=0; i<no_cap_facets; i++)
    {
        facet3D[0] = Vector((cos((theta - d_theta) *
        0.017453292)), (sin((theta - d_theta) *
    0.017453292)), 1.0);
        facet3D[0] = trans * facet3D[0];
```

```
        facet3D[1] = Vector((cos((theta + d_theta) *
        0.017453292)), (sin((theta + d_theta) *
    0.017453292)), 1.0);
        facet3D[1] = trans * facet3D[1];
        facet3D[2] = Vector((cos((180 - theta - d_theta) *
            0.017453292)), (sin((180 - theta - d_theta) *
            0.017453292)), 1.0);
        facet3D[2] = trans * facet3D[2];
        facet3D[3] = Vector((cos((180 - theta + d_theta) *
            0.017453292)), (sin((180 - theta + d_theta) *
            0.017453292)), 1.0);
        facet3D[3] = trans * facet3D[3];
        display_facet(facet3D,color);
        theta += 2*d_theta;
    }
    d_theta = 180/no_facets;
    theta = d_theta;
    for (i=0; i<no_facets; i++)
    {
        facet3D[0] = Vector((cos((theta - d_theta) *
            0.017453292)), (sin((theta - d_theta) *
            0.017453292)), -1.0);
        facet3D[0] = trans * facet3D[0];
        facet3D[1] = Vector((cos((theta + d_theta) *
            0.017453292)), (sin((theta + d_theta) *
            0.017453292)), -1.0);
        facet3D[1] = trans * facet3D[1];
        facet3D[2] = Vector((cos((theta + d_theta) *
            0.017453292)), (sin((theta + d_theta) *
            0.017453292)), 1.0);
        facet3D[2] = trans * facet3D[2];
        facet3D[3] = Vector((cos((theta - d_theta) *
            0.017453292)), (sin((theta - d_theta) *
            0.017453292)), 1.0);
        facet3D[3] = trans * facet3D[3];
        display_facet(facet3D,color);
        theta += 2*d_theta;
    }
}

/*

        toroid() = Displays a toroid on the screen

*/

void toroid(int type, int no_facets, float r1, float r2,
```

```
        int color)
    {
        int theta, d_theta, phi, d_phi,i, start, stop;
        float ctm, stm, ctp, stp, rcpm, rspm, rcpp, rspp;
        Vector facet3D[4];
        Vector temp1,temp2;
        Matrix trans;

        d_theta = 180/no_facets;
        d_phi = d_theta;
        if (type == 1)
        {
            start = d_theta + 90;
            stop = d_theta + 270;
        }
        else
        {
            start = d_theta + 270;
            stop =  d_theta + 450;
        }
        trans = transform(tr, sc, ro);
        for (theta=start; theta < stop; theta+=(2*d_theta))
        {
            ctm = cos((theta-d_theta)*0.017453292);
            stm = sin((theta-d_theta)*0.017453292);
            ctp = cos((theta+d_theta)*0.017453292);
            stp = sin((theta+d_theta)*0.017453292);
            for (phi=d_phi; phi<d_phi+360; phi+=(2*d_phi))
            {
                rcpm = r2*cos((phi-d_phi)*0.017453292);
                rspm = r2*sin((phi-d_phi)*0.017453292);
                rcpp = r2*cos((phi+d_phi)*0.017453292);
                rspp = r2*sin((phi+d_phi)*0.017453292);
                facet3D[0] = Vector((r1 + rcpm)*ctm,(r1 +
                rcpm)*stm,rspm);
                facet3D[0] = trans * facet3D[0];
                facet3D[1] = Vector((r1 + rcpm)*ctp,(r1 +
                rcpm)*stp,rspm);
                facet3D[1] = trans * facet3D[1];
                facet3D[2] = Vector((r1 + rcpp)*ctp,(r1 +
                rcpp)*stp,rspp);
                facet3D[2] = trans  * facet3D[2];
                facet3D[3] = Vector((r1 + rcpp)*ctm,(r1 +
                rcpp)*stm,rspp);
                facet3D[3] = trans * facet3D[3];
                display_facet(facet3D,color);
            }
        }
    }
```

```
/*
        solid_rev() = Displays a solid of revolution on
                          the screen
*/

void solid_rev(int type, int color)
{
    int i, j, theta, d_theta;
    float z_step, dz;
    Vector facet3D[4];
    Vector temp1,temp2;
    Matrix trans;
    float surface[60];

    if (type == 0)    /* pawn */
    {
        for (i=0; i<10; i++)
            surface[i] = 0.2 + sin(0.017453292 * (9 - i) *
                12.0) * 0.5;
        for (i=10; i<43; i++)
            surface[i] = 0.2;
        for (i=43; i<60; i++)
            surface[i] = sin(0.017453292 * (59 - i) * 9.0)
                * 0.6;
    }

    if (type == 1)    /* bishop */
    {
        for (i=0; i<10; i++)
            surface[i] = 0.2 + sin(0.017453292 * (9 - i) *
                12.0) * 0.5;
        for (i=9; i<38; i++)
            surface[i] = 0.3;
        for (i=38; i<60; i++)
            surface[i] = sin(0.017453292 * (59 - i) * 6) *
                0.45;
    }

    if (type == 2)   /* bowling pin */
    {
        for (i-0; i<38; i++)
            surface[i] = -0.65 + cos(0.017453292 * (i -
                16)*1.5);
        for (i=38; i<56; i++)
            surface[i] = 0.2;
        for (i=56; i<60; i++)
            surface[i] =  sin(0.017453292 * (59 - i) *
                30.0) * 0.2;
```

```
    }
    trans = transform(tr, sc, ro);
    d_theta = 3;
    theta = 93;
    dz = 1/60.0;

    for (i=0; i<60; i++)
    {
        z_step = dz - 1.0;
        for (j=0; j<60; j++)
        {
            facet3D[0] = Vector((cos((theta - d_theta) *
                0.017453292))* surface[j], (sin((theta -
                d_theta) * 0.017453292)) * surface[j],
            z_step - dz);
            facet3D[0] = trans * facet3D[0];
            facet3D[1] = Vector((cos((theta + d_theta) *
                0.017453292)) *surface[j],(sin((theta +
                d_theta) * 0.017453292)) * surface[j],
            z_step - dz);
            facet3D[1] = trans * facet3D[1];
            facet3D[2] = Vector((cos((theta + d_theta) *
                0.017453292)) *surface[j+1], (sin((theta
                + d_theta) * 0.017453292)) * surface[j+1],
                z_step + dz);
            facet3D[2] = trans * facet3D[2];
            facet3D[3] = Vector((cos((theta - d_theta) *
                0.017453292)) *surface[j+1], (sin((theta
                - d_theta) * 0.017453292)) * surface[j+1],
                z_step + dz);
            facet3D[3] = trans * facet3D[3];
            display_facet(facet3D,color);
            z_step += 2*dz;
        }
        theta += 2*d_theta;
    }
}

/*
         Cube() = Displays a cube on the screen
*/

void cube(int color)
{
    int i;
    Vector facet3D[4];
```

```
    facet3D[0] = Vector(1,1,1);
    facet3D[1] = Vector(-1,1,1);
    facet3D[2] = Vector(-1,-1,1);
    facet3D[3] = Vector(1,-1,1);
    cube_face(facet3D, color);
    facet3D[0] = Vector(1,1,-1);
    facet3D[1] = Vector(1,-1,-1);
    facet3D[2] = Vector(-1,-1,-1);
    facet3D[3] = Vector(-1,1,-1);
    cube_face(facet3D, color);
    facet3D[0] = Vector(1,1,1);
    facet3D[1] = Vector(1,-1,1);
    facet3D[2] = Vector(1,-1,-1);
    facet3D[3] = Vector(1,1,-1);
    cube_face(facet3D, color);
    facet3D[0] = Vector(-1,1,1);
    facet3D[1] = Vector(-1,1,-1);
    facet3D[2] = Vector(-1,-1,-1);
    facet3D[3] = Vector(-1,-1,1);
    cube_face(facet3D, color);
    facet3D[0] = Vector(1,1,1);
    facet3D[1] = Vector(1,1,-1);
    facet3D[2] = Vector(-1,1,-1);
    facet3D[3] = Vector(-1,1,1);
    cube_face(facet3D, color);
    facet3D[0] = Vector(1,-1,1);
    facet3D[1] = Vector(-1,-1,1);
    facet3D[2] = Vector(-1,-1,-1);
    facet3D[3] = Vector(1,-1,-1);
    cube_face(facet3D, color);
}

/*

            cube_face() = Displays face of cube

*/

void cube_face(Vector facet3D[], int color)
{
    Matrix trans;

    trans = transform(tr, sc, ro);
    facet3D[0] = trans * facet3D[0];
    facet3D[1] = trans * facet3D[1];
    facet3D[2] = trans * facet3D[2];
    facet3D[3] = trans * facet3D[3];
    display_facet(facet3D,color);
}
```

```
719    /*
        surface() = Displays a surface on the screen
721    */

722    void surface(int color)
723    {
724        Vector facet3D[4];
725        Vector temp1,temp2;
726        Matrix trans;

727        trans = transform(tr, sc, ro);
728        facet3D[0] = Vector(1,1,0);
729        facet3D[0] = trans * facet3D[0];
730        facet3D[1] = Vector(-1,1,0);
731        facet3D[1] = trans * facet3D[1];
732        facet3D[2] = Vector(-1,-1,0);
733        facet3D[2] = trans * facet3D[2];
734        facet3D[3] = Vector(1,-1,0);
735        facet3D[3] = trans * facet3D[3];
736        display_facet(facet3D,color);
737    }
```

Creating a Cone

Lines 450 through 474 create a cone. The parameters passed to the *cone* function are the number of facets and the cone color. The function begins in line 455 by dividing 180 degrees by the number of facets to obtain the angle increment (*d_theta*) that will be used to define each facet. Since integers are used at this point, you need to enter a number of facets that will divide evenly into 180. The function next finds a starting value for the angle (line 456) and then invokes the function *transform* (line 457) that creates a transformation matrix; *trans*, from the global vectors *tr*, for translation of the object; *sc*, for scaling of the object; and *ro*, for rotation of the object. These vectors are set to the proper values before the function is called. Next the function begins a *for* loop (line 458) that is repeated once for each facet that is to make up the cone. The four vertices of a facet are computed and placed in each of four vectors that make up *facet3D*. Note that the solid is designed to be centered at the origin and to fit into a box defined by the limits of -1 and +1 for each dimension. The matrix *trans* is then applied to change to the desired size, location, and orientation. These computations are performed in lines 460 through 471. For the cone, two of the vertices are spaced along the circumference of the circle that forms the base of the cone, and the other two are at the apex of the cone for every facet. (Therefore, in this case, the facets are actually triangles rather than quadrilaterals.) You should also note that numbers given for the z dimension are reversed, which makes the picture come out properly in the screen coordinate system, where y is the reverse of what is normally accepted. After all four vertices of each facet are computed, it is painted onto the screen in line 472. The angle is then increased in line 473 and the loop is iterated again for another facet.

Coloring and Displaying a Facet

The function *display_facet* (listed in lines 298 through 355) performs the operations necessary to determine the color of a facet and how to paint it to the screen. The function begins in line 309 by calculating a surface normal to the facet surface. This is accomplished by the function *surf_norm* (listed in lines 375 through 400). This function first finds a vector *dir1* between the first two vertices of the facet (line 379) and then finds another vector *dir2* between the first and last vertices of the facet (line 380). Next, the cross product of these two vectors is taken (line 381) to give a vector normal (at right angles) to the plane determined by the first two vectors (the facet surface). The length of the normal vector is then computed in line 382. In a similar manner, the normal to the vectors from the last vertex of the facet to the second and third vertices of the facet is determined and its length obtained (lines 382 through 386). Now, if the length of the first normal vector is 0, the second normal vector is normalized and the result becomes the surface normal vector for the facet (lines 387 and 388). If the first length isn't 0, the first surface normal vector is normalized and if the second normal has length 0, then the first normalized vector becomes the surface normal (line 391). If neither normal vector has 0 length, they are averaged to find the surface normal vector (lines 392 through 397). The function doesn't make any provision for what happens if both normal vectors have 0 length.

Getting back to *display_facet*, the function now computes the cosine of the angle between the viewer position vector and the facet surface normal vector *cos_beta* in lines 310 and 311. If the cosine of this angle is less than or equal to 0, the facet cannot be seen by the viewer, so the function returns without drawing it to the screen, or doing anything else, for that matter (line 312). Otherwise, the function computes the cosine of the angle between the light source position vector and the surface normal vector of the facet (*cos_theta*) by taking the dot product of the two vectors in line 314. If the cosine of this angle is less than or equal to 0, none of the light from the light source illuminates the facet, so its light intensity is set to that of ambient light (line

316). Otherwise, the surface normal vector is multiplied by *cos_theta* (line 319), the resulting vector is normalized and the light vector then subtracted from it (lines 320 and 321), and the resulting vector normalized again (line 322). The cosine of the angle between this vector and the viewer vector (*cos_alpha*) is then determined (line 323). The intensity of the facet color is the sum of the ambient light, the diffuse lighting from the surface multiplied by *cos_theta*, and the specular light from the surface multiplied by *cos_alpha* raised to the *glossiness* power (lines 324 through 326). This last term is the Phong shading, which creates the highlights that are seen in illuminating curved objects.

Now, if the intensity is greater than or equal to 1 (otherwise the facet is not illuminated so it need not be drawn), the *map* function is used to project each vertex of the facet onto the two-dimensional display screen (lines 330 and 331). Lines 332 and 333 make sure that the intensity is never greater than the maximum avilable for the selected color. Two possible display modes are incorporated in the program. If *dmode* is 1, the function *quad.draw* is called, which draws straight lines between adjacent vertices to outline each facet of the object. (Observe that for the class *Quadrilateral* we did not define the function *draw* so it inherits the *draw* function from the class *Polygon*, from which it was derived. If *dmode* is 2, the function *quad.fill* is called, which fills the quadrilateral with the proper shade of the designated color). Back in lines 48 through 63, we set up the palette of 256 colors to contain 36 shades of each of seven basic colors. The *intensity* value of 0 through 35 is added to the base color palette number to find the proper number of the palette color to be used.

Mapping to Two Dimensions

The *map* function (lines 360 through 370) converts a three-dimensional point from the world coordinates used to develop a scene to its two-dimensional projection onto the viewing screen. The geometry is illustrated in Figure 22-1. The viewer is looking at the origin of the world coordinate system; at some point between the viewer and the origin is the viewing screen, positioned at right angles to the view-to-origin vector. Lines 364 through 366 perform the conversion of the world coordinate system to one centered at the intersection of the screen with the view-to-origin vector. Then lines 367 and 368 convert the new coordinate location to its equivalent two-dimensional projection onto the viewing screen.

Creating a Cylinder

The function *cylinder* is listed in lines 479 through 535. It is just the same as the *cone* function, except that where the third and fourth vertices of the cone were both the same and were at a point above the

Figure 22-1. Geometry of Three-Dimensional to Two-Dimensional Conversion

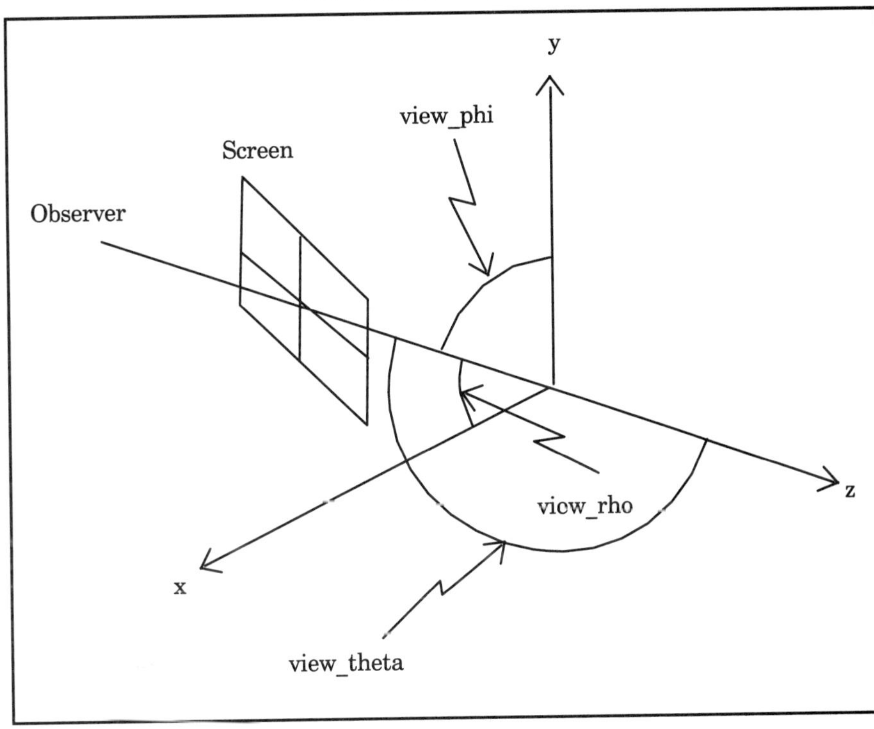

center of the cone base, the third and fourth vertices of the cylinder are directly above the first and second vertices.

Creating a Cube

The function *cube* is listed in lines 671 through 705. Lines 675 through 704 define the four vertices for each of the six sides of the cube. After each facet is defined, the function calls the function *cube_face*, which is listed in lines 709 through 718. It creates the transformation *trans* in line 712 and then applies it to each vertex in lines 713 through 716. The *display_facet* function is then called to display the facet on the screen.

Creating a Surface

The function *surface* is listed in lines 722 through 737. It simply creates the four vertices for a surface and then displays them on the screen.

Creating a Sphere

The function *sphere* is listed in lines 404 through 474. It is similar to the functions *cone* and *cylinder*, but instead of being able to use a single *for* loop to generate strips of the figure, it must use two nested *for* loops (lines 416 and 418) to generate small patches on the sphere's surface. This makes it much slower than the previous functions. The procedure is the same; generate a facet, transform it, and display it to the screen in the proper shade of color.

Creating A Solid of Revolution

The function to generate solids of revolution is listed in lines 592 through 667. If you look at lines 637 through 667, you'll see that this function is much like that for generating a sphere. Both (and the cylinder and cone functions as well) use a *for* loop to specify facet coordinates in steps around a circle in the (x,z) plane. However, where the sphere function computes the coordinate values for steps in the y direction, this function uses 60 steps that are stored in a coordinate array *surface*. You can fill this array with 60 arbitrary values or use some mathematics to compute the values. The function, as listed, computes the *surface* values for a chess pawn in lines 600 through 610, for a chess bishop in lines 611 through 621, and for a bowling pin in lines 622 through 632. Don't feel constrained by these cases, however; you can add any surfaces you want.

Creating a Torus

Lines 539 through 587 list a function to create a torus. It differs from previous functions in that we have added a parameter *type*. The function is then set up so that if *type* is 1, we draw the half of the torus that goes from 90 degrees to 270 degrees in the (x,z) plane, whereas for any other type value, the half from 270 to 450 degrees is drawn. This makes it possible to draw the back half of the torus, then insert some figure at its center, and then draw the front half. Some needed trigonometric functions for the torus are computed in lines 562 through 565. The needed mathematical parameters are computed in lines 568 through 571. The vertices for each facet are then computed in lines 572 through 583. You can check the mathematics against any solid geometry textbook.

The *solid.cpp* Program

This demonstration program paints a series of scenes on the screen that give some idea of the capabilities of the solid-modeling technique. With these as examples, you can define other pictures that you would like to create. You may have to experiment a little to get the proper size and position for each object. Lines 64 through 76 of the program set the screen to text mode and display the view-angle parameters. Then a number of parameters are initialized. The first screen created is simply a large magenta-colored cube (lines 94 through 100). We've used VESA mode 103H (800 pixels × 600 pixels × 256 colors), but you can change to any 256-color display mode that is supported by your VGA or Super VGA card by simply changing line 94. The program sets the display mode, sets the palette colors, sets up the translation, rotation, and scaling vectors, and then calls *cube* to place the cube on the screen. The next screen consists of three cylinders. The *cylinder* function paints only the top cap of the cylinder; if you change the viewing orientation such that the bottom cap of the cylinder is visible, you'll need to add a bottom cap to the function. This is listed in lines 104 through 117. The next scene shows a large sphere balanced upon three cones (lines 121 through 139). This is shown in Plate 23. The next scene shows 10 stacked cones (lines 143 through 162). In lines 143 through 152, 10 translation vectors are defined, which are used for positioning each cone and will also be used for the stacked-spheres and stacked-pyramids displays that follow. The spacing was adjusted to be correct for the cones; it isn't quite correct for the spheres and pyramids. You can change the values around if you like, to get them perfect for each display. The 10 stacked spheres are generated by lines 166 through 175. The 10 stacked pyramids are generated by lines 179 through 188. Note that the pyramids are generated by calling the *cone* function, specifying four facets. The next display is of 10 bowling pins and a bowling ball (lines 192 through 227). The very first thing that is generated in this display is a single facet that represents the bowling alley (lines 194 through 206). We could have used the *surface* function, but once the vertices of the facet were created in lines 198 through 205, it was just as easy to call *display_facet* to draw the surface. Lines 209 through 218 set up translation vectors for each of the 10 bowling pins. A *for* loop (line 219) is then used to properly position and draw each bowling pin using the *solid_rev* function. Line 226 uses *sphere* to draw the bowling ball, completing the picture. This scene is shown in Plate 24. The next scene is of a chessboard with two bishops and three pawns (lines 231 through 259). The bishops and pawns, as well as the bowling pins of the previous scene, were created with the *solid_of_rev* function (lines 247 through 259). By passing a type number to the function the proper profile for one of these three objects is selected. You can add more profiles if you desire to be able to make other symmetrical objects. At the beginning of this scene, two nested *for* loops are used to draw the alternate rows of red squares on the chessboard (lines 235 through 246). The resulting chessboard display is shown in Plate 25. The next scene is reminiscent of the Towers of Hanoi puzzle. The puzzle begins with seven rings stacked on a rod, each ring being smaller than the one below it. The goal is to move rings to the other two rods and back, until all seven rings are stacked on another of the rods. However, you can never put a bigger ring on top of a smaller one. To create this picture, we have to draw the back half of all of the tori and then draw the cylindrical rods. Finally the front half of each torus is drawn. The function *toroid* handles the tori, generating the back half of a torus when it is passed the type 1 and the front half when it is passed the type 0. The resulting display is shown in Plate 26.

23

Ray Tracing

Our experience with solid modeling has shown that it is somewhat complicated just to produce simple geometric objects with a reasonable shading of color. If we consider the possibility of scenes that contain not only objects but also shadows, reflections, and textured surfaces, the tools we've used so far are just not adequate to create a realistic scene. This is where a technique called ray tracing comes to our assistance to make complex scene representations possible. In ray tracing, we do the reverse of what actually happens when we view a scene. In real life, one or more light sources illuminate a scene with an infinite number of rays of light. Just a few of these rays are deflected off objects in the scene so that they impinge upon the observer's eye. Since these are the only rays we are interested in, we are going to trace them backward from the observer's eye to the objects they bounce off of and ultimately to each light source. At some point between the observer and the scene, we're going to insert a viewing screen. We'll trace a ray from the observer's eye to each pixel of the viewing screen and from there to whatever objects it hits on the way to the light sources. As a result of this process, we'll find out the color and intensity of the light as it hits the viewing screen, and it is this color and intensity that we'll assign to the pixel as we draw it on the screen. The final result will be that the colors and intensities that we've assigned to the screen will produce a picture just like a photograph would have done.

My book *Object Oriented Graphics Programming in C++* contains a full description of a simplified ray-tracing program. If you're interested in the mechanics of how such a program is put together, that's the place to look. Since even this simplified program uses almost a whole book, it's too big to include here. Besides, there is a very sophisticated ray-tracing program available for free. It's known as POV-Ray and is available from many bulletin boards. If you don't want the bother or expense of downloading it, you can get the whole thing and more on the POV-Ray CD-ROM for $39.95 which is available from:

Walnut Creek CD-ROM
041 Pike Lane Suite D
Concord, CA 94520-9909

Phone: (800) 786-9907

You can make some beautiful ray-traced images with this program. Plate 27 is a ray-traced image made with the program from my book.

Ray-Tracing Fundamentals

Figure 23-1 illustrates the geometry of ray tracing when just an object, a light source, and an observer are involved. A ray is projected from the observer position to a pixel on the screen. The ray then continues until it intersects with the closest object in the ray path. At this point, a new ray is created that goes from the point of intersection to the light source. If there is more than one light source, rays go from the object to each light source and the contributions from each light source are added together to determine the color at the point of intersection with the object. This color is displayed on the screen at the pixel where the ray passes through the screen.

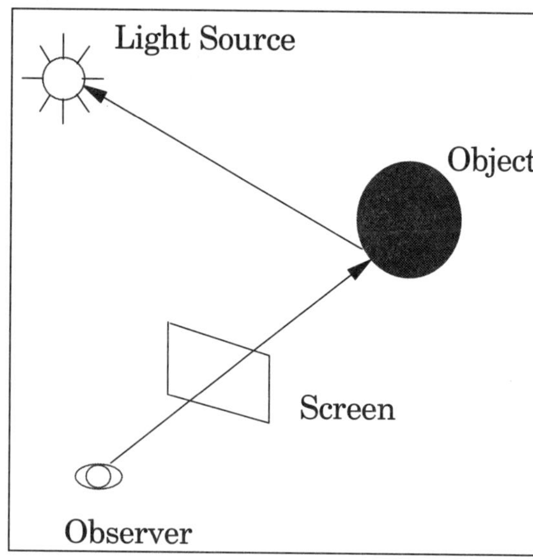

Figure 23-1. Ray-Tracing Geometry

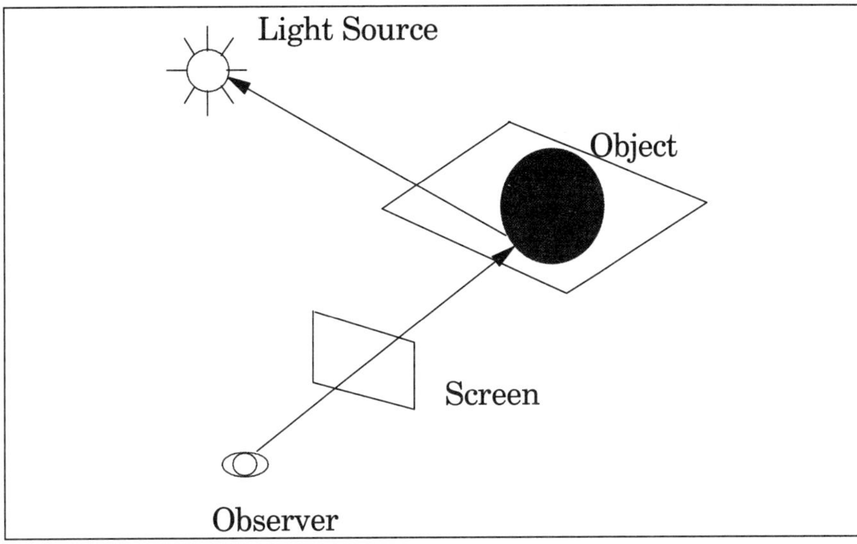

Figure 23-2. Ray-Tracing Geometry for Object in Shadow

Figure 23-2 shows what happens when an object interposes a shadow into the scene. In this figure, the ray first intersects with the plane that represents the ground or a floor within the picture. A new ray is then created from the point of intersection to the light source. However, an object is in the path of this ray, blocking it. Thus there is no contribution from the light source, so that part of the plane in the shadow area is darker than the part of the plane directly lit by the light source. The ray-tracing program automatically determines the proper color for the ray that impacts the shaded areas, thus creating the proper shadows for every object in the picture, without the need to specify and detail each shadow. Now let's see how this is done.

A typical ray-tracing program begins by setting up a ray structure that defines the ray starting point (the position of the observer's eye) and the ray direction. The direction is set to be such that the ray passes through the screen at the exact pixel location desired. The ray tracer then scans a list of objects that make up the scene and determines the nearest object intersected by the ray. If there is no intersection, the pixel is colored with a predetermined background color or texture. If a ray-object intersection is found, the ray tracer determines how any texture that applies to the object surface affects the light reflection and then begins to collect the components of the final color. The first component is the object color multiplied by the ambient color value, which is the amount of color produced by general overall illumination, excluding contributions from any light sources. Next, new rays are defined, having their origin at the intersection location and being directed toward each light source in the scene. The ray tracer checks whether there is a direct path to each light source. If an object interposes between the intersection and a light source, no additional light is added to the ambient light component. If there is a direct path to the light source, the ray tracer determines the cosine of the incident angle between the new ray and the surface normal of the object originally intersected. If this cosine is negative, the normal direction and the sign of the cosine are reversed. Then the light on the object from the light source is computed by multiplying the lamp strength by the cosine of the incident angle and dividing by the light source to object distance squared. The resulting value is multiplied by the object color value and added to the ambient contribution.

Specular reflection is the reflection of a light source highlight from a shiny surface, in the same color as the light source, regardless of the color of the surface itself. The highlight is reflected unequally in different directions, so that it appears to move as the observer's viewpoint of the object is changed. Figure 23-3 shows the geometry involved. The light is coming toward the surface along the vector L. This vector is at the incident angle θ to the surface normal. The reflected light leaves the surface in the direction of the vector R at an angle of θ on the other side of the normal, or a total angle of 2θ to the incoming light vector. The vector V represents the direction of the viewer. If the surface is a perfect mirror, light is reflected only in direction R, so that the viewer does not see a reflection unless the angle α is 0.

For nonperfect reflecting surfaces, rather than having a value only when α is 0, the specular reflection has a maximum when α is 0 and falls off sharply as $cos^n\alpha$ (where n is the *specular-reflection exponent* or *Phong exponent* of the material) when α is other than 0. This exponent can take on values from 1 to several hundred, with the reflection becoming more and more sharply concentrated around α as the exponent increases. This is the illumination model developed by Phong Bui-Tuong in 1975. When an object has a defined Phong coefficient, the ray tracer uses the above mathematics to determine

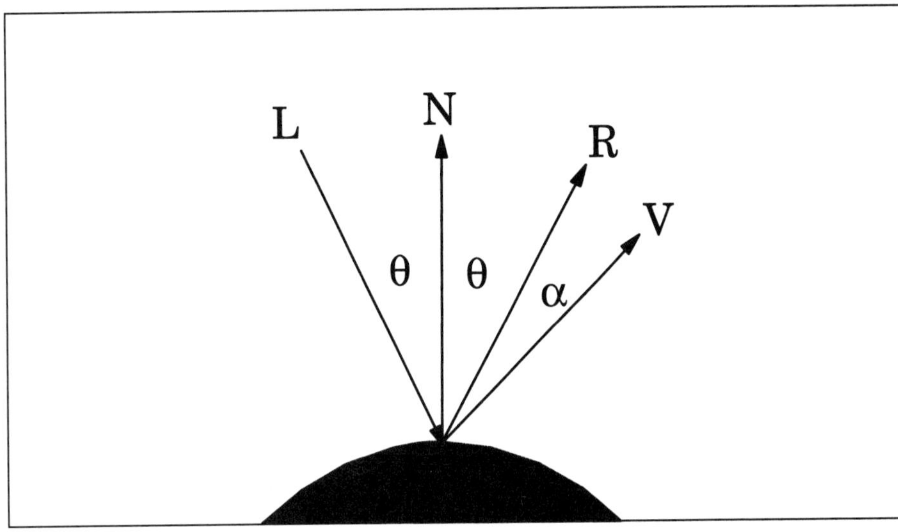

Figure 23-3. Geometry of Spectral Reflection

the light on a particular pixel. These color components are summed for all light sources, and the resulting light value becomes the color of the pixel. The same procedure is performed for every pixel of the viewing screen to produce a file of all the pixel color values that make up the scene.

As part of the definition of a surface texture of an object, there is a reflection coefficient that describes how much light is reflected by the obect. If there is a significant amount of reflected light, the ray tracer has to generate a new ray to represent this and trace it back to other objects or light sources. Doing this causes the final scene to include realistic reflections from mirrors and partially mirrored surfaces. The new vector has its origin at the intersection of the original ray and the object. The ray tracer then takes the incident angle between the viewer vector and the surface normal, doubles it, and multiplies by the surface normal. The result is added to the original ray direction to obtain the direction of the new vector.

The ray tracer must also consider objects that are at least partially transparent. The amount of transparency is specified in the object's texture data. It takes on values between 0.0 and 1.0. A value of 0.0 represents an object that is completely opaque and therefore requires no special action. A value of 1.0 represents an object that is completely transparent and therefore doesn't even appear in the picture. In between are partially transparent objects. For these, the ray tracer computes the cosine of the incident angle between the ray direction and the object surface normal. If this angle is less than or equal to 0, we are entering the transparent object.

Usually, when a light ray passes the boundary between two different media, it is bent in some way. This is the quality that makes lenses possible. The ray tracer should then apply a coefficient of refraction for bending light rays at the junction of two media. Then it sets up a new ray, which starts at the position of the intersection and has as its direction that of the original ray added to the surface normal and bent as specified by the coefficient of refraction. The final color is created by adding the original object color and the new color proportionally to the amount of transparency of the original object.

Object Textures

Most real-life objects are characterized by surfaces that are rough or have variegated colors. Attempting to define every point on the surface of an object as to exact position and color is an impossible task, but fortunately there are some fairly simple techniques for producing a very lifelike representation of an object with a textured surface or a surface that is varicolored. Using these techniques, we can produce an infinite number of different colored objects with smooth or interesting nonsmooth surfaces. One technique that is widely used to represent such objects is called *texture mapping*. This is accomplished by mapping the point on an object whose color we want to determine from a three-dimensional surface to a two-dimensional plane. The program has stored an array representing colors at points on this plane, so the color for the corresponding point is assigned to that particular ray/object intersection point and then processed through the ray-tracing program to obtain the exact color shade for the particular pixel being displayed.

Unfortunately, this technique has some pretty serious limitations. If you've ever compared a Mercator projection map of the world with a globe, you'll realize that considerable distortion is involved in mapping a sphere to a plane. The same thing occurs in reverse so that a texture-mapped sphere will have the texture pattern compressed at the poles of the sphere. A much less limited technique is *solid texturing*, in which a three-dimensional texture map is created, requiring no mapping of the solid; the appropriate color is obtained from the proper point in the three-dimensional texture representation. This process can be used to reproduce such varicolored materials as wood and marble and such irregular surfaces as that of an orange, waves in the ocean, or ripples in a pool.

A three-dimensional texture map can be expressed by explicitly defining the color for each point in a volume of space, but this uses up a huge amount of computer memory. On the other hand, the point in space being considered may be used to generate a *noise* value that is applied to a color or group of colors to determine what the color should be. This technique uses a minimal amount of memory and is quite efficient. The concepts were first developed by Ken Perlin and Darwin Peachey in 1985. The noise function used must have two distinct characteristics:

738. The noise must be defined continuously over three-dimensional space, so that no matter what set of three-dimensional coordinates is specified, a value of the noise exists for that point.

739. The correlation between two noise values must be proportional to the distance between spatial points, so that points that are close together have closely correlated noise values (the noise values are close together also) and points that are far apart have uncorrelated noise values.

The resulting noise function, as used in ray tracing, has a value between 0.0 and 1.0. The way we use this function to determine colors is to have a color table of sets of colors and the range of the noise function over which they apply. When a noise value is determined, we interpolate between the two colors whose ranges bracket that value to obtain the exact color for that noise value.

A major breakthrough in the modeling of rough surfaces occurred when Jim Blinn realized that a wrinkled surface, such as that of an orange, could be modeled by perturbing the surface normal randomly, rather than modeling every fold and bump in the surface itself. The same noise function that is used to produce color textures can be applied to the surface normal in such a way as to depict a bumpy surface. Modifications of this technique can be used to produce ripples in a surface that look like the ripples produced in a pool when a stone is thrown into it or waves in the ocean.

24

Anti-Aliasing

If you draw lines on a computer screen that are horizontal or vertical or have a slope of + or -1 (in terms of pixels), they look really good. But when you draw lines with other slopes, they have "jaggies," a step-like characteristic that makes them look more like tiny staircases than straight lines. Color Plate 28 shows a pattern of lines, many of which exhibit this objectionable characteristic. It comes about when we move one pixel along the major (longer) axis of such a line—we should only move a partial pixel along the minor axis, but we don't have this luxury, since we are working with a discrete number of pixel locations we must position at either the current pixel or the next one, whichever we think is the best approximation. There is a whole esoteric field of mathematics called *sampled data theory* that deals with this. Basically, it says that when you sample a continuous piece of information (such as a line) at discrete intervals, you not only lose some of the information about the line, but also introduce new and unwanted information at multiples of the sampling frequency. The result is those little extra steps that we don't want to see. Sampled data theory can tell us what sampling frequencies to select to get the best information from certain kinds of data, but, unfortunately, with a computer display the sampling frequency is determined by the display resolution and we are stuck with it. To be sure, if we get a better monitor and display adapter card, we can use a higher-resolution display mode, but this improves the situation only by reducing the size of the jaggies, not eliminating them altogether, and the price is the cost of more expensive equipment and more memory.

Does this make our search for improvement in drawing lines hopeless? Fortunately, no. While we can't actually improve the lines that we draw, we can use some tricks to fool the human eye into thinking that the line is much better than it actually is. Since the unwanted artifacts introduced by sampling are called *aliases*, the techniques for making them less obvious to the eye are known as *anti-aliasing*.

Anti-Aliasing in General

Generally speaking, the idea of anti-aliasing is that if a pixel must be located off the actual axis of a line, it should not be of the same color intensity as pixels that are exactly on the axis. When we think of lines, we ideally assume that they have no width, but as we actually draw one on a display screen, it must have a width of at least the pixel diameter. Suppose we visualize the rectangle produced by a one-pixel-wide line and then examine each pixel that we have drawn with our discrete location constraints. If the pixel is completely within the rectangle, we paint it with full color intensity; if it is only partially within the rectangle, we reduce the color intensity in porportion to the amount of the pixel that is within the rectangle. You might think that all this would do is cause us to see a bunch of dots with different color intensities, but actually the eye merges all this data and sees a straight line, without any jaggies. There are a lot of techniques for anti-aliasing. We're only going to show one, and we're going to limit it to the colors that we can make available with the 256-color display modes. If you're planning to use high color or true color display modes, you can vastly improve how you draw anti-aliased lines.

Wu Anti-Aliasing

This anti-aliasing technique was first proposed by Xiaolin Wu in July 1991. Like Bresenham's algorithm it moves along the major (longer) axis of a line a pixel at a time, but instead of using a decision function to determine whether to paint the pixel that is above or below the line if the line doesn't pass directly through a pixel, it paints both these pixels but uses the decision function to determine the intensity of each one. The demonstration program is given in Listing 24-1. The main program is listed in lines 107 through 134. As shown in line 111, we are running this program in VESA extended display mode 103H, but you can use any 256-color display mode that is compatible with your computer, monitor, and VGA card. Line 112 calls the function *SetPalette*. This function sets up the 256 palette colors to consist of 32 gamma-corrected shades of each of seven basic colors. The function starts on line 149 with a *for* loop that iterates once for each of the seven colors. Lines 151 through 159 set the maximum red, green, and blue levels for each pass through the *for* loop. Line 160 begins an inner *for* loop that iterates 32 times to create the 32 shades of color. Lines 162 through 170 compute the gamma-corrected color value for each of the red, green, and blue components. These are all proportional to the maximum values, so that if that is 0, then all shades are 0. Finally, in line 172, the function calls the *setVGApalette* function to transfer the array to the VGA registers. Note that these colors begin at palette number 32, so that the first 32 VGA colors remain unchanged.

Listing 24-1. Program for WU Anti-Aliasing

```
/*
        WULINES.CPP = PROGRAM TO DEMONSTRATE WU LINE
                        ANTIALIASING

                By Roger T. Stevens  2-17-96
*/

1    #include "c:\cpphbook\program\graphics.cpp"

2    unsigned char PALETTE[16]={0, 1, 2, 3, 4, 5, 20, 7, 56,
3        57, 58, 59, 60, 61, 62, 63};
4    unsigned char color_table[768];

5    void SetPalette(void);

6    /*
                        ALine class
8    */

9    class ALine : public Graphics
10   {
11       int xstart, ystart, xend, yend, color;

12       public:
13       void draw (int xstart, int ystart, int xend, int yend,
14           int color);
15   };
```

```
void ALine::draw (int xstart, int ystart, int xend, int
    yend, int color)
{
    unsigned int slope, decision;
    unsigned int old_decision, weight;
    int dx, dy, temp, x_sign;

    xstart = convert_x(xstart);
    ystart = convert_y(ystart);
    xend = convert_x(xend);
    yend = convert_y(yend);
    if (ystart > yend)
    {
        temp = ystart; ystart = yend; yend = temp;
        temp = xstart; xstart = xend; xend = temp;
    }
    plot(xstart, ystart, color);
    dx = xend - xstart;
    x_sign = dx >= 0 ? 1 : -1;
    dx *= x_sign;
    if ((dy = yend - ystart) == 0)
    {
        while (dx-- != 0)
        {
            xstart += x_sign;
            plot(xstart, ystart, color);
        }
        return;
    }
    if (dx == 0)
    {
        do
        {
            ystart++;
            plot(xstart, ystart, color);
        } while (--dy != 0);
        return;
    }
    if (dx == dy)
    {
        do
        {
            xstart += x_sign;
            ystart++;
            plot(xstart, ystart, color);
        } while (--dy != 0);
        return;
    }
    decision = 0;
    if (dy > dx)
    {
        slope = ((unsigned long) dx << 16) / (unsigned
        long) dy;
```

```
        while (--dy)
        {
            old_decision = decision;
            decision += slope;
            if (decision <= old_decision)
            {
                xstart += x_sign;
            }
            ystart++;
            weight = decision >> 11;
            plot(xstart, ystart, color + weight);
            plot(xstart + x_sign, ystart, color + (weight
                ^ 0x1F));
        }
    }
    else
    {
        slope = ((unsigned long) dy << 16) / (unsigned
        long) dx;
        while (--dx)
        {
            old_decision = decision;
            decision += slope;
            if (decision <= old_decision)
            {
                ystart++;
            }
            xstart += x_sign;
            weight = decision >> 11;
            plot(xstart, ystart, color + weight);
            plot(xstart, ystart + 1, color + (weight ^
            0x1F));
        }
    }
    plot(xend, yend, color);
}

ALine aLine;
Graphics graphic;
Line line;

void main()
{
   int CurrentColor, i, j;
   union REGS regset;

    graphic.setMode(0x103);
    SetPalette();
    for (i=-640; i<640; i += 40)
        aLine.draw(i/5, 288, i, -480, 32);
    for (i=-480; i<=480; i += 48)
```

```
            aLine.draw(-128, 384 + i/5, -640, i, 64);
        for (i=-480; i<=480; i += 48)
            aLine.draw(128, 384+i/5, 639, i, 96);
        for (i=-640; i<640; i += 40)
            aLine.draw(i/5, -480, i, 480, 192);
        getch();
        graphic.setMode(0x103);
        SetPalette();
        for (i=-640; i<640; i += 40)
            line.draw(i/5, 288, i, -480, 32);
        for (i=-480; i<=480; i += 48)
            line.draw(-128, 384 + i/5, -640, i, 64);
        for (i=-480; i<=480; i += 48)
            line.draw(128, 384+i/5, 639, i, 96);
        for (i=-640; i<640; i += 40)
            line.draw(i/5, -480, i, 480, 192);
        getch();
        graphic.setMode(3);
    }

    /*

        SetPalette() = Sets 256 color palette for Wu
                             antialiasing

    */


    void SetPalette(void)
    {
        int i, j;
        static unsigned char GammaTable[] = {0, 10, 14, 17,
            19, 21, 23, 24, 26, 27, 28, 29, 31, 32, 33, 34,
            35, 36, 37, 37, 38, 39, 40, 41, 41, 42, 43, 44,
            44, 45, 46, 46, 47, 48, 48, 49, 49, 50, 51, 51,
            52, 52, 53, 53, 54, 54, 55, 55, 56, 56, 57, 57,
            58, 58, 59, 59, 60, 60, 61, 61, 62, 62, 63, 63};
        unsigned char red, green, blue;
        for (i=1; i<8; i++)
        {
            red = 0;
            green = 0;
            blue = 0;
            if (i & 1)
                blue = 0x3F;
            if (i & 2)
                green = 0x3F;
            if (i & 4)
                red = 0x3F;
            for (j=0; j<32; j++)
```

```
161         {
162             color_table[96*(i-1)+3*j] =
163                 GammaTable[((double)red * (1.0 -
164                 (double)j / (double)31)) + 0.5];
165             color_table[96*(i-1)+3*j+1] =
166                 GammaTable[((double)green * (1.0 -
167                 (double)j / (double)31)) + 0.5];
168             color_table[96*(i-1)+3*j+2] =
169                 GammaTable[((double)blue * (1.0 -
170                 (double)j / (double)31)) + 0.5];
171         }
172         graphic.setVGApalette(32, 224, color_table);
173     }
174 }
```

Lines 113 through 120 of the main program include four *for* loops that call the *aline.draw* function to draw a pattern of anti-aliased straight lines. Note that we have set up the class *ALine*, which is compatible with the other *Graphics* classes, so that you can transfer this part of the program to your *graphics* module if you want to have it available at all times. It does require the particular set-up of palette registers to work properly, however. The anti-aliased draw function is listed in lines 16 through 103. It begins, in lines 22 through 25, by converting the starting and ending coordinates to screen coordinates, since values must be screen-pixel related for the function to work. Lines 35 through 52 cover the special cases of horizontal and vertical lines, where we can just draw the lines without any special computation. Lines 53 through 62 cover the special case where the line slope is +1 or -1; again, we only have to draw each pixel of the line. For other situations, the function first sets the decision variable to 0 in line 64. Then it performs one of two analogous routines, depending upon whether x or y is the major axis. The first of these is listed in lines 64 through 82 and the second in lines 83 through 101. Each routine begins by computing the slope shifted 16 places to the right (lines 66 and 67 or 85 and 86). This shift allows the program to avoid floating-point numbers in its calculations. For each advance of a pixel along the major axis, this slope value is added to the decision function (line 71 or 90). Lines 72 through 76 or 91 through 95 work just like Bresenham's algorithm to set up the line pixel values. In line 77 or 96, the *weight* parameter is taken as the five least significant bits of the decision function. These represent the amount that the minor axis pixel value is off the line, and thus the shade of color in which it should be drawn. Line 78 or 97 paints the pixel in that color and then lines 79 and 80 or 98 and 99 draw the pixel on the other side of the line in the shade whose value is the complement of *weight*. Thus, the two pixels have an intensity that sums to the maximum intensity of the selected color. Color Plate 28 shows the resulting line pattern. For comparison, lines 122 through 132 of the main program reset the display mode and palette and draw the same line pattern with ordinary aliased lines.

25

Creating Complex Displays

Some of the graphics screens created in the demonstration programs in previous chapters were pretty complex, but we just presented them without giving you any clues as to how to create such a display from scratch. In this chapter, we're going to give a couple of examples of how you can use the graphics tools we've developed together with a little ingenuity to create the displays you want. As examples, we're going to create displays of the flags of Tennessee and of Wales. We'll assume that you have a picture of each flag and want to reproduce them on your computer display. Listing 25-1 is a program that does this.

The Flag of Tennessee

Color Plate 30 shows the state flag of Tennessee. The picture is drawn by lines 44 through 52. Looking at the picture, we see that the flag background is red, so we clear the background to red in line 45. Then we note a wide vertical blue bar and a narrow vertical white bar at the right edge of the flag. If we measure the width of these bars as a proportion of the entire width of the flag and then convert to our world coordinate system, we find that the blue bar should have a width of 120 units and the white bar a width of 20 units. We then use the *line.draw* function to draw the two bars in lines 46 and 47. In addition to the color and width (which are the last two parameters passed to the function) we need the starting and ending coordinates for each line. These are pretty simple to find. The x starting and ending coordinate for the (center of the) blue bar is 60 units from the right edge of the flag, so that the right edge of the bar will just touch the edge of the flag. The x starting and ending coordinate for the center of the white bar is 10 units to the left of the start of the blue bar. Since for each bar the x starting and ending coordinate values are the same, a vertical line will be drawn. The y starting and ending coordinates are the top and bottom of the display for each bar. Next, we note two circles, which, upon measurement, turn out to be at the center of the world coordinate system. By measuring and converting, we find that the white circle has a radius of 300 units. We use the *circle.fill* function to paint the filled white circle in line 48. The blue circle is found to have a radius of of 270 units. Line 49 paints the filled blue circle.

The five-pointed "Betsy Ross" stars represent a more difficult problem. Because the star figure is used three times, we're going to create a function for star drawing. Let's suppose that the generic star has one point straight up. We'll consider this to be an unrotated star; if we want the star rotated from this position, we'll do so by passing a rotation parameter *angle* to the function. Looking at the geometry of the star, we can see that the points are equally spaced around the circumference of a circle. Thus it seems desirable to pass the x and y coordinates of this circle to the function. (Note also that this is the point around which any star rotation will take place.) Finally, we pass to the function the *radius* of the circle and the *color* of the star. Lines 76 through 80 make use of a *for* loop to compute the coordinates of each of the five points of the star. For an unrotated star, the first point is at an angle of 18 degrees from the x axis. Each succeeding point is then rotated an additional 72 degrees. If there is a rotation of the star, the rotation angle is added to the angle for each point of the star. Simple trig is used in lines 78 and 79 to compute the location of a point on the circle's circumference that is rotated from the x axis by the specified rotation. Lines 81 through 83 draw lines between each alternate pair of points of the star. When these operations are through, we have all of the lines that make up the star and a few extra ones besides. The drawn figure looks like a pentagon with a triangle extending from each of its sides, breaking the star up into six enclosed polygons. Now we're going to use the *polygon.floodfill* function to fill each polygon. The middle one is simple; we use a seed point at the figure's origin. For the other five polygons, we have to be careful what seed point we use, or the *floodfill* function may be outside the polygon and fill a huge unwanted portion of the screen. Lines 85 through 87 fill the other five polygons. If you're making a new function similar to this, instead of using the *floodfill* function at first, simply plot a seed point for each of the five polygons. You'll then see five dots; if any one of them is outside its associate polygon, you need to modify the point coordinates to be sure its inside at all times. When you're satisfied that this is true, you can replace the point-plotting function with the *floodfill* function and be sure of success. Lines 50 through 52 call the *star* function to draw the three stars on the flag. You can measure to determine the approximate radius (the same for each star), the center coordinates, and the tilt angle of each star, but you'll probably have to try a few times and make some minor trial and error modifications of these parameters before the flag begins to look good. This same technique can be applied to many complex pictures that are made up of largely geometric figures.

Listing 25-1. The Flags Demonstration Program

```
/*

        FLAGS.CPP = PROGRAM TO DRAW FLAGS WITH GRAPHICS
                            ROUTINES

              By Roger T. Stevens  3-18-96

*/

#include "c:\cpphbook\program\graphics.cpp"

void star (int x, int y, int radius, int angle, int
   color);

Polygon polygon;
Triangle tri;
Line line;
Circle circle;

void main (void)
{
   int i=0;
   int tail_hole[20] = {94, 6, 98, 4, 99, 0, 99, -5, 95,
      -6, 92, -5, 91, -3, 91, 2, 92, 4, -9999};
   int welch[333] = {-97, 60, -77, 59, -74, 64, -58, 60,
      -31, 66, -53, 20, -55, 15, -55, 10, -54, 6, -50,
      3, -47, 3, -28, 13, -29, 56, 0, 67, 8, 69, 20, 71,
      37, 79, 45, 80, 75, 91, 81, 92, 67, 82, 67, 73,
      77, 73,62, 60, 60, 53, 67, 48, 49, 39, 51, 29,
      40, 27, 30, 20, 25, 18, 20, 17, 10, 16, 16, 16,
      10, 11, 5, 9, 0, 7,  5, 7, -8, -1, 30, 13, 40, 15,
      45, 15, 50, 14, 56, 12, 75, 17, 80, 18, 85, 18,
      93, 16, 105, 27, 98, 34, 114, 34, 127, 39, 119,
      25, 112, 10, 107, 20, 100, 13, 105, 5, 108, 0,
   108, -7, 105, -10, 100, -15, 95, -17, 91, -17, 87,
```

```
        -15, 84, -10, 82, -5, 83, 0, 85, 6, 68, 0, 74, -5,
        62, -40, 73, -45, 73, -50, 71, -60, 67, -68, 75,
        -65, 80, -65, 82, -74, 75, -79, 70, -75, 60, -76,
        50, -76, 45, -74, 43, -74, 36, -76, 33, -68, 39,
        -65, 50, -67, 57, -62, 60, -58, 50, -57, 45, -55,
        40, -52, 37, -50, 42, -45, 41, -35, 32, -33, 22,
        -45, 24, -45, 25, -48, 30, -50, 31, -55, 28, -60,
        20, -65, 28, -68, 28, -73, 26, -77, 22, -74, 17,
        -76, 5, -76, -3, -75, -13, -76, -18, -66, 9, -64,
        14, -54, -2, -52, -5, -44, -35, -51, -47, -68,
    -42, -68, -32, -61, -27, -64, -25, -67, -32, -78,
    -37, -80, -42, -77, -59, -78, -65, -78, -73, -75,
    -78, -80, -84, -76, -84, -65, -77, -62, -65, -66,
    -60, -65, -56, -60, -53, -50, -61, -50, -74, -43,
            -79, -46, -98, -13, -102, -32, -113, -21, -108,
            -19, -113, -21, -108, -19, -112, -10, -115, -5,
            -115, 5, -114, 10, -110, 20, -114, 26, -101, 28,
            -97, 20, -99, 15, -99, 7, -85, -4, -82, 15, -72,
            33, -90, 33, -96, 29, -96, 42, -75, 43, -93, 46,
            -70, 48, -97, 51, -9999};

        polygon.setMode(0x12);
        polygon.cls(12);
        line.draw(580,-480,580,479,9,120);
        line.draw(510,-480,510,479,15,20);
        circle.fill(0,0,300, 15);
        circle.fill(0,0,270,9);
        star(0,148,135,180,15);
        star(125,-80,135,125,15);
        star(-125,-80,135,225,15);
        getch();
        polygon.setMode(0x12);
        polygon.set_screen(15,10,15);
        while(tail_hole[i] > -8000)
            tail_hole[i++] <<= 2;
        i = 0;
        while(welch[i] > -8000)
            welch[i++] <<= 2;
        polygon.draw(4,tail_hole);
        polygon.draw(4,welch);
        polygon.floodfill(0,0,4);
        tri.fill(-452,240,-412,216,-440,192,4);
        tri.fill(-400,188,-416,204,-424,196,4);
        tri.fill(-284,236,-268,232,-276,220,15);
        line.draw(-406,188,-372,184,4);
        line.draw(-640,479,-640,-480,0);
        line.draw(639,-480,0);
        line.draw(639,479,0);
```

```
71          line.draw(-640,479,0);
72          getch();
73      }
74      /*
        ┌─────────────────────────────────────────────────┐
        │        star() = Function to draw a star         │
        └─────────────────────────────────────────────────┘
76      */
77      void star (int x, int y, int radius, int angle, int color)
78      {
79          int i, j, xv[5], yv[5];
80          for (i=0, j=angle+18; i<5; i++,j+=angle=72)
81          {
82              xv[i] = x + radius * cos (0.017453292 * j);
83              yv[i] = y + radius * sin(0.017453292 * j);
84          }
85          for (i=0; i<5; i++)
86              line.draw(xv[i], yv[i], xv[(i + 2) % 5],
87                  yv[(i + 2) % 5], color);
88          polygon.floodfill(x,y,color);
89          for (i=0; i<5; i++)
90                  polygon.floodfill((x + xv[i]) / 2,(y + yv[i])
91                      / 2,color);
92      }
```

The Flag of Wales

The flag of Wales is shown in Color Plate 31. Normally, if you wanted to reproduce this flag, you would obtain a picture of it from an encyclopedia or some other source. This flag is typical of one that requires more than just simple combination of geometric figures. The flag is drawn by lines 54 through 71 of the program. Line 54 sets the screen to the 640 pixel × 480 pixel × 16-color graphics mode. In this mode, we can use the *polygon.set_screen* function to fill the background with two colors, specifying the top and bottom colors and the boundary (in character rows) point between them. The *set_screen* function doesn't work with some VESA-supported display modes; if you use one of these, you'll have to get a little more complicated with the *line.draw* functions to paint the background. Next, we have to cope with the figure of the dragon. To start with, we need to trace the entire figure onto a piece of grid paper so that we can easily read the coordinates of critical points along the outline of the figure. To create the main body of the dragon as an irregular polygon, I began at an arbitrary point, wrote down its coordinates, then moved in a straight line along the boundary of the dragon's body until I reached a point where the straight line began to depart from the boundary. Here I recorded another point on the boundary, then drew another straight line from it, and so forth, until I went all around the dragon and got back to the starting point. The dragon body polygon thus is approximated by a series of straight-line segments, which are of varying lengths. The resulting points to define this polygon are in the array of lines 13 through 43. The graph paper that I used came up with coordinates that were about one-forth of the length of coordinates in the world coordinate system we are using for graphics. Therefore, all of the coordinates for this polygon are left-shifted two places in lines 59 and 60, corresponding to a multiplication by 4. Note that the dragon's tail has a loop that results in a hole within the overall figure. A second polygon is obtained in the same manner to define this loop. It is in the array of lines 11 and 12, and is multiplied by 4 in lines 56 and 57. Lines 61 and 62 then use the *polygon.draw* function to draw the two polygons. When you are preparing such a program, don't implement the *floodfill* function yet; you want to see the figure outline to make sure you haven't made some mistakes in transcribing the coordinates. Such mistakes are almost inevitable; they're easily visible when you look at the outline of the whole figure, so you can trace through the coordinate array and correct them. When you're satisfied that the outline of the figure is correct, you can add the *polygon.floodfill* function to make it a solid color.

There are a couple more touches needed to complete the dragon. The flames issuing from his mouth are defined by two small triangles. I obtained the coordinates of these from the graph paper, multiplied them by 4, and then put these values into two *tri.fill* functions (lines 64 and 65) to draw the two filled triangles. There is also a line from the flames to the tongue. The coordinates were determined in the same way and the *line.draw* function used (line 67) to draw the line. Finally, the dragon has a triangular eye. After the rest of the figure was drawn, the *tri.fill* function was used to superimpose a white triangular eye, whose coordinates were obtained in the same way as the other triangles (line 66). Finally, since half the flag background is white, a black line was drawn around the border of the flag to differentiate from the white paper on which it is drawn (lines 68 through 71). This is a good example of how you can plot out a complex figure and represent it by a number of straight-line segments. Many more complex pictures can be produced by using combinations of simple geometric figures and sets of straight-line segments.

26

Warping and Morphing

Take a look at Color Plate 32. It is a picture of a tall building taken from ground level with a wide-angle lens. We have to tilt the camera upward to get the whole building into the picture. The end result is that the building appears to be leaning backward. Using a computer and a technique called warping, we can correct this distortion and produce a picture that looks more like what we expect to see when we look at such a building with the eye. The result is shown in Color Plate 33.

The Mathematics of Warping

Suppose we have a rectangular grid with grid lines at unit intervals. At each intersection of grid lines, we have a pixel that is assigned a color. The accumulation of pixels can be reproduced on the display screen as a picture. Now suppose we want to warp or distort this picture. Suppose our original rectangular grid is made of rubber and we stretch and/or compress it until it becomes some strange-shaped quadrilateral. We superimpose this quadrilateral on a new rectangular grid. This is shown in Figure 26-1. Note that the corners of the original rectangle are now the corners of the quadrilateral; in terms of the new grid, they have the coordinates (x_1,y_1), (x_2,y_2), (x_3,y_3) and (x_4,y_4). Given a point on the new grid (x,y) we can relate it to a position (u,v) on the original undistorted grid with the following equations:

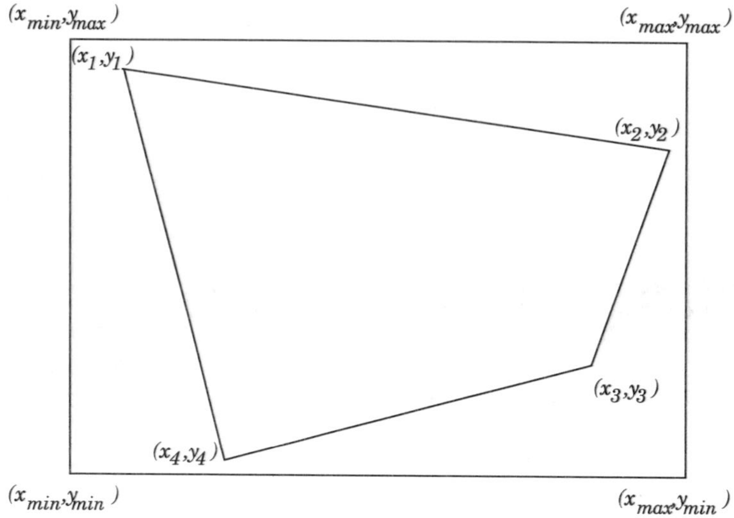

Figure 26-1. Warping Geometry

$$u = x_1 + \frac{(x_2 - x_1)x}{(x_{max} - x_{min})} + \frac{(x_4 - x_1)y}{(y_{max} - y_{min})} + \frac{x_1 - x_2 + x_3 + -x_4)xy}{(x_{max} - x_{min})(y_{max} - y_{min})}$$

(Equation 26-1)

and

$$v = y_1 + \frac{(y_2 - y_1)x}{(x_{max} - x_{min})} + \frac{(y_4 - y_1)y}{(y_{max} - y_{min})} + \frac{y_1 - y_2 + y_3 - y_4)xy}{(x_{max} - x_{min})(y_{max} - y_{min})}$$

(Equation 26-2)

You need to be aware that while the coordinates x and y are integers and therefore correspond to actual pixel locations, u and v are floating-point numbers, so if we have data that gives the colors of pixels located at integer coordinates on the old grid, we have to do some sort of interpolation to obtain the proper colors for u and v. There are many ways to interpolate; we're using one called bilinear interpolation. This makes use of the colors of the four integer locations surrounding the point (u,v). For example, for the point (25.56, 34.83), we would use color information stored for the integer points (25,34), (26,34), (25,35), and (26,35). We first find the color of an intermediate point along the u axis at the lower v integer value by weighting the colors of the first two points according to how close the actual point is to each. If f is the fractional part of the actual u location, then this is:

$$\text{color} = (1-\text{f})\mathit{color1} + \text{f}(\mathit{color2}) \qquad \text{(Equation 26-3)}$$

where *color1* is the color of the first integer point given above and *color2* is the color of the second integer point. The same procedure is used to find the intermediate point for the higher v value. Then a similar procedure is used along the v axis, making use of the second two intermediate points just calculated points to find the color of the actual point (u,v). This is the color used to paint the pixel at (x,y) on the screen.

The Warping Program

Listing 26-1 is the warping program. We are going to make use of a picture that is stored in the Targa (TGA) format, which will be described in more detail in Chapter 29. We are using the Targa format because it stores 24-bit color information without any compression, making it easy to go to the right place in the file to extract the color value of each of the four pixels surrounding each pixel value whose color we wish to find. Lines 78 through 81 define the rectangle in the final picture that we wish to warp. If you choose a rectangle smaller than the actual screen size, the program will warp the picture data within this rectangle and just transfer data outside the rectangle unchanged. (The edges of the rectangle may not match the outside picture perfectly, however.) For the sample picture, we have selected the entire screen as the warping rectangle. Lines 83 through 86 define the four corners of the quadrilateral into which the original picture is warped. Lines 88 and 89 open a file called *plate32.tga* and read its header. You must have this picture file in your default directory in order to run the program. By modifying line 65, you can change to another file name if you have a different file that you want to warp. Lines 90 and 91 set up the picture resolutions from the file header. In line 92 the display mode is set to mode 112H, the 640 pixel × 480 pixel × 16.8-million color mode. Lines 93 through 98 read the data for this mode from the VGA card. The most important thing here is *mode_data.BytesPerScanLine*, which we are going to use to determine where in display memory to place pixels. Some Super VGA cards use three bytes per pixel for this type of mode; others use four bytes per pixel with one byte blank. Lines 99 through 103 calculate offsets to be used to center the picture if the actual picture resolution is less than the screen resolution. Lines 103 through 111 compute parameters needed to transform a pixel from the original coordinates to the warped coordinates. In line 112, the display mode is set, and in line 113, the display memory bank is set to 0. The program now enters two nested *for* loops in lines 114 and 115. Together, these loops scan through every pixel location on the screen. Lines 117 through 125 compute the old (unwarped) pixel coordinates (as double floating-point numbers) for a given pixel location.

Listing 26-1. Program to Warp an Image

```
/*

        WARP.CPP = Program to warp a picture

             By Roger T. Stevens  3-16-96

*/

1   #include <dos.h>
2   #include <string.h>
3   #include <dir.h>
4   #include <stdio.h>
5   #include <conio.h>
6   #include <math.h>

7   #define max(a,b)     (((a) > (b)) ? (a) : (b))
8   #define min(a,b)     (((a) < (b)) ? (a) : (b))

9   void bilinear_interpolation(double x, double y);
10  void setBank(unsigned long int offset);
11  void setMode(int mode);

12  union REGS reg;
13  struct SREGS segregs;
14  struct REGPACK outregs;

15  struct
16  {
17      unsigned char id_length,
18                    color_map_type,
19                    image_type;
20      unsigned intcolor_map_start,
21                    color_map_length;
```

```
        unsigned charcolor_map_depth;
        unsigned intx_offset,
                    y_offset,
                    xres,
                    yres;
        unsigned char bits_per_pixel,
                    image_descriptor;
    } tga_header;
    struct
    {
        char signature[4];
        int version;
        long int far *OEM_string;
        char capabilities[4];
        long int far *Modes;
        int memory_size;
        char reserved[236];
    } info;

    struct
    {
        int     ModeAttributes;
        char    WinAAttributes;
        char    WinBAttributes;
        int     WinGranularity;
        int     WinSize;
        int     WinASegment;
        int     WinBSegment;
        long intWinFuncPtr;
        int         BytesPerScanLine;
        int         XResolution;
        int         YResolution;
        char    XCharSize;
        char    YCharSize;
        char    NumberOfPlanes;
        char    BitsPerPixel;
        char     NumberOfBanks;
        char    MemoryModel;
        char    BankSize;
        char    NumberOfImagePages;
        char    Reserved;
        char    Filler[225];
    } mode_data;

    int bytes_per_line, i, j, mode, color, xres, yres, ystop;
    char filename[16] = {"plate32.tga"};
    struct ffblk ffblk;
    long int col,row;
    FILE *read_file;
    unsigned char ch;
```

```
char red, green, blue;
unsigned int no_chars, old_bank, data;
char far * address;
int xoffset, yoffset, xright,xleft, ytop, ybottom,x,y,
    x1,y1,x2,y2,x3,y3,x4,y4,xa,ya,xb,yb,xab,yab;
double xmod,ymod,denom;
unsigned long int offset;

void main(void)
{
    xleft = 0;
    xright = 640;
    ytop = 0;
    ybottom = 480;
    x1 = 30;y1 = 0;
    x2 = 585;y2 = 90;
    x3 = 640;   y3 = 480;
    x4 = 0;   y4 = 480;
    segread(&segregs);
    read_file = fopen(filename,"rb");
    fread(&tga_header,1,18,read_file);
    xres =  tga_header.xres;
    yres = tga_header.yres;
    mode=0x112;
    outregs.r_ax = 0x4F01;
    outregs.r_cx = mode;
    segread(&segregs);
    outregs.r_es = segregs.ds;
    outregs.r_di = (unsigned int)&mode_data;
    intr(0x10,&outregs);
    xoffset = max (0,(mode_data.XResolution - xres -
    1)/2);
    yoffset = max(0,(mode_data.YResolution - yres - 1)/2);
    ystop = min(yres, mode_data.YResolution-yoffset);
    xa = x2 - x1;
    xb = x4 - x1;
    xab = x1 - x2 + x3 - x4;
    ya = y2 - y1;
    yb = y4 - y1;
    yab = y1 - y2 + y3 - y4;
    xmod = xright - xleft;
    ymod = ybottom - ytop;
    denom = xmod * ymod;
    setMode(mode);
    setBank(0);
    for (row=0; row<=ystop; row++)
        for (col=0; col < xres; col++)
        {
            if ((col > xleft) && (col < xright) && (row >
                ytop) && (row < ybottom))
            {
                x = x1 + (double(xa)*col)/xmod +
```

```
                (double(xb) * row) / ymod +
                    (double(xab)*col*row)/denom;
                y = y1 + (double(ya)*col)/xmod +
                (double(yb)*row)/ymod +
                    (double(yab)*col*row)/denom;
                bilinear_interpolation(x,y);
            }
            else
            {
                fseek(read_file,3L*xres*row + 3*col +
                18L,SEEK_SET);
                red = fgetc(read_file);
                green = fgetc(read_file);
                blue = fgetc(read_file);
            }
            offset = (row+yoffset) *
mode_data.BytesPerScanLine
                + 3 * (xoffset + col);
            setBank(offset);
            FP_SEG(address) = 0xA000;
            FP_OFF(address) =(unsigned int) offset++;
            *address = red;
            setBank(offset);
            FP_SEG(address) = 0xA000;
            FP_OFF(address) =(unsigned int) offset++;
            *address = green;
            setBank(offset);
            FP_SEG(address) = 0xA000;
            FP_OFF(address) =(unsigned int) offset;
            *address = blue;
        }
    fclose(read_file);
    getch();
    setMode(3);
}

/*

        setBank() = Sets video memory bank

*/

void setBank(unsigned long int offset)
{
    static int bank, old_bank;

    old_bank = reg.x.dx;
    bank = offset >> 16;
    if (bank == old_bank)
        return;
```

```
    reg.x.dx = bank;
    old_bank = bank;
    reg.x.ax = 0x4F05;
    reg.x.bx = 0;
    int86(0x10, &reg, &reg);
}

/*

              setMode() = Sets Video Mode

*/

void setMode(int mode)
{
    union REGS reg;
    if (mode > 0xFF)
    {
        reg.x.ax = 0x4F02;
        reg.x.bx = mode;
    }
    else
        reg.x.ax = mode;
    int86 (0x10,&reg,&reg);
}

/*

     bilinear_interpolation = Performs bilinear
                   interpolation.

*/

void bilinear_interpolation(double x, double y)
{
    double fraction_x, fraction_y, one_minus_x,
one_minus_y, tmp_double;
    int ceil_x, ceil_y, floor_x, floor_y;
    char red1, red2, red3, red4, redm1, redm2,
        green1, green2, green3, green4, greenm1, greenm2,
        blue1, blue2, blue3, blue4, bluem1, bluem2;

    floor_x = floor(x);
    floor_y = floor(y);
    ceil_x = ceil(x);
    ceil_y = ceil(y);
    fraction_x = x - floor(x);
    fraction_y = y - floor(y);
    one_minus_x = 1.0 - fraction_x;
```

```
206        one_minus_y = 1.0 - fraction_y;
207        fseek(read_file,3L*xres*floor_y + 3*floor_x +
208    18L,SEEK_SET);
209        red1 = fgetc(read_file);
210        green1 = fgetc(read_file);
211        blue1 = fgetc(read_file);
212        fseek(read_file,3L*xres*floor_y + 3*ceil_x +
213    18L,SEEK_SET);
214        red2 = fgetc(read_file);
215        green2 = fgetc(read_file);
216        blue2 = fgetc(read_file);
217        fseek(read_file,3L*xres*ceil_y + 3*floor_x +
218    18L,SEEK_SET);
219        red3 = fgetc(read_file);
220        green3 = fgetc(read_file);
221        blue3 = fgetc(read_file);
222        fseek(read_file,3L*xres*ceil_y + 3*ceil_x +
223    18L,SEEK_SET);
224        red4 = fgetc(read_file);
225        green4 = fgetc(read_file);
226        blue4 = fgetc(read_file);
227        redm1 = one_minus_x * (double)red1 + fraction_x *
228        (double)red2;
229        greenm1 = one_minus_x * (double)green1 + fraction_x *
230            (double)green2;
231        bluem1 = one_minus_x * (double)blue1 + fraction_x *
232            (double)blue2;
233        redm2 = one_minus_x * (double)red3 + fraction_x *
234            (double)red4;
235        greenm2 = one_minus_x * (double)green3 + fraction_x *
236            (double)green4;
237        bluem2 = one_minus_x * (double)blue3 + fraction_x *
238            (double)blue4;
239        red = one_minus_y * (double)redm1 +fraction_y *
240            (double)(redm2);
241        green = one_minus_y * (double)greenm1 +fraction_y *
242            (double)(greenm2);
243        blue = one_minus_y * (double)bluem1 + fraction_y *
244            (double)(bluem2);
245    }
```

In line 126, the function *bilinear_interpolation* is called to find the interpolated color. This function is listed in lines 191 through 245. Lines 199 through 202 compute the integer coordinates for the four points surrounding the desired pixel. Lines 203 and 204 compute the fractional parts of x and y, and lines 205 and 206 compute one minus each fractional part. Lines 207 through 226 get the red, green, and blue values for each of the four integer pixels from the file. Lines 227 through 238 compute the two intermediate pixel colors, and lines 239 through 244 compute the color of the final pixel.

Back in the main program, we now have the pixel colors in *red*, *green*, and *blue* if the warped pixel is within the selected rectangle. Lines 128 through 135 set *red*, *green*, and *blue* to the colors of the pixel in the file that is at the same location as the selected display pixel, if the pixel is outside the selected rectangle. Lines 136 through 151 determine the locations of the *red*, *green*, and *blue* colors for the selected pixel in display memory and store *red*, *green*, and *blue* in these locations. When the two nested *for* loops have finished, we have a new warped image displayed on the screen.

Control-Point Warping

The method of warping given above is the most useful when you are trying to correct a picture that has been distorted by lens effects. If you just want to distort a picture to produce some unusual effect, you don't need quite such precise control and you can specify the way a picture is warped by the use of a single control point. Figure 26-2 shows the geometry involved. In this case, the points (x_{min},y_{min}), (x_{min},y_{max}), (x_{max},y_{min}), and (x_{max},y_{max}) are the corners of both the original and the warped rectangles. The control point is (x_{cp},y_{cp}). (Don't try to visualize the figure as a three-dimensional representation; it is strictly two-dimensional.) The control point now divides the original picture into four quadrilaterals, each having two sides that are half the original sides of the rectangle and two sides created by drawing lines from the control point to the midpoints of two adjacent sides. We now treat each quarter of the original drawing separately, warping it into the corresponding quadrilateral as we did with the drawing in the

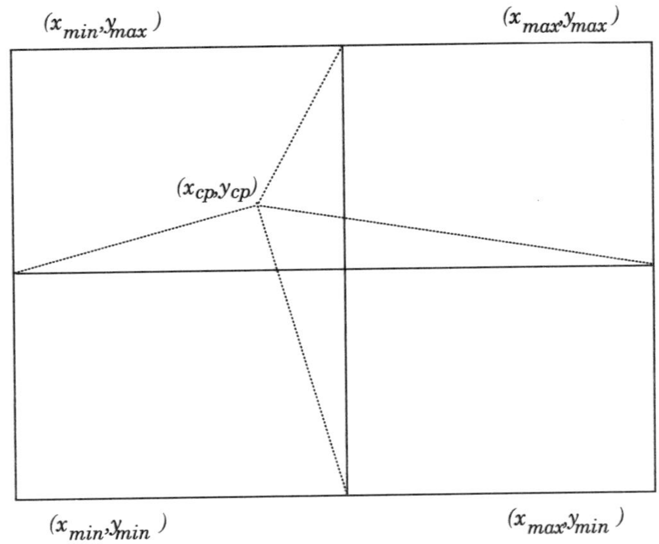

Figure 26-2. Control-Point Warping

program described above. This results in an interesting distortion of a picture.

Morphing

Morphing is the smooth transformation of one object or scene into another in a motion picture. In morphing, you select key features of the original and final images that are to match up. Next you use one of the warping techniques to warp the original in a series of steps until the key features match those of the final image. The same procedure is applied to the final image to warp the key features to the positions of those in the original image. Finally, a series of frames is created, each being a weighted average of the two images at a stage in the process. Assume that an image of a dog is to be morphed to that of a tiger. We warp the dog image in nine steps until the key points exactly match those on the tiger image. Then we morph the tiger image in ten steps until its key features exactly match the position of the dog's key features. Then we start with a first frame that is the dog's picture. The next frame is 90% of the first warped dog image added to 10% of the ninth warped tiger image. The next frame is 80% of the second warped dog image added to 20% of the eighth warped tiger image. This process continues until the last image is 100% of the tiger image. When projected as a motion picture, the dog seems to change smoothly into a tiger. If you've got a lot of time and enthusiasm, you can write modifications of the warping program we've already given to do some morphing for you. You can also find public domain or shareware programs on many bulletin boards that will do a credible job of morphing.

Part 7

Saving, Restoring and Converting Displays

27

Saving and Restoring Displays with the PCX Format

The next three chapters cover the general subject of saving the contents of a display screen to a disk file and then restoring that file to the screen. Many graphics displays require a good deal of computation, sometimes resulting in hours of computer usage to produce a single display. To avoid such a lengthy process every time we want to reproduce a display, it becomes important to have a technique for saving such pictures on disk and recalling them quickly. The *BMP* and *TGA* formats described in Chapters 30 and 31 store data directly, without compression, which can result in very large files for high-resolution multicolor displays. The *PCX* format described in this chapter uses run-length compression which works very well for 16-color displays, but often provides little improvement when a 16.8M display is saved. In this chapter, we're going to show one technique for dealing with the wide variety of screen resolutions and formats, and automatically selecting the best one for display.

The *PCX* file format was developed by:

ZSoft Corporation
450 Franklin Road, Suite 100
Marietta, GA 30067

Phone: (404) 428-0008

Z-Soft is now part of SoftKey International, but the address and phone number are still good. Shannon in their technical support group was most helpful to me in furnishing detailed specifications of this format. First developed with the PC Paintbrush painting program, *PCX* is one of the oldest and most widely used methods for storing and recovering graphics display information. To create a *PCX* file, the screen is scanned on a pixel-by-pixel basis. For multicolor displays, one line of each of the four color planes is scanned, then the next line for four color planes, etc. The program is capable of handling a 64K × 64K image size, but such large sizes are rarely used (they wouldn't fit on most floppy disks, for one thing). For very large pictures, our program will use the highest-resolution display mode available and show only as much of the top lefthand corner as will fit in the display. The format can handle monochrome displays, 16-color EGA/VGA displays, 256-color VGA displays, and 24-bit color displays (16.8 million colors). You may encounter any one of three *PCX* versions. Version 2.5 is the earliest. It supports 16-color EGA/VGA displays using the standard color palette only; no palette modifications are allowed. Version 2.8 supports 16-color EGA/VGA displays and contains palette information that allows each of the 16 colors to be selected from any of 64 available colors. Version 3.0 supports 256-color and 24-bit color EGA/VGA images, permitting definition of each of the 256 colors from 262,144 possible colors. The palette data is appended at the end of the *PCX* file for 256-color displays and direct writing of all 24-bit color information.

Preparing a Configuration File

Your Super VGA card has built into it information on the extended VESA display modes that it supports. The same information may be available for the regular EGA and VGA display modes, depending upon what brand of Super VGA card you have. Unfortunately, the fact that the Super VGA card supports a display mode does not guarantee that you will be able to display that mode; your monitor may not be capable of the frequencies and resolution needed for successful display. Some Super VGA cards allow you to store data that indicates whether a mode supported by the card is also supported by the monitor; others don't have this feature. To get around these difficulties, we've developed a program that will set up a configuration data file that determines which display modes are compatible with your system. This program is given in Listing 27-1. The three arrays *mode16*, *mode256*, and *modehi*, listed in lines 46 through 49, start out containing the display mode numbers for all EGA/VGA and VESA Super VGA display modes for 16 colors, 256 colors, and 16.8 million colors, respectively. Line 73 begins a *for* loop that iterates once for each of the 16-color VESA modes. It begins in line 75 by setting the parameter *ch* to *N*. In line 76 the function *getModeData* is called for the selected VESA function. This function returns a 1 if the mode is supported by the Super VGA card and a 0 if it is not supported. If the mode is supported, lines 78 through 80 display the mode information on the screen and permit the user to enter a *Y* or *y* if he wants to support this mode and an *N* or *n* if he doesn't want to support this mode (because he knows his monitor won't support it). The data that came with your monitor should tell you which resolutions it supports so that you can correctly make this decision. In lines 82 and 83, if the mode was not supported by the Super VGA card or if the user chose not to support it, that mode in the *mode16* array is reset to 0. Lines 85 through 96 perform these same operations for the 256-color VESA display modes. The 24-bit color is treated somewhat differently. The modes are set up by a *for* loop that begins at line 97. Each iteration begins by operating on a 24-bit color mode as was done for the previous modes. If the mode is not supported (by the Super VGA or by the user) the program tries again for the 64K-color mode having the same resolution. If this is supported, its mode number is inserted in the proper place in the *modehi* array. If this mode is not supported, the program tries again for the 32K-color mode having the same resolution. If this mode is supported, its mode number is entered in the *modehi* array. Only if none of the three multicolor modes at this resolution are supported does the program enter a 0 into the associated member of the *modehi* array. When all VESA graphics modes have been considered, the program opens a file called *vconfig.dat* (line 132) in the root directory of your hard drive and stores in it the contents of the three mode arrays (lines 133 through 135). (The file path and name are defined in line 43. Observe that we have to use a double backslash in order for a backslash to actually be written by the string.) The file is then closed (line 136) and an appropriate legend is displayed on the screen (line 137).

Listing 27-1. Program to Generate Configuration Data File

```
/*

    VCONFIG = CREATES A FILE CONTAINING GRAPHIC DISPLAY
            MODES AVAILABLE WITH A SUPER VGA CARD

                By Roger T. Stevens  3-23-96

*/

#include <stdio.h>
#include <string.h>
#include <dir.h>
#include <conio.h>
#include <dos.h>

int getModeData(int mode);

struct SREGS segregs;
struct REGPACK outregs;

struct
{
    char signature[4];
    int version;
    long int far *OEM_string;
    char capabilities[4];
    long int far *Modes;
    int memory_size;
    char reserved[236];
} info;

struct
{
    int     ModeAttributes;
    char    WinAAttributes;
    char    WinBAttributes;
    int     WinGranularity;
    int     WinSize;
    int     WinASegment;
    int     WinBSegment;
    long intWinFuncPtr;
    int         BytesPerScanLine;
    int         XResolution;
    int         YResolution;
    char    XCharSize;
    char    YCharSize;
    char    NumberOfPlanes;
    char    BitsPerPixel;
    char    NumberOfBanks;
    char    MemoryModel;
    char    BankSize;
    char    NumberOfImagePages;
```

```
        char    Reserved;
        char    Filler[225];
    } mode_data;

    char filename[32] = {"c:\\vconfig.dat"};
    FILE *config_file;
    unsigned char ch;
    unsigned int mode16[7] = {0x0D, 0x0E, 0x10, 0x12, 0x102,
            0x104,0x106},
        mode256[6] = {0x13, 0x100, 0x101, 0x103, 0x105,
        0x107};
        modehi[5] = {0x10F, 0x112, 0x115, 0x118, 0x11B};
    unsigned char string16[7][45]={"","","","",
        "102H (800 x 600 pixels x 16 colors).",
        "104H (1024 x 768 pixels x 16 colors).",
        "106H (1280 x 1024 pixels x 16 colors)."};
    unsigned char string256[6][45]={"",
        "100H (640 x 400 pixels x 256 colors).",
        "101H (640 x 480 pixels x 256 colors).",
        "103H (800 x 600 pixels x 256 colors).",
        "105H (1024 x 768 pixels x 256 colors).",
        "107H (1280 x 1024 pixels x 256 colors)."};
    unsigned char stringhi[5][45]={
        "H (320 x 200 pixels x ",
        "H (640 x 480 pixels x ",
        "H (800 x 600 pixels x ",
        "H (1024 x 768 pixels x ",
        "H (1280 x 1024 pixels x "};
    unsigned char stringcol[3][16] = {"16M colors).",
        "64K colors).",
        "32K colors)."};
    int i;

    void main(void)
    {
        clrscr();
        for (i=4; i<7; i++)
        {
            ch = 'N';
            if (getModeData(mode16[i]))
            {
                printf("\nYour Super VGA board supports ");
                printf("VESA mode %s\nUse (Y/N)?",
        string16[i]);
                ch = getch();
            }
            if ((ch == 'N') || (ch == 'n'))
                mode16[i] = 0;
        }
        for (i=1; i<6; i++)
        {
            ch = 'N';
            if (getModeData(mode256[i]))
            {
                printf("\nYour Super VGA board supports ");
                printf("VESA mode %s\nUse (Y/N)?",
        string256[i]);
```

```
            ch = getch();
        }
        if ((ch == 'N') || (ch == 'n'))
            mode256[i] = 0;
    }
    for (i=0; i<5; i++)
    {
        ch = 'N';
        if (getModeData(modehi[i]))
        {
            printf("\nYour Super VGA board supports ");
            printf("(VESA mode %x%s%s\nUse (Y/N)?",
                modehi[i], stringhi[i], stringcol[0]);
            ch = getch();
        }
        if ((ch == 'N') || (ch == 'n'))
        {
            modehi[i]--;
            if (getModeData(modehi[i]))
            {
                printf("\nYour Super VGA board supports");
                printf(" VESA mode %x%s%s\nUse (Y/N)?",
                    modehi[i], stringhi[i], stringcol[0]);
                ch = getch();
            }
            if ((ch == 'N') || (ch == 'n'))
            {
                modehi[i]--;
                if (getModeData(modehi[i]))
                {
                printf("\nYour Super VGA board supports");
                printf(" VESA mode %x%s%s\nUse (Y/N)?",
                    modehi[i], stringhi[i], stringcol[0]);
                    ch = getch();
                }
                if ((ch = 'N') || (ch == 'n'))
                    modehi[i] = 0;
            }
        }
    }
    config_file = fopen(filename,"wb");
    fwrite(mode16,2,7,config_file);
    fwrite(mode256,2,6,config_file);
    fwrite(modehi,2,5,config_file);
    fclose(config_file);
    printf("\nConfiguration file written
successfully...");
    getch();
}
```

```
/*

        getModeData() = Gets Super VGA data on a desired
                                mode

*/

int getModeData(int mode)
{

        segread(&segregs);
        outregs.r_ax = 0x4F01;
        outregs.r_cx = mode;
        outregs.r_es = segregs.ds;
        outregs.r_di =(unsigned int) &mode_data;
        intr(0x10,&outregs);
        if ((mode_data.ModeAttributes &0x01) == 1)
            return(1);
        return(0);
}
```

The PCX Header Format

The *PCX* header consists of 128 bytes at the beginning of the file. The contents of this header are described in Table 27-1. Most of the information is self-explanatory. A little further detail is required for the palette information, however. If you are writing a program to save a display screen as a *PCX* file, you will have two bits available to specify one of four levels for each of R, G, and B for every one of the 16 palettes. You can process this any way you want that will come up with a number within the proper range for the particular level for each palette triple. If you are writing for a VGA card, you can read the palette setting from the VGA registers. The corresponding registers in the EGA, however, are write-only. Therefore, when you are generating the color display initially, you need to be very careful to store somewhere the changes that you make in palette color settings, so that you have this information available for the *PCX* file header. Otherwise you will never be able to recover your original color settings. In the reverse direction, when you are writing a program to convert the disk file to a display screen, you have to carefully perform the conversion from the header triplets to the EGA/VGA palette numbers in such a way that the proper one of the four levels is obtained for every value within the range of numbers that represent that color level.

TABLE 27-1. *PCX* FILE HEADER CONTENTS

Byte #	Name	Description
0	Manufacturer ID	Always set to 0AH
1	Version number	0 = Version 2.5 1 = Version 2.8 2 = Version 2.8 with palette 3 = Version 3.0
2	Encoding technique	1 = Simple RLE. This is the normal setting for all PCX files. Other values are reserved for future encoding techniques that have not yet been implemented.
3	Bits per plane per pixel	Number of bits required in each plane to store 1 pixel. (Bit 65 gives the number of planes.) 1 = EGA/VGA 16-color modes 2 = CGA 4-color modes 8 = VGA 256-color modes
4-11	Window dimensions	4 integers (2 bytes each) defining top left and bottom right corners of the display box in the order *xl*, *yt*, *xr*, *yb*.
12-13	Horizontal resolution	Horizontal resolution of display device. Common values are 640 for EGA/VGA (16-color), 320 for CGA or for VGA (256- color) 720 for Hercules

TABLE 27-1. *PCX* FILE HEADER CONTENTS (CONT.)

Byte #	Name	Description
14-15	Vertical resolution	Vertical resolution of display device (rows). Common values are 480 for VGA 350 for EGA 200 for CGA or for VGA (256-color) 348 for Hercules
16-63	Color map	Sets EGA/VGA palette registers. Colors are specified as 16 RGB triplets. Each color number ranges from 0 to 255, but actually only four color levels are available. The numbers are therefore interpreted as follows: 0-63 = Level 0 64-127= Level 1 128-192 = Level 2 193-254 = Level 3
64	Reserved	Always set to 0
65	Number of bit planes	Bit planes used for representing a pixel. Normally 4 for EGA/VGA 16-color modes and 1 otherwise.
66-67	Bytes per scan line per plane	Number of bytes per scan-line per color plane. Must be an even number compatible with the window size definition (bytes 4-5 and 8-9).
68-69	Palette information	How to interpret palette 1 = color or B&W 2 = Gray scale (Usually ignored)
70-127	Filler	Blanks to fill out 128-byte header.

Information on 256 Colors

The VGA has the capability to display 256 out of 262,144 colors. To define the triplet for each of the 256-color registers requires more space than is available in the *PCX* header, so this information is appended at the end of the *PCX* file. First you should ascertain that the version number data in the header (byte 1) is 5 (version 3.0), since this is the only version that supports 256-color information. If the version is correct, you should go to the end of the file and then count back 769 bytes. If the value in this byte position is *0CH* (12 decimal), the information that follows is 256-color register data.

Run-Length Encoding

When storing data, it is read from the screen, horizontally from left to right, starting at the pixel position for the upper left corner. For 16-color EGA/VGA modes, pixel information must be read from four color memory planes. In these modes, a line is read from the red plane from the beginning to the end of the window boundary. Then the green information for the same line is read, then the blue, and finally the intensity information. The functions that we will develop below work only if the horizontal pixel boundaries are at a byte interface (the column number must be divisible by eight). Data is run-length encoded in the following way. A single byte that is unlike the ones on either side of it is written directly to the file if its two most significant bits are not 1. The two most significant bits being 1 represents a flag to indicated that repeated byte data is to follow. If the display contains a repeated series of the same byte, a count is made of the number of like bytes (up to 63) and this count is ANDed with *C0H* and the result written to the file, followed by the value of the byte. (Thus the byte that gives the count has its two most significant bits set to 1 by the *C0H*.) If there are more than 63 successive like bytes, the count for 63 and *C0H* (resulting in *FFH*) is written followed by the byte value. The count then begins all over again. (Note that a singular byte having the two most significant bits 1 is handled by writing a count byte with a count of 1 followed by the byte value. This is the only case where there is actually an expansion in size, one byte of the original being replaced by two bytes in the *compressed* code. Fortunately, the situation doesn't come up often so that the *compressed* file is almost always considerably smaller than the uncompressed data.)

Restoring PCX Files to the Screen

Listing 27-2 is a general-purpose program for restoring *PCX* files to the display screen. Our program begins with lines 100 through 104, which read the *vconfig* file from the root directory. We now have in the *mode16* array all of the available modes for 16-color display, in the *mode256* array all of the available modes for 256-color display, and in *modehi* all of the available colors for the 24-bit color display. (If certain display modes are not available in 24-bit color but are available for 64K colors or 32K colors, we substitute the corresponding mode having the highest number of colors. In lines 106 through 114, we use Borland C++ functions to create a list of file names having the extension *PCX*. We allow for 99 file names. If you have more than 99 *PCX* files in your default directory, you need to move some of them to another directory; otherwise some of them won't be accessed by this program. Lines 115 through 134 comprise a shell sort that puts all these file names in alphabetical order. Line 135 starts an infinite *for* loop that enables you to view these files until you hit the *ESC* key to leave the program. Lines 143 through 189 draw a double-line boundary around the display and separate it with single lines into five columns. At the top of the window is displayed the legend "Select file name with cursor arrows: ". Within these columns are placed the names of all of the *PCX* files. Lines 191 through 224 comprise a *while* loop that iterates until either a carriage return or an escape key is entered on the keyboard. With the foreground and background colors set for the normal display, in line 193 the cursor is positioned at the file name designated by *dir_index*, and in line 194 the name is rewritten. (This was the name that was last shown in reverse colors; it is now rewritten in normal colors.) The function then enters a *switch* statement (line 195) that changes the value of *dir_index* if an arrow key was selected. For an up or down arrow, the index is moved one line up or down. If it is already at the first line of the entire display and is moved up, it moves to the last line. If it is already at the bottom line of the entire display and moves down, it moves to the first line of the display. For right and left arrows, the index moves one column to the right or left if there is a file name in that location; otherwise it doesn't change. After leaving the *switch* operation, the colors are changed for reverse video and the line at the *dir_index* position is rewritten. The colors are then reset for the normal display by lines 219 and 220. The loop then gets a character from the keyboard (line 221) . If the character is a NULL (00) this indicates a key that has a two-character designation. In that case, the second character is read and 256 is added to it to distinguish it from ordinary alphanumeric key codes (lines 222 and 223). The *while* loop is then repeated to process this character. When the program breaks out of the *while* loop, line 225 copies the file name selected by *dir_index* to the string *filename*. In lines 226 and 227, the program breaks out of the infinite *for* loop and terminates if the last key struck was the *ESC* key.

Listing 27-2. Program to Display PCX Files

```
/*

        PCX = PROGRAM TO VIEW PCX GRAPHICS FILES
              USING REGULAR AND VESA MODES

              By Roger T. Stevens  3-22-96

*/

#include <dos.h>
#include <string.h>
#include <dir.h>
#include <stdio.h>
#include <conio.h>

#define UP_ARROW328
#define DOWN_ARROW336
#define LEFT_ARROW331
#define RIGHT_ARROW333
#define BACKSPACE  8
#define seq_out(register,val)  outport(0x3C4,val<<8\
                               | register);
#define max(a,b)    (((a) > (b)) ? (a) : (b))
#define min(a,b)    (((a) < (b)) ? (a) : (b))

int getModeData(int mode);
void setBank(unsigned long int offset);
void setEGApalette(int palette, int color);
void setVGApalette(unsigned char *buffer);
void setMode(int mode);

union REGS reg;
struct SREGS segregs;
struct REGPACK outregs;

struct
{
    char password;
    char version;
    char encoding;
    char bits_per_pixel;
    int xmin, ymin, xmax, ymax;
    int xres, yres;
```

```
    unsigned char palette[48];
    char reserved1;
    char no_of_planes;
    int bytes_per_line;
    int palette_type;
    char reserved2;
    int xsize;
    int ysize;
    char filler[53];
} pcx_header;

char directory[100][13];

struct
{
    char signature[4];
    int version;
    long int far *OEM_string;
    char capabilities[4];
    long int far *Modes;
    int memory_size;
    char reserved[236];
} info;

struct
{
    int     ModeAttributes;
    char    WinAAttributes;
    char    WinBAttributes;
    int     WinGranularity;
    int     WinSize;
    int     WinASegment;
    int     WinBSegment;
    long intWinFuncPtr;
    int     BytesPerScanLine;
    int     XResolution;
    int     YResolution;
    char    XCharSize;
    char    YCharSize;
    char    NumberOfPlanes;
    char    BitsPerPixel;
    char     NumberOfBanks;
    char    MemoryModel;
    char    BankSize;
    char    NumberOfImagePages;
    char    Reserved;
    char    Filler[225];
} mode_data;

typedef struct
{
    unsigned char color[3];
```

```
} COLOR;

int bytes_per_line, i, j, k, dir_index= 0, index, end,
mode, d, color, ch1 = NULL, xres, yres, ystop, type, flag,
memory_plane;
unsigned char palette_data[256][3];
char temp[13];
char filename[32];
int mode16[7], mode256[6], modehi[5];
struct ffblk ffblk;
long int col,row;
FILE *read_file;
FILE *config_file;
unsigned char ch;
COLOR buffer[1280];
unsigned int no_chars, old_bank, data;
char far * address;
int ix, xoffset, yoffset, planes;
unsigned long int offset;

void main(void)
{
    clrscr();
    config_file = fopen("c:\\vconfig.dat","rb");
    fread(mode16,2,7,config_file);
    fread(mode256,2,6,config_file);
    fread(modehi,2,5,config_file);
    fclose(config_file);
    segread(&segregs);
    index = 0;
    end = findfirst("*.pcx",&ffblk,0);
    while(!end)
    {
        strcpy(directory[index++],ffblk.ff_name);
        end = findnext(&ffblk);
        if (index > 99)
            break;
    }
    d = 4;
    while (d < index)
        d += d;
    d--;
    d /= 2;
    while (d >= 1)
    {
        for (j=1; j<index-d; j++)
        {
            for (i=j; i>=1; i-=d)
            {
                if (strcmp(directory[i+d],directory[i]) > 0)
                    break;
                strcpy(temp,directory[i]);
```

```
                strcpy(directory[i],directory[i+d]);
                strcpy(directory[i+d],temp);
            }
        }
        d /= 2;
    }
    for(;;)
    {
        type = 6;
        setMode(3);
        textbackground(1);
        textcolor(15);
        window(2,2,78,23);
        clrscr();
        gotoxy(1,1);
        putch(0xC9);
        for (i=1; i<19; i++)
        {
            if (i%15)
                putch(0xCD);
            else
                putch(0xD1);
        }
        cprintf(" Select file name with cursor arrows: ");
        for (i=12; i<30; i++)
        {
            if (i%15)
                putch(0xCD);
            else
                putch(0xD1);
        }
        putch(0xBB);
        for (i=2; i<22; i++)
        {
            for (j=1; j<79; j+=15)
            {
                gotoxy(j,i);
                if ((j==1) || (j == 76))
                    putch(0xBA);
                else
                    putch(0xB3);
            }
        }
        gotoxy(1,22);
        putch(0xC8);
        for (i=1; i<75; i++)
        {
            if (i%15)
                putch(0xCD);
            else
                putch(0xCF);
        }
```

```
putch(0xBC);
filename[0] = NULL;
gotoxy(19,1);
textcolor(7);
for (i=0; i<index; i++)
{
   gotoxy(3+(i/20)*15,(i%20)+2);
   cprintf("%s",directory[i]);
}
ch1 = 256;
while ((ch1 != 0x0D) && (ch1 != 0x1B))
{
   gotoxy(3+(dir_index/20)*15,(dir_index%20)+2);
   cprintf("%s",directory[dir_index]);
   switch(ch1)
   {
      case DOWN_ARROW:
         ++dir_index;
         dir_index = dir_index % index;
         break;
      case UP_ARROW:
         --dir_index;
         if (dir_index<0)
            dir_index = index - 1;
         break;
      case RIGHT_ARROW:
         if ((dir_index + 20) < index)
            dir_index += 20;
         break;
      case LEFT_ARROW:
         if (dir_index >= 20)
            dir_index -= 20;
         break;
   }
   textbackground(7);
   textcolor(1);
   gotoxy(3+(dir_index/20)*15,(dir_index%20)+2);
   cprintf("%s",directory[dir_index]);
   textbackground(1);
   textcolor(7);
   ch1 = getch();
   if (ch1 == 0x00)
      ch1 = getch() + 256;
}
strcpy(filename,directory[dir_index]);
if (ch1 == 0x1B)
   break;
read_file = fopen(filename,"rb");
fread(&pcx_header,1,128,read_file);
xres =  pcx_header.xmax - pcx_header.xmin + 1;
yres = pcx_header.ymax - pcx_header.ymin + 1;
if ((pcx_header.bits_per_pixel == 8) &&
```

```
            (pcx_header.no_of_planes == 3))
        {
            mode = modehi[0];
            if (((xres > 320) || (yres > 200)) &&
    modehi[1] != 0))
                mode = modehi[1];
            if (((xres > 640) || (yres > 480)) &&
    (modehi[2] != 0))
                mode = modehi[2];
            if (((xres > 800) || (yres > 600)) &&
    (modehi[3] != 0))
                mode = modehi[3];
            if (((xres > 1024) || (yres > 768)) &&
        (modehi[4] != 0))
                mode = modehi[4];
            if (mode == 0)
                continue;
            outregs.r_ax = 0x4F01;
            outregs.r_cx = mode;
            segread(&segregs);
            outregs.r_es = segregs.ds;
            outregs.r_di = (unsigned int)&mode_data;
            intr(0x10,&outregs);
            xoffset = max (0,(mode_data.XResolution -
        pcx_header.xmax - 1)/2);
            yoffset = max(0,(mode_data.YResolution -
    pcx_header.ymax - 1)/2);
            ystop = min(pcx_header.ymax + yoffset,
    mode_data.YResolution);
            setMode(mode);
            fseek(read_file,128L,SEEK_SET);
            row=yoffset;
            col = 0;
            planes = 0;
            setBank(0);
            while (row <= ystop)
            {
                ch = fgetc(read_file);
                if ((ch & 0xC0) != 0xC0)
                    no_chars = 1;
                else
                {
                    no_chars = ch & 0x3F;
                    ch = fgetc(read_file);
                }
                for (k=0; k<no_chars; k++)
                {
                    buffer[col++].color[planes] = ch;
                    if (col >= pcx_header.bytes_per_line)
                    {
```

```
                    planes++;
                    col = 0;
                    if (planes > 2)
                    {
                        planes = 0;
                        for (ix=0;
      ix<pcx_header.bytes_per_line;
                            ix++)
                        {
                            switch(mode)
                            {
                                case 0x10D:
                                    case 0x110:
                                case 0x113:
                                case 0x116:
                                case 0x119:
                                    data =
                  (int)(buffer[ix].color[0]
                                        & 0xF8) << 7 | (int)
                                        (buffer[ix].color[1] &
                                    0xF8) << 2 |
                            (int)(buffer[ix].color[2]
                            & 0xF8) >> 3;
                                    offset = row *
                            mode_data.BytesPerScanLine
                                        + 2 * (xoffset + ix);
                                    setBank(offset);
                                    FP_SEG(address) = 0xA000;
                                    FP_OFF(address) =(unsigned
                                        int) offset;
                                    *(address++)= data & 0xFF;
                                    *address = data >> 8;
                                    break;
                                case 0x10E:
                                case 0x111:
                                case 0x114:
                                case 0x117:
                                case 0x11A:
                                    data =
                        (int)(buffer[ix].color[0]
                                        & 0xF8) << 8 | (int)
                                        (buffer[ix].color[1] &
                                        0xFC) << 3 |
                            (int)(buffer[ix].color[2]
                            & 0xF8) >> 3;
                                    offset = row *
                            mode_data.BytesPerScanLine
                                        + 2 * (xoffset + ix);
                                    setBank(offset);
```

```
                                        FP_SEG(address) = 0xA000;
                                        FP_OFF(address) =(unsigned
                                           int) offset;
                                        *(address++)= data & 0xFF;
                                        *address = data >> 8;
                                        break;
                                    case 0x10F:
                                    case 0x112:
                                    case 0x115:
                                    case 0x118:
                                    case 0x11B:
                                        offset = row *
                              mode_data.BytesPerScanLine
                                           + 3 * (xoffset + ix);
                                        setBank(offset);
                                        FP_SEG(address) = 0xA000;
                                        FP_OFF(address) =(unsigned
                                           int) offset;
                                        *address =
                           buffer[ix].color[2];
                                        offset = row *
                              mode_data.BytesPerScanLine
                                           + 3 * (xoffset + ix) +
1;
                                        setBank(offset);
                                        FP_SEG(address) = 0xA000;
                                        FP_OFF(address) =(unsigned
                                           int) offset;
                                        *address =
                           buffer[ix].color[1];
                                        offset = row *
                              mode_data.BytesPerScanLine
                                           + 3 * (xoffset + ix) +
2;
                                        setBank(offset);
                                        FP_SEG(address) = 0xA000;
                                        FP_OFF(address) =(unsigned
                                           int) offset;
                                        *address =
                           buffer[ix].color[0];
                                 }
                              }
                              row++;
                           }
                        }
                     }
                  }
                  fclose(read_file);
               }
               else
               {
                  if ((pcx_header.bits_per_pixel == 0x01) ||
```

```
                (pcx_header.no_of_planes == 4))
                type = 0;
            else
            {
                fseek(read_file,-769L,SEEK_END);
                ch = fgetc(read_file);
                if (ch == 0x0C)
                type = 1;
            }
        if (type <2)
        {
            mode_data.XResolution = 320;
            mode_data.YResolution = 200;
            if (type == 1)
            {
                fseek(read_file,-768L,SEEK_END);
                fread(palette_data,768,1,read_file);
                for (i=0; i<256; i++)
                for (j=0; j<3; j++)
                        palette_data[i][j] >>= 2;
                mode = 0x13;
                mode_data.BytesPerScanLine = 320;
                if (((xres > 320) || (yres > 200)) &&
        (mode256[1] != 0))
                    mode = mode256[1];
                if ((yres > 400) && (mode256[2] != 0))
                    mode = mode256[2];
                if (((xres > 640) || (yres > 480)) &&
        (mode256[3] != 0))
                    mode = mode256[3];
                if (((xres > 800) || (yres > 600)) &&
        (mode256[4] != 0))
                    mode = mode256[4];
                if (((xres > 1024) || (yres > 768)) &&
            (mode256[5] != 0))
                    mode = mode256[5];
            }
            if (type == 0)
            {
                mode = mode16[0];
                mode_data.BytesPerScanLine = 40;
                mode = mode16[0];
                mode_data.XResolution = 320;
                mode_data.YResolution = 200;
                mode_data.BytesPerScanLine = 40;
                if (xres > 320)
                {
                    mode = mode16[1];
                    mode_data.XResolution = 640;
                    mode_data.YResolution = 200;
                    mode_data.BytesPerScanLine = 80;
```

```
                }
                if (yres > 200)
                {
                    mode = mode16[2];
                    mode_data.XResolution = 640;
                    mode_data.YResolution = 350;
                    mode_data.BytesPerScanLine = 80;
                }
                if (yres > 350)
                {
                    mode = mode16[3];
                    mode_data.XResolution = 640;
                    mode_data.YResolution = 480;
                    mode_data.BytesPerScanLine = 80;
                }
                if (((xres > 640) || (yres > 480)) &&
        (mode16[4] != 0))
                    mode = mode16[4];
                if (((xres > 800) || (yres > 600)) &&
        (mode16[5] != 0))
                    mode = mode16[5];
                if (((xres > 1024) || (yres > 768)) &&
            (mode16[6] != 0))
                    mode = mode16[6];
            }
            if (mode > 0xFF)
            {
                outregs.r_ax = 0x4F01;
                segread(&segregs);
                outregs.r_cx = mode;
                outregs.r_es = segregs.ds;
                outregs.r_di = (unsigned int) &mode_data;
                intr(0x10,&outregs);
            }
            xoffset = (max (0,(mode_data.XResolution -
        pcx_header.xmax - 1)/2)) >> 3;
            yoffset = max(0,(mode_data.YResolution -
    pcx_header.ymax - 1)/2);
            ystop = min(pcx_header.ymax + yoffset,
    mode_data.YResolution);
            setMode(mode);
            if (type == 0)
            {
                for (i=0; i<48; i+=3)
                {
                    k = i/3;
                    color = ((pcx_header.palette[i] & 0x40) >>
                        1) | ((pcx_header.palette[i] & 0x80) >>
                        5) | ((pcx_header.palette[i+1] & 0x40)
                        >> 2) | (pcx_header.palette[i+1] & 0x80)
```

```
                    >> 6 | ((pcx_header.palette[i+2] & 0x40)
                    >> 3) | ((pcx_header.palette[i+2]
            &   0x80) >> 7);
                setEGApalette(k,color);
            }
        }
        if (type == 1)
            setVGApalette(&palette_data[0][0]);
        fseek(read_file,128L,SEEK_SET);
        for (row=yoffset; row<ystop; row++)
        {
            col = 0;
            flag = 0;
            memory_plane = 0;
            if (type == 0)
                seq_out(2,(0x01 << memory_plane));
            while ((memory_plane < 4) && (flag < 1))
            {
                ch = fgetc(read_file);
                if ((ch & 0xC0) != 0xC0)
                    no_chars = 1;
                else
                {
                    ch &= 0x3F;
                    no_chars = ch;
                    ch = fgetc(read_file);
                }
                for (k=0; k<no_chars; k++)
                {
                    offset = (long)row *
    mode_data.BytesPerScanLine +
                        col + xoffset;
                    reg.x.dx = offset >> 16;
                    if (reg.x.dx != old_bank)
                    {
                        old_bank = reg.x.dx;
                        reg.x.ax = 0x4F05;
                        reg.x.bx = 0;
                        int86(0x10, &reg, &reg);
                    }
                    FP_SEG(address) = 0xA000;
                    FP_OFF(address) =(unsigned int) offset;
                    if ((col < mode_data.XResolution) ||
                    (type == 1))
                        *address = ch;
                    col++;
                    if (col >= pcx_header.bytes_per_line)
                    {
                        col = 0;
                        if (type == 0)
                            seq_out(2,(0x01 <<
```

```
                    ++memory_plane));
                              if (type == 1)
                                  flag = 1;
                          }
                      }
                  }
              }
          }
          fclose(read_file);
      }
      getch();
   }
}

/*

 setVGApalette() = Function to set all 256 color registers

*/

void setVGApalette(unsigned char *buffer)
{
   union REGS reg;
   struct SREGS inreg;

   reg.x.ax = 0x1012;
   segread(&inreg);
   inreg.es = inreg.ds;
   reg.x.bx = 0;
   reg.x.cx = 256;
   reg.x.dx = (int)&buffer[0];
   int86x(0x10,&reg,&reg,&inreg);
}

/*

   setEGApalette() = Sets the color for an EGA palette
                           number.

*/

void setEGApalette(int palette, int color)
{
   union REGS reg;

   reg.h.ah = 0x10;
   reg.h.al = 0;
   reg.h.bh = color;
   reg.h.bl = palette;
```

```
    int86(0x10,&reg,&reg);
}

/*
         setBank() = Sets video memory bank
*/

void setBank(unsigned long int offset)
{
    static int bank, old_bank;

    old_bank = reg.x.dx;
    bank = offset >> 16;
    if (bank == old_bank)
        return;
    reg.x.dx = bank;
    old_bank = bank;
    reg.x.ax = 0x4F05;
    reg.x.bx = 0;
    int86(0x10, &reg, &reg);
}

/*
   getModeData() = Gets Super VGA data on a desired mode
*/

int getModeData(int mode)
{
        segread(&segregs);
        outregs.r_ax = 0x4F01;
        outregs.r_cx = mode;
        outregs.r_es = segregs.ds;
        outregs.r_di =(unsigned int) &mode_data;
        intr(0x10,&outregs);
        if ((mode_data.ModeAttributes &0x01) == 1)
            return(1);
        return(0);
}

/*
          setMode() = Sets Video Mode
*/
```

```
609   void setMode(int mode)
610   {
611       union REGS reg;
612       if (mode > 0xFF)
613       {
614           reg.x.ax = 0x4F02;
615           reg.x.bx = mode;
616       }
617       else
618           reg.x.ax = mode;
619       int86 (0x10,&reg,&reg);
620   }
```

If the keystroke that terminated the *while* loop was a carriage return, the program continues on to line 228, which begins the process of displaying the selected file by opening the file. The program then reads the file header in line 229 and sets up the *x* and *y* resolutions from the file in lines 230 and 231. Lines 232 and 233 determine whether the file is a 24-bit color file. If so, lines 234 through 247 determine the lowest-resolution display mode that can contain the file data. Lines 248 and 249 end this iteration of the infinite *for* loop without any display if the system doesn't support any modes that can display the color from this file. Lines 252 through 255 obtain the data for the selected mode from the Super VGA card. From this data, the values for *xoffset*, *yoffset*, and *ystop* are obtained in lines 256 through 262. These parameters are used to center the picture on the screen if its resolution is less than that of the screen in either or both directions. Line 262 sets the video display mode. In line 263 the file pointer is set at the beginning of the pixel data. Line 268 begins a *while* loop that iterates once for each row of picture information. Lines 270 through 287 read and decode pixel data from the file and place it in a buffer. When a full line of red data is read, the parameter *planes* is incremented and then a full line of green data is read. This process is repeated for the blue data. When the buffer contains a full line of data for each of the three colors, the program begins the *for* loop at line 288. This loop assembles the color data in a single word, if so required by the display mode selected, and then writes the line of data to the correct place in display memory. All this takes place for each character in the *switch* statement consisting of lines 292 through 370. When the *while* statement is completed after the last row is displayed, the file is closed in line 377.

If the file was not a 24-bit color file, the program enters the *else* statement of line 379. Lines 381 through 384 check whether the file is a 16-color file; if so the parameter *type* is set to 0. Otherwise, the program goes to the end of the file in lines 386 through 389 and backs up to the place where a character 0CH should appear if the file is a 256-color file. If the 0CH is found, *type* is set to 1.

In lines 391 through 394, the display resolution parameters are set to 320 and 200 if a 16-color or 256-color file was found. Then, for 256-color files, the color palette is read from the end of the file in lines 397 through 401. Lines 402 through 418 then set the mode to the lowest-resolution mode that can contain the file resolution.

Lines 419 through 457 select the display mode and its parameters for 16-color files. Again, the mode is the lowest-resolution mode that will accomodate the file resolution. Lines 458 through 466 obtain the data for the selected mode from the Super VGA card. Since some Super VGA cards do not supply this data for the regular VGA modes, the proper settings for the critical data for these modes already were entered while the mode was being selected. From this data, the values for *xoffset*, *yoffset*, and *ystop* are obtained in lines 467 through 472. These parameters are used to center the picture on the screen if its resolution is less than that of the screen in either or both directions. Line 473 sets the video display mode. If the file is a 16-color one, lines 474 through 487 process the data for the 16 colors from the file and use it to set the EGA palette registers. If the file is a 256-color one, lines 489 and 490 set the VGA palette colors. In line 491 the file pointer is set at the beginning of the pixel data. Line 492 begins a *for* loop that iterates once for each row of picture information. Lines 494 through 541 read and decode pixel data from the file and send it to the proper location in display memory. When the *for* loop has completed for all rows of the display, the program waits at line 544 for the user to enter a keystroke. When you are finished looking at the display, this keystroke will return you to the display of file names, ready to select another picture for viewing.

Saving a Display as a *PCX* File

There are a number of programs available in the public domain or as shareware that purport to allow you to capture a picture from any display mode and store it as a *PCX* file. Some of these programs work, some work partially, and some don't work at all. For example, one program that I sent money for, since the freely distributed version printed their name across each file, worked well with my STB Super VGA board but drew a black horizontal bar across the display when used with my ATI Xpression board. So you can see that you may often need to create your own software to save a display. Listing 27-3 is a test program to show how this is done. The function *save_screen* can be inserted into your program at a point just after you have generated a graphics display. It will then save the display to a disk file. As written, it works only for display mode 103H (800 pixels × 600 pixels × 256 colors) but you can easily modify it to work for any display mode you wish to use. The main program is quite simple. Line 11 sets the display mode. Lines 12 through 14 are a *for* loop that generates a display of 15 horizontal bars of different colors. In line 15, the program calls *save_screen* to save the resulting display to a *PCX* file.

Listing 27-3. Example of Saving a Screen to a PCX File

```
        /*
        ┌──────────────────────────────────────────────────────┐
               SAVETEST = PROGRAM TO STORE PCX GRAPHICS FILES

                        By Roger T. Stevens  4-12-96
        └──────────────────────────────────────────────────────┘
        */
1       #include "c:\cpphbook\program\graphics.cpp"

2       void save_screen(char filename[13]);

3       unsigned char
4       PALETTE[16]={0,1,2,3,4,5,20,7,56,57,58,59,60,61,62,63};
5       char filename[13] = {"examp00.pcx"};
6       unsigned char color_table[768];
7       Line line;

8       void main(void)
9       {
10          int i;

11          line.setMode(0x103);
12          for (i=0; i<16; i++)
13              line.draw(-630, 480-(i*60), 630, 480-(i*60), i,
14                  50);
15          save_screen(filename);
16          getch();
17          line.setMode(3);
18      }

19      /*
        ┌──────────────────────────────────────────────────────┐
            save_screen() = Save display screen to PCX disk file
        └──────────────────────────────────────────────────────┘
21      */

22      void save_screen(char filename[13])
23      {
```

```
    union REGS reg;
    struct SREGS inreg;

    struct
    {
        char password;
        char version;
        char encoding;
        char bits_per_pixel;
        int xmin, ymin, xmax, ymax;
        int xres, yres;
        unsigned char palette[48];
        char reserved1;
        char no_of_planes;
        int bytes_per_line;
        int palette_type;
        char reserved2;
        int xsize;
        int ysize;
        char filler[53];
    } pcx_header;

    char far *address;
    int col, i, k, row, number, num_out, page=0,
old_page=0;
    unsigned char ch, old_ch, palette[768];
    FILE *write_file;
    unsigned long int offset;

    write_file = fopen(filename,"wb");
    pcx_header.password = 0x0A;
    pcx_header.version = 0x05;
    pcx_header.encoding = 0x01;
    pcx_header.bits_per_pixel = 0x08;
    pcx_header.xmin = 0;
    pcx_header.ymin = 0;
    pcx_header.xmax = 799;
    pcx_header.ymax = 599;
    pcx_header.xres = 800;
    pcx_header.yres = 600;
    for (i=0; i<16; i++)
    {
        k = 0;
        if ((PALETTE[i] & 0x20) != 0)
            k |= 1;
        if ((PALETTE[i] & 0x04) != 0)
            k |= 2;
            pcx_header.palette[3*i] = 84 * k;
        k = 0;
        if ((PALETTE[i] & 0x10) != 0)
            k |= 1;
        if ((PALETTE[i] & 0x02) != 0)
            k |= 2;
```

```
                pcx_header.palette[3*i+1] = 84 * k;
            k = 0;
            if ((PALETTE[i] & 0x08) != 0)
                k |= 1;
            if ((PALETTE[i] & 0x01) != 0)
                k |= 2;
                pcx_header.palette[3*i+2] = 84 * k;
        }
        pcx_header.reserved1 = 0;
        pcx_header.no_of_planes = 1;
        pcx_header.bytes_per_line = 800;
        pcx_header.palette_type = 0;
        pcx_header.reserved2 = 0;
        pcx_header.xsize = 800;
        pcx_header.ysize = 600;
        for (i=0; i<53; i++)
            pcx_header.filler[i] = 0x00;
        fwrite(&pcx_header,1,128,write_file);
        reg.x.dx = 0;
        reg.x.ax = 0x4F05;
        reg.x.bx = 1;
        int86(0x10, &reg, &reg);
        for (row=0; row<yres; row++)
        {
            number = 0;
            offset = (long) row * xres;
            for (col=0; col<=xres; col++)
            {
                if (col == xres)
                    ch = old_ch + 1;
                else
                {
                    page = offset >> 16;
                    if (page != old_page)
                    {
                        reg.x.dx = page;
                        reg.x.ax = 0x4F05;
                        reg.x.bx = 1;
                        int86(0x10, &reg, &reg);
                    }
                    FP_SEG(address) = 0xA000;
                    FP_OFF(address) =(unsigned int) offset;
                    offset++;
                    ch = *address;
                    if (col == 0)
                        old_ch = ch;
                }
                if ((ch == old_ch) && (number < 63))
                    number++;
                else
                {
                    num_out = ((unsigned char) number | 0xC0);
```

```
126                 if ((number != 1) || ((old_ch & 0xC0) ==
127                    0xC0))
128                    fputc(num_out,write_file);
129                 fputc(old_ch,write_file);
130                 old_ch = ch;
131                 number = 1;
132              }
133           }
134        }
135        fputc(0x0C,write_file);
136        reg.x.ax = 0x1017;
137        segread(&inreg);
138        inreg.es = inreg.ds;
139        reg.x.bx = 0;
140        reg.x.cx = 256;
141        reg.x.dx = (int)&palette[0];
142        int86x(0x10,&reg,&reg,&inreg);
143        for (i=0; i<768; i++)
144           palette[i] <<=2;
145        fwrite(palette,1,768,write_file);
146        fclose(write_file);
147     }
```

Lines 26 through 43 of the *save_screen* function set up a structure for the *PCX* file header. The function proper begins with line 50, which opens a file with the desired file name. This file name is defined in line 5 of the main program. You can use any file name acceptable to DOS, and you can have a new file name each time you use the *save_screen* function. Lines 51 through 90 load the header structure with the proper values. Lines 92 through 95 set the display memory page to 0. Note particularly line 94. Some Super VGA boards define two windows: window 0 for writing data to the display and window 1 for reading from it. The latter type boards require that register *bx* be set to 1 in this line. In line 96, the function begins a *for* loop that iterates once for each row of the display. At each iteration, the loop first gets the starting character for the line. (This is at an address that increases by *xres* bytes per line for 256-color modes.) Line 99 sets up an initial value for *offset*, the amount of offset from base display memory address at which the first color information is to be read. In line 100 a *for* loop begins that iterates once for each column of a display line. In lines 102 and 103, if the end of the row has already been reached, the character value is set to an arbitrary value of 1 less than the preceding character, forcing the buffer to be cleared out to the disk file at the end of each line. Otherwise, in lines 106 through 114, the display memory page value is computed and modified if it differs from the current memory page. Lines 114 and 115 set up the display memory address from which to read a pixel, and line 117 reads the pixel. In lines 118 and 119, we set *old_ch* to the same value as the character just read if this is the first character of a line. Next, if the character just read is the same same *old_ch*, a parameter called *number* is incremented, if number is less than 63 (lines 121 and 122). Otherwise (if the current character is different from the previous character or number is 63) *number* is modified to make its two most significant bits 1's (line 125). Line 128 sends the result to the disk file except when number is 1 and the previous character does not haves 1's as the two most significant bits. The previous character is then sent to the disk file and the current character replaces the previous character in *old_ch* (lines 129 and 130). Note that ordinarily we have two bytes sent to the file, one indicating the number of times a character is to be written and the next giving the value of the character itself. There is one exception to this. When the current value of *number* is 1 and the two most significant bits of the current character are not naturally 1, the numerical byte is not saved to the file; only the character byte is saved. All of this accomplishes the run-length compression that was described earlier. When all of the screen display data has been saved, lines 135 through 145 send *0CH* to the disk file, followed by the 768 bytes of color data for the 256-color registers.

28

Saving and Restoring Displays with the *BMP* Format

There are several varieties of graphics files having the *BMP* file extension. Several of them are associated with earlier versions of Windows and are now obsolete. We're going to concentrate on uncompressed 24-bit color *BMP* files. These are straightforward bit map files that don't use any form of data encoding. This makes them very large, but enables Windows to load very quickly.

The *BMP* File Header

Modern *BMP* files use a format developed for Windows 3.1. The header information, when expressed as a C++ structure, looks like this:

```
struct
{
      unsigned int           id;
      unsigned long int      file_size;
      unsigned int           reserved[2];
      unsigned long int      image_offset;
      unsigned int           header_size,
                             not_used;
      unsigned long int      xres,
                             yres;
      unsigned int           no_of_planes,
                             bits_per_pixel;
```

```
      unsigned long int      compression_method,
                             bit_map_size,
                             hor_res,
                             vert_res,
                             number_of_colors,
                             no_significant_colors;
}   bmp_header;
```

The **id** parameter identifies a bit-mapped file with the characters 42H and 4DH, which is ASCII code for the letters *BM*.

The **file_size** parameter is a long integer that contains the file size in bytes. It should agree with the file size reported by the file system.

The next two parameters (4 bytes) are reserved, meaning that MicroSoft may use them someday, but not now. They should be set to 0.

The next parameter, **image_offset**, is the number of bytes from the beginning of the file to the start of actual image data. Because color information of various sizes may reside between the header and the beginning of graphics data, this value is not the same for every *BMP* file. This parameter is used to position the file pointer prior to reading graphics data.

The next parameter, **header_size**, is the size of the part of the header from the beginning of this parameter to the end. For *BMP* files associated with MicroSoft Windows versions 3.XX, this size is always 40 bytes (28H).

The parameter **not_used** is currently not used.

The parameters **xres** and **yres** are long integers giving the width and height of the graphic image in pixels.

The parameter **no_of_planes** is always set to 1, since *BMP* files use only a single color plane.

The parameter **bits_per_pixel** is the number of bits used to represent the color of each pixel. Acceptable values are 1, 4, 8, and 24. We're only going to consider files having the value 24.

BMP files do not use compression, so the parameter **compression_method** is always 0.

The **bit_map_size** parameter is set to 0 for noncompressed files.

The **hor_res** and **vert_res** parameters are the horizontal and vertical resolutions of the generating device in pixels per meter. They may prove useful in determining how to print or display the image.

The **no_of_colors** parameter is the number of colors actually used in the picture. The maximum number of colors in a picture is one shifted left by the number of bits in the **bits_per_pixel** parameter. Thus 8 bits per pixel would allow a maximum of 256 colors. If **no_of_colors** is set to 0, the number of colors actually used in the picture is the maximum number.

The **no_of_significant_colors** gives the number of colors that appear frequently in the image. This is the number of colors that the display must be capable of reproducing to give a good-quality image.

BMP Image Data

The *BMP* image data is stored beginning at the lower left corner of the picture and working upward a line at a time. As you'll see in the program given below, it is a simple matter to paint the picture to the screen beginning at the bottom and moving upward.

Program to View 24-Bit Color *BMP* Files

Listing 28-1 is a program to view 24-bit color *BMP* files. Note that for this program to work properly, you must have created the *vconfig.dat* file in your root directory. Lines 1 through through 221 create the same directory of file names described in connection with Listing 27-2, except that *BMP* files are listed instead of *PCX* files. You are then able to select one of these files for display. The selected file is opened in line 222 and the header read in line 223. Lines 226 through 241 set up the display mode to be the lowest-resolution mode capable of displaying the file resolution, as with the previous program. Lines 256 through 259 set up a pair of nested *for* loops that read pixel red, green, and blue values for every row and column from the file. This reading of pixel color values takes place in lines 260 through 262. It is much simpler than the *PCX* program because no decoding is required. Once the color values are obtained, the program enters a *switch* statement (lines 263 through 326) that writes the pixel to display memory in the same way as for the program in listing 27-2. One thing that must be considered is that regardless of the value of *xres*, each scan line of the file must have a number of bytes that is divisible by four. If this isn't the case, the line is padded by zeroes to make it so. To take care of this situation, lines 328 through 332 form a *while* loop that reads and discards bytes from the file from the end of a scan line until the total number of bytes read for that line is divisible by four. When the nested *for* loops are complete, the desired picture is displayed upon the screen. The file is then closed in line 334. When the user enters a keystroke, the program returns to the beginning of the *for* loop of line 129 and again displays the list of file names, ready for another picture selection.

Listing 28-1. Program to Display BMP Files

```
/*

        BMP = PROGRAM TO VIEW .BMP GRAPHICS FILES
              USING REGULAR AND VESA MODES

              By Roger T. Stevens  3-31-96

*/

1     #include <dos.h>
2     #include <string.h>
3     #include <dir.h>
4     #include <stdio.h>
5     #include <conio.h>

6     #define UP_ARROW328
7     #define DOWN_ARROW      336
8     #define LEFT_ARROW      331
9     #define RIGHT_ARROW     333
10    #define BACKSPACE         8
11    #define seq_out(register,val)  outport(0x3C4,val<<8 | \
12                         register);
13    #define max(a,b)     (((a) > (b)) ? (a) : (b))
14    #define min(a,b)     (((a) < (b)) ? (a) : (b))

15    int getModeData(int mode);
16    void setBank(unsigned long int offset);
17    void setMode(int mode);
18    union REGS reg;
19    struct SREGS segregs;
20    struct REGPACK outregs;
```

```
struct
{
    unsigned int id;
    unsigned long intfile_size;
    unsigned intreserved[2];
    unsigned long intimage_offset;
    unsigned intheader_size,
                        not_used;
    unsigned long intxres,
                        yres;
    unsigned intno_of_planes,
                        bits_per_pixel;
    unsigned long intcompression_method,
                        bit_map_size,
                        hor_res,
                        vert_res,
                        number_of_colors,
                        no_significant_colors;
}   bmp_header;

char directory[100][13];

struct
{
    char signature[4];
    int version;
    long int far *OEM_string;
    char capabilities[4];
    long int far *Modes;
    int memory_size;
    char reserved[236];
} info;

struct
{
    int     ModeAttributes;
    char    WinAAttributes;
    char    WinBAttributes;
    int     WinGranularity;
    int     WinSize;
    int     WinASegment;
    int     WinBSegment;
    long intWinFuncPtr;
    int         BytesPerScanLine;
    int         XResolution;
    int         YResolution;
    char    XCharSize;
    char    YCharSize;
    char    NumberOfPlanes;
    char    BitsPerPixel;
    char    NumberOfBanks;
    char    MemoryModel;
    char    BankSize;
    char    NumberOfImagePages;
```

```
        char   Reserved;
        char   Filler[225];
    } mode_data;

    unsigned int mode16[7], mode256[6], modehi[5];
    int bytes_per_line, i, j, k, dir_index= 0, index, end,
    mode, d, color, ch1 = NULL, xres, yres, ystop, type,
    flag, memory_plane;
    unsigned char red, green, blue, palette_data[256][3];
    char temp[13];
    char filename[32];
    struct ffblk ffblk;
    long int col,row;
    FILE *read_file;
    FILE *config_file;
    unsigned int no_chars, old_bank, data;
    char far * address;
    int ix, xoffset, yoffset, planes;
    unsigned long int offset;

    void main(void)
    {
        clrscr();
        config_file = fopen("c:\\vconfig.dat","rb");
        fread(mode16,2,7,config_file);
        fread(mode256,2,6,config_file);
        fread(modehi,2,5,config_file);
        fclose(config_file);
        segread(&segregs);
        index = 0;
        end = findfirst("*.bmp",&ffblk,0);
        while(!end)
        {
            strcpy(directory[index++],ffblk.ff_name);
            end = findnext(&ffblk);
            if (index > 99)
                break;
        }
        d = 4;
        while (d < index)
            d += d;
        d--;
        d /= 2;
        while (d >= 1)
        {
            for (j=1; j<index-d; j++)
            {
                for (i=j; i>=1; i-=d)
                {
                    if (strcmp(directory[i+d],directory[i]) >
                        0)
```

```
                        break;
                    strcpy(temp,directory[i]);
                    strcpy(directory[i],directory[i+d]);
                    strcpy(directory[i+d],temp);
                }
            }
            d /= 2;
        }
        for(;;)
        {
            type = 6;
            setMode(3);
            textbackground(1);
            textcolor(15);
            window(2,2,78,23);
            clrscr();
            gotoxy(1,1);
            putch(0xC9);
            for (i=1; i<19; i++)
            {
                if (i%15)
                    putch(0xCD);
                else
                    putch(0xD1);
            }
            cprintf(" Select file name with cursor arrows: ");
            for (i=12; i<30; i++)
            {
                if (i%15)
                    putch(0xCD);
                else
                    putch(0xD1);
            }
            putch(0xBB);
            for (i=2; i<22; i++)
            {
                for (j=1; j<79; j+=15)
                {
                    gotoxy(j,i);
                    if ((j==1) || (j == 76))
                        putch(0xBA);
                    else
                        putch(0xB3);
                }
            }
            gotoxy(1,22);
            putch(0xC8);
            for (i=1; i<75; i++)
            {
                if (i%15)
                    putch(0xCD);
                else
```

```
        putch(0xCF);
}
putch(0xBC);
filename[0] = NULL;
gotoxy(19,1);
textcolor(7);
for (i=0; i<index; i++)
{
    gotoxy(3+(i/20)*15,(i%20)+2);
    cprintf("%s",directory[i]);
}
ch1 = 256;
while ((ch1 != 0x0D) && (ch1 != 0x1B))
{
    gotoxy(3+(dir_index/20)*15,(dir_index%20)+2);
    cprintf("%s",directory[dir_index]);
    switch(ch1)
    {
        case DOWN_ARROW:
            ++dir_index;
            dir_index = dir_index % index;
            break;
        case UP_ARROW:
            --dir_index;
            if (dir_index<0)
                dir_index = index - 1;
            break;
        case RIGHT_ARROW:
            if ((dir_index + 20) < index)
                dir_index += 20;
            break;
        case LEFT_ARROW:
            if (dir_index >= 20)
                dir_index -= 20;
            break;
    }
    textbackground(7);
    textcolor(1);
    gotoxy(3+(dir_index/20)*15,(dir_index%20)+2);
    cprintf("%s",directory[dir_index]);
    textbackground(1);
    textcolor(7);
    ch1 = getch();
    if (ch1 == 0x00)
        ch1 = getch() + 256;
}
strcpy(filename,directory[dir_index]);
if (ch1 == 0x1B)
    break;
read_file = fopen(filename,"rb");
fread(&bmp_header,1,54,read_file);
xres =  bmp_header.xres;
```

```
        yres = bmp_header.yres;
        mode = modehi[0];
        if (((xres > 320) || (yres > 200)) && (modehi[1]
            != 0))
            mode = modehi[1];
        if (((xres > 640) || (yres > 480)) && (modehi[2]
            != 0))
            mode = modehi[2];
        if (((xres > 800) || (yres > 600)) && (modehi[3]
            != 0))
            mode = modehi[3];
        if (((xres > 1024) || (yres > 768)) && (modehi[4]
            != 0))
            mode = modehi[4];
        if (mode == 0)
            continue;
        outregs.r_ax = 0x4F01;
        outregs.r_cx = mode;
        segread(&segregs);
        outregs.r_es = segregs.ds;
        outregs.r_di = (unsigned int)&mode_data;
        intr(0x10,&outregs);
        xoffset = max (0,(mode_data.XResolution -
    xres)/2);
        yoffset = max(0,(mode_data.YResolution - yres)/2);
        ystop = min(yres + yoffset,
mode_data.YResolution);
        setMode(mode);
        fseek(read_file,54L,SEEK_SET);
        planes = 0;
        setBank(0);
        for (row = yoffset; row <ystop; row++)
        {
            for (col=0; col < xres; col++)
            {
                red = fgetc(read_file);
                green = fgetc(read_file);
                blue = fgetc(read_file);
                switch(mode)
                {
                    case 0x10D:
                    case 0x110:
                    case 0x113:
                    case 0x116:
                    case 0x119:
                        data = (int)(blue & 0xF8) << 7 |
                            (int)(green & 0xF8) << 2 |
                            (int)(red & 0xF8) >> 3;
                        offset = (ystop-row+yoffset) *
                        mode_data.BytesPerScanLine
```

```
                    + 2 * (xoffset + col);
                setBank(offset);
                FP_SEG(address) = 0xA000;
                FP_OFF(address) =(unsigned
            int) offset;
                *(address++) = data & 0xFF;
                *address = data >> 8;
                break;
            case 0x10E:
            case 0x111:
            case 0x114:
            case 0x117:
            case 0x11A:
                data = (int)(blue & 0xF8) << 8 |
                    (int) (green & 0xFC) << 3 |
                    (int)(red & 0xF8) >> 3;
                offset = (ystop-row+yoffset) *
                mode_data.BytesPerScanLine
                    + 2 * (xoffset + col);
                setBank(offset);
                FP_SEG(address) = 0xA000;
                FP_OFF(address) =(unsigned int)
                    offset;
                *(address++) = data & 0xFF;
                *address = data >> 8;
                break;
            case 0x10F:
            case 0x112:
            case 0x115:
            case 0x118:
            case 0x11B:
                offset = (ystop-row+yoffset) *
                mode_data.BytesPerScanLine
                    + 3 * (xoffset + col);
                setBank(offset);
                FP_SEG(address) = 0xA000;
                FP_OFF(address) =(unsigned int)
                    offset;
                *address = red;
                offset++;
                setBank(offset);
                FP_SEG(address) = 0xA000;
                FP_OFF(address) =(unsigned int)
                    offset;
                *address = green;
                offset++;
                setBank(offset);
                FP_SEG(address) = 0xA000;
                FP_OFF(address) =(unsigned int)
                    offset;
```

```
                        *address = blue;
                    }
                }
                while (4*(col/4) < col)
                {
                    fgetc(read_file);
                    col++;
                }
            }
            fclose(read_file);
        getch();
        }
}

/*

            setBank() = Sets video memory bank

*/
void setBank(unsigned long int offset)
{
    static int bank, old_bank;

    old_bank = reg.x.dx;
    bank = offset >> 16;
    if (bank == old_bank)
        return;
    reg.x.dx = bank;
    old_bank = bank;
    reg.x.ax = 0x4F05;
    reg.x.bx = 0;
    int86(0x10, &reg, &reg);
}

/*

    getModeData() = Gets Super VGA data on a desired mode

*/

int getModeData(int mode)
{
        segread(&segregs);
        outregs.r_ax = 0x4F01;
        outregs.r_cx = mode;
        outregs.r_es = segregs.ds;
```

```
363          outregs.r_di =(unsigned int) &mode_data;
364          intr(0x10,&outregs);
365          if ((mode_data.ModeAttributes &0x01) == 1)
366              return(1);
367          return(0);
368      }

369      /*

                      setMode() = Sets Video Mode

371      */

372      void setMode(int mode)
373      {
374          union REGS reg;
375          if (mode > 0xFF)
376          {
377              reg.x.ax = 0x4F02;
378              reg.x.bx = mode;
379          }
380          else
381              reg.x.ax = mode;
382          int86 (0x10,&reg,&reg);
383      }
```

Saving a Display as a *BMP* File

Listing 28-2 is a program that displays a 24-bit color *PCX* file and then converts it to a *BMP* file. The primary purpose of this program is to show how you can use the function *save_bmp* to save a 24-bit color *BMP* file. You can use it to convert any 24-bit color *PCX* file, but you should be aware of a couple of things. First, if the resolution of the *PCX* file doesn't correspond to that of one of the display modes, the display program will use the next higher resolution mode and display the picture in the center of the screen with black space around it. The new *BMP* file will have as its resolution the resolution of the selected display mode, and the black space around the picture will be saved as part of the new file. (This will probably make the new file larger than the old one.) Second, if your display won't handle the required resolution in 24-bit color but instead uses 64K colors or 32K colors, even though the new *BMP* file will be written as 24-bit color, it actually will only contain 64K or 32K colors maximum, so some of the original color information will be lost.

Lines 1 through 371 are almost exactly the same as the program in the previous chapter for viewing *PCX* files, except that lines 110 through 113 open each file that is found to have a *PCX* extension, read its header, and perform a test to see whether it is a 24-bit color file. Only if it is, is it included in the directory display listing. Also, all parts of the program that handle the display of 16-color and 256-color files have been removed. One other difference is lines 368 through 371, which create a new file name, *outfile*, which is the same name as that of the file chosen for display, except that the extension is changed from *PCX* to *BMP*. Once the file is displayed, line 372 calls the *save_bmp* function to save the display as a new *BMP* file.

The *save_bmp* file begins at line 453. The output file is opened in this line. Lines 454 through 471 place the proper information in the header structure for the *BMP* file, and this header is written to disk in line 472. The function then begins a pair of nested *for* loops (lines 474 through 477), which iterate once for each pixel that makes up the display. In line 478, the function enters a *switch* statement. In this statement, the color data for a pixel is read from display memory and saved to the disk file. Lines 480 through 499 are the case for a 32K-color display. The correct display memory address and memory bank for the desired pixel are set up in lines 485 through 490. In lines 491 and 492 the two bytes of color data for the selected pixel are read into an integer called *data*. Lines 493, 495, and 497 convert *data* into three separate color bytes. These are written to the file by lines 494, 496, and 498. Lines 500 through 519 are used for the case of a 64K-color display. The code is very similar to the previous case except for the way in which the individual colors are extracted from *data*. Lines 520 through 537 are the case for 24-bit color display modes. Each of the three color bytes is read from display memory and sent to the file. At the end of each line, lines 551 through 555 make sure that the file line has enough bytes to be divisible by four by adding 00H bytes to the file until the proper number of bytes is reached. When the nested *for* loops end, line 557 closes the file, completing the function.

Listing 28-2. Program to Display a 24-Bit Color PCX File and Convert it to a BMP File

```
/*

    PCX2BMP = PROGRAM TO VIEW 24 BIT COLOR .PCX GRAPHICS
                FILE AND SAVE AS A .BMP FILE

                By Roger T. Stevens  4-13-96

*/

#include <dos.h>
#include <string.h>
#include <dir.h>
#include <stdio.h>
#include <conio.h>

#define UP_ARROW328
#define DOWN_ARROW336
#define LEFT_ARROW331
#define RIGHT_ARROW333
#define BACKSPACE  8
#define seq_out(register,val)  outport(0x3C4,val<<8 | \
                                 register);
#define max(a,b)     (((a) > (b)) ? (a) : (b))
#define min(a,b)     (((a) < (b)) ? (a) : (b))

int getModeData(int mode);
void save_bmp(char filename[32]);
void setBank(unsigned long int offset, int read_write);
void setEGApalette(int palette, int color);
void setVGApalette(unsigned char *buffer);
void setMode(int mode);

union REGS reg;
struct SREGS segregs;
struct REGPACK outregs;

struct
{
    char password;
    char version;
    char encoding;
    char bits_per_pixel;
    int xmin, ymin, xmax, ymax;
    int xres, yres;
    unsigned char palette[48];
    char reserved1;
    char no_of_planes;
    int bytes_per_line;
```

```
    int palette_type;
    char reserved2;
    int xsize;
    int ysize;
    char filler[53];
} pcx_header;

char directory[100][13];

struct
{
    char signature[4];
    int version;
    long int far *OEM_string;
    char capabilities[4];
    long int far *Modes;
    int memory_size;
    char reserved[236];
} info;

struct
{
    int     ModeAttributes;
    char    WinAAttributes;
    char    WinBAttributes;
    int     WinGranularity;
    int     WinSize;
    int     WinASegment;
    int     WinBSegment;
    long intWinFuncPtr;
    int     BytesPerScanLine;
    int     XResolution;
    int     YResolution;
    char    XCharSize;
    char    YCharSize;
    char    NumberOfPlanes;
    char    BitsPerPixel;
    char    NumberOfBanks;
    char    MemoryModel;
    char    BankSize;
    char    NumberOfImagePages;
    char    Reserved;
    char    Filler[225];
} mode_data;

typedef struct
{
    unsigned char color[3];
} COLOR;

int bytes_per_line, i, j, k, dir_index= 0, index, end,
```

```
mode, d, color, ch1 = NULL, length, xres, yres, ystop,
type, flag, memory_plane;
unsigned char palette_data[256][3];
char temp[13];
char filename[32], outfile[32];
int mode16[7], mode256[6], modehi[5];
struct ffblk ffblk;
long int col,row;
FILE *read_file;
FILE *config_file;
unsigned char ch;
COLOR buffer[1280];
unsigned int no_chars, old_bank, data;
char far * address;
int ix, xoffset, yoffset, planes;
unsigned long int offset;

void main(void)
{
    clrscr();
    config_file = fopen("c:\\vconfig.dat","rb");
    fread(mode16,2,7,config_file);
    fread(mode256,2,6,config_file);
    fread(modehi,2,5,config_file);
    fclose(config_file);
    segread(&segregs);
    index = 0;
    end = findfirst("*.pcx",&ffblk,0);
    while(!end)
    {
        read_file = fopen(ffblk.ff_name,"rb");
        fread(&pcx_header,1,128,read_file);
        if ((pcx_header.bits_per_pixel == 8) &&
            (pcx_header.no_of_planes == 3))
            strcpy(directory[index++],ffblk.ff_name);
        fclose(read_file);
        end = findnext(&ffblk);
        if (index > 99)
            break;
    }
    d = 4;
    while (d < index)
        d += d;
    d--;
    d /= 2;
    while (d >= 1)
    {
        for (j=1; j<index-d; j++)
        {
            for (i=j; i>=1; i-=d)
            {
                if (strcmp(directory[i+d],directory[i]) > 0)
```

```
                        break;
                    strcpy(temp,directory[i]);
                    strcpy(directory[i],directory[i+d]);
                    strcpy(directory[i+d],temp);
                }
            }
            d /= 2;
        }
        for(;;)
        {
            type = 6;
            setMode(3);
            textbackground(1);
            textcolor(15);
            window(2,2,78,23);
            clrscr();
            gotoxy(1,1);
            putch(0xC9);
            for (i=1; i<19; i++)
            {
                if (i%15)
                    putch(0xCD);
                else
                    putch(0xD1);
            }
            cprintf(" Select file name with cursor arrows: ");
            for (i=12; i<30; i++)
            {
                if (i%15)
                    putch(0xCD);
                else
                    putch(0xD1);
            }
            putch(0xBB);
            for (i=2; i<22; i++)
            {
                for (j=1; j<79; j+=15)
                {
                    gotoxy(j,i);
                    if ((j==1) || (j == 76))
                        putch(0xBA);
                    else
                        putch(0xB3);
                }
            }
            gotoxy(1,22);
            putch(0xC8);
            for (i=1; i<75; i++)
            {
                if (i%15)
                    putch(0xCD);
                else
```

```
        putch(0xCF);
}
putch(0xBC);
filename[0] = NULL;
gotoxy(19,1);
textcolor(7);
for (i=0; i<index; i++)
{
    gotoxy(3+(i/20)*15,(i%20)+2);
    cprintf("%s",directory[i]);
}
ch1 = 256;
while ((ch1 != 0x0D) && (ch1 != 0x1B))
{
    gotoxy(3+(dir_index/20)*15,(dir_index%20)+2);
    cprintf("%s",directory[dir_index]);
    switch(ch1)
    {
        case DOWN_ARROW:
            ++dir_index;
            dir_index = dir_index % index;
            break;
        case UP_ARROW:
            --dir_index;
            if (dir_index<0)
                dir_index = index - 1;
            break;
        case RIGHT_ARROW:
            if ((dir_index + 20) < index)
                dir_index += 20;
            break;
        case LEFT_ARROW:
            if (dir_index >= 20)
                dir_index -= 20;
            break;
    }
    textbackground(7);
    textcolor(1);
    gotoxy(3+(dir_index/20)*15,(dir_index%20)+2);
    cprintf("%s",directory[dir_index]);
    textbackground(1);
    textcolor(7);
    ch1 = getch();
    if (ch1 == 0x00)
        ch1 = getch() + 256;
}
strcpy(filename,directory[dir_index]);
if (ch1 == 0x1B)
    break;
read_file = fopen(filename,"rb");
fread(&pcx_header,1,128,read_file);
xres = pcx_header.xmax - pcx_header.xmin + 1;
```

```
        yres = pcx_header.ymax - pcx_header.ymin + 1;
        mode = modehi[0];
        if (((xres > 320) || (yres > 200)) && (modehi[1]
            != 0))
            mode = modehi[1];
        if (((xres > 640) || (yres > 480)) && (modehi[2]
            != 0))
            mode = modehi[2];
        if (((xres > 800) || (yres > 600)) && (modehi[3]
            != 0))
            mode = modehi[3];
        if (((xres > 1024) || (yres > 768)) && (modehi[4]
            != 0))
            mode = modehi[4];
        if (mode == 0)
            continue;
        outregs.r_ax = 0x4F01;
        outregs.r_cx = mode;
        segread(&segregs);
        outregs.r_es = segregs.ds;
        outregs.r_di = (unsigned int)&mode_data;
        intr(0x10,&outregs);
        xoffset = max (0,(mode_data.XResolution -
pcx_header.xmax - 1)/2);
        yoffset = max(0,(mode_data.YResolution -
pcx_header.ymax - 1)/2);
        ystop = min(pcx_header.ymax + yoffset,
mode_data.YResolution);
        setMode(mode);
        fseek(read_file,128L,SEEK_SET);
        row=yoffset;
        col = 0;
        planes = 0;
        setBank(0,0);
        while (row <= ystop)
        {
            ch = fgetc(read_file);
            if ((ch & 0xC0) != 0xC0)
                no_chars = 1;
            else
            {
                no_chars = ch & 0x3F;
                ch = fgetc(read_file);
            }
            for (k=0; k<no_chars; k++)
            {
                buffer[col++].color[planes] = ch;
                if (col >= pcx_header.bytes_per_line)
                {
                    planes++;
                    col = 0;
```

```
                    if (planes > 2)
                    {
                        planes = 0;
                        for (ix=0;
        ix<pcx_header.bytes_per_line;
                            ix++)
                        {
                            switch(mode)
                            {
                                case 0x10D:
                                case 0x110:
                                case 0x113:
                                case 0x116:
                                case 0x119:
                                    data =
                                        (int)(buffer[ix].color[0]
                                        & 0xF8) << 7 | (int)
                                        (buffer[ix].color[1]&0xF8)
                                        << 2 |
                (int)(buffer[ix].color[2] &
                                        0xF8) >> 3;
                                    offset = row *
                                        mode_data.BytesPerScanLine
                                        + 2 * (xoffset + ix);
                                    setBank(offset,0);
                                    FP_SEG(address) = 0xA000;
                                    FP_OFF(address) =(unsigned

                                        int) offset;
                                    *(address++) = data & 0xFF;
                                    *address = data >> 8;
                                    break;
                                case 0x10E:
                                case 0x111:
                                case 0x114:
                                case 0x117:
                                case 0x11A:
                                    data =
                (int)(buffer[ix].color[0]
                                        & 0xF8) << 8 | (int)
                                        (buffer[ix].color[1]&0xFC)
                                        << 3 |
                    (int)(buffer[ix].color[2] &
                                        0xF8) >> 3;
                                    offset = row *
                        mode_data.BytesPerScanLine
                                        + 2 * (xoffset + ix);
                                    setBank(offset,0);
                                    FP_SEG(address)= 0xA000;
                                    FP_OFF(address)=(unsigned int)
```

```
                                        offset;
                                    *(address++) = data & 0xFF;
                                    *address = data >> 8;
                                    break;
                                case 0x10F:
                                case 0x112:
                                case 0x115:
                                case 0x118:
                                case 0x11B:
                                    offset = row *
                        mode_data.BytesPerScanLine
                                        + 3 * (xoffset + ix);
                                    setBank(offset,0);
                                    FP_SEG(address)= 0xA000;
                                    FP_OFF(address)=(unsigned int)
                                        offset;
                                    *address= buffer[ix].color[2];
                                    offset = row *
                        mode_data.BytesPerScanLine
                                        + 3 * (xoffset + ix) + 1;
                                    setBank(offset,0);
                                    FP_SEG(address) = 0xA000;
                                    FP_OFF(address)=(unsigned int)
                                        offset;
                                    *address= buffer[ix].color[1];
                                    offset = row *
                        mode_data.BytesPerScanLine
                                        + 3 * (xoffset + ix) + 2;
                                    setBank(offset,0);
                                    FP_SEG(address) = 0xA000;
                                    FP_OFF(address =(unsigned int)
                                        offset;
                                    *address= buffer[ix].color[0];
                            }
                        }
                        row++;
                    }
                }
            }
        }
        fclose(read_file);
        strnset(outfile, NULL, 32);
        length = strcspn(filename, ".");
        strncpy(outfile, filename, length);
        strcat(outfile,".BMP");
        save_bmp(outfile);
    }
}
```

```
/*
            setBank() = Sets video memory bank
*/

void setBank(unsigned long int offset, int read_write)
{
    static int bank, old_bank;

    old_bank = reg.x.dx;
    bank = offset >> 16;
    if (bank == old_bank)
        return;
    reg.x.dx = bank;
    old_bank = bank;
    reg.x.ax = 0x4F05;
    reg.x.bx = read_write;
    int86(0x10, &reg, &reg);
}


/*
  getModeData() = Gets Super VGA data on a desired mode
*/

int getModeData(int mode)
{
        segread(&segregs);
        outregs.r_ax = 0x4F01;
        outregs.r_cx = mode;
        outregs.r_es = segregs.ds;
        outregs.r_di =(unsigned int) &mode_data;
        intr(0x10,&outregs);
        if ((mode_data.ModeAttributes &0x01) == 1)
            return(1);
        return(0);
}

/*
            setMode() = Sets Video Mode
*/

void setMode(int mode)
{
```

```
    union REGS reg;
    if (mode > 0xFF)
    {
        reg.x.ax = 0x4F02;
        reg.x.bx = mode;
    }
    else
        reg.x.ax = mode;
    int86 (0x10,&reg,&reg);
}

/*

    save_bmp() = Save display screen to .BMP disk file

*/

void save_bmp(char filename[32])
{
    unsigned char red, green, blue;
    union REGS reg;
    struct SREGS inreg;

    struct
    {
        unsigned int id;
        unsigned long intfile_size;
        unsigned intreserved[2];
        unsigned long intimage_offset;
        unsigned intheader_size,
                             not_used;
        unsigned long intxres,
                             yres;
        unsigned intno_of_planes,
                             bits_per_pixel;
        unsigned long intcompression_method,
                             bit_map_size,
                             hor_res,
                             vert_res,
                             number_of_colors,
                             no_significant_colors;
    }  bmp_header;
    char far *address;
    int col, i, k, row, number, num_out, page=0,
        old_page=0;
    unsigned char ch, old_ch, palette[768];
    FILE *write_file;
    unsigned long int offset;

    write_file = fopen(filename,"wb");
    bmp_header.not_used = 0x00;
```

```
        bmp_header.id = 0x4D42;
        bmp_header.file_size = 3 * mode_data.XResolution *
        mode_data.YResolution + 54;
        bmp_header.reserved[0] = 0;
        bmp_header.reserved[1] = 0;
        bmp_header.image_offset = 54;
        bmp_header.header_size = 40;
        bmp_header.xres = mode_data.XResolution;
        bmp_header.yres = mode_data.YResolution;
        bmp_header.no_of_planes = 1;
        bmp_header.bits_per_pixel = 24;
        bmp_header.compression_method = 0;
        bmp_header.bit_map_size = 0;
        bmp_header.hor_res = 0;
        bmp_header.vert_res = 0;
        bmp_header.number_of_colors = 1<<24;
        bmp_header.no_significant_colors = 0;
        fwrite(&bmp_header,1,54,write_file);
        setBank(0,1);
        for (row=mode_data.YResolution-1; row>=0; row--)
        {
            for (col=0; col<mode_data.XResolution; col++)
            {
                switch(mode)
                {
                    case 0x10D:
                    case 0x110:
                    case 0x113:
                    case 0x116:
                    case 0x119:
                        offset = (long)row *
                            mode_data.BytesPerScanLine
                            + 2 * col;
                        setBank(offset,1);
                        FP_SEG(address) = 0xA000;
                        FP_OFF(address) =(unsigned int) offset;
                        data = (unsigned char)*address++;
                        data |=  (unsigned char)(*address) << 8;
                        blue = (data << 3) & 0xF8;
                        fputc(blue,write_file);
                        green = (data >> 2) & 0xF8;
                        fputc(green,write_file);
                        red = (data >> 7) & 0xF8;
                        fputc(red,write_file);
                        break;
                    case 0x10E:
                    case 0x111:
                    case 0x114:
                    case 0x117:
                    case 0x11A:
                        offset = (long)row *
                            mode_data.BytesPerScanLine
```

```
                        + 2L * col;
                    setBank(offset,1);
                    FP_SEG(address) = 0xA000;
                    FP_OFF(address) =(unsigned int) offset;
                    data = (unsigned char)*address++;
                    data |=  (unsigned char)(*address) << 8;
                    blue = (data << 3) & 0xF8;
                    fputc(blue,write_file);
                    green = (data >> 3) & 0xFC;
                    fputc(green,write_file);
                    red = (data >> 8) & 0xF8;
                    fputc(red,write_file);
                    break;
                case 0x10F:
                case 0x112:
                case 0x115:
                case 0x118:
                case 0x11B:
                    offset = (long)row *
                        mode_data.BytesPerScanLine
                        + 3L * col;
                    setBank(offset,1);
                    FP_SEG(address) = 0xA000;
                    FP_OFF(address) =(unsigned int) offset;
                    fputc((*address++)&0xF8, write_file);
                    offset++;
                    setBank(offset,1);
                    fputc((*address++)&0xFC, write_file);
                    offset++;
                    setBank(offset,1);
                    fputc((*address)&0xF8, write_file);
            }
        }
        while (4*(col/4) < col)
        {
            fputc(0x00, write_file);
            col++;
        }
    }
    fclose(write_file);
}
```

29

Saving and Restoring Displays with the *TGA* Format

The 24-bit color *TGA* files are almost the same as *BMP* files except for the header. You can see how they are handled by comparing the code in Listings 29-1 and 29-2 with Listings 28-1 and 28-2. Only minor modifications are needed to work with *TGA* files rather than *BMP* files. One important difference is that *TGA* files may have the image origin at any one of the four corners of the viewing screen. We'll deal with this later.

The *TGA* File Header

The TGA header consists of 18 bytes. In the form of a C++ structure, it looks like this:

```
struct
{
      unsigned char         id_length,
                            color_map_type,
                            image_type;
      unsigned int          color_map_start,
                            color_map_length;
      unsigned char         color_map_depth;
```

```
        unsigned int            x_offset,
                                y_offset,
                                xres,
                                yres;
        unsigned char           bits_per_pixel,
                                image_descriptor;
    } tga_header;
```

The **id_length** parameter specifies the number of bytes in the image identification field, which can optionally follow the header. Our programs are only going to deal with *TGA* files that do not have an image identification field; for them this byte will be 0. If you want to handle files that have an image identification field, you need to decide how you want to handle the information in the field and program accordingly. Then make sure that you use this parameter to position the file pointer just following the image identification field before you start reading pixel data.

The next three fields, **color_map_start**, **color_map_length**, and **color_map_depth**, are for the color map specification, which is used to set up the display palette, if necessary. For 24-bit color files, this information is not required so all these parameters are set to 0.

The next two parameters, **x_offset** and **y_offset**, define the beginning of the image with respect to the origin of the display. The location of this origin is described in connection with the parameter **image_descriptor** below.

The parameters **x_res** and **y_res** are the image width and height, respectively, in pixels.

The parameter **bits_per_pixel** is the number of bits required for the color description of a pixel. For 24-bit color, this is set to 24.

The parameter **image_descriptor** contains two pieces of information. Bits 0 to 3 give the number of attribute bits per pixel. For 24-bit color no attribute bits are used so this is 0. Bits 4 and 5 define the location of the image origin, which can be any one of the four corners of the screen. When these bits are set to 00, the origin is the lower lefthand corner. When they are 01, the origin is the top lefthand corner. When 10, the origin is the top righthand corner. When 11, the origin is the bottom righthand corner.

TGA Image Data

The *TGA* image data begins at the origin defined by the **image_descriptor** parameter. The image is scanned one horizontal line at a time, row by row. The viewing program given in Listing 29-1 will handle files that begin at either the top left or bottom left corner of the image.

Program to View 24-Bit Color *TGA* Files

Listing 29-1 is a program to view 24-bit color *TGA* files. Note that for this program to work properly, you must have created the *vconfig.dat* file in your root directory. There are two main differences from the viewing program of Listing 28-1. First, the files that are selected for display in the directory are *TGA* files instead of *BMP* files. Second, the program is set up to display *TGA* files whose origin is either at the top left corner of the display or the bottom left corner. Lines 267 through 275 are typical of the code that does this. The *if* statement of lines 267 and 268 checks those bits in the *image_descriptor* parameter that indicate the display origin location. If the two bits are both 0 (origin at the bottom left corner), the program performs lines 269 through 271, which set the offset from the display memory base address at the bottom left beginning location for the display when the *for* loop of line 250 begins and moves upward line by line as further iterations of the loop take place. If the two bits contain other than 0, lines 273 through 275 are performed, which set the offset from the display memory base address at the top left beginning location for the display when the *for* loop of line 250 begins and moves downward line by line as further iterations of the loop take place. This code is used for 32K-color display modes. For 64K-color modes, similar code occurs in lines 291 through 299, and for 24-bit-color display modes, similar code occurs in lines 312 through 320.

Saving a Display as a *TGA* File

Listing 29-2 is a program that displays a 24-bit color *PCX* file and then converts it to a *TGA* file. The primary purpose of this program is to show how you can use the function *save_tga* to save a 24-bit color *TGA* file. You can use it to convert any 24-bit color *PCX* file, but you should be aware of a couple of things. First, if the resolution of the *PCX* file doesn't correspond to that of one of the display modes, the display program will use the next higher resolution mode and display the picture in the center of the screen with black space around it. The new *TGA* file will have as its resolution the resolution of the selected display mode, and the black space around the picture will be saved as part of the new file. (This will probably make the new file larger than the old one.) Second, if your display won't handle the required resolution in 24-bit color but instead uses 64K colors or 32K colors, even though the new *TGA* file will be written as 24-bit color, it actually will only contain 64K or 32K colors maximum, so some of the original color information will be lost. Except for the differences in the header contents, this function is just the same as the one for saving *BMP* files.

Listing 29-1. Program to Display TGA Files

```
/*

            TGA = PROGRAM TO VIEW .TGA GRAPHICS FILES
                  USING REGULAR AND VESA MODES

                  By Roger T. Stevens  4-17-96

*/
#include <dos.h>
#include <string.h>
#include <dir.h>
#include <stdio.h>
#include <conio.h>

#define UP_ARROW328
#define DOWN_ARROW336
#define LEFT_ARROW331
#define RIGHT_ARROW333
#define BACKSPACE  8
#define seq_out(register,val)  outport(0x3C4,val<<8 | \
                                register);
#define max(a,b)      (((a) > (b)) ? (a)  : (b))
#define min(a,b)      (((a) < (b)) ? (a)  : (b))

int getModeData(int mode);
void setBank(unsigned long int offset);
void setMode(int mode);

union REGS reg;
struct SREGS segregs;
struct REGPACK outregs;

struct
{
   unsigned char id_length,
```

```
                         color_map_type,
                         image_type;
    unsigned intcolor_map_start,
                         color_map_length;
    unsigned charcolor_map_depth;
    unsigned intx_offset,
                         y_offset,
                         xres,
                         yres;
    unsigned char bits_per_pixel,
                         image_descriptor;
} tga_header;

struct
{
    char signature[4];
    int version;
    long int far *OEM_string;
    char capabilities[4];
    long int far *Modes;
    int memory_size;
    char reserved[236];
} info;

struct
{
    int    ModeAttributes;
    char   WinAAttributes;
    char   WinBAttributes;
    int    WinGranularity;
    int    WinSize;
    int    WinASegment;
    int    WinBSegment;
    long intWinFuncPtr;
    int    BytesPerScanLine;
    int    XResolution;
    int    YResolution;
    char   XCharSize;
    char   YCharSize;
    char   NumberOfPlanes;
    char   BitsPerPixel;
    char   NumberOfBanks;
    char   MemoryModel;
    char   BankSize;
    char   NumberOfImagePages;
    char   Reserved;
    char   Filler[225];
} mode_data;

char directory[100][13];

unsigned int mode16[7], mode256[6], modehi[5];
```

```
int bytes_per_line, i, j, k, dir_index= 0, index, end,
mode, d, color, ch1 = NULL, xres, yres, ystop, type,
flag, memory_plane;
unsigned char red, green, blue, palette_data[256][3];
char temp[13];
char filename[32];
struct ffblk ffblk;
long int col,row;
FILE *read_file;
FILE *config_file;
unsigned int no_chars, old_bank, data;
char far * address;
int ix, xoffset, yoffset, planes;
unsigned long int offset;

void main(void)
{
    int start, stop;

    clrscr();
    config_file = fopen("c:\\vconfig.dat","rb");
    fread(mode16,2,7,config_file);
    fread(mode256,2,6,config_file);
    fread(modehi,2,5,config_file);
    fclose(config_file);
    segread(&segregs);
    index = 0;
    end = findfirst("*.tga",&ffblk,0);
    while(!end)
    {
        strcpy(directory[index++],ffblk.ff_name);
        end = findnext(&ffblk);
        if (index > 99)
            break;
    }
    d = 4;
    while (d < index)
        d += d;
    d--;
    d /= 2;
    while (d >= 1)
    {
        for (j=1; j<index-d; j++)
        {
            for (i=j; i>=1; i-=d)
            {
                if (strcmp(directory[i+d],directory[i]) > 0)
                    break;
                strcpy(temp,directory[i]);
                strcpy(directory[i],directory[i+d]);
                strcpy(directory[i+d],temp);
            }
```

```
        }
        d /= 2;
    }
    for(;;)
    {
        type = 6;
        setMode(3);
        textbackground(1);
        textcolor(15);
        window(2,2,78,23);
        clrscr();
        gotoxy(1,1);
        putch(0xC9);
        for (i=1; i<19; i++)
        {
            if (i%15)
                putch(0xCD);
            else
                putch(0xD1);
        }
        cprintf(" Select file name with cursor arrows: ");
        for (i=12; i<30; i++)
        {
            if (i%15)
                putch(0xCD);
            else
                putch(0xD1);
        }
        putch(0xBB);
        for (i=2; i<22; i++)
        {
            for (j=1; j<79; j+=15)
            {
                gotoxy(j,i);
                if ((j==1) || (j == 76))
                    putch(0xBA);
                else
                    putch(0xB3);
            }
        }
        gotoxy(1,22);
        putch(0xC8);
        for (i=1; i<75; i++)
        {
            if (i%15)
                putch(0xCD);
            else
                putch(0xCF);
        }
        putch(0xBC);
        filename[0] = NULL;
        gotoxy(19,1);
```

```
        textcolor(7);
        for (i=0; i<index; i++)
        {
            gotoxy(3+(i/20)*15,(i%20)+2);
            cprintf("%s",directory[i]);
        }
        ch1 = 256;
        while ((ch1 != 0x0D) && (ch1 != 0x1B))
        {
            gotoxy(3+(dir_index/20)*15,(dir_index%20)+2);
            cprintf("%s",directory[dir_index]);
            switch(ch1)
            {
                case DOWN_ARROW:
                    ++dir_index;
                    dir_index = dir_index % index;
                    break;
                case UP_ARROW:
                    --dir_index;
                    if (dir_index<0)
                        dir_index = index - 1;
                    break;
                case RIGHT_ARROW:
                    if ((dir_index + 20) < index)
                        dir_index += 20;
                    break;
                case LEFT_ARROW:
                    if (dir_index >= 20)
                        dir_index -= 20;
                    break;
            }
            textbackground(7);
            textcolor(1);
            gotoxy(3+(dir_index/20)*15,(dir_index%20)+2);
            cprintf("%s",directory[dir_index]);
            textbackground(1);
            textcolor(7);
            ch1 = getch();
            if (ch1 == 0x00)
                ch1 = getch() + 256;
        }
        strcpy(filename,directory[dir_index]);
        if (ch1 == 0x1B)
            break;
        read_file = fopen(filename,"rb");
        fread(&tga_header,1,18,read_file);
        xres = tga_header.xres;
        yres = tga_header.yres;
        mode = modehi[0];
        if (((xres > 320) || (yres > 200)) && (modehi[1]
            != 0))
            mode = modehi[1];
```

```
        if (((xres > 640) || (yres > 480)) && (modehi[2]
            != 0))
            mode = modehi[2];
        if (((xres > 800) || (yres > 600)) && (modehi[3]
            != 0))
            mode = modehi[3];
        if (((xres > 1024) || (yres > 768)) && (modehi[4]
            != 0))
            mode = modehi[4];
        if (mode == 0)
            continue;
        outregs.r_ax = 0x4F01;
        outregs.r_cx = mode;
        segread(&segregs);
        outregs.r_es = segregs.ds;
        outregs.r_di = (unsigned int)&mode_data;
        intr(0x10,&outregs);
        xoffset = max (0,(mode_data.XResolution -
    xres)/2);
        yoffset = max(0,(mode_data.YResolution - yres)/2);
        ystop = min(yres + yoffset,
            mode_data.YResolution);
        setMode(mode);
        setBank(0);
        for (row = yoffset; row <ystop; row++)
        {
            for (col=0; col < xres; col++)
            {
                blue = fgetc(read_file);
                green = fgetc(read_file);
                red = fgetc(read_file);
                switch(mode)
                {
                    case 0x10D:
                    case 0x110:
                    case 0x113:
                    case 0x116:
                    case 0x119:
                        data = (int)(red & 0xF8) << 7 |
                            (int)(green & 0xF8) << 2 |
                            (int)(blue & 0xF8) >> 3;
                        if ((tga_header.image_descriptor &
                            0x30) == 0)
                            offset = (ystop-row+yoffset) *
                                mode_data.BytesPerScanLine
                                + 2 * (xoffset + col);
                        else
                            offset = row *
        mode_data.BytesPerScanLine
                                + 2 * (xoffset + col);
                        setBank(offset);
                        FP_SEG(address) = 0xA000;
```

```
                  FP_OFF(address) =(unsigned
          int) offset;
                  *(address++) = data & 0xFF;
                  *address = data >> 8;
                  break;
              case 0x10E:
              case 0x111:
              case 0x114:
              case 0x117:
              case 0x11A:
                  data = (int)(red & 0xF8) << 8 |
                      (int) (green & 0xFC) << 3 |
                      (int)(blue & 0xF8) >> 3;
                  if ((tga_header.image_descriptor &
              0x30) == 0)
                      offset = (ystop-row+yoffset) *
                          mode_data.BytesPerScanLine
                          + 2 * (xoffset + col);
                  else
                      offset = row *
  mode_data.BytesPerScanLine
                          + 2 * (xoffset + col);
                  setBank(offset);
                  FP_SEG(address) = 0xA000;
                  FP_OFF(address) =(unsigned int)
          offset;
                  *(address++) = data & 0xFF;
                  *address = data >> 8;
                  break;
              case 0x10F:
              case 0x112:
              case 0x115:
              case 0x118:
              case 0x11B:
                  if ((tga_header.image_descriptor &
              0x30) == 0)
                      offset = (ystop-row+yoffset) *
                          mode_data.BytesPerScanLine
                          + 3 * (xoffset + col);
                  else
                      offset = row *
  mode_data.BytesPerScanLine
                          + 3 * (xoffset + col);
                  setBank(offset);
                  FP_SEG(address) = 0xA000;
                  FP_OFF(address) =(unsigned int)
          offset;
                  *address = blue;
                  offset++;
                  setBank(offset);
```

```
                        FP_SEG(address) = 0xA000;
                        FP_OFF(address) =(unsigned int)
                offset;
                        *address = green;
                        offset++;
                        setBank(offset);
                        FP_SEG(address) = 0xA000;
                        FP_OFF(address) =(unsigned int)
                offset;
                        *address = red;
                }
            }
        }
        fclose(read_file);
    getch();
    }
}

/*
        setBank() = Sets video memory bank
*/

void setBank(unsigned long int offset)
{
    static int bank, old_bank;

    old_bank = reg.x.dx;
    bank = offset >> 16;
    if (bank == old_bank)
        return;
    reg.x.dx = bank;
    old_bank = bank;
    reg.x.ax = 0x4F05;
    reg.x.bx = 0;
    int86(0x10, &reg, &reg);
}

/*
    getModeData() = Gets Super VGA data on a desired mode
*/

int getModeData(int mode)
{
    segread(&segregs);
    outregs.r_ax = 0x4F01;
    outregs.r_cx = mode;
```

```
    outregs.r_es = segregs.ds;
    outregs.r_di =(unsigned int) &mode_data;
    intr(0x10,&outregs);
    if ((mode_data.ModeAttributes &0x01) == 1)
        return(1);
    return(0);
}

/*
        setMode() = Sets Video Mode
*/

void setMode(int mode)
{
    union REGS reg;
    if (mode > 0xFF)
    {
        reg.x.ax = 0x4F02;
        reg.x.bx = mode;
    }
    else
        reg.x.ax = mode;
    int86 (0x10,&reg,&reg);
}
```

Listing 29-2. Program to Display a 24-Bit Color PCX File and Convert it to a BMP File

```
/*
    PCX2TGA = PROGRAM TO VIEW 24 BIT COLOR .PCX GRAPHICS
              FILE AND SAVE AS A .TGA FILE

              By Roger T. Stevens  4-18-96
*/

#include <dos.h>
#include <string.h>
#include <dir.h>
#include <stdio.h>
#include <conio.h>

#define UP_ARROW      328
#define DOWN_ARROW    336
```

```
#define LEFT_ARROW    331
#define RIGHT_ARROW   333
#define BACKSPACE       8
#define seq_out(register,val)  outport(0x3C4,val<<8 | \
                                 register);
#define max(a,b)     (((a) > (b)) ? (a) : (b))
#define min(a,b)     (((a) < (b)) ? (a) : (b))

int getModeData(int mode);
void save_tga(char filename[32]);
void setBank(unsigned long int offset, int read_write);
void setMode(int mode);

union REGS reg;
struct SREGS segregs;
struct REGPACK outregs;

struct
{
    char password;
    char version;
    char encoding;
    char bits_per_pixel;
    int xmin, ymin, xmax, ymax;
    int xres, yres;
    unsigned char palette[48];
    char reserved1;
    char no_of_planes;
    int bytes_per_line;
    int palette_type;
    char reserved2;
    int xsize;
    int ysize;
    char filler[53];
} pcx_header;

char directory[100][13];

struct
{
    char signature[4];
    int version;
    long int far *OEM_string;
    char capabilities[4];
    long int far *Modes;
    int memory_size;
    char reserved[236];
} info;

struct
{
    int    ModeAttributes;
```

```
    char   WinAAttributes;
    char   WinBAttributes;
    int    WinGranularity;
    int    WinSize;
    int    WinASegment;
    int    WinBSegment;
    long intWinFuncPtr;
    int         BytesPerScanLine;
    int         XResolution;
    int         YResolution;
    char        XCharSize;
    char        YCharSize;
    char        NumberOfPlanes;
    char        BitsPerPixel;
    char        NumberOfBanks;
    char        MemoryModel;
    char        BankSize;
    char        NumberOfImagePages;
    char        Reserved;
    char        Filler[225];
} mode_data;

typedef struct
{
    unsigned char color[3];
} COLOR;

int bytes_per_line, i, j, k, dir_index= 0, index, end,
mode, d, color, ch1 = NULL, length, xres, yres, ystop,
type, flag, memory_plane;
unsigned char palette_data[256][3];
char temp[13];
char filename[32], outfile[32];
int mode16[7], mode256[6], modehi[5];
struct ffblk ffblk;
long int col,row;
FILE *read_file;
FILE *config_file;
unsigned char ch;
COLOR buffer[1280];
unsigned int no_chars, old_bank, data;
char far * address;
int ix, xoffset, yoffset, planes;
unsigned long int offset;

void main(void)
{
    clrscr();
    config_file = fopen("c:\\vconfig.dat","rb");
    fread(mode16,2,7,config_file);
    fread(mode256,2,6,config_file);
    fread(modehi,2,5,config_file);
```

```
    fclose(config_file);
    segread(&segregs);
    index = 0;
    end = findfirst("*.pcx",&ffblk,0);
    while(!end)
    {
        read_file = fopen(ffblk.ff_name,"rb");
        fread(&pcx_header,1,128,read_file);
        if ((pcx_header.bits_per_pixel == 8) &&
            (pcx_header.no_of_planes == 3))
            strcpy(directory[index++],ffblk.ff_name);
        fclose(read_file);
        end = findnext(&ffblk);
        if (index > 99)
            break;
    }
    d = 4;
    while (d < index)
        d += d;
    d--;
    d /= 2;
    while (d >= 1)
    {
        for (j=1; j<index-d; j++)
        {
            for (i=j; i>=1; i-=d)
            {
                if (strcmp(directory[i+d],directory[i]) > 0)
                    break;
                strcpy(temp,directory[i]);
                strcpy(directory[i],directory[i+d]);
                strcpy(directory[i+d],temp);
            }
        }
        d /= 2;
    }
    for(;;)
    {
        type = 6;
        setMode(3);
        textbackground(1);
        textcolor(15);
        window(2,2,78,23);
        clrscr();
        gotoxy(1,1);
        putch(0xC9);
        for (i=1; i<19; i++)
        {
            if (i%15)
                putch(0xCD);
            else
                putch(0xD1);
```

```
            }
            cprintf(" Select file name with cursor arrows: ");
            for (i=12; i<30; i++)
            {
                if (i%15)
                    putch(0xCD);
                else
                    putch(0xD1);
            }
            putch(0xBB);
            for (i=2; i<22; i++)
            {
                for (j=1; j<79; j+=15)
                {
                    gotoxy(j,i);
                    if ((j==1) || (j == 76))
                        putch(0xBA);
                    else
                        putch(0xB3);
                }
            }
            gotoxy(1,22);
            putch(0xC8);
            for (i=1; i<75; i++)
            {
                if (i%15)
                    putch(0xCD);
                else
                    putch(0xCF);
            }
            putch(0xBC);
            filename[0] = NULL;
            gotoxy(19,1);
            textcolor(7);
            for (i=0; i<index; i++)
            {
                gotoxy(3+(i/20)*15,(i%20)+2);
                cprintf("%s",directory[i]);
            }
            ch1 = 256;
            while ((ch1 != 0x0D) && (ch1 != 0x1B))
            {
                gotoxy(3+(dir_index/20)*15,(dir_index%20)+2);
                cprintf("%s",directory[dir_index]);
                switch(ch1)
                {
                    case DOWN_ARROW:
                        ++dir_index;
                        dir_index = dir_index % index;
                        break;
                    case UP_ARROW:
                        --dir_index;
```

```
                if (dir_index<0)
                    dir_index = index - 1;
                break;
            case RIGHT_ARROW:
                if ((dir_index + 20) < index)
                    dir_index += 20;
                break;
            case LEFT_ARROW:
                if (dir_index >= 20)
                    dir_index -= 20;
                break;
        }
        textbackground(7);
        textcolor(1);
        gotoxy(3+(dir_index/20)*15,(dir_index%20)+2);
        cprintf("%s",directory[dir_index]);
        textbackground(1);
        textcolor(7);
        ch1 = getch();
        if (ch1 == 0x00)
            ch1 = getch() + 256;
    }
    strcpy(filename,directory[dir_index]);
    if (ch1 == 0x1B)
        break;
    read_file = fopen(filename,"rb");
    fread(&pcx_header,1,128,read_file);
    xres = pcx_header.xmax - pcx_header.xmin + 1;
    yres = pcx_header.ymax - pcx_header.ymin + 1;
    mode = modehi[0];
    if (((xres > 320) || (yres > 200)) && (modehi[1]
        != 0))
        mode = modehi[1];
    if (((xres > 640) || (yres > 480)) && (modehi[2]
        != 0))
        mode = modehi[2];
    if (((xres > 800) || (yres > 600)) && (modehi[3]
        != 0))
        mode = modehi[3];
    if (((xres > 1024) || (yres > 768)) && (modehi[4]
        != 0))
        mode = modehi[4];
    if (mode == 0)
        continue;
    outregs.r_ax = 0x4F01;
    outregs.r_cx = mode;
    segread(&segregs);
    outregs.r_es = segregs.ds;
    outregs.r_di = (unsigned int)&mode_data;
    intr(0x10,&outregs);
    xoffset = max (0,(mode_data.XResolution -
pcx_header.xmax - 1)/2);
```

```
        yoffset = max(0,(mode_data.YResolution -
    pcx_header.ymax - 1)/2);
        ystop = min(pcx_header.ymax + yoffset,
    mode_data.YResolution);
        setMode(mode);
        fseek(read_file,128L,SEEK_SET);
        row=yoffset;
        col = 0;
        planes = 0;
        setBank(0,0);
        while (row <= ystop)
        {
            ch = fgetc(read_file);
            if ((ch & 0xC0) != 0xC0)
                no_chars = 1;
            else
            {
                no_chars = ch & 0x3F;
                ch = fgetc(read_file);
            }
            for (k=0; k<no_chars; k++)
            {
                buffer[col++].color[planes] = ch;
                if (col >= pcx_header.bytes_per_line)
                {
                    planes++;
                    col = 0;
                    if (planes > 2)
                    {
                        planes = 0;
                        for (ix=0;
    ix<pcx_header.bytes_per_line;
                            ix++)
                        {
                            switch(mode)
                            {
                                case 0x10D:
                                case 0x110:
                                case 0x113:
                                case 0x116:
                                case 0x119:
                                    data =
        (int)(buffer[ix].color[0]
                                        & 0xF8) << 7 | (int)
                                        (buffer[ix].color[1]&0xF8)
                                        << 2 |
                (int)(buffer[ix].color[2]&
                                        0xF8) >> 3;
                                    offset = row *
                            mode_data.BytesPerScanLine
```

```
                                        + 2 * (xoffset + ix);
                                    setBank(offset,0);
                                    FP_SEG(address) = 0xA000;
                                    FP_OFF(address)=(unsigned int)
                                        offset;
                                    *(address++) = data & 0xFF;
                                    *address = data >> 8;
                                    break;
                                case 0x10E:
                                case 0x111:
                                case 0x114:
                                case 0x117:
                                case 0x11A:
                                    data =
                (int)(buffer[ix].color[0]
                                        & 0xF8) << 8 | (int)
                                        (buffer[ix].color[1]&0xFC)
                                        << 3 |
                    (int)(buffer[ix].color[2] &
                                        0xF8) >> 3;
                                    offset = row *
                        mode_data.BytesPerScanLine
                                        + 2 * (xoffset + ix);
                                    setBank(offset,0);
                                    FP_SEG(address) = 0xA000;
                                    FP_OFF(address)=(unsigned int)
                                        offset;
                                    *(address++) = data & 0xFF;
                                    *address = data >> 8;
                                    break;
                                case 0x10F:
                                case 0x112:
                                case 0x115:
                                case 0x118:
                                case 0x11B:
                                    offset = row *
                        mode_data.BytesPerScanLine
                                        + 3 * (xoffset + ix);
                                    setBank(offset,0);
                                    FP_SEG(address) = 0xA000;
                                    FP_OFF(address)=(unsigned int)
                                        offset;
                                    *address- buffer[ix].color[2];
                                    offset = row *
                        mode_data.BytesPerScanLine
                                        + 3 * (xoffset + ix) + 1;
                                    setBank(offset,0);
                                    FP_SEG(address) = 0xA000;
                                    FP_OFF(address)=(unsigned int)
                                        offset;
```

```
                                        *address= buffer[ix].color[1];
                                        offset = row *
                    mode_data.BytesPerScanLine
                                            + 3 * (xoffset + ix) + 2;
                                        setBank(offset,0);
                                        FP_SEG(address) = 0xA000;
                                        FP_OFF(address)=(unsigned int)
                                            offset;
                                        *address= buffer[ix].color[0];
                                }
                            }
                            row++;
                        }
                    }
                }
            }
            fclose(read_file);
            strnset(outfile, NULL, 32);
            length = strcspn(filename, ".");
            strncpy(outfile, filename, length);
            strcat(outfile,".TGA");
            save_tga(outfile);
        }
}

/*
            setBank() = Sets video memory bank
*/

void setBank(unsigned long int offset, int read_write)
{
    static int bank, old_bank;

    old_bank = reg.x.dx;
    bank = offset >> 16;
    if (bank == old_bank)
        return;
    reg.x.dx = bank;
    old_bank = bank;
    reg.x.ax = 0x4F05;
    reg.x.bx = read_write;
    int86(0x10, &reg, &reg);
}
```

```
/*
    getModeData() = Gets Super VGA data on a desired mode
*/

int getModeData(int mode)
{
        segread(&segregs);
        outregs.r_ax = 0x4F01;
        outregs.r_cx = mode;
        outregs.r_es = segregs.ds;
        outregs.r_di =(unsigned int) &mode_data;
        intr(0x10,&outregs);
        if ((mode_data.ModeAttributes &0x01) == 1)
            return(1);
        return(0);
}

/*
                  setMode() = Sets Video Mode
*/

void setMode(int mode)
{
    union REGS reg;
    if (mode > 0xFF)
    {
        reg.x.ax = 0x4F02;
        reg.x.bx = mode;
    }
    else
        reg.x.ax = mode;
    int86 (0x10,&reg,&reg);
}

/*
    save_tga() = Save display screen to .BMP disk file
*/

void save_tga(char filename[32])
{
    unsigned char red, green, blue;
    union REGS reg;
    struct SREGS inreg;
```

```
    struct
    {
        unsigned char id_length,
                        color_map_type,
                        image_type;
        unsigned intcolor_map_start,
                        color_map_length;
        unsigned charcolor_map_depth;
        unsigned intx_offset,
                        y_offset,
                        xres,
                        yres;
        unsigned char bits_per_pixel,
                        image_descriptor;
    } tga_header;

    char far *address;
    int col, i, k, row, number, num_out, page=0,
old_page=0;
    unsigned char ch, old_ch, palette[768];
    FILE *write_file;
    unsigned long int offset;

    write_file = fopen(filename,"wb");
    tga_header.id_length = 0x00;
    tga_header.color_map_type = 0x00;
    tga_header.image_type = 0x02;
    tga_header.color_map_start = 0x00;
    tga_header.color_map_length = 0x00;
    tga_header.color_map_depth = 0x00;
    tga_header.x_offset = 0x00;
    tga_header.y_offset = 0x00;
    tga_header.xres = mode_data.XResolution;
    tga_header.yres = mode_data.YResolution;
    tga_header.bits_per_pixel = 24;
    tga_header.image_descriptor = 0x00;
    fwrite(&tga_header,1,18,write_file);
    setBank(0,1);
    for (row=mode_data.YResolution-1; row>=0; row--)
    {
        for (col=0; col<mode_data.XResolution; col++)
        {
            switch(mode)
            {
                case 0x10D:
                case 0x110:
                case 0x113:
                case 0x116:
                case 0x119:
                    offset = (long)row *
mode_data.BytesPerScanLine
```

```
                        + 2 * col;
                    setBank(offset,1);
                    FP_SEG(address) = 0xA000;
                    FP_OFF(address) =(unsigned int) offset;
                    data = (unsigned char)*address++;
                    data |=  (unsigned char)(*address) << 8;
                    blue = (data << 3) & 0xF8;
                    fputc(blue,write_file);
                    green = (data >> 2) & 0xF8;
                    fputc(green,write_file);
                    red = (data >> 7) & 0xF8;
                    fputc(red,write_file);
                    break;
                case 0x10E:
                case 0x111:
                case 0x114:
                case 0x117:
                case 0x11A:
                    offset = (long)row *
        mode_data.BytesPerScanLine
                        + 2L * col;
                    setBank(offset,1);
                    FP_SEG(address) = 0xA000;
                    FP_OFF(address) =(unsigned int) offset;
                    data = (unsigned char)*address++;
                    data |=  (unsigned char)(*address) << 8;
                    blue = (data << 3) & 0xF8;
                    fputc(blue,write_file);
                    green = (data >> 3) & 0xFC;
                    fputc(green,write_file);
                    red = (data >> 8) & 0xF8;
                    fputc(red,write_file);
                    break;
                case 0x10F:
                case 0x112:
                case 0x115:
                case 0x118:
                case 0x11B:
                    offset = (long)row *
        mode_data.BytesPerScanLine
                        + 3L * col;
                    setBank(offset,1);
                    FP_SEG(address) = 0xA000;
                    FP_OFF(address) =(unsigned int) offset;
                    fputc((*address++)&0xF8, write_file);
                    offset++;
                    setBank(offset,1);
                    fputc((*address++)&0xFC, write_file);
                    offset++;
                    setBank(offset,1);
                    fputc((*address)&0xF8, write_file);
```

```
                }
            }
        }
        fclose(write_file);
    }
```

Index

About the CD-ROM

The CD-ROM packaged with this book contains about 150 megabytes of executable programs, source code, text, and a myriad of great pictures! All the tools necessary for developing a customized set of graphics routines are here at your finger tips. The code offers something for everyone—quick implementation for beginners and faster algorithms for advanced programmers.

System Requirements

Windows 3.1 and higher; preferably Windows 95; Borland C++ 6.0. This CD will run on just about any PC, but a Super VGA board is required to view some of the pictures.